The Additional Protocols
TO THE GENEVA CONVENTIONS
in Context

The Additional Protocols
TO THE GENEVA CONVENTIONS
in Context

ANNYSSA BELLAL AND STUART CASEY-MASLEN

OXFORD
UNIVERSITY PRESS

Great Clarendon Street, Oxford, OX2 6DP,
United Kingdom

Oxford University Press is a department of the University of Oxford.
It furthers the University's objective of excellence in research, scholarship,
and education by publishing worldwide. Oxford is a registered trade mark of
Oxford University Press in the UK and in certain other countries

© Annyssa Bellal and Stuart Casey-Maslen 2022

The moral rights of the authors have been asserted

First Edition published in 2022

Impression: 1

All rights reserved. No part of this publication may be reproduced, stored in
a retrieval system, or transmitted, in any form or by any means, without the
prior permission in writing of Oxford University Press, or as expressly permitted
by law, by licence or under terms agreed with the appropriate reprographics
rights organization. Enquiries concerning reproduction outside the scope of the
above should be sent to the Rights Department, Oxford University Press, at the
address above

You must not circulate this work in any other form
and you must impose this same condition on any acquirer

Public sector information reproduced under Open Government Licence v3.0
(http://www.nationalarchives.gov.uk/doc/open-government-licence/open-government-licence.htm)

Published in the United States of America by Oxford University Press
198 Madison Avenue, New York, NY 10016, United States of America

British Library Cataloguing in Publication Data

Data available

Library of Congress Control Number: 2022940290

ISBN 978-0-19-286890-9

DOI: 10.1093/law/9780192868909.001.0001

Printed and bound in the UK by
TJ Books Limited

Links to third party websites are provided by Oxford in good faith and
for information only. Oxford disclaims any responsibility for the materials
contained in any third party website referenced in this work.

Acknowledgements

The authors would like to thank the following for commenting on draft chapters for this work: Ms. Tamalin Bolus, Prof. Martha Bradley, Ms. Emanuela-Chiara Gillard, Dr. Sarah Mbeza, and Ms. Valérie Quéré. All feedback was given in an individual capacity and does not imply any endorsement of the final text for which the authors remain solely responsible.

Contents

Table of cases	xiii
Table of treaties	xix
About the authors	xxv

Introduction: The Development and Significance of the Additional Protocols	1
The aim of the book	5
1. The Scope of Application of the Three Additional Protocols	7
Introduction	7
The scope of application of the Additional Protocol I	7
Material scope of application	8
Geographical scope of application	15
Temporal scope of application	15
The scope of application of the Additional Protocol II	16
The existence of a non-international armed conflict	16
The additional criteria under the Additional Protocol II	20
Geographical scope of application	22
Who is bound by the Additional Protocol II?	22
Temporal scope of application	24
The scope of application of the Additional Protocol III	25
Concluding remarks and outlook	25
2. Fundamental Guarantees	26
Introduction	26
The prohibition of murder	28
The prohibition of denial of quarter	31
The prohibition of torture and other ill-treatment	31
The principle of non-discrimination	33
The prohibition of enslavement	34
The prohibition of collective punishment	36
The prohibition of hostage-taking	37
Fair-trial rights	38
Concluding remarks and outlook	39
3. The Protection of Women	41
Introduction	41
The prohibition of sexual violence in international humanitarian law	42
The prohibition of sexual violence under international criminal law	44
Sexual and gender-based violence as a war crime	45
Sexual and gender-based violence as a crime against humanity	46
Sexual and gender-based violence as genocide	48
Women and the death penalty	48
Concluding remarks and outlook	49

viii CONTENTS

4. **The Protection of Children** — 51
    - Introduction — 51
    - Child recruitment and use in hostilities — 51
        - The legal situation under international humanitarian law — 51
        - The legal situation under human rights law — 60
    - Child protection in armed conflict — 62
    - The prohibition of the death penalty for child offenders — 66
    - Concluding remarks and outlook — 67

5. **Protection of Detainees and Prisoner-of-War Status** — 68
    - Introduction — 68
    - Detention in international armed conflict — 69
        - The protection of civilian detainees — 70
        - The death penalty — 71
        - The duty and nature of humane treatment — 72
        - The treatment of detained combatants — 73
        - The right to POW status — 77
        - Release and return of POW — 82
    - Detention in non-international armed conflict — 85
        - Arbitrary deprivation of liberty — 85
        - The duty of humane treatment — 86
    - Concluding remarks and outlook — 88

6. **Relief Operations** — 89
    - Introduction — 89
    - The trigger for humanitarian relief operations — 90
    - Consent to humanitarian relief operations — 93
    - Implementation of relief operations and protection of humanitarian personnel — 96
    - International criminal law — 98
    - Armed non-State actors' perspectives on humanitarian relief operations — 99
    - Concluding remarks and outlook — 101

7. **The Distinctive Emblems** — 102
    - Introduction — 102
    - A brief (tormented) history of the emblems — 104
    - The protective functions of the distinctive emblems — 108
    - The indicative functions of the emblems — 110
    - Misuse of the emblems — 111
    - Concluding remarks and outlook — 112

8. **The Rule of Distinction (Objects)** — 113
    - Introduction — 113
    - The definition of 'civilian object' and 'military objective' — 114
        - The 'nature' of an object — 115
        - The 'location' of an object — 115
        - The 'use' of an object — 117
        - The 'purpose' of an object — 119
        - The requirement of definite military advantage — 120
    - Civilian objects — 121
    - The principle of distinction — 122
    - Special protection of hospitals — 126

Special protection of cultural property	128
Special protection of installations containing dangerous forces	130
Concluding remarks and outlook	131

9. The Rule of Distinction (Persons) — 132

Introduction	132
The definition of 'combatant' and 'civilian'	134
The definition of combatant	134
The definition of a civilian	139
The principle of distinction	140
Indiscriminate attacks	145
Loss of protection from attack as a consequence of direct participation in hostilities	147
Concluding remarks and outlook	149

10. The Rule of Proportionality — 151

Introduction	151
The treaty rules of proportionality in attack	152
Proportionality in attack under general international law	155
The interpretation and application of the rule	157
The war crime of disproportionate attacks	160
Disproportionate attacks affecting the natural environment	165
Concluding remarks and outlook	169

11. Precautions in Attack and Defence — 170

Introduction	170
Precautions in attack	172
The duty to verify a target is a lawful military objective	172
The duty to choose and use weapons and methods of attack with a view to minimising civilian harm	174
The duty to give an effective warning to civilians of an attack	176
Precautions in defence	177
The duty to remove civilians from the vicinity of military objectives	178
The duty to locate military objectives away from densely populated areas	179
Concluding remarks and outlook	180

12. Prohibited Weapons — 182

Introduction	182
The right of parties to use weapons is not unlimited	183
Weapons of a nature to cause superfluous injury	185
Inherently indiscriminate weapons	191
Weapons that may be inherently indiscriminate	194
Weapons causing widespread, severe, and long-term damage to the environment	202
Prohibited means and methods of warfare	203
The legality of weapons must be verified	204
Concluding remarks and outlook	206

13. Terrorism and Acts of Terror — 207

Introduction	207
Measures and acts of terrorism	209

Acts of violence intended to terrorise the civilian population	211
Terrorising civilians as a war crime under customary law	213
The definition of terrorism under international law	215
Threats to terrorise the civilian population	217
Counterterrorism operations	218
Concluding remarks and outlook	222
14. Starvation and Sieges	**223**
Introduction	223
The legality of sieges under international humanitarian law	225
The prohibition on starvation of civilians as a method of warfare	230
Concluding remarks and outlook	232
15. Reprisals	**233**
Introduction	233
The definition of reprisals and their exercise under customary law	235
Reprisals under the 1949 Geneva Conventions	236
Reprisals under the 1977 Additional Protocol I	240
Reprisals in non-international armed conflict	243
Reprisals and defences to war crimes charges	245
Concluding remarks and outlook	246
16. National Implementation	**247**
Introduction	247
The duty to adopt national implementing legislation	249
The duty to disseminate international humanitarian law	252
Orders to armed forces	254
Legal advisers in the armed forces	255
Duty to investigate possible breaches	256
Duty to suppress breaches of international humanitarian law	258
Concluding remarks and outlook	259
17. Application and Implementation by Armed Non-State Actors	**260**
Introduction	260
Armed non-State actors under the 1977 Additional Protocol I	263
Armed non-State actors under the 1977 Additional Protocol II	266
The problematic absence of a definition of 'organized armed groups'	267
Core rules and noteworthy normative silences	269
Armed non-State actors under customary international humanitarian law	271
Challenges	272
Lack of compliance	272
The counterterrorism narrative	273
Concluding remarks and outlook	274
18. Application of International Humanitarian Law to United Nations Operations	**276**
Introduction	276
When do United Nations forces become party to an armed conflict?	277
What rules apply to United Nations forces that are party to an armed conflict?	281
Implementation of international humanitarian law rules binding United Nations forces	284
Concluding remarks and outlook	286

19. International Criminal Law ... 287
   Introduction ... 287
   War crimes in the conduct of hostilities ... 290
      The war crime of attacking civilians ... 290
      The war crime of disproportionate attacks affecting civilians ... 291
      The war crime of attacking a person *hors de combat* ... 293
      The war crime of making perfidious use of the red cross or
         red crescent emblems ... 295
   Other war crimes ... 296
      The war crime of unjustifiable delay in the repatriation of prisoners of war ... 296
      The war crime of an unfair trial ... 298
   Alleged war crimes ... 299
   Concluding remarks and outlook ... 300

20. The Role of the International Committee of the Red Cross ... 301
   Introduction ... 301
   The humanitarian activities of the International Committee of the Red Cross
      under international humanitarian law ... 303
   The action of the International Committee of the Red Cross in
      'other situations of violence' ... 306
   Controversies and challenges ... 308
   Concluding remarks and outlook ... 310

Bibliography ... 313
Index ... 333

Table of cases

(References are to paragraph numbers)

AFRICAN COMMISSION ON HUMAN AND PEOPLES' RIGHTS

General Comment No. 3 on the African Charter on Human and Peoples' Rights: The Right to Life (Article 4), adopted at Banjul (fifty-seventh Ordinary Session), November 2015 .... 2.8

ERITREA-ETHIOPIA CLAIMS COMMISSION

Partial Award: Prisoners of War – Eritrea's Claim 17, 1 July 2003 .... 5.41
Partial Award: Western Front, Aerial Bombardment and Related Claims – Eritrea's Claims 1, 3, 5, 9–13, 14, 21, 25 & 26, 19 December 2005 .... 8.16, 8.20

EUROPEAN COURT OF HUMAN RIGHTS

Georgia v. *Russia (II)*, Judgment (Grand Chamber), 21 January 2021 .... 16.27
Hanan v. *Germany*, Judgment (Grand Chamber), 16 February 2021 .... 10.12, 16.26
Tagayeva and others v. *Russia*, Judgment (First Section), 13 April 2017 (as rendered final on 18 September 2017) 13.35, 13.36

INTER-AMERICAN COMMISSION ON HUMAN RIGHTS

Napoleon Beazley v. *United States*, Decision (Case 12.412), Report No. 101/03, 29 December 2003 .... 4.46, 5.11

INTER-AMERICAN COURT OF HUMAN RIGHTS

Santo Domingo massacre v. *Colombia*, Judgment (Preliminary Objections, Merits and Reparations), 30 November 2012 .... 11.16
Case of the 'Street Children' (Villagrán-Morales) v. *Guatemala*, Judgment (Merits), 19 November 1999 .... 9.18
Identidad de género, e igualdad y no discriminación a parejas del mismo sexo ['Gender identity, and equality and non-discrimination against same-sex couples'], Advisory Opinion OC-24/17, 24 November 2017, at: http://bit.ly/3sN2dRY 3.14

INTERNATIONAL COURT OF JUSTICE

Contentious cases

Case Concerning Military and Paramilitary Activities in and against Nicaragua (*Nicaragua* v. *United States of America*), Judgment (Merits), 27 June 1986 .... 1.18, 2.1, 6.13, 17.6
Case Concerning Application of the Convention on the Prevention and Punishment of the Crime of Genocide (*Bosnia and Herzegovina* v. *Serbia and Montenegro*), Judgment (Merits), 26 February 2007 .... 1.17, 1.18, 1.19

xiv TABLE OF CASES

Advisory Opinions

Legality of the Threat or Use of Nuclear Weapons, Advisory Opinion, 8 July 1996 .... 9.34, 10.40, 12.7, 12.27, 12.42, 12.51 13.41
Legality of the Threat or Use of Nuclear Weapons, Advisory Opinion, Written Statement of the United States, 20 June 1995 .... 10.21, 12.42
Legal Consequences of the Construction of a Wall in the Occupied Palestinian Territory, Advisory Opinion, 2004 .... 6.6

INTERNATIONAL CRIMINAL COURT

Prosecutor v. Bahar Idriss Abu Garda, Decision on the Confirmation of Charges, (Trial Chamber I) (Case No. ICC-02/05-02/09), 8 February 2010 .... 18.8
Prosecutor v. Ahmad Al Faqi Al Mahdi, Decision on the Confirmation of Charges (Pre-Trial Chamber I) (Case No. ICC-01/12-01/15), 24 March 2016 .... 8.44
Prosecutor v. Thomas Lubanga Dyilo, Judgment (Trial Chamber I) (Case No. ICC-01/04-01/06), 14 March 2012 .... 1.17, 4.12, 4.17
Prosecutor v. Thomas Lubanga Dyilo, Judgment (Appeals Chamber) (Case No. ICC-01/04-01/06 A 5), 1 December 2014 .... 4.12, 4.16, 4.21
Prosecutor v. Jean-Pierre Bemba Gombo, Decision pursuant to Article 61(7)(a) and (b) of the Rome Statute on the charges of the Prosecutor against Jean-Pierre Bemba Gombo (Pre-Trial Chamber II) (Case No. ICC-01/05-01/08), 15 June 2009 .... 3.13
Prosecutor v. Jean-Pierre Bemba Gombo, Judgment (Trial Chamber III) (Case No. ICC-01/05-01/08), 21 March 2016 .... 1.34
Prosecutor v. Germain Katanga, Judgment (Trial Chamber II) (Case No. ICC-01/04-01/07), 7 March 2014 .... 4.17, 4.21, 9.36, 9.37, 10.36, 10.37
Prosecutor v. Callixte Mbarushimana, Decision on the Confirmation of Charges (Trial Chamber) (Case No. ICC-01/04-01/10), 16 December 2011 .... 15.33
Prosecutor v. Bosco Ntaganda, Judgment (Trial Chamber IV) (Case No. ICC-01/04-02/06), 8 July 2019 .... 3.15, 3.16, 9.28, 9.29, 9.37
Prosecutor v. Bosco Ntaganda, Judgment (Appeals Chamber) (Case No. ICC-01/04-02/06-2666-Red), 30 March 2021 .... 3.16
Prosecutor v. Bosco Ntaganda, Judgment (Appeals Chamber) (Case No. ICC-01/04-02/06 A A2), 30 March 2021, Partly concurring opinion of Judge Chile Eboe-Osuji, 29 March 2021 .... 14.10
Prosecutor v. Dominic Ongwen, Judgment (Trial Chamber IX) (Case No. ICC-02/04-01/15), 4 February 2021 .... 3.15, 4.18, 18.11

International Criminal Tribunal for Rwanda (ICTR)

Prosecutor v. Akayesu, Judgment (Trial Chamber) (Case No. ICTR-96-4-T), 2 September 1998 .... 2.19, 17.16
Prosecutor v. Alfred Musema, Judgment and Sentence (Trial Chamber) (Case No. ICTR-96-13-T), 27 January 2000 .... 1.38
Prosecutor v. Muvunyi, Reasons for the Chamber's Decision on the Accused's Motion to Exclude Witness TQ (Case No. ICTR-2000-55), 15 July 2005 .... 20.25
Prosecutor v. Georges Anderson Nderubumwe Rutaganda, Judgement and Sentence (Trial Chamber I) (Case No. ICTR-96-3-T), 6 December 1999 .... 9.40

International Criminal Tribunal for the former Yugoslavia (ICTY)

ICTY Committee, 'Final Report to the Prosecutor by the Committee Established to Review the NATO Bombing Campaign Against the Federal Republic of Yugoslavia', 2000 .... 8.5, 8.9, 8.11, 11.34
Prosecutor v. Blagojević and Jokić, Judgment (Trial Chamber) (Case No. IT-02-60-T), 17 January 2005 .... 2.9

TABLE OF CASES   XV

Prosecutor v. *Brdjanin*, Decision on Interlocutory Appeal (Appeals Chamber)
(Case No. IT-99-36), 11 December 2002 .... 20.25
Prosecutor v. *Tihomir Blaškić*, Judgment (Trial Chamber) (Case No. IT-95-14-T),
3 March 2000 .... 9.33, 9.34, 9.36
Prosecutor v. *Tihomir Blaškić*, Judgment (Appeals Chamber) (Case No. IT-95-14-A),
29 July 2004 .... 9.33
Prosecutor v. *Boškoski and Tarčulovski*, Judgment (Trial Chamber) (Case No. IT-04-82-T),
10 July 2008 .... 1.33, 13.1, 17.16
Prosecutor v. *Delalić*, Judgment (Trial Chamber) (Case No. IT-96-21-T), 16 November 1998 ..... 2.9
Prosecutor v. *Furundžija*, Judgment (Trial Chamber) (Case No. IT-95-17/1-T),
10 December 1998 .... 2.17–2.18
Prosecutor v. *Furundžija*, Statement of the Trial Chamber at the Judgment Hearing,
Judgment Summary, The Hague, 10 December 1998 .... 2.18
Prosecutor v. *Galić*, Judgment and Opinion (Trial Chamber I) (Case No. IT-98-29-T),
5 December 2003 .... 8.36, 9.26, 9.27, 9.34, 9.35, 9.36,
10.29–10.31, 11.7, 12.29, 13.17, 13.20, 17.34, 19.10
Prosecutor v. *Galić*, Judgment and Opinion (Trial Chamber I), Dissenting Opinion of
Judge Nieto-Navia 10.32, 13.18
Prosecutor v. *Galić*, Judgment (Appeals Chamber) (Case No. IT-98-29-A),
30 November 2006 .... 9.35, 12.29, 13.17, 19.10
Prosecutor v. *Galić*, Judgment (Appeals Chamber), Dissenting Opinion of Judge Wolfgang
Schomburg 13.18
Prosecutor v. *Ante Gotovina and Mladen Markač* (Case No. IT-06-90-T), Prosecution's Public
Redacted Final Trial Brief, 2 August 2010 .... 8.27
Prosecutor v. *Ante Gotovina and Mladen Markač*, Judgment (Trial Chamber I)
(Case No. IT-06-90-T), 15 April 2011 .... 8.18, 8.26
Prosecutor v. *Ante Gotovina*, 'Application and Proposed Amicus Curiae Brief Concerning
the 15 April 2011 Trial Chamber Judgment and Requesting that the Appeals Chamber
Reconsider the Findings of Unlawful Artillery Attacks during Operation Storm',
Appeals Chamber, 13 January 2012 .... 8.28
Prosecutor v. *Gotovina and Markač*, Judgment (Appeals Chamber) (Case No. IT-06-90-A),
16 November 2012 .... 8.29
Prosecutor v. *Gotovina and Markač*, Judgment (Appeals Chamber), Dissenting
Opinion of Judge Fausto Pocar 8.29
Prosecutor v. *Hadzihasanovic and Kubura*, Decision on Joint Defence Interlocutory
Appeal of Trial Chamber Decision (Appeals Chamber) (Case No. IT-01-47-AR73.3),
11 March 2005 .... 8.33
Prosecutor v. *Haradinaj, Balaj, and Brahimaj*, Judgment (Trial Chamber)
(Case No. IT-04-84-T), 3 April 2008 .... 1.35
Prosecutor v. *Jokić*, Sentencing Judgment (Trial Chamber I) (Case No. IT-01-42/1-S),
18 March 2004 .... 8.43
Prosecutor v. *Radovan Karadžić*, Judgment (Trial Chamber) (Case No. IT-95-5/18-T),
24 March 2016 .... 13.19
Prosecutor v. *Dario Kordić and Mario Čerkez*, Judgment (Appeals Chamber)
(Case No. IT-95-14/2-A), 17 December 2004 .... 3.13
Prosecutor v. *Kunarac and others*, Judgment (Trial Chamber) (Case No. IT-96-23-T & IT-96-23/1-T),
22 February 2001 .... 2.22
Prosecutor v. *Kunarac*, Judgment (Appeals Chamber) (Case No. IT-96-23), 12 June 2002 .... 3.9
Prosecutor v. *Zoran Kupreškić and others*, Judgment (Trial Chamber)
(Case No. IT-95-16-T), 14 January 2000 .... 9.18, 9.31, 15.7, 15.30, 15.34
Prosecutor v. *Limaj, Bala, and Musliu*, Judgment (Trial Chamber) (Case No. IT-03-66-T),
30 November 2005 .... 1.35
Prosecutor v. *Milan Martić*, Review of Indictment Pursuant to Rule 61 (Trial Chamber)
(Case No. IT-95-11-R61), 8 March 1996 .... 15.31

Prosecutor v. *Milan Martić*, Judgment (Trial Chamber) (Case No. IT-95-11-T),
   12 June 2007 .... 15.32
Prosecutor v. *Milan Martić*, Judgment (Appeals Chamber) (Case No. IT-95-11-A),
   8 October 2008 .... 8.30, 12.7, 12.28, 15.31
Prosecutor v. *Dragomir Milošević*, Judgment (Trial Chamber III)
   (Case No. IT-98-29/1-T), 12 December 2007 .... 8.12, 8.13, 14.16
Prosecutor v. *Dragomir Milošević*, Judgment (Appeals Chamber)
   (Case No. IT-98-29/1-A), 12 November 2009 .... 8.13
Prosecutor v. *Mrkšić, Radić, and Šljivančin*, Judgment (Trial Chamber II)
   (Case No. IT-95-13/1-T), 27 September 2007 .... 1.35
ICTY, *Prosecutor* v. *Prlić*, Judgment (Appeals Chamber) (Case No. IT-04-74-A),
   29 November 2017 .... 13.13
Prosecutor v. *Simić*, Decision on the Prosecution Motion Under Rule 73 for a Ruling
   Concerning the Testimony of a Witness (Case No. IT-95-9), 27 July 1999 .... 20.25
Prosecutor v. *Pavle Strugar*, Judgment (Appeals Chamber) (Case No. IT-01-42-A),
   17 July 2008 .... 9.40
Prosecutor v. *Tadić (aka 'Dule')*, Decision on the Defence Motion for Interlocutory Appeal on
   Jurisdiction (Appeals Chamber) (Case No. IT-94-1), 2 October 1995 .... 0.10, 1.11, 1.28, 1.42,
                                                                1.48, 9.21, 12.16, 17.29
Prosecutor v. *Tadić (aka 'Dule')*, Judgment (Trial Chamber) (Case No. IT-94-1-T),
   7 May 1997 .... 1.28
Prosecutor v. *Tadić (aka 'Dule')*, Judgment (Appeals Chamber) (Case No. IT-94-1-A),
   15 July 1999 .... 1.16

INTERNATIONAL RESIDUAL MECHANISM FOR CRIMINAL TRIBUNALS

Prosecutor v. *Ratko Mladic*, Judgment (Appeals Chamber) (Case No. MICT-13-56-A),
   8 June 2021 .... 13.19

SPECIAL COURT FOR SIERRA LEONE

Prosecutor v. *Brima, Kamara, and Kanu*, Judgment (Trial Chamber II)
   (Case No. SCSL-04-16-T), 20 June 2007 .... 2.28, 4.15
Prosecutor v. *Sam Hinga Norman*, Decision on Preliminary Motion Based on Lack
   of Jurisdiction (Child Recruitment), (Appeals Chamber)
   (Case No. SCSL-2004-14-AR72(E)), 31 May 2004 .... 17.6
Prosecutor v. *Sesay, Kallon, and Gbao*, Judgment (Trial Chamber I) (Case No. SCSL-04-15-T),
   2 March 2009 .... 18.8
Prosecutor v. *Charles Ghankay Taylor*, Judgment (Trial Chamber) (Case No. SCSL-03-01-T),
   18 May 2012 .... 2.24
Prosecutor v. *Charles Ghankay Taylor*, Judgment (Appeals Chamber)
   (Case No. SCSL-03-01-A), 26 September 2013 .... 13.10

NATIONAL CASELAW

Israel

Military Court, *Military Prosecutor* v. *Omar Mahmud Kassem and others*, Ramallah,
   13 April 1969 .... 9.9

United Kingdom

Queen's Bench Divisional Court, *Rance* v. *Mid-Downs Health Authority* (1991) 1 All ER 801 .... 2.10

R v. Sergeant Alexander Wayne Blackman ("Marine A"), Case Reference: 2012CM00442,
  Sentencing Remarks by HHJ Jeff Blackett, Judge Advocate General, 6 December 2013 . . . . 2.11
Court Martial Appeal Court, *R v. Alexander Wayne Blackman*, Judgment
  (Case No. 2014/00049/B5), 22 May 2014 . . . . 19.21
Court Martial (Bulford), *R v. Alexander Blackman*, Sentencing Remarks
  (Case No. 2012CM00442) 19.21
Court Martial Appeal Court, *R v. Alexander Wayne Blackman*, Judgment, [2017]
  EW CA Crim 190, 15 March 2017 . . . . 19.21

HOUSE OF LORDS
AG Ref No. 3 of 1994 (1997) 3 All ER 936 . . . . 2.10

SUPREME COURT
Serdar Mohamed v. Ministry of Defence, Judgment, 17 January 2017, [2017] UKSC 2 . . . . 5.50
R v. Gul (Appellant), [2013] UKSC 64 . . . . 13.26

United States

SUPREME COURT
Hamdan v. Rumsfeld, 548 US 557 (2006) . . . . 1.30, 2.

Table of treaties

(References are to paragraph numbers)

1863

Instructions for the Government of Armies of the United States in the Field, General Order No 100, promulgated by the US Department of War on 24 April 1863 (Lieber Code) 12.9

1864

Convention for the Amelioration of the Condition of the Wounded in Armies in the Field; adopted at Geneva, 22 August 1864; entered into force, 22 June 1865 .... 7.5, 8.34

1868

Declaration Renouncing the Use, in Time of War, of Explosive Projectiles Under 400 Grammes Weight; adopted at St Petersburg, 11 December 1868; entered into force, 4 September 1900 .... 8.23, 9.20, 12.9

1899

Convention (II) with Respect to the Laws and Customs of War on Land; adopted at The Hague, 29 July 1899; entered into force, 4 September 1900 .... 16.17
Regulations concerning the Laws and Customs of War on Land annexed to Convention (II) with Respect to the Laws and Customs of War on Land; adopted at The Hague, 29 July 1899; entered into force, 4 September 1900 .... 2.12, 8.39, 12.5, 14.7

1907

Regulations concerning the Laws and Customs of War on Land, Annex to the Convention (IV) respecting the Laws and Customs of War on Land; adopted at The Hague, 18 October 1907; entered into force, 26 January 1910 .... 5.16, 5.33, 8.39, 8.43, 12.5, 14.7, 16.17
Convention (IX) concerning Bombardment by Naval Forces in Time of War; adopted at The Hague, 18 October 1907; entered into force, 26 January 1910 .... 8.43

1925

Protocol for the Prohibition of the Use of Asphyxiating, Poisonous or Other Gases, and of Bacteriological Methods of Warfare; adopted at Geneva, 17 June 1925; entered into force, 8 February 1928 .... 12.40

1926

Convention to Suppress the Slave Trade and Slavery; signed at Geneva, 25 September 1926; entered into force, 9 March 1927 .... 2.22

1929

Convention relative to the Treatment of Prisoners of War; adopted at Geneva,
27 July 1929; entered into force, 19 June 1931 .... 7.9, 15.3

1937

Convention for the Prevention and Punishment of Terrorism; adopted at Geneva,
16 November 1937; never entered into force 13.6

1945

Charter of the United Nations; adopted at San Francisco, 26 June 1945;
entered into force, 24 October 1945 .... 13.33, 18.1

1949

Convention (I) for the Amelioration of the Condition of the Wounded and
Sick in Armed Forces in the Field; adopted at Geneva, 12 August 1949;
entered into force, 21 October 1950. .... 6.8, 8.2, 9.10, 15.6, 16.1
Convention (II) for the Amelioration of the Condition of Wounded, Sick and
Shipwrecked Members of Armed Forces at Sea; adopted at Geneva,
12 August 1949; entered into force, 21 October 1950. .... 2.1, 15.11
Convention (III) relative to the Treatment of Prisoners of War; adopted at
Geneva, 12 August 1949; entered into force, 21 October 1950. .... 2.25, 4.9, 5.2, 5.3, 9.6, 15.4
Convention (IV) relative to the Protection of Civilian Persons in Time of War;
adopted at Geneva, 12 August 1949; entered into force,
21 October 1950. .... 1.2, 2.25, 3.4, 4.4, 5.3, 6.4, 8.2, 13.3, 14.2, 15.4

1954

Convention for the Protection of Cultural Property in the Event of Armed Conflict; adopted at
The Hague, 14 May 1954; entered into force, 7 August 1956 .... 8.2

1966

International Covenant on Civil and Political Rights; adopted at New York, 16 December 1966;
entered into force, 23 March 1976 .... 2.2, 2.8, 2.21, 5.9, 13.34
International Covenant on Economic, Social and Cultural Rights; adopted at New York, 16
December 1966; entered into force, 3 January 1976 .... 6.6

1976

Convention on the prohibition of military or any other hostile use of environmental modification
techniques; adopted at New York, 10 December 1976; entered into force, 5 October 1978 ... 12.50

1977

Protocol Additional to the Geneva Conventions of 12 August 1949, and relating to the Protection
of Victims of International Armed Conflicts (Protocol I); adopted at Geneva, 8 June 1977,
entered into force, 7 December 1978 .... 4.5, 4.10
Protocol Additional to the Geneva Conventions of 12 August 1949, and relating
to the Protection of Victims of Non-International Armed Conflicts (Protocol II);
adopted at Geneva, 8 June 1977, entered into force, 7 December 1978 (hereinafter,
1977 Additional Protocol II)........... 0.1, 1.1, 2.1, 3.1, 3.4, 5.1, 5.2, 8.1, 9.1, 10.1, 11.1, 11.2, 12.1,
13.2, 14.4, 15.2, 15.3, 16.1, 17.3, 18.1, 19.1, 19.3, 20.7

1979

International Convention Against the Taking of Hostages; adopted at New York, 17 December 1979; entered into force, 3 June 1983 .... 2.30

1980

Convention on Prohibitions or Restrictions on the Use of Certain Conventional Weapons which May Be Deemed to Be Excessively Injurious or to Have Indiscriminate Effects; adopted at Geneva, 10 October 1980; entered into force, 2 December 1983 .... 0.2, 0.7, 12.2

Protocol on Prohibitions or Restrictions on the Use of Mines, Booby-Traps and Other Devices (Protocol II) annexed to the Convention on Prohibitions or Restrictions on the Use of Certain Conventional Weapons which May Be Deemed to Be Excessively Injurious or to Have Indiscriminate Effects; adopted at Geneva, 10 October 1980; entered into force, 2 December 1983 .... 10.8

Protocol on Prohibitions or Restrictions on the Use of Incendiary Weapons (Protocol III) annexed to the CCW; adopted at Geneva, 10 October 1980; entered into force, 2 December 1983 .... 12.20

1984

Convention against Torture and Other Cruel, Inhuman or Degrading Treatment or Punishment; adopted at New York, 10 December 1984; entered into force, 26 June 1987 .... 2.14, 21.5

1989

Convention on the Rights of the Child; adopted at New York, 20 November 1989; entered into force, 2 September 1990 .... 4.5, 4.6

1992

Convention on the Prohibition of the Development, Production, Stockpiling and Use of Chemical Weapons and on their Destruction; adopted at Geneva, 3 September 1992; entered into force, 29 April 1997 .... 5.23, 12.40, 16.5

1994

Convention on the Safety of United Nations and Associated Personnel; adopted at New York, 9 December 1994; entered into force, 15 January 1999 .... 18.10

1995

Protocol to the Convention on Prohibitions or Restrictions on the Use of Certain Conventional Weapons which may be deemed to be Excessively Injurious or to have Indiscriminate Effects (Protocol IV, entitled Protocol on Blinding Laser Weapons); adopted at Vienna, 13 October 1995; entered into force, 30 July 1998 .... 12.19, 18.18

1996

Protocol on Prohibitions or Restrictions on the Use of Mines, Booby-Traps and Other Devices as amended on 3 May 1996 annexed to the CCW; adopted at Geneva, 3 May 1996; entered into force, 3 December 1998 .... 10.8, 12.10, 15.28

1997

Convention on the Prohibition of the Use, Stockpiling, Production, and Transfer of Anti-Personnel Mines and on their Destruction; adopted at Oslo, 18 September 1997; entered into force, 1 March 1999 .... 5.24, 12.43, 12.60, 15.28, 16.5

International Convention for the Suppression of Terrorist Bombings; adopted at New York, 15 December 1997; entered into force, 23 May 2001 .... 13.24, 13.25, 13.26, 13.41, 17.34

1998

Rome Statute of the International Criminal Court; adopted at Rome, 17 July 1998; entered into force, 1 July 2002 .... 0.12, 2.9, 2.13, 3.8, 3.10, 3.13, 3.17, 3.19, 4.8, 5.42, 6.22, 7.4, 7.28, 8.33, 8.38, 8.45, 9.3, 10.6, 10.10, 10.33, 12.16, 12.31, 12.39, 12.52, 13.11, 13.17, 14.4, 14.20, 15.4, 16.12, 18.10, 18.22, 19.3, 19.6, 19.9, 19.20, 19.23, 19.30

1999

International Convention for the Suppression of the Financing of Terrorism; adopted at New York, 9 December 1999; entered into force, 10 April 2002 .... 17.34

2000

Optional Protocol to the Convention on the Rights of the Child on the involvement of children in armed conflict; adopted at New York, 25 May 2000; entered into force, 12 February 2002 .... 4.23, 4.26, 4.48

2005

Protocol additional to the Geneva Conventions of 12 August 1949, and relating to the Adoption of an Additional Distinctive Emblem (Protocol III), adopted at Geneva, 8 December 2005; entered into force, 14 January 2007 .... 0.12, 7.1–7.31

Optional Protocol to the Convention on the Safety of United Nations and Associated Personnel; adopted at New York, 8 December 2005; entered into force, 19 August 2010 .... 18.10

International Convention for the Suppression of Acts of Nuclear Terrorism; adopted at New York, 13 April 2005; entered into force, 7 July 2007 .... 17.34

2008

Convention on Cluster Munitions; adopted at Dublin, 30 May 2008; entered into force, 1 August 2010 .... 12.60, 18.18

2013

Arms Trade Treaty; adopted at New York, 2 April 2013; entered into force, 24 December 2014 ... 1.8

2014

Protocol on Amendments to the Protocol on the Statute of the African Court of Justice and Human Rights; adopted at Malabo, 27 June 2014; not yet in force 3.17, 10.28

2017

Treaty on the Prohibition of Nuclear Weapons; adopted on 7 July 2017; entered into force, 22 January 2021 .... 12.41

Amendment to Article 8 of the Rome Statute of the International Criminal Court (Weapons which use microbial or other biological agents, or toxins); adopted at New York, 14 December 2017; entered into force, 2 April 2020 .... 12.39

Amendment to Article 8 of the Rome Statute of the International Criminal Court (Blinding laser weapons); adopted at New York, 14 December 2017; entered into force, 2 April 2020 .... 12.19

2019

Amendment to Article 8 of the Rome Statute of the International Criminal Court (Intentionally using starvation of civilians); adopted at The Hague, 6 December 2019; entered into force, 14 October 2021 .... 14.20

About the authors

Dr. Annyssa Bellal is a Senior Researcher at the Centre on Conflicts, Development and Peacebuilding at the Geneva Graduate Institute of International and Development Studies (Graduate Institute) and the Executive Coordinator of the Geneva Peacebuilding Platform. She was formerly Senior Research Fellow at the Geneva Academy of International Humanitarian Law and Human Rights. Dr. Bellal teaches at Sciences Po, Paris, the University of Bern, and at the Graduate Institute. Dr. Bellal formerly worked as a legal adviser for the Swiss NGO Geneva Call, the Office of the United Nations High Commissioner for Human Rights (OHCHR), the Swiss Department of Foreign Affairs, and International Committee of the Red Cross (ICRC). She was also an Assistant Professor in public international law at the Irish Centre for Human Rights in Galway, Ireland. She holds a PhD (summa cum laude) in Public International Law from the Graduate Institute and an LLM in Philosophy of Law from the University of Grenoble. She also holds a Master of Advanced Studies in International Relations and an MA in Law from the University of Geneva.

Stuart Casey-Maslen is Extraordinary Professor at the Centre for Human Rights of the University of Pretoria in South Africa where he teaches the law of armed conflict, international human rights law, counterterrorism law, and disarmament law. Stuart also teaches a course on international crime and punishment at Sciences Po Paris. He has a doctorate in international humanitarian law and master's degrees in international human rights law and forensic ballistics. Stuart represented the ICRC at the negotiation of the 1997 Anti-Personnel Mine Ban Convention and Norwegian People's Aid at the diplomatic conference that adopted the 2008 Convention on Cluster Munitions. He advised the Swiss government during the negotiation of the 2013 Arms Trade Treaty and the Austrian government during the negotiation of the 2017 Treaty on the Prohibition of Nuclear Weapons.

Introduction: The Development and Significance of the Additional Protocols

The two 1977 Additional Protocols to the four Geneva Conventions[1] were, and remain, a landmark in the development of the law of armed conflict, the branch of international law once called the law of war. The first two Additional Protocols were particularly important in developing and identifying the law governing the conduct of hostilities on land and in the air (but not at sea); many of the rules set out in them were being elaborated for the first time in a treaty. The third Additional Protocol on the protective emblems (concluded in 2005)[2] seeks to resolve long-standing concern as to the potential proliferation of protective symbols for neutral and impartial humanitarian relief agencies and operations; time will tell whether that aim has been achieved.

0.1

In the 1970s, the International Committee of the Red Cross (ICRC) and the Government of Switzerland were instrumental in promoting the progressive development of what has become widely referred to as international humanitarian law (IHL).[3] The ICRC hosted conferences of governmental experts in 1971 and 1972, along with separate consultations of national societies and non-governmental organisations, with the aim of considering what could become the content of new international legislation. The ICRC subsequently issued two draft texts of applicable rules, for the regulation of international armed conflicts and non-international armed conflicts, respectively.

0.2

As long ago as 1956, the ICRC had already promulgated Draft Rules for the Limitation of the Dangers incurred by the Civilian Population in Time of War,[4] conscious that the

0.3

---

[1] Protocol Additional to the Geneva Conventions of 12 August 1949, and relating to the Protection of Victims of International Armed Conflicts (Protocol I); adopted at Geneva, 8 June 1977; entered into force, 7 December 1978 (hereinafter, 1977 Additional Protocol I); and Protocol Additional to the Geneva Conventions of 12 August 1949, and relating to the Protection of Victims of Non-International Armed Conflicts (Protocol II); adopted at Geneva, 8 June 1977; entered into force, 7 December 1978 (hereinafter, 1977 Additional Protocol II).

[2] Protocol additional to the Geneva Conventions of 12 August 1949, and relating to the Adoption of an Additional Distinctive Emblem (Protocol III); adopted at Geneva, 8 December 2005; entered into force, 14 January 2007.

[3] The term was increasingly employed by the ICRC in particular. Although incorporated in the title of the diplomatic conference that adopted them, the two Additional Protocols do not incorporate the term 'international humanitarian law' in their provisions. It would, however, appear in the treaty that followed their conclusion: the 1980 Convention on Certain Conventional Weapons. Therein it is stipulated that: 'Nothing in this Convention or its annexed Protocols shall be interpreted as detracting from other obligations imposed upon the High Contracting Parties by international humanitarian law applicable in armed conflict.' Art. 2, Convention on Prohibitions or Restrictions on the Use of Certain Conventional Weapons which May Be Deemed to Be Excessively Injurious or to Have Indiscriminate Effects; adopted at Geneva, 10 October 1980; entered into force, 2 December 1983. See G. D. Solis, *The Law of Armed Conflict, International Humanitarian Law in War*, 3rd Edn, Cambridge University Press, Cambridge, 2021, p. 18 and related citations.

[4] ICRC, 'Draft Rules for the Limitation of the Dangers incurred by the Civilian Population in Time of War, ICRC, 1956', at: https://bit.ly/31DEDyv.

2 INTRODUCTION

focus of the 1949 Geneva Conventions on the protection of persons in the power of the enemy (so-called Geneva Law) left a need for corresponding codification of Hague Law on the conduct of hostilities.[5] As a whole, the 20 draft articles did not gain sufficient traction among States at the time, although many of the proposed provisions would ultimately find their way into the Protocols in some form. In addition, the harm to civilians occasioned by the Vietnam War through the late 1960s and early 1970s, especially as a result of the indiscriminate aerial bombing that often characterised United States (US) military operations, had become increasingly hard to ignore.[6]

0.4 The Swiss Government would organise and host the formal diplomatic conference that led to the successful adoption of the first two Additional Protocols in June 1977, taking the lead in its capacity as the depositary of the 1949 Geneva Conventions 'and in accordance with a hundred-year-old tradition'.[7] The Diplomatic Conference on the Reaffirmation and Development of International Humanitarian Law Applicable in Armed Conflicts met in Geneva over four long negotiating sessions: 20 February–29 March 1974, 3 February–18 April 1975, 21 April–11 June 1976, and finally 17 March–10 June 1977.[8] More than 100 States participated. The negotiations were ground-breaking in form due to the involvement in the diplomatic conference of eleven national liberation movements, including the African National Congress (ANC) and the Palestine Liberation Organization (PLO).[9]

0.5 The Rules of Procedure determined that all decisions on matters of substance taken by the plenary Assembly, and particularly the definitive adoption of articles, required a two-thirds majority among the participating States whenever consensus could not be achieved. In the drafting committees, however, only a simple majority was required.[10] In the negotiation of the Additional Protocol I on international armed conflict, many issues concerning the conduct of hostilities as well as on the extension of prisoner-of-war-status to fighters in guerrilla movements were highly contentious, as was the extension of scope of such conflict to encompass decolonisation struggles.

0.6 The Additional Protocol II on non-international armed conflict was also disputed, but this time the opposition came primarily from the Global South, with Pakistan leading opposition to what it termed 'interference' in internal affairs. Pakistan's steadfast refusal to countenance far-reaching rules restraining how States could suppress insurgencies

---

[5] Y. Sandoz, C. Swinarski, and B. Zimmermann (eds.), *Commentary on the Additional Protocols of 8 June 1977 to the Geneva Conventions of 12 August 1949*, ICRC/Martinus Nijhoff, Geneva, 1987, available at: https://bit.ly/3tgknhw (hereinafter, ICRC Commentary on the Two Additional Protocols of 1977), General Introduction, p. xxix. The last major revision of Hague Law had been in 1907 before the two World Wars and even before the use of military aircraft.

[6] See, e.g., T. McCormack, 'Negotiating the Two Additional Protocols of 1977: Interview with the Right Honourable Sir Kenneth Keith' in S. Linton, T. McCormack, and S Sivakumaran (eds.), *Asia-Pacific Perspectives on International Humanitarian Law*, Cambridge University Press, Cambridge, 18 October 2019, pp. 17–35, at: https://bit.ly/3Ga4gpF.

[7] ICRC Commentary on the Two Additional Protocols of 1977, p. xxxii.

[8] Ibid.

[9] Solis, *The Law of Armed Conflict, International Humanitarian Law in War*, 3rd Edn, p. 107; and see ICRC Commentary on the Two Additional Protocols of 1977, at: https://bit.ly/3q39QEF.

[10] ICRC Commentary on the Two Additional Protocols of 1977, p. xxxiii.

would lead to much of the ICRC's draft text, as revised by States during the negotiations, being gutted at the last minute. In order to secure the Protocol's adoption, informal negotiations were held at the Mission of Pakistan to the United Nations in Geneva.[11] Pakistan signed, but has never ratified, the Additional Protocol II.

But despite their tricky negotiation paths, the 1977 Additional Protocols have since attracted very wide adherence, with 174 States Parties to the Additional Protocol I (meaning only 23 States are not party[12] of which three are signatories[13]) and 169 States Parties to the Additional Protocol II (thus with 28 States not party,[14] of which, again, three are signatories.)[15] While many successes can be attributed to the two treaties, there were also failures, most notably to regulate any specific conventional weapons in either of the two 1977 Protocols. The ICRC had convened two sessions of a Conference of Government Experts, in Lucerne in 1974, and in Lugano in 1976 to discuss prohibitions or restrictions on the use of a range of weapons, particularly the use of napalm, agent orange, and landmines. But agreement proved elusive at the time, and the decision was taken to leave the regulation of specific weapons to the United Nations (UN). The UN would later convene further expert groups and then a diplomatic conference, leading to the adoption of the 1980 Convention on Certain Conventional Weapons.[16]

0.7

Today, much of the Additional Protocol I codifies customary rules that are binding on all States. As long ago as 1987, the US Department of State was declaring its view that 59 of the 91 substantive articles of the Protocol were of a customary nature.[17] The US opposed the recognition as customary law of several provisions, including the extension of scope of international armed conflict to wars of national liberation (in Article 1(4)); the prohibition on means or methods of warfare causing widespread, long-term, and severe damage to the environment (in Article 35(3)); the prohibition on the use of enemy emblems and uniforms during military operations (in Article 39); the relaxation of requirements contained in the 1949 Geneva Convention III concerning the

0.8

---

[11] A review of the Official Records of the diplomatic conference identifies frequent proposals by Pakistan to 'delete this article' with respect to proposed provisions in the Second Additional Protocol. See *Official Records of the Diplomatic Conference on the Reaffirmation and Development of International Humanitarian Law Applicable in Armed Conflicts, Geneva (1974–1977)*, Vol. IV, at: https://bit.ly/3zAkJAZ.

[12] Andorra, Azerbaijan, Bhutan, Eritrea, India, Indonesia, Iran, Israel, Kiribati, Malaysia, Marshall Islands, Myanmar, Nepal, Niue, Pakistan, Papua New Guinea, Singapore, Somalia, Sri Lanka, Thailand, Turkey, Tuvalu, and the United States.

[13] Iran, Pakistan, and the United States.

[14] Andorra, Azerbaijan, Bhutan, Eritrea, India, Indonesia, Iran, Iraq, Israel, Kiribati, Democratic People's Republic of Korea, Malaysia, Marshall Islands, Mexico, Myanmar, Nepal, Niue, Pakistan, Papua New Guinea, Singapore, Somalia, Sri Lanka, Syria, Thailand, Turkey, Tuvalu, the United States, and Vietnam.

[15] Again: Iran, Pakistan, and the United States. US President Ronald Reagan submitted the Second Additional Protocol for ratification in 1987 as did President Barack Obama in 2011, but in neither instance was the Senate minded to take action. Solis, *The Law of Armed Conflict, International Humanitarian Law in War*, 3rd Edn, pp. 119–20.

[16] As noted above, the formal title of the treaty, often called the CCW, is the Convention on Prohibitions or Restrictions on the Use of Certain Conventional Weapons which May Be Deemed to Be Excessively Injurious or to Have Indiscriminate Effects.

[17] M. Matheson, 'Additional Protocol I as Expressions of Customary International Law', *American University Journal of International Law and Policy*, Vol. 2, No. 2 (Fall 1987), p. 415. For a summary of the list of provisions and discussion of push back from certain quarters, see also Solis, *The Law of Armed Conflict, International Humanitarian Law in War*, 3rd Edn, p. 120 note 64.

4   INTRODUCTION

granting of prisoner-of-war status to members of irregular forces (in Articles 44 and 45 of the Protocol); a prohibition on the right of mercenaries to prisoner-of-war status (in Article 47); the prohibition on reprisals (in Articles 51 and 52); and the prohibition on targeting dikes, dams, and nuclear power stations (in Article 56).

0.9   Several of these rules have indeed not crystallised as custom. But the prohibition on means or methods of warfare causing significant damage to the environment,[18] the rules governing mercenaries,[19] and the prohibition on targeting dikes, dams, and nuclear power stations[20] are each customary law today. Moreover, it is not certain that the US is able persuasively to claim persistent objector status to these three customary rules.

0.10 Much if not all of the Additional Protocol II governing certain non-international armed conflicts is also now reflected in customary law. In 1995, in its decision on jurisdiction in the *Tadić* case, the International Criminal Tribunal for the former Yugoslavia (ICTY) held that while the Additional Protocol II did not reflect, *in toto*, customary law, many of its provisions were already, or were becoming, custom: 'Many provisions of this Protocol can now be regarded as declaratory of existing rules or as having crystallised emerging rules of customary law or else as having been strongly instrumental in their evolution as general principles.'[21]

0.11 Today, however, it is probable that all of the substantive rules constitute customary international law. This pertains to the fundamental guarantees (in Article 4); the treatment and protection of those in detention (in Article 5); fair-trial rights (in Article 6); the care and protection of the wounded or sick (in Articles 7 and 8); the protection of medical personnel and units (in Articles 9, 10, and 11); the protection of the emblem (in Article 12, as amended by State practice, including the conclusion and content of the 2005 Additional Protocol III); the protection of the civilian population, especially in the conduct of hostilities (in Articles 13–17); and the provision of humanitarian relief (in Article 18). Moreover, custom has not limited the application of these rules to the confined jurisdictional scope of the Protocol (both material and geographical), but applies them to all non-international armed conflicts.[22]

0.12 The extent to which the 2005 Additional Protocol III constitutes customary law is, however, far more debatable. Adherence to the Protocol remains relatively low, with only 79

---

[18] International Committee of the Red Cross (ICRC) Customary IHL Rule 45: 'Causing Serious Damage to the Natural Environment', at: https://bit.ly/3qPPYUO.
[19] ICRC Customary IHL Rule 108: 'Mercenaries', at: https://bit.ly/32N3uQN.
[20] ICRC Customary IHL Rule 42: 'Works and Installations Containing Dangerous Forces', at: https://bit.ly/3FSYbh3.
[21] ICTY, *Prosecutor v. Tadić (aka 'Dule')*, Decision on the Defence Motion for Interlocutory Appeal on Jurisdiction (Appeals Chamber) (Case No. IT-94-1), 2 October 1995, at: https://bit.ly/2YR8mzd, para. 117.
[22] In its study of customary IHL, the ICRC states that: 'In particular, the gaps in the regulation of the conduct of hostilities in Additional Protocol II have largely been filled through State practice, which has led to the creation of rules parallel to those in Additional Protocol I, but applicable as customary law to non-international armed conflicts.' See J.-M. Henckaerts and L. Doswald-Beck (eds.), *Customary International Humanitarian Law: Volume 1: Rules*, Cambridge University Press, Cambridge, 2005, p. xxxv.

States Parties at the time of writing[23] (leaving a total of 118 States not party). The red crystal was the first new symbol recognised under IHL since the adoption of the red lion and sun in 1923, a special symbol for Iran that has since fallen into desuetude. That said, as Chapter 7 describes, the fundamental norms on the protective use of the emblem, whether that be the red cross, the red crescent, or even the red crystal, are firmly part of customary law. For instance, under the 1998 Rome Statute of the International Criminal Court, attacking buildings, material, medical units, and transport, or personnel where the distinctive emblems are used 'in conformity with international law' is a war crime under the Court's jurisdiction in both international and non-international armed conflict.[24]

The aim of the book

The aim of the book is not to provide an article-by-article commentary of the three Additional Protocols. Work ongoing within the ICRC will produce new and detailed commentaries to supplement the one it published in 1987, to add to those written by leading academics Michael Bothe, Karl Josef Partsch, and Waldemar Solf, first in 1982,[25] and then, in a second edition, in 2013.[26] Our conviction is that the principal gap lies in contextualising the interpretation and application of the Protocols in practice, bringing together how the experience of the intervening 55 years, including the jurisprudence of the tribunals of international criminal law and of the regional human rights courts, has shaped our understanding of the provisions in the three Additional Protocols.   **0.13**

The book therefore takes a thematic approach. It first considers the scope of application of the three Additional Protocols (for each is, in its own way, innovative). It then looks at the fundamental guarantees laid down in the first two Additional Protocols, these 'human rights treaties' in miniature as they are sometimes termed. The specific protection of women and of children is then addressed in turn. The chapter on the protection of detainees and prisoner-of-war status considers how the Protocols have   **0.14**

---

[23] Albania, Argentina, Armenia, Australia, Austria, Belarus, Belgium, Belize, Brazil, Bulgaria, Burkina Faso, Cameroon, Canada, Chile, Cook Islands, Costa Rica, Croatia, Cyprus, Czechia, Denmark, Dominican Republic, Ecuador, El Salvador, Estonia, Fiji, Finland, France, Georgia, Germany, Greece, Guatemala, Guyana, Honduras, Hungary, Iceland, Israel, Italy, Kazakhstan, Kenya, Kyrgyzstan, Latvia, Lesotho, Liechtenstein, Lithuania, Luxembourg, Madagascar, Mexico, Moldova, Monaco, Nauru, Netherlands, New Zealand, Nicaragua, North Macedonia, Norway, Palestine, Panama, Paraguay, Peru, Philippines, Poland, Portugal, Romania, San Marino, Serbia, Singapore, Slovakia, Slovenia, South Sudan, Spain, Suriname, Sweden, Switzerland, Timor-Leste, Uganda, Ukraine, United Kingdom, United States, and Uruguay.
[24] Art. 8(2)(b)(xxiv) and (e)(ii), Rome Statute of the International Criminal Court; adopted at Rome, 17 July 1998; entered into force, 1 July 2002. As of 1 May 2022, 123 States were party to the Rome Statute.
[25] M. Bothe, K. J. Partsch, and W. A. Solf, with M. Eaton, *New Rules for Victims of Armed Conflicts: Commentary on the Two 1977 Protocols Additional to the Geneva Conventions of 1949*, Martinus Nijhoff, The Hague, 1982.
[26] M. Bothe, K. J. Partsch, and W. A. Solf, with M. Eaton, *New Rules for Victims of Armed Conflicts: Commentary on the Two 1977 Protocols Additional to the Geneva Conventions of 1949*, 2nd Edn, Martinus Nijhoff, Leiden, 2013.

built on—sometimes in controversial manner—that afforded since 1949 by Geneva Convention III and Common Article 3.

0.15 Relief operations are treated in a distinct chapter as are the distinctive emblems that seek to protect humanitarian personnel. The fundamental rules governing the conduct of hostilities—distinction (both for objects and persons), proportionality in attack, and precautions in attack and defence—are all described, followed by analysis of the general and specific prohibitions on weapons and terrorism and acts of terror. Starvation and sieges—a form of warfare once believed to belong to another era, but whose resurgence is beyond doubt—complete this section. The final part of the book looks at the different obligations, mechanisms, and actors that seek to implement the law, at both national and international level. The obligations on States, armed groups, and the United Nations in this regard are each addressed, along with an assessment of the tireless work of the ICRC.

0.16 This book would not be complete without consideration of international criminal law, which has both sprung from IHL and contributed to our understanding of how, when, and to whom the Protocols apply. As authors, we bring to our research and analysis a range of professional experience: as advisers to States; to international organisations; and to armed groups. We have been present in numerous armed conflicts as witnesses and documentarians. This work is therefore by nature a subjective appreciation, albeit one firmly grounded in scholarship and academic rigour. We hope that the readers find it both valuable and interesting.

1

The Scope of Application of the Three Additional Protocols

Introduction

The two Additional Protocols of 1977[1] and the Third Additional Protocol of 2005[2] have a differing scope of application. Common to each of the Protocols, however, is that certain provisions must be implemented in peacetime while most are limited to a situation of armed conflict: international armed conflict as defined in the Additional Protocol I, and a particular form of non-international armed conflict, as conditioned by the terms of the Additional Protocol II. The Third Additional Protocol applies in all situations falling within the scope of either of the first two Protocols.   1.1

While the Additional Protocol I is broader in scope than is Article 2 common to the four Geneva Conventions of 1949,[3] the Additional Protocol II has a narrower scope of application to non-international armed conflict than does Article 3 common to the 1949 Geneva Conventions. The Third Additional Protocol, governing the emblem, applies to all armed conflicts without distinction. This chapter discusses the differences of application and their legal implications, looking at the scope of application of each of the three Protocols in turn.   1.2

The scope of application of the Additional Protocol I

As its formal title makes explicit, the 1977 Additional Protocol I seeks to protect the victims of international armed conflict. The Protocol, to which 174 States were party at the time of writing, explicitly applies to all situations referred to in Article 2 common to the four Geneva Conventions of 1949, thus including certain provisions that must be   1.3

---

[1] Protocol Additional to the Geneva Conventions of 12 August 1949, and relating to the Protection of Victims of International Armed Conflicts (Protocol I); adopted at Geneva, 8 June 1977; entered into force, 7 December 1978 (hereinafter, 1977 Additional Protocol I); and Protocol Additional to the Geneva Conventions of 12 August 1949, and relating to the Protection of Victims of Non-International Armed Conflicts (Protocol II); adopted at Geneva, 8 June 1977; entered into force, 7 December 1978 (hereinafter, 1977 Additional Protocol II).

[2] Protocol additional to the Geneva Conventions of 12 August 1949, and relating to the Adoption of an Additional Distinctive Emblem (Protocol III); adopted at Geneva, 8 December 2005; entered into force, 14 January 2007.

[3] See, e.g., Art. 2, Convention (IV) relative to the Protection of Civilian Persons in Time of War; adopted at Geneva, 12 August 1949; entered into force, 21 October 1950.

implemented in peacetime.[4] But, controversially, the Protocol extends the notion of an international armed conflict within its scope to 'armed conflicts in which peoples are fighting against colonial domination and alien occupation and against racist régimes in the exercise of their right of self-determination'.[5] Without this express provision, such conflicts would be of a non-international character. As Jann Kleffner has observed, the distinction between international and non-international armed conflict generally rests upon the parties to the armed conflict.[6]

Material scope of application

In peacetime

1.4 A number of provisions of the Additional Protocol I apply not only during a situation of international armed conflict governed by the four Geneva Conventions and the Protocol itself, but also at all other times. This is so, for instance, with respect to the duties to disseminate the rules set out in these instruments and to conduct a legal review of new weapons. Also in time of peace, legal advisers must be appointed to the armed forces. According to Article 82 of the Protocol, its States Parties must ensure that such jurists are available 'at all times' to 'advise military commanders'. This obligation binds each State Party from the time the Protocol enters into force for it. There is, however, no corresponding obligation for armed groups to have legal advisers.[7]

1.5 That there is a duty to disseminate international humanitarian law (IHL) rules during peacetime is overt: the States Parties shall, 'in time of peace as in time of armed conflict', disseminate the Conventions and the Protocol 'as widely as possible in their respective countries'. It is further provided that the parties must include the study of IHL 'in their programmes of military instruction' and encourage its study by the civilian population, 'so that those instruments may become known to the armed forces and to the civilian population'.[8] It is considered that armed groups, like States, also have the obligation to encourage the teaching and dissemination of IHL to their members as well as to the civilians under their control.[9]

1.6 In contrast, it is only implicit that the duty to review the legality of new weapons set out in the Protocol applies also in peacetime as it does during a situation of international armed conflict.[10] Under Article 36, each State Party is obligated to determine whether

---

[4] Art. 1(3), 1977 Additional Protocol I.
[5] Ibid., Art. 1(4).
[6] J. K. Kleffner, 'Scope of Application of International Humanitarian Law', Chap. 3 in D. Fleck (ed.), *The Handbook of International Humanitarian Law*, 4th Edn, Oxford University Press, Oxford, 2021, p. 51.
[7] ICRC Customary IHL Rule 141, 'Legal Advisers for Armed Forces', at: https://bit.ly/3n80O6D.
[8] Art. 85(1), 1977 Additional Protocol I.
[9] Article 19, 1977 Additional Protocol II, and ICRC Customary IHL Rule 142 'Instruction in International Humanitarian Law within Armed Forces', at: https://bit.ly/3vp8IMM; and ICRC Customary IHL Rule 143, 'Dissemination of International Humanitarian Law among the Civilian Population', at: https://bit.ly/3jcSfGe.
[10] International Committee of the Red Cross (ICRC), Commentary on Article 3 of the 1977 Additional Protocol I, 1987, at: https://bit.ly/3sPiPJg, para. 149(b).

the use of a new weapon or method of warfare it develop or acquires 'would, in some or all circumstances, be prohibited' by the Protocol or by 'any other rule of international law applicable' to it. The reference to any other rule of international law clearly encompasses disarmament law,[11] whose prohibitions on use similarly apply at all times, including both peacetime and situations of armed conflict.[12]

More problematic is the claim that the Geneva Conventions—and by logical extension, also the Additional Protocols—also directly regulate the transfer of weapons under certain circumstances. Thus, in its 2020 commentary on the duty in the 1949 Geneva Convention III 'to respect and to ensure respect for the present Convention in all circumstances', the International Committee of the Red Cross (ICRC) avers that States Parties shall 'refrain from transferring weapons if there is an expectation, based on facts or knowledge of past patterns, that such weapons would be used to violate the Conventions'.[13] The corresponding duty in the Additional Protocol I to respect and ensure respect for the Protocol in all circumstances is set out in its Article 1(1). If correct, this would amount to incorporating an arms control prohibition on transfer into an IHL instrument. State practice favouring such a progressive interpretation appears, however, to be lacking.[14]

1.7

That said, compliance with IHL by a recipient of arms can certainly be a central factor in adjudging whether a transfer is permissible under international law. In this regard, the 2013 United Nations Arms Trade Treaty—an arms control agreement, to which 111 States were party at the time of writing[15]—applies at all times to regulate arms transfers, whether during peacetime or amid any armed conflict. The Treaty prohibits the granting by a State Party of authorisation to any actor within its jurisdiction to transfer conventional weapons or associated ammunition where it is known that they 'would be used' in the commission of 'grave breaches of the Geneva Conventions of 1949, attacks directed against civilian objects or civilians protected as such, or other war crimes as defined by international agreements' to which the transferring State is a party.[16] The Treaty further prohibits the granting of authorisation for a proposed export of conventional weapons where there is an overriding risk that they would be used to 'commit or facilitate a serious violation of international humanitarian law'.[17] Each State Party is obligated to 'establish and maintain a national control system' in order to implement

1.8

---

[11] ICRC, Commentary on Article 36 of the 1977 Additional Protocol I, 1987, at: https://bit.ly/3sMfWsR, para. 1472.

[12] See, e.g., S. Casey-Maslen and T. Vestner, *A Guide to International Disarmament Law*, Routledge, Abingdon, 2019, paras. 1.4, 4.1.

[13] ICRC, Commentary on Article 1 of the 1949 Geneva Convention III, 2020, at: https://bit.ly/3jivgKH, para. 195. See similarly M. Sassòli, *International Humanitarian Law Rules, Controversies, and Solutions to Problems Arising in Warfare*, Edward Elgar Publishing, Cheltenham, 2019, para. 10.97, pp. 528–29.

[14] It is also not the case that the duty to ensure respect obligates States Parties to the Geneva Conventions and/or Additional Protocols to ensure respect by all States. H. Duffy, *The 'War on Terror' and the Framework of International Law*, 2nd Edn, Cambridge University Press, Cambridge, 2015, p. 384.

[15] As of 1 May 2022. See the updated list in the UN Treaty Collection, at: http://bit.ly/2pDyXBm.

[16] Art. 6(3), Arms Trade Treaty; adopted at New York, 2 April 2013; entered into force, 24 December 2014.

[17] Ibid., Art. 7(1)(b)(i) and (3).

the provisions of the Treaty.[18] This covers transfers by State entities as well as corporate (non-State) actors within the jurisdiction of a State Party.

Military occupation

1.9 The Additional Protocol I applies to situations of 'partial or total' military occupation of a State by a State Party to the Protocol. Such belligerent occupation is a form of international armed conflict.[19] The rules of *jus ad bellum* determine whether the territorial State has validly consented to the presence of foreign military forces.[20] This is the case whether or not the occupation is actively opposed by the territorial State by military means. Thus, in the terms of Article 2 common to the four Geneva Conventions and also the Additional Protocol I, an occupation exists under IHL 'even if the said occupation meets with no armed resistance'.

1.10 At the time of writing, the following States Parties to the Additional Protocol I were occupying foreign territory: Armenia (with respect to territory in Azerbaijan); Morocco (with respect to territory in Western Sahara); the Russian Federation (with respect to territory in Georgia, Moldova, and Ukraine); and, more controversially,[21] Saudi Arabia and the United Arab Emirates (with respect to territory in Yemen).[22] The application of the pertinent rules under the Protocol is irrespective of the legality of the occupation under *jus ad bellum*. Further, even if an occupying State is not a party to the Additional Protocol I, it will nonetheless be bound by the rules codified therein that are of a customary nature. This would include, for instance, the duty in the Protocol to respect the remains of persons who died for reasons related to the occupation or during detention that was linked to the occupation.[23]

---

[18] Ibid., Art. 5(1).
[19] Elements of Crimes under the Rome Statute of the International Criminal Court, reproduced from Official Records of the Assembly of States Parties to the Rome Statute of the International Criminal Court, First Session, New York, 3–10 September 2002, note 34.
[20] S. Casey-Maslen, *Jus ad Bellum: The Law on Inter-State Use of Force*, Hart Publishing, Oxford, 2020, pp. 52–54 and 167–69.
[21] This position is not generally accepted, as some consider the Security Council's view of the legitimate executive of Yemen (in 2015) as authoritative. See UN Security Council Resolution 2216, adopted on 14 April 2015 by 14 votes to 0 with 1 abstention (Russia), eighth preambular para. But, absent an act of aggression, the issue under *jus ad bellum* is rather who has effective control over the country. In Afghanistan in 2001, only three States—and certainly not the UN Security Council, which described it as a 'faction'—had recognised the Taliban as the government of Afghanistan. See UN Security Council Resolution 1333, adopted on 19 December 2000 by 13 votes to 0 with 2 abstentions (China and Malaysia), seventh preambular para. Yet the US attack after 9/11 was undoubtedly an international armed conflict. Indeed, for example, Article 13(3) of the 1949 Geneva Convention I extends protection to 'Members of regular armed forces who profess allegiance to a Government or an authority not recognized by the Detaining Power'.
[22] For details on the extent of Saudi occupation of Yemen as of May 2021, see B. Riedel, 'Saudi Arabia and the UAE Consolidating Strategic Positions in Yemen's East and Islands', The Brookings Institution, Washington, D.C., 28 May 2021, at: https://brook.gs/3yiQpIW.
[23] Art. 34(1), 1977 Additional Protocol I. Under Rule 113 of the ICRC Study of Customary IHL: 'Each party to the conflict must take all possible measures to prevent the dead from being despoiled. Mutilation of dead bodies is prohibited.' ICRC Study of Customary IHL Rule 113: 'Treatment of the Dead', at: https://bit.ly/35CDtm9.

Active international armed conflict

1.11 Where two States Parties to the Additional Protocol I are engaged in an international armed conflict, the provisions of the Protocol will apply both to the conduct of hostilities and to the treatment of persons within their power. Under its 1995 decision on jurisdiction in the *Tadić* case, the Appeals Chamber of the International Criminal Tribunal for the former Yugoslavia (ICTY) issued a widely cited definition of when an international armed conflict exists—'whenever there is a resort to armed force between States'.[24]

1.12 While the minimum threshold of violence for such a conflict to exist is not settled in law, and the so-called 'first shot theory' is contested,[25] the requisite extent of use of force is certainly low.[26] The United States (US), for instance, interprets the notion of armed conflict in Common Article 2 of the 1949 Geneva Conventions to include 'any situation in which there is hostile action between the armed forces of two parties, regardless of the duration, intensity or scope of the fighting'.[27] It was reported that, on 3 January 2022, the border forces of two States Parties to the 1977 Additional Protocol—Afghanistan and Turkmenistan—clashed for several hours. According to the local population on the Afghan side of the border, the shooting between Turkmen and Taliban forces persisted for several hours, with Taliban fighters firing rockets at Turkmen positions during the clashes.[28] This could amount to a short-lived international armed conflict governed by the Protocol.

1.13 In the same way as applies under the Geneva Conventions, however, it is not necessary for the application of the Protocol that a State Party which has been attacked must respond in some manner by military means for an armed conflict to be occurring. That said, Solis believes that the unlawful use of force by Russian military operatives against civilians in Salisbury in 2018 involving a chemical means of warfare did not amount to an armed conflict. In his words, 'They are domestic crimes, rather than war crimes.'[29] That finding is, however, open to question. The better view is that they were the opening salvo in a short-lived international armed conflict between Russia and the United Kingdom (UK) as the two opposing parties.

---

[24] ICTY, *Prosecutor v. Tadić (aka 'Dule')*, Decision on the Defence Motion for Interlocutory Appeal on Jurisdiction (Appeals Chamber) (Case No. IT-94-1), 2 October 1995, at: https://bit.ly/2YR8mzd, para. 70. See generally also ICRC, 'How is the term "armed conflict" defined in international humanitarian law?', ICRC Opinion Paper, Geneva, March 2008; and S. Vité, 'Typology of Armed Conflicts in International Humanitarian Law: Legal Concepts and Actual Situations', *International Review of the Red Cross*, Vol. 91, No. 873 (March 2009), pp. 69–94.

[25] G. D. Solis, *The Law of Armed Conflict: International Humanitarian Law in War*, 3rd Edn, Cambridge University Press, Cambridge, 2021, p. 132. See also Kleffner, 'Scope of Application of International Humanitarian Law', p. 53.

[26] Ibid.; and see also Y. Dinstein, *The Conduct of Hostilities under the Law of International Armed Conflict*, 3rd Edn, Cambridge University Press, Cambridge, 2016, pp. 1–2, para. 2.

[27] US Department of Defense, *Department of Defense Law of War Manual*, Washington, D.C., June 2015 (Updated December 2016), § 3.4.2.

[28] B. Pannier, 'First Firefight: Turkmen, Taliban Engage in Border Shoot-Out', *Ghandara*, 5 January 2022, at: https://bit.ly/3qNuVC6.

[29] Solis, *The Law of Armed Conflict: International Humanitarian Law in War*, 3rd Edn, p. 624.

12   APPLICATION OF THE THREE ADDITIONAL PROTOCOLS

1.14   The ongoing hostilities in Yemen between Houthi armed forces and the armed forces of Saudi Arabia is a long-running international armed conflict to which the Additional Protocol I is fully applicable, with both States having adhered to it. In contrast, beginning in September 2020, Armenia and Azerbaijan fought a six-week-long armed conflict over territory occupied by Armenian forces within Azerbaijan. Armenia was a State Party to the Additional Protocol I (having adhered in 1993) but Azerbaijan was not. The Protocol was thus not formally applicable to that international armed conflict, although the many provisions therein that codify customary law were binding also on Azerbaijan.

1.15   There is an unresolved issue of classification of conflict when one State targets members of a non-State armed group on the territory of another State. For Sassòli, there is only a non-international armed conflict in play between the foreign State and the armed group.[30] This is, however, problematic. It implies that even if an act of aggression has been perpetrated by the foreign State under the rules of *jus ad bellum* (which can occur through bombardment of another State under the customary law definition),[31] no armed conflict exists between the two States. This does not appear logical, much less desirable. Moreover, the conditions may not be in place for a non-international armed conflict between the foreign State and the non-State armed group, either for want of intensity or of organisation of the group (or both).

Proxy armed conflicts

1.16   As determined by international tribunals, an international armed conflict exists also when proxy armed groups act as an agent of a foreign State in an armed conflict with a State. The 'overall control' test proposed by the ICTY in the *Tadić* case in 1999 is widely considered authoritative in this regard. In the words of the Tribunal: 'In order to attribute the acts of a military or paramilitary group to a State, it must be proved that the State wields overall control over the group, not only by equipping and financing the group, but also by coordinating or helping in the general planning of its military activity.'[32]

1.17   This test for the existence of a proxy international armed conflict has been endorsed to some degree by the International Court of Justice (ICJ). In its 2007 judgment in the Bosnian genocide case, the Court declared that 'it may well be that the test is

---

[30] Sassòli, *International Humanitarian Law Rules, Controversies, and Solutions to Problems Arising in Warfare*, paras. 6.09–6.11, pp. 171–72.
[31] Art. 3(b), Definition of Aggression, annexed to United Nations General Assembly Resolution 3314 (XXIX); adopted without a vote on 14 December 1974 (hereinafter, 1974 Definition of Aggression). See also Art. 8 *bis* (2)(b), Rome Statute of the International Criminal Court; adopted at Rome, 17 July 1998; entered into force, 1 July 2002.
[32] ICTY, *Prosecutor v. Tadić (aka 'Dule')*, Judgment (Appeals Chamber) (Case No. IT-94-1-A), 15 July 1999, para. 131.

applicable and suitable'.³³ More wholehearted in its support has been the International Criminal Court:

> As regards the necessary degree of control of another State over an armed group acting on its behalf, the Trial Chamber has concluded that the 'overall control' test is the correct approach. This will determine whether an armed conflict not of an international character may have become internationalised due to the involvement of armed forces acting on behalf of another State.³⁴

The Court further recalled in its judgment in the *Lubanga* case that a State 'may exercise the required degree of control when it "has a role in organising, coordinating or planning the military actions of the military group, in addition to financing, training and equipping or providing operational support to that group" '.³⁵

A different, higher threshold exists for State responsibility under international law for the unlawful acts of the armed group. In this regard, the ICJ has maintained that its 'effective control' test, which it first expounded in 1986 in its judgment on the merits in the *Nicaragua* case, represents the state of international law. Therein, the Court determined, 'it would in principle have to be proved that that State had effective control of the military or paramilitary operations in the course of which the alleged violations were committed'.³⁶ Such effective control is manifested for the purpose of State responsibility in the foreign State giving instructions 'in respect of each operation in which the alleged violations occurred, not generally in respect of the overall actions taken by the persons or groups of persons having committed the violations'.³⁷

1.18

The ICJ reaffirmed its 'effective control' standard in its 2007 judgment in the Bosnian genocide case.³⁸ The differential with the overall control test—and the awkward fragmentation of international legal order—has potentially unfortunate consequences. Thus, there may be actions by a proxy armed group in the context of an international armed conflict that violate IHL and even, in certain circumstances, amount to war crimes, but for which the foreign State which is party to the armed conflict has no responsibility in international law. This is so, even though the armed group is acting as its proxy. Where does that leave the obligation on that State to respect and ensure respect for IHL? Despite the difficulties this bifurcation of the law generates, the ICJ has sought to downplay the discrepancy between the two tests, claiming in this regard that:

1.19

---

[33] International Court of Justice, *Case Concerning Application of the Convention on the Prevention and Punishment of the Crime of Genocide (Bosnia and Herzegovina v. Serbia and Montenegro)*, Judgment (Merits), 26 February 2007, para. 404.
[34] International Criminal Court, *Prosecutor v. Thomas Lubanga Dyilo*, Judgment (Trial Chamber I) (Case No. ICC-01/04-01/06), 14 March 2012, para. 541.
[35] Ibid.
[36] International Court of Justice, *Case Concerning Military and Paramilitary Activities in and against Nicaragua (Nicaragua v. United States of America)*, Judgment (Merits), 27 June 1986, para. 115.
[37] International Court of Justice, *Case Concerning Application of the Convention on the Prevention and Punishment of the Crime of Genocide (Bosnia and Herzegovina v. Serbia and Montenegro)*, Judgment, 26 February 2007, para. 400.
[38] Ibid., paras. 399–400.

[t]he degree and nature of a State's involvement in an armed conflict on another State's territory which is required for the conflict to be characterized as international, can very well, and without logical inconsistency, differ from the degree and nature of involvement required to give rise to that State's responsibility for a specific act committed in the course of the conflict.[39]

National liberation struggles

1.20 In its Article 1(4), the Protocol extends the notion of international armed conflict within its scope to those armed conflicts in which 'peoples are fighting against colonial domination and alien occupation and against racist régimes in the exercise of their right of self-determination'.[40] The authority representing such a people 'may undertake' to apply the Geneva Conventions and the Additional Protocol I in an armed conflict 'by means of a unilateral declaration addressed to the depositary'.[41] If accepted, the binding effect on all the parties to the relevant conflict is 'immediate'.[42] The incorporation of these provisions was highly contested during the elaboration of the Protocol, especially by those States which felt themselves either directly or potentially targeted by it at the time: Israel, South Africa, the UK, and the US, in particular. The extension of the scope of international armed conflict to violent national liberation struggles does not constitute a rule of customary international law.[43] This 'fairly bold innovation' in the law[44] may, however, come to be considered *de lege ferenda*.

1.21 The provision in the Additional Protocol I does not appear to apply automatically to the UK. Upon its ratification of the Protocol in 1998, the UK government made a reservation to the salient provisions in the Protocol whereby:

> The United Kingdom will not, in relation to any situation in which it is itself involved, consider itself bound in consequence of any declaration purporting to be made under paragraph 3 of Article 96 unless the United Kingdom shall have expressly recognised that it has been made by a body which is genuinely an authority representing a people engaged in an armed conflict of the type to which Article 1, paragraph 4, applies.[45]

Thus, the depositary (Switzerland) may consider that a declaration is validly made (and thus that an international armed conflict exists) but the UK may take a different view.

1.22 To date, the provision has been effectively applied in only one instance. On 21 June 2015, the Polisario Front made a declaration on behalf of the people of Western Sahara that it undertook to apply the Conventions and the Additional Protocol to the conflict

---

[39] Ibid., para. 405.
[40] Art. 1(4), 1977 Additional Protocol I. See similarly Art. 7(4), 1980 Convention on Certain Conventional Weapons.
[41] Chapeau to Art. 96(3), 1977 Additional Protocol I.
[42] Ibid., Art. 96(3)(a) to (c).
[43] Dinstein, *The Conduct of Hostilities under the Law of International Armed Conflict*, 3rd Edn, p. 37, para. 103.
[44] Solis, *The Law of Armed Conflict: International Humanitarian Law in War*, 3rd Edn, p. 111.
[45] Declaration of the United Kingdom of 28 January 1998, text available at: http://bit.ly/2PC0crS.

between it and the Kingdom of Morocco. This was the first time that the Swiss Federal Council, as depositary of the Protocol, had accepted such a declaration by a national liberation movement and a non-State entity under international law.[46] (The Sahrawi Arab Democratic Republic is a member State of the African Union but is not recognised as a State by Switzerland[47] or indeed by the Secretary-General of the United Nations (UN).) But to the extent there is an ongoing armed conflict between Morocco and the Polisario Front—a fact denied by Morocco[48]—that conflict has been international in character under the Additional Protocol I since its formal recognition. This legal regulation would encompass the belligerent occupation by Morocco of the territory of Western Sahara.

Geographical scope of application

Although it is not made explicit therein, there is no geographical limit on the scope of application of the Additional Protocol I.[49] This is in stark contrast to both the situation with respect to the Additional Protocol II and non-international armed conflict more broadly. Thus, when two States Parties clash militarily, it does not matter whether they do so on metropolitan or non-metropolitan sovereign territory, on the territory of a foreign State, in the air, on the high seas, in outer space, or even in cyberspace. This is so, despite the seemingly limiting decision of the ICTY in the *Tadić* case, wherein it affirmed that IHL 'continues to apply in the whole territory of the warring States'.[50] For, as the US Department of Defense observes, 'law of war treaties and the customary law of war are understood to regulate the conduct of hostilities, regardless of where they are conducted'.[51] This statement holds good for all international armed conflict.[52]

1.23

Temporal scope of application

The Additional Protocol I is, however, explicit as to the temporal scope of its application. It begins once a situation covered by its Article 1 exists,[53] and persists through to the 'general close of military operations'.[54] Such a general close of military operations may occur after the 'cessation of active hostilities' referred to in Article 118 of the 1949

1.24

---

[46] See K. Fortin, 'Unilateral Declaration by Polisario under API Accepted by Swiss Federal Council', 2 September 2015, at: http://bit.ly/2NcA0lb.
[47] 'People from Western Sahara Deemed Stateless in Switzerland', Swissinfo.ch, 20 August 2021, at: https://bit.ly/3yoQqLe.
[48] A. Clapham, *War*, Oxford University Press, Oxford, 2021, p. 253.
[49] See *contra* Kleffner, 'Scope of Application of International Humanitarian Law', pp. 64–65.
[50] ICTY, *Prosecutor v. Tadić*, Decision on the Defence Motion for Interlocutory Appeal on Jurisdiction (Appeals Chamber), para. 70.
[51] US Department of Defense, *Department of Defense Law of War Manual*, Washington, D.C., June 2015 (Updated December 2016), § 14.10.2.2.
[52] Solis, *The Law of Armed Conflict: International Humanitarian Law in War*, 3rd Edn, p. 173 (sidebar).
[53] Art. 3(a), 1977 Additional Protocol I.
[54] Ibid., Art. 3(b).

Geneva Convention III: 'although a ceasefire, even a tacit ceasefire, may be sufficient for that Convention, military operations can often continue after such a ceasefire, even without confrontations.'[55]

1.25 In the case of occupied territories, the relevant provisions of the Protocol apply *in toto* until the end of the occupation. This goes beyond the temporal scope of application of the 1949 Geneva Convention IV.[56] In addition, the protection afforded to persons detained in connection with the armed conflict (including a belligerent occupation) continues until their final release, repatriation, or re-establishment, if any of these should take place thereafter.[57] As the ICRC clarifies, the 'expression "final release" means the end of captivity, detention, or other measures restricting a person's liberty as a result of armed conflict or occupation; "repatriation" refers to the return to the country of which a person is a national, or in some cases, to the country where he was normally resident; "re-establishment" means being established in another country, for whatever reason'.[58]

The scope of application of the Additional Protocol II

The existence of a non-international armed conflict

1.26 The Additional Protocol II, to which 169 States were party at the time of writing, applies to certain non-international armed conflicts only. It is thus narrower in scope than is the application of Article 3 common to the four 1949 Geneva Conventions.[59] It applies to all armed conflicts which are not subject to the Additional Protocol I and which take place 'in the territory' of a State Party 'between its armed forces and dissident armed forces or other organized armed groups which, under responsible command, exercise such control over a part of its territory as to enable them to carry out sustained and concerted military operations and to implement this Protocol'.[60]

1.27 The Protocol clarifies that 'situations of internal disturbances and tensions, such as riots, isolated and sporadic acts of violence and other acts of a similar nature' are not armed conflicts. This interpretive statement pertains to the definition of a non-international armed conflict in general and stands as a rule of customary law.[61] The ICRC explains

---

[55] ICRC, Commentary on Article 3 of the 1977 Additional Protocol I, 1987, para. 153.
[56] According to Article 6 of the 1949 Geneva Convention IV: 'In the case of occupied territory, the application of the present Convention shall cease one year after the general close of military operations; however, the Occupying Power shall be bound, for the duration of the occupation, to the extent that such Power exercises the functions of government in such territory, by the provisions of the following Articles of the present Convention: 1 to 12, 27, 29 to 34, 47, 49, 51, 52, 53, 59, 61 to 77, 143.'
[57] Art. 3(b), 1977 Additional Protocol I.
[58] ICRC, Commentary on Article 3 of the 1977 Additional Protocol I, 1987, para. 159.
[59] Y. Dinstein, *Non-International Armed Conflicts in International Law*, 2nd Edn, Cambridge University Press, Cambridge, 2021, p. 56, para. 146.
[60] Art. 1(1), 1977 Additional Protocol II.
[61] Dinstein, *Non-International Armed Conflicts in International Law*, 2nd Edn, p. 25, para. 66. See also Art. 8(2)(d), Rome Statute of the International Criminal Court; adopted at Rome, 17 July 1998; entered into force, 1 July 2002 (hereinafter, Rome Statute).

that while the terms used in this exclusionary provision are not formally defined in the Protocol (or indeed in international law more generally), the notion of internal disturbances and tensions includes violent demonstrations that occur 'without a concerted plan from the outset' and acts of violence that are not 'military operations carried out by armed forces or armed groups', as well as large-scale arrests of people 'for their activities or opinions'.[62]

Article 3 common to the four Geneva Conventions of 1949 omits to define what constitutes an 'armed conflict not of an international character'. This was the result of the inability of the negotiators to agree upon what the threshold—and associated criteria—should be. As is well known, in its 1995 decision in the *Tadić* case, the Appeals Chamber of the ICTY described such a non-international armed conflict as a situation where there was 'protracted armed violence between governmental authorities and organized armed groups or between such groups within a State'.[63] The use of the term 'protracted', with its ordinary meaning of long duration, was unfortunate. Indeed, despite a certain variance in its jurisprudence, the ICTY subsequently clarified that the term actually meant 'intense' violence rather than prolonged fighting: 'The test applied by the Appeals Chamber to the existence of an armed conflict for the purposes of the rules contained in Common Article 3 focuses on two aspects of a conflict: the intensity of the conflict and the organization of the parties to the conflict.'[64] This test may well reflect customary law. **1.28**

That said, not all States agree with this assessment. Germany, for instance, in its Defence Ministry's 2013 law of armed conflict manual, adds duration to the criteria for each non-international armed conflict, declaring that the violence must not only be intense but shall also be 'sustained' at such a level for a prolonged period of time.[65] This additional criterion does not appear to reflect the state of the law.[66] That said, of course a certain minimum duration at a high level of intensity is necessary given that 'isolated and sporadic acts of violence' are expressly excluded from the notion of an armed conflict.[67] **1.29**

Thus, if international law as it stands is applied rigorously, US prosecutorial affirmations, before the military commission judging Khalid Sheikh Mohammed and others, whereby an armed conflict existed between the US and al-Qaeda prior to the 9/11 attacks, will be exceptionally challenging to uphold. The intensity criterion is simply **1.30**

---

[62] ICRC, Commentary on Article 1 of the 1977 Additional Protocol II, 1987, para. 4474, at: https://bit.ly/3yi1kSV.
[63] ICTY, *Prosecutor v. Tadić (aka 'Dule')*, Decision on the Defence Motion for Interlocutory Appeal on Jurisdiction (Appeals Chamber), para. 70.
[64] ICTY, *Prosecutor v. Tadić (aka 'Dule')*, Judgment (Trial Chamber) (Case No. IT-94-1-T), 7 May 1997, para. 562.
[65] German Ministry of Defence, *Law of Armed Conflict Manual*, Joint Service Regulation (ZDv) 15/2, Berlin, 2013, para. 210.
[66] M. Schmitt (ed.), *Tallinn Manual on the International Law Applicable to Cyber Warfare*, 1st Edn, Cambridge University Press, Cambridge, 2013, Commentary on Rule 23, para. 6.
[67] Art. 1(2), 1977 Additional Protocol II.

not met based on the facts, while Helen Duffy also questions whether al-Qaeda fulfilled the 'organised' criterion for an armed group (discussed below).[68] In its 2006 judgment in *Hamdan v. Rumsfeld*, the US Supreme Court did 'not question the Government's position that the war commenced with the events of September 11, 2001'.[69] In his judgment for the majority, Justice Stevens observed that Justice Thomas in his dissenting opinion 'would treat Osama bin Laden's 1996 declaration of jihad against Americans as the inception of the war.... But even the Government does not go so far'.[70]

1.31 In December 2017, Sean Watts testified as an expert witness on behalf of the defence in the case against Khalid Sheikh Mohammed. Professor Watts testified that the existence of a non-international armed conflict was an objective analysis, and that neither the opinions of the State nor of the non-state party to an alleged conflict would normally be given much weight. In responding to a question from defence counsel on the violence between the US and al-Qaeda prior to the 9/11 attacks, he stated that it was 'almost quintessentially sporadic' and that few operations involved what would typically be considered combat. From an intensity perspective, Watts assessed that an armed conflict did not exist between the US and al-Qaeda until October 2001 when US forces entered Afghanistan.[71] Duffy avers that the 9/11 attacks amounted to an armed attack (for the purposes of *jus ad bellum* and specifically giving rise to the right of self-defence) but not an armed conflict (for the purposes of the application of IHL).[72]

1.32 After 9/11, and considering its forcible response, the US Government initially considered the global 'War on Terror' as an international armed conflict, but later accepted that it was engaged in a non-international armed conflict.[73] Conflict in Afghanistan with al-Qaeda from October 2001 did meet the necessary criteria for a non-international armed conflict, while the conflict between the US and the Taliban was international in character. But the unconstrained geographical scope of the War on Terror more broadly, as well as the lack of regular and intense hostilities with a non-State armed group, make the US Government's legal analysis of a global non-international armed conflict wholly unpersuasive.

1.33 In any armed conflict, it is assumed that a State armed force is sufficiently 'organised', but this is not necessarily the case with respect to a non-State armed group. Thus, an armed group must demonstrate certain qualities of an armed force, such as a functioning hierarchy—a chain of command—and must possess a reasonable degree of

---

[68] H. Duffy, *The 'War on Terror' and the Framework of International Law*, 2nd Edn, Cambridge University Press, Cambridge, 2015, pp. 135 and 396–99, although see also p. 394.
[69] US Supreme Court, *Hamdan v. Rumsfeld*, 548 US 557, 599 note 31 (2006). Solis affirms this claim but without adducing evidence. Solis, *The Law of Armed Conflict: International Humanitarian Law in War*, 3rd Edn, p. 539.
[70] US Supreme Court, *Hamdan v. Rumsfeld*, 548 US 557, 599 note 31 (2006).
[71] C. Mirasola, 'Last Week in the Military Commissions, 12/4-12/8: Was There an Armed Conflict Pre-9/11?', Lawfare, 14 December 2017, at: https://bit.ly/3AEl0Dq.
[72] H. Duffy, *The 'War on Terror' and the Framework of International Law*, 2nd Edn, Cambridge University Press, Cambridge, 2015, p. 348, but cf. also pp. 394–95.
[73] M. Sassòli, *International Humanitarian Law Rules, Controversies, and Solutions to Problems Arising in Warfare*, Edward Elgar Publishing, Cheltenham, 2019, para. 10.26, p. 498.

logistical capacity in addition to the ability to conduct military operations. In this regard, for instance, the Additional Protocol II refers to an organised armed group being 'under responsible command'.[74] Other criteria proposed by the ICTY as being relevant to the determination of whether a group is sufficiently organised are less persuasive—in particular, the ability of the group to 'speak with one voice'.[75] There is also no requirement that the members of an organised armed group wear a military uniform, although the existence and use of a uniform is assuredly evidence of a certain level of group organisation.

1.34 The requisite intensity of the violence is similarly not capable of simple definition. The International Criminal Court has recalled that the 'essential criterion is that it go beyond "isolated or sporadic acts of violence"', consonant with the exclusionary provision set out in the Additional Protocol II.[76] The *travaux préparatoires* of the negotiation of Common Article 3 support a relatively high threshold. During the negotiations, Monaco, which had a significant role in the drafting of the provision, noted the importance of distinguishing between a rebellion and a 'local uprising'.[77] Accordingly, in 1952, in his commentary on the 1949 Geneva Convention I, Jean Pictet wrote that an 'unorganised and short-lived insurrection' does not constitute an armed conflict.[78]

1.35 In its 2008 judgment in the *Haradinaj* case, the ICTY averred that indicative factors for an armed conflict include 'the number, duration and intensity of individual confrontations'.[79] In its judgment at trial in the *Mrkšić* case a year earlier, an ICTY Trial Chamber had referred to 'the seriousness of attacks and potential increase in armed clashes, their spread over territory and over a period of time'.[80] This notion of combat—direct conflict between two opposing armed groups—is important, helping to distinguish a situation of armed conflict from terrorist and counterterrorism activities.[81] Thus, in its judgment in the *Limaj* case, which concerned the situation within Kosovo, a Trial Chamber of the ICTY observed that by the end of May 1998 Kosovo Liberation Army (KLA) units

---

[74] Art. 1(1), 1977 Additional Protocol II.
[75] See ICTY, *Prosecutor v. Boškoski and Tarčulovski*, Judgment (Trial Chamber) (Case No. IT-04-82-T), 10 July 2008, paras. 199–203.
[76] International Criminal Court, *Prosecutor v. Jean-Pierre Bemba Gombo*, Judgment (Trial Chamber III) (Case No. ICC-01/05-01/08), 21 March 2016, para. 140.
[77] *Final Record of the Diplomatic Conference of Geneva of 1949*, Vol. II, Section B, Bern, 1949, p. 45.
[78] J. Pictet, Commentary on Article 3 of the 1949 Geneva Convention I, ICRC, 1952, at: https://bit.ly/3ykgpmZ, p. 50. In the ICRC's 2016 commentary on the provision, while the organisation seemed to row back on the criteria Pictet had listed as being 'merely indicative', this affirmation appeared to hold fast. ICRC, Commentary on Article 3 of the 1949 Geneva Convention I, 2016, at: https://bit.ly/3mEB2It, para. 420.
[79] ICTY, *Prosecutor v. Haradinaj, Balaj, and Brahimaj*, Judgment (Trial Chamber) (Case No. IT-04-84-T), 3 April 2008, para. 49.
[80] ICTY, *Prosecutor v. Mrkšić, Radić, and Šljivančin*, Judgment (Trial Chamber II) (Case No. IT-95-13/1-T), 27 September 2007, para. 407.
[81] J. K. Kleffner, 'The Legal Fog of an Illusion: Three Reflections on "Organization" and "Intensity" as Criteria for the Temporal Scope of the Law of Non-International Armed Conflict', *International Legal Studies*, Vol. 95 (2019), pp. 161–78, at p. 169; see also S. Casey-Maslen with S. Haines, *Hague Law Interpreted: The Conduct of Hostilities under the Law of Armed Conflict*, Hart Publishing, Oxford, 2018, p. 61.

'were constantly engaged in armed clashes with substantial Serbian forces' across the province.[82]

1.36 It is uncertain whether attacks perpetrated only in cyberspace could amount to an armed conflict, at least one that is non-international in character. Solis agrees with the assertion that cyber operations by non-State actors, 'absent accompanying kinetic attacks', would not amount to a non-international armed conflict.[83]

The additional criteria under the Additional Protocol II

Dissident armed forces or organised armed groups fighting against the State

1.37 Under a non-international armed conflict falling within the bounds of Common Article 3, one organised armed group may be a party to an armed conflict when it is fighting against another organised armed group (if, of course, the violence between them is sufficiently intense). This is not the case under the Additional Protocol II. The scope of application is expressly limited to those armed conflicts that take place in the territory of a State Party 'between its armed forces and dissident armed forces or other organized armed groups'.[84] Dissident armed forces are 'breakaway military units that have mutinied against the incumbent Government'.[85] Such a scenario may occur through a *coup d'état*, but an 'episodic mutiny hatched up by some disgruntled officers' will not be sufficient to meet the threshold in the Protocol.[86]

The armed group must exercise control over part of the territory of a State Party

1.38 Common Article 3 to the 1949 Geneva Conventions does not require territorial control by an armed group for its application. In contrast, the Additional Protocol II expressly demands that control be exercised over part of a State Party's territory such that the group is capable of mounting 'sustained and concerted' military operations and implementing the provisions of the Protocol. With respect to this latter element, it is not correct to infer that the ability to respect and ensure respect for IHL is dependent on territorial control.[87] Moreover, whether or not the opposition armed group in fact respects IHL is also not determinant. It is the *ability* to do that counts.[88] The extent of territory controlled is not the critical factor; rather, it is the quality of control that is

---

[82] ICTY, *Prosecutor v. Limaj, Bala, and Musliu*, Judgment (Trial Chamber) (Case No. IT-03-66-T), 30 November 2005, para. 172 [note omitted].
[83] Solis, *The Law of Armed Conflict: International Humanitarian Law in War*, 3rd Edn, p. 541, citing M. Schmitt, 'Law of Cyber Warfare: Quo Vadis?', Stanford Law and Policy Review, Vol. 25, No. 2 (June 2014), pp. 269–99, p. 292, at: https://stanford.io/3sWsJLc.
[84] Art. 1(1), 1977 Additional Protocol II.
[85] Dinstein, *Non-International Armed Conflicts in International Law*, 2nd Edn, p. 57, para. 150. See also S. Junod, 'Additional Protocol II: History and Scope', American University Law Review, Vol. 33 (1983), p. 30, at p. 36.
[86] Dinstein, *Non-International Armed Conflicts in International Law*, 2nd Edn, p. 57, para. 151.
[87] Casey-Maslen with Haines, *Hague Law Interpreted: The Conduct of Hostilities under the Law of Armed Conflict*, p. 64.
[88] Dinstein, *Non-International Armed Conflicts in International Law*, 2nd Edn, p. 65, para. 177.

exercised that is determinant.[89] And, as Dinstein further observes, there may be territorial 'ebb and flow' during a non-international armed conflict. What is 'indispensable' to fulfil the second criterion under the Protocol is that the armed opposition group retains control 'over some territory at any given time'.[90]

The ability to conduct sustained and concerted military operations

The Protocol only applies to situations where the relevant organised armed groups are able to exercise such control over a part of the territory of a State Party 'as to enable them to carry out sustained and concerted military operations' against its armed forces.[91] Military operations is a broad term, certainly one that is more expansive than is the notion of combat that occurs within the conduct of hostilities. According to the ICRC, albeit in relation to an interpretation of the term when employed in the Additional Protocol I, it pertains to 'all the movements and activities carried out by armed forces related to hostilities'.[92] Such operations thus include the transport and movement of fighters and associated personnel as well as military equipment across territory; intelligence and reconnaissance operations; and the building of fortifications. **1.39**

For the Additional Protocol II to apply, the military operations must be sustained—maintained 'more or less' continuously in Dinstein's words—even though 'intermittent pauses in the trail of violence are almost bound to transpire'.[93] Martha Bradley suggests that this dictate also informs the notion of intensity required for a non-international armed conflict, raising it above the ordinary threshold for a Common Article 3-type conflict by also requiring a prolonged duration of the hostilities.[94] In contrast, Andrew Clapham writes that 'today one could ask whether the Protocol really requires a greater level of intensity of violence than that required to trigger Common Article 3'.[95] In any event, the operations must be 'concerted', meaning that they are executed according to a plan.[96] **1.40**

These two strictures, whereby military operations must be both 'sustained' and 'concerted' are indeed 'rather rigorous'. The practical implications are that an insurgency will normally pass first through a Common Article 3-type conflict before burgeoning into one that is regulated also by the Additional Protocol II.[97] Crawford and Pert suggest that a notable exception is the conflict in Libya that erupted in February 2011, declaring that it is 'strongly arguable that it very quickly satisfied all the conditions' **1.41**

---

[89] The International Criminal Tribunal for Rwanda (ICTR) speaks of 'dominance' over territory: ICTR, *Prosecutor v. Alfred Musema*, Judgment and Sentence (Trial Chamber) (Case No. ICTR-96-13-T), 27 January 2000, para. 258.
[90] Ibid., p. 62, para. 169.
[91] Art. 1(1), 1977 Additional Protocol II.
[92] ICRC Commentary on Article 45 of the 1977 Additional Protocol I, 1987, para. 1936.
[93] Dinstein, *Non-International Armed Conflicts in International Law*, 2nd Edn, p. 64, para. 175.
[94] M. M. Bradley, 'Additional Protocol II: Elevating the minimum threshold of intensity?', *International Review of the Red Cross*, Vol. 102, No. 915 (2020), pp. 1125–52.
[95] Clapham, *War*, p. 256.
[96] ICRC, Commentary on Article 1 of the 1977 Additional Protocol II, 1987, para. 4469.
[97] Dinstein, *Non-International Armed Conflicts in International Law*, 2nd Edn, pp. 64–65, para. 175.

for the application of the Additional Protocol II.[98] Libya had already adhered to the Protocol in 1978.

Geographical scope of application

1.42 Once the criteria for application under Article 1(1) of the Additional Protocol II, its provisions will apply. Consonant with the broader application of IHL in a non-international armed conflict, the law governing the conduct of hostilities is limited to those areas where the fighting has reached a certain intensity. Thus, as the ICTY declared in its 1995 decision in the *Tadić* case with respect to Common Article 3-threshold conflicts: 'some of the provisions are clearly bound up with the hostilities and the geographical scope of those provisions should be so limited'.[99] In other areas, therefore, offensive action by State armed forces is conditioned by the law applicable to law enforcement operations. But with regard to persons in the power of the enemy anywhere on national territory (or indeed if they are moved abroad), the geographical scope of application is 'not so limited'.[100]

1.43 Whether or not the Protocol continues to apply where the conflict spills over into another State is not settled. Marco Pedrazzi has argued that fundamentally the scope of application of the Protocol is internal: geographically limited to sovereign territory of the territorial State fighting against an organised armed group. But he does not exclude that the conflict in question may spill over into the territory of adjacent States.[101] Bradley expresses her concern that 'less protection' may be afforded 'to those in a spill-over situation on the side of the border outside the territory in which the Additional Protocol II-type conflict originated'.[102]

Who is bound by the Additional Protocol II?

1.44 Overall, the question of who is bound by the Additional Protocol II is not as immediately obvious as might appear. Certainly, the State Party on whose territory the requisite

---

[98] E. Crawford and A. Pert, *International Humanitarian Law*, 2nd Edn, Cambridge University Press, Cambridge, 2020, p. 74.
[99] ICTY, *Prosecutor v. Tadić*, Decision on the Defence Motion for Interlocutory Appeal on Jurisdiction (Appeals Chamber), para. 68. This is so, even though Common Article 3 does not itself directly regulate the conduct of hostilities. N. Melzer, *Interpretive Guidance on the Notion of Direct Participation in Hostilities*, ICRC, Geneva, 2009, p. 28.
[100] ICTY, *Prosecutor v. Tadić*, Decision on the Defence Motion for Interlocutory Appeal on Jurisdiction (Appeals Chamber), para. 68.
[101] M. Pedrazzi, 'Additional Protocol II and Threshold of Application' in F. Pocar and G. L. Berute (eds.), *International Institute of Humanitarian Law: The Additional Protocols 40 Years Later: New Conflicts, New Actors, New Perspectives*, 40th Round Table on Current Issues of International Humanitarian Law, Franco Angeli, Milan, 2018, p. 51.
[102] M. M. Bradley, 'Classifying Non-International Armed Conflicts: The "Territorial Control" Requirement Under Additional Protocol II in an Era of Complex Conflicts', *Journal of International Humanitarian Legal Studies*, Vol. 11, No. 2 (2020), pp. 349–84, at p. 361.

armed conflict is occurring is constrained as a simple matter of treaty law: *pacta sunt servanda*. But what about the dissident armed forces or other armed group that is party to an armed conflict? After all, there is no stipulation as there is in Common Article 3 that 'each Party to the conflict shall be bound to apply, as a minimum, the following provisions'. Moreover, during the negotiation of the Protocol a number of participating States clearly believed that insurgent groups would not be bound by the instrument they were elaborating.[103] While customary IHL would unquestionably apply, this would leave aside any provisions in the Protocol that do not codify a customary rule. (As noted in the Introduction to this book, however, today it is hard to see which of the rules laid down in the Protocol are not of a customary nature.)

Also at issue is whether foreign forces assisting the territorial State in an Additional Protocol II armed conflict are also bound by the provisions. The question arose in Afghanistan, which adhered to the Additional Protocol II in November 2009, formally becoming a State Party on 10 May 2010. Until the last of the myriad of foreign forces that supported the Government of Afghanistan left the country at the end of August 2021, were they also subject to the provisions of the Protocol? Dinstein suggests that a 'more lenient deciphering' of Article 1(1) is necessary to decree that such an armed force, when the foreign State in question is itself party to the Protocol, is bound directly by it.[104] A number of authorities reject the application of the Protocol to such States Parties whose armed forces operate extraterritorially in an armed conflict falling within its scope.[105] But they tend to do so on a misreading of Article 1(1), fixating on the reference to 'its' armed forces. **1.45**

In this regard, it is important to recall that the 1977 Additional Protocol II applies to each *armed conflict* that meets the requisite criteria. Once an armed conflict has fulfilled all the requirements of the provision on application in the Protocol, it is logical (based on the ordinary wording of the provision) and indeed appropriate that all parties to that conflict, whether that be the territorial State party or a foreign State Party, be bound by its obligations. With respect to a foreign State whose armed force is participating in the conflict in support of the government of the territorial State, this is so where it is formally a Party to the Additional Protocol II. In the context of Afghanistan, many such foreign forces were a State Party to the Protocol at the salient time, including Australia, Czechia, Denmark, France, Germany, Georgia, Italy, the Netherlands, Norway, and the UK.[106] **1.46**

---

[103] L. Moir, *The Law of Internal Armed Conflict*, Cambridge University Press, Cambridge, 2002, p. 97.
[104] Dinstein, *Non-International Armed Conflicts in International Law*, 2nd Edn, p. 117, para. 318.
[105] See, e.g., R. Geiss and M. Siegrist, 'Has the Armed Conflict in Afghanistan Affected the Rules on the Conduct of Hostilities?', *International Review of the Red Cross*, Vol. 93, No. 881 (2011), pp. 11–46, at p. 16.
[106] For a list of foreign forces supporting the Government of Afghanistan as of 2018, see, e.g., Radio Free Europe/Radio Liberty, 'Which Countries Have Troops In Afghanistan?', 21 December 2018, at: https://bit.ly/3zo9URz.

Temporal scope of application

1.47 The Additional Protocol II does not set out in detail its temporal scope of application. That said, it is stipulated that even after the 'end of the armed conflict', certain provisions will continue to apply. Notably, these offer the protection of Articles 5 and 6 (on protection of detainees and on criminal prosecutions, respectively) to persons 'who have been deprived of their liberty or whose liberty has been restricted for reasons related to such conflict, as well as those deprived of their liberty or whose liberty is restricted after the conflict for the same reasons'.[107] With regard to others, however, the question still arises as to when the conflict is, in international legal terms, at an end.

1.48 In its 1995 *Tadić* decision, the ICTY Appeals Chamber had held that IHL applies in any non-international armed conflict 'until a peaceful settlement is achieved'.[108] This is not the case in law. As the ICRC has noted, 'armed confrontations may also dissipate without any ceasefire, armistice or peace agreement ever being concluded, or before the conclusion of such an agreement'. Accordingly, 'while the existence of such agreements may be taken into account when assessing all of the facts, they are neither necessary nor sufficient on their own to bring about the termination of the application of humanitarian law.'[109]

1.49 Emily Crawford affirms that what is at issue is whether a 'general close of military operations' has occurred, even while acknowledging that the determination 'can be difficult'.[110] For sure, few situations are as clear cut as was that in Afghanistan in August 2021, when the Taliban was unquestionably victorious over Afghan government forces and the armed conflict between them came to an end.[111] With the foreign militaries that had supported the former government forces for two decades now gone, at the time of writing it remained to be seen whether the Additional Protocol II would again become applicable to the conflict likely to arise between the Taliban regime—now the new Afghan government forces—and the armed opposition group, Islamic State Khorasan Province (IS-K).[112]

---

[107] Art. 2(2), 1977 Additional Protocol II.
[108] ICTY, *Prosecutor* v. *Tadić*, Decision on the Defence Motion for Interlocutory Appeal on Jurisdiction (Appeals Chamber), para. 70.
[109] ICRC commentary on Article 3 of the 1949 Geneva Convention I, 2016, para. 490.
[110] E. Crawford, 'The Temporal and Geographic Reach of International Humanitarian Law', Chap. 3 in B. Saul and D. Akande (eds.), *The Oxford Guide to International Humanitarian Law*, Oxford University Press, Oxford, 2020, p. 60.
[111] As noted above, those detained in connection with the erstwhile conflict, now or in the future, continue to be protected under the Second Additional Protocol until their release.
[112] See, e.g., F. Gardner, 'Afghanistan Airport Attack: Who Are IS-K?', BBC, 27 August 2021, at: https://bbc.in/3yjS7tz.

The scope of application of the Additional Protocol III

The scope of application of the Third Additional Protocol of 2005 is far easier to summarise. Its first article declares that it 'reaffirms and supplements the provisions of the four Geneva Conventions' and, 'where applicable, of their two Additional Protocols of 8 June 1977' pertaining to 'the distinctive emblems, namely the red cross, the red crescent and the red lion and sun, and shall apply in the same situations as those referred to in these provisions'.[113] The Third Additional Protocol applies of course during armed conflict, whether international or non-international in character, but the rules relating to the emblem also apply in peacetime. 'Their application therefore does not depend on the existence of an armed conflict.'[114]

1.50

The Red Crystal was the first new symbol recognised under IHL since the adoption of the Red Lion and Sun in 1923, a special symbol for Iran that, while still formally recognised, has not been used since 1980.[115] As of 1 May 2022, 79 States were party to the Third Additional Protocol.

1.51

Concluding remarks and outlook

The scope of application of the 1977 Additional Protocol I is clear even though its internationalisation of certain national liberation struggles remains controversial among a number of Western governments. Its application in relation to Western Sahara demonstrates that it will not be dead letter as a matter of law. The scope of application of the 1977 Additional Protocol II is less clear, in particular with respect to whether it applies to all parties to an armed conflict that takes place in the territory of a State Party between that State's armed forces and either dissident armed forces or other organised armed groups (where the opposition exercises sufficient territorial control to enable them to carry out sustained and concerted military operations). The better view, we have suggested, is that a foreign military force assisting that State Party, where it emanates from a State that has also adhered to the Protocol, is similarly bound. The crystallisation of the rules set out in the Additional Protocol II as custom has dented the significance of the treaty application, but it does not negate it.

1.52

---

[113] Art. 1(2), 2005 Additional Protocol III.
[114] ICRC, Commentary on Article 1 of the 2005 Additional Protocol III, 2007, at: https://bit.ly/3gF7tCN, para. 2.
[115] R. Giampietro, 'The Red Crystal', 2005, at: https://bit.ly/2WB6xIS.

2
Fundamental Guarantees

Introduction

2.1 In both of the 1977 Additional Protocols, an article is dedicated to what are termed, slightly curiously, 'fundamental guarantees'.[1] These are minimum standards of conduct and treatment below which no party to the salient armed conflict may lawfully fall with respect to any persons coming within their power. In the same way as the Article 3 common to the four Geneva Conventions of 1949 is termed a 'Convention in miniature',[2] so perhaps can these two provisions be considered. Moreover, each bears significant similarities with the obligations imposed on each party to the conflict under Common Article 3, while supplementing the protection afforded by that customary law provision.[3] But unusually for international humanitarian law (IHL), not only are certain acts prohibited *in bello* but so too are threats to commit any of those illegal acts.[4] In general, the additional legal protection afforded under Article 75 of the 1977 Additional Protocol I is substantially greater than that set out with regard to the non-international armed conflicts within the scope of Additional Protocol II in its Article 4.

2.2 While the provisions are primarily of IHL, they correspond closely with fundamental human rights, particularly those concerned with the protection of bodily integrity. Indeed, as the International Committee of the Red Cross (ICRC) has observed,[5] the provisions about fundamental guarantees in the Additional Protocol II of 1977 were in part 'inspired' by the 1966 International Covenant on Civil and Political Rights (ICCPR).[6] Protection of the rights to life, to freedom from torture and other ill-treatment, and to

---

[1] Art. 75, Protocol Additional to the Geneva Conventions of 12 August 1949, and relating to the Protection of Victims of International Armed Conflicts (Protocol I); adopted at Geneva, 8 June 1977; entered into force, 7 December 1978 (hereinafter, 1977 Additional Protocol I); and Art. 4, Protocol Additional to the Geneva Conventions of 12 August 1949, and relating to the Protection of Victims of Non-International Armed Conflicts (Protocol II); adopted at Geneva, 8 June 1977; entered into force, 7 December 1978 (hereinafter, 1977 Additional Protocol II).

[2] J. Pictet, Commentary on Article 3 of Convention (II) for the Amelioration of the Condition of Wounded, Sick and Shipwrecked Members of Armed Forces at Sea, International Committee of the Red Cross (ICRC), Geneva, 1960, p. 33, at: https://bit.ly/3nIq6sm.

[3] Common Article 3 applies to non-international armed conflicts, but in its judgment in the *Nicaragua* case, the International Court of Justice (ICJ) affirmed that there 'is no doubt that', in the event of international armed conflicts, the rules contained therein 'also constitute a minimum yardstick, in addition to the more elaborate rules which are also to apply to international conflicts'. ICJ, *Case Concerning Military and Paramilitary Activities in and against Nicaragua* (*Nicaragua v. United States of America*) Judgment (Merits), 27 June 1986, para. 218.

[4] Art. 75(2)(e), 1977 Additional Protocol I; and Art. 4(2)(h), 1977 Additional Protocol II.

[5] ICRC, Commentary on Article 4 of the 1977 Additional Protocol II, 1987, at: https://bit.ly/2IGhscP, para. 455.

[6] Art. 6(1), International Covenant on Civil and Political Rights; adopted at New York, 16 December 1966; entered into force, 23 March 1976 (ICCPR). As of 1 May 2022, 173 States were party to the Convention.

security are, appropriately, predominant in the fundamental guarantees set out in the two 1977 Additional Protocols.

Article 75 of the 1977 Additional Protocol I is one of the longest in the entire Protocol. **2.3** It was the object of 'lengthy discussion' in the formal sessions of the Diplomatic Conference itself, as well as in informal meetings of delegates.[7] In any situation of international armed conflict falling under the Additional Protocol I, the guarantees afforded extend beyond bodily integrity and security also to concern fair-trial rights and the protection and treatment of women in detention.

To the extent that those two issues are addressed in the 1977 Additional Protocol II, **2.4** this is achieved in separate provisions from those offering fundamental guarantees.[8] At the same time, child recruitment is addressed in the Additional Protocol II as a fundamental guarantee but is the subject of a distinct—although slightly narrower— prohibition elsewhere in the Additional Protocol I.[9] Slavery and the slave trade are explicitly prohibited in Article 4 of the 1977 Additional Protocol II, but not at all in the Additional Protocol I. Collective punishments are specifically outlawed in both the 1977 Additional Protocols.

This chapter considers the content of the principal fundamental guarantees in the **2.5** first two Additional Protocols. It does so in light of the evolution of customary IHL (see Table 2.1) as well as of customary human rights law. In 2006, a plurality on the US Supreme Court concluded that Article 75 of the Additional Protocol I *in toto* reflected customary law.[10] Furthermore, many of the provisions of general international law are also of a peremptory nature, as the chapter further discusses.

The prohibition of sexual violence against women is discussed in the following chapter **2.6** along with the treatment of women in detention (which can serve as a preventive measure). Of course, sexual violence is also perpetrated against men and boys[11] and is similarly outlawed under IHL and international criminal law. The prohibition on the recruitment of children under 15 years of age, set out in Article 4(3)(c) and (d) of the 1977 Additional Protocol II, is discussed in Chapter 4, along with the treatment of children in detention. The prohibition of acts of terrorism under the 1977 Additional Protocol II and the corresponding prohibition under the 1949 Geneva Convention IV are addressed in Chapter 13.

---

[7] ICRC, Commentary on Article 75 of the 1977 Additional Protocol I, 1987, at: https://bit.ly/3msyQDt, para. 3000.
[8] See Article 5 (on detention) and Article 6 (on penal prosecutions) in the 1977 Additional Protocol II.
[9] See Chapter 4 of this work for the details.
[10] US Supreme Court, *Hamdan v. Rumsfeld*, 548 US 557, 633 (2006); see G. D. Solis, *The Law of Armed Conflict: International Humanitarian Law in War*, 3rd Edn, Cambridge University Press, Cambridge, 2021, p. 110, and also p. 648.
[11] In 2013, the United Nations (UN) Security Council formally recognised for the first time that conflict-related sexual violence also affects men and boys. UN Security Council Resolution 2106, adopted by unanimous vote in favour on 24 June 2013, sixth preambular para.

Table 2.1 Summary of Fundamental Guarantees

Rule	AP I	Customary status (IAC)	AP II	Customary status (NIAC)
Prohibition of murder	Art. 75(2)(a)(i)	Yes	Art. 4(2)(a)	Yes
Prohibition of denial of quarter	Art. 40	Yes	Art. 4(1)	Yes
Prohibition of torture and other ill-treatment	Art. 75(2)(a)(ii) and (iii) and (iv) and 75(2)(b)	Yes	Art. 4(2)(a)	Yes
Prohibition of sexual violence	Art. 75(2)(b)	Yes	Art. 4(2)(e)	Yes
Non-discrimination	Art. 75(1)	Yes	Art. 4(1)	Yes
Prohibition of enslavement	No	Yes	Art. 4(2)(f)	Yes
Prohibition of collective punishment	Art. 75(2)(d)	Yes	Art. 4(2)(b)	Yes
Prohibition of hostage-taking	Art. 75(2)(c)	Yes	Art. 4(2)(c)	Yes
Treatment of women in detention	Art. 75(5)	Yes	Art. 5(2)(a)	Yes
Fair-trial rights	Art. 75(4) & (7)	Yes	Art. 6	Yes
Acts of terrorism	No	Yes	Art. 4(2)(d)	Yes
Treatment and protection of children	No	Yes	Art. 4(3)	Yes

The prohibition of murder

2.7 Both Additional Protocols expressly prohibit the murder of anyone in the power of a party to an armed conflict.[12] This prohibition is broad in scope, protecting all those who are fighters *hors de combat* because of wounds or sickness, as well as all detainees and civilians in occupied territory or in sovereign territory under the control of a party to an armed conflict. In fact, outside the conduct of hostilities, all intentional killings by State agents, whether military or civilian, will amount to murder unless the act is

---

[12] Art. 75(2)(a)(i), 1977 Additional Protocol I; and Art. 4(2)(a), 1977 Additional Protocol II.

perpetrated in lawful self-defence or defence of others.[13] The prohibition of murder is not only treaty-based—binding all States Parties to each of the Additional Protocols—it is also of a customary nature. Thus, in its study of customary IHL completed in 2005, the ICRC discerned a simple rule whereby, in all armed conflict that 'murder is prohibited'.[14]

2.8 The prohibition of murder is also at the core of the right to life, and particularly the prohibition of arbitrary deprivation of life set out in the ICCPR.[15] It is certainly a customary rule; indeed, the entire right to life is termed 'inherent' in the Covenant. As the Human Rights Committee, which oversees the treaty's implementation by its States Parties, has observed, the right to life is 'the supreme right from which no derogation is permitted, even in situations of armed conflict'.[16] Surprisingly, in its relatively recent consideration of peremptory international legal rules, the International Law Commission did not designate murder, or the arbitrary deprivation of life, as a norm of *jus cogens*.[17] In all likelihood, however, this prohibition has attained peremptory status in international law. Thus, for example, in 1987, in the Third Restatement of the Foreign Relations Law of the United States, the prohibition of 'murder' as a customary human rights rule was described as a norm of *jus cogens*.[18] The African Commission on Human and Peoples' Rights came to a similar conclusion with regard to the arbitrary deprivation of life in 2015.[19]

2.9 There is, however, no universal definition of what constitutes murder as a war crime, and national definitions of, especially, the requisite mental element for murder differ.[20] The key elements of the crime are not elucidated with great clarity either in the delineation of the relevant *actus reus* and *mens rea* under the 1998 Rome Statute of the International Criminal Court.[21] Therein, the key issue is whether the accused killed (or 'caused the death of') a person who was protected at the time from attack under IHL, whether as a civilian, a non-combatant,[22] or a fighter *hors de combat*. It is not,

---

[13] In non-international armed conflict, Common Article 3 provides that 'violence to life and person, in particular murder of all kinds' against anyone 'taking no active part in the hostilities' is 'and shall remain prohibited at any time and in any place whatsoever'.
[14] ICRC Customary IHL Rule 89: 'Violence to Life', at: https://bit.ly/2XZ2TJz.
[15] Art. 6(1), ICCPR.
[16] Human Rights Committee, General Comment No. 36: Article 6: right to life, UN doc. CCPR/C/GC/36, 3 September 2019, para. 2.
[17] International Law Commission (ILC), Annex to the text of the draft conclusions on peremptory norms of general international law (*jus cogens*), adopted by the ILC on first reading, in UN doc. A/74/10, 2019.
[18] See further D. T. Murphy, 'The Restatement (Third)'s Human Rights Provisions: Nothing New, but Very Welcome', *International Lawyer*, Vol. 24 (1990), 917, at p. 922; and H. Duffy, *The 'War on Terror' and the Framework of International Law*, 2nd Edn, Cambridge University Press, Cambridge, 2015, pp. 461–62, 918.
[19] African Commission on Human and Peoples' Rights, 'General Comment No. 3 on the African Charter on Human and Peoples' Rights: The Right to Life (Article 4)', adopted at Banjul (fifty-seventh Ordinary Session), November 2015, para. 5.
[20] See on this issue, e.g., K. J. Heller and M. D. Dubber (eds.), *The Handbook of Comparative Criminal Law*, Stanford University Press, Stanford CA, 2010.
[21] See, e.g., Elements of the war crime of murder under Article 8(2)(c)(i)-1 of the Rome Statute of the International Criminal Court; adopted at Rome, 17 July 1998; entered into force, 1 July 2002. The Elements of Crimes are reproduced from the *Official Records of the Assembly of States Parties to the Rome Statute of the International Criminal Court*, First Session, New York, 3–10 September 2002, Part II(B).
[22] K. Ipsen, 'Combatants and Non-Combatants', Chap. 5 in D. Fleck (ed.), *The Handbook of International Humanitarian Law*, 4th Edn, Oxford University Press, Oxford, 2021, Sections 5.13, p. 112.

30   FUNDAMENTAL GUARANTEES

however, stipulated whether murder can be committed only where there is an intent to kill, in contrast to an intent to cause serious bodily harm suffering. If the ICRC is correct that recklessness is sufficient to ground a war crimes conviction,[23] that would tend to sustain the broader scope of *mens rea*, as the International Criminal Tribunal for the former Yugoslavia (ICTY) held in its judgment in the *Delalić* case.[24] It later reaffirmed this stance, notably in its 2005 judgment at trial in the *Blagojević and Jokić* case: 'In the jurisprudence of both the Tribunal and the ICTR, murder has consistently been defined as the death of the victim which results from an act or omission by the accused, committed with the intent either to kill or to cause serious bodily harm with the reasonable knowledge that it would likely lead to death.'[25] In October 2021, a German woman and former member of Islamic State was convicted by a Munich court for letting a Yazidi girl enslaved in Iraq die of thirst. The defendant was found guilty of attempted murder and aiding and abetting the war crime of attempted murder by omission.[26]

2.10   Surprisingly, given its most serious nature, murder has never been defined by statute in the United Kingdom. Its common law definition in England and Wales comprises a number of elements, each of which must be present and proven beyond reasonable doubt if the accused is to be convicted. Thus, murder is committed where a natural person (a human being, not a body corporate), being of 'sound mind and discretion' (i.e. legally sane), unlawfully kills any human being ('reasonable creature') who is 'born alive and breathing through its own lungs'.[27] The killing must occur outside time of war (under 'the Queen's Peace'), and must be perpetrated with intent either to kill or to cause grievous bodily harm. Action in legitimate self-defence will preclude a conviction for murder.[28]

2.11   In 2011, Royal Marine Sergeant Alexander Blackman was convicted of murder for a killing he perpetrated amid the non-international armed conflict in Afghanistan. The intentional killing of a seriously wounded Afghan insurgent was not conducted in the heat of battle.[29] Indeed, Sergeant Blackman was recorded as saying, just after shooting the helpless insurgent in the chest, 'There you are, shuffle off this mortal coil you c---.' This declaration was followed a few seconds later by the explicit acknowledgement: 'I've just broke the Geneva Convention.'[30] In 2017, Mr Blackman's conviction

---

[23] ICRC Customary IHL Rule 156: 'Definition of War Crimes', at: http://bit.ly/32HjZb2, Interpretation, point (iii).
[24] ICTY, *Prosecutor v. Delalić*, Judgment (Trial Chamber) (Case No. IT-96-21-T), 16 November 1998, para. 437, 439. The ICTY cited the ICRC, Commentary on Article 85 of the Additional Protocol I as support for its holding.
[25] ICTY, *Prosecutor v. Blagojević and Jokić*, Judgment (Trial Chamber) (Case No. IT-02-60-T), 17 January 2005, para. 556.
[26] Euronews with AFP, 'German IS bride jailed in one of world's first trials for war crimes against Yazidis', Euronews, Updated 25 October 2021, at: https://bit.ly/3mDRmIX.
[27] Queen's Bench Divisional Court, *Rance v. Mid-Downs Health Authority* [1991] 1 All ER 801; and AG Ref No. 3 of 1994 [1997] 3 All ER 936.
[28] CPS, 'Homicide: Murder and Manslaughter', Legal Guidance, Last updated 18 March 2019, at: https://bit.ly/3o8Wrqh.
[29] *R v. Sergeant Alexander Wayne Blackman ("Marine A")*, Case Reference: 2012CM00442, Sentencing Remarks by HHJ Jeff Blackett, Judge Advocate General, 6 December 2013.
[30] S. Morris, 'Alexander Blackman shoots wounded Taliban fighter—transcript', *The Guardian*, 15 March 2017, at: https://bit.ly/3nCZQiM.

was reduced on appeal to manslaughter on the basis of his diminished responsibility at the salient time.[31]

The prohibition of denial of quarter

Denial of quarter is effectively an order or a threat to murder people *hors de combat* in an armed conflict. It is thus 'one of the fundamental rules on the conduct of combatants inspired by Hague law'.[32] As Yoram Dinstein has noted: '*Au fond*, the idea is that fighters must be given an opportunity to surrender.'[33] To 'declare that no quarter will be given' was already outlawed as a method of warfare in the Hague Regulations of 1899.[34] In the 1977 Additional Protocol II, the rule is expressly simply as a prohibition on ordering 'that there shall be no survivors'.[35] The corresponding prohibition in the Additional Protocol I, which is a little more elaborate, is not contained within the article on fundamental guarantees. Rather, Article 40 ('Quarter') stipulates that: 'It is prohibited to order that there shall be no survivors, to threaten an adversary therewith or to conduct hostilities on this basis.'

2.12

Identical text had been proposed for the 1977 Additional Protocol II, but was not ultimately adopted.[36] The absence of an explicit prohibition on 'threatening' to deny quarter in the Additional Protocol II is not of great consequence given the customary law on this issue that applies in all armed conflicts.[37] Under the Rome Statute of the International Criminal Court, 'declaring that no quarter will be given' is a war crime under the jurisdiction of the Court also in 'protracted' non-international armed conflicts.[38]

2.13

The prohibition of torture and other ill-treatment

As was the case with murder, torture had already been prohibited under Common Article 3 in 1949. Thus, Article 3(a) and (c) prohibited, respectively, 'mutilation, cruel treatment and torture' and 'outrages upon personal dignity, in particular humiliating

2.14

---

[31] For a considered view of this decision, see K. J. Heller, 'Bad Criminal Law in the Alexander Blackman Case (With Addendum)', *Opinio Juris*, 31 March 2017, at: https://bit.ly/2XZDMpR. Mr. Blackman has written about his experiences in Afghanistan and his subsequent trial in *Marine A: 'My Toughest Battle'*, Mirror Books, United Kingdom, 31 October 2019.
[32] ICRC, Commentary on Article 4 of the 1977 Additional Protocol II, 1987, para. 4525.
[33] Y. Dinstein, *Non-International Armed Conflicts in International Law*, 2nd Edn, Cambridge University Press, Cambridge, 2021, p. 185, para. 513.
[34] Art. 23(d), Regulations concerning the Laws and Customs of War on Land annexed to Convention (II) with Respect to the Laws and Customs of War on Land; adopted at The Hague, 29 July 1899 (hereinafter, 1899 Hague Regulations).
[35] Art. 4(1), 1977 Additional Protocol II.
[36] ICRC, Commentary on Article 4 of the 1977 Additional Protocol II, 1987, para. 4525.
[37] ICRC, Customary IHL Rule 46: 'Orders or Threats that No Quarter Will Be Given', at: https://bit.ly/3B6AsI7.
[38] Art. 2(e)(x), Rome Statute of the International Criminal Court.

and degrading treatment'. This encompassed acts such as waterboarding, prolonged sleep deprivation or hooding, beatings, or violent shakings.[39] Torture had not then been formally defined in international law, nor had the United Nations Convention against Torture been adopted[40] at the time the two Additional Protocols were negotiated.

2.15 That said, the Declaration on the Protection of All Persons from being Subjected to Torture had been promulgated by the UN General Assembly in 1975.[41] The Declaration, which was adopted by UN member States without a vote, stipulated that torture 'means any act by which severe pain or suffering, whether physical or mental, is intentionally inflicted by or at the instigation of a public official on a person for such purposes as obtaining from him or a third person information or confession, punishing him for an act he has committed or is suspected of having committed, or intimidating him or other persons'.[42] This would be the basis for the definition of torture incorporated in the Convention against Torture in 1984, except that this latter, more authoritative definition would expand the basis on which the severe pain or suffering was being inflicted: 'obtaining from him or a third person information or a confession, punishing him for an act he or a third person has committed or is suspected of having committed, or intimidating or coercing him or a third person, or for any reason based on discrimination of any kind'.[43]

2.16 The notion of involvement of a public official cannot be retained in the prohibition of torture in IHL or international criminal law, given that a non-State armed group may be party to an armed conflict. Thus, in the Elements of Crime for the war crime of torture under the Rome Statute in both international and non-international armed conflict, the *actus reus* of the offence includes simply a requirement to prove that the 'perpetrator' inflicted severe physical or mental pain or suffering upon one or more persons—those *hors de combat*, non-combatants, or civilians—and that he or she did so 'for such purposes as: obtaining information or a confession, punishment, intimidation or coercion or for any reason based on discrimination of any kind'.[44]

2.17 In its judgment in the *Furundžija* case, issued five months after the Rome Statute was adopted, the ICTY found that 'there is now general acceptance of the main elements contained in the definition set out in article 1 of the Torture Convention'.[45] The Trial Chamber considered that the elements of torture in an armed conflict require that

---

[39] See, e.g., Solis, *The Law of Armed Conflict: International Humanitarian Law in War*, 3rd Edn, pp. 513, 516–19.
[40] Convention against Torture and Other Cruel, Inhuman or Degrading Treatment or Punishment; adopted at New York, 10 December 1984; entered into force, 26 June 1987 (hereinafter, 1984 Convention against Torture).
[41] Declaration on the Protection of All Persons from being Subjected to Torture and Other Cruel, Inhuman or Degrading Treatment or Punishment, of 9 December 1975', adopted by UN General Assembly Resolution 3452 (XXX), resolution adopted without a vote.
[42] Art. 1(1), 1975 Declaration on the Protection of All Persons from being Subjected to Torture and Other Cruel, Inhuman or Degrading Treatment or Punishment.
[43] Art. 1(1), UN Convention against Torture. As of 1 May 2022, 173 States were party to the Convention.
[44] Elements of Crime for war crime of torture (Art. 8(2)(a)(ii) and (c)(i), 1998 Rome Statute of the International Armed Conflict).
[45] ICTY, *Prosecutor* v. *Furundžija*, Judgment (Trial Chamber) (Case No. IT-95-17/1-T), 10 December 1998, para. 161.

the crime: (i) consists of the infliction, by act or omission, of severe pain or suffering, whether physical or mental; (ii) this act or omission must be intentional; (iii) it must aim at obtaining information or a confession, or at punishing, intimidating, humiliating, or coercing the victim or a third person, or at discriminating, on any ground, against the victim or a third person; (iv) it must be linked to an armed conflict; and (v) at least one of the persons involved in the torture process must be a public official or must at any rate act in a non-private capacity, e.g. as a de facto organ of a State or any other authority-wielding entity.[46]

The accused, Anto Furundžija, was charged with the war crimes of torture and outrages upon personal dignity, including rape. Mr Furundžija was the local commander of a special unit of the military police of the Bosnian Croat army known as the 'Jokers'. He, and another soldier, interrogated a witness rubbing a knife against her inner thigh and lower stomach, while threatening to put the knife inside her vagina should she not tell the truth. The accused continued to interrogate the witness and a victim while they were beaten on the feet with a baton and stood by while the witness was forced to have oral and vaginal sexual intercourse with his co-accused.[47] In its judgment convicting Mr Furundžija, the Trial Chamber found that the prohibition against torture had attained the status of *jus cogens*.[48] This is also the long-standing position of the International Law Commission.[49]

2.18

Rape is a war crime in its own right,[50] but may also be prosecuted as torture in certain circumstances. In its judgment in *Akayesu*, the International Criminal Tribunal for Rwanda (ICTR) observed that:

2.19

> Like torture, rape is used for such purposes as intimidation, degradation, humiliation, discrimination, punishment, control or destruction of a person. Like torture, rape is a violation of personal dignity, and rape in fact constitutes torture when inflicted by or at the instigation of or with the consent or acquiescence of a public official or other person acting in an official capacity.[51]

The principle of non-discrimination

The prohibition of discrimination in the article on fundamental guarantees is distinct from the prohibitions therein on violence to life or health. Discrimination can be a

2.20

---

[46] Ibid., para. 162.
[47] ICTY, *Prosecutor v. Furundžija*, Statement of the Trial Chamber at the Judgment Hearing, Judgment Summary, The Hague, 10 December 1998, at: https://bit.ly/3CvB4HS, p. 1.
[48] ICTY, *Prosecutor v. Furundžija*, Judgment (Trial Chamber), para. 3.
[49] ILC, Annex to the text of the draft conclusions on peremptory norms of general international law (*jus cogens*), point (g).
[50] Art. 8(2)(b)(xxii) and (2)(e)(vi), Rome Statute of the International Criminal Court. See further Chapter 3 on this issue.
[51] ICTR, *Prosecutor v. Akayesu*, Judgment (Trial Chamber) (Case No. ICTR-96-4-T), 2 September 1998, para. 597.

personal motivation for a perpetrator to decide to torture his or her victim. What is at issue here, however, is sharply different in nature: what is envisaged is respect for other fundamental rights and guarantees. Thus, Article 4 of the 1977 Additional Protocol II stipulates that those protected by the provision 'shall in all circumstances be treated humanely, without any adverse distinction'. The notion of 'adverse distinction' is defined in Article 2 whereunder the Protocol 'shall be applied without any adverse distinction founded on race, colour, sex, language, religion or belief, political or other opinion, national or social origin, wealth, birth or other status, or on any other similar criteria' to 'all persons affected by an armed conflict' within its scope.[52] As Sandra Krähenmann observes, this prohibition is broad in scope such that it would apply to foreign ('terrorist') fighters.[53] Nationality is not an explicitly prohibited ground of discrimination under Common Article 3.[54]

2.21   As Dinstein recalls, the use of the adjective 'adverse' in relation to distinction is deliberate: 'in some situations "favourable distinctions may be made quite lawfully" in order to take into account special vulnerability'.[55] The language in the Protocols follows, and largely mirrors, the protection afforded under the 1966 ICCPR whereby the rights shall be respected and ensured by its States Parties 'without distinction of any kind, such as race, colour, sex, language, religion, political or other opinion, national or social origin, property, birth or other status'.[56] Underpinning all human rights are the notions of dignity and non-discrimination.[57] Religious or racial discrimination is common in time of armed conflict as it is in peacetime. The International Law Commission reiterated in 2019 that the prohibition of racial discrimination and *apartheid* was a peremptory norm of international law.[58]

The prohibition of enslavement

2.22   The prohibition of slavery and the slave trade 'in all their forms' in the 1977 Additional Protocol II is interesting. Termed, rather curiously, by the ICRC 'one of the "hard-core" fundamental guarantees, now reaffirmed in the Protocol',[59] as noted above, no similar

---

[52] Art. 2(1), 1977 Additional Protocol II.
[53] S. Krähenmann, 'Foreign fighters, terrorism and counter-terrorism', Chap. 17 in B. Saul (ed.), *Research Handbook on International Law and Terrorism*, 2nd Edn, Edward Elgar Publishing, Cheltenham, 2021, p. 242.
[54] In Common Article 3, prohibited grounds are ' … any adverse distinction founded on race, colour, religion or faith, sex, birth or wealth, or any other similar criteria'. Krähenmann affirms that nationality would fall within the rubric of 'any other similar criteria'. This may be open to question given that the 1949 Diplomatic Conference decided not to include nationality as a criterion, but the ICRC similarly opines that nationality 'cannot be regarded as affecting in any way the humanitarian law obligation of humane treatment'. ICRC, Commentary on Article 3 of the 1949 Geneva Convention III, 2020, at: https://bit.ly/34mhUpo, para. 608.
[55] Dinstein, *Non-International Armed Conflicts in International Law*, 2nd Edn, p. 311, para. 898.
[56] Art. 2(1), ICCPR.
[57] S. Casey-Maslen, *The Right to Life under International Law: An Interpretive Manual*, Cambridge University Press, Cambridge, 2021, para. 4.01.
[58] ILC, Annex to the text of the draft conclusions on peremptory norms of general international law (*jus cogens*), point (e).
[59] ICRC, Commentary on Article 4 of the 1977 Additional Protocol II, 1987, para. 4541.

prohibition exists in the Additional Protocol I. Under the ICCPR, it is stipulated that 'no one shall be held in slavery; slavery and the slave-trade in all their forms shall be prohibited'. This in turn is largely derived from the 1926 Slavery Convention, which defines slavery as 'the status or condition of a person over whom any or all of the powers attaching to the right of ownership are exercised'.[60] Indeed, the ICTY in its judgment at trial in the *Kunarac* case made it clear that the prohibition in the 1977 Additional Protocol II was based on Article 1 of the 1926 Convention.[61] The specific prohibition of 'slavery' is not only a customary rule of international law, it is also a peremptory norm.[62]

2.23 While chattel slavery is as old as humankind, today the practice is rare. The last nation in the world to formally abolish slavery was Mauritania, in 1981, although tens of thousands of people still live as bonded labourers there in what is sometimes termed 'modern slavery'.[63] But just as enslavement often occurred in wartime in history, armed conflict has been the scene for contemporary enslavement. In October 2021, a German woman who had joined Islamic State was convicted of enslavement. She and her husband, a fighter with Islamic State, 'purchased' a Yazidi woman and child as household slaves whom they held captive while living in occupied Mosul in Iraq, in 2015. Prosecutors charged that after the girl fell ill and wet her mattress, the husband of the accused chained her up outside as punishment and let the child die an agonising death by thirst in the scorching heat.[64]

2.24 Enslavement has often been of a sexual nature. In its judgment in the *Taylor* case, the Special Court for Sierra Leone affirmed that the *actus reus* of the war crime of sexual slavery comprises two elements, first, that the accused 'exercised any or all of the powers attaching to the right of ownership of a person or persons (the slavery element) and second, that the enslavement involved sexual acts (the sexual element)'. The *mens rea* for the crime consists in the intentional exercise of any or all of the powers attaching to the right of ownership, over the victim.[65] The Trial Chamber further observed that the primary characteristic of enslavement is the absence of the consent or free will of the victim. It held that there was no requirement that there be any payment or exchange in order to establish the exercise of ownership.[66]

---

[60] Convention to Suppress the Slave Trade and Slavery; signed at Geneva, 25 September 1926; entered into force, 9 March 1927. As of 1 May 2022, 99 States were party to the Convention. Kazakhstan was the most recent State to adhere to the Convention, in 2008.
[61] ICTY, *Prosecutor v. Kunarac and others*, Judgment (Trial Chamber) (Case No. IT-96-23-T & IT-96-23/1-T), 22 February 2001, para. 529; see also Dinstein, *Non-International Armed Conflicts in International Law*, 2nd Edn, p. 220, para. 622.
[62] ILC, Annex to the text of the draft conclusions on peremptory norms of general international law (*jus cogens*), point (f).
[63] 'The Unspeakable Truth about Slavery in Mauritania', *The Guardian*, 8 June 2018, at http://bit.ly/2Jrgjqd.
[64] 'German IS Bride Sentenced to 10 Years in Prison for Fatal Neglect of Yazidi Girl', *France24*, 25 October 2021, at: https://bit.ly/3GMDjcg.
[65] SCSL, *Prosecutor v. Taylor*, Judgment (Trial Chamber) (Case No. SCSL-03-01-T), 18 May 2012, para. 419.
[66] Ibid., para. 420.

The prohibition of collective punishment

2.25 A prohibition on collective punishment was set out in international armed conflict only under the 1949 Geneva Conventions: in Convention III with respect to prisoners of war[67] and, employing the term 'collective penalties', in Convention IV with respect to civilians protected as such (those in occupied territory and aliens in the territory of a party to an international armed conflict).[68] The prohibition was not defined in Geneva Convention III, but was originally devised at 'curbing the generalized abuses committed during the First World War, when [prisoner of war] camp commanders were all too frequently tempted to inflict collective punishments for acts committed by individuals, and were sometimes motivated by a spirit of vengeance'.[69]

2.26 The prohibition of collective penalties is analogous to, but potentially narrower than, that on collective punishment. Its origins can be traced back to the 1899 Hague Regulations, which specified that: 'No general penalty, pecuniary or otherwise, can be inflicted on the population on account of the acts of individuals for which it cannot be regarded as collectively responsible.'[70] As the ICRC commentary on the provision in Article 33 of the 1949 Geneva Convention IV explains:

> This does not refer to punishments inflicted under penal law, i.e. sentences pronounced by a court after due process of law, but penalties of any kind inflicted on persons or entire groups of persons, in defiance of the most elementary principles of humanity, for acts that these persons have not committed.[71]

2.27 The prohibition in the two 1977 Additional Protocols is simply and identically worded: 'collective punishments' are prohibited. Although the ICRC commentary on the prohibition in the Additional Protocol II links closely the notion with belligerent reprisals,[72] as Dinstein observes, collective punishments must be clearly distinguished.[73] Belligerent reprisals respond to earlier serious violations of IHL with proportionate measures that aim to forestall future violations. Collective punishments, which typically make no such claims, are wrought in a spirit of indiscriminate vengeance. As the Special Court for Sierra Leone declared in its judgment at trial in the *Brima* (AFRC) case, 'In other words, the punishments are imposed indiscriminately without establishing individual responsibility through some semblance of due process and without any real attempt to identify the perpetrators, if any'.[74]

---

[67] Art. 87, Convention (III) relative to the Treatment of Prisoners of War; adopted at Geneva, 12 August 1949; entered into force, 21 October 1950.
[68] Art. 33, Convention (IV) relative to the Protection of Civilian Persons in Time of War; adopted at Geneva, 12 August 1949; entered into force, 21 October 1950.
[69] ICRC, Commentary on Article 87 of the 1949 Geneva Convention III, 2020, at: https://bit.ly/3bwoD2o, paras. 3687, 3688.
[70] Art. 50, 1899 Hague Regulations.
[71] ICRC, Commentary on Article 33 of the 1949 Geneva Convention IV, 1958, at: https://bit.ly/2LbfkLJ, p. 225.
[72] ICRC, Commentary on Article 4 of the 1977 Additional Protocol II, 1987, para. 4531.
[73] Dinstein, *Non-International Armed Conflicts in International Law*, 2nd Edn, p. 187, para. 520.
[74] SCSL, *Prosecutor v. Brima, Kamara, and Kanu*, Judgment (Trial Chamber II) (Case No. SCSL-04-16-T), 20 June 2007, para. 680.

2.28 The accused in the *AFRC* case had been charged with perpetrating collective punishments 'to punish the civilian population for allegedly supporting the elected government of President Ahmed Tejan Kabbah and factions aligned with that government, or for failing to provide sufficient support to' the Armed Forces Revolutionary Council (who were on trial) and the Revolutionary United Front (RUF) in Sierra Leone.[75] The Special Court held that the following two elements constituted the war crime of collective punishments: a punishment imposed indiscriminately and collectively upon persons for acts that they have not committed; and intent on the part of the perpetrator indiscriminately and collectively to punish the persons for acts which form the subject of the punishment.[76] The Trial Chamber of the Special Court cited the 'extensive interpretation' in the ICRC commentary on the prohibition in Article 75 of the 1977 Additional Protocol I whereby collective punishments include 'not only penalties imposed in the normal judicial process, but also any other kind of sanction (such as confiscation of property)'. This is 'based on the intention to give the rule the widest possible scope, and to avoid any risk of a restrictive interpretation'.[77]

The prohibition of hostage-taking

2.29 The prohibition of hostage-taking is aligned to the prohibition on collective punishments. It had similarly been prohibited in the 1949 Geneva Convention IV whereunder it was a grave breach, as well as being prohibited in Common Article 3 in non-international armed conflict 'at any time and in any place whatsoever'. Dinstein firmly distinguishes human shields from hostages,[78] and it is true that the two concepts differ in some respects, but they do nonetheless overlap. A hostage may be taken and used to shield the hostage taker from being shot, but the shield is still a hostage. Thus, in its commentary on the prohibition of hostage-taking in the Additional Protocol II of 1977, the ICRC states that hostages 'are persons who are in the power of a party to the conflict or its agent, willingly or unwillingly, and who answer with their freedom, their physical integrity or their life for the execution of orders given by those in whose hands they have fallen, or for any hostile acts committed against them'.[79] In the Elements of Crimes under the Rome Statute of the International Criminal Court, the actus reus of the war crime of taking hostages provides, inter alia, that: 'The perpetrator seized, detained or otherwise held hostage one or more persons'; and that he or she 'threatened to kill, injure or continue to detain such person or persons'.[80]

---

[75] Ibid., para. 672.
[76] Ibid., para. 676.
[77] Ibid., para. 681, citing ICRC, Commentary on Article 75 of the 1977 Additional Protocol I, 1987, para. 1374.
[78] Dinstein, *Non-International Armed Conflicts in International Law*, 2nd Edn, p. 223, para. 630.
[79] ICRC, Commentary on Article 4 of the 1977 Additional Protocol II, 1987, para. 4537. See similarly the Commentary on Article 75 of the 1977 Additional Protocol I, 1987, para. 3052.
[80] Elements of the war crime of taking hostages under the Rome Statute of the International Criminal Court; see B. Saul, 'The Legal Nexus between Terrorism and Transnational Crime', Chap. 10 in B. Saul (ed.), *Research Handbook on International Law and Terrorism*, 2nd Edn, Edward Elgar Publishing, Cheltenham, 2021, p. 152.

2.30 The application of the International Convention Against the Taking of Hostages, adopted in 1979, two years after the conclusion of the two Additional Protocols, is precluded in international armed conflict when the 1977 Additional Protocol I applies to an incident of hostage-taking.[81] But as Dinstein astutely observes, the exclusionary clause in the Hostage-Taking Convention only applies when there is a duty to prosecute or hand over the hostage taker under the Protocols.[82] This would not exclude the application of the 1977 Additional Protocol II, given the lack of compulsory jurisdiction over serious violations thereunder. He notes that purely domestic instances of such terrorism in a non-international armed conflict would not be subject to the 1979 Hostage-Taking Convention, but this is only true 'where the offence is committed within a single State, the hostage and the alleged offender are nationals of that State and the alleged offender is found in the territory of that State'.[83] In many instances, this exclusion would not apply, as the number of foreign fighters and the extent of cross-border activities of groups such as Islamic State (in Iraq and Syria) and Boko Haram (in the nations of the Lake Chad Basin) was, and continues to be, significant. The 1979 Hostage-Taking Convention defines the crime, for the purpose of that Convention only, as follows:

> Any person who seizes or detains and threatens to kill, to injure or to continue to detain another person (hereinafter referred to as the 'hostage') in order to compel a third party, namely, a State, an international intergovernmental organization, a natural or juridical person, or a group of persons, to do or abstain from doing any act as an explicit or implicit condition for the release of the hostage commits the offence of taking of hostages ('hostage-taking') within the meaning of this Convention.[84]

Fair-trial rights

2.31 Common Article 3 to the four Geneva Conventions had employed the slightly awkward formulation of prohibiting 'the passing of sentences and the carrying out of executions without previous judgment pronounced by a regularly constituted court, affording all the judicial guarantees which are recognized as indispensable by civilized peoples'. It did not identify what precisely such 'civilized peoples' recognised as indispensable judicial guarantees. In international armed conflict, the article on fundamental guarantees in the 1977 Additional Protocol I sets out in detail many fair-trial rights, which the negotiating State now characterised as 'the generally recognized principles of regular judicial procedure':

- informing the accused without delay of the charges against him or her

---

[81] Art. 12, International Convention Against the Taking of Hostages; adopted at New York, 17 December 1979; entered into force, 3 June 1983. As of 1 May 2022, 176 States were party to the Convention.
[82] Dinstein, *Non-International Armed Conflicts in International Law*, 2nd Edn, p. 224, para. 632.
[83] Art. 13, 1979 Hostage-Taking Convention.
[84] Art. 1(1), 1979 Hostage-Taking Convention.

- ensuring the accused enjoys 'before and during his trial all necessary rights and means of defence'
- conviction only on the basis of individual penal responsibility
- respect for the principles of *nullum crimen sine lege*, *ne bis in idem*, and *nulla poena sine lege*
- the presumption of innocence until proved guilty 'according to law'
- the right of the accused to be tried in his presence
- the prohibition on self-incrimination
- the right to examine, or have examined, witnesses against the accused
- the right to have judgment pronounced publicly, and
- the right to be advised on conviction of judicial and other remedies and of the time-limits within which they may be exercised.[85]

2.32 The 1977 Additional Protocol II does not reproduce all of these valuable provisions. That said, Article 6 on 'penal prosecutions' does confirm many fundamental fair-trial provisions. There is a general exclusion of any sentence being passed and penalty executed on a person found guilty of an offence 'except pursuant to a conviction pronounced by a court offering the essential guarantees of independence and impartiality'.[86] The list of fair-trial rights is close to that in the Additional Protocol I, but does not comprise the right to examine, or have examined, witnesses against the accused, nor is the principle of *ne bis in idem* incorporated. It is further prohibited to impose the death penalty on persons who were under the age of 18 years at the time of the offence and to execute pregnant women or mothers of young children.[87]

2.33 Given that there is no combatant's privilege in non-international armed conflict,[88] there is only an obligation, at the 'end' of hostilities, to 'endeavour to grant the broadest possible amnesty to persons who have participated in the armed conflict'.[89] This does not preclude a prosecution being mounted by the authorities: for example, for treason, for rebellion, and for acts of violence by members of armed groups that are party to a non-international armed conflict.

Concluding remarks and outlook

2.34 The articles on fundamental guarantees in each of the two 1977 Additional Protocols set minimum standards for conduct and treatment of persons in the power of the enemy. While greater consistency between the provisions in the respective treaties would have been welcome, they are still immensely valuable, serving to supplement and

---

[85] Art. 75(4), 1977 Additional Protocol I.
[86] Art. 6(2), 1977 Additional Protocol II.
[87] Ibid., Art. 6(3).
[88] See, infra, paras. 5.1 and 5.16 for details of combatant's privilege in international armed conflict.
[89] Art. 6(5), 1977 Additional Protocol II.

complement the 'Convention in miniature' that is Common Article 3. Furthermore, international human rights law, which is markedly reflected in both Article 75 of the 1977 Additional Protocol I and Article 4 of the 1977 Additional Protocol II, continues to apply in parallel, offering additional legal protection to the most vulnerable. In the same way as serious violations of Common Article 3 are customary law war crimes, so it is with respect to the fundamental guarantees.

2.35 The practical significance of the fundamental guarantees should not be underestimated. Indeed, Gary Solis affirms that the due process provisions in Article 75 'have altered the way US warfighters treat captured enemy fighters' in non-international as well as international armed conflicts.[90]

---

[90] Solis, *The Law of Armed Conflict: International Humanitarian Law in War*, 3rd Edn, p. 648.

3
The Protection of Women

Introduction

The protection of women in armed conflicts is guaranteed under the 1977 Additional Protocols both in general—when women are civilians protected as such—but also specifically as women.[1] All civilians—men and boys, as well as women and girls—are at risk of sexual and gender-based violence during armed conflict. All are protected against such violence under international humanitarian law (IHL) during any armed conflict. But as the International Committee of the Red Cross (ICRC) has stated: 'While the prohibition of sexual violence applies equally to men and women, in practice women are much more affected by sexual violence during armed conflicts.'[2] This chapter then discusses the prohibition of sexual violence against women, both as a serious violation of IHL (see Table 3.1) and as a war crime (and potentially other international crime).[3]

3.1

In its landmark resolution 1325 (2000) on women, peace, and security, the United Nations (UN) Security Council called on 'all parties to armed conflict to take special measures to protect women and girls from gender-based violence, particularly rape and other forms of sexual abuse, and all other forms of violence in situations of armed conflict'.[4] Twenty years later, despite the persistently appalling prevalence of such violations, the UN Secretary-General declared that the past decade had seen a 'paradigm shift' in global understanding of the impacts of conflict-related sexual violence, 'particularly in terms of its relevance to international peace and security, the multisectoral services needed by survivors, the imperative need for gender-responsive security sector reform, and the necessity of tackling gender inequality as a root cause in times of war or conflict'.[5]

3.2

---

[1] Art. 75(5), Protocol Additional to the Geneva Conventions of 12 August 1949, and relating to the Protection of Victims of International Armed Conflicts (Protocol I); adopted at Geneva, 8 June 1977; entered into force, 7 December 1978 (hereinafter, 1977 Additional Protocol I); and Art. 5(2), Protocol Additional to the Geneva Conventions of 12 August 1949, and relating to the Protection of Victims of Non-International Armed Conflicts (Protocol II); adopted at Geneva, 8 June 1977; entered into force, 7 December 1978 (hereinafter, 1977 Additional Protocol II).

[2] ICRC, Customary IHL Rule 134: 'Women', at: http://bit.ly/2Tj99oS.

[3] Sexual violence refers to sexualised acts of violence, including rape, sexual assault, and sexual abuse, while gender-based violence refers to acts of violence perpetrated against a victim based on their gender identity or expression. That said, the differences between the two are not clear cut, as one's gender is often a huge factor in issues surrounding sexual violence and vice versa. C. Clemmer, 'Beyond the Definition: What Does "Sexual and Gender Based Violence" Really Mean?', *WeWillSpeakOut.US*, at: http://bit.ly/399Zhaq.

[4] UN Security Council Resolution 1325 adopted by unanimous vote on 31 October 2000, operative para. 10.

[5] Conflict-Related Sexual Violence, Report of the United Nations Secretary-General, UN doc. S/2020/487, 3 June 2020, at: https://bit.ly/2KJs2RT, para. 10.

Table 3.1 The Protection of Women

Rule	AP I	Customary status (IAC)	AP II	Customary status (NIAC)
Prohibition of sexual violence	Art. 75(2)(b)	Yes	Art. 4(2)(e)	Yes
Prohibition of (sexual) enslavement	No	Yes	Art. 4(2)(f)	Yes
Treatment of women in detention	Art. 75(5)	Yes	Art. 5(2)(a)	Yes
Prohibition of death penalty on pregnant women	Art. 76(3)	Yes	Art. 6(4)	Yes

3.3 The United Nations has been particularly active in this area. As part of its new system-wide approach to tackling the problem, in 2010 the UN Secretary-General appointed for the first time a Special Representative on Sexual Violence in Conflict.[6] The Office of the Special Representative drafts the annual reports of the Secretary-General on 'conflict-related sexual violence', each of which details parties to armed conflict that are credibly suspected of committing or being responsible for acts of rape or other forms of sexual violence.[7] All States repeatedly listed for conflict-related sexual violence are prohibited from participating in UN peacekeeping operations. In the Annual Reports, however, most of the listed parties are non-State armed groups.[8]

The prohibition of sexual violence in international humanitarian law

3.4 IHL has for a long time prohibited sexual violence, 'albeit implicitly and conservatively' and with treaty prohibitions often framed in 'rather archaic and discriminatory language'.[9] Thus, for example, in its regulation of international armed conflict, the 1949

---

[6] The Office of the Special Representative of the Secretary-General on Sexual Violence in Conflict was established by UN Security Council Resolution 1888 (2009).

[7] The system of monitoring, analysis, and reporting on conflict-related sexual violence was established pursuant to UN Security Council Resolution 1960 (2010). UN Security Council Resolution 1960, adopted by unanimous vote in favour on 16 December 2010, operative para. 8.

[8] Six of these having been designated as terrorist groups pursuant to Security Council resolutions 1267 (1999), 1989 (2011) and 2253 (2015), the ISIL (Da'esh, i.e. Islamic State), and al-Qaeda sanctions list. Conflict-Related Sexual Violence, Report of the UN Secretary General, UN doc. S/2019/280, 29 March 2019, paras. 4, 5.

[9] A. Priddy, 'Sexual Violence against Men and Boys in Armed Conflict', Chap. 2 in S. Casey-Maslen (ed.), *The War Report: Armed Conflict in 2013*, Oxford University Press, Oxford, 2014, pp. 271–96, at p. 279.

Geneva Convention IV stipulates that: 'Women shall be especially protected against any attack on their honour, in particular against rape, enforced prostitution, or any form of indecent assault.'[10] Considering such violence as attacks on women's 'honour' perpetuates discriminatory attitudes.[11] More neutral in its formulation of the protection of women is Common Article 3 to the 1949 Geneva Conventions, which prohibits sexual violence within the broad notion of 'outrages upon personal dignity, in particular humiliating and degrading treatment'; acts that are prohibited 'at any time and in any place whatsoever'. This language is largely reproduced in the fundamental guarantees for all in situations of international armed conflict falling under the 1977 Additional Protocol I.[12]

3.5 One form of practical protection is to detain women separately from men. Thus, under the 1949 Geneva Convention IV, when they are detained, women in occupied territories must be confined in separate quarters from men and under the direct supervision of women.[13] Whenever it is necessary, as 'an exceptional and temporary measure', to accommodate women internees who are not members of a family unit in the same internment facility as men, 'the provision of separate sleeping quarters and sanitary conveniences for the use of such women internees shall be obligatory.'[14] Reflected in both Additional Protocols,[15] the corresponding rule of customary IHL is thus applicable to all armed conflicts: 'Women who are deprived of their liberty must be held in quarters separate from those of men, except where families are accommodated as family units, and must be under the immediate supervision of women.'[16]

3.6 Further under the Geneva Convention IV, parties to an international armed conflict are further obligated to 'endeavour during the course of hostilities, to conclude agreements for the release, the repatriation, the return to places of residence, or the accommodation in a neutral country of pregnant women and mothers with infants and young children'.[17] It is also a customary rule in all armed conflicts that the specific protection, health, and assistance needs of women affected by armed conflict must be respected.[18] The ICRC offers the following interpretation of this rule:

---

[10] Art. 27, Convention (IV) relative to the Protection of Civilian Persons in Time of War; adopted at Geneva, 12 August 1949; entered into force, 21 October 1950.
[11] Priddy, 'Sexual Violence against Men and Boys in Armed Conflict', pp. 279–80 and note 65.
[12] Art. 75, Protocol Additional to the Geneva Conventions of 12 August 1949, and relating to the Protection of Victims of International Armed Conflicts; adopted at Geneva, 8 June 1977; entered into force, 7 December 1978 (hereinafter, 1977 Additional Protocol I).
[13] Art. 76, 1949 Geneva Convention IV.
[14] Ibid., Art. 85.
[15] Under the 1977 Additional Protocol II, parties to the non-international armed conflict must, 'within the limits of their capabilities', detain women in quarters separate from those of men and under the immediate supervision of women. This is so except when men and women of the same family are accommodated together. Art. 5(2)(1), 1977 Additional Protocol II.
[16] ICRC Customary IHL Rule 119: 'Accommodation for Women Deprived of Their Liberty', at: http://bit.ly/32wGtxc.
[17] Art. 132, 1949 Geneva Convention IV.
[18] ICRC Customary IHL Rule 134: 'Women', at: http://bit.ly/2Tj99oS.

44   THE PROTECTION OF WOMEN

The specific needs of women may differ according to the situation in which they find themselves—at home, in detention or displaced as a result of the conflict—but they must be respected in all situations. Practice contains numerous references to the specific need of women to be protected against all forms of sexual violence ... While the prohibition of sexual violence applies equally to men and women, in practice women are much more affected by sexual violence during armed conflicts.[19]

3.7 A specific example of respect for the specific needs of women cited by the ICRC is the requirement that pregnant women and mothers of young children, in particular nursing mothers, be treated with particular care. This requirement is found 'throughout the Fourth Geneva Convention', as well as in the 1977 Additional Protocol I.[20] These provisions require special care for pregnant women and mothers of young children with regard to the provision of food, clothing, medical assistance, evacuation, and transportation.[21]

The prohibition of sexual violence under international criminal law

3.8 International criminal law requires the prosecution of sexual or gender-based violence when it amounts to an international crime. In any armed conflict, sexual violence perpetrated by a belligerent on a member of the civilian population is a war crime. This covers rape, sexual slavery, enforced prostitution, forced pregnancy, and enforced sterilisation, and other serious forms of sexual violence.[22] Sexual violence may also amount to a crime against humanity.[23] The Statute of the International Criminal Court is said to contain 'one of the most modern and extensive lists of sexual and gender-based violence'.[24]

3.9 The Court remains an important forum for accountability for crimes of conflict-related sexual violence in States that are party to the Rome Statute or in situations referred to the Court by the UN Security Council.[25] The Elements of Crimes for the Statute defines sexual violence for the purpose of both war crimes and crimes against humanity as where a perpetrator 'committed an act of sexual nature against one or more persons or caused such person or persons to engage in an act of sexual nature by force, threat

---

[19] Ibid.
[20] Arts. 16–18, 21–23, 38, 50, 89, 91, and 127, 1949 Geneva Convention IV; and Arts. 70(1) and 76(2), 1977 Additional Protocol I.
[21] ICRC, Customary IHL Rule 134: 'Women'.
[22] Art. 8(2)(b)(xxii) and 2(e)(vi), Rome Statute of the International Criminal Court; adopted at Rome, 17 July 1998; entered into force, 1 July 2002. As of 1 May 2022, 123 States were party to the Statute.
[23] Article 7(1)(g) of the Statute concerns 'Rape, sexual slavery, enforced prostitution, forced pregnancy, enforced sterilization, or any other form of sexual violence of comparable gravity'.
[24] C. Stahn, *A Critical Introduction to International Criminal Law*, Cambridge University Press, Cambridge, 2019, p. 63.
[25] Conflict-Related Sexual Violence, Report of the UN Secretary General, 2019, para. 27.

of force or coercion, such as that caused by fear of violence, duress, detention, psychological oppression or abuse of power, against such person or persons or another person, or by taking advantage of a coercive environment such person's or persons' incapacity to give genuine consent'.[26] In any international crime of sexual violence, the use or threat of force or other forms of coercion preclude the possibility of genuine consent.[27] Whether or not the victim physically resisted is thus not determinative, and consent cannot be inferred from the absence of a struggle by the victim.[28]

Sexual and gender-based violence as a war crime

Under the Statute of the International Criminal Court, sexual violence is explicitly punishable in connection with both an international and a non-international armed conflict. With respect to international armed conflict, the Court has jurisdiction over the war crimes of 'rape, sexual slavery, enforced prostitution, forced pregnancy,[29] ... enforced sterilization, or any other form of sexual violence also constituting a grave breach of the Geneva Conventions'.[30] In the context of non-international armed conflict, the same list of war crimes is applied but the catch-all phrase at the end concerns rather a 'serious violation' of Common Article 3 (to reflect the fact that the grave breaches regime only applies in international armed conflict).[31]   **3.10**

The *actus reus* element of crime of rape under the Statute of the International Criminal Court is that the perpetrator 'invaded the body of a person resulting in penetration however slight, of any part of the body of the victim or of the perpetrator with a sexual organ, or the anal or genital opening of the victim with any object or any part of the body'. The *mens rea* of the offence is that the invasion was 'committed by force, or by threat of force or coercion, such as that caused by fear of violence, duress, detention, psychological oppression or abuse of power, against such a person on another person, or by taking advantage of a coercive environment, or the invasion was committed against a person incapable of giving genuine consent'.[32]   **3.11**

The distinction between enforced prostitution and sexual slavery is, legally speaking, a little 'blurred'.[33] Sexual slavery occurs where the 'perpetrator exercised any or all of the   **3.12**

---

[26] See Elements of Crimes, *Official Records of the Assembly of States Parties to the Rome Statute of the International Criminal Court, First session, New York, 3–10 September 2002* (hereinafter, ICC Elements of Crimes), pp. 10, 30, 38.
[27] International Criminal Tribunal for the former Yugoslavia (ICTY), *Prosecutor v. Kunarac*, Judgment (Appeals Chamber) (Case No. IT-96-23), 12 June 2002, para. 99.
[28] Ibid., para. 128; and Rule 70 of the International Criminal Court Rules of Procedure and Evidence, at: https://bit.ly/3QdyHjh.
[29] Forced pregnancy means 'the unlawful confinement of a woman forcibly made pregnant, with the intent of affecting the ethnic composition of any population or carrying out other grave violations of international law'. Art. 7(2)(f), Rome Statute of the International Criminal Court.
[30] Ibid., Art. 8(2)(b)(xxii).
[31] Ibid., Art. 8(2)(e)(vi).
[32] ICC Elements of Crimes, p. 28.
[33] Priddy, 'Sexual Violence against Men and Boys in Armed Conflict', p. 285.

powers attaching to the right of ownership over one or more person, such as by purchasing, selling, lending or bartering such a person or persons, or imposing on them a similar deprivation of liberty' and causing that person 'to engage in one or more acts of a sexual nature'.[34] In turn, enforced prostitution occurs where the perpetrator

> caused one or more persons to engage in one or more acts of a sexual nature by force, or by threat of force or coercion, such as that caused by fear of violence, duress, detention, psychological oppression or abuse of power, against such person or persons or another person, or by taking advantage of a coercive environment or such person's or persons' incapacity to give genuine consent

and the perpetrator or another person obtained or expected to obtain pecuniary or other advantage in exchange for or in connection with the acts of a sexual nature.[35] This latter requirement distinguishes the crime of enforced prostitution from that of slavery.[36]

Sexual and gender-based violence as a crime against humanity

3.13 Rape, sexual slavery, enforced prostitution, forced pregnancy, enforced sterilisation, and any other form of sexual violence 'of comparable gravity' are punishable by the International Criminal Court as crimes against humanity[37] if the underlying elements of a widespread or systematic attack against a civilian population and knowledge of the attack[38] can be established. The notion of a widespread attack comprises not only rape and other sexual violence occurring over a wide geographical area,[39] but also large numbers of rapes perpetrated in a localised area.[40] Crimes against humanity can be committed in peacetime as well as in armed conflict.

3.14 The Prosecutor of the International Criminal Court is obligated by the Statute to appoint advisers with legal expertise on specific issues, 'including, but not limited to, sexual and gender violence and violence against children'.[41] In Article 7(3) of the Statute, with respect to the crime against humanity of persecution based on gender it is stipulated that, for the purpose of the Statute, 'the term "gender" refers to the two sexes, male and female, within the context of society'. In its consideration of the need for a Convention on the prevention and repression of crimes against humanity, the International Law

---

[34] ICC Elements of Crimes, p. 28.
[35] Ibid., p. 29.
[36] Priddy, 'Sexual Violence against Men and Boys in Armed Conflict', p. 285.
[37] Art. 7(1)(g), Rome Statute of the International Criminal Court.
[38] Ibid., Art. 7(1) (chapeau).
[39] ICC, *Prosecutor* v. *Jean-Pierre Bemba Gombo*, Decision pursuant to Article 61(7)(a) and (b) of the Rome Statute on the charges of the Prosecutor against Jean-Pierre Bemba Gombo (Pre-Trial Chamber II) (Case No. ICC-01/05-01/08), 15 June 2009, paras. 117–24.
[40] ICTY, *Prosecutor* v. *Dario Kordić and Mario Čerkez*, Judgment (Appeals Chamber) (Case No. IT-95-14/2-A), 17 December 2004, para. 94.
[41] Art. 42(9), Rome Statute of the International Criminal Court.

Commission (ILC) observes that international understanding of the notion of gender has evolved since the Rome Statute was concluded, moving towards viewing gender as a socially constructed (rather than biological) concept.[42] This has been reflected, for instance, by the Inter-American Court of Human Rights in a 2017 Advisory Opinion.[43]

Trials before the International Criminal Court that have included charges of sexual violence are the *Ongwen* and *Ntaganda* cases. Dominic Ongwen was a former brigade commander of the Sinia Brigade of the Lord's Resistance Army (LRA). He was convicted of, among other international crimes, rape, sexual slavery, and outrages upon personal dignity as war crimes; and, as crimes against humanity, sexual slavery, rape, enslavement, and forced marriage as an inhumane act.[44] The Court found that a female LRA attacker raped a civilian resident of a military camp with a comb and a stick used for cooking, while the victim's husband was forced to watch. 'The assault was committed with such force that the victim started to bleed.'[45] The Court held that the crimes of rape and sexual slavery could be concurrent: 'the crime of rape requires the invasion of the body of a person by conduct resulting in penetration, however slight, committed under certain specific circumstances, while for the crime of sexual slavery any act of a sexual nature in which the victim is caused to engage would suffice without the need for penetration; conversely, the crime of sexual slavery requires the exercise by the perpetrator of any or all of the powers attaching to the right of ownership over the victim—an element which is not required for the commission of the crime of crime of rape.'[46]

3.15

In its judgment of 8 July 2019, the International Criminal Court found Bosco Ntaganda guilty of rape as a crime against humanity and a war crime, and guilty of sexual slavery as a crime against humanity and a war crime.[47] His conviction and sentence were confirmed on appeal.[48] One of the issues at trial was the 'delayed' reporting of rape by a number of victims. The Court relied heavily on the testimony of psychological expert Maeve Lewis in this regard. Ms. Lewis testified that delays in reporting rape are 'extremely common', regardless of where the rape occurred, but that women are particularly reluctant to report their sexual assaults in conflict or post-conflict areas where there is little trust in civil authorities, fear of stigmatisation, and fear of reprisals. The expert explained that one of the major reasons for delayed reporting of rape is the shame and stigma attached to it; the victims' fear that relationships will be broken; and their fear that they will be ostracised by their families. She further clarified that this fear

3.16

---

[42] ILC, Draft articles on Prevention and Punishment of Crimes Against Humanity, with commentaries, in UN doc. A/74/10, 2019, at: https://bit.ly/3odgLXD, commentary, para. 41, on Draft Article 2(2).

[43] Inter-American Court of Human Rights, *Identidad de género, e igualdad y no discriminación a parejas del mismo sexo* ['Gender identity, and equality and non-discrimination against same-sex couples'], Advisory Opinion OC-24/17, 24 November 2017, at: http://bit.ly/3sN2dRY, para. 32.

[44] ICC, *Prosecutor v. Dominic Ongwen*, Judgment (Trial Chamber IX) (Case No. ICC-02/04-01/15), 4 February 2021.

[45] Ibid., para. 2885.

[46] Ibid., para. 3037.

[47] ICC, *Prosecutor v. Bosco Ntaganda*, Judgment (Trial Chamber IV) (Case No. ICC-01/04-02/06), 8 July 2019.

[48] ICC, *Prosecutor v. Bosco Ntaganda*, Judgment (Appeals Chamber) (Case No. ICC-01/04-02/06-2666-Red), 30 March 2021.

is particularly prevalent in relation to female rape victims who fear rejection by their husbands.[49]

Sexual and gender-based violence as genocide

3.17 In certain circumstances, sexual violence may amount to genocide, the so-called 'crime of crimes'.[50] When the underlying crime is rape or forced pregnancy, in order for it to amount to an act also of genocide, the intent to destroy, in whole or in part, a minority group must accompany the intent to commit the underlying crime.[51] With respect to the Statute of the International Criminal Court, the elements of crimes determine that the genocidal act of 'causing serious bodily or mental harm' under Article 6(b) of the Rome Statute may include rape and sexual violence.[52] The Court has, however, yet to prosecute any individual for rape as an act of genocide.[53] In Africa, the Statute of the African Criminal Court explicitly lists 'acts of rape or any other form of sexual violence' as genocidal acts, but the treaty has not yet entered in force.[54]

Women and the death penalty

3.18 The 1977 Additional Protocol I requires that parties to an international armed conflict 'endeavour, to the maximum extent feasible' to avoid imposing the death penalty on pregnant women or mothers having dependent infants for any offence related to the armed conflict. In any event, the death penalty may not be executed on such women.[55] This rule applies to all persons convicted for an offence related to the armed conflict, whether or not they enjoy protected status under the Geneva Conventions and Additional Protocol 1.

3.19 In any non-international armed conflict, the death penalty 'shall not be carried out on pregnant women or mothers of young children'.[56] Unusually, this provision is stricter than the corresponding treaty provision pertaining to women in a situation of

---

[49] ICC, *Prosecutor* v. *Bosco Ntaganda*, Judgment (Trial Chamber IV), para. 187 and note 192.
[50] See, e.g., W. A. Schabas, *Genocide in International Law: The Crime of Crimes*, 2nd Edn, Cambridge University Press, Cambridge, 2009.
[51] G. Mettraux, 'Crimes Against Humanity in the Jurisprudence of the International Criminal Tribunals for the Former Yugoslavia and for Rwanda', *Harvard International Law Journal*, Vol. 43, No. 1 (2002), pp. 237–316, at pp. 295–96; see also J. M. Short, 'Sexual Violence as Genocide: The Developing Law of the International Criminal Tribunals and the International Criminal Court', *Michigan Journal of Race and Law*, Vol. 8 (2003), pp. 503–27, at pp. 505–506.
[52] Elements of Crime for Article 6(b) (Genocide by causing serious bodily or mental harm), Element 1, note 3.
[53] See, e.g., T. Altunjan, 'The International Criminal Court and Sexual Violence: Between Aspirations and Reality', *German Law Journal*, Vol. 22, No. 5 (2021), 878–93.
[54] Art. 28B(f), Protocol on Amendments to the Protocol on the Statute of the African Court of Justice and Human Rights; adopted at Malabo, 27 June 2014; not yet in force. As of 1 May 2022, 15 States had signed the Protocol, but none of these had also ratified it.
[55] Art. 76(3), Additional Protocol I.
[56] Art. 6(4), 1977 Additional Protocol II.

international armed conflict. In addition, under Common Article 3, 'the passing of sentences and the carrying out of executions without previous judgment pronounced by a regularly constituted court, affording all the judicial guarantees which are recognized as indispensable by civilized peoples' is a serious violation of IHL. The imposition of a death sentence at the issue of an unfair trial is a war crime within the jurisdiction of the International Criminal Court.[57]

There is, however, no customary law prohibition on the *imposition* of the death penalty on a pregnant woman, nor its execution on her once her child has been born, at least after a period of nursing the baby. There is also no general prohibition on the imposition and execution of the death penalty on women who are not pregnant or nursing an infant.[58] This is despite the fact that, as the UN Secretary-General has reported:

3.20

> The application of the death penalty often also violates the right to equality and the principle of non-discrimination. The decision about whether to sentence a convict to death or to lesser punishment is often arbitrary and does not necessarily follow predictable, rational criteria. In that judicial lottery, the odds are often stacked against the poor, minorities and other common targets of discrimination, including women.[59]

Concluding remarks and outlook

The claim made in 2020 by the UN Secretary-General that the past decade had seen a 'paradigm shift' in global understanding of the impacts of conflict-related sexual violence may be true, at least within the UN system, but this has not translated into better treatment of women by parties to armed conflict. Abuse comes at the hands of State armed forces and non-State armed groups alike. In Nigeria, for example, in some communities even the security forces, supposedly there for the protection of women, are said to prey on widows and young girls, exploiting them for sex when they go to fetch water or firewood. The women concerned are either too afraid to report to their parents or the men in the community are too scared to confront the perpetrators as the security forces are usually armed. Internally displaced persons (IDPs) are particularly vulnerable to being raped.[60]

3.21

In September 2021, the Office of the Special Representative of the Secretary-General on Sexual Violence in Conflict published an anthology of 'voices of survivors of

3.22

---

[57] Art. 8(2)(c)(iv), Rome Statute. In the corresponding elements of crimes, the Court is asked to consider whether, 'in the light of all relevant circumstances, the cumulative effect of factors with respect to guarantees deprived the person or persons of a fair trial'. ICC Elements of Crimes, p. 34.

[58] A woman will be protected in the same way as would a man if she had committed a capital offence while under 18 years of age.

[59] 'Capital punishment and the implementation of the safeguards guaranteeing protection of the rights of those facing the death penalty: Yearly supplement of the Secretary-General to his quinquennial report on capital punishment', 2015, para. 55.

[60] UN Protection Cluster, *Protection Analysis Report*, Protection Sector North-East, June 2021, pp. 9, 15.

conflict-related sexual violence',[61] which laid bare in harrowing testimony the suffering that women continue to endure in situations of armed conflict. The consequences can last a lifetime. In Burundi, one woman said:

> I was raped by three men who left me to die. They were armed men affiliated with the ruling party of that time … In peace negotiations no one mentioned rape or what happened during the war. I did not have a platform to tell my story. I never received any reparations. I believe people, state army and politicians need to be educated on not using women as weapon of war. Also, in peace negotiations, they need to document what happened during war for accountability and a better future.[62]

---

[61] *Voices of Survivors of Conflict-Related Sexual Violence and Service-Providers*, Office of the Special Representative of the Secretary-General on Sexual Violence in Conflict, New York, September 2021, at: https://bit.ly/3nMcwny.

[62] Ibid., p. 19.

4
The Protection of Children

Introduction

Under customary and conventional international humanitarian law (IHL), all parties to any armed conflict are prohibited from recruiting children under the age of 15 in their armed forces and from using them in the conduct of hostilities. When children are detained in connection with an armed conflict, parties must both respect and protect them, ensuring that they receive the 'special' care and aid they require. No one may be executed for conduct perpetrated during an armed conflict if he or she was under the age of 18 years when committing the criminal act or acts. These rules apply whether the armed conflict is international or non-international in character. **4.1**

This chapter discusses the protection of children under the two 1977 Additional Protocols, provisions that are reflected also in customary law. The key rules are summarised in Table 4.1. Certain treatment of children is punishable as a war crime. The protection of children is also substantively enhanced by international human rights law; indeed, this is an area of IHL in which the complementarity of human rights law is particularly marked. **4.2**

The chapter first addresses the recruitment of children into the armed forces or into armed groups and their use in the conduct of hostilities in a situation of armed conflict. The provisions in the two Additional Protocols are considered in the light of customary IHL, international human rights law, and international criminal law. The second part of the chapter describes the nature of the duty to ensure the special respect and protection of all children affected by armed conflict. The chapter concludes with consideration of the prohibition on the imposition of the death penalty for acts committed while under 18 years of age. **4.3**

Child recruitment and use in hostilities

The legal situation under international humanitarian law

No provisions on the age of recruitment were incorporated in the four 1949 Geneva Conventions, primarily on the basis that this was considered a matter for national law and practice. That said, a particular focus on the protection of children under 15 years of age in the Fourth Convention on the Protection of Civilians indicated an age **4.4**

52 THE PROTECTION OF CHILDREN

Table 4.1 Summary of Rules Protecting Children in Armed Conflict

Rule	AP I	Customary status (IAC)	AP II	Customary status (NIAC)
Prohibition on recruiting children under 15 years of age	Art. 77(2)	Yes	Art. 4(2)(c)	Yes
Obligation of special respect and protection of all children	Art. 77(1)	Yes	Art. 4(3)	Yes
Prohibition on executing anyone for acts committed while under 18 years of age	Art. 77(5)	Yes	Art. 6(4)	Yes

threshold between those who were not expected to be enrolled in armed forces and those who might either join voluntarily or even be conscripted. Thus, for example, it is stipulated that, after the outbreak of hostilities, parties to an international armed conflict 'may establish in their own territory and, if the need arises, in occupied areas, hospital and safety zones and localities so organized as to protect from the effects of war, wounded, sick and aged persons, [and] children under fifteen'.[1] In its commentary on the provision, the International Committee of the Red Cross (ICRC) stated: 'These various categories among the civilian population are based on a very simple criterion: they are persons who are taking no part in the hostilities and whose weakness makes them incapable of contributing to the war potential of their country; they thus appear to be particularly deserving of protection.'[2] While the tone of the ICRC commentary of 1958 appears rather paternalistic today, it was reflecting prevailing views of the period and it does serve to underline the importance of child protection during armed conflict.

4.5 The issue of child recruitment and their participation in hostilities is addressed directly in both 1977 Additional Protocols. In the Additional Protocol I, Article 77 is dedicated to the protection of children.[3] As the subsequent ICRC commentary on the article explains:

---

[1] Art. 14, Convention (IV) relative to the Protection of Civilian Persons in Time of War; adopted at Geneva, 12 August 1949; entered into force, 21 October 1950.
[2] ICRC, Commentary on Article 14 of 1949 Geneva Convention IV, 1958, at: http://bit.ly/3lBHr3n, p. 126.
[3] Art. 77, Protocol Additional to the Geneva Conventions of 12 August 1949, and relating to the Protection of Victims of International Armed Conflicts (Protocol I); adopted at Geneva, 8 June 1977; entered into force, 7 December 1978.

In view of its character, this article serves as a development of both the fourth Convention and of other rules of international law which govern the protection of fundamental human rights in time of armed conflict, particularly the International Covenant of 1966 on Civil and Political Rights and the Declaration of the Rights of the Child, adopted unanimously in 1959 by the United Nations General Assembly. At the present time a Draft Convention on the Rights of the Child is under discussion in the United Nations.

While the specific issue of recruitment into the armed forces was not addressed in either the 1959 Declaration of the Rights of the Child or the International Covenant on Civil and Political Rights (ICCPR),[4] the Declaration did stipulate that: 'The child shall not be admitted to employment before an appropriate minimum age; he shall in no case be caused or permitted to engage in any occupation or employment which would prejudice his health or education, or interfere with his physical, mental or moral development.'[5] That 'appropriate minimum age' was not determined; nor indeed was any age attributed in the Declaration at which a child would become an adult.

4.6 That the UN Convention on the Rights of the Child (CRC) had not yet been adopted—it is today the most widely ratified human rights treaty in history[6]—led the ICRC to aver in 1987 that no definition existed of a child in international law. Nonetheless, it concluded that there was 'no doubt that all human beings under fifteen should, within the meaning of the Fourth Convention and this Protocol, be considered and treated as children'.[7] With respect to the participation of children in hostilities, the ICRC declared that:

> Recent conflicts have all too often shown the harrowing spectacle of boys, who have barely left childhood behind them, brandishing rifles and machine-guns and ready to shoot indiscriminately at anything that moves. Participation of children and adolescents in combat is an inhumane practice and the ICRC considered that it should come to an end. It entails mortal danger for the children themselves, but also for the many people who are exposed to their erratic [behaviour].[8]

4.7 The second paragraph of Article 77 concerns recruitment and use in hostilities. This provides in full:

> The Parties to the conflict shall take all feasible measures in order that children who have not attained the age of fifteen years do not take a direct part in hostilities and, in particular, they shall refrain from recruiting them into their armed forces. In

---

[4] International Covenant on Civil and Political Rights; adopted at New York, 16 December 1966; entered into force, 23 March 1976. As of 1 May 2022, 173 States were party to the ICCPR.
[5] Principle 9, UN Declaration on the Rights of the Child; proclaimed by UN General Assembly Resolution 1386 (XIV) of 20 November 1959; text available at: http://bit.ly/38hKYji.
[6] As of 1 May 2022, 196 of 197 States were party to the Convention, while the United States was a signatory.
[7] ICRC, Commentary on Article 77 of the 1977 Additional Protocol I, 1987, at: http://bit.ly/37qwSJq, pp. 899–900, para. 3179.
[8] Ibid., p. 900, para. 3183.

recruiting among those persons who have attained the age of fifteen years but who have not attained the age of eighteen years, the Parties to the conflict shall endeavour to give priority to those who are oldest.

The ICRC explains that their proposals encountered opposition, as governments did not wish to undertake unconditional obligations to prevent children under 15 from participating directly in hostilities. The ICRC had suggested that the Parties to the conflict take 'all necessary measures' to prevent such participation, but this was watered down in the final text to a duty to take 'all feasible measures' with a view to doing so.[9] Moreover, although the obligation to refrain from recruiting children under 15 years of age remained, that of refusing their voluntary enrolment was no longer explicitly mentioned. In fact, according to the Rapporteur of the Committee charged with drafting the provision, 'sometimes, especially in occupied territories and in wars of national liberation, it would not be realistic to totally prohibit voluntary participation of children under fifteen'.[10]

4.8 While, nonetheless, the duty to refrain from recruiting children under 15 years of age into armed forces on a voluntary as well as a compulsory basis was clear-cut ('shall refrain from recruiting them'), in the Additional Protocol I the duty to prevent such participation in hostilities was made primarily one of due diligence—reasonable effort—rather than one of result. Subsequently, however, the nature of that duty has evolved into one that is absolute, and which encompasses accepting any underage children in armed forces. Thus, the 1998 Rome Statute of the International Criminal Court grants the Court jurisdiction in international armed conflict over the war crime of 'conscripting or enlisting children under the age of fifteen years into the national armed forces or using them to participate actively in hostilities'.[11] The corresponding elements of crime confirm that the *actus reus* of the offence is simply that the perpetrator 'conscripted or enlisted one or more persons into the national armed forces or used one or more persons to participate actively in hostilities'.[12]

4.9 The Additional Protocol I confirms that should, in breach of international law, a child under 15 years of age participate directly in hostilities and be captured, then he or she shall be entitled to prisoner-of-war status in the same manner and according to the same criteria as any older combatant.[13] Thus, the ICRC confirms that there is no age limit for the right to such treatment: 'Theoretically prisoners of war may be very young or very old.'[14] It noted, however, that according to the Third Geneva Convention of

---

[9] Ibid., p. 900, para. 3184.
[10] Ibid.
[11] Art. 8(2)(b)(xxvi), Rome Statute of the International Criminal Court; adopted at Rome, 17 July 1998; entered into force, 1 July 2002 (hereinafter, Rome Statute).
[12] Element 1, Elements of Crime for Article 8(2)(b)(xxvi): war crime of using, conscripting or enlisting children, in *Official Records of the Assembly of States Parties to the Rome Statute of the International Criminal Court, First session, New York, 3–10 September 2002*, Part II(B).
[13] Art. 77(3), Additional Protocol I.
[14] ICRC, Commentary on Article 77 of the 1977 Additional Protocol I, 1987, p. 902, para. 3194.

1949, age is a factor which justifies privileged treatment.[15] On 'many occasions', the ICRC noted, it 'has intervened in favour of very young prisoners of war, requesting privileged treatment for them during captivity and priority during repatriation'.[16]

4.10 The corresponding provision in the 1977 Additional Protocol II with respect to recruitment and use of children in non-international armed conflicts falling within the scope of application of the Protocol is, exceptionally, framed in stricter terms than it is in the Additional Protocol I. According to the Additional Protocol II: 'Children who have not attained the age of fifteen years shall neither be recruited in the armed forces or groups nor allowed to take part in hostilities'.[17] Absent is the language of 'all feasible measures' and a prohibition is imposed on all participation in hostilities, whether that be direct or indirect. Thus, the ICRC commentary on the provision concludes that not only can a child not be conscripted or voluntarily enlist, but he will also not be ' "allowed to take part in hostilities", i.e., to participate in military operations such as gathering information, transmitting orders, transporting ammunition and foodstuffs, or acts of sabotage'.[18] The ICRC confirms that the 'principle of non-recruitment also prohibits accepting voluntary enlistment'.[19]

4.11 Under customary international criminal law, the minimum age for recruitment and use of children as direct participants in hostilities is 15 years irrespective of the classification of the conflict.[20] The Rome Statute replicates the language used with respect to international armed conflict under the 1977 Additional Protocol I in the war crime of 'conscripting or enlisting children under the age of fifteen years into armed forces or groups or using them to participate actively in hostilities' in non-international armed conflict.[21] It adds reference to armed groups to address the different realities of such conflicts. The same *actus reus* and *mens rea* elements as in the provision applicable in international armed conflict are incorporated, *mutatis mutandis*, in the corresponding elements of crimes.

---

[15] Art. 16, Convention (III) relative to the Treatment of Prisoners of War; adopted at Geneva, 12 August 1949; entered into force, 21 October 1950. In its 2020 commentary on the provision, the ICRC notes that whether they are recruited lawfully or unlawfully, children in the power of an adverse Party remain entitled to special respect and protection. In a prisoner-of-war camp setting, such special treatment includes access to education appropriate to their age and separate accommodation (except where families are accommodated together as units). Treatment may also consist of a 'distinct disciplinary or judicial regime' and 'special arrangements for family contacts'. A balance must be found 'between accommodating families together and the potential need to separate minors from all adult prisoners of war. Any such measures must also take into account cultural norms relating to the way in which families live together, for instance regarding the sharing of rooms by family members of different genders'. ICRC, Commentary on Article 16 of 1949 Geneva Convention III, 2020, at: http://bit.ly/30vZsaJ, para. 1755.
[16] ICRC, Commentary on Article 77 of the 1977 Additional Protocol I, 1987, p. 902, para. 3194.
[17] Art. 4(3)(c), Protocol Additional to the Geneva Conventions of 12 August 1949, and relating to the Protection of Victims of Non-International Armed Conflicts (Protocol II); adopted at Geneva, 8 June 1977; entered into force, 7 December 1978.
[18] ICRC, Commentary on Article 4 of the 1977 Additional Protocol II, 1987, at: https://bit.ly/2IGhscP, p. 1380, para. 4557.
[19] Ibid.
[20] Y. Dinstein, *Non-International Armed Conflicts in International Law*, 2nd Edn, Cambridge University Press, Cambridge, 2021, p. 242, para. 686.
[21] Art. 8(2)(e)(vii), Rome Statute.

4.12 The first case adjudged by the International Criminal Court concerned alleged recruitment and use of children as a war crime. Thomas Lubanga Dyilo was found guilty by a trial chamber, in March 2012, of the war crimes of enlisting and conscripting children under the age of 15 years and using them to participate actively in hostilities.[22] Mr. Lubanga's command—he was the President of the Union of Congolese Patriots (UPC)—existed partially in a situation of international armed conflict (a military occupation by proxy) and later in a situation of non-international armed conflict. In July 2012, Mr. Lubanga was sentenced to a total of 14 years of imprisonment for his actions in non-international armed conflict. Both the verdict and the resultant sentence were confirmed by the Appeals Chamber of the Court in December 2014.[23]

4.13 In its judgment at trial, the Court observed that the prohibition of recruitment (in international armed conflict) was based on Article 77(2) of the Additional Protocol I.[24] The crimes specifically charged were, however, committed only in the later context of non-international armed conflict. The Court noted that Article 4(3)(c) of the 1977 Additional Protocol II 'includes an absolute prohibition against the recruitment and use of children under the age of 15 in hostilities.'[25] It determined, bearing in mind the inclusion of the word 'or' in Article 8(2)(e)(vii) of the Rome Statute, that the three alternatives set out in the war crime—conscription, enlistment, and use in hostilities—are separate offences.[26] While this is a logical conclusion and a robust appreciation of the law, concerns have arisen as a result of the Court's broad interpretation of the war crime of using children to participate 'actively' in hostilities.

4.14 The Court opines that the prohibition against using children under the age of 15 years to participate actively in hostilities 'is not dependent on the individuals concerned having been earlier conscripted or enlisted into the relevant armed force or group'.[27] Therefore, it concludes, 'a child can be "used" for the purposes of the Statute without evidence being provided as regards his or her earlier "conscription" or "enlistment" into the relevant armed force or group'.[28] This is problematic as it suggests that a formal process is demanded for recruitment into an armed group (as it is for a State armed force). But this may simply not be the case. A child may be forcibly abducted by an armed group and then used to participate in hostilities without any formal ceremony but has still been enrolled in its ranks. (The consequences of any attempt to escape the clutches of the group will, indeed, be made painfully clear to him or her.)

4.15 But the Court went further, seeking to draw an uncomfortable distinction between 'actively' participating in hostilities (which it qualified as a broad term applicable to any

---

[22] International Criminal Court, *Prosecutor v. Thomas Lubanga Dyilo*, Judgment (Trial Chamber I) (Case No. ICC-01/04-01/06), 14 March 2012, at: https://bit.ly/3ekkS2P (hereinafter, *Lubanga* Trial Judgment).

[23] International Criminal Court, *Prosecutor v. Thomas Lubanga Dyilo*, Judgment (Appeals Chamber) (Case No. ICC-01/04-01/06 A 5), 1 December 2014, at: https://bit.ly/3t0bIfT (hereinafter, *Lubanga* Appeals Judgment).

[24] *Lubanga* Trial Judgment, para. 542.
[25] Ibid., para. 604.
[26] Ibid., para. 609.
[27] Ibid., para. 620.
[28] Ibid.

form of participation) and 'directly' participating in hostilities (which it deemed to be a significantly narrower concept).[29] In this it quoted extensively from the judgments of the Special Court for Sierra Leone, which observed in its judgment at trial in the so-called AFRC (Armed Forces Revolutionary Council) case that an armed force or group

> requires logistical support to maintain its operations. Any labour or support that gives effect to, or helps maintain, operations in a conflict constitutes active participation. Hence carrying loads for the fighting faction, finding and/or acquiring food, ammunition or equipment, acting as decoys, carrying messages, making trails or finding routes, manning checkpoints or acting as human shields are some examples of active participation as much as actual fighting and combat.[30]

These dicta by the Special Court mix direct and indirect participation in hostilities.[31] Collecting food, cooking food, cleaning, and other acts required of many children in an armed group, such as providing sexual services to fighters on demand, are not direct participation in hostilities (even though the use of children in this way may nonetheless be criminal).

4.16 In its judgment on the appeal by Mr. Lubanga against his conviction for the use of children as soldiers, the Court clarified its position, declaring that the term 'participate actively in hostilities' in Article 8(2)(e)(vii) of the Statute 'does not have to be given the same interpretation as the terms active or direct participation in the context of the principle of distinction between combatants and civilians, as set out, in particular, in Common Article 3 of the Geneva Conventions'.[32] The Court argued that its approach was supported by the provisions in IHL dealing specifically with children in armed conflict, namely Article 77(2) of the 1977 Additional Protocol I and Article 4(3)(c) of the 1977 Additional Protocol II.[33] Its mistake—if such it is—was to analyse the broad wording of Article 4(3)(c), which does not refer to *direct* participation but to any form of participation, and apply this to the Rome Statute. It also means that active participation as designated in Article 8(2)(c) of the Statute—'persons taking no active part in the hostilities'—is defined differently from the wording in subparagraph (b) and (e) of Article 8(2).

4.17 In the second case adjudged by the International Criminal Court, *Prosecutor v. Germain Katanga*, the trial chamber appeared to pull back a little from its position in *Lubanga* (while denying that it was doing so). In its judgment in *Katanga*, the Court said that 'whereas "active participation" in hostilities does refer to direct participation in hostilities, viz. combat ... it also encompasses active participation in activities linked to

---

[29] As Dinstein observes, 'there is not even slender evidence in the practice of States for this assertion'. Dinstein, *Non-International Armed Conflicts in International Law*, 2nd Edn, p. 80, para. 214.
[30] Special Court for Sierra Leone, *Prosecutor v. Brima, Kamara, and Kanu*, Judgment (Trial Chamber II) (Case No. SCSL-04-16-T), 20 June 2007, para. 737.
[31] Dinstein, *Non-International Armed Conflicts in International Law*, 2nd Edn, p. 243, para. 688.
[32] International Criminal Court, *Prosecutor v. Thomas Lubanga Dyilo*, Judgment (Appeals Chamber) (Case No. ICC-01/04-01/06 A 5), 1 December 2014, para. 324.
[33] Ibid., para. 325.

combat, including support functions within military operations ... However, a child is not actively participating in hostilities if the activity which he or she is performing is "clearly unrelated to hostilities".[34] This position would exclude, at the least, 'finding and/or acquiring food'.

4.18 In February 2021, the International Criminal Court issued its judgment in the *Ongwen* case. Dominic Ongwen, a former commander of one of the brigades of the Lord's Resistance Army, was charged with 70 counts (combined) of war crimes and crimes against humanity. This case posed a further challenge to the Court. While the list of crimes allegedly perpetrated by Dominic Ongwen was both long and shocking, it was agreed by all relevant parties that he himself had been forcibly recruited as a young child, at an age of somewhere between eight and fourteen years.[35] He was thus victim as well as perpetrator. That said, as Carsten Stahn has observed, the victims of atrocities at the hands of children 'find little comfort in the fact that child soldiers are themselves victims'.[36]

4.19 Although the Rome Statute precludes the prosecution before it of those who were under 18 years of age at the commission of the offence,[37] those recruited as children who committed international crimes as adults may be charged and convicted. Mr. Ongwen was charged with international crimes committed against civilians in Northern Uganda when aged in his twenties. The time frame began on 1 July 2002—the time of the Rome Statute's entry into force—and ended on 31 December 2005.[38] But he assuredly committed international crimes before he reached his 18th birthday.

4.20 Often miscast as encapsulating a comprehensive prohibition on holding children criminally responsible for international crimes or acts of terrorism, the soft-law Paris Principles of 2007[39] do not exclude such liability. They merely observe, correctly, that children should be considered *primarily* as victims of offences against international law and not only as perpetrators. Such children must be treated in accordance with international law in a framework of restorative justice and social rehabilitation, consistent with international law which offers children special protection through numerous agreements and principles.[40]

4.21 As concerns the use of recruited children, the Court reiterated in its *Ongwen* trial judgment that 'to "participate actively in hostilities" ranges from direct participation in hostilities to other supporting combat-related activities'.[41] Conversely, the Court

---

[34] International Criminal Court, *Prosecutor v. Germain Katanga*, Judgment (Trial Chamber II) (Case No. ICC-01/04-01/07), 7 March 2014, para. 1044.

[35] International Criminal Court, *Prosecutor v. Dominic Ongwen*, Judgment (Trial Chamber IX) (Case No. ICC-02/04-01/15), 4 February 2021 (hereinafter, *Ongwen* Trial Judgment), paras. 28–29.

[36] C. Stahn, *A Critical Introduction to International Criminal Law*, Cambridge University Press, Cambridge, 2019, p. 314.

[37] Art. 26, Rome Statute.

[38] *Ongwen* Trial Judgment, para. 32.

[39] Principles and Guidelines on Children Associated with Armed Forces or Armed Groups (Paris Principles), Paris, February 2007.

[40] Ibid., para. 3.6.

[41] *Ongwen* Trial Judgment, para. 2770.

said, citing the *Katanga* trial judgment, activities unrelated to hostilities fall outside of Article 8(2)(e)(vii) of the Rome Statute: 'When assessing whether the role of the child is to be treated as active participation, what matters is a case-by-case assessment of the link between the activity undertaken by the child and the hostilities in which the armed force or group for which he or she is acting is engaged.'[42]

4.22 We are left by the Court with a broad notion of child participation under international criminal law but a—potentially—narrow understanding of recruitment. Arguably, the Court would have stayed closer to an accurate appreciation of IHL if it had taken a broader understanding of what amounts to recruitment, starting with an abduction by an armed group. In doing so, it would still be ensuring accountability for the abuse of children. Such an approach would be balanced with a narrower conception of active/direct participation in hostilities: one that is consonant with IHL's general protection against attack afforded to all civilians. There may of course be present at camps the children of fighters, who play no role in hostilities and are certainly not members of the group. These children are civilians, entitled to immunity from attack.

4.23 A final note on the prohibition on child recruitment under IHL is warranted. While, by definition, the war crime of enlistment into the armed forces is limited to acts that have direct nexus to an armed conflict, the provision in Article 77(2) of the 1977 Additional Protocol I is not so limited, applying also in peacetime. Article 1(3) of the Additional Protocol I explicitly applies the Protocol *in toto* to the situations referred to in Article 2 common to the four 1949 Geneva Conventions. Therein, reference is made to 'the provisions which shall be implemented in peacetime'. The prohibition on recruitment of children into State armed forces applies also in peacetime. That this is so is reinforced by the language of the Optional Protocol to the CRC on the involvement of children in armed conflict, which applies at all times, including peacetime.[43]

4.24 The situation with respect to the provision in Article 4(2) of the 1977 Additional Protocol II is more complicated given its limited scope of application. While recruitment into the State armed forces remains covered by the rule in the Additional Protocol I, it is to customary law that one turns to cover the acts of 'dissident armed forces or other organized armed groups' at all times, including in 'situations of internal disturbances and tensions, such as riots, isolated and sporadic acts of violence and other acts of a similar nature'.[44] Rule 136 of the ICRC's Study of customary IHL stipulates simply that children 'must not be recruited into armed forces or armed groups'. While there is not a 'uniform practice with respect to the minimum age for recruitment', there is 'agreement', the ICRC states, 'that it should not be below 15 years of age'.[45]

---

[42] Ibid., citing the *Lubanga* Appeals Judgment, paras. 333, 340.
[43] Optional Protocol to the Convention on the Rights of the Child on the involvement of children in armed conflict; adopted at New York, 25 May 2000; entered into force, 12 February 2002 (hereinafter, Optional Protocol to the CRC on children in armed conflict).
[44] Art. 1(2), 1977 Additional Protocol II.
[45] ICRC Customary IHL Rule 136: 'Recruitment of Child Soldiers', at: http://bit.ly/2PAzhgS.

The legal situation under human rights law

4.25 The failure to raise the minimum age for recruitment and use of children in hostilities in the negotiation of the CRC in the late 1980s was unacceptable to many governments. The Convention, which determined that a child was, as a general rule, anyone under the age of 18,[46] not only retained 15 years as the minimum age for recruitment into the armed forces, but also adopted the weaker standard incorporated in the 1977 Additional Protocol I. Thus, Article 38(2) of the CRC stipulated that: 'States Parties shall take all feasible measures to ensure that persons who have not attained the age of fifteen years do not take a direct part in hostilities.' Paragraph 3 provided that: 'States Parties shall refrain from recruiting any person who has not attained the age of fifteen years into their armed forces.'

4.26 Following a campaign by a coalition of non-governmental organisations[47] and work by a number of key governments, an Optional Protocol to the CRC on the involvement of children in armed conflict was adopted by States Parties to the CRC in 2000.[48] The Protocol—a human rights instrument not an IHL treaty[49]—stipulates that States Parties 'shall take all feasible measures to ensure that members of their armed forces who have not attained the age of 18 years do not take a direct part in hostilities'.[50] It is further prohibited to recruit children compulsorily into the armed forces.[51] With respect to non-State armed groups: 'Armed groups that are distinct from the armed forces of a State should not, under any circumstances, recruit or use in hostilities persons under the age of 18 years.'[52] The 'jarring' use of the term 'should not', when juxtaposed with 'under any circumstances',[53] is intended to distinguish a politically binding exhortation to non-State armed groups from the international legal obligations imposed on States Parties.[54]

4.27 In this regard, as a result of objections by a number of States, particularly the United Kingdom and the United States, it was only required that States 'raise the minimum age for the voluntary recruitment of persons into their national armed forces from that set out' in the CRC (i.e. to at least 16 years).[55] The minimum age for enlistment into the UK armed forces is 16 years,[56] while in the United States it is 17 years of age.[57]

---

[46] Art. 1, Convention on the Rights of the Child; adopted at New York, 20 November 1989; entered into force, 2 September 1990: 'For the purposes of the present Convention, a child means every human being below the age of eighteen years unless under the law applicable to the child, majority is attained earlier.'

[47] Coalition to Stop the Use of Children as Soldiers, later renamed Child Soldiers International. The coalition closed in 2019, for want of funding, although some of their work was taken by the Romeo Dallaire Child Soldiers Initiative, at: http://bit.ly/3cjgKgK. Child Soldiers International, 'Child Soldiers International Announcement', 12 April 2019, at: http://bit.ly/3v71nk6.

[48] As of 1 May 2022, 172 States were party to the Optional Protocol.

[49] A fact described by Yoram Dinstein as a 'quaint phenomenon'. Dinstein, *Non-International Armed Conflicts in International Law*, 2nd Edn, p. 309, para. 889.

[50] Art. 1, Optional Protocol to the CRC on children in armed conflict.

[51] Ibid., Art. 2.

[52] Ibid., Art. 4(1).

[53] Dinstein, *Non-International Armed Conflicts in International Law*, 2nd Edn, p. 211, para. 594.

[54] This is because some States do not accept that non-State armed groups may be the bearers of obligations under international human rights law.

[55] Art. 3(1), Optional Protocol to the CRC on children in armed conflict.

[56] A child between the age of 16 and 18 years of age may join the British Army, but to be accepted he or she must have parental consent to do so. British Army, 'Can I Join?', at: https://bit.ly/37cL5eJ.

[57] USA.Gov, 'Join the Military', at: https://bit.ly/3yx8IL9.

4.28 All of the 172 States Parties to the Optional Protocol as of writing have accepted the prohibition on conscription of anyone under the age of 18 years into their armed forces, a rule that appears to have passed into customary law. The minimum age for voluntary enlistment under international law is 16 years. A minimum age of 18 years for voluntary recruitment may be considered no more than *de lege ferenda*.

4.29 States must further take all feasible measures to ensure that members of their armed forces who have not attained the age of 18 years do not take a direct part in hostilities. It is uncertain whether, given the protective aim of the provision, the notion of direct participation in hostilities is to be considered broadly or in line with the general understanding in IHL. In its Resolution 2427 (2018), the UN Security Council strongly condemned 'all violations of applicable international law involving the recruitment and use of children by parties to armed conflict'.[58] The slightly awkward formulation of its condemnation reflected the fact that four of the five permanent members of the Council—China, France, the United Kingdom, and the United States—continue to recruit children into their armed forces.[59]

4.30 The Council also stressed the need 'to pay particular attention to the treatment of children associated or allegedly associated with all non-State armed groups, including those who commit acts of terrorism, in particular by establishing standard operating procedures for the rapid handover of these children to relevant civilian child protection actors'.[60] Reflecting the language of the 2007 Paris Principles, the Council emphasised that children 'who have been recruited in violation of applicable international law by armed forces and armed groups and are accused of having committed crimes during armed conflicts should be treated primarily as victims of violations of international law'.[61]

4.31 As the Committee on the Rights of the Child has observed in its General Comment No. 24 on the CRC:

> When under the control of such groups, children may become victims of multiple forms of violations, such as conscription; military training; being used in hostilities and/or terrorist acts, including suicide attacks; being forced to carry out executions; being used as human shields; abduction; sale; trafficking; sexual exploitation; child

---

[58] UN Security Council Resolution 2427, adopted by unanimous vote in favour on 9 July 2018, operative para. 1.
[59] For China and France, as well as the United States, the minimum age for voluntary recruitment is 17 years. Other States that are believed to accept children aged 17 years into their armed forces include Algeria, Australia, Austria, Azerbaijan, Cabo Verde, Cuba, Cyprus, the Democratic People's Republic of Korea, Germany, Guinea-Bissau, Ireland, Israel, Italy, Luxembourg, Malaysia, New Zealand, the Philippines, São Tomé and Príncipe, Saudi Arabia, Turkmenistan, and the United Arab Emirates. Other States beside the United Kingdom that continue to recruit children aged 16 years into their armed forces include Brazil, Canada, Chile, the Dominican Republic, Egypt, El Salvador, India, Jordan, Pakistan, and Singapore. The situation with respect to Oman remains unclear. See: http://bit.ly/2SLXZKV. Iran, a signatory to the Optional Protocol, appears to allow voluntary enlistment into the *Basij* at 15 years of age.
[60] UN Security Council Resolution 2427, adopted by unanimous vote in favour on 9 July 2018, operative para. 19.
[61] Ibid., operative para. 20.

marriage; being used for the transport or sale of drugs; or being exploited to carry out dangerous tasks, such as spying, conducting surveillance, guarding checkpoints, conducting patrols or transporting military equipment. It has been reported that non-State armed groups and those designated as terrorist groups also force children to commit acts of violence against their own families or within their own communities to demonstrate loyalty and to discourage future defection.[62]

Under customary law, the use of any civilians as human shields in any armed conflict is prohibited.[63] The rule is codified in Article 51(7) of the 1977 Additional Protocol I: 'The Parties to the conflict shall not direct the movement of the civilian population or individual civilians in order to attempt to shield military objectives from attacks or to shield military operations.'

Child protection in armed conflict

4.32 In the course of the conduct of hostilities in an armed conflict, the fundamental principles of distinction and proportionality in attack apply to child civilians in any armed conflict, just as they do to any other civilians. Thus, as is the case with adults, children will be protected from attack by these IHL principles unless and for such time as they participate directly in hostilities. This is true under customary law whether the conflict is international or non-international in character.

4.33 The UN Assistance Mission in Afghanistan (UNAMA) issues detailed and carefully researched annual reports on the protection of civilians, including children. In its report covering calendar year 2020, Afghanistan was said to be 'one of the deadliest places in the world to be a child'.[64] Children are killed and maimed in ground engagements (comprising almost one-half of all child casualties), or in blasts of landmines or unexploded ordnance, during aerial attacks, and by abductions. Children continue to be subjected to recruitment and used in combat and support roles by parties to the conflict, and to sexual exploitation and violence. Confirmed child casualties in 2020 (totalling 760 killed and 1,859 injured) made up 30 per cent of all civilian casualties.[65]

4.34 IHL also has provisions detailing the duty to ensure the special protection of children in situations of armed conflict. Thus, under the Additional Protocol I: 'Children shall be the object of special respect and shall be protected against any form of indecent

---

[62] Committee on the Rights of the Child, General Comment No. 24 (2019) on children's rights in the child justice system, UN doc. CRC/C/GC/24, 18 September 2019 (reissued for technical reasons on 11 November 2019), available at: https://bit.ly/3rAv9vo, para. 98.
[63] ICRC Customary IHL Rule 97: 'Human Shields', at: https://bit.ly/3F1BTsf.
[64] UNAMA, *Protection of Civilians in Armed Conflict, Annual Report 2020*, Kabul, February 2021, at: https://bit.ly/3eoqMjh, p. 30.
[65] Ibid.

assault. The Parties to the conflict shall provide them with the care and aid they require, whether because of their age [not stipulated] or for any other reason.'[66] The ICRC's commentary of 1987 on the provision offers little insight into the kind of care required other than to remark that the duty 'may seem self-evident, but it is just as well to state it in black and white'.[67]

Considerably more detail is provided in the wording of the Additional Protocol II of 1977 on this issue. Under Article 4(3) of the Protocol, it is similarly stipulated that children must be provided with the care and aid they require. It is further specified that this includes an education, 'including religious and moral education', in keeping with the wishes of their parents or, in the absence of parents, of those responsible for their care.[68] In addition, all appropriate steps must be taken to facilitate the reunion of families temporarily separated.[69] Measures must be taken, 'if necessary, and whenever possible with the consent' of their parents or guardians, 'to remove children temporarily from the area in which hostilities are taking place to a safer area within the country and ensure that they are accompanied by persons responsible for their safety and well-being'.[70]

4.35

Further comment is provided on these provisions by the ICRC, which observes that as children are 'particularly vulnerable', they require 'privileged treatment in comparison with the rest of the civilian population'. That is why, the ICRC states, 'they enjoy specific legal protection'.[71] The subparagraph on the provision of education was not contained in the ICRC draft for the Protocol, which was limited to the material aspect of protection, and was the result of an amendment. In its view, however, it 'answers the concern' to ensure continuity of education 'so that children retain their cultural identity and a link with their roots'. The rule seeks to remove the risk that children separated from their family by armed conflict 'might be uprooted by being initiated into a culture, religion or moral code which may not correspond with the wishes of their parents, and in addition could in this way become political pawns'. The word 'education' should be understood in its broadest sense.[72]

4.36

While schools do not benefit from special protection under IHL—as do, for instance, medical facilities—efforts have been made at a policy level to reduce attacks on educational facilities and to minimise their use by parties to armed conflict. The Safe Schools Declaration commits signatory States[73] to the *Guidelines for protecting schools and universities from military use during armed conflict*.[74] These soft-law guidelines, agreed

4.37

---

[66] Art. 77(1), 1977 Additional Protocol I.
[67] ICRC, Commentary on Article 77 of the 1977 Additional Protocol I, 1987, p. 900, para. 3182.
[68] Art. 4(3)(a), 1977 Additional Protocol II.
[69] Ibid., Art. 4(3)(b).
[70] Art. 4(3)(e), 1977 Additional Protocol II.
[71] ICRC, Commentary on Article 4 of the 1977 Additional Protocol II, 1987, at: https://bit.ly/2IGhscP, p. 1377, para. 4544.
[72] Ibid., p. 1378, para. 4552.
[73] As of 8 March 2022, 114 States had signed the Declaration. See the Norwegian government's list of signatories, at: http://bit.ly/2k3LOtS.
[74] Available at: http://bit.ly/2lY5ZtM.

upon in 2014, do not affect existing obligations under international law.[75] They are, however, intended 'to lead to a shift in behaviour that will lead to better protections for schools and universities in times of armed conflict and, in particular, to a reduction in their use by the fighting forces of parties to armed conflict in support of the military effort'.[76]

4.38 Armed conflict is both a cause of disability and the context for further abuse and neglect. The Additional Protocols do not specifically address the impact of disability on children, but it is generally agreed that this impact can be devastating.[77] For instance, children with disabilities have been found in certain research to be up to four times more likely to be subjected to violence than other children.[78] In many countries, children with disabilities are frequently placed in institutions, where they are at heightened risk of abuse, exploitation, and neglect. Such facilities often have low standards of care and lack independent monitoring, with the result that perpetrators of violence and abuse are rarely held to account.[79] Placement in residential facilities also increases the risk of trafficking of children with disabilities. Girls with disabilities are at particular risk of being trafficked.[80]

4.39 Children with disabilities who become separated from caregivers are especially endangered. Family members may have been the only persons to know how to care for a child's specific physical requirements or how to communicate with a child.[81] Children with disabilities may be unable to communicate information that is essential for family tracing and reunification. Unaccompanied children with disabilities may be excluded from traditional systems of care if local families do not accept them.

4.40 Neither Additional Protocol of 1977 addresses the rehabilitation and reintegration of children associated with armed forces or armed groups. While one may consider that this is subsumed within the general notions of care and aid, it is regrettable that it was not expressly addressed. Under human rights law, the CRC obligates all States Parties to take 'all appropriate measures to promote physical and psychological recovery and social reintegration of a child victim of ... armed conflicts'.[82] Such recovery and reintegration, the Convention stipulates, 'shall take place in an environment which fosters

---

[75] *Commentary on the Guidelines for Protecting Schools and Universities from Military Use During Armed Conflict*, at: http://bit.ly/2m6212t, p. 5.

[76] Ibid. See S. Haines, 'Developing International Guidelines for Protecting Schools and Universities from Military Use During Armed Conflict', *International Legal Studies*, Vol. 97 (2021), pp. 573–620, at: https://bit.ly/3lCdZva. See also UN Children's Fund (UNICEF), 'Education under attack', 18 February 2021, at: http://uni.cf/3bvd7oO.

[77] That said, Article 8(a) of the First Additional Protocol stipulates that for the purposes of the Protocol, 'wounded' and 'sick' mean persons, whether military or civilian, who, because of trauma, disease or other physical or mental disorder or disability, need medical assistance or care and who refrain from any act of hostility.

[78] K. Hughes and others, 'Prevalence and Risk of Violence against Adults with Disabilities: a Systematic Review and Meta-analysis of Observational Studies', *The Lancet*, Vol. 379, No. 9826, 2012, pp. 1621–29, at: http://bit.ly/3rLt0xn.

[79] African Child Policy Forum, *The African Report on Violence against Children*, 2014.

[80] Leonard Cheshire Disability, *Still Left Behind: Pathways to Inclusive Education for Girls with Disabilities*, 2017.

[81] UNICEF, *State of the World's Children: Children with Disabilities*, 2013.

[82] Art. 39, CRC.

the health, self-respect and dignity of the child'.[83] A Group of Friends on Reintegration, comprising 27 UN member States,[84] was created to increase support to the reintegration of former child soldiers, acknowledging that durable peace cannot be achieved if children are left behind and not fully reintegrated into civilian life.

4.41 The Machel Study on the Impact of Armed Conflict on Children, requested by the UN Committee on the Rights of the Child, was presented to the UN General Assembly in 1996.[85] The report, which paid particular attention to the problem of child soldiers, led to the adoption of General Assembly Resolution 51/77, which created the mandate of a Special Representative of the Secretary-General on the impact of armed conflict on children.[86] The resolution requested that the Special Representative prepare reports on the situation of children affected by armed conflict to be presented to the UN General Assembly and Human Rights Council (formerly, the Commission on Human Rights).[87]

4.42 In 2018, the Global Coalition for Reintegration of Child Soldiers—an alliance of Member States, UN agencies, the World Bank, civil society organisations, and academia—was launched with a view to developing new ideas to 'sustainably address support for child reintegration programmes'. The Global Coalition is co-chaired by the Office of the Special Representative of the UN Secretary-General for Children and Armed Conflict and the UN Children's Fund (UNICEF).[88] Research conducted for the Coalition recommended that reintegration support should be provided to former child soldiers for a minimum of between three and five years per child.[89] As such, it relied on policy recommendations for the demobilisation and reintegration of former child soldiers originally issued by the United Nations in 2006.[90]

4.43 The UN has identified six grave violations committed against children during armed conflicts.[91] One is the prohibition on recruiting and using children as soldiers, discussed above. The other five are as follows:

- killing and maiming children
- sexual violence against children
- abduction of children

---

[83] Ibid.
[84] Andorra, Argentina, Belgium, Canada, China, Djibouti, Dominican Republic, France (Co-chair), Germany, Indonesia, Ireland, Japan, Kazakhstan (Co-chair), Lebanon, Liechtenstein, Malta (Co-chair), Mexico, Poland, Qatar, Republic of Korea, Saudi Arabia, Spain, Sri Lanka, Türkiye, United Arab Emirates, United Kingdom, and Uruguay.
[85] 'Impact of Armed Conflict on Children', UN doc. A/51/306, 26 August 1996, at: https://bit.ly/3bvC0AR.
[86] UN General Assembly Resolution 51/77; adopted on 12 December 1996 without a vote, operative para. 35.
[87] Ibid., operative para. 37.
[88] Office of the Special Representative of the Secretary-General for Children and Armed Conflict, 'Global Coalition for Reintegration of Child Soldiers', undated but accessed 1 March 2021 at: http://bit.ly/3l0xiOQ.
[89] Global Coalition for Reintegration of Child Soldiers, 'Improving Support to Child Reintegration: Summary of Findings from Three Reports', New York, 2020, at: https://bit.ly/2OfMjjF, p. 2.
[90] 'Demobilization and reintegration programmes for children should be expected to extend over a period of five years or more'. Integrated Disarmament, Demobilization and Reintegration Standards (IDDRS), Standard 5.30: Children and DDR, 1 August 2006, at: https://bit.ly/2Ozbc9N, p. 6, §5.2.
[91] UN Security Council Resolution 1261, adopted by unanimous vote in favour on 25 August 1999, operative para. 2.

- attacks against schools or hospitals and
- denial of humanitarian access for children.

While they are often categorised as grave violations of child rights, most find their legal source in IHL.

4.44 In 2005, to document and report on these grave violations, the UN established the Monitoring and Reporting Mechanism (MRM)[92] pursuant to Security Council Resolution 1612.[93] On the basis of this information, the UN Secretary-General names parties to conflict who commit such acts in an annual report on children and armed conflict, with the goal of ending these violations. In addition to the Secretary-General's annual report to the UN Security Council, the Council's Working Group on Children and Armed Conflict reviews the country reports stemming from the MRM and makes recommendations on how better to protect children in specific country situations.

4.45 The credibility of the UN Secretary-General's reporting, however, came under intense scrutiny in 2017, after it emerged that Saudi Arabia had put pressure on the Secretariat to keep its name off the list of those engaged in grave violations against children (in the context of the armed conflict in which it was involved in Yemen).[94] Saudi Arabia threatened to pull funding to the UN, so, 'as a compromise', the Secretary-General's report now has two levels of actor: one level outlining those committing grave violations and a second containing those actors that have put a plan in place to stop them from happening again.[95]

The prohibition of the death penalty for child offenders

4.46 Under customary international law it is prohibited merely to impose (and thus a fortiori to carry out) the death penalty on any person who was under 18 years of age at the time a capital offence was committed.[96] For a State to act otherwise amounts to an arbitrary deprivation of life. The prohibition is codified in both the ICCPR[97] and the CRC.[98]

---

[92] United Nations Children's Fund (UNICEF), the UN Department of Peacekeeping Operations (DPKO), and the Office of the Special Representative of the Secretary-General for Children and Armed Conflict (OSRSG-CAAC) have launched a website dedicated to the MRM: www.mrmtools.org. See: UNICEF, OSRSG-CAAC, and DPKO, *Monitoring and Reporting Mechanism (MRM) on Grave Violations Against Children in situations of Armed Conflict*, Field Manual, New York, June 2014.

[93] UN Security Council Resolution 1612; adopted unanimously on 26 July 2005, operative para. 3.

[94] See, e.g., 'UN Again Blacklists Saudi-Led Forces for Yemen Child Killings. Coalition Blacklisted for Third Year Over Killing and Wounding of 729 Children But Critics Say Measure Is Not Enough', *Aljazeera*, 28 July 2019, at: http://bit.ly/2w0rM9r.

[95] See, e.g., R. Blume, 'The 'Children and Armed Conflict' Report on Grave Violations Is Vital in Protecting Children, and Here's Why', *War Child*, 26 June 2018, at: http://bit.ly/32mLWX6.

[96] Inter-American Commission on Human Rights, *Napoleon Beazley* v. *United States*, Decision, citing with approval its views in *Michael Domingues* v. *United States*, Decision (Case 12.285), Report 62/02 para. 84. See also N. Peterson, 'Life, Right to, International Protection', *Max Planck Encyclopedia of Public International Law*, Last updated October 2012, at: http://bit.ly/2u2adEK.

[97] Article 6(5) of the ICCPR specifies that the death penalty 'shall not be imposed for crimes committed by persons below eighteen years of age'.

[98] Article 37(a) of the CRC provides that: 'Neither capital punishment nor life imprisonment without possibility of release shall be imposed for offences committed by persons below eighteen years of age.'

This general prohibition applies also in all armed conflict. The imposition of the death penalty on those under 18 years of age is prohibited by the 1949 Geneva Convention IV in situations of military occupation: 'the death penalty may not be pronounced against a protected person who was under eighteen years of age at the time of the offence'.[99] The Additional Protocol I of 1977 stipulates that 'the death penalty for an offence related to the armed conflict shall not be executed on persons who had not attained the age of eighteen years at the time the offence was committed'.[100] In its 1987 commentary on the provision, the ICRC stated that: '[W]ith regard to time of armed conflict and offences related to conflicts, it can be said that the death penalty for persons under eighteen years of age is ruled out completely.'[101] With respect to the non-international armed conflicts within its scope, the 1977 Additional Protocol II prohibits the imposition of the death penalty on anyone under 18 years of age at the time of the offence.[102]

4.47

Concluding remarks and outlook

The protection of children was significantly enhanced under the two 1977 Additional Protocols. That said, the need to improve legal protection led to the adoption in 2000 of the Optional Protocol to the CRC on the involvement of children in armed conflicts. This human rights instrument is evidence that customary law now prohibits all conscription of children into armed forces (and non-State armed groups) and demands that all feasible measures be taken to ensure that children do not take part in combat. But the Protocol did not outlaw all child enlistment in the armed forces, which remains a work in progress under international law. Moreover, in practice, many non-State armed groups continue to recruit—typically by force—very young children into their ranks.[103] The grave problem of using children as soldiers will persist.

4.48

---

[99] Art. 68(4), Geneva Convention IV.
[100] Art. 77(5), Additional Protocol I.
[101] ICRC commentary on Article 77 of the 1977 Additional Protocol I, 1987, para. 3202, at: http://bit.ly/37qwSJq.
[102] Art. 6(4), Additional Protocol II.
[103] With respect to continuing child recruitment in Syria, see, e.g., Syria Justice and Accountability Centre, 'One Year After Banning the Practice, the SDF Is Still Recruiting Children', 23 July 2020, at: https://bit.ly/3fFvx87.

5

Protection of Detainees and Prisoner-of-War Status

Introduction

5.1 Under customary and conventional international humanitarian law (IHL), all detainees must be treated humanely. That means they must be both respected by those detaining them and protected from harm, while their basic needs are met. In addition, in an international armed conflict, certain individuals and members of specific groups are entitled to the status of prisoner of war (POW), which gives them additional rights. These are, most notably, for combatants, the right to immunity from prosecution for their direct participation in hostilities ('combatant's privilege').[1] Certain civilians are also entitled to POW status, but they could be prosecuted for taking direct part in hostilities as they are not similarly authorised to do so.

5.2 This chapter discusses the protection IHL affords to different categories of detainees and the criteria for adjudging POW status under the 1949 Geneva Convention III,[2] the two 1977 Additional Protocols, and customary law. The broadening in the 1977 Additional Protocol I of the right to POW status for members of irregular forces who meet certain less stringent conditions[3] is especially controversial. The notion of prisoner of war does not exist in non-international armed conflict as a matter of international law, although the 1977 Additional Protocol II does urge the authorities to grant the broadest possible amnesty to persons who have participated in an armed conflict falling within its purview.[4] In non-international armed conflict, a contentious issue is whether IHL implicitly grants the power to detain and intern.

5.3 The key rules governing the treatment of detainees set out in the two 1977 Additional Protocols are summarised in Table 5.1.

---

[1] Article 43 of the First Additional Protocol refers to combatant members of the armed forces as having the 'right to participate directly in hostilities'. Art. 43(2), Protocol Additional to the Geneva Conventions of 12 August 1949, and relating to the Protection of Victims of International Armed Conflicts (Protocol I); adopted at Geneva, 8 June 1977; entered into force, 7 December 1978 (hereinafter, 1977 Additional Protocol I). See, e.g., A. Clapham, *War*, Oxford University Press, Oxford, 2021, p. 273.

[2] Convention (III) relative to the Treatment of Prisoners of War; adopted at Geneva, 12 August 1949; entered into force, 21 October 1950 (hereinafter, 1949 Geneva Convention III).

[3] Art. 44(3), 1977 Additional Protocol I.

[4] Art. 6(5), Protocol additional to the Geneva Conventions of 12 August 1949, and relating to the protection of victims of non-international armed conflicts (Protocol II); adopted at Geneva, 8 June 1977; entered into force, 7 December 1978 (hereinafter, 1977 Additional Protocol II).

Table 5.1 Summary of Rules on the Treatment of Detainees

Rule	AP I	Customary status (IAC)	AP II	Customary status (NIAC)
Right to POW status	Art. 44(1)	Yes	No	No
National liberation movement fighters who carry their arms openly are entitled to POW status	Art. 44(3)	No	No	No
Right of POWs to release upon cessation of active hostilities	Art. 85(4)(b) (Art. 118, GC III)	Yes	N/A	N/A
Right of detainees to humane treatment	Arts. 10(2) and 75(1)	Yes	Art. 4(1)	Yes
Right of wounded and sick to protection	Arts. 10(1) and 11(1)	Yes	Art. 8	Yes
Children shall not be sentenced to death	Art. 77(5)	Yes	Art. 6(4)	Yes
Pregnant women shall not be executed	Art. 76(3)	Yes	Art. 6(4)	Yes

The detail of protection set out in the two Additional Protocols adds to and complements that afforded under the 1949 Geneva Conventions III and IV to, respectively, military and civilian detainees in international and non-international armed conflict.[5]

Detention in international armed conflict

While all detainees must be treated humanely in all circumstances, the specifics of protection and treatment of those detained in relation to an international armed conflict depend on two issues: whether a person is believed to have participated directly in hostilities or not; and what function, if any, he or she was attributed by the party to the conflict to which that person belongs. The protection of civilians is discussed first below, followed by that of combatants and others who may be entitled to POW status. For the purpose of this chapter, civilians are any persons who are not combatant (or non-combatant)[6] members of the armed forces.[7]

5.4

---

[5] 1949 Geneva Convention III; and Convention (IV) Relative to the Protection of Civilian Persons in Time of War; adopted at Geneva, 12 August 1949; entered into force, 21 October 1950.
[6] E.g. religious and medical personnel who are members of the armed forces, who do not have the right to participate directly in hostilities.
[7] K. Dörmann, 'The Legal Situation of "Unlawful/Unprivileged Combatants"', *International Review of the Red Cross*, Vol. 85, No. 849, (2003), pp. 45–74, at p. 49.

The protection of civilian detainees

5.5 In general, civilians in occupied territory and aliens in the territory of a party to an international armed conflict may not be interned or placed in assigned residence.[8] There are, however, exceptions to this rule. With respect to situations of military occupation, the 1949 Geneva Convention IV determines that such assigned residence or internment may occur only where the occupying power considers the action 'necessary, for imperative reasons of security'.[9] Besides occupied territories, civilian 'aliens' in the territory of a party to an international armed conflict may be interned or placed in assigned residence 'only if the security of the Detaining Power makes it absolutely necessary'.[10] Anyone so treated is entitled to have their internment or placement in assigned residence 'reconsidered as soon as possible by an appropriate court or administrative board designated by the Detaining Power for that purpose'.[11]

5.6 As Sassòli observes, it may appear 'strange' to classify heavily armed 'terrorists' who are captured in an international armed conflict and who do not benefit from combatant or POW status as 'civilians'.[12] But the granting of such status does not lead to 'absurd results'. Such individuals can be prosecuted for participating in hostilities; depending on the circumstances they may lawfully be administratively detained; and they must be prosecuted for any war crimes they may have committed.[13]

5.7 The 1977 Additional Protocol I stipulates that anyone detained or interned in relation to the armed conflict must be informed promptly, in a language he or she understands, of the reasons for such measures.[14] The Protocol adds that the 'physical or mental health and integrity' of internees or detainees held in connection with an international armed conflict 'shall not be endangered by any unjustified act or omission'.[15] Furthermore, unless arrested for a criminal offence, detainees and internees must be released 'with the minimum delay possible'.[16]

5.8 Civilians in occupied territory who commit an offence against the occupying power, but which is not an attack on their personnel, a serious damage to their property, or a grave collective danger may be interned or imprisoned as long as their duration is proportionate to the offence committed.[17] In any event, persons detained on suspicion of having committed a criminal offence related to an armed conflict must be accorded

---

[8] Art. 79, 1949 Geneva Convention IV.
[9] Ibid., Art. 78.
[10] Ibid., Art. 42.
[11] Art. 43, 1949 Geneva Convention IV.
[12] M. Sassòli, *International Humanitarian Law Rules, Controversies, and Solutions to Problems Arising in Warfare*, Edward Elgar Publishing, Cheltenham, 2019, p. 505, para. 10.46.
[13] Ibid.
[14] Art. 77(3), 1977 Additional Protocol I.
[15] Ibid., Art. 11(1).
[16] Ibid., Art. 77(3).
[17] Art. 68, 1949 Geneva Convention IV.

fair-trial rights in any prosecution. The list of such rights is said to be 'almost identical' under IHL and international human rights law.[18]

The death penalty

Under the Fourth Geneva Convention, the death penalty may only be imposed on a protected person[19] where he or she is guilty of espionage, 'serious' acts of sabotage against the military installations of the occupying power, or of 'intentional' offences which have caused the death of one or more persons. Moreover, such offences must have been punishable by death under the law of the occupied territory in force before the occupation began.[20] It is questionable, however, whether such broad grounds for the imposition of the death penalty persist today. It is probable that the evolution in international human rights law since the adoption of the International Covenant on Civil and Political Rights (ICCPR) precludes, even in a situation of armed conflict, a capital sentence for any but the 'most serious crimes'.[21] These are decreed by the United Nations (UN) Human Rights Committee to be only those that involve the perpetration of unlawful homicide by the accused.[22] This is arguably so, whether or not a State is party to the ICCPR, on the basis that this rule has crystallised as custom.[23]

5.9

Those who were under 18 years of age when they committed a criminal offence, no matter its seriousness, may not be sentenced to death. This is also a rule of customary law, which is applicable in peacetime as it is in all armed conflict.[24] The prohibition was first included in the 1949 Geneva Convention IV, although it was limited there to a situation of military occupation.[25]

5.10

The 1977 Additional Protocol I provides more narrowly that 'the death penalty for an offence related to the armed conflict shall not be *executed* on persons who had not attained the age of eighteen years at the time the offence was committed'.[26] This rule applies to all persons convicted for an offence related to the armed conflict, whether or not

5.11

---

[18] ICRC, 'Internment in Armed Conflict: Basic Rules and Challenges', Opinion Paper, Geneva, November 2014, p. 2.
[19] Protected persons are those who, in an international armed conflict or occupation, are in the power ('hands') of a Party to the conflict or occupying power of which they are not nationals. But nationals of a neutral State and nationals of a co-belligerent State are not protected persons while the State of which they are nationals has normal diplomatic representation in the State in whose power they are. Art. 4, 1949 Geneva Convention IV.
[20] Art. 68, 1949 Geneva Convention IV.
[21] Art. 6(2), International Covenant on Civil and Political Rights; adopted at New York, 16 December 1966; entered into force, 23 March 1976. No derogation is possible to this provision.
[22] As of 1 May 2022, 173 States were party to the ICCPR. States not party were Bhutan, Brunei, China (a signatory), Comoros (a signatory), Cook Islands, Cuba (a signatory), Holy See, Kiribati, Malaysia, Micronesia, Myanmar, Nauru (a signatory), Niue, Oman, Palau (a signatory), St Kitts and Nevis, St Lucia (a signatory), Saudi Arabia, Singapore, the Solomon Islands, South Sudan, Tonga, Tuvalu, and the United Arab Emirates.
[23] Human Rights Committee, 'General Comment No. 36: Article 6: right to life', UN doc. CCPR/C/GC/36, 3 September 2019, para. 35.
[24] Art. 6(5), ICCPR; Art. 37(a), Convention on the Rights of the Child; adopted at New York, 20 November 1989; entered into force, 2 September 1990.
[25] Art. 68, 1949 Geneva Convention IV.
[26] Art. 77(5), 1977 Additional Protocol I (emphasis added).

they enjoyed protected status under the Geneva Conventions and Additional Protocol 1. It is narrower than the rule that exists in customary human rights law whereby no death sentence shall be *imposed* in any circumstances on a person who was under 18 years of age at the time of the commission of the offence.[27] In its 1987 commentary on the provision in the 1977 Additional Protocol I, the International Committee of the Red Cross (ICRC) had already asserted that: 'with regard to time of armed conflict and offences related to conflicts, it can be said that the death penalty for persons under eighteen years of age is ruled out completely'.[28]

5.12 The Additional Protocol I also requires that parties to a conflict 'endeavour, to the maximum extent feasible' to avoid imposing the death penalty on pregnant women or mothers having dependent infants for any offence related to the armed conflict. In any event, the death penalty may not be executed on such women.[29] That pregnant women may not be executed under any circumstances—although it is not unlawful per se to impose upon them the death penalty—is also a human rights treaty rule[30] and a customary norm of international law applicable at all times and in all armed conflict.[31] The treaty rule was 'inspired by humanitarian considerations and by consideration for the interests of the unborn child'.[32] Under domestic law, seemingly only one State in the world (St Kitts and Nevis) formally allows a pregnant woman to be executed,[33] and this appears to be largely a theoretical possibility. The last execution in St Kitts occurred in 2008; the condemned was a man, convicted of killing his wife.[34]

The duty and nature of humane treatment

5.13 The duty of humane treatment means that a detainee must be both respected—not harmed by the detaining power—and also protected from violence at the hands of others. This is a 'fundamental guarantee' granted under Article 75 of the Additional Protocol I to all persons who are 'arrested, detained or interned for reasons related to the armed conflict'. They 'shall enjoy the protection provided by this Article until final release, repatriation or re-establishment, even after the end of the armed conflict'.[35] In its General Comment on Article 4 of the ICCPR, the Human Rights Committee

---

[27] See, e.g., Inter-American Commission on Human Rights, *Napoleon Beazley v. United States*, Decision (Case 12.412), Report No. 101/03, 29 December 2003, para. 30; see also N. Peterson, 'Life, Right to, International Protection', *Max Planck Encyclopedia of Public International Law*, Last updated October 2012, at: http://bit.ly/2u2adEK.
[28] ICRC, Commentary on Article 77 of the 1977 Additional Protocol I, 1987, at: http://bit.ly/37qwSJq, para. 3202.
[29] Art. 76(3), Additional Protocol I.
[30] Art. 6(5), ICCPR.
[31] See further on this issue, S. Casey-Maslen, *The Right to Life under International Law: An Interpretive Manual*, Cambridge University Press, Cambridge, 2021, para. 21.46.
[32] 'Draft International Covenants on Human Rights', UN doc. A/2929, 1 July 1955, 'Article 6', at p. 85, para. 10.
[33] Cornell Center on the Death Penalty Worldwide, 'Pregnant Women', Last updated 25 January 2012.
[34] A. Bright, 'India Uses Death Penalty: 5 other Places Where It's Legal But Rare', *Christian Science Monitor*, 29 August 2012, at: http://bit.ly/325oxLY.
[35] Art. 75(6), Additional Protocol I.

declared that the requirement in the Covenant that persons deprived of their liberty be treated with humanity and with respect for the inherent dignity of the human person was non-derogable and therefore applicable at all times, including in armed conflict.[36]

A rule discerned by the ICRC in its detailed study of customary IHL stipulates that: 'Persons deprived of their liberty must be provided with adequate food, water, clothing, shelter and medical attention.'[37] Under the 1949 Geneva Convention IV, parties to an international armed conflict who intern protected persons must ensure their sustenance free of charge and grant them all necessary medical attention.[38] The 1977 Additional Protocol I adds to the duties specified in Article 55 of Convention IV concerning the provision of food and medical supplies in a situation of military occupation. Thereunder, the occupying power must, 'to the fullest extent of the means available to it and without any adverse distinction', provide 'clothing, bedding, means of shelter, other supplies essential to the survival of the civilian population of the occupied territory and objects necessary for religious worship'.[39]

5.14

The treatment of detained combatants

Protection of prisoners of war

Once accorded POW status (see below), the 1949 Geneva Convention III is said by the ICRC to provide a sufficient legal basis for the 'internment' of a POW. That an 'additional domestic law basis' is not required is 'generally uncontroversial'.[40] As the ICRC recalls, during the Vietnam War, North Vietnam refused to grant POW status to captured American pilots because, as 'aggressors', they had allegedly committed war crimes.[41] Such a denial of a combatant's fundamental rights violates customary law. In any event, under the Convention, POWs 'must at all times be humanely treated'.[42] Further, POWs 'must at all times be protected, particularly against acts of violence or intimidation and against insults and public curiosity'. Reprisals against POWs are comprehensively prohibited, without exception or the possibility of lawful reservation.[43] North Vietnamese forces wilfully mistreated many US pilots, often engaging in torture and other forms of ill treatment.[44]

5.15

---

[36] Human Rights Committee, General Comment No. 29 on States of Emergency (Article 4 of the ICCPR), UN doc. CCPR/C/21/Rev.1/Add.11, 31 August 2001, para. 13(a).

[37] ICRC, Customary IHL Rule 118: 'Provision of Basic Necessities to Persons Deprived of Their Liberty', at: http://bit.ly/2YmIoTS.

[38] Art. 81, 1949 Geneva Convention IV.

[39] Art. 69(1), 1977 Additional Protocol I.

[40] ICRC, 'Internment in Armed Conflict: Basic Rules and Challenges', Opinion Paper, 2014, p. 4.

[41] ICRC, 'The International Committee and the Vietnam Conflict', *International Review of the Red Cross*, Vol. 6, No. 65 (1966), pp. 399–418, at p. 403.

[42] Art. 13, 1949 Geneva Convention III.

[43] Ibid.

[44] See, e.g., M. Pribbenow, 'Treatment of American POWs in North Vietnam', Research Paper, Cold War International History Project, Wilson Center, Washington, D.C., at: http://bit.ly/340NTuj.

5.16 Those who are detained but who do not have the status of POW must also be treated humanely, as Article 75 of the 1977 Additional Protocol I (and customary law) requires. They do not, however, benefit from the 'combatant's privilege', a customary rule[45] that prohibits their trial on charges of direct participation in hostilities or for lawful acts of war.[46] The rule is not formally codified in either the Geneva Convention III or the Additional Protocol I, although the Protocol does make it explicit that members of the armed forces of a party to a conflict are 'combatants, that is to say, they have the right to participate directly in hostilities'.[47] Despite claims by certain commentators (and the United States), this right does not equate to a 'right to kill'. As the ICRC has observed, 'the fact that a particular category of persons is not protected against offensive or defensive acts of violence is not equivalent to a legal entitlement to kill such persons without further considerations'.[48]

5.17 The primary exceptions to the right to POW status are military medical and dedicated religious personnel who are 'non-combatants' in accordance with Article 33 of the 1949 Geneva Convention III. They must be accorded similar treatment to POWs, although they are not entitled to participate directly in hostilities.[49] They may use force but only in individual self-defence as well as, in the case of military medical personnel, with a view to protecting their patients from attack. Should they comply with these rules, they may not be targeted during the conduct of hostilities nor put on trial subsequent to capture.

5.18 Women must be given specific treatment as POWs. According to Article 14 of Geneva Convention III, for instance, it is stipulated that: 'Women shall be treated with all the regard due to their sex and shall in all cases benefit by treatment as favourable as that granted to men.' In a blog post in December 2020, Heleen Hiemstra and Vanessa Murphy recall some of the more unacceptable remarks in the ICRC's 1960 commentary on the provision, welcoming the approach in the 2020 Commentary to 'gendered assumptions, norms, harm and specificity'.[50] These 'progressions' were, they affirmed, 'badly needed, as elements of the original 1960 Commentary ... do not meet today's international legal standards related to gender-based discrimination'. A 'particularly eye-watering' example, they note, 'was the 1960 Commentary's statement that the "regard" that was due to women in Article 14(2) must take into account three

---

[45] See, e.g., G. D. Solis, *The Law of Armed Conflict: International Humanitarian Law in War*, 3rd Edn, Cambridge University Press, Cambridge, 2021, p. 37. As he recalls, the 1907 Hague Regulations (and indeed the earlier 1899 Regulations) expressed this in terms of the 'laws, rights, and duties of war'. Art. 1, Regulations concerning the Laws and Customs of War on Land, Annex to the Convention (IV) respecting the Laws and Customs of War on Land; adopted at The Hague, 18 October 1907; entered into force, 26 January 1910.

[46] ICRC, 'Internment in Armed Conflict: Basic Rules and Challenges', Opinion Paper, p. 4. See also Swiss Federal Department of Foreign Affairs, *ABC of International Humanitarian Law*, Bern, 2009, p. 13.

[47] Art. 43(2), 1977 Additional Protocol I.

[48] N. Melzer, *Interpretive Guidance on the Notion of Direct Participation in Hostilities*, ICRC, Geneva, 2009, p. 78.

[49] Orderlies and chaplains' assistants, however, are combatants who may be targeted but upon capture are entitled to POW status. G. D. Solis, *The Law of Armed Conflict: International Humanitarian Law in War*, 3rd Edn, Cambridge University Press, Cambridge, 2021, p. 175.

[50] H. Hiemstra and V. Murphy, 'GCIII Commentary: I'm a Woman and a POW in a Pandemic. What Does the Third Geneva Convention Mean for Me?', ICRC Blog, 8 December 2020, at: http://bit.ly/3f5bVuz.

considerations: their "weakness", "honour and modesty", and "pregnancy and childbirth".' The earlier commentary also referred to women as 'the weaker sex'.[51]

Child combatants, even if they have been recruited illegally while underage, are still entitled to POW status. As Chapter 4 explained, the minimum age for recruitment and direct participation in hostilities in international armed conflict as stipulated in IHL and international criminal law treaties is 15 years.[52] The minimum age for conscription and for direct participation in hostilities has been raised to 18 years under international human rights law by an Optional Protocol to the UN Convention on the Rights of the Child.[53] In practice, humanitarian agencies such as the UN Children's Fund (UNICEF) are likely to intervene to secure the release of all child POWs and to support their early repatriation and rehabilitation.[54] **5.19**

A combatant who is granted the status of POW may yet be convicted—and even potentially sentenced to death, where domestic law in force already provided for that penalty—for the commission of a war crime. Examples of such crimes would be the wilful killing of civilians or of fighters *hors de combat*. A POW may also be sentenced for the wilful killing of a prison guard or another prisoner during his or her detention. In contrast, a POW who attempts to escape and is recaptured before having made good his escape is liable only to a disciplinary punishment for this act. This is so, even if it is a repeated offence.[55] **5.20**

Security measures may of course be taken to prevent their escape. The 1949 Geneva Convention III stipulates that the use of weapons—meaning firearms—against escaping POWs 'shall constitute an extreme measure, which shall always be preceded by warnings appropriate to the circumstances'.[56] In its 1960 commentary on the provision, the ICRC stipulated that these warnings may either be verbal (using, for instance, a whistle or a bell) or may be made by means of a warning shot.[57] The commentary appeared to endorse a broad use of firearms, suggesting that: 'One cannot require the Detaining Power to reinforce the sentry units indefinitely at the expense of its active combat forces. The only remaining alternative is therefore to adopt very strict measures in order to intimidate prisoners of war.'[58] The commentary further stated that: 'In any **5.21**

---

[51] Ibid., citing C. O'Rourke, 'Geneva Convention III Commentary: What Significance for Women's Rights?', *Just Security*, 21 October 2020, at: http://bit.ly/3gFMKxz.

[52] Art. 77(2), 1977 Additional Protocol I; and Art. 8(2)(b)(xxvi), Rome Statute of the of the International Criminal Court; adopted at Rome, 17 July 1998; entered into force, 1 July 2002.

[53] Optional Protocol to the Convention on the Rights of the Child on the involvement of children in armed conflict; adopted at New York, 25 May 2000; entered into force, 12 February 2002.

[54] This is despite challenges in appreciation of the applicable law by some. In February 2020, for instance, UNICEF reported that 15 children associated with armed forces and armed groups in South Sudan had been released, claiming that boys 'ranging from 16 to 18 years of age were taken as *prisoners of war* during clashes in the northern parts of the country in 2019'. UNICEF UK, '15 Children Associated With Armed Forces, Released in South Sudan', 26 February 2020, at: http://bit.ly/3melWpg (emphasis added). The conflict in South Sudan is, however, non-international in character and the children were not therefore POWs, nor were they accorded such status by the parties to the conflict.

[55] Art. 93, 1949 Geneva Convention III.

[56] Ibid., Art. 42.

[57] ICRC Commentary on Article 42 of the 1949 Geneva Convention III, p. 247, at: http://bit.ly/37s3mn5.

[58] Ibid.

case, if the guards or sentinels have to open fire on prisoners of war, they should first aim low, unless they are themselves in imminent danger, so as to avoid inflicting fatal wounds.'[59]

5.22 This rule must today be interpreted in light of the rules governing the use of firearms in the 1990 Basic Principles on the Use of Force and Firearms by Law Enforcement Officials.[60] Indeed, in its 2020 commentary on Article 42 of Geneva Convention III, the ICRC stated that: 'Any use of firearms against a person is potentially lethal irrespective of what is being aimed at (e.g. legs, knees or chest) ... "Shoot to wound", such as aiming low (e.g. at legs) cannot be considered as a warning or as a preventive step; it is an actual use of potentially lethal force, which is strictly limited under Article 42.'[61] United Nations guidance on the use of less-lethal weapons in law enforcement, issued by the Office of the High Commissioner for Human Rights (OHCHR) in 2020, is valuable in this regard.[62]

5.23 Only upon a successful escape would a detained POW become targetable under the far more permissive IHL rules governing the use of force in the conduct of hostilities.[63] This is consonant with the limited State practice on the issue. The United States, for instance, considers that the use of tear gas against rioting POWs or those in the process of escaping is not a violation of the 1992 Chemical Weapons Convention.[64] The Convention explicitly prohibits the use of riot control agents as a method of warfare[65] but allows their use for law enforcement.[66]

5.24 In its commentary of 2020 on Article 42 of Geneva Convention III, the ICRC surprisingly suggests that laying anti-personnel mines outside a POW camp might be lawful in circumstances where prisoners are informed of their presence:

> Where the Detaining Power has placed anti-personnel mines outside a prisoner-of-war camp without marking them or informing the prisoners of their presence, this

---

[59] Ibid. Aiming at the lower limbs is not generally accepted as good law enforcement practice owing to the risk of missing the target and hitting an unintended bystander. Most, although not all, law enforcement agencies around the world train their officers to aim at the main body mass of a target. Casey-Maslen, *The Right to Life under International Law: An Interpretive Manual*, paras. 10.17 et seq. and 7.68–7.73.

[60] Principle 9, Basic Principles on the Use of Force and Firearms by Law Enforcement Officials; adopted by the Eighth United Nations (UN) Congress on the Prevention of Crime and the Treatment of Offenders at Havana, 27 August to 7 September 1990.

[61] ICRC Commentary on Article 42 of the 1949 Geneva Convention III, 2020, at: http://bit.ly/3hvie99, para. 2548 (footnote omitted).

[62] OHCHR, United Nations Human Rights Guidance on Less-Lethal Weapons in Law Enforcement, Geneva, 2020, at: http://bit.ly/367c0ac.

[63] See ICRC, *International Humanitarian Law and the Challenges of Contemporary Armed Conflicts*, Report for the 32nd International Conference of the Red Cross and Red Crescent, Geneva, October 2015, p. 36.

[64] United States (US) Department of Defense, *Department of Defense Law of War Manual*, Washington, D.C., June 2015 (Updated December 2016), §9.22.6.1. For details of other relevant State practice along the same lines, see E. Hoffberger-Pippan, 'Non-Lethal Weapons and International Law: A Three-Dimensional Perspective', PhD Thesis, Johannes Kepler University, Linz, Austria, 2018, pp. 100–101.

[65] Art. I(5), Convention on the Prohibition of the Development, Production, Stockpiling and Use of Chemical Weapons and on their Destruction; adopted at Geneva, 3 September 1992; entered into force, 29 April 1997 (hereinafter, 1992 Chemical Weapons Convention).

[66] Art. II(9), 1992 Chemical Weapons Convention.

may—depending on the circumstances—amount to the use of weapons without warning against an escaping prisoner. Placing such mines in these conditions may also amount to violations of other international rules governing their use.[67]

The emplacement of anti-personnel mines is, however, an intentional lethal use of force.[68] Given that use of firearms is already considered an 'extreme measure', the suggestion that landmines may lawfully be laid to prevent escape is not robust.[69]

The right to POW status

The right to POW status is generally articulated in Article 4 of the 1949 Geneva Convention III, but is explicitly set out in the Additional Protocol I. Therein it is stated that: 'Any combatant, as defined in Article 43 [of the Protocol], who falls into the power of an adverse Party shall be a prisoner of war.'[70] This codifies customary law. It does not matter for the purpose of POW status whether a combatant is a man, woman, or a child.[71] The broadening of the right to POW status in Article 44 is, however, controversial, as discussed below.

5.25

The 1949 Geneva Convention III determines that members of certain groups and other individuals are entitled to POW status. First and foremost, under Article 4(A)(1) of the 1949 Convention, members of the armed forces of a party to an international armed conflict have the right to be granted the status of prisoner of war and treated accordingly, as do 'members of militias or volunteer corps forming part of such armed forces'.[72] With respect to the members of the armed forces, as the ICRC observed in its commentary of 2020: 'These are likely to constitute the most significant category of prisoners of war and historically the least controversial of the subcategories of Article 4A'.[73]

5.26

Beyond the army, navy, and air force of a State, Article 43(3) of the 1977 Additional Protocol I obligates parties to an international armed conflict to notify each other of the incorporation of law enforcement bodies into their armed forces. Thus, upon their respective ratification of the Protocol, both Belgium and France issued notifications

5.27

---

[67] ICRC, Commentary on Article 42 of the 1949 Geneva Convention III, 2020, para. 2550.
[68] Principle 9 (final sentence), Basic Principles on the Use of Force and Firearms by Law Enforcement Officials.
[69] One hundred and sixty-four States are party to the 1997 Anti-Personnel Mine Ban Convention, which outlaws use of the weapons in all circumstances, including in all armed conflict. Art. 1(1)(a), Convention on the Prohibition of the Use, Stockpiling, Production, and Transfer of Anti-Personnel Mines and on their Destruction; adopted at Oslo, 18 September 1997; entered into force, 1 March 1999. Moreover, a total ban on the use of anti-personnel mines, and even the criminalisation of all use, is considered by some to be *de lege ferenda* under customary law. R. Cryer, H. Friman, D. Robinson, and E. Wilmshurst, *An Introduction to International Criminal Law and Procedure*, 3rd Edn, Cambridge University Press, Cambridge, 2014, pp. 299–300. However, see also Y. Dinstein, *Non-International Armed Conflicts in International Law*, 2nd Edn, Cambridge University Press, Cambridge, 2021, p. 274, para. 778.
[70] Art. 44(1), 1977 Additional Protocol I.
[71] See, e.g., K. Ipsen, 'Combatants and Non-Combatants', Chap. 5 in D. Fleck (ed.), *The Handbook of International Humanitarian Law*, 4th Edn, Oxford University Press, Oxford, 2021, Sections 5.05 and 5.06.
[72] Art. 4(A)(1), 1949 Geneva Convention III. This is so unless the captured soldier is a national of the detaining power. Dinstein, *Non-International Armed Conflicts in International Law*, 2nd Edn, p. 143, para. 394.
[73] ICRC Commentary on Article 4 of the 1949 Geneva Convention III, 2020, at: http://bit.ly/2KaLSof, para. 975.

to the effect that their *gendarmerie* would form part of their armed forces in the event of an armed conflict.[74] In contrast, as noted above, military medical and religious personnel are non-combatants. In accordance with the 1949 Geneva Convention III, while they 'shall not be considered as prisoners of war', they must 'receive as a minimum the benefits and protection of the … Convention, and shall also be granted all facilities necessary to provide for the medical care of, and religious ministration to prisoners of war'.[75]

5.28 POW status must be granted to members of 'regular armed forces who profess allegiance to a government or an authority' even where it is not recognised by the Detaining Power.[76] For example, in 1999 the Taliban was recognised as the legitimate government of Afghanistan by only three States: Pakistan, Saudi Arabia, and the United Arab Emirates.[77] In 2000, in its Resolution 1333, the UN Security Council strongly condemned 'the continuing use of the areas of Afghanistan under the control of the Afghan faction known as Taliban, which also calls itself the Islamic Emirate of Afghanistan'.[78] A year later, however, Taliban forces were in control of around 90 per cent of the country, making them the sovereign authority in Afghanistan.[79]

5.29 The United States, however, refused to grant POW status to Taliban fighters it captured after its invasion in late 2001, giving them the moniker of 'unlawful (enemy) combatants'.[80] The United States acknowledged that the Taliban were the armed forces of Afghanistan and that their capture occurred in the context of an international armed conflict between the United States and Afghanistan.[81] But they determined that POW status would not be accorded, since 'the Taliban armed forces failed to wear a distinctive uniform and routinely disregarded the laws and customs of war'.[82] This was, the ICRC

---

[74] Ibid., para. 982.
[75] Art. 33, 1949 Geneva Convention III.
[76] Art. 4(A)(3), 1949 Geneva Convention III.
[77] See, e.g., K. Gannon, 'Pakistan, Saudis, UAE Join US–Taliban Talks', *AP News*, 17 December 2018, at: http://bit.ly/2y9tMtO.
[78] UN Security Council Resolution 1333, adopted on 19 December 2000 by 13 votes to 0 with 2 abstentions (China and Malaysia), seventh preambular para.
[79] Dinstein, *Non-International Armed Conflicts in International Law*, 2nd Edn, p. 130, para. 354; see also S. Casey-Maslen, *Jus ad Bellum: The Law on Inter-State Use of Force*, Hart Publishing, Oxford, 2020, p. 42.
[80] See, e.g., J. P. Bialke, 'Al-Qaeda & Taliban—Unlawful Combatant Detainees, Unlawful Belligerency, and the International Laws of Armed Conflict', *Air Force Law Review*, Vol. 55 (2004), p. 1; and G. S. Corn, 'Thinking the Unthinkable: Has the Time Come to Offer Combatant Immunity to Non-State Actors?', *Stanford Law & Policy Review*, Vol. 22, No. 1 (2011), pp. 253–94, at: http://stanford.io/3oxIG5d. See also US Department of Justice, 'Application of Treaties and Laws to al Qaeda and Taliban Detainees', Memorandum for Alberto R. Gonzales, Counsel to the President, and William J. Haynes II, General Counsel of the Department of Defense, Washington, D.C., 22 January 2002, p. 31. Following adverse rulings in a series of court cases, the Obama administration did change the nomenclature they chose to apply from 'unlawful combatant' (in its Military Commissions Act of 2006) to 'unprivileged enemy combatants' (in its Military Commissions Act of 2009). E. Crawford and A. Pert, *International Humanitarian Law*, 2nd Edn, Cambridge University Press, Cambridge, 2020, p. 113 and note 90.
[81] As the ICRC has stated: 'The expression "members of the armed forces" refers to all military personnel under a command that is responsible to a Party to the conflict.' ICRC commentary on Article 4 of 1949 Geneva Convention III, 2020, at: http://bit.ly/2KaLSof, para. 976.
[82] Corn, 'Thinking the Unthinkable: Has the Time Come to Offer Combatant Immunity to Non-State Actors?', p. 263.

declared, a 'potential exception' to the general practice of recognising POW status both during the Second World War and 'in most international armed conflicts since'.[83]

That said, members of the armed forces are indeed obligated to distinguish themselves from the civilian population during military operations.[84] Under customary IHL, the ICRC declares, 'the failure of individual combatants to distinguish themselves while engaged in an attack or in a military operation preparatory to an attack means they forfeit the right to prisoner-of-war status'.[85] Thus, under the Additional Protocol I, a member of the armed forces who, out of uniform (or wearing an enemy uniform), gathers or attempts to gather information,[86] may be treated as a spy not a POW and prosecuted on that basis. Espionage during and in relation to armed conflict is not, however, 'in itself unlawful under international law'.[87] There is also 'a well-established practice' that saboteurs are treated in the same way as spies with regard to POW status.[88] Under Additional Protocol I[89]—and, despite US opposition,[90] customary international law[91]—, mercenaries[92] are also not entitled to POW status. If they have participated directly in hostilities, they are 'unprivileged belligerents'[93] and may thus be prosecuted for criminal offences under applicable domestic law. As 'civilians' they are entitled to the protection afforded by fundamental guarantees.[94]

5.30

In case of doubt about the right to POW status of a captured belligerent, Article 5 of the Geneva Convention III provides that he or she is protected as such until his or her status has been determined by a 'competent tribunal'. The ICRC notes that 'little guidance' exists as to what is meant by a 'competent tribunal' under this provision, and in practice the status of individuals has been decided by a variety of mechanisms, such as military tribunals, courts, or boards of inquiry, as well as, in specific circumstances, civilian courts.[95] In the United States, for instance, the relevant Army regulation holds that three officers are required for a competent tribunal, whose senior member must hold at least the rank of major.[96] Under the Additional Protocol I, any person in the

5.31

---

[83] ICRC, Commentary on Article 4 of 1949 Geneva Convention III, 2020, para. 1035.
[84] ICRC, Customary IHL Rule 106 stipulates that: 'Combatants must distinguish themselves from the civilian population while they are engaged in an attack or in a military operation preparatory to an attack. If they fail to do so, they do not have the right to prisoner-of-war status.' ICRC Customary IHL Rule 106: 'Conditions for Prisoner-of-War Status', at: https://bit.ly/3aXJwlc.
[85] ICRC, Commentary on Article 4 of 1949 Geneva Convention III, 2020, para. 983.
[86] Art. 46(1) and (2), 1977 Additional Protocol I.
[87] ICRC, Commentary on Article 4 of 1949 Geneva Convention III, 2020, para. 988.
[88] Ibid., para. 990.
[89] Art. 47(1), 1977 Additional Protocol I.
[90] See supra the Introduction to this work.
[91] ICRC, Commentary on Article 4 of 1949 Geneva Convention III, 2020, para. 998.
[92] A mercenary is any person who is specially recruited locally or abroad in order to fight in an armed conflict; participates directly in hostilities; is motivated to do so 'essentially by the desire for private gain' and is paid significantly more than combatant members of the armed forces of a similar rank; is neither a national of a party to the conflict nor a resident of territory controlled by a party to the conflict; is not a member of the armed forces of a party to the conflict; and has not been sent by a State which is not a party to the conflict on official duty as a member of its armed forces. Art. 47(2), 1977 Additional Protocol I.
[93] Solis, *The Law of Armed Conflict, International Humanitarian Law in War*, 3rd Edn, p. 110 and note 18.
[94] See supra Chapter 2 for a discussion of these guarantees.
[95] ICRC commentary on Article 5 of the 1949 Geneva Convention III, 2020, at: http://bit.ly/3qTpQHv, paras. 1123 and 1126.
[96] Solis, *The Law of Armed Conflict, International Humanitarian Law in War*, 3rd Edn, p. 188.

power of the enemy who is not held as a POW and is to be tried for an offence arising from the hostilities has the right to assert their entitlement to POW status before a judicial tribunal and have the matter freshly decided.[97]

Irregular forces

5.32 The most controversial issue in POW determination comes from the circumstances in which the status is to be accorded to members of 'other militias' or 'other volunteer corps', including organised resistance movements, which belong to a party to an international armed conflict. Status is dependent, under the 1949 Geneva Convention III, on their fulfilling four conditions: being under the command of a person 'responsible for his subordinates'; having a fixed distinctive sign recognisable at a distance; carrying arms openly;[98] and conducting their operations in accordance with IHL.[99] This customary rule is a high threshold for irregular forces to meet in practice.

5.33 An ordinary reading of Article 4 would suggest that members of regular armed forces do not need to meet the four criteria, but this is a position which is firmly rejected by the United States.[100] Case law is indeed conflicting, although the Military Court at Hamburg adjudged in the *von Lewinski* case (with respect to the equivalent criteria in Article 1 of the 1907 Hague Regulations)[101] that: 'Regular soldiers are so entitled without any of the four requirements set out in Article 1; they are requisite in order to give the Militia and Volunteer Corps the same privileges as the Army.'[102] The criteria are, the ICRC concludes correctly, 'obligations' and not 'collective conditions for prisoner-of-war status to be granted to regular Article 4A(1) armed forces or militias or volunteer corps forming part of them'.[103]

5.34 Two alternative interpretations have been offered of the impact of the cumulative criteria that could be applied by analogy to claims for POW status by irregular forces: one whereby if large numbers of a force (or an entire unit or group) fail to meet all four criteria, each of those persons would lose POW status; or, alternatively, that the force as a whole would not be entitled to POW status in the face of substantial non-compliance with any of the conditions in subparagraph 2.[104]

---

[97] Art. 45(2), 1977 Additional Protocol I.
[98] On the nuanced difference between carrying weapons 'openly' and 'visibly', see, e.g., Crawford and Pert, *International Humanitarian Law*, 2nd Edn, p. 101. The ICRC's new commentary on the provision describes the notion of carrying weapons openly as meaning 'without concealment'. ICRC commentary on Article 4 of 1949 Geneva Convention III, 2020, para. 1021, citing as reference the Twelfth Edition of the *Concise Oxford English Dictionary* published by Oxford University Press.
[99] Art. 4(A)(2), 1949 Geneva Convention III.
[100] USDOD December 2016 *Law of War Manual*, §4.6.
[101] Art. 1, Regulations concerning the Laws and Customs of War on Land, Annex to the Convention (IV) respecting the Laws and Customs of War on Land; adopted at The Hague, 18 October 1907; entered into force, 26 January 1910.
[102] Military Court at Hamburg, *von Lewinski* case, Judgment, 1949, pp. 515–16.
[103] ICRC, Commentary on Article 4 of 1949 Geneva Convention III, 2020, para. 1039.
[104] Ibid., paras. 1029, 1030.

Under its Article 44, the 1977 Additional Protocol I loosens the four criteria for POW status for irregular forces in one of the Protocol's most controversial provisions. Combatants are still 'obliged to distinguish themselves from the civilian population while they are engaged in an attack or in a military operation preparatory to an attack'.[105] But the Protocol explicitly recognises that 'there are situations in armed conflicts where, owing to the nature of the hostilities an armed combatant cannot so distinguish himself'. In such situations, a combatant shall 'retain his status as a combatant' and therefore be entitled to POW status as long as he or she carries his arms openly during each military engagement as well as 'during such time as he is visible to the adversary while he is engaged in a military deployment preceding the launching of an attack in which he is to participate'.[106] Ipsen states that these rules apply only to occupied territories and armed conflicts of national liberation, as set forth in Article 1(4) of the Additional Protocol I.[107]

5.35

As Crawford and Pert observe, the adoption of these new rules for the determination of combatantcy was intensely criticised by States such as India, Israel, Pakistan, and the United States.[108] Thirteen other States have adhered to the Protocol with a reservation to Article 44.[109] The rules were also condemned by many commentators, with Douglas Feith describing them as 'law in the service of terror'.[110] He further termed them 'endorsement, in the politically potent form of a legal instrument, of both the rhetoric and anti-civilian practices of terrorist organizations that fly the banner of self-determination'.[111] Yoram Dinstein has labelled Article 44 a 'dismaying composite picture'.[112]

5.36

Crawford and Pert suggest that the ICRC concluded in 2005 that the rules were of a customary nature,[113] an assessment which should, they say, 'be treated with some caution'. In truth, neither Rule 4 nor Rule 106 of the ICRC customary IHL study which they cite makes the claim that all of the rules in Article 44 reflect general international law. Indeed, the lack of adequate *opinio juris*, including among specially affected States, means that this is not the case. Article 44 remains binding on States Parties to the Protocol who have not made a lawful reservation to it, but not on other States.

5.37

---

[105] Art. 44(3), 1977 Additional Protocol I.
[106] Ibid.
[107] K. Ipsen, 'Combatants and Non-Combatants', Chap. 5 in D. Fleck (ed.), *The Handbook of International Humanitarian Law*, 4th Edn, Oxford University Press, Oxford, 2021, p. 105.
[108] Crawford and Pert, *International Humanitarian Law*, 2nd Edn, p. 103.
[109] Argentina, Australia, Canada, France, Germany, Ireland, Italy, Japan, the Netherlands, New Zealand, South Korea, Spain, and the United Kingdom.
[110] D. Feith, 'Law in the Service of Terror—the Strange Case of the Additional Protocol', *National Interest*, Vol. 1 (1985), pp. 36–47. See also Solis, *The Law of Armed Conflict, International Humanitarian Law in War*, 3rd Edn, pp. 113–14.
[111] Feith, 'Law in the Service of Terror—the Strange Case of the Additional Protocol', p. 47.
[112] Y. Dinstein, *The Conduct of Hostilities under the Law of International Armed Conflict*, Cambridge University Press, Cambridge, 2016, p. 62.
[113] Crawford and Pert, *International Humanitarian Law*, 2nd Edn, p. 104.

82 DETAINEES AND PRISONER-OF-WAR STATUS

5.38 The Additional Protocol determines that a situation of international armed conflict exists where 'peoples are fighting against colonial domination and alien occupation and against racist régimes in the exercise of their right of self-determination'.[114] As Chapter 1 discusses, this is also a contested provision and one that, to date, has only been applied once: in the case of Morocco and the Polisario Front. The Polisario Front made a formal declaration under Article 96(3) of the Protocol, which was circulated among the States Parties and only objected to by Morocco. A three-decade-long truce has been in place, and largely respected, although in November 2020 the Polisario Front claimed that Morocco had broken the ceasefire and 'ignited war'. The exchange of fire, which posed the biggest risk in decades of a new phase of armed conflict in Western Sahara, led the Polisario to claim: 'We have declared a return to the armed struggle'.[115] Polisario Front fighters captured in any new conflict would be entitled to assert their right to POW status.

Others entitled to prisoner-of-war status

5.39 There are also certain individuals who are entitled to POW status but who do not have the right to participate directly in hostilities, namely those 'who accompany the armed forces without actually being members thereof'. This includes, but is not expressly limited to, 'civilian members of military aircraft crews, war correspondents, supply contractors, members of labour units or of services responsible for the welfare of the armed forces'. Their right exists so long as they were duly authorised by the armed forces and provided with an identity card for this purpose, similar to a model annexed to the Geneva Convention III.[116] Merchant marine crews and the crews of civil aircraft of the parties to the conflict, if they do not benefit from more favourable treatment under international law, are also entitled to POW status.[117] These civilians are entitled to POW status but 'not entitled to combatant status, immunity or privileges'.[118] As Solis explains, personnel belonging to the erstwhile Blackwater Worldwide company, when operating in Iraq, would not have been entitled to POW status as the company's contract was with the US Department of State not the Department of Defense and Blackwater personnel were accompanying diplomats, not the US armed forces.[119]

Release and return of POW

5.40 Under the 1949 Geneva Convention III, 'Prisoners of war shall be released and repatriated without delay after the cessation of active hostilities.'[120] The term 'without delay' is

---

[114] Art. 1(4), 1977 Additional Protocol I.
[115] Reuters, 'Fears grow of new Western Sahara war between Morocco and Polisario Front', 13 November 2020, at: http://reut.rs/2Wdk5Xm.
[116] Art. 4(A)(4), 1949 Geneva Convention III. The model is included in Annex IV(A).
[117] Art. 4(A)(5), 1949 Geneva Convention III.
[118] ICRC Commentary on Article 4 of 1949 Geneva Convention III, 2020, para. 1045.
[119] Solis, *The Law of Armed Conflict, International Humanitarian Law in War*, 3rd Edn, p. 181.
[120] Art. 118, 1949 Geneva Convention III.

a 'strict' notion, to be equated with 'prompt' (although not immediate).[121] As the ICRC further recalls, the action to be taken is limited to what is feasible in the circumstances. It may depend on factors such as the actual number of prisoners, the location of the camps, and the logistical means available to the Detaining Power at the end of active hostilities, as well as the security situation and the ability of a State to receive the repatriated prisoners.[122]

The Eritrea-Ethiopia Claims Commission held that a three-month delay in the repatriation of POWs by Ethiopia, without providing any explanation for the delay, was a violation of the obligation set out in Article 118 of the 1949 Geneva Convention III. According to the Commission: 'While Eritrea promptly released and repatriated its remaining POWs in late August 2002, Ethiopia waited three months, until November 29, 2002, to release the remainder of its POWs and to repatriate those desiring repatriation. This three-month delay was not explained ... In these circumstances, the Commission concludes that Ethiopia did not meet its obligation promptly to repatriate the POWs it held, as required by law.'[123]

5.41

The Additional Protocol I makes an 'unjustifiable delay in the repatriation of prisoners of war' a grave breach,[124] and therefore a war crime.[125] Under the Draft Code of Crimes against the Peace and Security of Mankind, concluded by the International Law Commission (ILC) in 1991, an 'unjustifiable delay in the repatriation of prisoners of war after the cessation of hostilities' is an 'exceptionally serious war crime.'[126] It is not, however, a war crime within the jurisdiction of the International Criminal Court and its customary status is uncertain.

5.42

The duty to repatriate POWs is a stand-alone obligation and not one that is dependent on reciprocity. As the ICRC observes in its customary law study commentary on the war crime of 'unjustifiable delay in the repatriation of prisoners of war or civilians', the legislation of numerous States specifies that it is a war crime, including Azerbaijan, which is a State not party to Additional Protocol I.[127] In the course of the international armed conflict between Armenia and Azerbaijan in September to November 2020, prisoners were captured by both States' armed forces.[128] According to Article 8 of the Ceasefire Agreement, signed on 9 November 2020, all POWs were to be 'exchanged'. In the Joint Statement issued the following day by the President of the Republic of Azerbaijan, the Prime Minister of the Republic of Armenia, and the President of the

5.43

---

[121] ICRC, Commentary on Article 118, Geneva Convention III, 2020, paras. 4462, 4463, at: http://bit.ly/3hERVhy.
[122] Ibid., para. 4462.
[123] Eritrea-Ethiopia Claims Commission, Partial Award: Prisoners of War—Eritrea's Claim 17, 1 July 2003, text available at: http://bit.ly/38YrjEu, paras. 157–58. See further on this issue Chapter 15 of this work on the issue of reprisals.
[124] Art. 85(4)(b), 1977 Additional Protocol I.
[125] Ibid., Art. 85(5).
[126] Art. 22(2)(a), ILC Draft Code of Crimes against the Peace and Security of Mankind, UN doc. A/46/10, 1991.
[127] ICRC, Customary IHL Rule 156: 'War Crimes', at: http://bit.ly/32HjZb2.
[128] Radio Free Europe (RFE)/Radio Liberty (RL), 'Azerbaijan, Armenia Swap Prisoners As Part Of Nagorno-Karabakh Truce Deal', 14 December 2020, at: http://bit.ly/3ndXbd6.

Russian Federation reaffirmed that: 'The Parties shall exchange prisoners of war, hostages and other detained persons, and dead bodies.'[129] Azerbaijani authorities said the sides had agreed to an all-for-all exchange of prisoners, and that an aircraft with several of those detained had landed in Azerbaijan on 14 December 2020.[130]

5.44 In March 2021, Armenia accused Azerbaijan of 'dragging its feet' on the repatriation of the Armenian POWs it was holding. At a press conference, President Ilham Aliyev claimed that Azerbaijan had returned all the POWs but claimed that other detainees were 'saboteurs'. This concerned 62 Armenian soldiers captured by Azerbaijani forces in December, a month after the ceasefire agreement was signed. That agreement stipulated that the two sides would return all POWs, but Azerbaijan has said that since the soldiers were captured on Azerbaijani territory after the formal end of hostilities, they can 'in no way' be considered POWs.[131] Even the exact number of Armenian detainees was disputed.[132] There were also allegations of ill treatment of the Armenian prisoners, detailed by Human Rights Watch.[133]

5.45 Consonant with the two States' IHL obligations, Russia, 'the only third party wielding significant authority on both sides', called on the two sides to exchange prisoners on an 'all-for-all' basis.[134] In June 2021, however, Azerbaijan put on trial 26 individuals described as 'members of an armed terrorist group consisting of Armenian citizens'. A series of charges were made against the men, including acts of terrorism.[135] It is not known if the accused were regular Armenian soldiers in uniform. A few days later, Armenian Prime Minister Nikol Pashinyan declared:

> We have not exchanged the maps for POWs, but rather we took a step for a step, and we are prepared to take another step for another step. Seeing that Azerbaijan halted the return of POWs, we also halted the return of maps. If the return of POWs was not halted, there would not be so many casualties on landmines in Azerbaijan.[136]

5.46 The ICRC stipulates that: 'In case a delay in the repatriation of prisoners of war or civilians is unjustifiable, in practice there would no longer exist a legal basis for their deprivation of liberty and it would amount to unlawful confinement.' Thus, in addition to amounting to a war crime, such detention would also constitute arbitrary deprivation of liberty in violation of international human rights law, including Article 9 of the

---

[129] Text available at: http://bit.ly/3rVjJ6m.
[130] RFE/RL, 'Azerbaijan, Armenia Swap Prisoners as Part of Nagorno-Karabakh Truce Deal'.
[131] J. Kucera, 'Post-war Report: Armenia Accuses Azerbaijan of Dragging Feet on POWs', *EurasiaNet*, 5 March 2021, at: https://bit.ly/3sk5eta.
[132] J. Kucera, 'Prisoners of the Caucasus: Post-War Report', *EurasiaNet*, 23 April 2021, at: https://bit.ly/3z0tYsU.
[133] Human Rights Watch, 'Azerbaijan: Armenian POWs Abused in Custody', 19 March 2021, at: https://bit.ly/3iRw2hv.
[134] Kucera, 'Post-war Report: Armenia Accuses Azerbaijan of Dragging Feet on POWs'.
[135] Azerbaijan State Security Service, 'Joint Information of the Press Services of the State Security Service and the Prosecutor General's Office', 10 June 2021, at: https://bit.ly/3g1GaCr.
[136] L. Avedian, 'Armenian POWs Stand Trial', *The Armenian Weekly*, 30 June 2021, at: https://bit.ly/3AJoTFP.

ICCPR.[137] The prohibition of arbitrary deprivation of liberty is certainly of a customary nature and is arguably even a peremptory norm.[138]

Detention in non-international armed conflict

The issue of detention in non-international armed conflict is contentious. This is not with regard to the rules governing the treatment of detainees, who must, under customary law[139] as well as the Additional Protocol II,[140] be treated humanely in all circumstances, meaning that they must be both respected and protected. Rather, the principal controversy surrounds the nature of arbitrary deprivation of liberty in non-international armed conflict. The ICRC has argued that there is an implied power to detain on the basis of IHL.[141] The better view is that an explicit domestic legal basis for such action is always necessary.[142] The failure to ensure such a legal basis would mean that the detention would be inherently arbitrary and therefore unlawful.   5.47

What is not contested is that the protection afforded by the Additional Protocol II to those detained in the course of and in connection to a non-international armed conflict extends beyond the end of the armed conflict.[143] This is made explicit in the Protocol.[144]   5.48

Arbitrary deprivation of liberty

In an Opinion Paper issued in 2014, the ICRC claimed that 'both customary and treaty IHL contain an inherent power to intern and may in this respect be said to provide a legal basis for internment in [non-international armed conflict]'.[145] This position is, the ICRC states, 'based on the fact that internment is a form of deprivation of liberty which is a common occurrence in armed conflict', and is 'not prohibited by Common Article 3' while the 1977 Additional Protocol II 'refers explicitly to internment'.[146] This is not persuasive.[147] Article 5 of the 1977 Additional Protocol II addresses the treatment of   5.49

---

[137] See, e.g., Human Rights Committee, General Comment No. 35: Article 9 (Liberty and security of person), UN doc. CCPR/C/GC/35, 16 December 2014, paras. 10–12 and 64–67.
[138] See, e.g., Report of the Working Group on Arbitrary Detention, 'Deliberation No. 9 concerning the definition and scope of arbitrary deprivation of liberty under customary international law', UN doc. A/HRC/22/44, 24 December 2012, paras. 47–51), in which the Working Group reiterated its view that the prohibition of all forms of arbitrary deprivation of liberty constitutes not only customary international law but is also a peremptory norm.
[139] ICRC, Customary IHL Rule 87: 'Humane Treatment', at: http://bit.ly/380xuqV.
[140] Arts. 4 and 5, 1977 Additional Protocol I.
[141] For a useful discussion of this issue see, e.g., Sassòli, *International Humanitarian Law Rules, Controversies, and Solutions to Problems Arising in Warfare*, paras. 10.17 and 10.18, pp. 494–95.
[142] See ibid., para. 10.42, p. 504.
[143] Dinstein, *Non-International Armed Conflicts in International Law*, 2nd Edn, p. 47, para. 125.
[144] Art. 2(2), 1977 Additional Protocol II.
[145] ICRC, 'Internment in Armed Conflict: Basic Rules and Challenges', Opinion Paper, 2014, p. 7.
[146] Ibid.
[147] See, e.g., A. Conte, 'The Legality of Detention in Armed Conflict', in A. Bellal and S. Casey-Maslen (eds.), *The War Report 2014*, Oxford University Press, Oxford, 2015; see also A. Conte, 'The UK Court of Appeal in Serdar

internees (as does Common Article 3) but without regulating when internment may start and when it may end. Further, given the principle of equality of belligerents, presumably non-State armed groups are also given an implicit power to detain.

5.50 In its 2020 commentary on 1949 Geneva Convention III, the ICRC reaffirmed its stance, while acknowledging that the question whether IHL provides inherent authority or power to detain is 'still subject to debate'.[148] It did conceded, however, that '*additional* authority related to the grounds and procedure for deprivation of liberty in non-international armed conflict must in all cases be provided, in keeping with the principle of legality'.[149] In the United Kingdom Supreme Court's 2017 judgment in the *Serdar Mohamed* case,[150] Lord Mance concluded that there were 'substantial arguments both for and against the contention that the Geneva Conventions or their Protocols implicitly confer authority under international law for detention in non-international armed conflicts'. His 'current view, based on the submissions in the present case, is that the arguments against that contention ... are cumulatively the more persuasive'.[151]

The duty of humane treatment

5.51 In the 1977 Additional Protocol II, detail is added to the general requirement of humane treatment 'in all circumstances' and the specific prohibitions on inhumane treatment set out in Common Article 3. Indeed, Part II of the Additional Protocol II is entitled 'Humane Treatment'. It covers fundamental guarantees (Article 4, applicable as a baseline to all those not or no longer participating directly in hostilities), persons whose liberty has been restricted (Article 5), and penal prosecutions (Article 6).

5.52 Under Article 4(1), anyone not or no longer participating directly in hostilities, 'whether or not their liberty has been restricted', is entitled to 'respect for their person, honour and convictions and religious practices'. They shall, the provision continues, be treated humanely 'in all circumstances' and 'without any adverse distinction'.

5.53 Article 5 adds specific protection to those who are interned or otherwise detained in connection with the conflict. The wounded and sick must be respected and protected.[152] All must be provided with food and drinking water and be 'afforded safeguards as regards health and hygiene and protection against the rigours of the climate

---

Mohammed: Treaty and Customary IHL Provides No Authority for Detention in Non-international Armed Conflicts', *EJIL: Talk!*, 6 August 2015, at: http://bit.ly/3gHWozG.

[148] ICRC, Commentary on Article 3, 1949 Geneva Convention III, 2020, at: http://bit.ly/3qV1NYI, paras. 764–65.
[149] Ibid., para. 765, citing ICRC, 'Internment in Armed Conflict: Basic Rules and Challenges', Opinion Paper, 2014, p. 8 (emphasis added).
[150] UK Supreme Court, *Serdar Mohamed v. Ministry of Defence*, Judgment, 17 January 2017, [2017] UKSC 2, para. 258.
[151] Ibid., para. 274.
[152] Article 5 contains a renvoi to Article 7 of the Protocol.

and the dangers of the armed conflict', at the least 'to the same extent as the local civilian population'.[153] They may be compelled to work, but if they are, they must be accorded working conditions and safeguards 'similar to those enjoyed by the local civilian population'.[154]

Specific provisions govern the detention itself, as stipulated in Article 5(2). Places of internment and detention must not be located close to a combat zone. If fighting moves nearby, and it is possible to move those detained in reasonable safety, they must be transported to a safer area.[155] Except when men and women of a family are accommodated together, women must be held separately from men and under the immediate supervision of women warders.[156] While those detained must benefit from medical examinations, it is prohibited to subject them 'to any medical procedure which is not indicated by the state of health of the person concerned, and which is not consistent with the generally accepted medical standards applied to free persons under similar medical circumstances'.[157]

5.54

The obligations in Article 5(2) are not absolute in nature but are to be performed by detaining authorities only 'within the limits of their capabilities'.[158] The ICRC implies, but does not make it explicit, that this caveat is reflected in the customary rule. In its discussion of the customary rule whereby women deprived of their liberty 'must be held in quarters separate from those of men',[159] reference is made to the limiting factor under the Protocol, while noting that separation of men and women in detention 'generally occurs'. If, sometimes, 'only minimal separation is provided, this is not because of a lack of acceptance of this rule but rather a result of limited resources available to the detaining authorities'.[160]

5.55

Article 6 governs penal prosecutions of detainees, specifying that: 'No sentence shall be passed and no penalty shall be executed on a person found guilty of an offence except pursuant to a conviction pronounced by a court offering the essential guarantees of independence and impartiality'.[161] There is no combatant immunity from domestic prosecution for armed groups under international law.[162] Consonant with customary international human rights law, as noted above, the death penalty shall not be pronounced on anyone who was under 18 years of age at the time of the offence and shall not be carried out on pregnant women.[163] The prohibition on executing 'mothers of

5.56

---

[153] Art. 5(1)(b), 1977 Additional Protocol II.
[154] Ibid., Art. 5(1)(e).
[155] Ibid., Art. 5(2)(c).
[156] Ibid., Art. 5(2)(a).
[157] Ibid., Art. 5(2)(d).
[158] Ibid., Art. 5(2) chapeau.
[159] ICRC, Customary IHL Rule 119: 'Accommodation for Women Deprived of Their Liberty', at: http://bit.ly/32wGtxc.
[160] Ibid.
[161] Art. 6(2) chapeau, 1977 Additional Protocol II.
[162] Clapham, *War*, p. 277.
[163] Art. 6(4), 1977 Additional Protocol II.

young children', also included in the relevant provision in the Protocol,[164] is *de lege ferenda* under customary international law.

Concluding remarks and outlook

5.57 Two significant legal issues remain to be settled with respect to POWs and detainees under IHL. First, to what extent are fighters engaged in a struggle for self-determination entitled to POW status as a matter of customary law? If such a rule does exist—not the view of the current authors—to what extent do those States that have most vociferously opposed the rule meet the criteria for persistent objection? Secondly, is a domestic legal basis for internment or detention in connection with a non-international armed conflict always required by virtue of applicable international human rights law and the prohibition of arbitrary deprivation of liberty? We believe that the preponderance of evidence indicates that it is. That said, given the controversy over the applicability of human rights law to non-State armed groups, a more nuanced approach with regard to the legality, under international law, of the detention or internment by these actors should also be considered, for instance by including their own 'laws' and practices in the analysis.

---

[164] Ibid.

6
Relief Operations

Introduction

For several years, there has been a steady increase of the number of people in the world in need of humanitarian assistance. According to the United Nations Office for the Coordination of Humanitarian Affairs (OCHA), 235 million people were in need of such assistance in 2021.[1] Of course, not all humanitarian needs are created by armed conflicts—natural disasters or disease are a major concern, as recent history has shown all too graphically—but the humanitarian needs induced by armed conflicts account for most of the overall statistic. In particular, conflict remains the principal driver of massive population displacement: an estimated 51 million people were internally displaced in 2021, while the number of refugees had doubled to 20 million. At least 77 million people across 22 war-torn countries are suffering acute hunger, creating immense humanitarian needs.[2] Given the sobering facts, it is crucial to understand the rules governing humanitarian relief operations under international humanitarian law (IHL).[3]   **6.1**

In addition to IHL, human rights law, and notably the norms pertaining to the rights to life, to food, to water, and to health, is also directly relevant. Both bodies of law offer a broad-based regulation of humanitarian relief operations and access to populations in need, despite some inherent limits. Of course, IHL binds both States and armed non-State actors, but its application is limited to situations of armed conflicts as legally defined.[4] In contrast, human rights law applies in all situations, including outside situations of armed conflict, but its binding force on armed non-State actors remains disputed.[5] Under human rights law, the primary responsibility to ensure conflict-affected populations falls upon the territorial State. Under IHL, that responsibility falls to either the territorial State or an occupying foreign power, but also to a salient non-State armed group that controls territory in an armed conflict.[6] The norms related to humanitarian relief are of a more general nature with no specific mandate falling upon humanitarian organisations.   **6.2**

---

[1] OCHA, *Global Humanitarian Overview 2021*, New York, 2021, available at: https://bit.ly/2ZXDGQ4, p. 8.
[2] Ibid.
[3] E. Massingham and K. Thynne, 'Humanitarian Relief Operations', in B. Saul and D. Akande (eds.), *The Oxford Guide to International Humanitarian Law*, Oxford University Press, Oxford, 2020, p. 320.
[4] On the legal qualification of armed conflicts generally, see, e.g., S. Vité, 'Typology of Armed Conflicts in International Humanitarian Law: Legal Concepts and Actual Situations', *International Review of the Red Cross*, Vol. 91, No. 873 (March 2009), pp. 69–74.
[5] See generally K. Fortin, *The Accountability of Armed Groups under Human Rights Law*, Oxford University Press, Oxford, 2017; see also J.-M. Henckaerts and C. Wiesener, 'Human Rights Obligations of Non-State Armed Groups: An Assessment Based on Recent Practice', in E. Heffes, M. D. Kotlik, and M. J. Ventura (eds.), *International Humanitarian Law and Non-State Actors: Debates, Law and Practice*, Springer, The Hague, 2020, pp. 195–227.
[6] See further D. Akande and E.-C. Gillard, *Oxford Guidance on the Law Relating to Humanitarian Relief Operations in Situations of Armed Conflicts*, University of Oxford and OCHA, 2016, available at: https://bit.ly/3BN62tM (hereinafter, 2016 Oxford Guidance), Section B.

Table 6.1 Summary of Rules on Humanitarian Relief Operations

Rule	AP I	Customary status (IAC)	AP II	Customary status (NIAC)
Basic needs in occupied territory	Art. 69	Yes	No	No
Relief actions	Art. 70	Yes	Art. 18(2)	Yes
Personnel participating in relief actions	Art. 71	Yes	No	Yes

6.3   In the manner in which it is used in the 1949 Geneva Conventions, the term *relief* 'mostly applies to activities to address humanitarian needs arising in emergency situations'. Within the context of the 1977 Additional Protocol I, however, the term needs to be read in conjunction with the broader term 'assistance' in its Article 81(1), 'which seeks also to cover longer-term as well as recurrent and even chronic needs'.[7] The relevant rules of IHL governing relief operations can be articulated around four main issues: (1) when should humanitarian relief operations take place; (2) who must consent to humanitarian relief operations; (3) how are humanitarian relief operations to be implemented, including conditions that may be imposed, along with the duty to respect and protect humanitarian personnel; and (4) given that most armed conflicts involve armed non-State actors, how do they understand and perceive humanitarian relief operations? The rules set out in the two 1977 Additional Protocols[8] are summarised in Table 6.1 above.

The trigger for humanitarian relief operations

6.4   The first sentence of Article 70 of the 1977 Additional Protocol I establishes that:

> If the civilian population of any territory under the control of a Party to the conflict, other than occupied territory, is not adequately provided with the supplies mentioned in Article 69, relief actions which are humanitarian and impartial in character and conducted without any adverse distinction shall be undertaken, subject to the agreement of the Parties concerned in such relief actions.[9]

---

[7] ICRC, Commentary on Article 3 of the 1949 Geneva Convention III, 2020, at: https://bit.ly/34mhUpo, para. 858.
[8] Protocol Additional to the Geneva Conventions of 12 August 1949, and relating to the Protection of Victims of International Armed Conflicts (Protocol I); adopted at Geneva, 8 June 1977; entered into force, 7 December 1978 (hereinafter, 1977 Additional Protocol I); and Protocol Additional to the Geneva Conventions of 12 August 1949, and relating to the Protection of Victims of Non-International Armed Conflicts (Protocol II); adopted at Geneva, 8 June 1977; entered into force, 7 December 1978 (hereinafter, 1977 Additional Protocol II).
[9] Art. 70 (1), 1977 Additional Protocol I.

As expressed in this provision, the trigger for humanitarian relief operations in international armed conflict is when the civilian population is 'not adequately provided' with the supplies mentioned in the preceding article, which in turn refers back to the 1949 Geneva Convention IV, which addresses the obligation of an occupying power to provide for food and medical supplies to the population living under its control.[10] Read together, these treaty provisions highlight that the basic needs that must be met are: food, medical supplies, clothing, bedding, means of shelter, other supplies essential to the survival of the civilian population, and objects necessary for religious worship. The extent to which these basic needs are not 'adequately provided' must be assessed on a case-by-case basis.[11]

In non-international armed conflicts, the relevant obligation is worded slightly differently. Thus, Article 18(2) of the 1977 Additional Protocol II stipulates that: **6.5**

> If the civilian population is suffering undue hardship owing to a lack of the supplies essential for its survival, such as foodstuffs and medical supplies, relief actions for the civilian population which are of an exclusively humanitarian and impartial nature and which are conducted without any adverse distinction shall be undertaken subject to the consent of the High Contracting Party concerned.

The words 'such as' indicate that the list is not exhaustive. Because 'the suffering and the needs of civilian populations are much the same, irrespective of the type of conflict',[12] clothing, bedding, means of shelter, other supplies essential to the survival of the civilian population, and objects necessary for religious worship must be provided for in non-international armed conflicts; otherwise, relief operations must take place.

International human rights law also identifies the basic needs of persons (better framed here in terms of their *rights* of course) for the purpose of humanitarian relief. Of notable relevance are Articles 11 and 12 of the International Covenant on Economic, Social and Cultural Rights (ECSR) of 1966,[13] which recognise, respectively, 'the right of everyone to an adequate standard of living for himself and his family, including adequate food, clothing and housing, and to the continuous improvement of living conditions' and 'the right of everyone to the enjoyment of the highest attainable standard of physical and mental health'. It has been confirmed that these rights apply in situations of armed conflict despite the absence of a derogation clause in the treaty.[14] **6.6**

---

[10] Art. 55, Convention (IV) relative to the Protection of Civilian Persons in Time of War; adopted at Geneva, 12 August 1949; entered into force, 21 October 1950.
[11] ICRC Commentary on Article 70 of the 1977 Additional Protocol I, 1987, para. 2794.
[12] ICRC, Commentary on Article 18 of the 1977 Additional Protocol II, 1987, para. 4870.
[13] International Covenant on Economic, Social and Cultural Rights; adopted at New York, 16 December 1966; entered into force, 3 January 1976.
[14] International Court of Justice (ICJ), *Legal Consequences of the Construction of a Wall in the Occupied Palestinian Territory, Advisory Opinion*, ICJ Reports 2004, p. 136; and see also G. Giacca, *Economic, Social, and Cultural Rights in Armed Conflict*, Oxford University Press, Oxford, 2014; and A. Breitegger, 'The Legal Framework

6.7 In any armed conflict, the belligerent parties are responsible under international law for ensuring the civilian population living under their control is adequately provided with the basic goods necessary for its survival.[15] It has been suggested that the mandatory wording used in Article 70 of the Additional Protocol I and Article 18 of the Additional Protocol II—relief actions '*shall be* undertaken'—could also be interpreted as a collective '*right* of the civilian population in need to receive humanitarian relief'.[16] As to the question as to whom this right may be addressed,[17] an analogy can be made with Article 30 of the fourth Geneva Convention, which recalls that: 'Protected persons shall have every facility for making application to the Protecting Powers, the International Committee of the Red Cross, the National Red Cross (Red Crescent, Red Lion and Sun) Society of the country where they may be, as well as to any organization that might assist them.'[18]

6.8 In the context of a non-international armed conflict, paragraph 2 of Common Article 3 to the 1949 Geneva Conventions provides that: 'An impartial humanitarian body, such as the International Committee of the Red Cross, may offer its services to the Parties to the conflict.' The term 'such as' indicates that the organisations that may thus offer their services to the parties to the conflicts, including armed groups, are not limited to the ICRC, but can be any humanitarian entity, including those linked to States, provided that they act in an impartial manner.[19] Furthermore, Article 18(1) of the Additional Protocol II of 1977 envisages that relief societies located in the territory of the High Contracting Party, as well as the civilian population, may offer to provide for humanitarian relief, including to collect and care for the wounded, the sick, and the shipwrecked.

6.9 Rules pertaining to humanitarian relief are of a customary international law nature in international and non-international armed conflict. The ICRC's study of customary law departs slightly from the wording of the two Protocols, framing the rules rather in terms of access (as in Rule 55)[20] and freedom of movement for humanitarian relief personnel (in Rule 56).[21] In addition, since its completion the law is said to have evolved

Applicable to Insecurity and Violence Affecting the Delivery of Health Care in Armed Conflicts and Other Emergencies', *International Review of the Red Cross*, Vol. 95, No. 889 (2013), pp. 83–127.

[15] F. Lattanzi, 'Humanitarian Assistance', in A. Clapham, P. Gaeta, and M. Sassòli (eds.), *The 1949 Geneva Conventions: A Commentary*, Oxford University Press, Oxford, 2015, p. 232, para. 3.

[16] ICRC, Customary IHL Rule 55: 'Access for Humanitarian Relief to Civilians in Need', at: https://bit.ly/3GQEkjr (emphasis added).

[17] In relation to the word 'shall', the ICRC Commentary on Article 70 of the 1977 Additional Protocol I notes (at para. 2796): 'As in the case of relief actions intended for occupied territories, the question arises as "to whom" this apparent "obligation" is addressed.'

[18] See in that regard ICRC Customary IHL Rule 55.

[19] See the ICRC's 2016 commentary on Article 3 of Convention (I) for the Amelioration of the Condition of the Wounded and Sick in Armed Forces in the Field; adopted at Geneva, 12 August 1949; entered into force, 21 October 1950. The commentary, which is at: https://bit.ly/3mEB2It, is set out in paras. 779, 791, and 861.

[20] ICRC Customary IHL Rule 55: 'The parties to the conflict must allow and facilitate rapid and unimpeded passage of humanitarian relief for civilians in need, which is impartial in character and conducted without any adverse distinction, subject to their right of control.'

[21] ICRC Customary IHL Rule 56: 'Freedom of Movement of Humanitarian Relief Personnel', at: https://bit.ly/2ZW4ro1: 'The parties to the conflict must ensure the freedom of movement of authorized humanitarian relief

further.[22] The *Oxford Guidance on the Law relating to Humanitarian Relief Operations in Situations of Armed Conflicts* of 2016, an expert document commissioned by the United Nations Office for the Coordination of Humanitarian Affairs (OCHA), seeks to encapsulate key elements of that normative evolution.

Consent to humanitarian relief operations

The issue of consent, or rather the refusal to give consent to offers to provide humanitarian aid, along with the conditions that are imposed on its provision by the relevant parties to an armed conflict, are at the heart of many humanitarian crises in contemporary armed conflicts. Thus, Partsch and Solf have noted that the provision on humanitarian relief, especially in non-international armed conflict, was among the most debated draft provisions in the final plenaries of the diplomatic conference that adopted the 1977 Additional Protocols, maybe because 'relief was often equated with foreign intervention, with foreign assistance to rebellion, or at least with a danger of these things happening'.[23] 6.10

In international armed conflict, and more specifically in the context of occupation, Article 59 of the 1949 Geneva Convention IV stipulates that 'if the whole or part of the population of an occupied is inadequately supplied the occupying power, the Occupying Power *shall agree* to relief schemes on behalf of the said population, and *shall facilitate* them by all the means at its disposal'. In other words, an occupying power cannot refuse external humanitarian assistance for the benefit of the occupied territory's population if it is unable to provide the civilian population directly with the basic supplies necessary for its survival. 6.11

In all situations other than occupied territories, the 'agreement' (Additional Protocol I) and 'consent' (Additional Protocol II) to humanitarian relief operations is required. The difference in wording was not happenstance. As a matter of law and important in practice, it is not settled whether the consent of the relevant State Party is required in a non-international armed conflict if operations do not have to transit under areas under its control. The ICRC's study of customary IHL stated in its commentary on Rule 55, however, that it was 'self-evident that a humanitarian organization cannot operate without the consent of the party concerned'.[24] 6.12

---

personnel essential to the exercise of their functions. Only in case of imperative military necessity may their movements be temporarily restricted.'

[22] Email from Emanuela Chiara-Gillard, Senior Research Fellow at the Oxford Institute for Ethics, Law and Armed Conflict, 10 January 2022.
[23] M. Bothe, K. Partsch, and W. Solf, *New Rules for Victims of Armed Conflict, Commentary on the two 1977 Protocols Additional to the Geneva Conventions of 1949*, 2nd Edn, Martinus Nijhoff, Leiden, 2013, p. 799.
[24] ICRC, Customary IHL Rule 55, 'Consent'.

6.13 Under public international law, foreign non-governmental organisations (NGOs), States, and international organisations would all need the authorisation of the territorial sovereign State that was party to the relevant conflict to enter and operate on its territory. For similar reasons of territorial sovereignty, consent is also required from the adverse State, as well as from the neutral State through whose territory the assistance must pass or from where the assistance is initiated. It is worth noting, however, that in its judgment on the merits in the *Nicaragua* case, the International Court of Justice was adamant that 'the provision of strictly humanitarian aid to persons or forces in another country, whatever their political affiliations or objectives, cannot be regarded as unlawful intervention, or as in any other way contrary to international law'.[25]

6.14 While the texts of the relevant articles do not elaborate on this issue, the ICRC commentary notes that consent to humanitarian access cannot be arbitrarily withheld.[26] The question then is what are the circumstances where withholding of consent can be considered arbitrary and thus illegal under IHL? For Sassòli, there are two simple and clear scenarios where consent can be lawfully denied: 'either the civilian population does not actually need the humanitarian assistance or if the entity offering it is unable to carry out relief actions that are exclusively humanitarian and impartial in character without any adverse distinction'.[27] The 2016 Oxford Guidance elaborates on the notion, suggesting that consent would be withheld arbitrarily 'if it is withheld ... in circumstances that result in a violation of obligations under international law ... with respect to the civilian population in question, including, in particular, obligations under international humanitarian law and international human rights law ... in violation of the principles of necessity and proportionality; or ... in a manner that is unreasonable, or that may lead to injustice or lack of predictability, or that is otherwise inappropriate.'[28]

6.15 In the context of the armed conflicts in Syria, the UN Security Council went a step further and required the Syrian authorities to allow humanitarian relief operations to take place on Syria's territory. In its Resolution 2139, adopted on 22 February 2014, the Council first noted that 'arbitrary denial of humanitarian access and depriving civilians of objects indispensable to their survival, including wilfully impeding relief supply and access, can constitute a violation of international humanitarian law'. It then *demanded* 'that all parties, in particular the Syrian authorities, promptly allow rapid, safe and unhindered humanitarian access for United Nations humanitarian agencies and their implementing partners, including across conflict lines and across borders, in order to ensure that humanitarian assistance reaches people in need through the most direct routes.'[29] In a further resolution, a few months later, the Security Council was even more

---

[25] International Court of Justice, *Military and Paramilitary Activities in and against Nicaragua (Nicaragua v. United States)*, Judgment (Merits), 27 June 1986, para. 242.
[26] ICRC, Commentary on Article 70 of the 1977 Additional Protocol I, 1987, para. 2805.
[27] M. Sassòli, *International Humanitarian Law Rules, Controversies, and Solutions to Problems Arising in Warfare*, Edward Elgar Publishing, Cheltenham, 2019, p. 579, para. 10.208.
[28] 2016 Oxford Guidance, p. 25, Rule (E)(ii). See further, with examples, pp. 21–25.
[29] UN Security Council Resolution 2139, adopted by unanimous vote in favour on 22 February 2014, operative para. 6.

specific, *deciding* that 'all Syrian parties to the conflict shall enable the immediate and unhindered delivery of humanitarian assistance directly to people throughout Syria'.[30] Through the wording of the resolution ('shall') as well as the inclusion of a reminder of Article 25 of the UN Charter in the text,[31] the Council made it clear that it was imposing an obligation on the parties to the conflicts to accept humanitarian relief operations in the country, despite a persistent denial of consent on the part of the Syrian authorities.

In situations of non-international armed conflict, Common Article 3 does not detail by whom, nor how, an offer of humanitarian assistance is to be responded to. In contrast, Article 18(2) of the 1977 Additional Protocol II explicitly addresses the requirement to obtain the consent 'of the High Contracting Party concerned'. This issue of who can give consent in non-international armed conflict can indeed prove especially problematic in situations where humanitarian relief needs to be provided to a territory under the control of an armed group. What if the armed group in control of territory accepts humanitarian access, but the State on whose territory the armed group operates refuses? 6.16

In this regard, the 2016 ICRC commentary on Common Article 3 notes that despite the provision's 'silence', it 'is clear from the logic underpinning international law in general, and humanitarian law in particular, that, in principle, an impartial humanitarian organization will only be able to carry out the proposed humanitarian activities if it has consent to do so'.[32] Interestingly, the commentary adds: 6.17

> Consent may be manifested through a written reply to the organization which has made the offer but can also be conveyed orally. In the absence of a clearly communicated approval, an impartial humanitarian organization can make sure that the 'Party to the conflict' concerned consents at least implicitly, by acquiescence, to the proposed humanitarian activities duly notified to that Party in advance.[33]

Thus, the ICRC commentary of 2016 on Common Article 3 only speaks about the modalities of obtaining the consent of the 'party to the conflict' and not the 'High Contracting Party', which is the wording in the 1977 Additional Protocol II.

There are differing interpretations of the issues of consent and access to territory controlled by an armed non-State actor. One commentator argues that under Common Article 3, a humanitarian body may proceed with humanitarian assistance if an armed group has accepted it even if the host State withheld its consent.[34] Other authors maintain that an armed group's consent for humanitarian relief operations in area under its 6.18

---

[30] UN Security Council Resolution 2165, adopted by unanimous vote in favour on 14 July 2014, operative para. 6.
[31] Art. 25, Charter of the United Nations; adopted at San Francisco, 26 June 1945; entered into force, 24 October 1945.
[32] ICRC, Commentary on Article 3 of 1949 Geneva Convention I, 2016, para. 867.
[33] Ibid., para. 868.
[34] See N. Nishat, 'The Right of Initiative of the ICRC and Other Impartial Humanitarian Bodies', in A. Clapham, P. Gaeta, and M. Sassòli (eds.), *The 1949 Geneva Conventions: A Commentary*, p. 501, para. 20.

control might be legally required.[35] To overcome the express wording of the Additional Protocol II, which requires the consent of the State 'concerned' for relief actions, some authorities argue that the territorial State is not 'concerned' if the relief does not need to pass through territory controlled by its government.[36]

6.19 The 2016 Oxford Guidance provides that:

> In situations of non-international armed conflict, where a humanitarian relief operation is intended for civilians in territory under the effective control of an organised armed group, and this territory can be reached without transiting through territory under the effective control of the state party to the conflict, the consent of the state is nonetheless required, but it has a narrower range of grounds for withholding consent.[37]

The Guidance also, rightly, underlines that:

> Whatever the legal position, as a matter of operational practice, the agreement or acquiescence of all parties to an armed conflict to humanitarian relief operations intended for civilians in territory under their effective control or transiting through such territory will be required to conduct the operations in a safe and unimpeded manner.[38]

Implementation of relief operations and protection of humanitarian personnel

6.20 If consent is given and relief operations can proceed, parties to the conflict as well as each 'High Contracting Party' (the term traditionally used in IHL for State Party) 'shall allow and facilitate rapid and unimpeded passage of all relief consignments, equipment and personnel'.[39] They may, however, prescribe the technical arrangements, including search, or make such permission conditional on the distribution of the assistance under the local supervision of a protecting power.[40] Relief consignments may obviously not be diverted and parties to the conflict must protect them and facilitate their rapid distribution.[41]

6.21 The duty to facilitate rapid and unimpeded passage of humanitarian relief supplies, equipment, and personnel in Article 70(2) of the 1977 Additional Protocol I covers initial entry into the country as well as movement within it.[42] So-called 'technical

---

[35] F. Bouchet-Saulnier, 'Consent to Humanitarian Access: An Obligation Triggered by Territorial Control, Not States' Rights', *International Review of the Red Cross*, Vol. 96, No. 893 (2014), pp. 207–17; see also T. Gal, 'Territorial Control by Armed Groups and the Regulation of Access to Humanitarian Assistance', *Israel Law Review*, Vol. 50, No. 1 (2017), pp. 25–47.
[36] Bothe, Partsch, and Solf, *New Rules for Victims of Armed Conflicts*, p. 801.
[37] 2016 Oxford Guidance, Rule D(ii).
[38] Ibid., para. 31.
[39] Art. 70(2), 1977 Additional Protocol I.
[40] Ibid., Art. 70(3).
[41] Ibid., Art. 70(4).
[42] 2016 Oxford Guidance, Rule 59.

arrangements' permissible to a party to an international armed conflict[43] 'may include the search of consignments to check they do not contain weapons, other military equipment or items that may be used for military purposes; and the requirement that relief convoys use prescribed routes at specific times to ensure that they do not hamper and are not endangered by military operations'.[44] There is no specific provision on the modalities of humanitarian relief operations in the 1977 Additional Protocol II, including on the freedom of movement of authorised humanitarian personnel. The ICRC study of customary IHL concluded that, once parties to an armed conflict have given consent and if the condition of impartiality is fulfilled, they are obligated to facilitate rapid and unimpeded passage of humanitarian relief for civilians in need, *subject to their right of control*, in international and non-international armed conflict alike.[45]

6.22 The obligation to respect and protect humanitarian relief personnel is set out in Article 71(2) of the Additional Protocol I. They are in any event civilians protected as such, unless and until they participate directly in hostilities (hardly a common occurrence). Freedom of movement of humanitarian relief personnel is protected in Article 71(3), although it can be suspended temporarily on the basis of imperative dictates of security. While there is no equivalent provision in the Additional Protocol II, general protections for humanitarian relief personnel in non-international armed conflict are part of the corpus of customary international law.[46]

6.23 Optimistically, the 2016 Oxford Guidance stipulates that: 'Administrative procedures and formalities and other technical arrangements must be applied in good faith and their nature, extent, and impact must not prevent the rapid delivery of humanitarian relief in a principled manner.'[47] Examples abound, however, of States as well as armed non-State actors imposing a variety of administrative hurdles to restrict humanitarian access in practice. For instance, the requirement for a work permit and other bureaucratic impediments and restrictions have significantly impacted humanitarian relief operations in situations of non-international armed conflict in Myanmar, Syria, and Yemen, among others.[48] The *Aid Worker Security Report* has further highlighted that, in 2020, 484 aid workers were victims of major attacks in 41 countries, noting that the worst of the violence took place in the Democratic Republic of Congo, South Sudan, and Syria.[49]

---

[43] Art. 70(3)(a), 1977 Additional Protocol I. The term is from the 2016 Oxford Guidance.
[44] 2016 Oxford Guidance, Rule 67. The Guidance further observes that the practical arrangements for passage will usually be the subject of special agreements between the parties to an armed conflict and the actors conducting the humanitarian relief operations.
[45] See ICRC Customary IHL Rule 55.
[46] Ibid., Rules 31 and 56.
[47] 2016 Oxford Guidance, Rule 55.
[48] Report of the UN Secretary-General on the protection of civilians in armed conflicts, UN doc. S/2021/423, May 2021, para. 39.
[49] Aid Worker Security Database 2021, Figures at a glance 2021, at: https://bit.ly/3k8xn3C.

6.24 Given the intensity of attacks against hospitals, medical personnel, and humanitarian workers in recent conflicts, in 2016 the UN Security Council adopted an important resolution (2286) on health care in armed conflict. In it, the Council urged:

> States and all parties to armed conflict to develop effective measures to prevent and address acts of violence, attacks and threats against medical personnel and humanitarian personnel exclusively engaged in medical duties, their means of transport and equipment, as well as hospitals and other medical facilities in armed conflict, including, as appropriate, through the development of domestic legal frameworks to ensure respect for their relevant international legal obligations, the collection of data on obstruction, threats and physical attacks on medical personnel and humanitarian personnel exclusively engaged in medical duties, their means of transport and medical facilities, and to share challenges and good practice in this regard.[50]

It remains to be seen whether this call will be heeded by belligerents.

International criminal law

6.25 Intentionally using starvation of civilians as a method of warfare by wilfully impeding relief supplies is a war crime in international armed conflicts under the jurisdiction of the International Criminal Court.[51] Since an amendment to the Statute in 2019 (see below), the crime is punishable also in non-international armed conflict. In addition, the 'deprivation of access to food and medicine, calculated to bring about the destruction of part of a population', can be considered as an extermination,[52] defined as 'the intentional infliction' of such 'conditions of life'[53] and constitute a crime against humanity when committed as part of a widespread or systematic attack directed against any civilian population, with knowledge of the attack.

6.26 Starvation caused by blocking humanitarian access, especially during sieges, has been a common feature of contemporary armed conflicts. In Yemen, famine has been caused by the blockades of airports and seaports and obstructing humanitarian aid.[54] In South Sudan, acute hunger has been the consequence of regular and intentional attacks by

---

[50] UN Security Council Resolution 2286 (2016), adopted by unanimous vote in favour on 3 May 2016, operative para. 4.

[51] Art. 8(2)(b)(xxv), Rome Statute of the International Criminal Court; adopted at Rome, 17 July 1998; entered into force, 1 July 2002. Starvation as a method of warfare is also prohibited by the Article 54(1) of the First Additional Protocol and Article 14 of the Second Additional Protocol, as well as under the ICRC Customary IHL Rule 53. See further Chapter 14 of this book.

[52] Art. 7(1)(b), Rome Statute of the International Criminal Court.

[53] Ibid., Art. 7(2)(b).

[54] M. Mundy, 'The Strategies of the Coalition in the Yemen War: Aerial Bombardment and Food War', World Peace Foundation, 2018, available at: https://bit.ly/3vCEVBh, at pp. 7, 11. See also L. Graham, 'Prosecuting Starvation Crimes in Yemen's Civil War', *Case Western Reserve Journal of International Law*, Vol. 52, No. 1 (2020), pp. 267–86, available at: https://bit.ly/3EMdAPh.

government soldiers and allied militias, not only on food supplies but also on humanitarian agencies working in the country.[55]

It remains extremely difficult, however, to prosecute individuals for the war crime of starvation by wilfully impeding humanitarian access. Until recently, the war crime as such, when committed in non-international armed conflict, was not included in the Rome Statute of the International Criminal Court. In December 2019, however, the proposal to amend the Statute was accepted by the Assembly of the States Parties to the International Criminal Court.[56] But even if consent to offers to conduct relief operations cannot be arbitrarily refused, the relevant authorities can still come up with plausible excuses to delay humanitarian assistance. Finally, the interpretation of the threshold required to constitute the war crime of starvation by restricting humanitarian access might explain the difficulty. As Rogier Bartels explains, 'humanitarian goods are often seized by one of the warring parties as a pay-off to let the goods pass. It has been questioned what level of relief supplies have to be diverted to the opposition for a party to legitimately deny the deliverance of relief. One author considers that it is only when an "excessively large portion of aid" is diverted to the opposition that access could be denied, but this threshold appears to be far too high—especially in the context of a criminal trial'.[57]

Armed non-State actors' perspectives on humanitarian relief operations

In a study published by the NGO Geneva Call, 19 armed non-State actors that were consulted generally expressed support for humanitarian relief operations and certain underlying principles, namely neutrality, impartiality, and independence.[58] In another study published by Aid Worker Security in 2017, a more critical perception of humanitarian aid and workers was reported, perhaps because of the types of the groups interviewed for the study: al-Shabaab in Somalia, and the Taliban and Haqqani Network in Afghanistan.[59] In addition, the Aid Worker Security research sought to include Islamic State and al-Qaeda viewpoints through a review of their public statements and

---

[55] See, e.g., Amnesty International, 'South Sudan's Man-Made Hunger Crisis', February 2016, at: https://bit.ly/3CQfIF1.

[56] See ICC Press Release, 'Assembly of States Parties concludes its eighteenth session', 6 December 2019, at: https://bit.ly/3BEoKr5. Amendments to the Rome Statute of the International Criminal Court must be proposed, adopted, and ratified in accordance with Articles 121 and 122 of the Statute. According to Article 121(5) of the Statute, any amendment to Articles 5, 6, 7, or 8 of the Statute only enters into force for States Parties that have ratified the amendment. A State Party which ratifies an amendment to Articles 5, 6, 7, or 8 is legally bound by that amendment one year after ratifying it, regardless of how many other States Parties have also ratified it. As of 1 May 2022, eight States had ratified the amendment (Andorra, Croatia, Liechtenstein, the Netherlands, New Zealand, Norway, Portugal, and Romania). See the UN Treaty Collection at: https://bit.ly/3k8WSl8.

[57] R. Bartels, 'Denying Humanitarian Access as an International Crime in Times of Non-International Armed Conflict: The Challenges to Prosecute and Some Proposals for the Future', *Israel Law Review*, Vol. 48, No. 3 (2015), pp. 281–307, at p. 289.

[58] A. Jackson, *In their Words: Perceptions of Armed Non-State Actors on Humanitarian Action*, Geneva Call, Geneva, 2016, at: https://bit.ly/3BHtqZC.

[59] *Aid Worker Security Report 2017*, Behind the Attacks: A Look at the Perpetrators of Violence against Aid Workers, Humanitarian Outcomes.

English-language publications. The general conclusion the report draws with regard to the perception of humanitarian aid is that 'armed groups view aid organisations as potential threats to their authority as well as useful proxy targets. When attempting to govern territory and provide some measure of public services, armed groups have incentives to grant aid organisations secure access, but this often requires the aid groups to accept conditions that compromise humanitarian principles'.[60]

6.29 Some armed non-State actors also issue positive declarations in favour of humanitarian assistance, such as the Declaration of Commitment on Compliance with IHL and the Facilitation of Humanitarian Assistance by the National Coalition of Syrian Revolution and Opposition Forces.[61] Others have adopted formal policies regulating humanitarian aid, such as, for instance, the Karen National Union (KNU) in Myanmar (which it and other armed groups prefer to call Burma), which issued a Policy for Humanitarian Assistance in June 2014.[62]

6.30 While these texts and declarations usually comply with IHL, the interpretations that some armed non-State actors have concerning humanitarian principles are problematic. This is the case with regard to the type of entity that can provide humanitarian assistance. Common Article 3 states that an impartial humanitarian body, such as the International Committee of the Red Cross, may offer its services to the Parties to the conflict. Offers to conduct humanitarian relief operations may thus be made by States, international organisations, or NGOs. Some of these actors are perceived by armed groups as not meeting the criteria of neutrality, impartiality, and independence. Unsurprisingly, 'national aid organizations' fall into that category. In the context of Sudan, the Sudan People's Liberation Movement—North (SPLM-N) has even asserted that 'no actors fulfil all three principles'.[63]

6.31 Apart from the fact that national aid organisations are said to be in some instances 'infiltrated by the government',[64] perhaps more worryingly, humanitarian assistance, even when provided by independent and neutral NGOs, can be perceived as partial, because, according to a specific mandate, they might target aid towards a certain population. For example, the Democratic Forces for the Liberation of Rwanda (FDLR), active in the north-east of the Democratic Republic of Congo, criticised the partiality of organisations that distributed aid only to the Congolese population and excluded the Rwandan refugees.[65] The perception of the absence of neutrality is particularly problematic for humanitarian access, as it can justify, in the eyes of an armed non-State actor, refusal of consent to access the zones under its control.

---

[60] Ibid., Summary of key findings.
[61] The document is available at: https://bit.ly/3bHhw7B.
[62] The document is available online at: http://theirwords.org/media/transfer/doc/knu_s_policy_for_humanitarian_assistance_2014-be64212cf1a6b6dffd134dee3e7e6a25.pdf
[63] Jackson, *In their Words*, p. 12.
[64] Ibid.
[65] Ibid.

Concluding remarks and outlook

In recent armed conflicts, restrictions on and impediments to humanitarian relief operations have had a tremendously negative impact on the civilian population. It has been rightly noted that attacks on hospitals, medical personnel, or humanitarian workers are not a new phenomenon. These attacks have often been used by parties to a conflict as a military strategy: depriving entire populations of vital assistance does indeed 'allow the parties to the conflict to assert their power in an effective and symbolic manner'.[66] It then becomes crucial to enhance the accountability framework for the violations of the norms on humanitarian relief operations, especially in non-international armed conflicts. It is wholly unacceptable that as of writing only eight States have ratified the amendment to the Rome Statute on the war crime of starvation in non-international armed conflict. Even if parties to an armed conflict could be held accountable by other means, notably for a violation of the principle of distinction for instance, symbolically and in practice States as well as armed groups must commit more firmly to respecting these principles.

6.32

---

[66] C. Abu Sa'Da, F. Duroch, and B. Taith, 'Attacks on Medical Missions: Overview of a Polymorphous Reality: the Case of Médecins Sans Frontières', *International Review of the Red Cross*, Vol. 95, No. 890 (2013), pp. 309–33, at p. 312. Bartels notes that 'access to populations in need is also frequently withheld by one or more of the warring parties, seemingly on purpose. During conflicts that are fought along ethnic and/or religious lines, one side may wish to deny access to humanitarian aid to the civilians who are seen as belonging to the opposing side, yet share the same nationality'. Bartels, 'Denying humanitarian access', p. 282.

7
The Distinctive Emblems

Introduction

7.1 To protect those who are dedicated to collecting and caring for the wounded soldiers on the battlefield from being killed, shot at, or harmed, the idea was simple—to create an emblem which was the same for all warring parties and which was visible from afar that would signal the presence of doctors and nurses near the soldiers and shield them from attack. To fulfil its protective role, from the outset two characteristics were deemed key for the emblem: it had to be *uniform* as well as *universal*. In 1863, as François Bugnion has recalled,

> [t]he International Committee for Aid to Wounded Soldiers—the future International Committee of the Red Cross—set as one of its principal objectives the adoption of a single distinctive sign to indicate both the army medical services and volunteers of aid societies for the relief of wounded soldiers ... Thus, from the very start the protective function of the emblem was closely linked to its universality.[1]

7.2 Despite this original ambition of universality, the path of the distinctive emblem has not run entirely smoothly. In fact, the issue of which emblems may be employed in armed conflicts has been marred by political disputes and cultural relativism. A century and a half after the creation of the Red Cross emblem, the adoption, in 2005, of the Third Additional Protocol to the Geneva Conventions[2] seems to have largely ended these tensions and the current problems regarding emblems are linked to their misuse rather than to the scope of their cultural or religious significance.

7.3 Four emblems are recognised in contemporary international humanitarian law (IHL): the red cross, the red crescent, the red crystal, and the red sun and lion. The last of these, however, has fallen into desuetude.[3] As this chapter discusses, they are the fruit

---

[1] F. Bugnion, *Red Cross, Red Crescent, Red Crystal*, International Committee of the Red Cross (ICRC), Geneva, 2007, pp. 5–6.

[2] Protocol additional to the Geneva Conventions of 12 August 1949, and relating to the Adoption of an Additional Distinctive Emblem (Protocol III); adopted at Geneva, 8 December 2005; entered into force, 14 January 2007.

[3] As discussed below, the Red Lion and Sun was an emblem used by Persia and is explicitly recognised by the 1949 Geneva Conventions, but is no longer used by any State. The Islamic Republic of Iran uses the red crescent as its protective emblem. Analysis of the legal obligations pertaining to the blue shield emblem applied to cultural property and archaeological heritage, which is regulated by the 1954 Hague Convention for the Protection of Cultural Property in the Event of Armed Conflict, is not considered in this chapter.

Table 7.1 Summary of Rules on the Protective Emblems in the 1977 Additional Protocols

Rule	AP I	Customary status (IAC)	AP II	Customary status (NIAC)
General protection of medical personnel and units	Art. 8(l)	Yes	No	No
Identification of medical personnel and units	Art. 18	Yes	Art. 12	Yes
Misuse of the emblem	Art. 38	Yes	No	No
Perfidious use of the emblem as a war crime	Art. 85(f)	Yes	No	Yes

of a rather tormented history. They each have a protective function as established in law, in international as well as in non-international armed conflicts. They also have an indicative function, the source of which can be found in the Statutes of the Movement of the Red Cross and Red Crescent societies. One may question, however, whether, irrespective of their legal significance, the use of emblems is as protective as in the past, given the high numbers of attacks against medical services in contemporary armed conflicts. This might be one of the great challenges the Movement has to face.

7.4 The rules on the emblems found in the Geneva Conventions and the two 1977 Additional Protocols, as well as in customary IHL, are summarised in Table 7.1 below. The entire 2005 Additional Protocol III relates to the red crystal emblem, so the rules are not summarised therein. The extent to which the rules laid down under Additional Protocol III are also part of customary IHL is debatable given that the protocol was only adopted in 2005 and adherence is not general, much less universal among States. That said, the fundamental norms on the protective use of the emblem, whether that be the red cross, the red crescent, or the red crystal, are firmly part of customary law. Furthermore, under the 1998 Rome Statute of the International Criminal Court, making improper use of the distinctive emblems of the Geneva Conventions is a war crime in international armed conflict (where it results in death or serious personal injury).[4] Attacking buildings, material, medical units, and transport, or personnel using the distinctive emblems 'in conformity with international law' is a war crime under the Court's jurisdiction in both international and non-international armed conflict.[5]

---

[4] Art. 8(2)(b)(vii), Rome Statute of the International Criminal Court; adopted at Rome, 17 July 1998; entered into force, 1 July 2002. As of 1 May 2022, 123 States were party to the Rome Statute.

[5] Art. 8(2)(b)(xxiv) and (e)(ii), Rome Statute.

A brief (tormented) history of the emblems

7.5 The development of the red cross emblem is closely linked to the drafting of the first Geneva Convention to protect the wounded on the battlefield and the creation of aid societies that would provide relief to wounded soldiers. Article 7 of the first Geneva Convention of 1864 thus required that:

> A distinctive and uniform flag shall be adopted for hospitals, ambulances and evacuation parties. It should in all circumstances be accompanied by the national flag. An armlet may also be worn by personnel enjoying neutrality, but its issue shall be left to the military authorities. Both flag and armlet shall bear a red cross on a white ground.[6]

7.6 Why this emblem—a red cross on a white ground—was chosen at that time has not been recorded in the minutes of the international diplomatic conference, but it has been noted that:

> Since the dawn of time, the white flag had been recognized as a sign of the wish to negotiate or of surrender; firing on anyone displaying it in good faith was forbidden. With the addition of a red cross, the flag's message was taken a stage further, demanding respect for the wounded and for anyone coming to their aid. Furthermore, the resulting sign had the advantage of being easy to make and recognizable at a distance because of its contrasting colours.[7]

7.7 In addition, as the emblem was intended as the visible expression of the neutral status enjoyed by the army medical services and the protection conferred upon them, the emblem was also chosen by reversing the colours of the Swiss flag, a permanent neutral country recognised as such internationally since 1815.[8] The first Geneva Convention of 1949 (in its Article 38) thus reminds that: 'As a compliment to Switzerland, the heraldic emblem of the red cross on a white ground, formed by reversing the Federal colours, is retained as the emblem and distinctive sign of the Medical Service of armed forces.'

7.8 Despite the (apparent) absence of a religious significance to the red cross as protective emblem,[9] the Ottoman Empire, which was a party to the 1864 Geneva Convention and was involved in the Russo-Turkish War of 1876–78, said the red cross emblem was offensive to Muslim soldiers and declared unilaterally it would use the red crescent on a white flag instead.[10]

---

[6] Art. 7, Convention for the Amelioration of the Condition of the Wounded in Armies in the Field; adopted at Geneva, 22 August 1864; entered into force, 22 June 1865.

[7] Bugnion, *Red Cross, Red Crescent, Red Crystal*, p. 8. With regard to the choice of the red cross, the author adds that: 'The sign of the cross has been seen in different civilizations from time immemorial. It is generally considered to be a symbol of the human being and his place in the world, the horizontal bar symbolizing arms extended towards the cardinal points (relationship to the world) and the vertical axis symbolizing the relationship with the divinity. The early Christians adopted a symbol which long predated Christianity and identified it with the instrument of Christ's passion.'

[8] E. Andrews, 'Why Is Switzerland a Neutral Country?', *History*, Last updated 22 August 2018, at: http://bit.ly/2NItJzF.

[9] Bugnion, *Red Cross, Red Crescent, Red Crystal*, p. 9.

[10] Ibid.

Along the same lines of reasoning and cultural relativism, the Ottoman Empire, Persia, and Siam requested formal recognition of other emblems during the negotiations of the 1899 and 1907 Hague Peace conferences: the red crescent for the Ottoman Empire, the red lion and sun for Persia, and the red flame for Siam. The Conference did not grant the request, but authorised the lodging of reservations to the provision related to the red cross emblem, which the Ottoman Empire and Persia duly did. At the diplomatic conference of 1929, the red crescent and the red lion and sun were formally recognised as protective emblems, but only for those States already using them.[11] This solution was intended to limit the proliferation of emblems. But in 1931, the International Committee of the Red Cross (ICRC) was informed that a relief society in Palestine was using as its emblem the Red Shield of David (Magen David Adom), thereby preventing the national society from entering the Movement.[12]

During the negotiation of the 1949 Geneva Conventions, Israel requested formal recognition of the Magen David Adom as a protective emblem. After heated debates, the request was rejected, partly because there was an obvious need to avoid the proliferation of protective emblems, which could weaken their protective force.[13] In addition, recognising the Magen David Adom would discredit the argument that the distinctive signs had no religious significance.[14] As a consequence, Article 38 of the first Geneva Convention only admitted that 'in the case of countries which already use as emblem, in place of the red cross, the red crescent or the red lion and sun on a white ground, those emblems are also recognized by the terms of the present Convention'.

Israel did not submit another request of recognition at the conferences in 1974–77. It had nevertheless lodged a reservation when signing the Geneva Conventions in 1951.[15] In 1980, the Islamic Republic of Iran declared that it was waiving its right to use the red lion and sun. Eventually, the sign fell in desuetude.[16]

The use of the Magen David Adom, and particularly the refusal to recognise it, raised a number of issues, not least the impossibility for the Israeli National Society to join the movement. This is because, until 2006, the Statutes of the Movement set use of the red

---

[11] See Article 19 of the Geneva Convention for the Amelioration of the Condition of the Wounded and Sick in Armies in the Field of 27 July 1929: 'As a compliment to Switzerland, the heraldic emblem of the red cross on a white ground, formed by reversing the Federal colours, is retained as the emblem and distinctive sign of the medical service of armed forces. Nevertheless, in the case of countries which already use, in place of the red cross, the red crescent or the red lion and sun on a white ground as a distinctive sign, these emblems are also recognized by the terms of the present Convention.' Bugnion, *Red Cross, Red Crescent, Red Crystal*, pp. 10–12.

[12] Ibid., p. 13. The International Red Cross and Red Crescent Movement is composed of the ICRC, the International Federation of Red Cross and Red Crescent Societies, and the individual National Societies. Each has its own legal identity and role, but they are all united by seven Fundamental Principles (humanity, impartiality, neutrality, independence, voluntary service, unity and universality). See: https://bit.ly/3sOUZ2s.

[13] Bugnion, *Red Cross, Red Crescent, Red Crystal*, p. 14.

[14] See also J.-F. Quéguiner, 'Commentary on the Protocol Additional to the Geneva Conventions of 12 August 1949, and Relating to the Adoption of an Additional Distinctive Emblem (Protocol III)', *International Review of the Red Cross*, Vol. 89, No. 865 (March 2007), 175–207, at p. 177.

[15] The text of the reservation stated that: 'Subject to the reservation that, while respecting the inviolability of the distinctive signs and emblems of the Convention, Israel will use the Red Shield of David as the emblem and distinctive sign of the medical services of her armed forces.' Available at: https://bit.ly/3JBoFWS.

[16] Bugnion, *Red Cross, Red Crescent, Red Crystal*, p. 17.

cross or red crescent as a necessary condition for the recognition of a National Society.[17] In addition to the religious connotation of the emblem engendered by the recognition of the red crescent in 1929 and 1949, another problem was linked to the fact that certain National Societies were using emblems side by side instead of replacing one with the other as requested by the Geneva Conventions.[18]

7.13 Taken together, these practices were defeating the purposes of the protective emblem; namely to be neutral as well as universal. As noted by Bugnion,

> [p]robably the most serious consideration was that the coexistence of two emblems—or three if the Israeli reservation was taken into account—undermined their protective value, especially if each adversary used a different one. Instead of appearing as a symbol of neutrality, the distinctive sign became identified with one or other of the parties to the conflict.[19]

7.14 Several attempts to find a solution were made in the 1970s, but without success. It was the publication in the *International Review of the Red Cross* of an article in 1992 by the then President of the ICRC, Cornelio Sommaruga, which would spark the process that led to the Diplomatic Conference of 2005.[20] Therein, the President warned of

> the danger of the proliferation of emblems that is inherent in the existence of two emblems each identified with a particular religion. When such connotations become fixed in the mind, requests for the recognition of other emblems are bound to arise, although every increase in the number of emblems would have the effect of diminishing their protective value. In the worst case, partisan emblems would become targets. Accordingly, the adoption of one or more new signs with a specific connotation, which would be valid only in one country or in a small number of countries, would contribute to dividing the Movement and weakening the protective value of the emblem.

President Sommaruga outlined a possible solution:

> [t]he ICRC has come to the conclusion that a third sign would offer considerable advantages and would be a solution worth examining in depth within the Movement. If the Movement were to agree that a new, third sign be made available to the States and National Societies wishing to have it, the disadvantages mentioned above with regard to the existing emblems could probably be avoided. This sign would have to meet the requirements of visibility, be free from any religious, political, cultural or other connotations and be chosen with the utmost care.

---

[17] Quéguiner, 'Commentary on the Protocol Additional to the Geneva Conventions of 12 August 1949, and Relating to the Adoption of an Additional Distinctive Emblem (Protocol III)', p. 178.
[18] Ibid.
[19] Bugnion, *Red Cross, Red Crescent, Red Crystal*, p. 28.
[20] C. Sommaruga, 'Unity and Plurality of the Emblems', *International Review of the Red Cross*, Vol. 32, No. 289 (1992), at: https://bit.ly/3HlIaR4.

7.15 The idea of replacing existing emblems by another had been systematically rejected by States during the different consultations that took place in the years that followed.[21] In December 2005, States eventually agreed to adopt, after intense negotiations, the Third Additional Protocol to the 1949 Geneva Conventions creating an *additional* emblem, devoid of any religious connotation: the red crystal, a red, four-sided, diamond-shaped sign with thick borders.[22] The 2005 Diplomatic Conference was followed by the 29th International Conference of the Red Cross and Red Crescent Movement, during which the Magen David Adom and the Palestinian Red Crescent were finally recognised formally as national societies and admitted to the Movement.[23]

7.16 At the time of writing, 79 States have ratified the Third Additional Protocol, including Israel and the United States. Further turmoil was provoked, however, when Israel lodged a reservation to the Protocol when ratifying it in 2007, declaring that 'the ratification or the implementation of this protocol does not affect any rights acquired pursuant to reservations made by Israel to the Geneva Conventions of 12 August 1949'.[24] Switzerland, as the depositary of the Geneva Conventions, and also Sweden commented on the reservation, as well as on the subsequent communication issued by Israel in 2008, whereby Israel recognised that 'under the terms of the Protocol, the Red Crystal, when used as a protective emblem, may not incorporate any additional emblems or combine them as part of the protective emblem'. In their communications, Switzerland and Sweden made clear their understanding of Israel's initial reservation as not preventing it from respecting 'the Protocol III in its entirety' and that Israel would 'solely use the Additional Emblem (Red Crystal) as the distinctive emblem in accordance with said Protocol'.[25] Nonetheless, Israel's armed forces still appear to be using the Magen David Adom, contrary to what is stipulated by the 2005 Additional Protocol III.[26]

---

[21] There were eight conferences prior to the adoption of the third protocol discussing notably this issue: the Council of Delegates meetings in 1995, 1997, 1999, 2001, 2003, and 2005, as well as the 27th (1999) and 28th (2003) International Conferences of the Red Cross. See ICRC Blog, Cross Files, 'Drafting history of the 2005 Additional Protocol', 8 February 2021, at: https://bit.ly/3sPcgsm.

[22] The negotiation of the Third Additional Protocol took place in the highly sensitive context of the conflict in the Middle East, linked notably to the occupation of the Palestinian territories and the Syrian Golan Heights by Israel. This explains why the Protocol was adopted by vote (passing by 98 votes to 27, with 10 abstentions) demonstrating an unfortunate split in the international community about an IHL treaty. For a detailed historical account of the negotiations and adoption of the Third Additional Protocol, see Bugnion, *Red Cross, Red Crescent, Red Crystal*, at pp. 48–55. On the politics surrounding the negotiations of the protocols, see also G. Solis, *The Law of Armed Conflict*, 1st Edn, Cambridge University Press, Cambridge, 2010, p. 137.

[23] Bugnion, *Red Cross, Red Crescent, Red Crystal*, p. 64.

[24] The declaration read in full as follows: 'The Government of Israel declares that while respecting the inviolability of the additional distinctive emblem provided for in the "Protocol additional to the Geneva Conventions of 12 August 1949, and relating to the Adoption of an Additional Distinctive Emblem (Protocol III)", it is the understanding of the Government of Israel that the ratification or the implementation of this protocol does not affect any rights acquired pursuant to reservations made by Israel to the Geneva Conventions of 12 August 1949.' Text available at: https://bit.ly/3eE31Tx.

[25] Text also available at: https://bit.ly/3eE31Tx.

[26] T. Pileggi, 'Red Cross Asked to Expel MDA over Emblem Violation', *Times of Israel*, 20 September 2015, at: https://bit.ly/3EK09z1; see also M. Sassòli, *International Humanitarian Law, Rules, Controversies, and Solutions to Problems arising in Warfare*, Edward Elgar Publishing, Cheltenham, 2019, para. 8.38, p. 244.

The protective functions of the distinctive emblems

7.17 The protective function of the emblem was established very early in the development of the law of armed conflict. As a cardinal operational tool, in order to protect, collect, and care for the wounded and sick on the battlefield or at sea, medical services had to be protected as well. One of the challenges that the drafters of the Geneva Conventions faced was that, while wounded and sick soldiers *hors de combat* were not able to participate in hostilities, medical personnel belonging to the armed forces of a State could very well be able or be used to engage in combat.[27] It was thus essential to secure their protection by clearly identifying them on the battlefield with a neutral and visible sign, while also criminalising improper use of the protective emblem, notably when it constituted perfidy.

7.18 The 1949 Geneva Conventions thus stipulate that parties to an international armed conflict must use the emblem clearly to mark their medical units and transports on the ground, at sea, and in the air and, further, that medical personnel must wear armlets and carry identity cards displaying the emblem.[28] The same logic underpins Article 18 of the 1977 Additional Protocol I, Article 12 of the 1977 Additional Protocol II, and Article 2 of the 2005 Additional Protocol III.

7.19 In international armed conflicts, Article 18 of the Additional Protocol I provides, in paragraphs 1 and 2, that parties to the conflict shall endeavour 'to ensure that medical and religious personnel and medical units and transports are identifiable' and to 'adopt and to implement methods and procedures which will make it possible to recognize medical units and transports which use the distinctive emblem and distinctive signals'. In situations of military occupation, however, and 'in areas where fighting is taking place or is likely to take place, civilian medical personnel and civilian religious personnel should be recognizable by the distinctive emblem and an identity card certifying their status'.[29]

7.20 The use of the protective emblems must be authorised by the relevant party to the conflict to which the individuals or units belong. Thus, the authorised users of the protected emblems are the persons falling within IHL definitions of medical personnel, units, and vehicles,[30] namely the medical services of armed forces, the medical personnel units and transports of National Societies that have been duly recognised and authorised by their governments to assist the medical services of the armed forces, authorised NGOs, and authorised hospitals (whether public or private). The ICRC and the International Federation of Red Cross and Red Crescent Societies may use the emblem for protective purposes (and at all times) in armed conflicts without further restrictions.[31]

---

[27] See ICRC Commentary of 1987 on Article 18 of the 1977 Additional Protocol I, para. 734.
[28] See Arts. 39–44 of 1949 Geneva Convention I; and Arts. 22–23, 26–28, 34–37, 39, and 41–44 of 1949 Geneva Convention II.
[29] Art. 18(3), 1977 Additional Protocol I.
[30] See Art. 8 of the 1977 Additional Protocol I for the definitions of medical personnel, units, and vehicles.
[31] Art. 44, 1949 Geneva Convention I.

In situations of non-international armed conflicts, Article 12 of the Additional Protocol **7.21**
II is more straightforward. It states that:

> Under the direction of the competent authority concerned, the distinctive emblem of the red cross, red crescent or red lion and sun on a white ground shall be displayed by medical and religious personnel and medical units, and on medical transports. It shall be respected in all circumstances. It shall not be used improperly.

Article 12 thus confirms that authorised users of the protected emblems are also the medical services of organised armed groups. As highlighted by the ICRC Commentary on the provision:

> The protection conferred by the distinctive emblem requires that its use be subject to the authorization and supervision of the competent authority concerned. It is up to each responsible authority to take the measures necessary to ensure that such control be effective. The competent authority may be civilian or military. For those who are fighting against the legal government this will be the de facto authority in charge. It should be recalled that the threshold for application of the Protocol requires a certain degree of organization in general, and in particular the ability of the insurgents to apply the rules of the Protocol.[32]

There are unfortunately very few studies of the use, practice, and understanding of the **7.22**
emblems by armed groups. In the Geneva Call Deed of Commitment, while signatory armed groups commit to respect and protect health care personnel, facilities, and transports in accordance with IHL, they also commit: 'To respect the distinctive emblems of the red cross, red crescent and red crystal, and not to use them for purposes not related to the provision of health care.'[33]

The Third Additional Protocol does not add obligations with respect to the protective **7.23**
function of the emblems, apart from proposing the use of the red crystal. Article 2(3) recalls that: 'The conditions for use of and respect for the third Protocol emblem are identical to those for the distinctive emblems established by the Geneva Conventions and, where applicable, the 1977 Additional Protocols.' However, under Article 4 of the 2005 Additional Protocol III it is noted that the ICRC and the International Federation of Red Cross and Red Crescent Societies may use the red crystal only 'in exceptional circumstances and to facilitate their work'. Under the First and Second Additional Protocol, as well as under the Geneva Conventions, they may use the red cross and red crescent emblems without restrictions and at all times. As noted by Quéguiner:

> Article 44(3) of the First Geneva Convention permits the international Red Cross organizations and their duly authorized personnel to make use, at all times, of the

---

[32] ICRC, Commentary of 1987 on Article 12 of Additional Protocol II, available at: https://bit.ly/3sIOj5U, para. 4746.
[33] Deed of Commitment under Geneva Call for the Protection of Health Care in Armed Conflict, available at: https://www.genevacall.org/. Unfortunately, only two armed groups so far have signed the deed: the APCLS from the Democratic Republic of the Congo and the Free Syrian Army from Syria, both of which signed in 2019.

110   THE DISTINCTIVE EMBLEMS

emblem of the red cross. A similarly worded previous draft of Additional Protocol III authorized the international components of the Movement to avail themselves of the third Protocol emblem whenever it seemed necessary. However, Article 4 as it now stands follows a different logic. It must be read in conjunction with the last paragraph of the preamble (which did not appear in previous versions) expressing the determination of the ICRC, the International Federation and the Movement to retain their current names and distinctive emblems.[34]

7.24 Finally, it is important to highlight that the protection afforded by IHL to medical personnel, transport, or units is not conferred by the emblems, which are 'only' used to facilitate their identification. In other words, medical personnel, transport, and units are protected against attacks by the Geneva Conventions and the Protocols because of the functions they are performing *and not* because they use the emblems. As Marco Sassòli eloquently observes: 'If an adversary knows that a State identifies its ambulances with green frogs, it would be as unlawful to attack them as if they were identified with a recognized emblem or even with no emblem at all.'[35]

The indicative functions of the emblems

7.25 In contrast, the indicative use of the emblems is intended to show that persons or objects are linked to the Red Cross and Red Crescent Movement and it is relevant *only in times of peace*.[36] The authorised users are: national Red Cross and Red Crescent societies and ambulances and first-aid stations operated by third parties, when exclusively assigned to provide free treatment to the wounded and sick, as an exceptional measure, on condition that the emblem is used in conformity with national legislation and that the national society has expressly authorised such use.[37] The ICRC and the International Federation may use the emblem for indicative purposes without restriction.[38]

7.26 While the protective emblem must be identifiable from as far away as possible, and may be as large as necessary to ensure recognition,[39] the indicative emblem must be comparatively small in size and may not be placed on armlets or on the roofs of buildings.[40] Finally, under the Additional Protocol III, for indicative purposes only, a State adopting the red crystal as its protective emblem may add its own smaller emblem to the interior of the open diamond.[41]

---

[34] Quéguiner, 'Commentary on the Protocol Additional to the Geneva Conventions of 12 August 1949, and Relating to the Adoption of an Additional Distinctive Emblem (Protocol III)', p. 194.
[35] Sassòli, *International Humanitarian Law, Rules, Controversies, and Solutions to Problems arising in Warfare*, para. 8.39, pp. 244–45.
[36] See Art. 44, 1949 Geneva Convention I.
[37] Ibid., Art. 44(2) and (4).
[38] Ibid., Art. 44(3).
[39] Ibid., Arts. 39–44; and Art. 18, 1977 Additional Protocol I.
[40] Art. 44(2), 1949 Geneva Convention I.
[41] Article 3(1) of the 2005 Additional Protocol III highlights the different possibilities: 'National Societies of those High Contracting Parties which decide to use the third Protocol emblem may, in using the emblem in

Misuse of the emblems

7.27 In addition to being the subject of controversy over its meaning, the emblems have also been misused. Because of the protective value of the emblems, the Movement has long focused on the problem of its improper use. To this end, a thorough study was commissioned to address the operational and commercial use of the emblems.[42] The core objective of the study was to ensure greater respect for the emblem, by improving the understanding of the rules governing its use. Indeed,

> [m]isuse of the emblem, whenever committed, creates confusion and distrust in the public mind in general, and especially in the parties to an armed conflict ... This undermines confidence in the entities entitled to use the emblem, such as the components of the Movement or the armed forces' medical services, which in turn threatens their access to victims and even their own security.[43]

7.28 The illicit use of the emblem commonly covers perfidy and usurpation (the use of the emblem by unauthorised entities or persons), as well as imitation (the use of any sign that could potentially be confused with the emblem).[44] Perfidy comprises acts that invite 'the confidence of an adversary to lead him to believe that he is entitled to, or is obliged to accord, protection under the rules of international law applicable in armed conflict, with intent to betray that confidence'.[45] The perfidious use of the emblem is prohibited by Article 85(f) of the 1977 Additional Protocol I. As noted above, perfidious use of the emblem is a war crime within the jurisdiction of the International Criminal Court in international armed conflict (where death or serious injury results), while attacking buildings, material, medical units, and transports or personnel displaying the distinctive emblems are war crimes under the Court's jurisdiction in both international and non-international armed conflicts.[46] Under customary law, killing or wounding an adversary by resort to perfidy, including through misuse of the protective emblems, is a war crime also in non-international armed conflict.[47]

7.29 A famous example of usurpation of the emblem occurred in the context of a Colombian non-international armed conflict in 2008. The then President of Colombia admitted that during a military operation to rescue hostages taken by an armed group, a military

---

conformity with relevant national legislation, choose to incorporate within it, for indicative purposes: (a) a distinctive emblem recognized by the Geneva Conventions or a combination of these emblems; or (b) another emblem which has been in effective use by a High Contracting Party and was the subject of a communication to the other High Contracting Parties and the International Committee of the Red Cross through the depositary prior to the adoption of this Protocol.'

[42] ICRC, Study on the use of the Emblems, Geneva, 2009, at: https://bit.ly/34ePK1J.
[43] B. Rolle and E. Lafontaine, 'The Emblem that Cried Wolf: ICRC Study on the Use of the Emblems', *International Review of the Red Cross*, Vol. 91, No. 876 (December 2009), pp. 759–78, at p. 763.
[44] S. Zelada, 'A Controversial Emblem', ICRC blog cross-files, 21 April 2021, available at: https://bit.ly/342urjI.
[45] Art. 37, 1977 Additional Protocol I.
[46] Art. 8(2)(b)(vii) and (xxiv), Rome Statute.
[47] ICRC Customary IHL Rule 156: 'Definition of War Crimes', (iv) 'Other serious violations of international humanitarian law committed during a non-international armed conflict', at: https://bit.ly/3sON6K8.

112   THE DISTINCTIVE EMBLEMS

intelligence officer wore the Red Cross bib over his jacket, contrary to the stipulations of the Geneva Conventions (and customary law).[48] This case is discussed further in Chapter 19.[49]

Concluding remarks and outlook

7.30 Apparently a simple concept and idea, the use of the emblems in IHL has been caught by the ideological and religious tensions of the conflicts in which they were devised to offer protection. History will tell us if the 2005 Additional Protocol III and the creation of red crystal is a lasting solution to these tensions. However, an undisputable positive outcome of the treaty has been to allow the Movement to reach universal membership.

7.31 The development of new technologies might represent both a challenge and an opportunity for the emblems. In that regard, the 2016 ICRC Commentary on Geneva Convention I noted that 'the marking of medical facilities might also involve the communication of GPS coordinates to other Parties in addition to, or in lieu of, marking them with the distinctive emblem'.[50] Finally, the use of the emblem should also be re-examined in the context of cyberwarfare. Taking the example of the codification of non-physical infrastructures, such as light and radio signals to protect the operations of medical units and other objects identified by the recognised emblems, it was thus recommended that States 'should today redouble their efforts to provide legal protection to certain cyber infrastructures by marking them with distinctive emblems. States may seek to extend similar protection to websites, networks and servers by marking them through electronic emblems'.[51]

---

[48] K. Penhaul, 'Uribe: Betancourt Rescuers Used Red Cross Emblem in Rescue', *CNN*, 16 July 2008, at: https://cnn.it/3pHSpJs.

[49] See, infra, paras. 19.24–19.25. See, for other examples, *Misuse of the Emblem* in the ICRC database, *How Does Law Protect in War*, at: https://bit.ly/3qLPBuq.

[50] L. Cameron, B. Demeyere, J.-M. Henckaerts, E. La Haye, and H. Niebergall-Lackner, 'The Updated Commentary on the First Geneva Convention—A New Tool for Generating Respect for International Humanitarian Law', *International Review of the Red Cross*, Vol. 97, No. 900 (2015), pp. 1209–26, at p. 1222.

[51] A. Iaria, 'E-Emblems: Protective Emblems and the Legal Challenges of Cyber Warfare', Instituto Affari Internazionali, 18 June 2018, at: https://bit.ly/3qHLXBp.

8

The Rule of Distinction (Objects)

Introduction

The principle of distinction is the fundamental rule governing the conduct of hostilities in international humanitarian law (IHL), 'the single most important principle for the protection of the victims of armed conflict' in the words of Helen Duffy.[1] This chapter discusses the rule governing the targeting of objects under the two 1977 Additional Protocols, other IHL treaties, and customary law.[2] The overarching obligation to distinguish between civilian objects and military objectives in the conduct of hostilities is set out explicitly only in the 1977 Additional Protocol I,[3] although a more limited prohibition on attacking certain civilian objects is incorporated in the 1977 Additional Protocol II.[4] An attack is unlawful not only if it is targeted against a civilian object, but also if it is *not* targeted at a lawful military objective, in which case it amounts to an indiscriminate attack.[5]   8.1

The key rules governing the principle of distinction with respect to objects set out in the two 1977 Additional Protocols are summarised in Table 8.1.   8.2

A number of objects are also given special protection under IHL through other instruments, notably military hospitals (protected under 1949 Geneva Convention I),[6] civilian hospitals (protected under 1949 Geneva Convention IV),[7] and cultural objects

---

[1] H. Duffy, *The 'War on Terror' and the Framework of International Law*, 2nd Edn, Cambridge University Press, Cambridge, 2015, p. 363.

[2] The United States military describes targeting as 'the process of selecting enemy objects to be attacked, assigning priorities to those objects, and matching appropriate weapons to them to assure their destruction', cited in G. D. Solis, *The Law of Armed Conflict: International Humanitarian Law in War*, 3rd Edn, Cambridge University Press, Cambridge, 2021, pp. 397–98.

[3] Art. 48, Protocol Additional to the Geneva Conventions of 12 August 1949, and relating to the Protection of Victims of International Armed Conflicts (Protocol I); adopted at Geneva, 8 June 1977; entered into force, 7 December 1978 (hereinafter, 1977 Additional Protocol I).

[4] Arts. 14 and 16, Protocol additional to the Geneva Conventions of 12 August 1949, and relating to the protection of victims of non-international armed conflicts (Protocol II); adopted at Geneva, 8 June 1977; entered into force, 7 December 1978 (hereinafter, 1977 Additional Protocol II).

[5] According to Article 51(4) of 1977 Additional Protocol I and under customary IHL, indiscriminate attacks include those that are not directed at a specific military objective, and which are consequently 'of a nature to strike military objectives and civilians or civilian objects without distinction'. International Committee of the Red Cross (ICRC) Customary IHL Rule 12: 'Definition of Indiscriminate Attacks', at: http://bit.ly/2lJ2V4y.

[6] Convention (I) for the Amelioration of the Condition of the Wounded and Sick in Armed Forces in the Field; adopted at Geneva, 12 August 1949; entered into force, 21 October 1950.

[7] Convention (IV) Relative to the Protection of Civilian Persons in Time of War; adopted at Geneva, 12 August 1949; entered into force, 21 October 1950.

Table 8.1 Summary of Rules on the Principle of Distinction (Objects)

Rule	AP I	Customary status (IAC)	AP II	Customary status (NIAC)
Basic rule	Art. 48	Yes	No	Yes
General protection of civilian objects	Art. 52(1)	Yes	No	Yes
Definition of civilian object	Art. 52(1)	Yes	No	Yes
Definition of military objective	Art. 52(2)	Yes	No	Yes
Protection of cultural objects and places of worship	Art. 53	Yes	Art. 16	Yes

(protected under the 1954 Hague Convention and its Protocols).[8] Special protection is also afforded to 'works or installations containing dangerous forces, namely dams, dykes and nuclear electrical generating stations'.[9] (The customary law nature of the latter prohibition is contested by the United States and a number of commentators.[10]) The intentional destruction of objects indispensable to the survival of the civilian population for the specific purpose of denying the civilian population their use, which is specifically prohibited in both the 1977 Additional Protocols, is discussed in Chapter 14.

The definition of 'civilian object' and 'military objective'

8.3 Before turning to the content of the rules governing the conduct of hostilities, the definitions of civilian object and of military objective (with respect to objects) are first addressed. The former is straightforward; the latter more complicated. Under Article 52(1) of the 1977 Additional Protocol I, a civilian object is simply any object that is not a military objective. The term is therefore defined in the negative. According to paragraph 2 of the same article, 'military objectives are limited to those objects which by their nature, location, purpose or use make an effective contribution to military action and whose total or partial destruction, capture or neutralization, in the circumstances ruling at the time, offers a definite military advantage'.

---

[8] Convention for the Protection of Cultural Property in the Event of Armed Conflict; adopted at The Hague, 14 May 1954; entered into force, 7 August 1956 (hereinafter, 1954 Hague Convention); and the Second Protocol to the 1954 Hague Convention; adopted at The Hague, 26 March 1999; entered into force, 9 March 2004. As of 1 May 2022, 133 States were party to the 1954 Convention and 84 States were party to the 1999 Protocol.
[9] Art. 56(4), 1977 Additional Protocol I.
[10] See Solis, *The Law of Armed Conflict: International Humanitarian Law in War*, 3rd Edn, p. 411.

These two definitions, which reflect customary international law, apply in both international and non-international armed conflict.[11]

8.4 The definition of military objective comprises two main elements. First, the nature, location, purpose, or use of an object must make an effective contribution to military action. Secondly, the object's partial or total destruction, capture, or neutralisation must, in the circumstances ruling at the time, offer a definite military advantage. Unless an object, in the circumstances ruling at the time, fulfils both criteria, it is a civilian object protected from attack. The twin elements and their constituents are discussed in turn.

The 'nature' of an object

8.5 Certain objects will be, by their nature, military objectives. Thus, for instance, in the words of the Committee of the International Criminal Tribunal for the former Yugoslavia (ICTY) that was established to review the legality of the bombing of the Federal Republic of Yugoslavia in 1999 by the North Atlantic Treaty Organization (NATO): 'Everyone will agree that a munitions factory is a military objective.'[12] Military weapons and weapons systems generally, along with military barracks, transportation vehicles, and storage facilities, will likewise fall into the category of objects whose nature makes them a lawful military target. Military command-and-control centres are similarly military objectives by nature.[13] Yoram Dinstein considers the nature of the following objects would also tend to make them military objectives: military ports, shipyards, and dry-docks; raw materials for military use; military repair facilities; military research and development facilities; intelligence-gathering facilities (even when not run by the military); and the Ministry of Defence.[14]

The 'location' of an object

8.6 As the International Committee of the Red Cross (ICRC) observes in its 1987 commentary on Article 51(2) in the 1977 Additional Protocol I, certain objects 'by their nature' have 'no military function' but, by virtue of their location, make an effective contribution to military action:

---

[11] ICRC Customary IHL Rule 9: 'Definition of Civilian Objects', at: http://bit.ly/3ajxsLn; and Customary IHL Rule 8: 'Definition of Military Objectives', at: http://bit.ly/2X2mHqu. On the status of the latter definition, see also, e.g., International Criminal Court (ICC), *Prosecutor v. Bosco Ntaganda*, Judgment (Trial Chamber VI) (Case No. ICC-01/04-02/06), 8 July 2019, para. 1146, note 3156.

[12] ICTY Committee, 'Final Report to the Prosecutor by the Committee Established to Review the NATO Bombing Campaign Against the Federal Republic of Yugoslavia', 2000, para. 37.

[13] United Kingdom (UK) Ministry of Defence, *The Manual of the Law of Armed Conflict*, Oxford University Press, Oxford, 2004, para. 5.4.4(c).

[14] Y. Dinstein, *The Conduct of Hostilities under the Law of International Armed Conflict*, 3rd Edn, Cambridge University Press, Cambridge, 2016, para. 296(a)–(p).

116   THE RULE OF DISTINCTION (OBJECTS)

This may be, for example, a bridge or other construction, or it could also be ... a site which is of special importance for military operations in view of its location, either because it is a site that must be seized or because it is important to prevent the enemy from seizing it, or otherwise because it is a matter of forcing the enemy to retreat from it.[15]

Dinstein asserts that military objectives 'by nature' comprise transportation arteries of strategic importance, including railways, bridges, roads, navigable rivers and canals, and tunnels, but this is not persuasive. Depending on the prevailing circumstances, however, such objects are better understood as having military value by reason of their location, or potentially their use.[16] This may extend to civilian objects that are not being used for military purposes. According to Solis, 'if military necessity dictates that a civilian house be seized or destroyed to clear a field of fire or block an enemy avenue of approach, the house ceases to be a civilian object and may be considered a military objective'.[17]

8.7   An area of land is an object[18] that can be a military objective purely by virtue of its location (or, alternatively, its use or purpose).[19] When it ratified the 1977 Additional Protocol I, the United Kingdom entered a statement of understanding whereby 'a specific area of land may be a military objective if, because of its location or other reasons specified in Article 52, its total or partial destruction, capture or neutralisation in the circumstances ruling at the time offers definite military advantage'.[20] Similar understandings have been made by Canada,[21] France,[22] Germany,[23] Italy,[24] and New Zealand,[25] among others. This interpretation, the ICRC recalls, was 'not discussed' during the Diplomatic Conference that negotiated the Protocol; 'nevertheless', the organisation has asserted, this position appears to be 'reasonable'.[26] Of course, such an area 'can only be of a limited size'. Furthermore, this concept 'is only valid in the combat area'.[27] That said, the potential terrain of hostilities for an international armed conflict is not geographically limited.

---

[15] ICRC, Commentary on the 1977 Additional Protocols, 1987, para. 2021.
[16] Dinstein, *The Conduct of Hostilities under the Law of International Armed Conflict*, 3rd Edn, para. 296(q).
[17] Solis, *The Law of Armed Conflict: International Humanitarian Law in War*, 3rd Edn, p. 399.
[18] According to the ICRC, it 'is clear that in both English and French the word [object] means something that is visible and tangible'. ICRC Commentary on the 1977 Additional Protocols, 1987, para. 2008. Objects include land, buildings, livestock, and the natural environment. The issue of data is discussed below.
[19] For instance, in the view of the United Kingdom (citing as evidence the ICRC commentary on the 1977 Additional Protocol I), location 'includes areas which are militarily important because they must be captured or denied to the enemy or because the enemy must be made to retreat from them'. UK Ministry of Defence, *The Manual of the Law of Armed Conflict*, para. 5.4.4(d), citing ICRC, Commentary on the 1977 Additional Protocols, 1987, para. 2022.
[20] UK Statement of Understanding, 28 January 1998, para. j, at: http://bit.ly/2PC0crS.
[21] Canadian Statement of Understanding, 20 November 1990, at: http://bit.ly/2RaSqV4.
[22] French Statement of Understanding, 11 April 2001, para. 12, at: http://bit.ly/2OQfTGD.
[23] German Statement of Understanding, 14 February 1991, para. 7, at: http://bit.ly/2RvEEeE.
[24] Italian Statement of Understanding, 27 February 1986, at: http://bit.ly/36bOaJf.
[25] New Zealand Statement of Understanding, 8 February 1988, para. 4, at: http://bit.ly/2G4MW7Q.
[26] ICRC, Commentary on the 1977 Additional Protocols, 1987, para. 2026.
[27] Ibid.

The 'use' of an object

Any civilian object may become a military objective as a consequence of its use for military functions. Stationing troops or placing weapons, military intelligence assets, or military *matériel* in or on an object may all transform it into a lawful military objective insofar as an effective contribution to military action is thereby made. Thus, for example, the ICTY held that the fact of stationing ethnic Serb police (who were participating directly in hostilities) in a monastery in the Croatian town of Knin during the 1995 conflict in the Krajina had transformed what had been a protected civilian object into a military objective.[28]

8.8

Many objects will be used for both civilian and military purposes. During the 1999 Kosovo conflict between NATO member States and the Federal Republic of Yugoslavia, a NATO aircraft launched two laser-guided bombs at a railway bridge in eastern Serbia. Although the railway was also used to carry trains bearing civilian passengers, the bridge was 'part of the integrated communications supply network in Serbia', used to re-supply Serb forces in Kosovo.[29] Accordingly, the ICTY Committee was of the 'opinion' that the bridge was a 'legitimate' military objective.[30]

8.9

The same principle applies to other objects. If they have a dual use that includes military as well as civilian activities, they become a military objective by virtue of their use. This pertains to, among other objects, roads, electricity generating plants, and schools. With respect to the latter, in 2015, Norway and Argentina led the development of the Safe Schools Declaration, an intergovernmental political agreement that seeks to restrict use of schools and universities for military purposes.[31] As of December 2021, a total of 113 States had endorsed the soft-law Declaration.[32] According to the associated *Guidelines for Protecting Schools and Universities from Military Use During Armed Conflict*: 'Functioning schools and universities should not be used by the fighting forces of parties to armed conflict in any way in support of the military effort.'[33] The Guidelines further call for restraint by attackers, while accepting that such use transforms the school into a lawful military objective:

8.10

> While the use of a school or university by the fighting forces of parties to armed conflict in support of their military effort may, depending on the circumstances, have the effect of turning it into a military objective subject to attack, parties to armed conflict

---

[28] ICTY, *Prosecutor v. Ante Gotovina and Mladen Markač*, Judgment (Trial Chamber I) (Case No. IT-06-90-T), 15 April 2011, para. 1213.

[29] ICTY Committee, 'Final Report to the Prosecutor by the Committee Established to Review the NATO Bombing Campaign Against the Federal Republic of Yugoslavia', 2000, paras. 59, 58.

[30] Ibid., para. 62.

[31] Global Coalition to Protect Education from Attack (GCPEA), 'The Safe Schools Declaration', 2020, at: http://bit.ly/2TDzWy3.

[32] See the Norwegian government's list of signatories, at: http://bit.ly/2k3LOtS. See also GCPEA, 'The Safe Schools Declaration', 2020, and see also 'Third International Conference on Safe Schools, 27–29 May 2019, Palma de Mallorca, Spain, Conclusions', 2019, p. 1, at: http://bit.ly/2txwuuc.

[33] *Guidelines for Protecting Schools and Universities from Military Use During Armed Conflict*, Guideline 1, at: http://bit.ly/2lY5ZtM.

should consider all feasible alternative measures before attacking them, including, unless circumstances do not permit, warning the enemy in advance that an attack will be forthcoming unless it ceases its use.[34]

8.11 Whether an object is being used for military purposes may be contested. Moreover, certain military activities do not suffice to transform a civilian object into a military objective. Notable among these is the dissemination of propaganda. During the 1999 Kosovo conflict, NATO forces bombed the Serbian TV and Radio Station (RTS) in Belgrade killing up to 17 people.[35] At a press conference in the aftermath of the bombing, NATO officials justified the attack on the basis that '[m]ost of the commercial system serves the military and the military system can be put to use for the commercial system'.[36] If RTS was indeed being used as a command and control centre by the military, this would render it a lawful military objective. 'More controversially', however, as the ICTY Committee recalled, the attack 'was also justified on the basis of the propaganda purpose to which it was employed'.[37] According to NATO: 'Strikes against TV transmitters and broadcast facilities are part of our campaign to dismantle the FRY propaganda machinery which is a vital part of President Milosevic's control mechanism'.[38] The then UK Prime Minister, Tony Blair, in Washington, D.C. at the time of the bombing, claimed that bombing television stations was 'entirely justified' since they were part of the 'apparatus of dictatorship and power of Milosevic'.[39] This is incorrect as a matter of international law.

8.12 Indeed, the treatment of this incident contrasts starkly with that pertaining to an attack on a TV building in Sarajevo on 28 June 1995 during the armed conflicts in Bosnia and Herzegovina. This attack is one of the acts for which Dragomir Milošević, the commander of the Bosnian Serb forces above the city at that time, was convicted of war crimes. Commander Milošević had written in a letter: 'Our artillery forces are responding with precision to the Muslim artillery attacks. In one such response on 28 June they hit the BH Radio and Television Centre, the centre of media lies against the just struggle of the Serbian people.'[40] In a letter dated 30 June 1995, Colonel Robert Meille of the UN Protection Force (UNPROFOR) lodged a protest with General Milošević regarding attacks on civilian targets in the city of Sarajevo on 28 and 29 June 1995, in particular, the shelling of the TV building.[41]

---

[34] *Guidelines for Protecting Schools and Universities from Military Use During Armed Conflict*, Guideline 4.
[35] ICTY Committee, 'Final Report to the Prosecutor by the Committee Established to Review the NATO Bombing Campaign Against the Federal Republic of Yugoslavia', 2000, para. 71.
[36] Ibid., para. 72.
[37] Ibid., para. 74.
[38] Remarks by Colonel Konrad Freytag, 'Press Conference by NATO Spokesman, Jamie Shea and Colonel Konrad Freytag, SHAPE', Press Conference, Washington, D.C., 23 April 1999, at: http://bit.ly/2NCPtdR.
[39] Reported in R. Norton-Taylor, 'Serb TV Station Was Legitimate Target, Says Blair', *The Guardian*, 24 April 1999, at: http://bit.ly/3692RwJ.
[40] ICTY, *Prosecutor v. Dragomir Milošević*, Judgment (Trial Chamber III) (Case No. IT-98-29/1-T), 12 December 2007, para. 836.
[41] Ibid., para. 852.

In its judgment against Mr Milošević, the ICTY Trial Chamber found 'abundant evidence of the Accused planning and ordering the shelling of civilian areas, including, in particular, the TV Building'.[42] In their judgment on his appeal, the Appeals Chamber declared that it

8.13

> cannot accept Milošević's argument that the shelling incident could have been a legitimate military action since the TV Building was clearly a civilian object. Witnesses testified at trial that there were neither any military targets or activity, nor any ABiH [Army of Bosnia and Herzegovina] military equipment inside or around the TV Building.[43]

Faulty intelligence may also lead to a civilian object being targeted in the mistaken belief that it is being used for military activities at the time. During the 1991 Gulf War, a bunker in the Amariyah suburb of south-western Baghdad was targeted and destroyed by United States (US) forces in the mistaken belief that it was purely a military command-and-control centre and therefore a lawful military objective. In fact, civilians were sheltering in the bunker at night and more than 200 people, most, if not all of whom were civilians, were killed by the US airstrike.[44] Extensive reconnaissance had failed to identify the fact that each night the wives and children of the Iraqi secret police sheltered from US air raids in the basement of the bunker.[45] Had US forces known this, they would have had to either target the bunker during the day when it was being used for military purposes or conduct a proportionality assessment that would appropriately consider the very significant civilian casualties expected to result from a night attack.

8.14

It is important to recall that any loss of protection of a civilian object is temporary, being limited to the period during which it is used for hostile action. As Dinstein records: 'Once military use of a civilian object has ceased, the object reverts to its initial status, which is not tainted by past military use.'[46]

8.15

The 'purpose' of an object

The purpose of an object is its intended future use.[47] The Eritrea-Ethiopia Claims Commission considered the case of Ethiopia's bombing in May 2000 of an Eritrean power plant at Hirgigo. While the construction of the plant had been completed, it was still in the 'testing and commissioning phase'.[48] Eritrea had asserted that, as of May

8.16

---

[42] Ibid., para. 964.
[43] ICTY, *Prosecutor v. Dragomir Milošević*, Judgment (Appeals Chamber) (Case No. IT-98-29/1-A), 12 November 2009, para. 250.
[44] G. D. Solis, *The Law of Armed Conflict: International Humanitarian War in Law*, 2nd Edn, Cambridge University Press, New York, 2016, p. 275.
[45] Ibid.
[46] Dinstein, *The Conduct of Hostilities under the Law of International Armed Conflict*, 3rd Edn, p. 112, para. 299.
[47] UK Ministry of Defence, *The Manual of the Law of Armed Conflict*, para. 5.4.4(e); ICRC commentary on the 1977 Additional Protocols, 1987, para. 2022.
[48] Eritrea-Ethiopia Claims Commission, *Partial Award: Western Front, Aerial Bombardment and Related Claims—Eritrea's Claims 1, 3, 5, 9–13, 14, 21, 25 & 26*, 19 December 2005, at: http://bit.ly/2NGdLU4, para. 111.

2000, the Hirgigo plant was not yet producing power for use in Eritrea and that Eritrea's military forces had their own electric generating equipment and did not depend on general power grids in Eritrea. Eritrea also submitted evidence in support of its assertion that its Ministry of Defence used no more than 4 per cent of Eritrea's non-military power supply and that Eritrean manufacturing companies did not produce significant military equipment.[49]

8.17 The Claims Commission agreed with Ethiopia's assertion in its pleadings that electricity generating stations 'are generally recognized to be of sufficient importance to a State's capacity to meet its wartime needs of communication, transport and industry so as usually to qualify as military objectives during armed conflicts'.[50] The Commission also endorsed Ethiopia's interpretation of the law whereby a State engaged as a party to an armed conflict should not have to wait until an object is put into use, when its purpose is such that 'it will make an effective contribution to military action once it has been tested, commissioned and put to use'.[51]

8.18 In its judgment in the *Gotovina* case, an ICTY Trial Chamber appeared to accept documentary evidence that a civilian factory producing bolts, screws, and other metal products would be used to produce ammunition at a future point in time as sufficient to render the object a lawful military objective.[52] There must, however, be hard evidence that an object is to be put to a military use in the future, not merely a suspicion that this will be the case, much less a hypothetical risk.[53] In this regard, Dinstein cautions against targeting based on a 'worst case scenario'.[54]

The requirement of definite military advantage

8.19 The second part of the definition of a military objective demands that not only must an object's nature, location, purpose, or use make an effective contribution to military action, but also that its destruction, capture, or neutralisation must, in the circumstances ruling at the time, offer a definite military advantage. As a consequence, 'it is not legitimate to launch an attack which only offers potential or indeterminate advantages. Those ordering or executing the attack must have sufficient information available to take this requirement into account'.[55]

---

[49] Ibid., para. 117.
[50] Ibid.
[51] Ibid., para. 120. The Hirgigo Power Plant finally opened in 2003, becoming the largest in the country and providing electricity to five of the country's largest cities, including Asmara, Massawa, and Keren. The plant increased national electrical capacity more than threefold. 'New Power Plant Opens in Massawa', *The New Humanitarian*, 28 March 2003, at: http://bit.ly/2Rd8QfQ.
[52] ICTY, *Prosecutor v. Ante Gotovina and Mladen Markač*, Judgment (Trial Chamber I) (Case No. IT-06-90-T), paras. 1208, 1216.
[53] Solis thus is incorrect to speak of '*possible* use' as sufficient grounds for attack without further qualification [emphasis in original]. Solis, *The Law of Armed Conflict: International Humanitarian Law in War*, 3rd Edn, p. 403.
[54] Dinstein, *The Conduct of Hostilities under the Law of International Armed Conflict*, 3rd Edn, para. 306.
[55] ICRC, Commentary on the 1977 Additional Protocols, 1987, para. 2024.

8.20 Despite criticism from some quarters,[56] the definition of military objective in the Protocol 'excludes the general industrial and agricultural potential of the economy. Targets must offer a more specific military advantage'.[57] According to the Eritrea-Ethiopia Claims Commission, the infliction of economic losses from attacks against lawful military objectives is 'a lawful means of achieving a definite military advantage, and there can be few military advantages more evident than effective pressure to end an armed conflict that, each day, added to the number of both civilian and military casualties on both sides of the war'.[58] This is not persuasive. It suggests that a purely financial impact from attacking an object may constitute a definite military advantage.

Civilian objects

8.21 As Article 52(1) of the Additional Protocol I makes clear, any object that does not meet the twin criteria for a military objective is a civilian object and is thereby protected from attack. Article 52(3) provides that, in case of doubt, objects are to be considered civilian. It is questionable whether this provision exists as a rule of customary law. Indeed, based on its appreciation of State practice, the ICRC concluded in its customary law study only that it 'cannot automatically be assumed that any object that appears dubious may be subject to lawful attack'.[59] The US, in particular, has consistently made clear its opposition to the crystallisation of this specific treaty rule as custom.[60]

8.22 Moreover, within the provisions in the 1977 Additional Protocol I on precautions in attack, it is only required that those who plan or decide upon an attack must 'do everything feasible to verify that the objectives to be attacked are neither civilians nor civilian objects'.[61] The standard of feasibility for precautionary measures is a relatively low one in international law. Italy stated in a declaration submitted upon ratification of the 1977 Additional Protocol I that 'feasible' must be understood to mean that which is 'practicable or practically possible, taking into account all circumstances ruling at the time, including humanitarian and military considerations'.[62]

---

[56] See, e.g., A. Hays Parks, 'Air War and the Law of War', *Air Force Law Review*, Vol. 32, No. 1 (1990), p. 1, at p. 135.
[57] A. P. V. Rogers, *Law on the Battlefield*, 3rd Edn, Manchester University Press, Manchester, 2012, p. 110.
[58] Eritrea-Ethiopia Claims Commission, *Partial Award: Western Front, Aerial Bombardment and Related Claims—Eritrea's Claims 1, 3, 5, 9–13, 14, 21, 25 & 26*, 19 December 2005, para. 121.
[59] ICRC, Customary IHL Rule 10: 'Civilian Objects' Loss of Protection from Attack', at: http://bit.ly/367anrP.
[60] See, e.g., US Department of Defense, *Law of War Manual*, June 2015 (Updated December 2016), at: http://bit.ly/30D0xN8 (hereinafter, USDOD December 2016 *Law of War Manual*), §5.4.3.2; see also on this issue Dinstein, *The Conduct of Hostilities under the Law of International Armed Conflict*, 3rd Edn, paras. 301, 379.
[61] Art. 57(2)(a)(i), 1977 Additional Protocol I.
[62] Statements of Understanding by Italy, 27 February 1986. Several States have submitted similar declarations pertaining to the 1977 Additional Protocol I, with no objections raised by other States Parties. (See Statements of Understanding of Belgium (20 May 1986), The Netherlands (26 June 1987), Spain (21 April 1989), Canada (20 November 1990), Germany (14 February 1991), Australia (21 June 1991), and Egypt (9 October 1992).

The principle of distinction

8.23 The principle of distinction was first set out in a binding IHL treaty in 1977: in the Basic Rule in Article 48 of the Additional Protocol I. That said, already in 1868, the Saint Petersburg Declaration,[63] which outlawed the use of exploding bullets against military personnel, had affirmed in its preamble that 'the only legitimate object which States should endeavour to accomplish during war is to weaken the military forces of the enemy'. This was at the least a philosophical underpinning of the future rule of distinction with respect to objects.[64]

8.24 Article 48 of the 1977 Protocol I ('Basic Rule') stipulates that in 'order to ensure respect for and protection of' civilian objects, the parties to an international armed conflict 'shall at all times distinguish ... between civilian objects and military objectives and accordingly shall direct their operations only against military objectives'. As the ICRC stated in its commentary on the provision:

> The basic rule of protection and distinction is confirmed in this article. It is the foundation on which the codification of the laws and customs of war rests: the civilian population and civilian objects must be respected and protected in armed conflict, and for this purpose they must be distinguished from combatants and military objectives.[65]

In particular, this means that attacks must be directed only against lawful military objectives and not against civilian objects. This is made explicit in Article 52(1) wherein it is stipulated that: 'Civilian objects shall not be the object of attack or of reprisals.' In addition to the prohibition on attacking civilian objects, also unlawful is an indiscriminate attack, which is to say, an attack that is not directed against a lawful military objective. Article 52(4) stipulates that indiscriminate attacks are prohibited. Indiscriminate attacks are those which are not directed at a specific military objective, or which involve the use of an indiscriminate weapon, and that consequently 'are of a nature to strike military objectives and civilians or civilian objects without distinction'.

8.25 But while there is no doubt as to the binding nature of the principle of distinction in all armed conflict, nor indeed as to its fundamental nature, the practical application of both the basic rule and the general protection of civilian objects continues to be immensely challenging. In particular, it is unclear how accurate an attack must be if it is to comply with this duty. Certainly, a party to an armed conflict does not need to hit what it is aiming at. The ICRC's 1987 commentary on Article 52(1) does not consider the issue, devoting only a single paragraph to the prohibition on attacking civilian objects.[66] This lacuna will surely be rectified when the new commentary is published in years to come.

---

[63] Declaration Renouncing the Use, in Time of War, of Explosive Projectiles Under 400 Grammes Weight; adopted at St Petersburg, 11 December 1868; entered into force, 4 September 1900.
[64] ICRC, Commentary on the 1977 Additional Protocols, 1987, para. 1863.
[65] Ibid.
[66] Ibid., para. 2011.

The interpretation and application of the rule, at least with respect to artillery, were tested perhaps more than in any other forum before the ICTY, in its considerations in the *Gotovina* case. The Trial Chamber found that, on 4 and 5 August 1995, Croatian army artillery units fired artillery shells and rockets at the so-called 'four towns' in the Krajina (Benkovac, Gračac, Knin, and Obrovac). After comparing the evidence on the locations of impacts in these towns with the locations of possible military targets, the Trial Chamber concluded that Croatian forces had targeted certain areas that did not contain military objectives. 8.26

Owing to the lack of an established standard in IHL, the Trial Chamber determined, for reasons that remain obscure, that any object which fell 200 metres from a military objective would be considered the result of an unlawful attack.[67] Such a standard did not appear in the Prosecution's Trial Brief, which held the seemingly inconsistent position that attacks on Knin involved the use of indiscriminate weapons (meaning they could not be targeted with the requisite accuracy) while also asserting that civilians were being directly attacked.[68] Moreover, the Trial Chamber judgment appeared to employ a simple *ex-post-facto* impact assessment as evidence of violations during the attacks. 8.27

But the judgment's holding on this issue was explicitly overridden on appeal. In an *amicus curiae* brief, it was argued that 200 metres was an 'unrealistic operational standard' (for shelling by artillery). The *Amici*[69] encouraged the Appeals Chamber to 'carefully consider whether this 200-meter radius of acceptable error is: (1) sufficiently established by the Trial record, and if so (2) whether that radius is inherently inconsistent with the nature of artillery and indirect fire capabilities and employment'.[70] The Amici advocated the adoption by the Appeals Chamber of a 400-metre standard, as 'proposed' during evidence before the Trial Chamber and based on the realities of operational artillery employment.[71] 8.28

In fact, the Appeals Chamber held, Judges Agius and Pocar dissenting, that absent 'an established range of error', it could not exclude the possibility 8.29

> that all of the impact sites considered in the Trial Judgement were the result of shelling aimed at targets that the Trial Chamber considered to be legitimate. The fact that a relatively large number of shells fell more than 200 metres from fixed artillery targets could be consistent with a much broader range of error. The spread of shelling

---

[67] ICTY, *Prosecutor v. Ante Gotovina and Mladen Markač*, Judgment (Trial Chamber I) (Case No. IT-06-90-T), 15 April 2011, para. 1898.
[68] ICTY, *Prosecutor v. Ante Gotovina and Mladen Markač* (Case No. IT-06-90-T), Prosecution's Public Redacted Final Trial Brief, 2 August 2010, para. 488 *et seq*. The Prosecution was, however, following established jurisprudence in the judgments of the ICTY.
[69] Laurie R. Blank, Bill Boothby, Geoffrey S. Corn, William J. Fenrick, Professor C. H. B. Garraway CBE, Dean Donald J. Guter, Walter B. Huffman, Eric Talbot Jensen, Mark E. Newcomb, Major General Thomas J. Romig, USA (Ret.), Colonel Raymond C. Ruppert, and Gary Solis.
[70] ICTY, *Prosecutor v. Ante Gotovina*, 'Application and Proposed Amicus Curiae Brief Concerning the 15 April 2011 Trial Chamber Judgment and Requesting that the Appeals Chamber Reconsider the Findings of Unlawful Artillery Attacks during Operation Storm', (Appeals Chamber), 13 January 2012, pp. 20–21.
[71] Ibid., p. 21.

124   THE RULE OF DISTINCTION (OBJECTS)

across Knin is also plausibly explained by the scattered locations of fixed artillery targets ... along with the possibility of a higher margin of error. Although evidence on the record suggests that individual units of the HV aimed artillery in the general direction of the Four Towns rather than at specific targets, the Trial Chamber found that this evidence was not wholly conclusive when considered alone ... and was indicative of an unlawful attack only in the context of the Trial Chamber's application of the 200 Metre Standard.[72]

The Appeals Chamber unanimously agreed that a 200-metre standard for artillery and rocket attacks in populated areas did not exist in IHL at the time. But it did not articulate, as it was required to do under the ICTY's own Statute, the correct legal standard. In drawing attention to this failing in his dissenting opinion, Judge Pocar asked: 'Does the Majority consider that the correct legal standard was a 400-metre standard? A 100-metre standard? A 0-metre standard?' The Appeals Chamber judgment, he observed, 'provides no answer to this question.'[73]

8.30   As Chapter 12 describes,[74] the Second World War-era V-2 rocket launched by the Germans is widely considered to be an inherently indiscriminate weapon. In later, more accurate variants, its circular error probable (CEP)—the radius within which half of all projectiles fired at the same target are expected to land—was significantly reduced, but only down to about one mile (1.6 kilometres). The post-war Soviet R-11 (Scud A) ballistic missile, which was partly based on the V-2, was similarly inaccurate.[75] In its judgment in the *Martić* case, the ICTY Trial and Appeal Chambers held that a weapon (a Yugoslav cluster munition) that would land up to 1,000 metres from the target with an area of dispersion for the submunitions of about 20,000 metres could not lawfully be used to target specific sites in a heavily populated area.[76] More modern rockets that may be inherently indiscriminate include some of those fired by Palestinian armed groups from Gaza. The UN Commission of Inquiry on the 2014 Gaza conflict reported that the Fajr-5109 and similar J-80 and M-75 rockets can land as far as three kilometres from any intended target. Longer-range rockets, such as the R-160 variant, can land as far as six kilometres away from the target because their accuracy decreases with range.[77]

8.31   If one were to take one kilometre as the lawful upper limit of three CEP[78] for long-range artillery, this means that around half of the munitions fired in attacks using such

---

[72] ICTY, *Prosecutor v. Gotovina and Markač*, Judgment (Appeals Chamber) (Case No. IT-06-90-A), 16 November 2012, para. 65.
[73] ICTY, *Prosecutor v. Gotovina and Markač*, Judgment (Appeals Chamber), Dissenting Opinion of Judge Fausto Pocar, para. 13.
[74] See, infra, paras. 12.33 and 12.34.
[75] See S. Zaloga, *The Scud and Other Russian Ballistic Missiles*, Concord Publications, Hong Kong, 2000.
[76] ICTY, *Prosecutor v. Milan Martić*, Judgment (Trial Chamber) (Case No. IT-95-11), 12 June 2007, para. 462. ICTY, *Prosecutor v. Milan Martić*, Judgment (Appeals Chamber) (Case No. IT-95-11-A), 8 October 2008, para. 247.
[77] See, infra, para. 12.35.
[78] The figure of three CEP equates to the area within which approximately 95 per cent of all projectiles fired at the same target from the same position are expected to land. See, e.g., 'Comments by LTG (Ret.) Wilson A. Shoffner on The Report by Major General Robert H. Scales on Croatian Army ("HV") Use of Artillery and Rockets on Targets Based in Knin, Croatia, August 4–5, 1995', p. 3, in *Prosecutor v. Ante Gotovina*, 'Application and Proposed Amicus Curiae Brief Concerning the 15 April 2011 Trial Chamber Judgment and Requesting that the Appeals

methods would need to land within a 333-metre radius of a military objective in order to comply with IHL. It is to be hoped that jurisprudence will either confirm a limit or otherwise identify what the legal threshold is. A similar limit might be appropriate for aerial bombing using gravity ordnance while the upper limit for mortar fire would be far lower.

Despite doubts as to its practical application, that the principle of distinction is of a customary nature is beyond doubt. Rule 7 of the ICRC's customary IHL study holds that: 'The parties to the conflict must at all times distinguish between civilian objects and military objectives. Attacks may only be directed against military objectives. Attacks must not be directed against civilian objects.'[79] State practice establishes the rule as a norm of customary international law applicable in both international and non-international armed conflicts.[80] **8.32**

It is highly probable that the IHL principle of distinction is also a peremptory norm of international law (*jus cogens*). As the Special Rapporteur of the International Law Commission (ILC) on the issue of peremptory norms has stated: 'The *jus cogens* status of basic rules of international humanitarian law has been affirmed in the jurisprudence of international courts and tribunals.'[81] It is surprising that the 1977 Additional Protocol I does not make attacks on civilian objects a war crime, as it does with respect to attacks against the civilian population or individual civilians. Nonetheless, under the Statute of the International Criminal Court, in an international armed conflict, intentionally directing attacks against civilian objects, 'that is, objects which are not military objectives', is a war crime subject to the Court's jurisdiction.[82] The omission of the corresponding war crime under the Court's jurisdiction in non-international armed conflict—whose status as a customary law war crime has been confirmed by the ICTY[83]—can be traced back to its deletion from the final draft of the 1977 Additional Protocol II before its conclusion, along with many other conduct of hostilities rules.[84] **8.33**

Chamber Reconsider the Findings of Unlawful Artillery Attacks during Operation Storm', Appeals Chamber, 13 January 2012.

[79] ICRC, Customary IHL Rule 7: 'The Principle of Distinction between Civilian Objects and Military Objectives', at: http://bit.ly/2G8to2w.
[80] Ibid.
[81] ILC, 'Fourth report on peremptory norms of general international law (*jus cogens*) by Dire Tladi, Special Rapporteur', UN doc. A/CN.4/727, 31 January 2019, para. 117. Rapporteur Tladi later affirms that the *jus cogens* status of these basic rules 'is also generally recognized in the literature'. Ibid., para. 120.
[82] Art. 8(2)(b)(ii), Rome Statute. No directly corresponding war crime is within the Court's jurisdiction in non-international armed conflict, a lacuna that Dinstein justly considers 'particularly deplorable'. Y. Dinstein, *Non-International Armed Conflicts in International Law*, 2nd Edn, Cambridge University Press, Cambridge, 2021, p. 245, para. 702.
[83] ICTY, *Prosecutor v. Hadzihasanovic and Kubura*, Decision on Joint Defence Interlocutory Appeal of Trial Chamber Decision (Appeals Chamber) (Case No. IT-01-47-AR73.3), 11 March 2005, para. 30; see Dinstein, *Non-International Armed Conflicts in International Law*, 2nd Edn, p. 281, para. 798.
[84] The prohibition on attacking civilian objects is one of those that is 'sorely missing' from the 1977 Additional Protocol II. Dinstein, *Non-International Armed Conflicts in International Law*, 2nd Edn, p. 182, para. 583.

Special protection of hospitals

8.34 The highest level of protection afforded to a civilian object by IHL is for hospitals (and similar medical facilities). Exceptionally, their protection from attack during the conduct of hostilities was addressed in the 1949 Geneva Conventions (as a general rule, these instruments focus on assistance to those in the power of the enemy who do not or who no longer participate actively in hostilities: so-called Geneva Law). The principle of immunity from attack is, however, long-standing: already the first Geneva Convention of 1864[85] had proclaimed the neutrality of military hospitals and 'as such', they were to be 'protected and respected by the belligerents as long as they accommodate wounded and sick'.[86] The 1949 Geneva Convention I protects both fixed establishments, including military hospitals, and mobile medical units (including field hospitals),[87] while Geneva Convention IV accords protection to civilian hospitals.[88] The scope of protection from attack is provided to all types of medical units, whether military or civilian, under the 1977 Additional Protocol I.[89]

8.35 Under the 1949 Geneva Convention I, fixed and mobile military medical units 'may in no circumstances be attacked, but shall at all times be respected and protected by the Parties to the conflict'.[90] The prohibition on attacking fixed establishments and mobile medical units of the military medical services confirms that these are civilian objects.[91] Similarly, according to the 1949 Geneva Convention IV, civilian hospitals giving care to the wounded and sick, the infirm, and maternity cases, 'may in no circumstances be the object of attack, but shall at all times be respected and protected'.[92] The scope of protection was expanded in the 1977 Additional Protocol I to cover civilian medical units in addition to military medical units; protection applies 'in all circumstances' during an armed conflict.[93] In sum, medical units exclusively assigned to medical purposes must be respected and protected in all circumstances.[94]

8.36 The protection afforded to medical units is only lost if 'they are being used, outside their humanitarian function, to commit acts harmful to the enemy'.[95] It is explicit in the

---

[85] Convention for the Amelioration of the Condition of the Wounded in Armies in the Field; adopted at Geneva, 22 August 1864; entered into force, 18 June 1865.

[86] Art. 1, 1864 Geneva Convention. See E. Mikos-Skuza, 'Hospitals' in A. Clapham, P. Gaeta, and M. Sassòli (eds.), *The Geneva Conventions in Context: A Commentary*, Oxford University Press, Oxford, 2015, pp. 207–29, at p. 209.

[87] Art. 19, 1949 Geneva Convention I.

[88] Art. 18, 1949 Geneva Convention IV.

[89] Arts. 12, 14, and 21–27, 1977 Additional Protocol I.

[90] Art. 19, 1949 Geneva Convention I. As the ICRC has noted, 'the specific mention of a prohibition of attack is important within the framework of the codification, in Additional Protocol I, of the rule of distinction between civilian objects and military objectives in the conduct of hostilities'. ICRC commentary on the 1949 Geneva Convention I, 2016, para. 1793.

[91] ICRC, Commentary on the 1949 Geneva Convention I, 2016, para. 1795.

[92] Art. 18, 1949 Geneva Convention IV.

[93] Art. 12, 1977 Additional Protocol I.

[94] ICRC Customary IHL Rule 28: 'Medical Units', at: http://bit.ly/2sFDvc0.

[95] Ibid.

1949 Geneva Convention IV that the fact that sick or wounded members of the armed forces are being cared for in hospitals, and that small arms and ammunition taken from such combatants have not yet been handed 'to the proper service' do not constitute 'acts harmful to the enemy'.[96] Moreover, the loss of protection only takes effect 'after due warning has been given, naming, in all appropriate cases, a reasonable time limit, and after such warning has remained unheeded'.[97] What constitutes a reasonable time limit will depend on the extent of the violation and the acts that are required to remedy it. Certain States have explicitly stated that there may be situations where a warning is 'not due' owing to overriding military necessity or the exercise of the right of combatants' self-defence. This might occur when combatants approaching a military medical establishment or unit come under fire from persons inside it.[98]

Despite the prohibition on attacking hospitals, history is replete with examples where such serious violations of IHL have occurred. In its judgment in the *Galić* case, the ICTY Trial Chamber declared itself 'satisfied beyond reasonable doubt' that the Koševo hospital in Sarajevo, 'was regularly targeted' by Bosnian Serb forces. The Chamber was also satisfied that Bosniak army mortar fire 'originated from the hospital grounds or from its vicinity and that these actions may have provoked' Bosnian Serb counter-fire. The Chamber was unable to establish what damage and which casualties resulted from exchange of fire, but 'the evidence does reveal that, on occasions, the Koševo hospital buildings themselves were directly targeted, resulting in civilian casualties, and that this fire was certainly not aimed at any possible military target'. The Trial Chamber held that the direct attacks on the hospital 'constitute examples of the campaign of attacks on civilians'.[99]

8.37

The duty to respect and protect in all circumstances medical units exclusively assigned to medical purposes is a rule of customary law applicable in all armed conflicts.[100] Moreover, under the 1998 Rome Statute of the International Criminal Court, intentionally directing attacks against 'hospitals and places where the sick and the wounded are collected, provided they are not military objectives' and against 'medical units ... using the distinctive emblems of the Geneva Conventions in conformity with international law' constitute war crimes in both international and non-international armed conflicts.[101]

8.38

---

[96] Art. 19, 1949 Geneva Convention IV.
[97] Art. 21, 1949 Geneva Convention I; Art. 19, 1949 Geneva Convention IV.
[98] ICRC, Commentary on the 1949 Geneva Convention I, 2016, para. 1848, citing inter alia Australia's 2006 *Manual of the Law of Armed Conflict*, para. 9.69; and the US Department of Defense, *Law of War Manual*, Update December 2016, §7.10.3.2.
[99] ICTY, *Prosecutor v. Galić*, Judgment and Opinion (Trial Chamber I) (Case No. IT-98-29-T), 5 December 2003, para. 509.
[100] ICRC, Customary IHL Rule 28: 'Medical Units'.
[101] Art. 8(2)(b)(ix) and (2)(e)(ii) and (iv), Rome Statute.

Special protection of cultural property

8.39 The protection of cultural objects (and places of worship), which is set out in the 1977 Additional Protocols, is a long-standing concern of IHL. Already in the Regulations annexed to the 1899 Hague Convention II, it was stipulated that: 'In sieges and bombardments all necessary steps should be taken to spare as far as possible edifices devoted to religion, art, science, and charity ... provided they are not used at the same time for military purposes.'[102] A similar provision was incorporated in the corresponding Regulations in 1907, although protection was extended also to 'historic monuments'.[103] After the Second World War, the Netherlands proposed to the United Nations Educational, Scientific and Cultural Organization (UNESCO) the elaboration of a treaty dedicated to the protection of cultural property during armed conflict. In 1951, UNESCO decided to convene a committee of governmental experts to draft a convention on the issue.

8.40 The outcome of their work was the 1954 Hague Convention on the Protection of Cultural Property. Under the Convention, States Parties undertake to respect cultural property during armed conflict and to refrain from directing any act of hostility against such property.[104] It is also stipulated, however, that this obligation could be 'waived' (i.e. ignored) in case of imperative military necessity.[105] However, no definition was provided of what would constitute such necessity (this 'vaguely defined' concept, in Solis' words).[106] Moreover, the 1977 Protocol I makes it explicit that only 'more clearly defined and more carefully selected'[107] military objectives could be made the object of attack. To prevent an inconsistent approach in international law, a new (second) protocol to the 1954 Hague Convention was negotiated and adopted in 1999. Under Article 6 of the new protocol, imperative military necessity could only permit an act of hostility against cultural property 'when and for as long as' that property had become a military objective and no feasible alternative existed to the use of force.[108] The 1999 Protocol also applied in non-international armed conflicts.[109]

8.41 In summarising the core rules protecting cultural property in armed conflict under customary IHL, the ICRC stated as follows:

---

[102] Art. 27, Regulations Respecting the Laws and Customs of War on Land, annexed to Convention (II) with Respect to the Laws and Customs of War on Land; adopted at The Hague, 29 July 1899; entered into force, 4 September 1900.
[103] Art. 27, Regulations Respecting the Laws and Customs of War on Land, annexed to Convention (IV) with Respect to the Laws and Customs of War on Land; adopted at The Hague, 18 October 1907; entered into force, 26 January 1910.
[104] Art. 4(1), 1954 Hague Convention. As of 1 May 2022, 133 States were party to the Convention.
[105] Art. 4(2), 1954 Hague Convention.
[106] Solis, *The Law of Armed Conflict: International Humanitarian Law in War*, 3rd Edn, p. 239. He caveats the observation, though, by recalling that it is no more vaguely defined than the civilian legal system's 'reasonable person' or 'gross negligence'.
[107] ICRC, 'Second Protocol to the Hague Convention of 1954 for the Protection of Cultural Property in the Event of Armed Conflict. The Hague, 26 March 1999', at: http://bit.ly/2NK9Dmb.
[108] Art. 6, 1999 Second Protocol to the 1954 Hague Convention.
[109] Ibid., Art. 22.

Each party to the conflict must respect cultural property:

A. Special care must be taken in military operations to avoid damage to buildings dedicated to religion, art, science, education or charitable purposes and historic monuments unless they are military objectives.

B. Property of great importance to the cultural heritage of every people must not be the object of attack unless imperatively required by military necessity.[110]

This latter rule 'should not be confused' with the prohibition on attacking cultural property in Article 53(1) of Additional Protocol I and Article 16 of Additional Protocol II, which do not provide for a waiver in case of imperative military necessity.[111]

That said, Article 53(1) states that, 'without prejudice' to the provisions of the 1954 Hague Convention for the Protection of Cultural Property, it is prohibited 'to commit any acts of hostility directed against the historic monuments, works of art or places of worship which constitute the cultural or spiritual heritage of peoples'.[112] Similar language is included in Article 16 of the 1999 Second Protocol to the 1954 Hague Convention. These articles 'were meant to cover only a limited amount of very important cultural property, namely that which forms part of the cultural or spiritual heritage of 'peoples' (i.e., humankind), while the scope of the Hague Convention is broader and covers property which forms part of the cultural heritage of 'every people'.[113] At the Diplomatic Conference leading to the adoption of the 1977 Additional Protocols, several States indicated that even highly important cultural property could become the object of attack in the event it was used, illegally, for military purposes.[114]

8.42

The *Jokić* case concerned naval and land bombardment of the Old Town of Dubrovnik in Croatia in 1991 during the conflicts in the former Yugoslavia.[115] In its judgment, the ICTY noted that the destruction and damage inflicted on the Old Town were 'very serious crimes'. It found that 'since it is a serious violation of international humanitarian law to attack civilian buildings, it is a crime of even greater seriousness to direct an attack on an especially protected site, such as the Old Town'.[116] The Old Town of Dubrovnik had been inscribed on UNESCO's World Heritage List in 1975.

8.43

---

[110] ICRC Customary IHL Rule 38: 'Attacks Against Cultural Property', at: http://bit.ly/2GjRKqp.
[111] Ibid.
[112] See on this issue Solis, *The Law of Armed Conflict: International Humanitarian Law in War*, 3rd Edn, pp. 582–83.
[113] ICRC Customary IHL Rule 38. The property covered by the Additional Protocols must be of such importance that it will be recognised by everyone, even without being marked.
[114] Ibid., citing statements by West Germany, the Netherlands, the United Kingdom, and the United States.
[115] With respect to naval bombardment, the 1907 Hague Convention IX requires that: 'In bombardments by naval forces all the necessary measures must be taken by the commander to spare as far as possible sacred edifices, buildings used for artistic, scientific, or charitable purposes, historic monuments, hospitals, and places where the sick or wounded are collected, on the understanding that they are not used at the same time for military purposes.' Art. 5, Convention (IX) concerning Bombardment by Naval Forces in Time of War; adopted at The Hague, 18 October 1907; entered into force, 26 January 1910.
[116] ICTY, *Prosecutor v. Jokić*, Sentencing Judgment (Trial Chamber I) (Case No. IT-01-42/1-S), 18 March 2004, para. 53.

8.44 In 2016, Ahmad Al Faqi Al Mahdi pleaded guilty before the International Criminal Court to the charge of intentionally directing attacks against historic monuments and buildings dedicated to religion as a war crime committed in a non-international armed conflict. He was sentenced to nine years' imprisonment for his involvement in the destruction of nine mausoleums and one mosque in Timbuktu, Mali, in June and July 2012. In the earlier confirmation of charges, a Pre-Trial Chamber had found that the buildings and structures that had been destroyed 'were regarded and protected as a significant part of the cultural heritage of Timbuktu and of Mali'.[117]

8.45 The rule prohibiting attacks on cultural property other than in case of imperative military necessity is a norm of customary law applicable in all armed conflicts.[118] Under Article 15(1) of the 1999 Second Protocol to the 1954 Hague Convention, a person commits an offence if that person intentionally and in violation of the Convention or the Protocol makes cultural property under enhanced protection the object of attack. Such an act is a serious violation of the Protocol. It is a war crime under the jurisdiction of the International Criminal Court to intentionally direct attacks against buildings dedicated to religion, education, art, science or charitable purposes, or historic monuments, 'provided they are not military objectives'.[119]

Special protection of installations containing dangerous forces

8.46 Special protection is afforded under the 1977 Additional Protocol I to installations that contain 'dangerous forces' (dams, dykes, and nuclear power stations). The ICRC has found that a corresponding customary rule in all armed conflict stipulates that: 'Particular care must be taken if works and installations containing dangerous forces, namely dams, dykes and nuclear electrical generating stations, and other installations located at or in their vicinity are attacked, in order to avoid the release of dangerous forces and consequent severe losses among the civilian population.'[120] The three installations are listed to the exclusion of others – a factory producing toxic chemicals, for instance, is not accorded similar protection.[121]

8.47 The special protection against attack provided under Article 56(1) of the 1977 Additional Protocol I and customary law cease if the dam, dyke, or nuclear power station if they are used in regular, significant, and direct support of military operations, and if attack is the only feasible way to terminate such support.[122] Dinstein has argued

---

[117] ICC, *Prosecutor v. Ahmad Al Faqi Al Mahdi*, Decision on the Confirmation of Charges (Pre-Trial Chamber I) (Case No. ICC-01/12-01/15), 24 March 2016, para. 36.
[118] ICRC Customary IHL Rule 38: 'Attacks Against Cultural Property'.
[119] Art. 8(2)(b)(ix) and 2(e)(iv), Rome Statute.
[120] ICRC, Customary IHL Rule 42: 'Works and Installations Containing Dangerous Forces', at: https://bit.ly/3m6koj4.
[121] Dinstein, *The Conduct of Hostilities under the Law of International Armed Conflict*, 3rd Edn, para. 227.
[122] Art. 56(2)(a) and (b), 1977 Additional Protocol I.

that better protection would have been afforded to the civilian population if a duty of passive precautions had been imposed in the Protocol on parties to an armed conflict, such as to oblige a belligerent with nuclear reactors to shut them down during hostilities or switch off any hydroelectric facility linked to a dam, so as to 'extinguish any military rationale for attack by the enemy'.[123] Whether this is realistic for a State that is highly reliant on nuclear power or hydroelectric power is debatable. France, for example, derives about 70 per cent of its electricity from nuclear energy (although Government policy as of 2021 was to reduce this to 50 per cent by 2035).[124]

Concluding remarks and outlook

The provisions in the 1977 Additional Protocol I on the protection of civilian objects are clearly reflected in customary international law. Regrettably, the 1977 Additional Protocol II does not incorporate the general rule prohibiting attacks on any civilian object, but this customary rule certainly applies in all non-international armed conflict and therefore also binds non-state armed groups. Special protection against attack is afforded to hospitals and other medical facilities, whether fixed or mobile. Attacks against cultural property where an object has become a lawful military objective can only be lawful in a situation of imperative military necessity.

8.48

A critical challenge for the future is to clarify the degree of accuracy required to comply with the principle of distinction. To have such a lack of clarity in the practical application of such a fundamental rule is astonishing: this lacuna clearly impedes the rule's effective implementation in all armed conflicts.

8.49

---

[123] Dinstein, *The Conduct of Hostilities under the Law of International Armed Conflict*, 3rd Edn, para. 229.
[124] World Nuclear Association, 'Nuclear Power in France', Last updated January 2021, at: https://bit.ly/39OM9XN.

9
The Rule of Distinction (Persons)

Introduction

9.1 This chapter discusses the rules governing the targeting of persons under the Additional Protocols during the conduct of hostilities. The 'cardinal' principle of distinction[1] is the most fundamental rule governing the conduct of hostilities in international humanitarian law (IHL). Integral to the principle is the obligation upon each party to an armed conflict to 'distinguish' in their military operations between civilians, on the one hand, and combatants (or civilians directly participating in hostilities) on the other, and to target only the latter. This obligation is explicit in both 1977 Additional Protocols.[2]

9.2 Attacks may thus only be directed against combatants or against civilians who are directly participating in hostilities. An attack is unlawful not only if it is targeted against one or more civilians, or the civilian population more broadly, but also if it is *not* directed at a lawful target, in which case it amounts to an indiscriminate attack.[3] Making the civilian population or individual civilians the object of attack is a war crime under the Additional Protocol I.[4] This is only so, however, according to the provisions of the Protocol, when the attack is committed wilfully, in violation of the relevant provisions of the Protocol, *and* where that attack causes death or serious injury to body or health.[5]

9.3 Under customary international law, however, the war crime is broader in scope. Thus, under the 1998 Rome Statute of the International Criminal Court (Rome Statute), for the war crime of attacking civilians[6] it is necessary only to prove that the *object* of the attack 'was a civilian population as such or individual civilians not taking direct part in

---

[1] International Court of Justice (ICJ), *Legality of the Threat or Use of Nuclear Weapons*, Advisory Opinion, July 1996 (hereinafter, ICJ, Nuclear Weapons Advisory Opinion), para. 78.
[2] Arts. 48 and 51(2) and (3), Protocol Additional to the Geneva Conventions of 12 August 1949, and relating to the Protection of Victims of International Armed Conflicts (Protocol I); adopted at Geneva, 8 June 1977; entered into force, 7 December 1978 (hereinafter, 1977 Additional Protocol I); and Art. 13(2) and (3), Protocol additional to the Geneva Conventions of 12 August 1949, and relating to the protection of victims of non-international armed conflicts (Protocol II); adopted at Geneva, 8 June 1977; entered into force, 7 December 1978 (hereinafter, 1977 Additional Protocol II).
[3] According to Article 51(4) of 1977 Additional Protocol I and under customary IHL, indiscriminate attacks include those that are not directed at a specific military objective, and which are consequently 'of a nature to strike military objectives and civilians or civilian objects without distinction'. See further International Committee of the Red Cross (ICRC) Customary IHL Rule 12: 'Definition of Indiscriminate Attacks', at: http://bit.ly/2lJ2V4y.
[4] Art. 85(3)(a), 1977 Additional Protocol I.
[5] Ibid., Art. 85(3).
[6] Art. 8(2)(b)(i) and 2(e)(i), Rome Statute of the International Criminal Court; adopted at Rome, 1998; entered into force, 2002 (hereinafter, Rome Statute).

INTRODUCTION 133

Table 9.1 Summary of Rules on the Principle of Distinction (Persons)

Rule	AP I	Customary status (IAC)	AP II	Customary status (NIAC)
Basic rule	Art. 48	Yes	No	Yes
General protection of civilians	Art. 52(1)	Yes	Art. 13(1)	Yes
Definition of civilians	Art. 50	Yes	No	Yes
Prohibition on attacking civilians	Art. 51(2)	Yes	Art. 13(2)	Yes
Loss of protection during direct participation in hostilities	Art. 51(3)	Yes	Art. 13(3)	Yes
Attacking civilians is a war crime	Art. 85(3)	Yes	No	Yes

hostilities'.[7] A war crime can thus be committed even if civilians are not in fact killed or injured. This is the case whether the armed conflict is international or non-international in character. Customary law also encompasses the war crime of 'launching an indiscriminate attack resulting in loss of life or injury to civilians',[8] although this is not incorporated, per se, in the Rome Statute.

9.4 The key rules governing the principle of distinction with respect to persons set forth in the two 1977 Additional Protocols are summarised in Table 9.1. The content of the Additional Protocol II pertaining to this principle is significantly reduced compared to the Additional Protocol I. This is due to the fact that a number of States, led by Pakistan, were unwilling to accept more comprehensive protection in non-international armed conflicts, even in the context of the limited scope of application of the Additional Protocol II.[9]

The prohibition of acts or threats of violence whose primary purpose is to terrorise the civilian population[10] is discussed in Chapter 13.

---

[7] Element 2, Elements of Crime for Article 8(2)(b)(i) and (e)(i): war crime of attacking civilians, in *Official Records of the Assembly of States Parties to the Rome Statute of the International Criminal Court, First session, New York, 3–10 September 2002*, Part II(B).
[8] ICRC, Customary IHL Rule 156: 'Definition of War Crimes', at: http://bit.ly/2v9zCgg. The war crime exists in non-international as well as international armed conflict.
[9] ICRC, Commentary on the 1977 Additional Protocol II, 1987, paras. 4412–14, 4416.
[10] Art. 51(2), 1977 Additional Protocol I; Art. 13(2), 1977 Additional Protocol II.

The definition of 'combatant' and 'civilian'

9.5 Before turning to the content of the rules governing the principle of distinction in conduct of hostilities, the definitions of combatant and civilian under IHL need to be clarified. As the term civilian is defined in the negative (as someone who is not a member of the armed forces), the notion of combatant is first defined. The term 'combatant' is only used in treaty law with respect to international armed conflict. The definition of a civilian in a situation of non-international armed conflict is less clear and more contested given the existence of non-State armed groups.

The definition of combatant

International armed conflict

9.6 In broad terms, and within the context of an international armed conflict, a combatant is any member of the armed forces of a party to the conflict, except for dedicated medical or religious personnel.[11] According to Article 43(1) of the 1977 Additional Protocol I, the armed forces 'consist of all organized armed forces, groups and units which are under a command responsible to that Party for the conduct of its subordinates'. This remains the case even if that party is represented by a government or an authority that is not recognised by the enemy.[12] Members of 'militias' or 'volunteer corps' that form part of the armed forces are also deemed combatants.[13] Whenever a party to an international armed conflict incorporates a paramilitary or armed law enforcement agency into its armed forces, it is specifically obligated to notify the other parties to the armed conflict of that fact.[14] France, when ratifying Additional Protocol I in 2001, made a declaration whereby its armed forces include 'on a permanent basis' its national *gendarmerie*.[15]

9.7 Members of militias and volunteer corps, including those of organised resistance movements, which belong to a party to an international armed conflict, but which are *not* part of the armed forces, are nonetheless combatants if they meet a set of criteria laid down in the 1949 Geneva Convention III. They must be commanded by a person responsible for his subordinates; have a fixed distinctive sign recognisable at a distance; carry their arms openly; and conduct their operations in accordance with the laws and customs of war.[16] The 1977 Additional Protocol I, however, has added a controversial rule whereby in a situation in armed conflicts where, 'owing to the nature of the hostilities', an armed combatant cannot distinguish himself from the civilian, he or she

---

[11] See ICRC, Customary IHL Rule 3: 'Definition of Combatants', at: http://bit.ly/2GYnRfC.
[12] Art. 43(1), 1977 Additional Protocol I. See for the definition in customary IHL Article 4(3) of the Convention (III) relative to the Treatment of Prisoners of War; adopted at Geneva, 12 August 1949; entered into force, 21 October 1950 (hereinafter, 1949 Geneva Convention III).
[13] Art. 4(2), 1949 Geneva Convention III.
[14] Art. 43(3), 1977 Additional Protocol I.
[15] Declaration of France, 11 April 2001, para. 7, text available at: http://bit.ly/2OQfTGD.
[16] Art. 4(2), 1949 Geneva Convention III.

retains his status as a combatant, provided that, in such situations, he carries his arms openly, both during each military engagement and during such time as he is visible to the enemy while engaged in military deployment preceding an attack.[17]

The type of situations envisaged by the drafters were 'in occupied territory and in wars of national liberation in which a guerrilla fighter could not distinguish himself [from the civilian population] throughout his military operations and still retain any chance of success'.[18] The ICRC commentary on the provision acknowledged that 'it is a fact that no delegation at the Conference finally got precisely the terms it wished'.[19] Foremost among those States that were most critical of the outcome text is the United States, which cited the provision as one of the bases for its decision not to ratify the Protocol.[20] It is probable that the norm has not attained the status of customary law.

9.8

Finally, inhabitants of a non-occupied territory who, on the approach of the enemy, spontaneously take up arms to resist the invading forces are also combatants. Those participating in such a *'levée en masse'*[21] are entitled to prisoner-of-war status, provided that they carry their arms openly and respect the laws and customs of war.[22] According to the United Kingdom (UK) Joint Service Manual of the Law of Armed Conflict: 'Under the law of armed conflict, members of the civilian population lose their civilian protection when they participate [directly] in hostilities.' However, when they take part in the exceptional circumstances of a levée en masse, while they also lose their civilian status and become targetable combatants, they are entitled to prisoner-of-war status.[23] While relatively infrequent these days, Gary Solis offers the example from 2008 of Georgian citizens who spontaneously rose up to confront the invading Russian forces.[24]

9.9

Medical and religious personnel within the armed forces[25] are non-combatants,[26] that is to say, they do not have the right to participate directly in hostilities. They are not,

9.10

---

[17] Art. 44(3), 1977 Additional Protocol I.
[18] See report on the drafting in the ICRC commentary on Article 44(3), at: http://bit.ly/31wjgKS, at para. 1698.
[19] Ibid., para. 1714.
[20] A. D. Sofaer, 'The Rationale for the United States Decision', *American Journal of International Law*, Vol. 82, No. 4 (1988), p. 784, at p. 786. See further, L. Hill-Cawthorne, 'Persons Covered by International Humanitarian Law: Main Categories', Chap. 5 in B. Saul and D. Akande (eds.), *The Oxford Guide to International Humanitarian Law*, Oxford University Press, Oxford, 2020, pp. 101–102.
[21] See the excerpts from the judgment by the Israeli Military Court sitting in Ramallah in 1969: 'We can be brief. The Organization to which the defendants belong [Popular Front for the Liberation of Palestine] does not answer even the most elementary criteria of a *levée en masse*. We have not to do with the population of an area which an enemy is approaching or invading. In October 1969 we were not approaching an area whose population was not yet under our effective control and we were certainly not invading new areas, and there cannot be the least doubt that, in the period from 5 June 1967 to October 1968, that 'population' had time to 'form itself' into regular armed units.' Israeli Military Court, *Military Prosecutor* v. *Omar Mahmud Kassem and others*, Ramallah, 13 April 1969. Originally cited in E. Lauterpacht (ed.), *International Law Reports*, Vol. 42 (1971), Grotius Publications, Cambridge, pp. 470–83; reproduced in *How Does Law Protect in War?*, ICRC, at: http://bit.ly/2Oy7YAF.
[22] Art. 4(6), 1949 Geneva Convention III.
[23] UK Ministry of Defence, *Joint Service Manual of the Law of Armed Conflict* (as amended in 2010), London, para. 4.2.2.
[24] G. D. Solis, *The Law of Armed Conflict: International Humanitarian Law in War*, 3rd Edn, Cambridge University Press, Cambridge, 2021, p. 183.
[25] See Art. 33, 1949 Geneva Convention III.
[26] Art. 43(2), 1977 Additional Protocol I. According to the US Department of Defense: 'In contemporary parlance', the term "non-combatant" should generally be used to mean military medical and religious personnel,

however, considered civilians under IHL.[27] Medical personnel in the armed forces may carry small arms for their own protection and for the protection of their patients and medical facilities. Should they use their weapon other than in self-defence or defence of other medical personnel or persons *hors de combat* who are under direct attack, they commit acts harmful to the enemy and may themselves be targeted.[28] The mere carriage of small arms does not constitute an act harmful to the enemy.

9.11 In the US army, chaplains do not carry a weapon, but their assistants may do so.[29] As the UK *Manual on the Law of Armed Conflict* observes, the Geneva Conventions 'are silent on whether chaplains may be armed'. UK *policy*, the Manual recalls, is that chaplains should be unarmed.[30] Controversially, Dinstein declares that it is 'hard to assail the conclusion' that religious personnel who are engaged in recruiting new members (of a non-State armed group) in a non-international armed conflict are directly participating in hostilities.[31] Presumably, the same principle would apply in international armed conflict. If so, State practice is lacking. As a US Navy chaplain famously said during the Japanese attack on Pearl Harbour in December 1941: 'Praise the Lord and pass the ammunition'.[32]

9.12 Also considered non-combatants are members of the armed forces who are 'permanently assigned and exclusively devoted' to civil defence. This is so, as long as they meet the following criteria: they must not perform any other military duties during a conflict; they must be clearly distinguishable from the other members of the armed forces by 'prominently displaying the international distinctive sign of civil defence'; they must have a valid identity card certifying their status; they may be equipped only with small arms (for the purpose of maintaining order or for self-defence); they must not participate directly in hostilities or otherwise commit acts harmful to the enemy; and they may perform their civil defence tasks only within the national territory of their party.[33] While Article 43(2) of the Additional Protocol I otherwise implies that they are combatants (and thereby entitled to participate directly in hostilities), the final provisions of Article 67(1) make it clear that it is prohibited for any members of the armed forces

---

'but also can include those combatants placed hors de combat'. US Department of Defense, *Law of War Manual*, June 2015 (Updated December 2016), Washington, D.C., 2016 (hereinafter, USDOD 2016 *Law of War Manual*), §4.1.1.1.

[27] Thus, it is not strictly correct to say that if a person 'is not a combatant, by default he or she is a civilian'. B. Saul, 'Terrorism and International Humanitarian Law', Chap. 14 in B. Saul (ed.), *Research Handbook on International Law and Terrorism*, 2nd Edn, Edward Elgar Publishing, Cheltenham, 2021, p. 201.
[28] 'The protection to which fixed establishments and mobile medical units of the Medical Service are entitled shall not cease unless they are used to commit, outside their humanitarian duties, acts harmful to the enemy.' Art. 21, Convention (I) for the Amelioration of the Condition of the Wounded and Sick in Armed Forces in the Field; adopted at Geneva, 12 August 1949; entered into force, 21 October 1950 (hereinafter, 1949 Geneva Convention I).
[29] UK Ministry of Defence, *Joint Service Manual of the Law of Armed Conflict*, para. 7.30.
[30] Ibid.
[31] Y. Dinstein, *Non-International Armed Conflicts in International Law*, 2nd Edn, Cambridge University Press, Cambridge, 2021, p. 195, para. 543.
[32] Oxford Learner's Dictionary, 'Praise the Lord and Pass the Ammunition', at: https://bit.ly/37mqIfd.
[33] Art. 67(1), 1977 Additional Protocol I.

who are permanently assigned and exclusively devoted to civil defence to participate directly in hostilities. Should they do so, the enemy may target them.

Non-international armed conflict

In a situation of non-international armed conflict, the term combatant *stricto sensu* is not appropriate, at the least with respect to non-State armed forces.[34] This is explained by the fact that the granting of prisoner-of-war status is only obligated in a situation of international armed conflict. At particular stake is the associated 'combatant's privilege', which precludes prosecution by the enemy for the fact of having taken up arms against it (and even killing many of their number, as long as this was in accord with IHL rules). States remain implacably opposed to accepting any legal requirement to grant such prisoner-of-war status to members of non-State armed opposition groups in non-international armed conflict. According to the ICRC's 2005 customary study of IHL, for purposes of the principle of distinction, members of State armed forces 'may be considered combatants in both international and non-international armed conflicts. Combatant status, on the other hand, exists only in international armed conflicts'.[35] State practice, the ICRC declared, is 'not clear' as to the status of members of armed opposition groups: as civilians directly participating in hostilities or as persons who have lost their civilian status and are to be treated as *de facto* combatants.[36]

9.13

In its 2009 Interpretive Guidance on the notion of direct participation in hostilities, however, the ICRC argued that in non-international armed conflict, 'organized armed groups constitute the armed forces of a non-State party to the conflict and consist only of individuals whose continuous function it is to take a direct part in hostilities ("continuous combat function")'.[37] The concept of continuous combat function (or 'CCF', as it is sometimes abbreviated) is highly controversial.[38] While the approach has its adherents,[39] it is certainly not the case, as has been argued, that 'consensus exists that organized armed groups may be targeted' on this basis and rather that only 'a persistent controversy surrounds whether *any* members of the group continue to benefit from the prohibition on targeting civilians'.[40] As Gary Solis observes: 'The concept of

9.14

---

[34] Although see on this issue dicta from Germany to the contrary reported in European Court of Human Rights, *Hanan v. Germany*, Judgment (Grand Chamber), 16 February 2021, para. 33.
[35] ICRC, Customary IHL Rule 3: 'Definition of Combatants'.
[36] Ibid.
[37] N. Melzer, *Interpretive Guidance on the Notion of Direct Participation in Hostilities*, ICRC, Geneva, 2009 (hereinafter, ICRC Interpretive Guidance on DPH), Chap. II.
[38] A. Clapham, *War*, Oxford University Press, Oxford, 2021, pp. 426–32.
[39] Including, among leading commentators, Michael Schmitt and Marco Sassòli. See, e.g., M. Sassòli, *International Humanitarian Law Rules, Controversies, and Solutions to Problems Arising in Warfare*, Edward Elgar Publishing, Cheltenham, 2019, p. 504, para. 10.41.
[40] M. N. Schmitt, 'International Humanitarian Law and the Conduct of Hostilities', Chap. 7 in B. Saul and D. Akande (eds.), *The Oxford Guide to International Humanitarian Law*, Oxford University Press, Oxford, 2020, p. 157 (emphasis added). Writing in the same volume, Hill-Cawthorne is more cautious on the issue: 'it might be argued that it is now accepted that the law of NIAC does not prohibit the targeting of members of armed opposition groups on the basis of that status alone'. L. Hill-Cawthorne, 'Persons Covered by International Humanitarian Law: Main Categories', in B. Saul and D. Akande (eds.), *The Oxford Guide to International Humanitarian Law*, Oxford University Press, Oxford, 2020, p. 106.

continuous combat function does not enjoy either universal state practice or universal acceptance.'[41] The Special Rapporteur on extrajudicial, summary, or arbitrary executions wrote in 2010: 'Creation of the CCF category also raises the risk of erroneous targeting of someone who, for example, may have disengaged from their function. If States are to accept this category, the onus will be on them to show that the evidentiary basis is strong.'[42]

9.15 The issue was at the forefront of the considerations by the United Nations (UN) Commission of Inquiry into the protests in Gaza in the Occupied Palestinian Territory that began in March 2018.[43] According to one interpretation of the law that favours continuous combat function, military members of Hamas present in the crowd protesting near the fence surrounding Gaza could be targeted with lethal force without warning. Civilians in the crowd would be protected, as such, from direct attack, but the IHL rule of proportionality in attack (discussed in the following chapter) would potentially admit that a number may lawfully suffer incidental harm when Hamas fighters were being duly targeted.

9.16 The Commission report acknowledged that the notion of continuous combat function 'has been the object of criticism'.[44] This comprises the notion per se while, from other quarters, it is not its existence that is at issue but the fact that it is limited to only the military members of an organised armed group. The Commission stated tactfully that it 'does not opine on the recognition of CCF, nor its lawfulness as an IHL-based status', before proceeding, implicitly, to do just that. It noted that continuous combat function does not appear anywhere in an IHL treaty and concluded that the concept 'remains unsettled when assessed as custom'.[45] In such circumstances, the Commission stated, while legal approaches 'accepted by only a small group of countries are not necessarily wrong', they are 'best not applied ... until there is further acceptance by the international community'.[46] The Commission held that during a situation of armed conflict, demonstrations are to be managed according to the rules governing law enforcement. International human rights law, the Commission affirmed, 'prohibits the targeting of individuals in the crowd with lethal force if based purely on their membership in an armed group'.[47]

---

[41] Solis, *The Law of Armed Conflict: International Humanitarian Law in War*, 3rd Edn, p. 439.
[42] Report of the Special Rapporteur on extrajudicial, summary or arbitrary executions, Philip Alston, Addendum, UN doc. A/HRC/14/24/Add.6, 28 May 2010, para. 66.
[43] 'Report of the detailed findings of the independent international Commission of inquiry on the protests in the Occupied Palestinian Territory', UN doc. A/HRC/40/CRP.2, 18 March 2019. The Commission was initially chaired by David Michael Crane of the United States, an international law expert who served for more than 30 years in the Federal Government, including as Senior Inspector General in the US Department of Defense.
[44] 'Report of the detailed findings of the independent international Commission of inquiry on the protests in the Occupied Palestinian Territory', UN doc. A/HRC/40/CRP.2, at: https://bit.ly/2OWLcph, para. 104 and note 130.
[45] Ibid., para. 105.
[46] Ibid.
[47] Ibid., para. 106.

9.17 In the summary of its findings, the report by the Commission stated that even had it accepted the notion of continuous combat function, with its 'permissive approach to targeting members of armed groups', it believed that the Israeli Security Forces would have had 'difficulty' in complying with the principles of precautions and proportionality in attack:[48]

> Given the proximity, even intermingling, of armed group members with the demonstrating civilian crowd, harm to civilians is not only foreseeable, but nearly impossible to avoid. Indeed the more than 1,500 demonstrators wounded by shrapnel attest to the danger of civilians being injured by mistake, by ricochets, by bullet fragmentation and by shots going through one body to enter another, when snipers fire high-velocity live ammunition into a demonstrating crowd.[49]

9.18 We do not believe that the notion of continuous combat function represents the state of the law today. As the Commission noted, it is not found in the two 1977 Additional Protocols (or anywhere else in an IHL treaty). From a policy and legal point of view, its formal adoption by States runs the risk of significantly increasing loss of life, not only among military members of armed opposition groups when they are legitimate targets of attack, but also more broadly among the civilian population. A low standard of feasibility is demanded for precautionary measures in attack in an international armed conflict. Thereby, a party to the conflict must only do 'everything feasible to verify that the objectives to be attacked are neither civilians nor civilian objects'.[50] If applied also to situations of non-international armed conflict, this would hardly mitigate the risk.[51] It may be, however, that international human rights law requires a higher standard in such a situation, given the asserted *jus cogens* nature of the prohibition on arbitrary deprivation of life.[52] In any event, as Gary Solis affirms: 'Even civilians known to have a continuous combat function cannot be shot in cold blood, but they may be apprehended.'[53]

The definition of a civilian

9.19 According to the terms of Article 50 of the 1977 Additional Protocol I, a civilian is any person who is neither a combatant (as defined broadly above) nor a non-combatant member of the armed forces. Thus, Rule 5 of the ICRC's customary IHL study suggests

---

[48] See on these principles, infra, Chapters 11 and 10, respectively.
[49] 'Report of the detailed findings of the independent international Commission of inquiry on the protests in the Occupied Palestinian Territory', para. 696.
[50] Art. 57(2)(a)(i), 1977 Additional Protocol I. See further Chapter 11.
[51] In its judgment in the *Kupreškić* case, the ICTY endorsed the view, subsequently confirmed by the ICRC in its customary IHL study, that the precautionary rules applied also in non-international armed conflict as a matter of custom. International Tribunal for the Prosecution of Persons Responsible for Serious Violations of International Humanitarian Law Committed in the Territory of the Former Yugoslavia since 1991 (ICTY), *Prosecutor v. Zoran Kupreškić and others*, Judgment (Trial Chamber) (Case No. IT-95-16-T), 14 January 2000, paras. 49 and 132.
[52] Inter-American Court of Human Rights, *Case of the 'Street Children' (Villagrán-Morales) v. Guatemala*, Judgment (Merits), 19 November 1999, para. 139. See also 'Fourth report on peremptory norms of general international law (*jus cogens*) by Dire Tladi, Special Rapporteur', UN doc. A/CN.4/727, 31 January 2019, para. 128.
[53] Solis, *The Law of Armed Conflict: International Humanitarian Law in War*, 3rd Edn, p. 453.

that civilians 'are persons who are not members of the armed forces'.[54] That said, the term civilian also includes persons who formally accompany the armed forces without actually being members thereof, such as civilian members of military aircraft crews, war correspondents, and supply contractors. If, however, they have received formal authorisation from the armed forces (including an identity card in due form), they shall nonetheless be entitled to prisoner-of-war status in the event of capture.[55] The same rule applies to all the crew members of merchant vessels and civil aircraft of the Parties to the conflict, but only to the extent that they do not benefit from more favourable treatment under any other provisions of international law.[56] Finally, there is a specific issue with respect to children and the notion of CCF. Dinstein has suggested that 'unlike adults', in the conduct of hostilities, 'underage children' will not lose their protection from attack 'on account of mere membership in an armed group'.[57] He does not define what constitutes an underage child, but presumably this is the IHL limit of 15 years of age.

The principle of distinction

9.20 The principle of distinction was first set out in a binding IHL treaty only in 1977: in the Basic Rule in Article 48 of the Additional Protocol I. That said, already in 1868 the Saint Petersburg Declaration,[58] which outlawed the use of exploding bullets against military personnel, affirmed in its preamble that 'the only legitimate object which States should endeavour to accomplish during war is to weaken the military forces of the enemy'. This was at the least a philosophical underpinning of the future rule of distinction with respect to persons.[59]

9.21 While the Saint Petersburg Declaration applied to international armed conflict, in its 1995 decision on admissibility in the *Tadić* case, the Appeals Chamber of the International Criminal Tribunal for the Former Yugoslavia (ICTY) noted that the 'first rules' that evolved in relation to internal armed conflicts

> were aimed at protecting the civilian population from the hostilities. As early as the Spanish Civil War (1936–39), State practice revealed a tendency to disregard the distinction between international and internal wars and to apply certain general principles of humanitarian law, at least to those internal conflicts that constituted large-scale civil wars.[60]

---

[54] ICRC, Customary IHL Rule 5: 'Definition of Civilians', at: http://bit.ly/34KPPVO.
[55] Art. 4(4), 1949 Geneva Convention III.
[56] Ibid., Art. 4(5).
[57] Dinstein, *Non-International Armed Conflicts in International Law*, 2nd Edn, p. 244, para. 690.
[58] Declaration Renouncing the Use, in Time of War, of Explosive Projectiles Under 400 Grammes Weight; adopted at St Petersburg, 11 December 1868; entered into force, 4 September 1900.
[59] ICRC, Commentary on the 1977 Additional Protocols, 1987, para. 1863.
[60] ICTY, *Prosecutor v. Dusko Tadić a/k/a 'Dule'*, Decision on the Defence Motion for Interlocutory Appeal on Jurisdiction (Appeals Chamber), 2 October 1995, para. 100.

Subsequent State practice, the ICTY Appeals Chamber observed, 'indicates that the Spanish Civil War was not exceptional in bringing about the extension of some general principles of the laws of warfare to internal armed conflict'.[61] In 1968, UN General Assembly Resolution 2444 on 'Respect of human rights in armed conflict' recognised the obligation to apply basic humanitarian principles in all armed conflicts, and affirmed that 'it is prohibited to launch attacks against the civilian populations as such',[62] presaging the rules that would be incorporated in the two 1977 Additional Protocols.

9.22 Article 48 of the 1977 Additional Protocol I ('Basic Rule') stipulates that in 'order to ensure respect for and protection of the civilian population', the parties to an international armed conflict 'shall at all times distinguish ... between combatants and civilians ... and accordingly shall direct their operations only against military objectives'. As the ICRC has said in its 1987 commentary on the provision:

> The basic rule of protection and distinction is confirmed in this article. It is the foundation on which the codification of the laws and customs of war rests: the civilian population and civilian objects must be respected and protected in armed conflict, and for this purpose they must be distinguished from combatants and military objectives.[63]

In particular, this means that attacks must be directed only against lawful military objectives and not against civilians. In addition to the prohibition on directly attacking civilians, also unlawful is an indiscriminate attack, which is to say, an attack that is not directed against a combatant or other lawful military objective.

9.23 In case of doubt whether a person is a civilian, the Additional Protocol I declares that he or she 'shall be considered to be a civilian'.[64] The United States, not a party to the Protocol, contests that this stipulation reflects a customary norm. In the December 2016 edition of its Law of War Manual, the Department of Defense avers that: 'Under customary international law, no legal presumption of civilian status exists for persons or objects, nor is there any rule inhibiting commanders or other military personnel from acting based on the information available to him or her in doubtful cases.'[65] The manual concedes, however, that attacks 'may not be directed against civilians or civilian objects based on merely hypothetical or speculative considerations regarding their possible current status as a military objective'.[66] Gary Solis, a former Professor of Law at the US Military Academy at Westpoint, sets the bar substantively higher when it concerns a so-called targeted killing based on a 'signature' (pattern of conduct) strike. He affirms as follows:

---

[61] Ibid., para. 102.
[62] UN General Assembly Resolution 2444 (XXIII), adopted by 111 votes to nil on 19 December 1968, para. 1(b). (After the vote was taken, Gabon stated that it had intended to vote against the resolution.)
[63] ICRC, Commentary on the 1977 Additional Protocols, 1987, para. 1863.
[64] Art. 50(1), 1977 Additional Protocol I.
[65] USDOD December 2016 *Law of War Manual*, §5.4.3.2. See also on this issue R. Goodman, 'Clear Error in the Defense Department's Law of War Manual: On Presumptions of Civilian Status', *Just Security*, 9 February 2022, at: https://bit.ly/3Lz9Apu.
[66] USDOD December 2016 *Law of War Manual*, §5.4.3.2.

When invoking the state's targeted killing apparatus to kill a human target whose name is unknown, without signals intelligence or human intelligence to independently confirm the target's status as an enemy fighter before he is killed, or the ability to make on-the-ground after-action assessments, or confirm the reliability of the signature targeting process, the basic requirement of distinction cannot be satisfied.[67]

9.24 In its analysis of the application of the principle of distinction, reference is made by the United States Department of Defense to the UK Manual on the Law of Armed Conflict whereby:

In the practical application of the principle of civilian immunity and the rule of doubt, (a) commanders and others responsible for planning, deciding upon, or executing attacks necessarily have to reach decisions on the basis of their assessment of the information from all sources which is available to them at the relevant time, (b) it is only in cases of substantial doubt, after this assessment about the status of the individual in question, that the latter should be given the benefit of the doubt and treated as a civilian, and (c) the rule of doubt does not override the commander's duty to protect the safety of troops under his command or to preserve the military situation.[68]

The UK is a State Party to the 1977 Additional Protocol I, but has not made a reservation to Article 50(1).

9.25 For an attack to be deemed to have been directed against civilians in violation of the Protocols, there must be certainty as to both the author of the attack and the fact that one or more civilians were in fact being targeted (and not a lawful military objective nearby):

In general, an individual who is hit by a ricochet or is caught in crossfire during combat between two parties to an armed conflict (if a lawful military objective is being targeted) cannot be said either to have been under attack as a civilian or to have been the victim of an indiscriminate attack. This is also the case where an individual is accidentally hit by a shell or by shrapnel (shell fragmentation), unless the targeting was reckless or involved the use of an indiscriminate weapon.[69]

In the case of a violation of the primary rule of distinction, whether or not an attacked was 'directed' against civilians can be adduced from the circumstances of the attack. In case of an alleged war crime, the requisite mens rea must of course be proven.

9.26 General Stanislav Galić, as commander of Bosnian Serb forces above Sarajevo in 1992 to 1994 during the armed conflicts in Bosnia and Herzegovina, was accused before the International Criminal Tribunal for the former Yugoslavia (ICTY) of having led 'a coordinated and protracted campaign of sniper attacks upon the civilian population of

---

[67] Solis, *The Law of Armed Conflict: International Humanitarian Law in War*, 3rd Edn, p. 489.
[68] UK 2004 *Manual of the Law of Armed Conflict*, para. 5.3.4.
[69] S. Casey-Maslen with S. Haines, *Hague Law Interpreted: The Conduct of Hostilities under the Law of Armed Conflict*, Hart Publishing, Oxford, 2018, p. 146.

Sarajevo, killing and wounding a large number of civilians of all ages and both sexes, such attacks by their nature involving the deliberate targeting of civilians with direct fire weapons'.[70] He was further indicted for conducting 'a coordinated and protracted campaign of artillery and mortar shelling onto civilian areas of Sarajevo and upon its civilian population. The campaign of shelling resulted in thousands of civilians being killed or injured'.[71] One witness, a Bosnian Serb soldier, testified that his mortar battery had been ordered to target ambulances, a marketplace, funeral processions, and cemeteries.[72]

In one of a number of incidents which underpinned General Galić's conviction for the war crime of attacking civilians, Nafa Tarić went out to get schoolbooks with her eight-year-old daughter, Elma. There was no combat ongoing at the time. They crossed a street behind a line of containers that had been installed to provide protection against Bosnian Serb snipers, but as they emerged from the cover of the containers, they were hit by rifle fire. A single bullet hit Ms. Tarić's left thigh and grazed her daughter's hand, penetrating her stomach. Ms. Tarić stated that another bullet 'whizzed past' their bodies as they lay there. They managed to crawl away and were taken to hospital where they were treated.[73] The Trial Chamber noted Ms. Tarić's testimony that no other military action was occurring at the time of the incident and that neither soldiers nor any items of military equipment were in the vicinity (according to the witness, the closest Bosniak army command post was between 500 and 800 metres from the neighbourhood in which she and her daughter were walking). In addition, that a second shot was fired at them as they lay wounded, revealed, the Chamber stated, that they were deliberately targeted and not wounded by accident.[74] The Chamber was 'satisfied beyond reasonable doubt' that Nafa and Elma Tarić, both civilians, were deliberately targeted from a Bosnian Serb-controlled position.[75]

9.27

In its judgment in the *Ntaganda* case, the International Criminal Court found the defendant responsible, as indirect co-perpetrator, for commanding an attack against civilians in a village in eastern Democratic Republic of Congo.[76] In finding him criminally responsible, the Trial Chamber cited the provision in Article 57(2) of the Additional Protocol I, which refers to 'those who plan or decide an attack'. 'Read in conjunction with Article 51 [of the Protocol],' the Court stated, 'which forms the basis of the present war crime as included in Article 8 of the [Rome] Statute, the direct perpetrator of any use of artillery must be understood as being the person deciding on the attack (i.e. the commander who selected the target and ordered the firing on it), as opposed to the

9.28

---

[70] ICTY, *Prosecutor v. Galić*, Judgment and Opinion (Trial Chamber) (Case No. IT-98-29-T), 5 December 2003, para. 14.
[71] Ibid., para. 15.
[72] Ibid., para. 217.
[73] Ibid., para. 267.
[74] Ibid., para. 269.
[75] Ibid., para. 271.
[76] International Criminal Court, *Prosecutor v. Bosco Ntaganda*, Judgment (Trial Chamber VI) (Case No. ICC-01/04-02/06), 8 July 2019, para. 743.

person who operated the weapon system'.[77] On this basis, the Chamber found that the notion of 'directing' an attack against civilians means 'selecting the intended target and deciding on the attack'.[78]

9.29 The object of the attack, the Chamber further held, may be either a '"civilian population", in other words, a group of civilians', or individual civilians not taking a direct part in hostilities.[79] Specifically, during one assault, the Court found that Mr. Ntaganda had ordered the firing 'with a grenade launcher at the slope of the mountain where men and women wearing civilian clothing were walking in a single file; these individuals were clearly not taking any part in hostilities when they were attacked'.[80] On the basis of the circumstances at the time, the Chamber held, 'Mr Ntaganda necessarily knew that these persons could not be legitimately targeted and were entitled to protection as civilians under IHL'.[81]

9.30 That the principle of distinction is of a customary nature is beyond doubt. Indeed, the very first rule of the ICRC's customary IHL study holds that: 'The parties to the conflict must at all times distinguish between civilians and combatants. Attacks may only be directed against combatants. Attacks must not be directed against civilians.'[82] The ICRC records that State practice establishes the rule as a norm of customary international law applicable in both international and non-international armed conflicts.

9.31 Deliberately attacking civilians is also a war crime under both customary and conventional law. The provision in Article 85(3)(a) of the 1977 Additional Protocol I was cited in the introduction above.[83] Under the Rome Statute, in both an international and a non-international armed conflict, 'intentionally directing attacks against the civilian population as such or against individual civilians not taking direct part in hostilities' is a war crime subject to the Court's jurisdiction.[84] According to the ICRC customary IHL study, 'making the civilian population or individual civilians, not taking a direct part in hostilities, the object of attack' is a war crime in both international and non-international armed conflicts.[85] It is enough to launch an attack on civilians, 'even if something unexpectedly prevented the attack from causing death or serious injury'.[86] Furthermore, under general international law, the prohibition on deliberately attacking civilians who are not directly participating in hostilities is a norm of *jus cogens*.[87]

---

[77] Ibid., para. 744, note 2300.
[78] Ibid., para. 744.
[79] Ibid., para. 921.
[80] Ibid., para. 1182.
[81] Ibid.
[82] ICRC, Customary IHL Rule 1: 'The Principle of Distinction between Civilians and Combatants', at: http://bit.ly/32rIER0.
[83] See, *supra*, para. 9.2.
[84] Art. 8(2)(b)(i) and 2(e)(i), Rome Statute.
[85] ICRC Customary IHL Rule 156: 'Definition of War Crimes'.
[86] Ibid.
[87] ICJ, Nuclear Weapons Advisory Opinion, para. 79. Although the Court, in para. 83, seemingly declines to pronounce on the jus cogens nature of the fundamental principles of IHL, it is hard to interpret the reference to 'intransgressible' rules in para. 79 in any other manner. See further on this issue International Law Commission (ILC), 'Fourth report on peremptory norms of general international law (*jus cogens*) by Dire Tladi, Special

Indiscriminate attacks

Both the ICTY and the International Criminal Court appear to have conflated indiscriminate attacks with attacks directed against civilians. These are distinct rules in the 1977 Additional Protocol I[88] and under customary law[89] and should therefore be treated as two distinct war crimes. In a number of cases, however, the indiscriminate use or nature of the weapon used has been the basis for the finding that an attack had been directed against civilians. As noted above, indiscriminate attacks, at the least where they result in civilian harm, are distinct war crimes under customary law.

9.32

In its judgment in the *Blaškić* case, an ICTY Trial Chamber 'inferred from the arms used that the perpetrators of the attack had wanted to affect Muslim civilians'.[90] The so called 'baby-bombs' were 'home-made mortars' that 'are difficult to guide accurately'. Since, the Chamber found, their trajectory is 'irregular' and 'non-linear', they 'are likely to hit non-military targets. In this case, these blind weapons were sent onto [the town of] Stari Vitez where they killed and injured many Muslim civilians'.[91] The Defence did not deny that Bosnian Croat troops were responsible for some of the attacks on Stari Vitez but argued that they had attacked military targets and were always acting in response to an Bosniak army attack.[92] On appeal, the Appeals Chamber, considering that the fact of civilian casualties was regarded by the Trial Chamber as part of the proof of the illegal nature of the attack, cited evidence whereby in fact the casualties from the artisanal mortars were low and damage to civilian property largely resulted from a subsequent 'fierce fight' with Bosniak army units holding out in Stari Vitez.[93] It reversed the holding at trial that a crime against humanity had been committed by an attack on civilians.[94]

9.33

In its judgment in the *Galić* case, the Trial Chamber cited the trial judgment in *Blaškić*.[95] It also cited the view of the International Court of Justice in its Advisory Opinion on the Legality of the Threat or Use of Nuclear Weapons, whereby States may not make civilians the object of attack and must '*consequently* never use weapons that are incapable of distinguishing between civilian and military targets'.[96] The Court's formulation

9.34

Rapporteur', UN doc. A/CN.4/727, 31 January 2019, paras. 117–118; and ICTY, *Prosecutor v. Zoran Kupreškić and others*, Judgment (Trial Chamber), paras. 520, 521.

[88] The prohibition is 'sorely missing' from the 1977 Additional Protocol II. Dinstein, *Non-International Armed Conflicts in International Law*, 2nd Edn, p. 182, para. 583.
[89] Ibid., p. 282, para. 805.
[90] ICTY, *Prosecutor v. Tihomir Blaškić*, Judgment (Trial Chamber) (Case No. IT-95-14-T), 3 March 2000, para. 512.
[91] Ibid.
[92] Ibid., para. 514.
[93] ICTY, *Prosecutor v. Tihomir Blaškić*, Judgment (Appeals Chamber) (Case No. IT-95-14-A), 29 July 2004, para. 464.
[94] Ibid., para. 466.
[95] ICTY, *Prosecutor v. Galić*, Judgment and Opinion (Trial Chamber) (Case No. IT-98-29-T), 5 December 2003, para. 57.
[96] ICJ, Nuclear Weapons Advisory Opinion, para. 78 (emphasis added).

is unfortunate. In fact, the word 'consequently' follows, and should be explicitly linked to, the Court's reference earlier in the same paragraph of its Opinion to the 'cardinal principle' establishing 'the distinction between combatants and non-combatants'.[97] Based in part on the poor wording in the Advisory Opinion, the ICTY Trial Chamber concluded that 'indiscriminate attacks, that is to say, attacks which strike civilians or civilian objects and military objectives without distinction, may qualify as direct attacks against civilians'.[98]

9.35 General Galić's lawyers contested the finding on appeal, arguing, correctly in law, that the Trial Chamber had conflated two war crimes. In response, the Appeals Chamber, offering circuitous logic and referring back to other legally flawed decisions within the ICTY on the issue, concluded simply that: 'In principle, the Trial Chamber was entitled to determine on a case-by-case basis that the indiscriminate character of an attack can assist it in determining whether the attack was directed against the civilian population.'[99] To be clear, the 1977 Additional Protocol I specifically prohibits both attacking the civilian population as such (as well as individual civilians not participating directly in hostilities),[100] *and*, separately, indiscriminate attacks, that is to say: attacks that are not directed at a specific military objective or which involve the use of a weapon that cannot be directed at a specific military objective.[101] Both are unlawful and both can be war crimes, but they are distinct, and for good reason as they involve different conduct (actus reus) and associated mental states (mens rea) in criminal law terms.

9.36 The error committed by the ICTY has been repeated by the International Criminal Court in its jurisprudence. In its judgment in the *Katanga* case, a Trial Chamber cited the *Galić* trial and appeals chamber judgments to underpin its holding that indiscriminate attacks 'may qualify as intentional attacks against the civilian population or individual civilians'.[102] The Chamber did qualify its statement that this was 'especially' the case 'where the damage caused to civilians is so great that it appears to the Chamber that the perpetrator meant to target civilian objectives'.[103] But the Trial Chamber went on to cite the *Blaškić* trial judgment in holding further that 'the use of weaponry that has indiscriminate effects may, inter alia, show that the attack was directed at the civilian population or individual civilians'.[104]

9.37 The most recent case adjudged by the International Criminal Court confirms this trend. Referring back to its judgment at trial in *Katanga*, in finding Mr. Ntaganda criminally

---

[97] One might also note that there is no such thing in IHL as civilian 'targets'.
[98] ICTY, *Prosecutor v. Galić*, Judgment and Opinion (Trial Chamber), para. 57.
[99] ICTY, *Prosecutor v. Galić*, Judgment (Appeals Chamber) (Case No. IT-98-29-A), 30 November 2006, paras. 131, 132.
[100] Art. 51(2) and (3), 1977 Additional Protocol I.
[101] Ibid., Art. 51(4)(a) and (b).
[102] International Criminal Court, *Prosecutor v. Germain Katanga*, Judgment (Trial Chamber II) (Case No. ICC-01/04-01/07), 7 March 2014, para. 802.
[103] Ibid.
[104] Ibid.

responsible for a direct attack on civilians, a Trial Chamber held in July 2019 that the crime under the Rome Statute

> may encompass attacks that are carried out in an indiscriminate manner, that is by targeting an area, as opposed to specific objects, or not targeting specific military objects or persons taking a direct part in hostilities, so long as the perpetrator was aware of the presence of civilians in the relevant area. It may also include attacks that are launched without taking necessary precautions to spare the civilian population or individual civilians.[105]

The Trial Chamber asserted: 'Therefore, the use of weapons that have inherently indiscriminate effects in an area where civilians are present may constitute an attack directed at the civilian population or individual civilians.'[106]

Loss of protection from attack as a consequence of direct participation in hostilities

Civilians are protected from direct attack as well as from indiscriminate attack 'unless and for such time as they take a direct part in hostilities'.[107] More ink has been spilt on these last four words than perhaps any others in IHL over the last decade or so. The reason is clear: without being overly melodramatic, civilians will live or die, depending on how the concept is interpreted. **9.38**

If the ICRC's 2009 Interpretive Guidance on direct participation in hostilities (DPH) is controversial for the concept it elaborated of 'continuous combat function', it is so also for its broad interpretation of what constitutes such 'DPH'. The ICRC identified three components: threshold of harm to the enemy; direct causation; and belligerent nexus, largely mirroring the words 'participation', 'direct', and 'in hostilities'. Overall, this approach is 'both logical and reasonable and does not appear to be contested'.[108] But the devil is in the detail. The problem arises from the low threshold of harm on which the ICRC decided as being sufficient for DPH, which was certainly substantially below the position it expressed in its 1987 commentary on the wording in the two 1977 Additional Protocols. A review of key caselaw highlights some of the potential consequences. **9.39**

In its 1999 judgment in the *Rutaganda* case, the International Criminal Tribunal for Rwanda (ICTR) explicitly applied the ICRC's commentary on the 1977 Additional Protocols as its basis for determining that direct participation in hostilities is constituted by 'acts of war which by their nature or purpose are likely to cause actual harm **9.40**

---

[105] International Criminal Court, *Prosecutor v. Bosco Ntaganda*, Judgment (Trial Chamber VI), para. 921.
[106] Ibid.
[107] Art. 51(3), 1977 Additional Protocol I; Art. 13(3), 1977 Additional Protocol II.
[108] Casey-Maslen, *Hague Law Interpreted*, p. 138.

to the personnel and equipment of the enemy armed forces'.[109] The *Stragar* case was first adjudicated before the ICTY in 2005. In the Appeals Chamber judgment, issued a year before the ICRC's Interpretive Guidance, it was observed that 'the notion of active participation in hostilities encompasses armed participation in combat activities'.[110] In 2009, however, the ICRC's Interpretive Guidance averred that participation in hostilities can be founded by an act which either does, or is likely: adversely to affect the military operations of a party to an armed conflict; adversely to affect the military capacity of a party to an armed conflict; to kill or injure civilians protected against direct attack; or to destroy (or damage) civilian objects protected against direct attack.[111] No longer is actual harm a requisite criterion: adverse effects are sufficient. The consequences of such a broad interpretation of harm can be seen reflected in the International Criminal Court's 2019 trial chamber judgment in the *Ntaganda* case.

9.41 During an attack on the village of Kobu, a group, mostly of women, all of whom were in civilian clothing were 'singing, shouting, and hitting on pans'.[112] They were all, it seems, unarmed. The opposing armed groups fired at them, after which they dispersed. The Chamber noted that 'it appears from the circumstances' that the group making noise 'may have been purposely distracting' those armed groups in order for ethnic Lendu fighters to be able to attack them from a closer-by position. 'If this would have been the case, these civilians may be considered as directly participating in hostilities during that relevant time, and firing at them to disperse the group would have been lawful.'[113] In addition to the remarkably low threshold set for the use of lethal force, the Chamber does not seem to have considered Chapter IX of the ICRC's Interpretive Guidance, which may serve to mitigate the effects of such a low threshold of harm. Therein the ICRC affirm that 'the kind and degree of force which is permissible against persons not entitled to protection against direct attack must not exceed what is actually necessary to accomplish a legitimate military purpose in the prevailing circumstances'.[114]

9.42 The mere provision of funding does not amount to direct participation in hostilities in the view of a number of leading academic authorities.[115] In theory—if not necessarily

---

[109] ICTR, *Prosecutor v. Georges Anderson Nderubumwe Rutaganda*, Judgement and Sentence (Trial Chamber I) (Case No. ICTR-96-3-T), 6 December 1999, para. 100; see Y. Sandoz, C. Swinarski, and B. Zimmermann (eds.), *Commentary on the Additional Protocols of 8 June 1977 to the Geneva Conventions of 12 August 1949*, Martinus Nijhoff, Geneva, 1987, paras. 1944, 4788 (hereinafter, ICRC, Commentary on the 1977 Additional Protocols). In para. 1944, it is stated: 'Thus "direct" participation means acts of war which by their nature or purpose are likely to cause actual harm to the personnel and equipment of the enemy armed forces.'
[110] ICTY, *Prosecutor v. Pavle Strugar*, Judgment (Appeals Chamber) (Case No. IT-01-42-A), 17 July 2008, para. 176.
[111] ICRC, Interpretive Guidance on DPH, p. 47.
[112] International Criminal Court, *Prosecutor v. Bosco Ntaganda*, Judgment (Trial Chamber VI), para. 575.
[113] Ibid., para. 925.
[114] ICRC, Interpretive Guidance on DPH, Chap. IX.
[115] Dinstein, *Non-International Armed Conflicts in International Law*, 2nd Edn, p. 82, para. 220; and Saul, 'Terrorism and International Humanitarian Law', p. 203, citing the *Tallinn Manual on the International Law Applicable to Cyber Warfare*, Cambridge University Press, Cambridge, 2013, p. 120.

in practice—the United States Department of Defense appears to take a similar view. With respect to the notion in international armed conflict, the Department of Defense holds that 'taking a direct part in hostilities does not encompass the general support that members of the civilian population provide to their State's war effort, such as by buying war bonds'.[116] This contrasts with the department's view that (at the least prior to the Taliban assuming full control of the country in August 2021), it was lawful, on the basis of military necessity, to target the opium crop in Afghanistan because of the substantial funding the Taliban derived from opium production and trade.[117] Presumably, those civilians engaged in growing opium, as well as those refining it, remained protected civilians. This assessment is not certain to be true, however, especially with respect to those who sell drugs. For in 2009, the US Senate Committee on Foreign Relations confirmed that US forces in Afghanistan were authorised to kill drug traffickers in Afghanistan with links to the Taliban: 'two U.S. generals in Afghanistan said that the ROE [Rules of Engagement] and the internationally recognized Law of War have been interpreted to allow them to put drug traffickers with proven links to the insurgency on a kill list'.[118]

9.43 Surprisingly, Ben Saul says only that targeting drug traffickers '*may* ... raise legal questions where such targets are not strictly military objectives under IHL'.[119] If a target is not a lawful military objective, an attack against it is a violation of IHL. For, notwithstanding dispute as to its proper interpretation (and opposition from the United States to its formulation in the Additional Protocol I),[120] that civilians are protected against attack, unless and for such time as they take a direct part in hostilities, is a clear rule of customary international law applicable in all armed conflicts.[121] Schmitt affirms, correctly, that the rule is 'generally accepted'.[122]

Concluding remarks and outlook

9.44 The provisions in the 1977 Additional Protocol I on the protection of civilians are reflected in customary international law. So too are those governing loss of immunity from attack, when and for such time as a civilian participates directly in hostilities. The

---

[116] USDOD December 2016 *Law of War Manual*, §5.8.3.
[117] Ibid., §5.17.2.3; and see Solis, *The Law of Armed Conflict: International Humanitarian Law in War*, 3rd Edn, p. 400.
[118] *Afghanistan's Narco War: Breaking the Link Between Drug Traffickers and Insurgents. A Report to the Committee on Foreign Relations*, US Senate, 10 August 2009, at: https://bit.ly/3r6k1sq, p. 15, and cf. also p. 16 for recognition of NATO concerns as to this interpretation.
[119] B. Saul, 'The legal nexus between terrorism and transnational crime', Chap. 10 in B. Saul (ed.), *Research Handbook on International Law and Terrorism*, 2nd Edn, Edward Elgar Publishing, Cheltenham, 2021, p. 145.
[120] USDOD December 2016 *Law of War Manual*, §5.8.1.2.
[121] ICRC, Customary IHL Rule 6: 'Civilians' Loss of Protection from Attack', at: http://bit.ly/2UxOq2T.
[122] Schmitt, 'International Humanitarian Law and the Conduct of Hostilities', p. 156.

controversies as to the existence or not of the notion of continuous combat function and the interpretation to be given to the concept of 'direct participation in hostilities' persist. Given the lack of consensus among States, judicial authorities, and scholars on this notion, the challenges for non-State armed groups to both interpret and apply the law must not be underestimated.

10

The Rule of Proportionality

Introduction

In armed conflict, civilians 'almost always suffer when hostilities are raging'.[1] Indeed, incidental harm to civilians and damage to civilian objects is, as the United States (US) Department of Defense has observed, 'unfortunate and tragic' but also 'inevitable'.[2] The question becomes how much foreseeable civilian harm international humanitarian law (IHL) permits. It is clear, however, that while IHL requires parties to armed conflict to take 'all feasible precautions' in attack with a view to 'avoiding, and in any event to minimizing, incidental loss of civilian life',[3] it does not render illegal all incidental killing and wounding of civilians. The content of the rule of proportionality—sometimes termed a 'principle' in order to reflect its fundamental character—was first elaborated in the modern era in the context of the two 1977 Additional Protocols. 10.1

In simple terms, by virtue of the proportionality rule, all parties to armed conflict are prohibited from launching attacks which 'may be expected' to cause 'excessive' civilian harm when compared to the 'concrete and direct military advantage anticipated'. These rules apply as a matter of custom irrespective of whether the armed conflict is international or non-international in character. In treaty law, however, the rule is set forth only in the Additional Protocol I of 1977 and not also the Additional Protocol II. The key rules are summarised in Table 10.1. 10.2

This chapter discusses the interpretation and application of the rule of proportionality in attack under the 1977 Additional Protocols, and under the corresponding rule of customary law. The chapter first addresses the rule as set out in the Additional Protocol I of 1977. It then considers the treaty rule in the light of customary IHL and international criminal law. A disproportionate attack is punishable as a war crime under certain circumstances in both international and non-international armed 10.3

---

[1] Y. Dinstein, *The Conduct of Hostilities under the Law of International Armed Conflict*, 3rd Edn, Cambridge University Press, Cambridge, 2016, p. 149, para. 397.

[2] US Department of Defense, *Law of War Manual*, June 2015 (Updated December 2016), available at: http://bit.ly/30D0xN8, §2.4.1.2.

[3] Art. 57(2)(a)(ii), Protocol Additional to the Geneva Conventions of 12 August 1949, and relating to the Protection of Victims of International Armed Conflicts (Protocol I); adopted at Geneva, 8 June 1977; entered into force, 7 December 1978 (hereinafter, 1977 Additional Protocol I); International Committee of the Red Cross (ICRC) Customary IHL Rule 15: 'Principle of Precautions in Attack', at: http://bit.ly/2m6mCnj. See generally on the issue of precautions Chapter 11.

152   THE RULE OF PROPORTIONALITY

Table 10.1 The Rules of Proportionality in Attack

Rule	AP I	Customary status (IAC)	AP II	Customary status (NIAC)
Proportionality in attack	Art. 51(5)(b)	Yes	No	Yes
Duty to refrain from disproportionate attacks	Art. 57(2)(a)(iii) Art. 57(2)(b)	Yes	No	Yes
Launching an indiscriminate attack knowing it will cause excessive civilian harm is a war crime	Art. 85(3)(b)	Yes	No	Yes

conflict. The final part of the chapter considers the rule in the context of environmental protection.

The treaty rules of proportionality in attack

10.4   The primary rule governing proportionality in attack is set out in Article 57(5)(b) of the 1977 Additional Protocol I.[4] This provision stipulates as follows:

> Among others, the following types of attacks are to be considered as indiscriminate: ... an attack which may be expected to cause incidental loss of civilian life, injury to civilians, damage to civilian objects, or a combination thereof, which would be excessive in relation to the concrete and direct military advantage anticipated.

There are six main elements to this rule. First, there must be an 'attack'. (This is defined elsewhere in the Protocol in broad terms as 'acts of violence against the adversary, whether in offence or in defence'.[5]) In addition, the attack must have been subject to some form of prior planning. Secondly, the attack must be directed at a lawful military objective, meaning that the principle of distinction is complied with. Thirdly, in the requisite assessment conducted at the planning stage, the standard of foreseeability of harm from the attack is relatively low ('which may be expected'). This is also an objective, not a subjective standard. Fourthly, the expected harm must be to civilians (involving death or physical injury) or concern damage to civilian objects (or be a combination of such foreseen consequences). Fifthly, the civilian harm foreseen by the attacking party must be compared to the anticipated 'concrete and direct' military advantage.[6] The final element is that the attack is unlawful under the proportionality rule

---

[4] Art. 51(5)(b), 1977 Additional Protocol I.
[5] Art. 49(1), 1977 Additional Protocol I.
[6] Military advantage may, in the view of the US Department of Defense, include: denying the enemy the ability to benefit from the object's effective contribution to its military action (e.g. using this object in its military

where that foreseen civilian harm would be 'excessive' in comparison to the expected military advantage.[7]

10.5 The fact that civilians have been killed in any attack demands that an inquiry be conducted to assess whether the rule of proportionality in attack was complied with. But it is essential to bear in mind that compliance with proportionality is not adjudged on the situation pertaining after an attack (*ex post facto*), based, for instance, on the number of civilians it harmed or civilian objects it destroyed. Rather consideration of compliance with the rule of proportionality in attack is judged *ex ante*, looking back in time at the situation when the attack was launched. What did the commander know about the risk to civilians at that time, or what should he or she be reasonably expected to have known? And based on that knowledge, was the attack justified because of the military benefit it was likely to bring? Would a reasonable commander have come to a similar decision to proceed with the attack? There is thus no obligation under IHL to '*ensure* [i.e. as an outcome] that civilian losses are not disproportionate to the direct and concrete military advantage anticipated to result from the attack'.[8]

10.6 The notion of comparison inheres in the rule, as very significant anticipated military advantage may allow foreseeable civilian harm also to be substantial. It is therefore incorrect to say that: 'The Protocol does not provide any justification for attacks which cause extensive civilian losses and damages. Incidental losses and damages should never be extensive.'[9] As Rogers notes, such an interpretation would make 'nonsense of the rule of proportionality, the whole idea of which is to achieve a balance between the military advantage and the incidental loss'.[10] Michael Schmitt disavows the notion of a balancing, terming it a misinterpretation, while noting the importance of parsing the text to understand the rule fully. But in correctly stressing the importance of the notion of excessiveness in determining whether an attack is unlawful, he suggests that this will only be the case when there is a 'significant imbalance' between expected military advantage and the civilian harm foreseen.[11] This is a less protective standard than the ordinary wording of the rule and must be rejected. Indeed, it is akin to the threshold set in the Rome Statute of the International Criminal Court for individual criminal

---

operations); improving the security of the attacking force; and diverting the enemy's resources and attention. US Department of Defense, *Law of War Manual*, Washington, D.C., June 2015 (Updated December 2016), §5.12.2.

[7] Hayashi suggests that the standard is 'manifestly disproportionate collateral damage' but this is too restrictive. N. Hayashi, 'General Principles of International Law', Chap. 4 in D. Fleck (ed.), *The Handbook of International Humanitarian Law*, 4th Edn, Oxford University Press, Oxford, 2021, p. 88.

[8] H. Duffy, *The 'War on Terror' and the Framework of International Law*, 2nd Edn, Cambridge University Press, Cambridge, 2015, p. 373 (emphasis added).

[9] ICRC, Commentary on Article 51 of the 1977 Additional Protocols, 1987, at: https://bit.ly/30PnnD8, p. 626, para. 1980.

[10] A. P. V. Rogers, *Law on the Battlefield*, 3rd Edn, Manchester University Press, Manchester, 2012, p. 31.

[11] M. N. Schmitt, 'International Humanitarian Law and the Conduct of Hostilities', Chap. 7 in B. Saul and D. Akande (eds.), *The Oxford Guide to International Humanitarian Law*, Oxford University Press, Oxford, 2020, p. 153.

154   THE RULE OF PROPORTIONALITY

responsibility for a disproportionate attack, which requires that the civilian harm foreseen must have been 'clearly excessive' not just excessive.[12] This issue is discussed further below.

10.7 The rule of proportionality in attack is reiterated twice more in the Additional Protocol I, on both occasions in relation to the precautions to be taken in attack. States Parties are further obligated to 'refrain from deciding to launch any attack which may be expected to cause incidental loss of civilian life, injury to civilians, damage to civilian objects, or a combination thereof, which would be excessive in relation to the concrete and direct military advantage anticipated'.[13] This provision in Article 57 is thus, in effect, a repetition of the primary rule set forth earlier in the Protocol. In its 1987 commentary on this later provision, the International Committee of the Red Cross (ICRC) observed that the rule 'allows for a fairly broad margin of judgment'. While, during the negotiations, several States regretted this imprecision, others 'commended the fact that in future military commanders would have a universally recognized guideline as regards their responsibilities to the civilian population during attacks against military objectives'.[14] The duty to refrain from a disproportionate attack is reinforced once more in the Protocol, in the subsequent subparagraph of Article 57, according to which an attack 'shall be cancelled or suspended' should it become 'apparent' that excessive civilian harm will result.[15]

10.8 In addition to the general treaty provision in the Additional Protocol I, the rule of proportionality in attack is also applied to certain specific weapons. It was incorporated in the Protocol II to the 1980 Convention on Certain Conventional Weapons, an instrument negotiated under United Nations (UN) auspices following the failure to agree upon rules regulating specific weapons in the Protocol. Therein, it is explicitly prohibited to emplace landmines and booby-traps where they 'may be expected to cause incidental loss of civilian life, injury to civilians, damage to civilian objects, or a combination thereof, which would be excessive in relation to the concrete and direct military advantage anticipated'.[16] The original Protocol II applied only in international armed conflict. But the rule is repeated in the 1996 Amended Protocol II where it applies also to situations of non-international armed conflict.[17]

---

[12] Art. 8(2)(b)(iv), Rome Statute of the International Criminal Court; adopted at Rome, 17 July 1998; entered into force, 1 July 2002. As of 1 May 2022, 123 States were party to the Rome Statute.
[13] Art. 57(2)(a)(iii), 1977 Additional Protocol I.
[14] ICRC, Commentary on Art. 57(2)(a)(iii), 1977 Additional Protocol I, 1987, at: http://bit.ly/3t60yWZ, p. 684, para. 2210.
[15] Art. 57(2)(b), 1977 Additional Protocol I.
[16] Protocol on Prohibitions or Restrictions on the Use of Mines, Booby-Traps and Other Devices (Protocol II) annexed to the Convention on Prohibitions or Restrictions on the Use of Certain Conventional Weapons which May Be Deemed to Be Excessively Injurious or to Have Indiscriminate Effects; adopted at Geneva, 10 October 1980; entered into force, 2 December 1983 (CCW). As of 1 May 2022, 95 States were party to Protocol II.
[17] Art. 3(8)(c), Protocol on Prohibitions or Restrictions on the Use of Mines, Booby-Traps and Other Devices as amended on 3 May 1996 annexed to the CCW; adopted at Geneva, 3 May 1996; entered into force, 3 December 1998. As of 1 May 2022, 106 States were party to the 1996 Amended Protocol II.

Proportionality in attack under general international law

10.9 While in the 1977 Additional Protocol I (and in the protocols on landmines annexed to the 1980 Convention on Certain Conventional Weapons), proportionality is articulated as a form of indiscriminate attack, it is better—and more generally—understood as an autonomous principle. This is because the essence of an indiscriminate attack is that it is not targeted at a lawful military objective. In contrast, in a disproportionate attack the target is a lawful one, but the expected incidental civilian harm is too high, rendering the attack unlawful. The rule is approached in these independent terms under general international law. Thus, the ICRC determined that a separate customary rule, aside from and additional to the general prohibition on indiscriminate attacks that results inevitably from the principle of distinction,[18] dictates that: 'Launching an attack which may be expected to cause incidental loss of civilian life, injury to civilians, damage to civilian objects, or a combination thereof, which would be excessive in relation to the concrete and direct military advantage anticipated, is prohibited.'[19] State practice establishes the rule as a norm of customary international law applicable in both international and non-international armed conflicts.[20]

10.10 The customary nature of the rule is attested to, inter alia, by its specific inclusion as a war crime in the Rome Statute of the International Criminal Court. Consonant with the inclusion of the rule only in the Additional Protocol I of 1977, however, the corresponding war crime in the Statute is provided for only in a situation of international armed conflict.[21] The evidence adduced for the customary nature of the rule of proportionality in non-international armed conflict is indeed rather weaker. Thus, it was affirmed in 2005 that while the 1977 Additional Protocol II does not contain an explicit reference to the principle of proportionality in attack, 'it has been argued that it is inherent in the principle of humanity which was explicitly made applicable to the Protocol in its preamble and that, as a result, the principle of proportionality cannot be ignored in the application of the Protocol'.[22] This is a surprisingly flimsy argument for such a fundamental principle.

10.11 State practice and *opinio juris* have, however, combined to confirm the customary status of the rule in all armed conflict.[23] The Rome Statute, adopted in 1998, does not generally provide for prosecution of indiscriminate attacks in any armed conflict. But, as noted above, a disproportionate attack can be prosecuted in an international armed conflict when the expected harm is 'clearly excessive'. To date, no one has been explicitly prosecuted under this war crime, perhaps in part in consequence of the high evidentiary

---

[18] ICRC, Customary IHL Rule 11: 'Indiscriminate Attacks', at: http://bit.ly/2kmcrdT.
[19] ICRC, Customary IHL Rule 14: 'Proportionality in Attack', at: http://bit.ly/2k9mrHh.
[20] Ibid.
[21] Art. 8(2)(b)(iv), Rome Statute.
[22] ICRC, Customary IHL Rule 14: 'Proportionality in Attack'.
[23] Y. Dinstein, *Non-International Armed Conflict in International Law*, 2nd Edn, Cambridge University Press, Cambridge, 2021, p. 283, para. 808.

bar that must be passed. It appeared from the wording of the Court's judgment in the *Katanga* case, however, that it had found that a disproportionate attack had occurred in the prevailing non-international armed conflict.[24] Moreover, in its 2019 judgment in the *Ntaganda* case, a Trial Chamber of the International Criminal Court held that the crime under the Rome Statute of attacking civilians 'may encompass attacks that are carried out in an indiscriminate manner'.[25] The Trial Chamber further opined that the crime 'may also include attacks that are launched without taking necessary precautions to spare the civilian population or individual civilians'.[26] These dicta may open the door to a future prosecution for a disproportionate attack in a non-international armed conflict, albeit one that is subsumed—on questionable grounds[27]—within the war crime of attacking civilians.

10.12 In its 2021 judgment in the *Hanan* case, the Grand Chamber of the European Court of Human Rights reiterated the customary nature of the rule in the non-international armed conflict in Afghanistan to which the case specifically pertained.[28] Germany was alleged to have perpetrated a disproportionate attack in the Kunduz region in 2009. Although a parliamentary commission of inquiry found procedural irregularities in the decision to launch the attack,[29] the investigating authorities in the German Ministry of Defence accepted the commander's assertion that he both honestly and reasonably believed at the time that no civilians were present in the area being targeted by the attack.[30] The Commentary on the *Harvard Manual on International Law Applicable to Air and Missile Warfare* stipulates that 'harm to civilians and civilian objects that the attacker did not expect is not collateral damage included in proportionality calculations, so long as the lack of expectation of harm was reasonable in the circumstances'.[31] The key question with regard to such harm is, the Commentary observes, 'whether there is compliance with the requirement to take feasible precautions in attack'.[32]

10.13 In its annual report on the protection of civilians in Afghanistan covering 2020, the UN Assistance Mission in Afghanistan (UNAMA) reminded 'Pro-Government Forces' engaged in the ongoing non-international armed conflict against the Taliban that the failure by one party to the conflict to respect IHL 'does not absolve an opposing

---

[24] International Criminal Court, *Prosecutor* v. *Germain Katanga*, Judgment (Trial Chamber II) (Case No. ICC-01/04-01/07), 7 March 2014, paras. 865 and 1218.
[25] International Criminal Court, *Prosecutor* v. *Bosco Ntaganda*, Judgment (Trial Chamber VI) (Case No. ICC-01/04-02/06), 8 July 2019, para. 921.
[26] Ibid.
[27] See on this issue, supra, Chapter 9.
[28] European Court of Human Rights, *Hanan* v. *Germany*, Judgment (Grand Chamber), 16 February 2021, para. 80. In a renvoi to para. 77 of its judgment, however, the Court appears to confuse proportionality *in bello* with proportionality *ad bellum*.
[29] Ibid., para. 69. See further Deutscher Bundestag, Drucksache 17/7400: *Beschlussempfehlung und Bericht des Verteidigungsausschusses als 1. Untersuchungsausschuss gemäß Artikel 45a Absatz 2 des Grundgesetzes*, Berlin, 25 October 2011.
[30] European Court of Human Rights, *Hanan* v. *Germany*, Judgment (Grand Chamber), paras. 36–40.
[31] *Commentary on the Harvard Manual on International Law Applicable to Air and Missile Warfare*, Cambridge University Press, Cambridge, 2013, p. 33, para. 4.
[32] Ibid.

party from its obligations under international law, including ... to respect the principle of proportionality in attack, including when gathering intelligence about the civilian status of targets and choosing means and methods to be used'.[33] UNAMA further declared the principle of proportionality 'applies regardless of whether airstrikes are conducted as part of a planned, deliberate targeting operation or whether they are conducted in support of forces on the ground'.[34] A total of 146 children were killed and a further 153 were injured in airstrikes in Afghanistan in 2020, according to data collated and verified by UNAMA.[35]

The interpretation and application of the rule

The manifest difficulty with proportionality, whether under custom or treaty, is that its interpretation, and especially the notion of what is to be considered 'excessive' civilian harm, continues to be extremely unclear. This inevitably renders its practical application even more challenging. Indeed, at the Diplomatic Conference in 1977 that concluded the Additional Protocols, France voted against the adoption of Article 51 because it deemed that paragraph 5 by its 'very complexity' would 'seriously hamper the conduct of defensive military operations against an invader and prejudice the inherent right of legitimate defence'.[36] **10.14**

In its 1996 Advisory Opinion on the legality of the threat or use of force, the International Court of Justice did not discuss the principle of proportionality *in bello* in any depth. It made only passing references, including in relation to the protection of the environment during armed conflict (cited below).[37] This omission from the Court's Opinion, in which it did address other 'intransgressible'—i.e. *jus cogens*—norms of IHL,[38] is unfortunate. **10.15**

In 2016, the ICRC convened an international expert meeting to seek to clarify the interpretation of the proportionality rule, but made little headway on the issue.[39] As stated in the report, the experts 'noted the difficulty in assessing and discussing what is "excessive".'[40] They did, however, agree that, under the proportionality assessment, civilian life would be valued higher than civilian property: **10.16**

---

[33] UNAMA, *Protection of Civilians in Armed Conflict Report: 2020*, Kabul, February 2021, p. 60.
[34] Ibid., p. 68.
[35] Ibid., p. 31.
[36] ICRC, Customary IHL Rule 14: 'Proportionality in Attack'.
[37] International Court of Justice, *Legality of the Threat or Use of Nuclear Weapons*, Advisory Opinion, 8 July 1996, para. 30.
[38] Ibid., paras. 78–79.
[39] See L. Gisel, *The Principle of Proportionality in the Rules Governing the Conduct of Hostilities under International Humanitarian Law*, Report of an International Expert Meeting in Quebec, 22–23 June 2016, ICRC, Geneva, August 2018, at: http://bit.ly/397bsor, Part III. It is worth noting that, unfortunately, the perspective of non-State armed groups, though bound by the rule, was not considered at all.
[40] Ibid., p. 62.

158   THE RULE OF PROPORTIONALITY

For example, it was suggested that if a belligerent could spare 10 civilians by using a weapon that would destroy 30 stores, every commander would choose to do so. However, the experts disagreed on whether, exceptionally, property damage could be so serious as to 'weigh' more in terms of incidental civilian harm than a single life. One expert considered it could be the case depending on the circumstances, while another discarded the idea even for specially protected or significant property, such as cultural property.[41]

10.17 In its latest iteration of its *Law of War Manual*, the US Department of Defense similarly asserts that: 'In light of the humanitarian objectives of the law of war, the expected loss of civilian life and injury to civilians should be given greater consideration than the expected damage to civilian objects.'[42] It does, however, qualify that stance by clarifying that 'expected damage to civilian objects (such as schools, hospitals, and religious facilities) should be given greater consideration when such damage is expected to involve the risk of harming civilians present inside such objects'. It also asserts that expected damage to cultural property 'should be afforded greater consideration than expected damage to ordinary property.'[43]

10.18 There is also a limited measure of agreement that while all life is valuable, the lives of certain civilians may be accorded greater weight in the proportionality assessment. According to Dinstein, for example, those who benefit from special protection from attack, such as the wounded and sick, or, 'even more so', medical personnel, 'do not seem to be counted on a par with ordinary civilians. Differently put, a dozen civilians dining in a restaurant do not weigh as much as a dozen patients and doctors in an infirmary. Otherwise, what is the real meaning of the special protection accorded to the latter?'[44]

10.19 A broadly similar approach was taken by some of the experts at the 2016 ICRC meeting. They postulated that vulnerable groups, such as children, the mentally ill, the elderly, or the wounded and sick, might be privileged for protection because these individuals are seen as being less able to cope with the harm.[45] In a similar vein, Dinstein suggests that 'intuitively', adult men 'in their prime' are not seen in the same light as women, children, and the elderly, who are more vulnerable. When an air strike or an artillery barrage leaves a trail of civilian deaths behind, nobody would equate a score of adult men in a pub with a score of toddlers in a kindergarten.[46] However, the experts at the ICRC meeting did not generally endorse the notion of according particular importance to medical personnel in the proportionality assessment.[47]

---

[41] Ibid., p. 63.
[42] US Department of Defense, *Law of War Manual*, Washington, D.C., June 2015 (Updated December 2016), §5.12.1.1.
[43] Ibid.
[44] Dinstein, *The Conduct of Hostilities under the Law of International Armed Conflict*, 3rd Edn, pp. 159–60, para. 428(a).
[45] Gisel, *The Principle of Proportionality in the Rules Governing the Conduct of Hostilities under International Humanitarian Law*, p. 63.
[46] Dinstein, *The Conduct of Hostilities under the Law of International Armed Conflict*, 3rd Edn, p. 160, para. 428(b).
[47] Ibid., p. 61.

A Committee of the International Criminal Tribunal for the former Yugoslavia (ICTY) **10.20**
was set up to assess the legality of bombings against the Federal Republic of Yugoslavia by North Atlantic Treaty Organization (NATO) member States in 1999. In its final report, the Committee stated that: 'The main problem with the principle of proportionality is not whether or not it exists but what it means and how it is to be applied. It is relatively simple to state that there must be an acceptable relation between the legitimate destructive effect and undesirable collateral effects.'[48] The Committee usefully identified four questions 'which remain unresolved once one decides to apply the principle of proportionality':

(a) What are the relative values to be assigned to the military advantage gained and the injury to non-combatants and or the damage to civilian objects?
(b) What do you include or exclude in totaling your sums?
(c) What is the standard of measurement in time or space? ...
(d) To what extent is a military commander obligated to expose his own forces to danger in order to limit civilian casualties or damage to civilian objects?

The answers to these questions, the Committee observes rather unhelpfully, 'are not simple'.[49]

Although the US is not a party to the 1977 Additional Protocol I, it has never questioned the customary nature of the proportionality rule.[50] That said, US lawyers tend to have a far more permissive appreciation of the proportionality rule in practice than is the case in most other nations. In 2015, the US Department of Defense asserted in its *Law of War Manual* that 'a *very significant military advantage* would be necessary to justify the collateral death or injury to *thousands* of civilians'.[51] This shocking and legally unsustainable claim was amended and narrowed in the Department's revised *Law of War Manual*, which it issued in December 2016. In coming substantially closer to the state of IHL, it was now affirmed that 'an *extraordinary* military advantage would be necessary to justify an operation posing risks of collateral death or injury to thousands of civilians'.[52] In much smaller-scale operations, Michael Schmitt suggests that it is only **10.21**

---

[48] Final Report to the Prosecutor by the Committee Established to Review the NATO Bombing Campaign Against the Federal Republic of Yugoslavia, 2000, at: https://bit.ly/3l9mNZl, para. 48.

[49] Ibid., para. 49. But the Committee blotted its copy book by declaring that 'bombing a refugee camp is obviously prohibited if its only military significance is that people in the camp are knitting socks for soldiers'. Ibid., para. 48. Refugees knitting socks for soldiers are not, under any credible analysis, directly participating in hostilities. They are civilians protected from attack, pure and simple. By definition, therefore, this scenario is not one that is deserving of a proportionality assessment, because such an attack would be directly targeting civilians and would constitute a war crime.

[50] The US Department of Defense changed its Field Manual in 1976, prior to the formal adoption of the Protocol, to reflect the rule's enunciation in the First Additional Protocol. 1956 FM 27-10 (Change No. 1 1976). The US Department of State referred to the rule in its written statement to the International Court of Justice in connection with the Advisory Opinion on the legality of nuclear weapons. International Court of Justice, *Legality of the Threat or Use of Nuclear Weapons*, Advisory Opinion, Written Statement of the United States, 20 June 1995, at: https://bit.ly/2N5Fd0v, p. 23.

[51] US Department of Defense, *Law of War Manual*, June 2015, §5.12.4 (emphasis added).

[52] US Department of Defense, *Law of War Manual*, June 2015 (Updated December 2016), §5.12.3 (emphasis added).

160   THE RULE OF PROPORTIONALITY

'arguably' disproportionate to attack a 'single low-level soldier far from the battlefield' when 'harm would befall even a few civilians'.[53] In contrast, Solis declares that 'to kill a sniper in a crowded orphanage with a mere hand grenade could easily be a violation of proportionality because of the close presence of so many civilians'.[54]

10.22 Rogers constructs a scenario of a counterattack on an enemy stronghold in a village. If the commander directs his attack at the stronghold, the risk of excessive incidental civilian loss is, he argues, 'minimal'. But if he destroys the whole village, 'there is a much greater risk of infringing the proportionality rule'.[55] He suggests that the following factors should be considered in assessing the legality of a planned attack:

- the military importance of the target
- the density of the civilian population in the target area
- the likely incidental effects of the attack, including the possible release of hazardous substances
- the types of weapon available to attack the target and their accuracy
- whether the defenders are deliberately exposing civilians or civilian objects to risk
- the mode of attack, and
- the timing of the attack, especially in the case of a mixed target.[56]

This serves as a useful guide to a commander conducting a proportionality assessment of a planned attack. Furthermore, the rule applies to 'all those who exercise a degree of control over an attack. In particular, it extends to attack planners, commanders who authorize the attack, and individuals who conduct the operation'.[57]

The war crime of disproportionate attacks

10.23 There is no doubt that intentionally launching a disproportionate attack is not only a violation of IHL, but it may also amount to a war crime. But both the *actus reus* and the *mens rea* elements of this international crime are a matter of dispute. The 'default standard' is set out in Article 85(3) of the Additional Protocol I to which 174 States were party as of 1 May 2022. When the act is committed wilfully, and when it results in death or serious physical or mental injury, it is a war crime to launch an indiscriminate attack affecting the civilian population or civilian objects 'in the knowledge that such attack will cause excessive loss of life, injury to civilians or damage to civilian objects, as defined in Article 57(2)(a)(iii)' of the Protocol.[58]

---

[53] Schmitt, 'International Humanitarian Law and the Conduct of Hostilities', p. 154.
[54] Solis, *The Law of Armed Conflict, International Humanitarian Law in War*, 3rd Edn, p. 232.
[55] Rogers, *Law on the Battlefield*, 3rd Edn, p. 26.
[56] Ibid., p. 27.
[57] Schmitt, 'International Humanitarian Law and the Conduct of Hostilities', p. 155.
[58] Art. 85(3)(b), 1977 Additional Protocol I.

10.24 While the formulation of the war crime in the Protocol is rather clumsy, it clearly identifies the elements of *actus reus* and *mens rea* that constitute the offence. The *actus reus* demands proof that an indiscriminate attack affected the civilian population or civilian objects, and resulted in death or serious physical or mental injury or damage to civilian objects. Under the Protocol, even if the attack impacted on civilian objects, it must also have resulted in death or serious injury. This sets a substantially higher standard than in the primary rule of proportionality in attack in the Protocol.

10.25 The *mens rea* of a disproportionate attack is that it must have been committed wilfully (i.e. deliberately and either with intent that the harm would result, or recklessly as to the risk of the harm occurring), in the knowledge that the attack would cause civilian harm that was excessive when compared to the concrete and direct military advantage anticipated. According to the ICRC commentary on the term 'wilful', the accused 'must have acted consciously and with intent, i.e., with his mind on the act and its consequences, and willing them'. This encompasses the concept of 'recklessness'.[59] Negligence on the part of the accused is not sufficient.

10.26 The intentional launching of a disproportionate attack is a war crime under customary law. But one formulation of the crime in international armed conflict differs from that in non-international armed conflict. The ICRC identifies as a war crime in international armed conflict the launching of an attack 'in the knowledge that such attack will cause incidental loss of civilian life, injury to civilians or damage to civilian objects which would be clearly excessive in relation to the concrete and direct military advantage anticipated'.[60] This standard, reflecting the wording of the Rome Statute, differs materially from that set out in the Additional Protocol I of 1977: the civilian harm must be not just excessive but *clearly* excessive.

10.27 Taken together, these requirements set the bar extremely high for any prosecution, effectively making it highly unlikely that any conviction would be secured. Indeed, potentially only in a scenario where a party destroys an entire village to kill a single sniper[61] would the standard be met in practice. The inclusion of the modifier 'clearly' is justified on the basis that it 'follows more closely the wording' found in the Rome Statute. As Article 10 of the Statute explains, however, nothing in the articulation of the crimes falling under the jurisdiction of the Court 'shall be interpreted as limiting or prejudicing in any way existing or developing rules of international law for purposes other than this Statute'. Indeed, in its 2016 report on its experts meeting on proportionality, the ICRC remarks that: 'Contrary to the IHL standard, the war crime of disproportionate attack under the Rome Statute requires the expected incidental harm

---

[59] ICRC, Commentary on Article 85 of the 1977 Additional Protocol I, 1987, at: http://bit.ly/3ciLeQ9, p. 994, para. 3474.
[60] ICRC, Customary IHL Rule 156: 'Definition of War Crimes', at: http://bit.ly/32HjZb2, (ii) 'Other serious violations of international humanitarian law committed during an international armed conflict', point (ii).
[61] See Dinstein, *The Conduct of Hostilities under the Law of International Armed Conflict*, 3rd Edn, p. 156, para. 418.

162   THE RULE OF PROPORTIONALITY

to be clearly excessive in comparison with the direct and concrete military advantage anticipated.'[62]

10.28   In the context of a non-international armed conflict, the ICRC affirms that the corresponding war crime in customary law is the launching of an indiscriminate attack resulting in death or injury to civilians, 'or an attack in the knowledge that it will cause excessive incidental civilian loss, injury or damage'.[63] Here, the word 'clearly' is omitted, suggesting that the standard for the customary law war crime is lower in a non-international armed conflict than it is in an international armed conflict. It is unclear on what basis this assertion is made, although the African Union has sustained this distinction in its 2014 Protocol for the African Court of Justice and Human Rights (not yet in force).[64] The crime in international armed conflict reflects the wording in the Rome Statute while in non-international armed conflict, the African Union provides for the Court's jurisdiction over the war crime of 'launching an indiscriminate attack resulting in death or injury to civilians, or an attack in the knowledge that it will cause excessive incidental civilian loss, injury or damage'.[65]

10.29   Where, however, agreement is widespread is that the 'reasonable commander' standard is pertinent to determining whether an individual has committed the war crime of a disproportionate attack in any armed conflict. In its judgment in the *Galić* case, an ICTY Trial Chamber stated: 'In determining whether an attack was proportionate it is necessary to examine whether a reasonably well-informed person in the circumstances of the actual perpetrator ... making reasonable use of the information available to him or her, could have expected excessive civilian casualties to result from the attack.'[66]

10.30   The *Galić* case has offered the most extensive discussion of the war crime of launching a disproportionate attack. One of the attacks for which the former commander of Bosnian Serb forces over Sarajevo was convicted was against off-duty soldiers playing a football match. On 1 June 1993, a group of residents of the Dobrinja district in the capital decided to organise a football tournament. The residents looked for a safe place to hold the matches. The football pitch was in the corner of a car park, bounded by six-storey apartment blocks on three sides and by a hill on the fourth side; it was not visible from any point on the Bosnian Serb side of the confrontation line. Some 200 spectators, among whom were women and children, gathered to watch the games.[67] About 15 minutes into the second game, a shell landed among the players in the centre of the pitch.

---

[62] Gisel, *The Principle of Proportionality in the Rules Governing the Conduct of Hostilities under International Humanitarian Law*, p. 54, note 195.

[63] ICRC, Customary IHL Rule 156: 'Definition of War Crimes', (iv) 'Other serious violations of international humanitarian law committed during a non-international armed conflict', point (ii).

[64] Art. 28D(b)(iv), Protocol on Amendments to the Protocol on the Statute of the African Court of Justice and Human Rights; adopted at Malabo, 27 June 2014; not yet in force.

[65] Art. 28D(e)(xviii), Protocol on Amendments to the Protocol on the Statute of the African Court of Justice and Human Rights; and see A. Clapham, *War*, Oxford University Press, Oxford, 2021, p. 493.

[66] ICTY, *Prosecutor v. Galić*, Judgment and Opinion (Trial Chamber I) (Case No. IT-98-29-T), 5 December 2003, para. 58.

[67] Ibid., para. 372.

Eleven young men were on the ground, eight of whom had died instantly. Three players were 'totally dismembered'; only their tracksuits held them together, and many people around the pitch lay on the ground.[68] The referee was hit by shrapnel, sustaining serious injuries in both legs as well as in other parts of his body. A second shell, which landed at almost the same spot within seconds of the first shell, fell in front of a young man and tore his leg off.[69]

10.31 General Galić's defence counsel submitted that the intended target of this attack was a legitimate military objective, arguing, inter alia, that the Bosnian government army had headquarters located close to the car park and that a system of trenches ran only a dozen metres away from that site.[70] In addition, a number of army soldiers were at the football match. The commander of a local brigade acknowledged that off-duty soldiers amounted to around half of the casualties.[71] The Majority of the Trial Chamber nonetheless held that, although the number of soldiers present at the game was significant, an attack on a crowd of approximately 200 people, including numerous children, would clearly be expected to cause incidental loss of life and injuries to civilians excessive in relation to the direct and concrete military advantage anticipated.[72]

10.32 Judge Nieto-Navia dissented from the holding of the Majority in respect of its conclusion of an indiscriminate (disproportionate) attack, both on the basis that it had not been proven beyond a reasonable doubt that the shell was fired by Bosnian Serb forces, and that the foreseeable incidental civilian harm was not excessive compared to the anticipated military advantage.[73] This advantage included the possible targeting of objects as well as personnel that constituted lawful military objectives.

10.33 As noted above, the Statute of the International Criminal Court has set a high threshold for the prosecution of the war crime of a disproportionate attack. Article 8(2)(b)(iv) accords the Court jurisdiction over the war crime of:

> Intentionally launching an attack in the knowledge that such attack will cause incidental loss of life or injury to civilians or damage to civilian objects or widespread, long-term and severe damage to the natural environment which would be clearly excessive in relation to the concrete and direct overall military advantage anticipated.

10.34 The associated elements of crime (with the footnotes in the original text) are as follows:

1. The perpetrator launched an attack.
2. The attack was such that it would cause incidental death or injury to civilians or damage to civilian objects ... and that such death, injury or damage would be

---

[68] Ibid., para. 373.
[69] Ibid., para. 374.
[70] Ibid., para. 382.
[71] Ibid., para. 386.
[72] Ibid., para. 387.
[73] ICTY, *Prosecutor v. Galić*, Judgment and Opinion (Trial Chamber I), Dissenting Opinion of Judge Nieto-Navia, paras. 63–65.

of such an extent as to be clearly excessive in relation to the concrete and direct overall military advantage anticipated.[74]

3. The perpetrator knew that the attack would cause incidental death or injury to civilians or damage to civilian objects ... and that such death, injury or damage would be of such an extent as to be clearly excessive in relation to the concrete and direct overall military advantage anticipated.[75]

4. The conduct took place in the context of and was associated with an international armed conflict.

5. The perpetrator was aware of factual circumstances that established the existence of an armed conflict.

In contradistinction to its formulation in the 1977 Additional Protocol I, damage to civilian objects without accompanying death or injury would be sufficient for the Court potentially to have jurisdiction to prosecute the war crime.

10.35 In its judgment in the *Katanga* case, a Trial Chamber of the Court held that the civilians who fled the safety of a building in the village of Bogoro that had been attacked were killed intentionally. This is despite the fact that civilians and soldiers were fleeing together and that the soldiers 'at that moment may have constituted a military target for the attackers'. The Trial Chamber's conclusion was that 'the loss of human life ensuing from the shots fired at the group of fleeing persons was excessive in relation to the military advantage which the attackers could have anticipated, specifically given that the ... soldiers were already fleeing'. By 'shooting indiscriminately at fleeing persons', the attackers, the Chamber said, 'showed scant regard for the fate of the civilians among the ... soldiers in the mêlée and knew that their death would occur in the ordinary course of events'. The Chamber thus found that they 'intended to cause their death'.[76]

10.36 The attack had occurred in the context of a non-international armed conflict. It appears therefore that the Court will treat what appears to be a disproportionate attack as one that involves directly attacking civilians. This latter war crime exists under the Rome Statute in non-international armed conflict.[77] The Trial Chamber convicted Germain Katanga, by majority, of acting as an accessory to an '[a]ttack against a civilian population as such or against individual civilians not taking direct part in hostilities, as a war crime under article 8(2)(e)(i) of the Statute'.[78]

---

[74] 'The expression "concrete and direct overall military advantage" refers to a military advantage that is foreseeable by the perpetrator at the relevant time. Such advantage may or may not be temporally or geographically related to the object of the attack. The fact that this crime admits the possibility of lawful incidental injury and collateral damage does not in any way justify any violation of the law applicable in armed conflict. It does not address justifications for war or other rules related to *jus ad bellum*. It reflects the proportionality requirement inherent in determining the legality of any military activity undertaken in the context of an armed conflict.'

[75] '[T]his knowledge element requires that the perpetrator make the value judgement as described therein. An evaluation of that value judgement must be based on the requisite information available to the perpetrator at the time.'

[76] International Criminal Court, *Prosecutor v. Germain Katanga*, Judgment (Trial Chamber II), para. 865.

[77] Art. 8(2)(e)(i), Rome Statute.

[78] International Criminal Court, *Prosecutor v. Germain Katanga*, Judgment (Trial Chamber II), p. 659.

10.37 In her dissenting minority opinion, Judge Christine Van den Wyngaert criticised the holding of the majority in the Trial Chamber. Although she miscast the conviction as being one of attacking civilians in a situation of international armed conflict, certain of her arguments would resonate no matter the classification. 'Civilians were killed in that attack', she acknowledged, but she saw 'no evidence establishing, beyond reasonable doubt, that it was an attack against the civilian population'.[79] Some of her arguments were forensic in nature—the lack of birth certificates or other identification documentation for the alleged 130 or more of those killed—while others were evidentiary ('for a majority of cases, the Chamber only has the word of one witness').[80] Specifically on the shooting of those fleeing civilians, however, she complained that the Majority did not

> indicate how many civilians there were among the fleeing ... soldiers. Yet, this is an essential piece of information, without which it seems impossible to form any opinion about the disproportionality of the action. Second, the Majority—unable to identify who fired at the fleeing people and from what distance—is not in a position to know whether those who fired the lethal shots knew that there were civilians among the group of fleeing ... soldiers.[81]

One is left rather with the perception that some on the bench in the Court's judgment in the *Katanga* case did not rigorously reflect the dictates of the Statute and the core tenets of international criminal law in confirming the verdict. The judgment at trial was, however, final, as three months later, in June 2014, both the Defence and Prosecution withdrew their notice of appeal.[82]

Disproportionate attacks affecting the natural environment

10.38 The natural environment is ordinarily a civilian object.[83] Thus, an attack directed at the natural environment is also an attack directed against a civilian object. That said, an area of land may be a lawful military objective, for instance on the basis of its use or location by a party to an armed conflict.[84] Article 35(3) of the Additional Protocol I further stipulates that: 'It is prohibited to employ methods or means of warfare which are intended, or may be expected, to cause widespread, long-term and severe damage to the natural environment.' Cymie Payne suggests that IHL protection of the environment

---

[79] Ibid., Minority Opinion of Judge Christine Van den Wyngaert, at: https://bit.ly/3ckojnv, para. 175.
[80] Ibid., paras. 177–78.
[81] Ibid., para. 184.
[82] International Criminal Court, 'Katanga Case', undated but accessed 1 March 2021 at: http://bit.ly/30xCMHf.
[83] As Dinstein observes, although the natural environment is not formally designated as a civilian object, unless it or its constituent elements are a military objective, it is protected from attack. Dinstein, *The Conduct of Hostilities under the Law of International Armed Conflict*, 3rd Edn, p. 237, para. 641.
[84] Art. 52(2), 1977 Additional Protocol I.

has 'developed from the principle of protection of civilians, and it has similar motives and goals'.[85]

10.39 The *Harvard Manual on International Law Applicable to Air and Missile Warfare* states that the destruction of the natural environment 'carried out wantonly is prohibited'.[86] In the accompanying commentary on the rule, it is stated that: 'Despite the lack of a generally recognized definition of the term "natural environment", there is evidence in State practice of the customary character of the prohibition laid down in this Rule.'[87] But while no universally accepted definition of the 'natural environment' exists in IHL, the ICRC explains that the term refers to the 'system of inextricable interrelations between living organisms and their inanimate environment'.[88] In fact, Payne suggests that the lack of an agreed definition 'should not pose a serious problem' as the main elements, broadly defined, are well known: 'soil, land, water, air, the living and non-living elements, and physical processes'.[89]

10.40 What is clear that the protection of the environment from the effects of armed conflict has risen in importance in recent decades, and is an element of the proportionality equation insofar as the natural environment is a civilian object. While the US has not 'accepted' the provisions on environmental protection set out in the 1977 Additional Protocol I,[90] the ICRC believes that certain rules have crystallised as customary law. Thus, Rule 43 of its Customary Law Study provides as follows:

A. No part of the natural environment may be attacked, unless it is a military objective.
B. Destruction of any part of the natural environment is prohibited, unless required by imperative military necessity.
C. Launching an attack against a military objective which may be expected to cause incidental damage to the environment which would be excessive in relation to the concrete and direct military advantage anticipated is prohibited.[91]

---

[85] C. Payne, 'Protection of the Natural Environment', Chap. 9 in B. Saul and D. Akande (eds.), *The Oxford Guide to International Humanitarian Law*, Oxford University Press, Oxford, 2020, p. 205.

[86] Program on Humanitarian Policy and Conflict Research at Harvard University, *HPCR Manual on International Law Applicable to Air and Missile Warfare*, 1st Edn, Cambridge University Press, New York, 2013, Rule 88.

[87] *Commentary on the Harvard Manual on International Law Applicable to Air and Missile Warfare*, 2010, p. 206, para. 1.

[88] ICRC, Commentary on Article 35 of the 1977 Additional Protocol I, 1987, at: https://bit.ly/3dMJqBg, para. 1451.

[89] Payne, 'Protection of the Natural Environment', p. 208.

[90] US Department of Defense, *Law of War Manual*, June 2015, §6.10.3.1, citing US Response to the ICRC Customary IHL Study: 'France and the United States repeatedly have declared that Articles 35(3) and 55 of AP I, from which the Study derives the first sentence of rule 45, do not reflect customary international law.' John B Bellinger, III, Legal Adviser, Department of State, and William J Haynes II, General Counsel, Department of Defense, Letter to Dr. Jacob Kellenberger, President, ICRC, Regarding Customary International Humanitarian Law Study, 3 November 2006, reprinted in *International Legal Materials*, Vol. 46 (2007), p. 514, at p. 521.

[91] ICRC, Customary IHL Rule 43: 'Application of General Principles on the Conduct of Hostilities to the Natural Environment', at: http://bit.ly/3vfV1iI.

These rules apply in all armed conflict in the view of the ICRC.[92] In its 1996 Advisory Opinion on the Legality of the Threat or Use of Nuclear Weapons, the International Court of Justice had stated that: 'States must take environmental considerations into account when assessing what is necessary and proportionate in the pursuit of legitimate military objectives. Respect for the environment is one of the elements that goes into assessing whether an action is in conformity with the principles of necessity and proportionality.'[93]

10.41 It is also significant that the Rome Statute includes the war crime of intentionally launching an attack in the knowledge that such attack will cause widespread, long-term, and severe damage to the natural environment 'which would be clearly excessive in relation to the concrete and direct overall military advantage anticipated'.[94] As noted above, the Court's jurisdiction over this war crime is, however, limited to international armed conflict. In the application of the rule, the United Kingdom Ministry of Defence's *Manual of the Law of Armed Conflict* stipulates that the provisions in the Additional Protocol I (and by extension also the Rome Statute) 'do not automatically prevent certain types of military objectives such as nuclear submarine or supertankers from being legitimate targets nor do they automatically prevent the use of certain means of warfare such as herbicides or chemical agents. The effects of attacking these targets or using these means must be considered'.[95]

10.42 The formulation in the 1977 Additional Protocol I and the Rome Statute is of environmental damage that is widespread, long-term, *and* severe, that is to say, the elements of the prohibition are cumulative. The polluting effects of hostilities in the short or medium term (days, months, or years) will not meet the definition. During the negotiation of Article 35 of the Protocol, the Rapporteur from the Working Group that discussed the provision stated:

> The time or duration required (i.e., long-term) was considered by some to be measured in decades. References to twenty or thirty years were made by some representatives as being a minimum. Others referred to battlefield destruction in France in the First World War as being outside the scope of the prohibition. The Biotope report states that 'Acts of warfare which cause short-term damage to the natural environment, such as artillery bombardment, are not intended to be prohibited by the article', and continues by stating that the period might be perhaps for ten years or more. However, it is impossible to say with certainty what period of time might be involved. It appeared to be a widely shared assumption that battlefield damage incidental to conventional warfare would not normally be proscribed by this provision.[96]

---

[92] Ibid.
[93] International Court of Justice, *Legality of the Threat or Use of Nuclear Weapons*, Advisory Opinion, 8 July 1996, para. 30.
[94] Art. 8(2)(b)(iv), Rome Statute.
[95] United Kingdom Ministry of Defence, *The Manual of the Law of Armed Conflict*, Oxford University Press, Oxford, 2005, para. 5.29.3 (notes omitted).
[96] Cited in ICRC, Commentary on Article 35 of the 1977 Additional Protocol I, 1987, para. 1454.

168   THE RULE OF PROPORTIONALITY

10.43 At the time of writing, there had been no prosecution before the International Criminal Court for disproportionate harm caused to the environment in international armed conflict. It is hard to see how even a creative approach by the Court could serve to convict a person for corresponding harm in non-international armed conflict, at least until the war crime of attacking civilian objects is added to the list of crimes within its jurisdiction when committed in such conflicts.[97]

10.44 In 2019, the International Law Commission transmitted Draft Principles on the Protection of the Environment in relation to Armed Conflicts to the UN General Assembly for its consideration.[98] The Draft Principles were the result of six years' work by the Commission. Draft Principle 13(3) provides that: 'No part of the natural environment may be attacked, unless it has become a military objective.' This principle 'underlines the inherently civilian nature of the natural environment'.[99] The Commission further notes in its commentary on paragraph 3 of Draft Principle 13 that it is 'based on the first paragraph of rule 43 of the ICRC study on customary international humanitarian law'.[100]

10.45 According to Draft Principle 14: 'The law of armed conflict, including the principles and rules on distinction, proportionality, military necessity and precautions in attack, shall be applied to the natural environment, with a view to its protection.' In its commentary on the Draft Principle, the Commission explained that: 'As the environment is often indirectly rather than directly affected by armed conflict, rules relating to proportionality are of particular importance in relation to the protection of the natural environment in armed conflict.'[101] Draft Principle 15 stipulates that: 'Environmental considerations shall be taken into account when applying the principle of proportionality and the rules on military necessity.' The Commission makes no distinction between international and non-international armed conflict for the purpose of the Draft Principles.

10.46 More recently, Philippe Sands QC and Dior Fall Sow have been co-chairing an international expert drafting panel on the legal definition of 'ecocide' as a potential—and distinct—international crime. Launched with preparatory work in November 2020, the panel has been convened by the Stop Ecocide Foundation at the request of parliamentarians from governing parties in Sweden.[102] The draft definition of the crime was published by the panel in June 2021: 'unlawful or wanton acts committed with knowledge

---

[97] Only in international armed conflict is the war crime of 'intentionally directing attacks against civilian objects, that is, objects which are not military objectives' within the Court's jurisdiction. Art. 8(2)(b)(ii), Rome Statute.
[98] International Law Commission (ILC), 'Text of the draft principles on protection of the environment in relation to armed conflicts, adopted by the Commission on first reading', Chap. IV, Section C, in UN doc. A/74/10, 2019, at: https://bit.ly/3qAI7bj.
[99] ILC, Commentary, para. 10, on Draft Principle 13.
[100] ILC, Commentary, para. 12, on Draft Principle 13.
[101] ILC, Commentary, para. 7, on Draft Principle 14.
[102] Stop Ecocide Foundation, 'Top international lawyers to draft definition of "Ecocide"', undated but accessed 1 March 2021, at: http://bit.ly/3rHyrx5.

that there is a substantial likelihood of severe and widespread or long-term damage to the environment being caused by those acts'.[103] The drafters hope that the crime will be proposed and eventually adopted as an amendment to the Rome Statute.[104]

Concluding remarks and outlook

The rule of proportionality *in bello* desperately needs interpretive clarification, as this chapter has sought to demonstrate. In particular, what amounts to 'excessive' civilian harm during a planned military operation needs far better elucidation. The solution, we have suggested, is to be found not in conflating disproportionate attacks with indiscriminate attacks, much less with direct attacks on civilians. The convening of a broad-based expert group to look at vectors in the application of the rule of proportionality in attack, especially in the course of sieges, seems long overdue, and could complement the ongoing work of States and civil society on the use of explosive weapons in populated areas. At the time of writing, the Political Declaration issued by the Irish Department of Foreign Affairs merely recalled at one point the prohibition of disproportionate attacks, but no more.[105] In the ICRC's view, use in populated areas of explosive weapons 'with a wide impact area' should be avoided, 'due to the significant likelihood of indiscriminate effects and despite the absence of an express legal prohibition for specific types of explosive weapons'.[106] In its latest report on the issue, published in January 2022, the ICRC did not seek to define what amounts to a wide impact area.

10.47

---

[103] H. Siddique, 'Legal Experts Worldwide Draw Up "Historic" Definition of Ecocide', *The Guardian*, 22 June 2021, at: https://bit.ly/3wDMWUu.

[104] 'Is It Time for "Ecocide" to Become an International Crime?', *The Economist*, 28 February 2021, at: http://econ.st/3crovS9.

[105] Department of Foreign Affairs of Ireland, *Political Declaration on Strengthening the Protection of Civilians from the Humanitarian Consequences arising from the use of Explosive Weapons in Populated Areas*, Final, May 2022, at: https://bit.ly/3zvdOcK, para. 2.3.

[106] ICRC, *Explosive Weapons With Wide Area Effects: A Deadly Choice in Populated Areas*, Geneva, January 2022, at: https://bit.ly/3H6VBo9, p. 22.

11
Precautions in Attack and Defence

Introduction

11.1 The requirement imposed upon attacker and defender to take all feasible precautions to protect civilians is a vital underpinning of the principles of distinction and proportionality in attack. The overriding aim of such precautions is to minimise civilian harm, either by seeking to ensure that few if any civilians are not present when an attack strikes or by limiting the ambient effects of an attack to a military objective. The level of protection afforded by the salient precautionary rules under international humanitarian law (IHL) is, however, quite limited. Humanitarian considerations bend to military utility to a large degree under the rules laid down in the 1977 Additional Protocol I.[1]

11.2 As the International Committee of the Red Cross (ICRC) recalls, these provisions—specifically those governing precautions in attack—were the subject of protracted and difficult negotiations in the diplomatic conference that adopted the Protocol, and the text that emerged was 'the fruit of laborious compromise'.[2] No similar provisions on precautionary measures are incorporated in the 1977 Additional Protocol II,[3] although generically the duty to take precautions in attack is reflected in customary IHL and applies to all armed conflicts.[4] The rules are summarised in Table 11.1.

11.3 The nature of precautions in attack (set out in Article 57 of the 1977 Additional Protocol I) involve, in particular, a duty to seek to verify that an attack is targeting military objectives; selecting weapons that are likely to minimise the risks to civilians and civilian objects, and then using them in a manner that does so, including by timing an attack to minimise the risk of civilian harm; and issuing an effective warning to the civilian population of an impending or future attack. The prohibition on launching a disproportionate attack, a rather incongruous provision in the context of Article 57,[5] is the

---

[1] Protocol Additional to the Geneva Conventions of 12 August 1949, and relating to the Protection of Victims of International Armed Conflicts (Protocol I); adopted at Geneva, 8 June 1977; entered into force, 7 December 1978 (hereinafter, 1977 Additional Protocol I).

[2] ICRC Commentary on Article 57 of the 1977 Additional Protocol I, 1987, para. 2184.

[3] Protocol Additional to the Geneva Conventions of 12 August 1949, and relating to the Protection of Victims of Non-International Armed Conflicts (Protocol II); adopted at Geneva, 8 June 1977; entered into force, 7 December 1978 (hereinafter, 1977 Additional Protocol II).

[4] 'All feasible precautions must be taken to avoid, and in any event to minimize, incidental loss of civilian life, injury to civilians and damage to civilian objects.' ICRC Customary IHL Rule 15: 'Principle of Precautions in Attack', at: http://bit.ly/2m6mCnj.

[5] Art. 57(2)(a)(iii), 1977 Additional Protocol I.

Table 11.1 Summary of Precautionary Measures

Rule	AP I	Customary status (IAC)	AP II	Customary status (NIAC)
Do everything feasible to verify that a target is lawful	Art. 57(2)(a)(i)	Yes	No	Yes
Take all feasible precautions in the choice of means and methods of attack to minimise civilian harm	Art. 57(2)(a)(ii)	Yes	No	Yes
Warn civilians of an imminent attack, unless circumstances do not permit	Art. 57(2)(c)	Yes	No	Yes
Keep civilians away from military objectives to the maximum extent feasible	Art. 58(1)(a)	Yes	No	Yes
Locate military objectives away from populated areas to maximum extent feasible	Art. 58(1)(b)	Yes	No	Yes

corollary of Article 51(5)(b) of the Additional Protocol I, whose interpretation and application were discussed in the previous chapter.

11.4 Precautions 'against the effects of attacks' (set out in Article 57)—typically concerning, in practice, defensive actions and positions—include a duty to 'the maximum extent feasible' to 'endeavour' to remove civilians from the vicinity of military objectives; to not locate military objectives within or near densely populated areas; and, more generically, to take 'other necessary precautions' to protect civilians.[6]

11.5 The chapter discusses, in turn, precautionary measures in attack and in defence. The typically low threshold of the duties imposed—to take 'all feasible' measures, so not 'all possible' measures, much less 'all necessary' measures—demonstrates how little is legally required of the parties to an armed conflict. While the term 'feasible' is not

---

[6] Art. 58(1), 1977 Additional Protocol II.

11.6 Furthermore, ostensibly the failure to take precautionary measures does not, per se, render an attack indiscriminate or otherwise unlawful.[8] This is so under the Additional Protocol I, even though a general duty is set out in the provisions on precautionary measures, obligating that the conduct of military operations take 'constant care' to 'spare' civilians and civilian objects.[9] It is also noteworthy that a disproportionate attack is a grave breach when it is launched 'in the knowledge' that it will cause excessive loss of life, injury to civilians or damage to civilian objects, 'as defined in' Article 57(2)(a)(iii).

formally defined in the Protocol, several States followed Italy's lead in interpreting 'feasible' upon its ratification as meaning that which is 'practicable or practically possible, taking into account all circumstances ruling at the time, including humanitarian and military considerations'.[7] This renders the concept intentionally vague, with a large measure of discretion entrusted to the parties to an armed conflict to determine what is, or is not, feasible in the circumstances as they perceive them.

11.7 In its 2019 judgment at trial in the *Ntaganda* case, the International Criminal Court held that the war crime of directly attacking civilians in the Rome Statute may include 'attacks that are launched without taking necessary precautions to spare the civilian population or individual civilians'.[10] In 2003, the International Criminal Tribunal for the former Yugoslavia (ICTY), in its judgment at trial in *Galić*, had indicated that in the case of a crime against humanity, whether the civilian population was the primary object of the attack could be determined by a number of factors including 'the extent to which the attacking force may be said to have complied or attempted to comply with the precautionary requirement of the laws of war'.[11]

Precautions in attack

The duty to verify a target is a lawful military objective

11.8 The principle of distinction dictates that the parties to an armed conflict 'at all times distinguish between the civilian population and combatants and between civilian objects and military objectives' and that they 'direct their operations only against military

---

[7] Statements of Understanding of Italy, 27 February 1986. Other States that followed this approach include Australia, Belgium, Canada, Egypt, Germany, The Netherlands, and Spain.

[8] At one point in its judgment in *Galić*, referred to further below, the Trial Chamber of the International Criminal Tribunal for the former Yugoslavia (ICTY) had held that if the Bosnian Serb forces had 'launched two shells into a residential neighbourhood at random, without taking feasible precautions to verify the target of the attack, they would have unlawfully shelled a civilian area'. ICTY, *Prosecutor v. Galić*, Judgment and Opinion (Trial Chamber I) (Case No. IT-98-29-T), 5 December 2003, para. 387. It is, however, the randomness of the shelling rather than the failure to take precautions that renders the attack unlawful.

[9] Art. 57(1), 1977 Additional Protocol I.

[10] International Criminal Court, *Prosecutor v. Bosco Ntaganda*, Judgment (Trial Chamber VI) (Case No. ICC-01/04-02/06), 8 July 2019, para. 921.

[11] ICTY, *Prosecutor v. Galić*, Judgment and Opinion (Trial Chamber I), para. 142.

objectives'.[12] Respect for this 'basic' rule, which applies in all armed conflicts,[13] requires, in turn, that the parties must seek to ensure that the persons or objects they are targeting are lawful under IHL. Of course, no commander 'could ever be absolutely sure that an objective to be attacked was a military objective unless he inspected it himself which, of course, is quite impracticable'.[14]

Article 57 of the 1977 Additional Protocol I sets the standard to be met for such an identification of a lawful military objective. It stipulates that those who plan or decide upon an attack must 'do everything feasible to verify that the objectives to be attacked are neither civilians nor civilian objects and are not subject to special protection but are military objectives' as defined in Article 52(2) of the Protocol; and it must further be established that it is not otherwise prohibited under the Protocol to attack them. This is both a factual and a legal obligation, requiring that, in the case of an object, its nature and use be first established as well as any contribution to military action; while in the case of a person, his or her status, function, and participation (if any) in the hostilities must similarly be determined.[15] Elsewhere, the Protocol stipulates that in 'case of doubt whether a person is a civilian, that person shall be considered to be a civilian'.[16] The United States (US) does not consider this obligation to be of a customary nature: 'Under customary international law, no legal presumption of civilian status exists for persons or objects, nor is there any rule inhibiting commanders or other military personnel from acting based on the information available to him or her in doubtful cases'.[17]

11.9

The US attack on a Médecins sans Frontières (MSF) hospital in 2015 demonstrates how serious a failure to verify the target can be. On 3 October 2015, at around 2 o'clock in the morning, a US Air Force AC-130 gunship attacked MSF's Trauma Centre in the city of Kunduz in northern Afghanistan. It is estimated that the airstrikes lasted at least one hour.[18] Doctors and other medical staff were reportedly shot by the aircraft's gunners while running to safety in a different part of the compound, while MSF was repeatedly calling the US forces in Kabul to plead with them to call off the attack. According to MSF's internal report on the air strike, the total number of dead was 'known to be at least 30, including: 10 known patients, 13 known staff, and 7 more bodies that were burnt beyond recognition'.[19] Subsequently, it was reported that 42 people had been killed and 37 wounded.[20]

11.10

---

[12] Art. 48, 1977 Additional Protocol I.
[13] ICRC Customary IHL Rule 1: 'The Principle of Distinction between Civilians and Combatants', at: http://bit.ly/32rIER0; and Rule 7: 'The Principle of Distinction between Civilian Objects and Military Objectives', at: http://bit.ly/2G8to2w.
[14] A. P. V. Rogers, *Law on the Battlefield*, 2nd Edn, Manchester University Press, Manchester, 2004, p. 97.
[15] S. Casey-Maslen with S. Haines, *Hague Law Interpreted: The Conduct of Hostilities under the Law of Armed Conflict*, Hart Publishing, Oxford, 2018, p. 199.
[16] Art. 50(1), 1977 Additional Protocol I.
[17] US Department of Defense, *Law of War Manual*, June 2015 (Updated December 2016), Washington, D.C., 2016, §5.4.3.2.
[18] MSF, 'Initial MSF Internal Review: Attack on Kunduz Trauma Centre, Afghanistan', November 2015, p. 7.
[19] Ibid., pp. 10, 12.
[20] I. Ali, 'US Strike on Afghan Hospital in 2015 Not a War Crime: Pentagon', *Reuters Canada*, 29 April 2016, at: https://reut.rs/3mplwjw.

11.11 The US investigation into the tragedy concluded that a combination of factors had caused both the ground force commander and the air crew to believe mistakenly that the air crew was firing on the intended target, an insurgent-controlled site approximately 400 metres away from the MSF Trauma Centre. Remarkably, as Brian Cox recalled in a blog post five years later, 'the factual record indicates that the aircrew observed the target compound, which was in fact the MSF trauma center, for 68 minutes before initiating the attack'.[21]

11.12 General Joseph Votel, the commander of US Central Command, said that the investigation had concluded that a number of personnel had failed to comply with the rules of engagement and the law of armed conflict. 'However, the investigation did not conclude that these failures amounted to a war crime.'[22] General Votel did, however, reveal that the official investigation had identified 16 personnel 'whose conduct warranted consideration for appropriate administrative or disciplinary action, including a general officer'. The administrative measures adopted ranged from 'suspension and removal from command, letters of reprimand, formal counseling and extensive retraining'.[23]

The duty to choose and use weapons and methods of attack with a view to minimising civilian harm

11.13 The 1977 Additional Protocol I also dictates that those who plan or decide upon an attack 'shall take all feasible precautions in the choice of means and methods of attack with a view to avoiding, and in any event to minimizing, incidental loss of civilian life, injury to civilians and damage to civilian objects'.[24] This concerns both the weapons that are used in an attack and the manner in which they are used. And as the Protocol also provides elsewhere, in any armed conflict, the right of the Parties to the conflict to choose methods or means of warfare is not unlimited.[25] This means that parties to an armed conflict are restricted by applicable treaty and customary rules in the weapons they may lawfully use, as well as in the way they may lawfully use them. Furthermore, according to the ICRC, military necessity 'cannot justify any derogation from rules which are drafted in a peremptory manner'.[26] Thus, an inherently indiscriminate weapon may never be used. Customary international law also prohibits

---

[21] B. L. Cox, 'Five Years On: Military Accountability and the Attack on the MSF Trauma Center in Kunduz', *Just Security*, 3 October 2020, at: https://bit.ly/3mjZGhg.
[22] 'News Transcript: Department of Defense Press Briefing by Army General Joseph Votel, commander, US Central Command, Press Operations, Army General Joseph Votel, commander, US Central Command', 29 April 2016.
[23] Cox, 'Five Years On: Military Accountability and the Attack on the MSF Trauma Center in Kunduz'.
[24] Art. 57(2)(a)(ii), 1977 Additional Protocol I.
[25] Ibid., Art. 35(1).
[26] ICRC, Commentary on Article 35 of the 1977 Additional Protocol I, 1987, para. 1405.

the use of weapons that are of a nature to cause superfluous injury or unnecessary suffering.[27]

But the precautionary measures laid down in the Additional Protocol I go beyond the confines of these customary prohibitions on weapons to call for greater restraint to the benefit of the civilian population. Even if the use of a particular weapon is not prohibited under IHL, or even if its specific use in the prevailing circumstances is not unlawful, Article 57 and customary international law is calling for all feasible precautions to minimise civilian harm. This may mean using an alternative weapon or a different manner or timing of an attack.

11.14

There is no obligation on parties to an armed conflict to use precision-guided munitions.[28] But it may still be feasible to use a precision-guided munition rather than gravity ordnance in order to reduce the risk of incidental civilian harm. Remotely piloted aircraft (drones) possess a real-time video link, the quality of whose imaging has increased manifold over the last 20 years. Drones can be used to fire precision-guided missiles or bombs once it has been verified that civilians are not close to the strike zone. It is clear that for some armed groups, the fulfilment of this obligation will be more challenging as their strategic options are more limited. As noted by Sassòli: 'how can (armed groups) choose the means causing the least damage when they have at their disposal only one weapon capable of reaching the enemy?'[29]

11.15

The obligation on each party to an armed conflict to use weapons that minimise the risk of civilian harm was at issue in the *Santo Domingo* case before the Inter-American Court of Human Rights in 2012. In its judgment, the Court found that a violation of fundamental human rights had occurred by applying the customary duty to take precautions to the non-international armed conflict between Colombia and the non-State armed group, the Colombian Revolutionary Armed Forces (FARC).[30] The case concerned the dropping by the Colombian Air Force of a Second World War-era cluster bomb containing six explosive submunitions on the hamlet of Santo Domingo on 13 December 1998. The attack killed 17 civilians, including 6 children, and injured 27 others, including 9 children. The Court held that given the lethal capacity and limited precision of the device used, its launch over the hamlet was contrary to the duty of precautions in attack.[31] Based in particular on this finding, the Court found a violation of the right to life of those who were killed and a violation of the prohibition of inhumane treatment with respect to the injured.[32]

11.16

---

[27] ICRC, Customary IHL Rule 70: 'Weapons of a Nature to Cause Superfluous Injury or Unnecessary Suffering', at: http://bit.ly/2CyqlPC.
[28] See, infra, para. 12.46.
[29] M. Sassòli, *International Humanitarian Law Rules, Controversies, and Solutions to Problems Arising in Warfare*, Edward Elgar Publishing, Cheltenham, 2019, para. 8.349, p. 373.
[30] Inter-American Court of Human Rights, *Santo Domingo massacre v. Colombia*, Judgment (Preliminary Objections, Merits and Reparations), 30 November 2012.
[31] Ibid. para. 229.
[32] Ibid. para. 230.

The duty to give an effective warning to civilians of an attack

11.17 The 1907 Hague Regulations had required that the officer in command of an attacking force should, 'before commencing a bombardment, except in cases of assault, do all in his power to warn the authorities'.[33] The duty under the 1977 Additional Protocol I goes considerably further, obligating the provision of 'an effective advance warning' of 'attacks which may affect the civilian population'. This is so, 'unless circumstances do not permit'.[34] As the ICRC observe: 'In the case of bombardment by long-distance projectiles or bombs dropped from aircraft, giving warning may be inconvenient when the element of surprise in the attack is a condition of its success.'[35]

11.18 In the 2014 Gaza conflict, on numerous occasions the Israel Defence Forces (IDF) used a controversial warning technique known as 'roof knocking'. This typically involved use of a low-yield or even non-explosive munition, which was dropped on the roof of a building with a view to warning the inhabitants that a major strike against the building was imminent. In some instances, this was accompanied by text or phone warnings to the inhabitants. Israel believes that the procedure used by the IDF was 'highly effective, preventing many civilian injuries and deaths' during the conflict.[36]

11.19 The United Nations (UN) Commission of Inquiry on the 2014 conflict noted in its report that four buildings had been totally destroyed in the latter days of hostilities following use of this procedure without consequent loss of life.[37] But it expressed considerable concern in relation to a number of other attacks. The Commission stated that sometimes the warnings were not understood; that the direction of safety for escaping civilians was often unclear; or the time given for evacuation between the warning and the actual strike was insufficient.[38]

11.20 The technique was again employed in the 2021 conflict in Gaza, and it was again criticised. An air force officer, who spoke to Agence France-Presse on condition of anonymity, said in May 2021 that 1,000 strikes had hit the enclave, but that a warning had not been issued in all cases. 'When it's infrastructure, we can use this technique, but not if eliminating terrorists. We fire a small, empty missile to knock on the roof and make the civilians understand they must leave. As soon as we have the most assurances possible that the building has been evacuated, we fire.'[39] Amnesty International noted that: 'In many cases, key elements of effective warning have been missing, including timelines, informing civilians where it is safe to flee, and providing safe passage and

---

[33] Art. 26, 1907 Hague Regulations.
[34] Art. 57(2)(c), 1977 Additional Protocol I.
[35] ICRC, Commentary on Article 57 of the 1977 Additional Protocol I.
[36] Israeli Ministry of Foreign Affairs, *IDF Conduct of Operations during the 2014 Gaza Conflict*, at: https://bit.ly/3ybru9Q, p. 37.
[37] Report of the detailed findings of the independent commission of inquiry established pursuant to Human Rights Council resolution S-21/1, UN doc. A/HRC/29/CRP.4, 22 June 2015, paras. 210–11.
[38] Ibid., paras. 235–38.
[39] AFP, '"Roof Knocking": Israel Warning System under Scrutiny in Gaza Conflict', *France24*, 20 May 2021, at: https://bit.ly/3B4pke9.

sufficient time to flee before an attack. Amnesty also noted that it had documented cases of civilians being killed or injured by the missiles used to warn civilians of an impending attack 'in previous Israeli military operations'.[40]

Israeli media defended the practice, noting that 'Israel could have taken the easy way out and attacked without phone calls or warning strikes. But it didn't.'[41] An article in *The Jerusalem Post* in March 2021 noted that IDF personnel who called Palestinians at risk

11.21

> had a standard text they read in Arabic that went something like this: 'How are you? Is everything okay? This is the Israeli military. We need to bomb your home and we are making every effort to minimize casualties. Please make sure that no one is nearby since in five minutes we will attack.' The line would then go dead.

In 'every case', the report stated, 'an Israeli drone would be hovering above, watching what was happening in the home and nearby. Once it saw people running out of the building, IAF headquarters would give the fighter pilot or attack helicopter the green light to drop their bomb'.[42]

In May 2021, the Human Rights Council held a special session on 'the Grave Human Rights Situation in the Occupied Palestinian Territory, including East Jerusalem' and adopted a resolution under which it decided to 'urgently establish an ongoing, independent, international commission of inquiry to investigate, in the occupied Palestinian territory, including East Jerusalem, and in Israel, all alleged violations and abuses of international human rights law leading up and since 13 April 2021'. The commission of inquiry is mandated to report to the Human Rights Council and to the General Assembly on an annual basis as from June 2022 and September 2022, respectively.[43] The Commission, which is chaired by former UN High Commissioner for Human Rights, Navi Pillay, was expected to again consider the practice of roof knocking in its report on compliance with international law during the conflict in Gaza in May 2021.

11.22

Precautions in defence

The 1977 Additional Protocol I also lays down precautions 'against the effects of attacks' in its Article 58—what the ICRC terms 'passive precautions'.[44] These obligations

11.23

---

[40] Ibid.
[41] Y. Katz, 'How the IDF Invented "Roof Knocking", the Tactic that Saves Lives in Gaza', *The Jerusalem Post*, 25 March 2021, at: https://bit.ly/3z9OVlb.
[42] Ibid.
[43] Office of the High Commissioner for Human Rights (OHCHR), 'The United Nations Independent International Commission of Inquiry on the Occupied Palestinian Territory, including East Jerusalem, and in Israel', at: https://bit.ly/3DbvPhh.
[44] ICRC, Commentary on Article 58 of the 1977 Additional Protocol I, 1987, at: https://bit.ly/3ze7BAC, para. 2241.

constitute customary law, at the least in international armed conflict.[45] But there is also good evidence to suggest that they also apply in toto in non-international armed conflict. As the ICRC has noted, the obligation to take all feasible precautions to protect the civilian population and civilian objects against the effects of attacks was included in the draft of Additional Protocol II but was dropped at the last moment. While the Additional Protocol II does not explicitly require such precautions, Article 13(1) requires that 'the civilian population and individual civilians shall enjoy general protection against the dangers arising from military operations'. It would, the ICRC observes, 'be difficult to comply with this requirement without taking precautions against the effects of attack'.[46]

11.24 Such precautions are especially important in the case of defensive positions, for instance in a city or populated area that is besieged or under direct assault. One important precautionary measure is the duty to remove civilians from the proximity of military objectives; a second concomitant obligation is to locate military objectives away from populated areas. These are discussed in turn.

The duty to remove civilians from the vicinity of military objectives

11.25 The 1977 Additional Protocol I requires that the Parties to the conflict, 'to the maximum extent feasible ... endeavour to remove the civilian population, individual civilians and civilian objects under their control from the vicinity of military objectives'.[47] This obligation is limited insofar as it does not require a party to a conflict 'to arrange its armed forces and installations in such a way as to make them conspicuous to the benefit of the adversary'.[48]

11.26 The duty to remove civilians from the vicinity of military objectives should be implemented in such a way as to protect the most vulnerable or the most at risk, such as children, mothers, the elderly, or the sick.[49] This is especially important in a besieged area. Certain objects such as buildings cannot be removed and civilians are therefore endangered as a result of being in the vicinity of them, when they constitute military objectives.[50]

11.27 The siege of Mosul, Iraq's second largest city, constituted a nine-month-long effort in 2016–17 by Iraqi government forces with international support, especially from US forces, to overwhelm the Islamic State forces controlling the city. The Battle for Mosul was the first large-scale combat operation involving US forces since the 2003 invasion

---

[45] Eritrea Ethiopia Claims Commission, *Partial Award, Western Front, Aerial Bombardment and Related Claims*, Eritrea's Claims 1, 3, 5, 9–13, 14, 21, 25 & 26, The Hague, 19 December 2005, para. 95.
[46] ICRC, Customary IHL Rule 22: 'Principle of Precautions against the Effects of Attacks', at: https://bit.ly/2UQXRg4.
[47] Art. 58(a), 1977 Additional Protocol I.
[48] ICRC, Commentary on Article 58 of the 1977 Additional Protocol I, 1987, para. 2246.
[49] Ibid., para. 2247.
[50] Ibid., para. 2250.

of Iraq.[51] Iraqi special forces first entered Mosul on 1 November 2016. But progress slowed as troops encountered fierce resistance from Islamic State, including snipers, suicide bombers, and shelling.[52] By late March 2017, Lieutenant-General Stephen Townsend, the top US-led coalition commander, was describing the fight as 'the most significant urban combat to take place since World War II'.[53]

11.28 Following the recapture of the eastern part of the city in January 2017, thousands of people remained in the densely populated west of the city, with food supplies reported to be very low and clean drinking water in short supply. The United Nations claimed that almost half of all the casualties in Mosul during the offensive in the east of the city had been civilians. The Iraqi government had asked civilians to remain in place to prevent large-scale displacement.[54] By late May, however, the United Nations was warning that civilians were not only enduring severe shortages of food, water, medicine, and electricity, but Islamic State militants were also shooting those who tried to escape.[55] Some would remain until the end of the assault to stay with infirm family members.[56] By the time the siege was over, in July, many thousands of civilians had died.

11.29 The threat to civilians from the forces attacking the city was sharply exacerbated by the atrocities committed within. Islamic State used civilians as both cannon fodder and as shields. The UN High Commissioner for Human Rights referred to the group's 'depraved, cowardly strategy', seeking to use 'the presence of civilians to render certain points, areas or military forces immune from military operations, effectively using tens of thousands of women, men and children as human shields'.[57] Islamic State fighters also shot at and killed civilians as they tried to flee the city. In their joint report on the siege, information gathered by the United Nations 'strongly suggests that international crimes may have been perpetrated' by Islamic State in Mosul.[58]

The duty to locate military objectives away from densely populated areas

11.30 Article 58 of the 1977 Additional Protocol I also obligates a party to an armed conflict 'to the maximum extent feasible … [to] avoid locating military objectives within

---

[51] Maj. T. D. Arnold and Maj. Nicolas Fiore, 'Five Operational Lessons from the Battle for Mosul', *Military Review*, January–February 2019, at: https://bit.ly/3kmFQRE, p. 58.
[52] BBC, 'How the Battle for Mosul Unfolded', 10 July 2017.
[53] J. Michaels, 'Iraqi Forces in Mosul See Deadliest Urban Combat Since World War II', *USA Today*, 29 March 2017, at: https://bit.ly/3klGxea.
[54] 'Coalition "Failing to Protect Civilians" in Mosul', Forces.net, 28 March 2017, at: https://bit.ly/3zJdu8q.
[55] 'UN Warns Mosul Civilians in Grave Danger', Forces.net, 27 May 2017, at: https://bit.ly/2VhrOpN.
[56] J. Verini, *They Will Have to Die Now: Mosul and the Fall of the Caliphate*, OneWorld Publications, London, 2019, p. 87.
[57] S. Nebehay, 'Islamic State Using Tens of Thousands as Human Shields in Mosul: U.N.', *Reuters*, 28 October 2016, at: https://reut.rs/2UK9GVy.
[58] UN Assistance Mission for Iraq (UNAMI) and OHCHR, *Report on the Protection of Civilians in the context of the Ninewa Operations and the retaking of Mosul City, 17 October 2016–10 July 2017*, Baghdad, 2017, available at: https://bit.ly/3OSzEwt, p. 2.

or near densely populated areas'. This covers both permanent and mobile objectives. Authorities should endeavour—already in peacetime—to find places away from densely populated areas to site permanent objectives. For example, as the ICRC suggests, a barracks or a store of military equipment or ammunition should not be built in the middle of a town.[59] As regards mobile objectives, care should be taken, in particular during the conflict, to avoid placing troops, equipment, or transports in densely populated areas.[60]

11.31 Optimistically, the organisation suggests that: 'In both cases it is likely that governments are sufficiently concerned with sparing their own population and that they will therefore act in the best interests of that population.'[61] But, as Dinstein observes: 'Some intermingling of civilians/civilian objects with combatants/military objectives is virtually inevitable.'[62] In any event, pursuant to Article 51(7) of the Protocol, the failure of a defender to comply with this obligation does not affect the attacker's duty to take active precautions nor does it affect the application of the rule of proportionality in attack.[63]

Concluding remarks and outlook

11.32 The notion of precautionary measures has not been accorded great attention in both case law and academic commentary. Yet with the increasing importance of siege warfare, as discussed further in Chapter 14, this will need to change. The ongoing discussion on the use of explosive weapons in populated areas (EWIPA) is one aspect of this.[64] Thus, the UN Secretary-General has called on all parties to conflict—State armed forces and non-State armed groups alike—to avoid using explosive weapons with wide-area effects in populated areas and has called on States to develop an international political declaration as one means of addressing the humanitarian impact of such use.[65] This would certainly be an important step forward. But the need for other precautionary measures to be taken by both attacker and defender is also of ever greater importance.

11.33 Jonathan Horowitz puts particular emphasis on the importance of information gathering to enable the commander to make an informed decision prior to launching an attack. 'Most importantly', he notes, 'this information should be up-to-date and should not rely on outdated data from old census figures or city maps, especially when

---

[59] ICRC, Commentary on Article 58 of the 1977 Additional Protocol I, 1987, para. 2251.
[60] Ibid., para. 2252.
[61] Ibid., para. 2253.
[62] Y. Dinstein, *The Conduct of Hostilities under the Law of International Armed Conflict*, 3rd Edn, Cambridge University Press, Cambridge, 2016, p. 174, para. 467.
[63] M. N. Schmitt, 'International Humanitarian Law and the Conduct of Hostilities', Chap. 7 in B. Saul and D. Akande (eds.), *The Oxford Guide to International Humanitarian Law*, Oxford University Press, Oxford, 2020, p. 169.
[64] See, supra, para. 10.47.
[65] UN Office for the Coordination of Humanitarian Affairs (OCHA), 'Explosive Weapons in Populated Areas', at: https://bit.ly/2UFDzXf.

information that is more accurate can be collected.'[66] He refers with approval to the ICTY's *Final Report to the Prosecutor by the Committee Established to Review the NATO Bombing Campaign Against the Federal Republic of Yugoslavia*, which declared that: 'A military commander must set up an effective intelligence gathering system to collect and evaluate information concerning potential targets.'[67]

Accurate and timely information is certainly a critical means to enhance precautionary measures. But with a low legal standard both for the implementation of such measures and a lack of clarity as to the implementation of the principles of distinction and proportionality in attack, an authoritative interpretation, and probably also changes to the law are urgently needed. In 2000, the ICTY Committee set up to assess NATO's 1999 bombing campaign against Yugoslavia over the issue of Kosovo declared that: 'If precautionary measures have worked adequately in a very high percentage of cases then the fact they have not worked well in a small number of cases does not necessarily mean they are generally inadequate.'[68] That is true as a statement of theory. Much practice, sadly, would tell a different story.

11.34

---

[66] J. Horowitz, 'Joint Blog Series: Precautionary Measures in Urban Warfare: A Commander's Obligation to Obtain Information', ICRC Joint Blog Series, 10 January 2019, at: https://bit.ly/383cQqT.
[67] ICTY Committee, 'Final Report to the Prosecutor by the Committee Established to Review the NATO Bombing Campaign Against the Federal Republic of Yugoslavia', 2000, at: https://bit.ly/3l9mNZl, para. 29.
[68] Ibid.

12
Prohibited Weapons

Introduction

12.1 This chapter discusses the treatment of weapons under the two Additional Protocols of 1977.[1] The term 'weapon' is employed on numerous occasions in the 1977 Additional Protocol I[2] but is not found in the 1977 Additional Protocol II. It is not defined in the Protocols.

12.2 Where prohibitions are imposed on weapons in the two Protocols these are general in nature. Whether the rules in the Protocol apply directly to weapons of mass destruction, in particular nuclear weapons, is disputed. As States were unable to agree upon the prohibition of specific weapons during the negotiation of the 1977 Additional Protocol I, this task was handed over to the United Nations (UN), under whose auspices States adopted in 1980 the so-called Convention on Certain Conventional Weapons.[3] A notable innovation in the 1977 Additional Protocol I, set out in Article 36, obligates States Parties to determine the legality of any new weapon prior to its acquisition by any means.

12.3 The key rules governing weapons set out in the two 1977 Additional Protocols are summarised in Table 12.1. The six rules in the Table are addressed in turn in this chapter.

12.4 Before turning to a discussion of the rules, however, we will first discuss the definition of a weapon under international law. While there is no generally agreed definition of what constitute either weapons or arms, a 'weapon' is widely understood as a term that is broader in scope than is an 'armament'.[4] The following has been proposed by one of the authors as a working definition for a weapon:

> Any device constructed, adapted, or used to kill, harm, disorient, incapacitate, or affect a person's behaviour against their will, or to damage or destroy buildings or *matériel*.

---

[1] Protocol Additional to the Geneva Conventions of 12 August 1949, and relating to the Protection of Victims of International Armed Conflicts (Protocol I); adopted at Geneva, 8 June 1977; entered into force, 7 December 1978 (hereinafter, 1977 Additional Protocol I); Protocol Additional to the Geneva Conventions of 12 August 1949, and relating to the Protection of Victims of Non-International Armed Conflicts (Protocol II); adopted at Geneva, 8 June 1977; entered into force, 7 December 1978 (hereinafter, 1977 Additional Protocol II).

[2] In Arts. 13(2)(a), 25, 28(3), 35(2), 36, 56(5), 59(2)(a), 60(3)(a), 65(3), 67(1)(d), 1977 Additional Protocol I.

[3] Convention on Prohibitions or Restrictions on the Use of Certain Conventional Weapons which May Be Deemed to Be Excessively Injurious or to Have Indiscriminate Effects; adopted at Geneva, 10 October 1980; entered into force, 2 December 1983.

[4] Arms effectively denote weapons and weapons systems which are produced in a factory, especially when destined for the military. S. Casey-Maslen and T. Vestner, *A Guide to International Disarmament Law*, Routledge, Abingdon, 2019, para. 131.

Table 12.1 Summary of Weapons Law Rules

Rule	AP I	Customary status (IAC)	AP II	Customary status (NIAC)
Choice of weapons not unlimited	Art. 35(1)	Yes	No	Yes
Use of weapons causing superfluous injury prohibited	Art. 35(2)	Yes	No	Yes
Use of indiscriminate weapons prohibited	Art. 51(4)(b) and (c)	Yes	No	Yes
Weapons causing severe, long-term damage to the environment prohibited	Art. 35(3)	Yes (arguably)	No	Yes (arguably)
Legality of weapons must be verified	Art. 36	Yes (arguably)	No	Yes (arguably)
Martens clause	Art. 1(2)	Yes	No	Yes (arguably)

A weapon acts through the application of kinetic force or of other means, such as the transmission of electricity, the diffusion of chemical substances or biological agents or sound, or the direction of electromagnetic energy. The term 'weapon' includes offensive cyber operations that damage or interrupt the normal operation of computer systems and networks or result in physical harm to people or objects.[5]

This definition will be used for the purpose of this chapter without prejudice to any definition that is subsequently adopted by States under international law.

The right of parties to use weapons is not unlimited

Under Article 35(1) of the 1977 Additional Protocol I: 'In any armed conflict, the right of the Parties to the conflict to choose methods or means of warfare is not unlimited.' This is one of the longest standing rules of international humanitarian law (IHL). Thus, in the Regulations annexed to both the 1899 Hague Convention II and then again in the 1907 Hague Convention IV, it is stipulated that: 'The right of belligerents to adopt means of injuring the enemy is not unlimited.'[6] This followed a provision in the Oxford Manual of 1880 whereby: 'The laws of war do not recognize in belligerents an unlimited

12.5

---

[5] S. Casey-Maslen (ed.), *Weapons Under International Human Rights Law*, Cambridge University Press, Cambridge, 2014, p. xx.

[6] Art. 22, Regulations concerning the Laws and Customs of War on Land annexed to Convention (II) with Respect to the Laws and Customs of War on Land; adopted at The Hague, 29 July 1899; entered into force, 4 September 1900; and Art. 22, Regulations concerning the Laws and Customs of War on Land annexed to 1907 Hague Convention (IV) respecting the Laws and Customs of War on Land; adopted at The Hague, 18 October 1907; entered into force, 26 January 1910.

liberty as to the means of injuring the enemy.'[7] In an unopposed resolution in 1968, the UN General Assembly reaffirmed more broadly that 'the right of the parties to a conflict to adopt means of injuring the enemy is not unlimited'.[8] This formulation applies to all armed conflicts, whether international or non-international in character.

12.6 The rule holds that parties to an armed conflict are restricted by applicable treaty and customary rules in the weapons they may lawfully use, as well as in the way they may lawfully use them. As the International Committee of the Red Cross (ICRC) has duly observed: 'Military necessity cannot justify any derogation from rules which are drafted in a peremptory manner'.[9] Thus, for example, use of lawful weapons must comply with the rules of distinction and proportionality in attack, while inherently indiscriminate weapons and those of a nature to cause superfluous injury or unnecessary suffering may never be used. Thus, if a party to an armed conflict has only prohibited weapons in its arsenal, the rule whereby parties to a conflict do not have an unlimited choice of weapons makes it clear that such unlawful weapons may not be used. This is so, even if the likely result will be military defeat.[10]

12.7 In its 1996 Advisory Opinion on the *Legality of the Threat or Use of Nuclear Weapons*, the International Court of Justice (ICJ) reaffirmed that States 'do not have unlimited freedom of choice of means in the weapons they use'.[11] But the Court then, incorrectly, limited the principle to the rule prohibiting use of weapons that cause unnecessary suffering to combatants. This error of law notwithstanding, the general rule that the right of the parties to an armed conflict to use weapons is not unlimited is unquestionably one with customary law status.[12] The United Kingdom, for example, observes in its Manual on the Law of Armed Conflict that it is a 'general principle' which 'is firmly rooted in the law of armed conflict'.[13] In its own Manual, the French Ministry of Defence notes that the rule applies in 'every armed conflict',[14] while Canada affirms that it is of 'general application'.[15]

---

[7] Art. 4, *The Laws of War on Land*, Manual published by the Institute of International Law (Oxford Manual), adopted by the Institute of International Law at Oxford, 9 September 1880, available at: https:// bit.ly/3vtDYd8.
[8] UN General Assembly Resolution 2444 (XXIII), adopted on 19 December 1968 by 111 votes to 0, para. 1.
[9] ICRC, Commentary on the 1977 Additional Protocols, 1987, para. 1405.
[10] Thus, in rejecting Milan Martić's appeal against conviction for war crimes for attacks on Zagreb in early May 1995 using cluster munitions, the Appeals Chamber of the International Criminal Tribunal for the former Yugoslavia (ICTY) stated that: 'Whether the RSK had another artillery system at its disposal is irrelevant as regards the inquiry into whether the Trial Chamber erred when it considered the M-87 Orkan to be an indiscriminate weapon.' ICTY, *Prosecutor v. Martić*, Judgment (Appeals Chamber) (Case No. IT-95-11-A), 8 October 2008, para. 248.
[11] ICJ, *Legality of the Threat or Use of Nuclear Weapons*, Advisory Opinion, 8 July 1996 (hereinafter, '1996 Nuclear Weapons Advisory Opinion'), para. 78.
[12] This is despite the fact that the ICRC did not include the rule in its list of 161 customary IHL rules published in 2005.
[13] United Kingdom (UK) Ministry of Defence, *Joint Service Manual of the Law of Armed Conflict*, Joint Service Publication 383, 2004, para. 2.1, note 1 (hereinafter, 'UK Manual of the Law of Armed Conflict').
[14] 'Dans tout conflit armé, le choix des méthodes et moyens de combats n'est pas illimité.' French Ministry of Defence, *Manuel de Droit des Conflits Armés*, Ministère de la Défense, Paris, 2012, p. 44 (hereinafter, 'French Manual of the Law of Armed Conflict').
[15] Canada Ministry of National Defence, *Manual of the Law of Armed Conflict at the Operational and Tactical Levels*, Joint Doctrine Manual, Doc. B-GJ-005-104/FP-021, Ottawa, 2001, pp. 1–2 (hereinafter, 'Canadian 2001 Manual of the Law of Armed Conflict').

12.8 The rule may also possess the peremptory status attributed to it by the ICRC in its commentary of 1987. It is certainly one of the basic principles of IHL, with the implications that has for *jus cogens* status.[16] For Canada, for instance, it is one of the fundamental principles of the law of armed conflict.[17] And in the view of the United States (US) Department of Defense, accepting that there are legal limits that govern the conduct of hostilities 'is a prerequisite for the existence and operation of the law of war in the way that the principle of *pacta sunt servanda* ... provides a necessary foundation for treaties to exist and operate as instruments that are legally binding on States'.[18]

Weapons of a nature to cause superfluous injury

12.9 Article 35(2) of the 1977 Additional Protocol I provides that: 'It is prohibited to employ weapons, projectiles and material and methods of warfare of a nature to cause superfluous injury or unnecessary suffering.' The superfluous injury rule (to use a convenient short form), which protects those fighting in armed conflict, was first found in hard international law in Article 23(e) of the Regulations annexed to the 1899 Hague Convention II. It was derived from Article 13(e) of the abortive 1874 Brussels Declaration,[19] although its inspiration derives initially from the US Government's 1863 Lieber Code, which instructed the Union forces during the American Civil War: 'Whoever intentionally inflicts additional wounds on an enemy already wholly disabled, or kills such an enemy, or who orders or encourages soldiers to do so, shall suffer death, if duly convicted.'[20] It was then reflected indirectly in the 1868 Saint Petersburg Declaration,[21] whose preamble observed that since the only 'legitimate object' States should endeavour to accomplish through warfare is 'to weaken the military forces of the enemy', this objective 'would be exceeded by the employment of arms which uselessly aggravate the sufferings of disabled men, or render their death inevitable'. As Germany's Ministry of Defence has written, the Saint Petersburg Declaration 'codified the customary principle that the use of weapons that cause unnecessary suffering is prohibited, which is still valid today'.[22]

---

[16] See, e.g., T. Kleinlein, 'Jus Cogens as the "Highest Law"? Peremptory Norms and Legal Hierarchies', *Netherlands Yearbook of International Law*, Vol. 46 (2015), pp. 173–210, at p. 197.

[17] Canadian 2001 *Manual of the Law of Armed Conflict*, para. 203.

[18] US Department of Defense, *Law of War Manual*, Washington, D.C., June 2015 (Updated December 2016) (hereinafter, 'USDOD December 2016 *Law of War Manual*'), §2.6.2.1.

[19] Project of an International Declaration concerning the Laws and Customs of War; adopted at Brussels, 27 August 1874; never entered into force. According to Article 9(a) of the 1880 Oxford Manual, it was forbidden to 'employ arms, projectiles, or materials of any kind calculated to cause superfluous suffering, or to aggravate wounds'.

[20] Art. 71, Instructions for the Government of Armies of the United States in the Field, General Order No. 100, promulgated by the US Department of War on 24 April 1863 (hereinafter, '1863 Lieber Code').

[21] Declaration Renouncing the Use, in Time of War, of Explosive Projectiles Under 400 Grammes Weight; adopted at Saint Petersburg, 11 December 1868; entered into force the same day.

[22] German Ministry of Defence, *Law of Armed Conflict Manual*, Joint Service Regulation (ZDv) 15/2, Berlin, 2013, para. 119 and see also para. 401.

12.10 Under Article 23(e) of the 1899 Hague Regulations, it is especially prohibited to 'employ arms, projectiles, or material of a nature to cause superfluous injury'. The French original and authentic version of the provision states that: 'il est notamment 'interdit' d'employer des armes, des projectiles ou des matières propres à causer des maux superflus'. This French text was unamended in the 1907 Hague Regulations. In the English version of the corresponding provision in the 1907 Hague Regulations, however, the formulation changed to the following: 'To employ arms, projectiles, or material *calculated* to cause *unnecessary suffering*'.[23] The two changes are explained by an attempt to render better the meaning in the French original. First, it was felt that the phrase 'propres à' should be construed so as to encapsulate a notion of intent. In fact, this is a poor rendition of the more objective French standard, which means 'likely to' or 'liable to'.[24] Secondly, the reference to unnecessary suffering sought to broaden the prohibited harm to beyond the purely physical. In the 1977 Additional Protocol I, the formulation adopts the more objective standard 'of a nature to' and combines superfluous injury and unnecessary suffering in the alternative, amounting to a broad norm.[25]

12.11 Thus, the superfluous injury rule prohibits the use of weapons whose innate characteristics are such that they would inflict gratuitous harm, which is to say, injury or suffering beyond what is necessary to render a fighter *hors de combat*.[26] Injury describes both identifiable wounds and other physical harm to limbs, organs, senses, or other parts of the body, including through burns. Such injuries may render a person temporarily incapacitated or with a permanent disability, such as through loss of sight or hearing, or a soldier may become a single, double, triple or even quadruple amputee. Suffering denotes primarily pain, but also extends to encompass severe psychological distress.[27] The ICRC has argued that a relevant factor in establishing whether a weapon causes superfluous injury or unnecessary suffering 'is the inevitability of serious permanent disability'.[28]

---

[23] Emphasis added.
[24] *Oxford Hachette French Dictionary*.
[25] In Article 3(3) of the 1996 Protocol on Protocol on Prohibitions or Restrictions on the Use of Mines, Booby-Traps and Other Devices as Amended on 3 May 1996 (Amended Protocol II), annexed to the Convention on Prohibitions or Restrictions on the Use of Certain Conventional Weapons which May Be deemed to Be Excessively Injurious or to Have Indiscriminate Effects (with Protocols I, II and III); adopted at Geneva, 10 October 1980; entered into force, 2 December 1983: 'It is prohibited in all circumstances to use any mine, booby-trap or other device *which is designed or of a nature* to cause superfluous injury or unnecessary suffering' (emphasis added). The words 'is designed' were added at the behest of an idiosyncratic academic on the Italian delegation.
[26] In its Advisory Opinion on the Legality of the Threat or Use of Nuclear Weapons, the ICJ defined unnecessary suffering as 'a harm greater than that unavoidable to achieve legitimate military objectives'. ICJ 1996 Nuclear Weapons Advisory Opinion, para. 78. This principle does not concern the indiscriminate nature of any weapon, as is sometimes averred. See H. Duffy, *The 'War on Terror' and the Framework of International Law*, 2nd Edn, Cambridge University Press, Cambridge, 2015, p. 376. Hayashi suggests that harm must be 'clearly excessive' in relation to the military advantage sought, but this sets the threshold too high. N. Hayashi, 'General Principles of International Law', Chap. 4 in D. Fleck (ed.), *The Handbook of International Humanitarian Law*, 4th Edn, Oxford University Press, Oxford, 2021, Section 4.02.
[27] See, e.g., Y. Dinstein, *The Conduct of Hostilities under the Law of International Armed Conflict*, 3rd Edn, Cambridge University Press, Cambridge, 2016, p. 74.
[28] ICRC, Customary IHL Rule 70: 'Weapons of a Nature to Cause Superfluous Injury or Unnecessary Suffering', at: http://bit.ly/2CyqlPC.

12.12 The US Department of Defense believes the test to be used in applying the rule to any given weapon is 'whether the suffering caused by the weapon provides no military advantage or is otherwise clearly disproportionate to the advantage reasonably expected from the use of the weapon'.[29] This is, however, a very narrow understanding of the rule. The UK Ministry of Defence believes rather that: 'The correct criterion is whether the use of a weapon is of a nature to cause injury or suffering greater than that required for its military purpose'.[30] For Germany, means and methods of warfare cause superfluous injury or unnecessary suffering 'if the expected impairment does not serve any military purpose or if injuries or suffering are caused by the effects of weapons or projectiles that are not necessary to neutralise the adversary forces'.[31] But while there are differences in the expression of the test in State practice, it is clear that a balancing is required of the military advantage from the use of the weapon and its expected humanitarian effects. As Boothby has observed, 'both adjectives, "unnecessary" and "superfluous", are comparative, not absolute, concepts'.[32]

12.13 The prohibition of weapons causing superfluous injury is one of the very few rules of IHL that protects combatants while they are fighting. Thus, despite occasional suggestions to the contrary, the rule is not intended for the direct protection of civilians (unless of course they are participating directly in hostilities).[33] Precisely which weapons are of a nature to cause superfluous injury or unnecessary suffering is not the subject of consensus among States in their practice or doctrine, nor between commentators.[34] Indeed, two authorities even argued in 2001 that the rule is 'too vague to produce by itself a great many practical results'. They further noted that States 'have not been known to lightly decide unilaterally to discard a weapon, once introduced into their arsenals, because it is considered to cause unnecessary suffering'.[35]

12.14 The superfluous injury rule is undoubtedly of customary status.[36] It is a 'cardinal principle' of IHL according to the International Court of Justice.[37] The UK Ministry of Defence terms it a guiding principle,[38] while the US Department of Defense considers it to be one of the two fundamental prohibitions in customary international law that apply to all weapons during armed conflict (although it frames the prohibition as one on the use of weapons 'calculated to cause superfluous injury').[39] According to the ICRC, the superfluous injury rule is expressed simply in customary law as follows: 'The

---

[29] USDOD December 2016 *Law of War Manual*, para. 6.6.3.
[30] UK *Manual of the Law of Armed Conflict*, para. 6.2.
[31] German *Manual of the Law of Armed Conflict*, para. 402.
[32] W Boothby, *Weapons and the Law of Armed Conflict*, 1st Edn, Oxford University Press, Oxford, 2009, p. 62.
[33] S. Casey-Maslen with S. Haines, *Hague Law Interpreted: The Conduct of Hostilities under the Law of Armed Conflict*, Hart Publishing, Oxford, 2018, pp. 22, 208.
[34] Ibid., p. 209.
[35] F. Kalshoven and L. Zegveld, *Constraints on the Waging of War: An Introduction to International Humanitarian Law*, 3rd Edn, ICRC, Geneva, 2001, pp. 41–42.
[36] ICRC, Customary IHL Rule 70: 'Weapons of a Nature to Cause Superfluous Injury or Unnecessary Suffering'.
[37] ICJ, 1996 Nuclear Weapons Advisory Opinion, para. 78.
[38] UK *Manual of the Law of Armed Conflict*, para. 6.1.
[39] USDOD December 2016 *Law of War Manual*, para. 6.4.1.

188 PROHIBITED WEAPONS

use of means and methods of warfare which are of a nature to cause superfluous injury or unnecessary suffering is prohibited.'[40]

12.15 The use of weapons of a nature to cause superfluous injury is also identified as a war crime under the Rome Statute of the International Criminal Court.[41] The Court, however, only has possible future jurisdiction for the war crime of 'employing weapons, projectiles and material and methods of warfare which are of a nature to cause superfluous injury or unnecessary suffering' during an international armed conflict. Even in such a case, jurisdiction is dependent on a specific weapon being included in an annex to the Statute.[42] This had not occurred at the time of writing. The Statute of the International Criminal Tribunal for the former Yugoslavia (ICTY) included jurisdiction for the war crime of the 'employment of poisonous weapons or other weapons calculated to cause unnecessary suffering'.[43] No prosecution of this crime occurred during the life of the Tribunal.[44]

12.16 The prohibition is also inscribed as a war crime in numerous military manuals and domestic criminal jurisdictions. China's 1946 Law Governing the Trial of War Criminals provides that 'employment of inhuman weapons' constitutes a war crime.[45] In Nicaragua, it is a crime under military law for any soldier to use or order the use of weapons 'designed to cause unnecessary suffering or superfluous injury'.[46] In Rwandan law, a war crime is defined as encompassing the use in an armed conflict of 'poisonous weapons or other weapons calculated to cause unnecessary suffering'.[47] Spain's Military Criminal Code sanctions 'any soldier who uses, or orders the use of, means or methods of combat which are prohibited or destined to cause unnecessary suffering or superfluous injury'.[48] The US 1996 War Crimes Act treats violations of Article 23(e) of the 1907 Hague Regulations as potential war crimes.[49]

12.17 In its commentary, published in 1987, on Article 35(2) of the 1977 Additional Protocol I, the ICRC asserted that any use of the following weapons would be unlawful under the superfluous injury rule:

---

[40] ICRC, Customary IHL Rule 70: 'Weapons of a Nature to Cause Superfluous Injury or Unnecessary Suffering'.
[41] Art. 8(2)(b)(xx), Rome Statute of the International Criminal Court; adopted at Rome, 17 July 1998; entered into force, 1 July 2002.
[42] Under Article 8(2)(b)(xx), the jurisdiction of the Court is limited to 'such weapons, projectiles and material and methods of warfare [that] are the subject of a comprehensive prohibition and are included in an annex to th[e] Statute, by an amendment in accordance with the relevant provisions set forth in articles 121 and 123'.
[43] Art. 3(a), Statute of the International Tribunal for the Prosecution of Persons Responsible for Serious Violations of International Humanitarian Law Committed in the Territory of the Former Yugoslavia since 1991, approved by UN Security Council Resolution 827, adopted by unanimous vote in favour on 25 May 1993. See also ICTY, *Prosecutor v. Tadić*, Decision on the Defence Motion for Interlocutory Appeal on Jurisdiction (Appeals Chamber) (Case No. IT-94-1), 2 October 1995, para. 127.
[44] S. O'Connor, 'Nuclear Weapons and the Unnecessary Suffering Rule', in G. Nystuen and others (eds.), *Nuclear Weapons under International Law*, Cambridge University Press, Cambridge, 2014, pp. 128–47, at p. 135.
[45] Art. 3(13), China Law Governing the Trial of War Criminals, 1946.
[46] Art. 51, 1996 Nicaragua Military Penal Code.
[47] Art. 10(1), Rwanda Law Repressing the Crime of Genocide, Crimes against Humanity and War Crimes, 2003.
[48] Art. 70, Spain Military Criminal Code, 1985.
[49] S. 2441(c)(2), US 1996 War Crimes Act.

- explosive bullets
- projectiles filled with glass
- bullets which easily expand or flatten in the human body
- poison and poisoned weapons
- weapons containing any substance intended to aggravate a wound
- asphyxiating or deleterious gases
- bayonets with a serrated edge and lances with barbed heads.[50]

This list is largely uncontentious aside, perhaps, from the inclusion of expanding ammunition.[51] The ICRC also claimed in its 1987 commentary that 'hunting shotguns are the object of some controversy, depending on the nature of the ammunition and its effect on a soft target'.[52]

In its subsequent study of customary IHL, published in 2005, the ICRC stated that a customary law prohibition it identified on the use of blinding laser weapons was 'inspired by the consideration that deliberately causing permanent blindness in this fashion amounted to the infliction of superfluous injury or unnecessary suffering'.[53] In support of this assertion, it cited the declaration made by Sweden upon adoption in 1995 of Protocol IV to the 1980 Convention on Certain Conventional Weapons, which outlawed the use of lasers specifically designed to blind.[54] Also of note is the position of a number of governments during the negotiation of the 1995 Protocol IV, whereby they would have preferred to also see incorporated in the text the prohibition of blinding as a method of warfare.[55] The US has accepted the treaty prohibition and is a State Party to the 1995 Protocol IV. It has, however, used 'dazzling' lasers in situations of armed conflict, notably at checkpoints in Afghanistan and Iraq.[56]

12.18

---

[50] ICRC, Commentary on the 1977 Additional Protocols, para. 1419.

[51] The United States may perhaps lay claim to persistent objector status to a customary prohibition of the use of expanding ammunition in armed conflict. The legal situation is complicated because such ammunition is routinely used by many police forces against their own citizens in law enforcement operations. New Zealand argues in its new manual on the law of armed conflict that 'match-grade' ammunition, which has a small aperture in the nose, is not caught by the IHL prohibition, as the aim of the opening is to enhance the stability of the bullet in flight, not to promote its expansion upon entering the body. New Zealand, *Manual of Armed Forces Law, Vol. 4: Law of Armed Conflict*, 2019, para. 7.6.3. It further avers that 'using a soft nosed bullet to kill a terrorist in a crowded market is not a war crime because it does not uselessly aggravate the suffering of the terrorist; rather it usefully does so'. Ibid., para. 7.6.5, note 69. 'Nevertheless', Solis observes, 'internationally it is widely agreed that hollow-point bullets are prohibited'. Solis, *The Law of Armed Conflict, International Humanitarian Law in War*, 3rd Edn, p. 49.

[52] ICRC, Commentary on the 1977 Additional Protocols, para. 1419.

[53] ICRC, Customary IHL Rule 70. An amendment to the Rome Statute, adopted by States Parties in 2017, accords jurisdiction to the International Criminal Court over the war crime of using blinding laser weapons: 'Employing laser weapons specifically designed, as their sole combat function or as one of their combat functions, to cause permanent blindness to unenhanced vision, that is to the naked eye or to the eye with corrective eyesight devices'. The Amendment first entered into force on 2 April 2020 in regard to Luxembourg one year after the deposit of its instrument of ratification, in accordance with Article 121(5) of the Statute. As of 1 May 2022, ten States had ratified the amendment: Czechia, Croatia, Latvia, Luxembourg, the Netherlands, New Zealand, Norway, Romania, Slovakia, and Switzerland.

[54] Additional Protocol to the Convention on Prohibitions or Restrictions on the Use of Certain Conventional Weapons which may be deemed to be Excessively Injurious or to have Indiscriminate Effects (Protocol IV, entitled Protocol on Blinding Laser Weapons); adopted at Vienna, 13 October 1995; entered into force, 30 July 1998.

[55] The ICRC cites statements in this regard by Australia, Austria, Belgium, Denmark, Ecuador, Finland, France, Germany, Iran, Mexico, the Netherlands, Norway, Poland, Romania, the Russian Federation, and Sweden.

[56] See, e.g., USDOD December 2016 *Law of War Manual*, para. 6.15.1.2 and note 385.

12.19 Incendiary weapons[57] are also controversial when used against military personnel. The ICRC customary IHL study identified a rule whereby the 'anti-personnel use of incendiary weapons is prohibited, unless it is not feasible to use a less harmful weapon to render a person *hors de combat*'.[58] It further affirmed that State practice establishes the rule as a norm of customary international law applicable in both international and non-international armed conflicts.[59] The evidence for this assertion is, however, rather scant. The US firmly rejects the prohibition in international law. In the December 2016 edition of its Law of War Manual, the US Department of Defense affirms instead that: 'The use of incendiary weapons is permissible, but subject to certain restrictions in order to reduce the risk of incidental harm to civilians.'[60] The UK Ministry of Defence holds that, although incendiary weapons 'can cause severe injury to personnel, their use is lawful provided the military necessity for their use outweighs the injury and suffering which their use may cause'.[61] The French Ministry of Defence states that incendiary weapons 'are not prohibited by the law of armed conflict but their use is controlled'.[62]

12.20 Given the challenges in identifying which weapons were of a nature to cause superfluous injury or unnecessary suffering, in the mid-1990s, the ICRC established within its headquarters in Geneva the SIrUS project (an acronym for Superfluous Injury or Unnecessary Suffering). The aim of the Project, which was led by Dr. Robin Coupland along with key lawyers in the Legal Division, was to elaborate criteria that could be applied to any weapon to make an evidence-based determination of whether or not its use was lawful under the superfluous injury rule. The ICRC identified four alternative criteria by which a weapon's legality could be determined when applied to the foreseeable effects of weapons used against people:

- Specific disease, specific abnormal physiological state, specific abnormal psychological state, specific and permanent disability, or specific disfigurement (Criterion 1), or
- Field mortality of more than 25 per cent or a hospital mortality of more than 5 per cent (Criterion 2), or
- Grade 3 wounds as measured by the Red Cross wound classification (Criterion 3), or
- Effects for which there is no well-recognised and proven treatment (Criterion 4).[63]

---

[57] The Protocol III on Incendiary Weapons defining incendiary weapon as 'any weapon or munition which is primarily designed to set fire to objects or to cause burn injury to persons through the action of flame, heat, or combination thereof, produced by a chemical reaction of a substance delivered on the target.' Art. 1(1), Protocol on Prohibitions or Restrictions on the Use of Incendiary Weapons (Protocol III) annexed to the CCW; adopted at Geneva, 10 October 1980; entered into force, 2 December 1983.

[58] ICRC, Customary IHL Rule 85: 'The Use of Incendiary Weapons against Combatants', at: http://bit.ly/2O4AJ73.

[59] Ibid.

[60] USDOD December 2016 *Law of War Manual*, para. 6.14.

[61] UK *Manual on the Law of Armed Conflict*, para. 6.12.1.

[62] French *Manual of the Law of Armed Conflict*, p. 21: 'Les armes incendiaires ne sont pas interdites par le droit des conflits armés mais leur utilisation est réglementée.'

[63] *The SIrUS Project: Towards a determination of which weapons cause 'superfluous injury or unnecessary suffering*, ICRC, Geneva, 1997, p. 23.

12.21 Criterion 1 would apply to a weapon designed to disorientate, confuse, induce calm, or precipitate seizures or psychosis causing a known neuroendocrine response to an agent or energy form, but without the infliction of physical injury (which would represent a specific normal physiological response). It would also encompass weapons whose method of wounding would predictably demand a blood transfusion. With respect to Criterion 2, the ICRC argued that the use of weapons whose design renders death inevitable is already prohibited as part of the same legal concept that prohibits those causing superfluous injury or unnecessary suffering. According to the ICRC, the figures of 25 per cent and 5 per cent for field and hospital mortality, respectively, were proposed 'as limits which are on the conservative side of the established baseline'.[64]

12.22 Criterion 3 applied to weapons which, without targeting a particular part of the body, simply inflict large wounds, such as is the case for exploding and expanding bullets.[65] Grade 3 wounds under the Red Cross classification denote skin wounds of 10 centimetres or more with a cavity.[66] Criterion 4 (effects for which no well-recognised and proven treatment exists) is closely linked to Criterion 1. This would apply, for instance, to blindness for, as the ICRC specifically observed, 'for laser-damaged retina there is no known successful treatment even in the best facilities'.[67]

12.23 Falling foul of any of the four criteria, the ICRC argued, would mean that the weapon in question was indeed of a nature to cause superfluous injury or unnecessary suffering. Its approach, while valuable, failed to take account of the military advantage element of the equation and was sharply criticised as a result, especially by the US.[68] This led to the ICRC prematurely ditching the project in early 2001. Regrettably, it has still not been revived.

Inherently indiscriminate weapons

12.24 A treaty prohibition on inherently indiscriminate weapons was first instituted in the 1977 Additional Protocol I. It is derived from the customary IHL principle of distinction. According to Article 51(4)(b) and (c), an indiscriminate attack includes one that employs a weapon which either 'cannot be directed at a specific military objective' or whose effects 'cannot be limited' as the Protocol requires, and consequently 'is of a nature to strike military objectives and civilians or civilian objects without distinction'.

---

[64] Ibid., p. 24.
[65] Ibid.
[66] Ibid., p. 15. Grade 1 denotes skin wounds of less than 10cm without a cavity, while Grade 2 denotes skin wounds of less than 10cm but with a cavity.
[67] Ibid., p. 25.
[68] As the US Library of Congress noted, criticism of 'this well-intentioned, but flawed methodology' was raised at the ICRC meeting of experts in May 1999. Growing opposition led to the ICRC announcing the withdrawal of the project in January 2001. US Library of Congress, 'The SIrUS Project: Towards a Determination of Which Weapons Cause 'Superfluous Injury or Unnecessary Suffering''', 16 July 2010, at: http://bit.ly/34U0MEO.

Any weapon that systematically breaches either of these prohibitions is inherently indiscriminate and may not be used in an armed conflict.

12.25 There are two alternative elements to the test for an inherently indiscriminate weapon: either the weapon cannot be targeted with sufficient accuracy, or its effects are initially targeted against a military objective but then spread out in an indiscriminate manner. There is a particular lack of clarity as to how inaccurate a weapon must be before its use is always unlawful, and military manuals do not offer much guidance in this regard. That said, as the US Department of Defense has observed, a weapon does not need to be able to pinpoint enemy combatants in order to be lawful: 'if the weapon could be directed at specific areas [that constitute military objectives], it would be unlikely that the weapon would be considered inherently indiscriminate'.[69] Thus, the use of certain weapons would amount to an indiscriminate attack in certain situations and against certain point targets but could be targeted with sufficient accuracy in other situations and against large area targets, meaning that the weapon would not be inherently indiscriminate. A weapon that is activated by the 'victim', such as a landmine or a sea mine, also poses challenges for targeting law.

12.26 As the International Court of Justice explained in its 1996 Nuclear Weapons Advisory Opinion, the rule of distinction means that the use of any weapon that is 'incapable of distinguishing between civilian and military targets'[70] is unlawful. The Court described this as a 'cardinal' principle of the law of armed conflict.[71] In 2005, the ICRC study of customary IHL concluded that: 'The use of weapons which are by nature indiscriminate is prohibited.'[72] The US Department of Defense considers the rule one of two fundamental prohibitions in customary international law that apply to all weapons.[73] The customary rule is applicable in all armed conflicts.[74]

12.27 In its judgment in the *Martić* case, which concerned the firing of cluster munitions against Zagreb in early May 1995, an ICTY Trial Chamber observed that the weapon, the M-87 Orkan, was a high-dispersion weapon fired 'from the extreme of its range'. The Trial Chamber held that the Orkan was 'an indiscriminate weapon, the use of which in densely populated civilian areas, such as Zagreb, will result in the infliction of severe casualties'.[75] The Trial Chamber had based its decision on the fact that Orkan was a non-guided artillery system that was 'incapable of hitting specific targets'. The maximum firing range of the Orkan was 50 kilometres and the dispersion error when fired at its maximum range was affirmed in testimony to be about 1,000 metres in any direction. Thus, given its inaccuracy, the Orkan was suitable for use against troops in the

---

[69] USDOD December 2016 *Law of War Manual*, para. 6.7.2.
[70] ICJ, 1996 Nuclear Weapons Advisory Opinion, para. 78. The Court's formulation is a little clumsy, given that it implies there may be civilian 'targets'. A better formulation would have been 'incapable of distinguishing between civilians and civilian objects and military objectives'.
[71] ICJ, 1996 Nuclear Weapons Advisory Opinion, para. 78.
[72] ICRC, Customary IHL Rule 71: 'Weapons That Are by Nature Indiscriminate', at: http://bit.ly/36VUeHp.
[73] USDOD December 2016 *Law of War Manual*, para. 6.4.1.
[74] ICRC, Customary IHL Rule 71: 'Weapons That Are by Nature Indiscriminate'.
[75] ICTY, *Prosecutor v. Milan Martić*, Judgment (Trial Chamber) (Case No. IT-95-11), 12 June 2007, para. 463.

open, but not for point targeting military objectives in areas populated by civilians. It was not therefore an inherently indiscriminate weapon, but one that was used in an indiscriminate manner in the circumstances. Accordingly, the Appeals Chamber would clarify that the Trial Chamber had in fact and in law concluded that the Orkan 'was *used* as an indiscriminate weapon'.[76]

Milan Martić's conviction at trial for, inter alia, attacks on civilians was confirmed by the Appeals Chamber. This is, however, problematic from an international legal standpoint, as it appears to conflate a direct attack on civilians with an indiscriminate attack (an issue addressed in earlier chapters of this work). In relation to the war crime for which he was convicted and sentenced regarding the attacks on Zagreb, the Appeals Chamber held that the Trial Chamber had 'correctly stated the applicable law' when it held that 'a direct attack against civilians can be inferred from the indiscriminate weapon used'.[77] In doing so, it cited the jurisprudence in the earlier *Galić* case. In that case, the Trial Chamber had held that indiscriminate or disproportionate attacks may amount to direct attacks against civilians.[78] General Galić appealed against his conviction for war crimes, arguing that the Trial Chamber had conflated a set of distinct war crimes. The Appeals Chamber rejected this argument, however, holding that the Trial Chamber's finding 'that disproportionate attacks "may" give rise to the inference of direct attacks on civilians is ... a justified pronouncement on the evidentiary effects of certain findings, not a conflation of different crimes'.[79]

12.28

The Appeals Chamber also affirmed that the Trial Chamber had 'limited itself to attacks on civilians pursuant to Article 51(2) of Additional Protocol I, which only contemplates direct attacks against the civilian population'.[80] The Protocol envisages two war crimes: 'making the civilian population or individual civilians the object of attack'; and launching an indiscriminate attack affecting the civilian population or civilian objects.[81] The apparent conflation of war crimes has persisted within the jurisprudence of the International Criminal Court. Under the Rome Statute, the war crime exists under the ICC's jurisdiction in non-international armed conflict of 'Intentionally directing attacks against the civilian population as such or against individual civilians not taking direct part in hostilities'.[82] Most recently, in the judgment at trial in the *Ntaganda* case, the Court stated that the crime:

12.29

> may encompass attacks that are carried out in an indiscriminate manner, that is by targeting an area, as opposed to specific objects, or not targeting specific military

---

[76] ICTY, *Prosecutor v. Milan Martić*, Judgment (Appeals Chamber) (Case No. IT-95-11-A), 8 October 2008, para. 247 (emphasis added).
[77] Ibid., para. 260, citing the Trial Judgment, para. 69.
[78] ICTY, *Prosecutor v. Galić*, Judgment and Opinion (Trial Chamber I), 5 December 2003, para. 57.
[79] ICTY, *Prosecutor v. Galić*, Judgment (Appeals Chamber) (Case No. IT-98-29-A), 30 November 2006, para. 133.
[80] Ibid., para. 134. Article 51(2) provides that: 'The civilian population as such, as well as individual civilians, shall not be the object of attack.'
[81] Art. 85(3)(a) and (b), 1977 Additional Protocol.
[82] Art. 8(2)(e)(i), Rome Statute.

objects or persons taking a direct part in hostilities ... so long as the perpetrator was aware of the presence of civilians in the relevant area. It may also include attacks that are launched without taking necessary precautions to spare the civilian population or individual civilians ... Therefore, the use of weapons that have inherently indiscriminate effects in an area where civilians are present may constitute an attack directed at the civilian population or individual civilians.[83]

12.30 The situation is complicated because there is no war crime of indiscriminate attacks under the Rome Statute and the war crime of disproportionate attacks only exists with respect to international armed conflict. Moreover, the International Criminal Court only has possible future jurisdiction for the war crime, still only in international armed conflict, of 'employing weapons, projectiles and material and methods of warfare ... which are inherently indiscriminate in violation of the international law of armed conflict'. Even in such a case, jurisdiction is dependent on a specific weapon being included in an annex to the Statute.[84] This had yet to occur at the time of writing. With respect to war crimes in non-international armed conflict under customary law, the ICRC has been overly tentative, noting in its customary law study only that: 'As most States define a "war crime" as being a "violation" or a "serious violation" of international humanitarian law ... it is reasonable to conclude that they would consider the use of prohibited weapons in non-international armed conflicts to fall within this category.'[85]

Weapons that may be inherently indiscriminate

12.31 There is no consensus among States as to which weapons are inherently indiscriminate. As the UK's Manual of the Law of Armed Conflict describes, there are two alternative tests: if a weapon cannot be targeted against a specific military objective (for instance, because it has a rudimentary guidance system), or if its effects cannot be limited to a military objective, it is an indiscriminate weapon and may not be used in armed conflict.[86] An obvious example of the former is a highly inaccurate rocket or missile,[87] whereas a weapon whose effects cannot be limited as international law requires includes biological weapons as their effects spread indiscriminately even when they are targeted initially at combatants.

---

[83] ICC, *Prosecutor v. Bosco Ntaganda*, Judgment (Trial Chamber) (Case No. ICC-01/04-02/06), 8 July 2019, para. 921 (footnotes omitted).
[84] Under Article 8(2)(b)(xx), the jurisdiction of the Court is limited to 'such weapons, projectiles and material and methods of warfare [that] are the subject of a comprehensive prohibition and are included in an annex to th[e] Statute, by an amendment in accordance with the relevant provisions set forth in articles 121 and 123'.
[85] ICRC, Customary IHL Rule 156: 'Definition of War Crimes', at: http://bit.ly/32HjZb2.
[86] UK *Manual of the Law of Armed Conflict*, para. 6.4.
[87] In a military context, a rocket is an unguided, rocket-powered weapon, with no steering ability. A missile is a self-propelled weapon, which is often, but not always, rocket-powered and that has an incorporated guidance system to direct it in flight towards its target. See, e.g., Cambridge English Dictionary, at: http://bit.ly/2rFncew.

Inaccurate rockets and missiles

12.32 It is widely agreed that the V-1 flying bombs and V-2 rockets used by the Nazis in 1944 and 1945 against London were inherently indiscriminate weapons.[88] According to the US Department of Defense, for instance, 'German long-range rockets without guidance systems used during World War II' were illegal.[89] The UK Ministry of Defense has affirmed that the V-1 is an example of a weapon 'likely to be caught by' the prohibition on inherently indiscriminate weapons.[90] Indeed, at the time, British Prime Minister Winston Churchill called the V-1 'a weapon literally and essentially indiscriminate'.[91] Even the German commanding officer for the programme cautioned that the V-1 was 'of use only as an instrument of terror, and not for attacking military objectives'.[92] Writing in a similar vein shortly after the end of the War, James Spaight said that the V-1 was a weapon 'which cannot really be aimed at all'.[93]

12.33 The V-2[94] was the world's first long-range guided ballistic missile. With respect to the V-2, Spaight stated that, under the law applicable at the time: 'While such a weapon is not banned in terms by any international convention, the use of it could not be regarded as compatible with the observance of certain rules which are the subject of definite international agreement, such as those forbidding the bombardment "by any means" of undefended towns and villages'.[95] The intent of the German rocket programme, which had begun before the outbreak of the Second World War, had been to develop a long-range ground-launched weapon. It did not, however, achieve any reasonable degree of accuracy until late 1944 when, as a result of the incorporation of an updated radio beam guidance system, the 'theoretical' circular error probable radius was brought down from around four miles to one.[96] On the final day of V-2 rocket attacks against London, a single rocket fell on a block of flats in Stepney, killing more than 130 people, all seemingly civilians.[97] The ICRC has affirmed that the V-2 is an example of a weapon that cannot be directed against a military objective.[98]

12.34 More modern rockets that may be indiscriminate include those fired by Palestinian armed groups from Gaza. The UN Commission of Inquiry on the 2014 Gaza conflict reported that most of the projectiles fired by Palestinian armed groups during that armed conflict were rockets 'that at best were equipped with only rudimentary

---

[88] See, e.g., G. Solis, *The Law of Armed Conflict. International Humanitarian Law in War*, 2nd Edn, Cambridge University Press, New York, 2016, p. 525.
[89] USDOD December 2016 *Law of War Manual*, para. 6.7.3.
[90] UK *Manual of the Law of Armed Conflict*, para. 6.4.1.
[91] See D. Irving, *The Mare's Nest*, Panther Books, London, 1985, p. 258.
[92] Ibid., pp. 313–14.
[93] J. M. Spaight, *Air Power and War Rights*, 3rd Edn, Longman's, London, p. 215.
[94] The V stood for 'Vergeltungswaffe' (meaning 'retribution weapon'), although its technical name was Aggregat 4 (A4). See generally, M. J. Neufeld, *The Rocket and the Reich: Peenemünde and the Coming of the Ballistic Missile Era*, The Free Press, New York, 1995.
[95] Ibid., p. 214.
[96] Irving, *The Mare's Nest*, pp. 316–17; Astronautix, 'V-2', undated but accessed 1 November 2019, at: http://bit.ly/2QbqRec.
[97] Irving, *The Mare's Nest*, p. 318.
[98] ICRC, Commentary on the Additional Protocols, 1987, para. 1958.

guidance systems and in the vast majority of cases had none at all'.[99] The rockets available to armed groups in Gaza at the time 'were unguided and inaccurate'. Estimates, confirmed by the Commission, indicated that the Fajr-5109 and similar J-80 and M-75 rockets can land as far as three kilometres from any intended target. The longer-range rockets, such as the R-160, can land as far as six kilometres away from the target because their accuracy decreases with range.[100]

12.35 The Commission concluded that the rockets could not be directed at a specific military objective and therefore were indiscriminate attacks in violation of the customary rule codified in Article 51(4) of the Additional Protocol I of 1977. The fact that Palestinian armed groups did not possess more accurate weapons was rejected as a justification for their failure to attack precisely military targets. As the Commission noted, the 'military capacity of the parties to a conflict is irrelevant to their obligation to respect the prohibition against indiscriminate attacks'.[101] It stated that the launching of rockets by Palestinian armed groups may therefore amount to war crimes.[102]

12.36 In January 2022, the ICRC launched a new report on the use of explosive weapons with wide area effects in populated areas.[103] The report does not identify which weapons may not be lawfully used in such areas, although it declares that 'area weapons' are 'not suitable for use against point targets located in populated areas'.[104] It further notes that: 'The use of unguided air-delivered bombs, rockets and other munitions in populated areas is also of serious concern, in view of their lack of accuracy and the large destructive radius of most air-delivered munitions'.[105]

Biological weapons

12.37 The biological weapon is the example of an inherently indiscriminate weapon on the basis that, while it can be initially targeted at a military objective, its effects may spread far beyond that in both time and space. Thus, the US Air Force's 1976 *Manual on International Law* cites biological weapons as a 'universally agreed illustration of... an indiscriminate weapon'. The document observed that the uncontrollable effects from such weapons 'may include injury to the civilian population of other states as well as injury to an enemy's civilian population'.[106] These uncontrolled effects exist not only spatially but also over time. More recently, the US Department of Defense has affirmed that: 'Bacteriological or biological warfare is prohibited... because it can have massive,

---

[99] Report of the detailed findings of the independent commission of inquiry established pursuant to Human Rights Council resolution S-21/1, UN doc. A/HRC/29/CRP.4, 22 June 2015 (hereinafter 'UN Commission of Inquiry on the 2014 Gaza Conflict'), para. 97.
[100] Amnesty International, *Unlawful and deadly. Rocket and Mortar Attacks by Palestinian Armed Groups during the 2014 Gaza/Israel Conflict*, March 2015, p. 10.
[101] UN Commission of Inquiry on the 2014 Gaza Conflict, para. 97.
[102] Ibid., para. 98, citing Article 8 of the Rome Statute.
[103] ICRC, *Explosive Weapons With Wide Area Effects: A Deadly Choice in Populated Areas*, Geneva, January 2022, at: https://bit.ly/3H6VBo9, p. 22.
[104] Ibid., p. 63.
[105] Ibid., p. 64.
[106] See US Department of the Air Force, *International Law—The Conduct of Armed Conflict and Air Operations*, Air Force Pamphlet 110-31, 1976, §6-3(c).

unpredictable, and potentially uncontrollable consequences'.[107] According to Canada, 'bacteriological and biological weapons are prohibited because they cause unnecessary suffering and may affect the civilian population in an indiscriminate fashion'.[108] This indicates that biological weapons fall foul of both general prohibitions on the use of weapons as a method of warfare.

In the preamble to a resolution adopted in 1969, the UN General Assembly stated that biological (and chemical) weapons 'are inherently reprehensible because their effects are often uncontrollable and unpredictable'.[109] In December 2017, States Parties to the International Criminal Court amended the Rome Statute to confer potential jurisdiction on the Court for the war crime of using biological weapons in both international and non-international armed conflict.[110] **12.38**

Poison

Poison is similarly prohibited as both a means and method of warfare[111] as it is considered both of a nature to cause superfluous injury and has indiscriminate effects. As the ICRC has observed, 'poison is unlawful in itself, as would be any weapon which would, by its very nature, be so imprecise that it would inevitably cause indiscriminate damage'.[112] It is a long-standing prohibition with the Regulations annexed to both the 1899 Hague Convention II and the 1907 Hague Convention IV codifying the prohibition of the employment in warfare of 'poison or poisoned arms'.[113] The prohibition of poison and poisoned weapons exists in customary law in all armed conflicts, whether international or of a non-international character.[114] The ICRC affirms that it exists independently of the prohibition of chemical weapons: although the 1925 Geneva Gas Protocol[115] was 'inspired by the existing prohibition of the use of poison', it observes that sufficient separate practice establishes a 'specific rule on poison and poisoned weapons'.[116] The ICTY saw the prohibition in terms of its effect on combatants rather than its indiscriminate nature. Article 3 of the Statute gave the Tribunal the power to prosecute persons violating the laws or customs of war, which **12.39**

---

[107] USDOD December 2016 *Law of War Manual*, para. 6.9.1.
[108] Canadian 2001 *Manual of the Law of Armed Conflict*, commentary para. 1 on rule 516.
[109] UN General Assembly Resolution 2603A (XXIV), adopted on 16 December 1969 by 80 votes to 3 with 36 abstentions. The ICRC observes that, although 3 States did vote against this resolution and a further 36 abstained, their opposition was primarily in relation to the issue of herbicides and not the general principles.
[110] Art. 8(2)(b)(xxvii) and Art. 8(2)(e)(xvi), Rome Statute. The Amendment first entered into force on 2 April 2020 in regard to Luxembourg one year after the deposit of its instrument of ratification, in accordance with Article 121(5) of the Rome Statute. As of 1 May 2022, twelve States had ratified the amendment: Croatia, Czechia, Latvia, Liechtenstein, Luxembourg, the Netherlands, New Zealand, Norway, Romania, Slovakia, Sweden, and Switzerland.
[111] In the ICRC commentary on the Protocol, poison is cited as a means of warfare, while poisoning wells is a method of warfare. ICRC commentary on the 1977 Additional Protocols, 1987, paras. 1402, 1963.
[112] Ibid., para. 1402.
[113] Art. 23(a), 1899 Hague Convention II; and Art. 23(a), 1907 Hague Convention IV. This latter provision replaces 'arms' with 'weapons'.
[114] ICRC, Customary IHL Rule 72: 'Poison and Poisoned Weapons', at: http://bit.ly/2Xhoc4m.
[115] Protocol for the Prohibition of the Use of Asphyxiating, Poisonous or Other Gases, and of Bacteriological Methods of Warfare; adopted at Geneva, 17 June 1925; entered into force, 8 February 1928.
[116] ICRC, Customary IHL Rule 72: 'Poison and Poisoned Weapons'.

included 'employment of poisonous weapons or *other* weapons calculated to cause unnecessary suffering'.[117]

Nuclear weapons

12.40 As is the case with poison and chemical weapons, it is argued that nuclear weapons are illegal both on the grounds that they cause unnecessary suffering and that they are inherently indiscriminate. The indiscriminate nature of nuclear weapons derives primarily from the huge area that is devastated by the extreme heat and blast effects they engender through fission or fusion.[118] Moreover, most strategic nuclear weapons are also targeted at the cities of a potential adversary, intended not to target military objectives but to riposte against a first strike against its own cities.

12.41 During the pleadings in relation to the ICJ's 1996 Nuclear Weapons Advisory Opinion, nuclear-armed States offered examples of submarines on the high seas or troops massed in the desert as potentially lawful uses of a small-yield ('tactical') nuclear weapon. In his dissenting opinion from the Court's 1996 Opinion, then Vice-President Stephen Schwebel discussed the use of 'tactical' nuclear weapons 'against discrete military or naval targets so situated that substantial civilian casualties would not ensue'. He affirmed that:

> the use of a nuclear depth-charge to destroy a nuclear submarine that is about to fire nuclear missiles, or has fired one or more of a number of its nuclear missiles, might well be lawful. By the circumstance of its use, the nuclear depth-charge would not give rise to immediate civilian casualties. It would easily meet the test of proportionality; the damage that the submarine's missiles could inflict on the population and territory of the target State would infinitely outweigh that entailed in the destruction of the submarine and its crew. The submarine's destruction by a nuclear weapon would produce radiation in the sea, but far less than the radiation that firing of its missiles would produce on and over land. Nor is it as certain that the use of a conventional depth-charge would discharge the mission successfully; the far greater force of a nuclear weapon could ensure destruction of the submarine whereas a conventional depth-charge might not.[119]

This is a narrow instance where a nuclear weapon's use would likely comply with the rules of IHL, but it is still a credible example.[120] Thus, although the preamble to the Treaty on the Prohibition of Nuclear Weapons considers 'that any use of nuclear weapons would be contrary to the rules of international law applicable in armed

---

[117] Art. 3, ICTY Statute (emphasis added).
[118] At ground zero, temperatures are as hot as the surface of the sun (3,800°C), resulting in immolation, asphyxiation, and burns. *Vienna Conference on the Humanitarian Impact of Nuclear Weapons, 8–9 December 2014, Conference Report*, Austrian Federal Ministry for Europe, Integration and Foreign Affairs, Vienna, 2015, pp. 24–25.
[119] ICJ, *Legality of the Threat or Use of Nuclear Weapons*, Advisory Opinion, Dissenting Opinion of Vice-President Schwebel, pp. 320–21.
[120] See, e.g., S. Casey-Maslen, *Treaty on the Prohibition of Nuclear Weapons: A Commentary*, Oxford University Press, Oxford, 2019, paras. 0.107–0.108.

conflict, in particular the principles and rules of international humanitarian law',[121] this is not a robust statement of the law. It is possible, albeit in highly circumscribed circumstances, to use nuclear weapons without violating IHL.

The other main result from the detonation of a nuclear weapon is radiation. The US argues that radioactivity is not to be considered when assessing the legality of nuclear weapons because it is not an intended effect of the weapons, but rather merely a by-product.[122] This is a difficult argument to sustain with any degree of seriousness.[123] Moreover, the huge emission of poisonous radiation by the detonation of a high-yield nuclear weapon, where it has been 'salted' by surrounding the bomb with, for example, cobalt-60 or gold-198, would surely violate the prohibition on inherently indiscriminate weapons. In such a case, any claim that radiation was merely a by-product would be palpably false.

12.42

Landmines

A weapon that has frequently been cited as 'indiscriminate' is the landmine. In its commentary on Article 51 of the 1977 Additional Protocol I, the ICRC stated that '[f]rom the point of view of the protection of civilians', the use of landmines (or sea mines) 'raises some problems'.[124] At the heart of the concern is the fact that the mine is activated by the victim rather than the soldier. An anti-personnel mine cannot 'distinguish', at the moment of triggering, between the footfall of a soldier or that of a civilian: either will detonate the weapon. This would tend to suggest that its effects are indiscriminate.[125] However, it is possible to use anti-personnel mines in a discriminate manner, by emplacing them in a marked and fenced area, especially where military personnel patrol the exterior of the area. This can effectively ensure that the victims of any explosion are predominantly, if not exclusively, military and not civilian.[126] That this is rarely the case in practice justifies their prohibition by treaty,[127] but not the assertion that they are inherently indiscriminate weapons.[128] A distinct prohibition on the use of anti-personnel mines is *de lege ferenda*,[129] but has not crystallised as a customary norm given

12.43

---

[121] Treaty on the Prohibition of Nuclear Weapons; adopted on 7 July 2017; entered into force, 22 January 2021, preambular para. 10.

[122] ICJ, *Legality of the Threat or Use of Nuclear Weapons*, Advisory Opinion, Written Statement of the United States, 1995, at: https://bit.ly/2N5Fd0v, pp. 23–24.

[123] See, e.g., C. J. Moxley Jr, J. Burroughs, and J. Granoff, 'Nuclear Weapons and Compliance with International Humanitarian Law and the Nuclear Non-Proliferation Treaty', *Fordham International Law Journal*, Vol. 34, No. 4 (2011), pp. 595–696, at: http://bit.ly/354K855.

[124] ICRC, Commentary on the 1977 Additional Protocols, para. 1959.

[125] Casey-Maslen with Haines, *Hague Law Interpreted: The Conduct of Hostilities under the Law of Armed Conflict*, p. 21.

[126] Ibid., p. 22.

[127] As of 1 May 2022, 164 States were party to the 1997 Anti-Personnel Mine Ban Convention, which outlaws all use of anti-personnel mines. Art. 1(1)(a), Convention on the Prohibition of the Use, Stockpiling, Production and Transfer of Anti-Personnel Mines and on their Destruction, adopted at Oslo, 18 September 1997; entered into force, 1 March 1999.

[128] Moreover, any State that believes that anti-personnel mines are inherently indiscriminate must surely accept that any use of an anti-vehicle mine is similarly unlawful, since such mines do not distinguish between, for instance, a tank and a school bus.

[129] Cryer and others affirm that among weapons frequently mentioned as a candidate for a comprehensive prohibition, '[p]erhaps the closest to achieving the status as a war crime is the use of anti-personnel mines'. R.

the opposition, or at least lack of requisite *opinio juris*, of a number of specially affected States.[130]

Autonomous weapons

12.44   There are ongoing discussions as to the legality of weapons that are able to select targets, and to fire weapons against those targets, without human intervention.[131] Certainly, any weapon that cannot comply with the rules of distinction and proportionality in attack will be inherently indiscriminate. Indeed, Gary Solis believes that a weapon 'without a human in the fire/not fire loop … would be indiscriminate'.[132] The ICRC has called upon States to adopt legally binding rules to prohibit 'unpredictable' autonomous weapon systems, 'notably because of their indiscriminate effects'.[133] That said, an autonomous weapon system does not need to be 'error-free' in order to be lawful.[134] It has been suggested that the 'yardstick should be the conduct of human beings who would otherwise be taking the decisions'.[135]

12.45   It is also asserted by some that such weapon systems might even be designed to comply with the law in a manner that is better than humans.[136] Robots may delay the attack until the most appropriate moment, thereby taking 'additional precautionary measures that IHL would never expect humans to take because they are too dangerous'.[137] Sassòli further opines that, one day, autonomous weapons systems 'may be able to select and engage targets without human intervention in an open environment under circumstances that are unstructured and dynamic'. That said, 'no weapon system possesses such capabilities at the present time'.[138] Gary Solis agrees: 'Presently, there are no tools that would allow autonomous weapons systems to meet the requirements of distinction or, especially, proportionality'.[139] The ICRC has exhorted States not to allow use of

Cryer, H. Friman, D. Robinson, and E. Wilmshurst, *An Introduction to International Criminal Law and Procedure*, Cambridge University Press, Cambridge, 2010, p. 305.

[130] Notably China, India, Pakistan, the Russian Federation, and the United States.
[131] A useful definition is offered by the US Department of Defense: 'A weapon system that, once activated, can select and engage targets without further intervention by a human operator. This includes human-supervised autonomous weapons systems that are designed to allow human operators to override operation of the weapon system but can select and engage targets without further human input after activation.' US Department of Defense, *Autonomy in Weapons Systems*, Directive 3000.09 (as amended), Glossary. An *automated* weapon is one that simply follows a script; an *autonomous* weapon makes choices on its own. See Solis, *The Law of Armed Conflict, International Humanitarian Law in War*, 3rd Edn, pp. 465–66.
[132] Ibid., p. 415.
[133] 'International Committee of the Red Cross (ICRC) position on autonomous weapon systems: ICRC position and background paper', in *International Review of the Red Cross*, Vol. 102, No. 915 (2020), pp. 1335–49, at p. 1336.
[134] See generally, e.g., N. Weizmann and M. Costas Trascasas, *Autonomous Weapon Systems under International Law*, Academy Briefing No. 8, Geneva Academy of International Humanitarian Law and Human Rights, Geneva, November 2014; and M. Brehm, *Defending the Boundary: Constraints and Requirements on the Use of Autonomous Weapon systems under International Humanitarian and Human Rights Law*, Academy Briefing No. 9, Geneva Academy of International Humanitarian Law and Human Rights, Geneva, May 2017.
[135] 'Report of the Special Rapporteur on Extrajudicial, Summary Or Arbitrary Executions', UN doc. A/HRC/23/47, 9 April 2013, para. 63.
[136] Ibid., para. 64.
[137] M. Sassòli, *International Humanitarian Law Rules, Controversies, and Solutions to Problems Arising in Warfare*, Edward Elgar Publishing, Cheltenham, 2019, para. 10.81, p. 522.
[138] Ibid., para. 10.73, p. 517.
[139] Solis, *The Law of Armed Conflict, International Humanitarian Law in War*, 3rd Edn, p. 470.

autonomous weapon systems to target human beings. It argues that this duly reflects 'ethical considerations to safeguard humanity' as well as to uphold IHL rules for the protection of civilians and combatants *hors de combat*.[140]

Cyber operations

Cyber operations are not inherently indiscriminate. In certain circumstances, their conduct may be indiscriminate or have indiscriminate effects (and would therefore be unlawful) but, as with other weapons, this would not render all cyber attacks inherently indiscriminate.[141] The leading authority on cyber operations as a means or method of warfare—for no specific treaty rules existed at the time of writing—is the *Tallinn Manual on the International Law Applicable to Cyber Warfare*, the Second Edition of which was issued in 2017.[142] According to this interpretive expert document, indiscriminate cyber attacks would encompass weaponised cyber operations that are of a nature to generate effects that spread uncontrollably, such as where they were introduced into civilian computers and networks or that create an uncontrollable chain of events.[143] Scrambling the banking system in another country would, as the US claims to be within its powers, would also be an indiscriminate attack.[144] As Sassòli observes, however, it is controversial whether mere deletion of data constitutes damage and destruction and also whether data can constitute a military objective as it is 'intangible'.[145]

12.46

Perhaps the best known cyber attack was the one employing the 'Stuxnet' virus against an Iranian nuclear reactor at Natanz. The virus (malware), which was reportedly developed in a joint initiative by Israel and the US[146] (although neither has ever formally accepted responsibility), affected the computers regulating the centrifuges used to enrich uranium, causing the centrifuges to spin out of control. The first infection is said to have occurred in June 2009. In 2010, the International Atomic Energy Agency (IAEA) reported that almost 1,000 centrifuges had been shut down for several days.[147]

12.47

Gravity ordnance

Finally, it is occasionally suggested that the development of precision-guided munitions renders the use of gravity ordnance unlawful.[148] This is incorrect. There is not

12.48

---

[140] 'International Committee of the Red Cross (ICRC) position on autonomous weapon systems: ICRC position and background paper', p. 1336.
[141] M. Schmitt (ed.), *Tallinn Manual on the International Law Applicable to Cyber Warfare*, 2nd Edn, Cambridge University Press, Cambridge, 2017, Rule 105 and related commentary, pp. 455–57.
[142] A third edition of the Manual is in the process of being elaborated.
[143] *Tallinn Manual on the International Law Applicable to Cyber Warfare*, 2nd Edn, Commentary para. 4 on Rule 105.
[144] See Solis, *The Law of Armed Conflict, International Humanitarian Law in War*, 3rd Edn, p. 537.
[145] Sassòli, *International Humanitarian Law Rules, Controversies, and Solutions to Problems Arising in Warfare*, p. 538, Box 10.6, p. 532; and para. 10.121.
[146] Solis, *The Law of Armed Conflict, International Humanitarian Law in War*, 3rd Edn, p. 472.
[147] See, e.g., D. Albright, P. Brannan, and C. Walrond, 'Did Stuxnet Take Out 1,000 Centrifuges at the Natanz Enrichment Plant? Preliminary Assessment', Report, Institute for Science and International Security, 22 December 2010, at: https://bit.ly/3qW5m1J.
[148] J.-F. Quéguiner, 'Precautions under the Law Governing the Conduct of Hostilities', *International Review of the Red Cross*, Vol. 88, No. 864 (December 2006), pp. 801–802.

even a general obligation under IHL to use precision-guided munitions where a State's armed forces have them in significant quantities in their arsenals.[149] That said, there will certainly be scenarios where, given the risk of civilian harm, only an attack using precision-guided munitions is likely to be lawful under IHL.[150]

Weapons causing widespread, severe, and long-term damage to the environment

12.49 Article 35(3) of the 1977 Additional Protocol I stipulates that: 'It is prohibited to employ methods or means of warfare which are intended, or may be expected, to cause widespread, long-term and severe damage to the natural environment.' This provision is a progressive development in IHL, reflecting the growing importance of the protection of the environment from the effects of armed conflict (and now, of course, more broadly). Its antecedent can be seen in the Environmental Modification Convention adopted a year before the 1977 Additional Protocol I.[151] Although the natural environment is not formally designated as a civilian object, unless it or its constituent elements are a military objective, it is protected from attack.[152] No accepted definition of the 'natural environment' exists in the law of armed conflict, although the ICRC explains that the term refers to the 'system of inextricable interrelations between living organisms and their inanimate environment'.[153] If it may lawfully be attacked, the expected incidental harm on civilians or civilian objects must also be part of the proportionality equation in any event. This is so, notwithstanding the provision in Article 35(3).

12.50 The elements of the prohibition in the 1977 Additional Protocol I are cumulative, and the rule is therefore narrow in ambit, especially given the fact that nuclear weapons are not formally governed by the provision. The polluting effects of hostilities in the short or medium term (i.e. days, months, or years) will clearly not meet the definition. However, it is impossible to say with certainty what period of time might be involved.[154] It further appeared to be a widely shared assumption that battlefield damage incidental

---

[149] USDOD December 2016 *Law of War Manual*, para. 5.2.3.2, also citing the military manuals of Australia, Canada, and Germany.

[150] Dinstein, *The Conduct of Hostilities under the Law of International Armed Conflict*, 3rd Edn, paras. 447 and 453. See also, e.g., C. Dunlap, 'No, the Law of War Does Not Always Require the Use of Precision Munitions—and That's a Good Thing for the US', *Lawfare*, 25 February 2016, at: http://bit.ly/2Oocelt.

[151] Convention on the prohibition of military or any other hostile use of environmental modification techniques; adopted at New York, 10 December 1976; entered into force, 5 October 1978.

[152] Dinstein, *The Conduct of Hostilities under the Law of International Armed Conflict*, 3rd Edn, para. 641.

[153] ICRC, Commentary on the 1977 Additional Protocols, para. 1451.

[154] During the negotiations, the Rapporteur from the Working Group that discussed the provision stated that: 'The time or duration required (i.e., long-term) was considered by some to be measured in decades. References to twenty or thirty years were made by some representatives as being a minimum. Others referred to battlefield destruction in France in the First World War as being outside the scope of the prohibition.' The Biotope report states that 'Acts of warfare which cause short-term damage to the natural environment, such as artillery bombardment, are not intended to be prohibited by the article', and continues by stating that the period might be perhaps for 10 years or more.

to conventional warfare would not normally be proscribed by this provision.[155] The ICRC affirms that under customary law: 'The use of methods or means of warfare that are intended, or may be expected, to cause widespread, long-term and severe damage to the natural environment is prohibited. Destruction of the natural environment may not be used as a weapon.' It states that this applies in international armed conflict and arguably also non-international armed conflict.[156] The US has 'repeatedly expressed the view' that these provisions are 'overly broad and ambiguous' and 'not a part of customary law'.[157] The ICRC affirms the customary nature of the prohibition, but identifies the US as a persistent objector. It notes, however, that there exists 'a certain amount of practice that indicates doubt as to the customary nature of the rule'.[158] Indeed, in its 1996 Nuclear Weapons Advisory Opinion, the International Court of Justice 'appeared to consider the rule not to be customary as it only referred to the applicability of this provision to 'States having subscribed to these provisions''.[159]

12.51 Despite doubts as to its customary status, the International Criminal Court has jurisdiction over the war crime, in international armed conflict only, of '[i]ntentionally launching an attack in the knowledge that such attack will cause ... widespread, long-term and severe damage to the natural environment which would be clearly excessive in relation to the concrete and direct overall military advantage anticipated'.[160] The inclusion of the modifying adverb 'clearly' sets the bar for any possible prosecution very high.

Prohibited means and methods of warfare

12.52 Iraq's releasing of oil into the Persian Gulf and its subsequent setting fire to the oil wells in Kuwait in 1991 is often cited as an instance where the rule in Article 35(3) of the 1977 Additional Protocol I was violated. In fact, as Dinstein records, while the environmental effects were undoubtedly severe (and the action itself probably wanton), the action fails this particular test by virtue of the relatively short duration of the impact.[161] The most

---

[155] Cited in ICRC, Commentary on the 1977 Additional Protocols, para. 1454.
[156] ICRC, Customary IHL Rule 45: 'Causing Serious Damage to the Natural Environment', at: http://bit.ly/2ph87yR.
[157] USDOD 2016 *Law of War Manual*, §6.10.3.1, citing US Response to the ICRC, Customary IHL Study: 'France and the United States repeatedly have declared that Articles 35(3) and 55 of AP I, from which the Study derives the first sentence of rule 45, do not reflect customary international law.' J. B Bellinger, III, Legal Adviser, Department of State, and W. J. Haynes II, General Counsel, Department of Defense, Letter to Dr. Jacob Kellenberger, President, ICRC, Regarding Customary International Humanitarian Law Study, 3 November 2006, reprinted in *International Legal Materials*, Vol. 46 (2007), p. 521. See similarly Solis, *The Law of Armed Conflict. International Humanitarian Law in War*, 2nd Edn, p. 513; Dinstein, *The Conduct of Hostilities under the Law of International Armed Conflict*, 3rd Edn, para. 644.
[158] ICRC, Customary IHL Rule 45.
[159] ICJ, 1996 Nuclear Weapons Advisory Opinion, para. 31.
[160] See also the duty of care installed by Article 55 of the Additional Protocol, which focuses on the potential dangers for the civilian population of environmental damage. ICRC commentary on the 1977 Additional Protocols, para. 1449.
[161] Dinstein, *The Conduct of Hostilities under the Law of International Armed Conflict*, 3rd Edn, paras. 666–71.

obvious armaments whose use could meet the test are evidently high-yield nuclear weapons, particularly those whose explosive yield is greater than half a megaton.

12.53 In its official response to the ICRC Customary IHL Study, and particularly Rule 45, the US offers the example of State A, which has hidden its chemical and biological weapons arsenal in a large rainforest, and plans imminently to launch the arsenal at State B. Under the ICRC customary rule, State B could not launch a strike against that arsenal if it expects that such a strike may cause widespread, long-term, and severe damage to the rainforest, even if it has evidence of State A's imminent launch, and knows that such a launch itself would cause environmental devastation.[162]

The legality of weapons must be verified

12.54 Article 36 of the Additional Protocol I also represents a development of the law. In its commentary on the provision the ICRC observed that there was a need for a link between the basic rule laid down in Article 35 and the prohibitions on weapons of a nature to cause superfluous injury or unnecessary suffering or which have indiscriminate effects.[163] The provision that emerged from the diplomatic conference amounted to a compromise among negotiating States, some of whom sought 'the creation of a special body, a committee responsible for drawing up a list of weapons or methods of use' which would fall under the prohibitions of means or methods of warfare causing superfluous injury and of inherently indiscriminate weapons.[164] Other delegations, however, objected to the proposal on the grounds that it 'seemed to imply disarmament, a subject which was outside the scope of the Diplomatic Conference'.[165]

12.55 The result of the negotiations was a purely national duty to conduct a legal review of weapons prior to their acquisition or deployment. Article 36 thus provides that:

> In the study, development, acquisition or adoption of a new weapon, means or method of warfare, a High Contracting Party is under an obligation to determine whether its employment would, in some or all circumstances, be prohibited by this Protocol or by any other rule of international law applicable to the High Contracting Party.

The aim of Article 36 is thus to 'prevent the use of weapons that would violate international law in all circumstances and to impose restrictions on the use of weapons that would violate international law in some circumstances, by determining their lawfulness before they are developed, acquired or otherwise incorporated into a State's arsenal'.[166]

---

[162] US Response to the ICRC, Customary IHL Study, p. 528, endnote 30.
[163] ICRC commentary on the 1977 Additional Protocols, para. 1463.
[164] Ibid. The ICRC further notes that: 'For small countries this was a fundamental point, essential for their security. Some even seemed to be inclined to make it a condition of accepting the Protocol in its entirety.'
[165] Ibid., para. 1464.
[166] K. Lawand with R. Coupland and P. Herby, *A Guide to the Legal Review of New Weapons, Means and Methods of Warfare, Measures to Implement Article 36 of Additional Protocol I of 1977*, ICRC, Geneva, January 2006, p. 4. See also generally S. Casey-Maslen, N. Corney, and A. Dymond-Bass, 'The review of weapons under international

The ICRC does not consider the rule to be of customary status.[167] This is despite the fact that the principle of distinction dictates that parties to an armed conflict must at all times distinguish between the civilian population and combatants and between civilian objects and military objectives and direct their operations only against military objectives. As discussed above, it is further prohibited to launch an indiscriminate attack, which includes the use of any weapon that cannot be directed at a specific military objective or whose effects cannot be limited as required by the Protocol. How can a State comply with this prohibition without first assessing the targeting and effects of the weapon? Indeed, as the ICRC's commentary on the Additional Protocol observes, if the requisite determination is not made, the State will be 'responsible in any case for any wrongful damage ensuing'.[168]

12.56

More persuasive are the arguments in favour of the generally binding nature of the obligation in Article 36. According to Schmitt, 'the obligation to conduct legal reviews of new means of warfare before their use is generally considered reflective of customary international law'.[169] Experts involved in drafting the 2013 Tallinn Manual on the International Law Applicable to Cyber Warfare were divided as to whether the rule is customary with respect to methods of warfare.[170] Boothby has suggested that it is 'decidedly arguable that the obligation to conduct such a review is customary and binds all States'.[171] The US Department of Defense has a 'policy' of conducting legal reviews of weapons but does not make it explicit that this is a requirement under international law.[172] This would be significant as the US has not adhered to the 1977 Additional Protocol I. In 2007, India, also not a State Party to the Protocol, referred to 'a need for renewed debate and discussion on strengthening the obligations of all

12.57

---

humanitarian law and human rights law', Chapter 14 in S. Casey-Maslen (ed.), *Weapons Under International Human Rights Law*, Cambridge University Press, Cambridge, 2014, pp. 411–47.

[167] See J.-M. Henckaerts and L. Doswald-Beck (eds.), *Customary International Humanitarian Law—Volume 1: Rules*, Cambridge University Press, 2005, Cambridge, p. 250 and note 102. Sassòli suggests that they have accepted that the obligation is implicitly binding on all States through their substantive obligations, but this rather overstates the ICRC position, which is only that it is 'arguably' so binding. See M. Sassòli, *International Humanitarian Law Rules, Controversies, and Solutions to Problems Arising in Warfare*, Edward Elgar Publishing, Cheltenham, 2019, para. 8.375, p. 385; and ICRC, *A Guide to the Legal Review of New Weapons, Means and Methods of Warfare: Measures to Implement Article 36 of Additional Protocol I of 1977*, Geneva, 2006, p. 4. In 2021, the ICRC issued new guidance on national implementation of IHL, which observes merely that it is '*in the interest of every State* to review the legality of new weapons, means and methods of warfare prior to their deployment'. ICRC, *Bringing IHL Home: Guidelines on the National Implementation of International Humanitarian Law*, Geneva, May 2021, at: https://bit.ly/3u3FVyt, p. 21 (emphasis added). The guidance does, however, go on to state that: 'Carrying out such reviews also flows from the obligation to ensure respect for IHL.'

[168] ICRC, Commentary on the 1977 Additional Protocols, para. 1466.

[169] M. Schmitt, 'Autonomous Weapon Systems and International Humanitarian Law: A Reply to the Critics', *Harvard National Security Journal*, Features Online, 2013, p. 28.

[170] Commentary, para. 2, on Rule 110, in M. N. Schmitt (ed.), *Tallinn Manual 2.0 on the International Law Applicable to Cyber Operations*, Cambridge University Press, Cambridge, 2017, p. 465. See also N. Weizmann and M. Costas Trascasas, *Autonomous Weapon Systems under International Law*, Academy Briefing No. 8, p. 17 and note 98.

[171] W. Boothby, *Conflict Law: The Influence of New Weapons Technology, Human Rights and Emerging Actors*, TMC Asser Press, The Hague, 2014, p. 171.

[172] USDOD 2016 *Law of War Manual*, §6.2.

States to consider whether the adoption of new weapons systems of methods of warfare should, in some circumstances, be prohibited under the applicable rules of international law'.[173]

Concluding remarks and outlook

12.58 The provisions in the 1977 Additional Protocol I governing weapons are largely general in nature and, for the most part, reflect customary international law. Regrettably, the 1977 Additional Protocol II does not even incorporate the fundamental rules. Relatively few weapons have been prohibited directly under the two main IHL principles that pertain to means of warfare: the prohibition of use in armed conflict of weapons of a nature to cause superfluous injury or unnecessary suffering and the prohibition of inherently indiscriminate weapons. Moreover, the criteria by which the determination is to be made of legality in each case remains unclear. The ICRC would serve the international community well by resuscitating its SIrUS project and incorporating an additional element to look at the level of accuracy that weapons must meet to avoid the prohibition on those with indiscriminate effects. How much can you miss by and still comply with IHL is clearly weapons-dependent but clarification of the standards, primarily through international criminal law jurisprudence, has been piecemeal and fragmentary.

12.59 The legal gap in IHL on weapons regulation since the mid-1990s has largely been filled by disarmament treaties. The consensus rule within the UN Convention on Certain Conventional Weapons has precluded effective and decisive action on anti-personnel mines and cluster munitions. The result was the adoption in 1997 of the Anti-Personnel Mine Ban Convention (which had 164 States Parties at the time of writing) and the adoption in 2008 of the Convention on Cluster Munitions[174] (which had 110 States Parties at the time of writing).

12.60 Many challenges remain, not least how to tackle the implications of 3D printing of weapons, artificial intelligence, and non-kinetic attacks such as cyber warfare for the future of warfare. While the principles the 1977 Additional Protocol I espouses remain valid and valuable, without sustained action to promote their effective implementation, we may find ourselves closing the stable door after the horse has bolted.

---

[173] Statement of India to the Annual Meeting of States Parties to the UN Convention on Certain Conventional Weapons, Geneva, 7 November 2007.
[174] Convention on Cluster Munitions; adopted at Dublin, 30 May 2008; entered into force, 1 August 2010.

13

Terrorism and Acts of Terror

Introduction

Under customary and conventional international humanitarian law (IHL), all parties to an armed conflict are prohibited, in the conduct of hostilities, from threatening or perpetrating acts of violence where the primary purpose of such action is to terrorise civilians. They are also prohibited from committing acts of terrorism against civilians who are in their power.[1] This is so, whether the armed conflict is international or non-international in character. It is important to bear in mind, however, that the fact that a government designates a specific non-State armed group as 'terrorist' or that certain of its acts are termed 'terrorist' has no relevance to the determination of an armed conflict.[2] The impact of the current States' counter-terrorism narratives with regard to non-State armed groups and NIACs will be further discussed in Chapter 17.

13.1

The notion of terrorism in relation to armed conflict is, in certain respects, considerably narrower than is the case in peacetime. During the conduct of hostilities, this is rendered inevitable by virtue of the underlying principle of distinction, which stipulates that parties to any armed conflict 'shall direct their operations only against military objectives'.[3] Thus, under IHL, acts of terror during combat can only be conducted against civilians or the civilian population as such.[4] Combatants too may often be terrorised by attacks upon them but this reality is not covered by the prohibition on acts of terror.[5]

13.2

---

[1] As Yoram Dinstein observes, the two 'edicts' in this regard set out in the 1977 Additional Protocol II 'have to be disencumbered from each other'. Y. Dinstein, *Non-International Armed Conflict in International Law*, 2nd Edn, Cambridge University Press, Cambridge, 2021, p. 196, para. 547.

[2] See, e.g., ICTY, *Prosecutor v. Ljube Boškoski and Johan Tarčulovski*, Judgment (Trial Chamber) (Case No. IT-04-82-T), 10 July 2008, esp. paras. 185, 187, and 189–93. See Chap. 17 for a discussion of the impact of counter-terrorism measures on armed groups.

[3] Art. 48, Protocol Additional to the Geneva Conventions of 12 August 1949, and relating to the Protection of Victims of International Armed Conflicts (Protocol I); adopted at Geneva, 8 June 1977; entered into force, 7 December 1978 (hereinafter, 1977 Additional Protocol I); and see International Committee of the Red Cross (ICRC) Customary IHL Rule 1: 'The Principle of Distinction between Civilians and Combatants', at: http://bit.ly/32rIER0.

[4] See International Criminal Tribunal for the former Yugoslavia (ICTY), *Prosecutor v. Galić*, Judgment and Opinion (Trial Chamber) (Case No. IT-98-29-T), 5 December 2003, para. 135.

[5] One might, though, perceive some sort of equivalence for combatants during the conduct of hostilities through the prohibition on 'denial of quarter': threatening, ordering, or ensuring that there are no survivors from an attack, even if combatants seek to surrender or are otherwise *hors de combat* through wounds or sickness. See Art. 40, 1977 Additional Protocol I; and also Art. 4(1), Protocol additional to the Geneva Conventions of 12 August 1949, and relating to the protection of victims of non-international armed conflicts (Protocol II); adopted at Geneva, 8 June 1977; entered into force, 7 December 1978 (hereinafter, 1977 Additional Protocol II). Denial of quarter is discussed *supra* in Chapter 2 of this work.

Table 13.1 Summary of Prohibitions of Acts or Threats of Terror

Prohibition	AP I	Customary status (IAC)	AP II	Customary status (NIAC)
Threatening or acting to terrorise the civilian population	Art. 51(2)	Yes	Art. 13(2)	Yes
Acts of terrorism against civilians	Art. 33, GC IV	Yes	Art. 4(2)	Yes

13.3 This chapter discusses the prohibition of terrorism under the two 1977 Additional Protocols[6] as well as under the 1949 Geneva Convention IV;[7] provisions that are reflected also in customary law.[8] The key rules are summarised in Table 13.1. As evidenced therein, the prohibitions in the two Additional Protocols complement the protection afforded under the 1949 Geneva Convention IV, which prohibits 'measures' of terrorism against protected civilians in international armed conflict.[9] The prohibition on acts of terrorism in the 1977 Additional Protocol II serves to protect not only civilians but also persons who were—but who are no longer—taking a direct part in hostilities.

13.4 The chapter first addresses acts and 'measures' of terrorism under Geneva Law. It then describes the notion of acts of terror in the conduct of hostilities (i.e. Hague Law). Finally, the chapter addresses the lawful conduct of counterterrorism operations by States during situations of armed conflict, seeking to clarify when Hague Law rules will apply and when law enforcement rules are applicable, as complemented by human rights law principles of legality and precaution. Since the 9/11 attacks in the United States, there has been a growing tendency in certain quarters to refer to responsive US actions in situations of armed conflict as counterterrorism rather than counterinsurgency or action taken to quell an insurrection. The moniker applied by a State in its public pronouncements does not affect the applicable law or the applicable rules, which are rooted in the prevailing circumstances of each case.

---

[6] Art. 51(2), 1977 Additional Protocol I; and Art. 13(2), 1977 Additional Protocol II.
[7] Convention (IV) Relative to the Protection of Civilian Persons in Time of War; adopted at Geneva, 12 August 1949; entered into force, 21 October 1950 (hereinafter, 1949 Geneva Convention IV).
[8] ICRC, Customary IHL Rule 2: 'Violence Aimed at Spreading Terror among the Civilian Population', at: http://bit.ly/2ONFTT7.
[9] Art. 33, 1949 Geneva Convention IV.

Measures and acts of terrorism

IHL prohibits terrorism against persons in the power of the enemy in both international and non-international armed conflict in two dedicated treaty provisions. Under Article 33 of the 1949 Geneva Convention IV, 'measures' of terrorism are prohibited in international armed conflict against civilians in occupied territory and aliens in the territory of a party to an international armed conflict. The slightly strange choice of wording—'measures'—encompasses, but is not limited to, acts of violence, including those perpetrated under colour of law applicable domestically or extraterritorially in occupied territory against protected civilians. The prohibition thus concerns acts by States and their agents, especially but not only their armed forces.[10]

13.5

The 1958 commentary on the provision in Article 33[11] did little to elucidate the precise meaning of 'terrorism' therein, leading two commentators to describe the notion as 'vague in view of the lack of a generally recognized definition' of the term.[12] Kretzmer considers the term in broad terms as extending to mass arrests or detentions and even house searches, where their primary purpose is to terrorise the population in an occupied territory.[13] That said, the earlier definition of terrorism that States inserted in the 1937 Convention for the Prevention and Punishment of Terrorism—a League of Nations treaty that never entered into force—referred to 'criminal acts *directed against a State* and intended or calculated to create a state of terror in the minds of particular persons or a group of persons or the general public'.[14] This implied actions by non-State actors and was not directly transposable to acts perpetrated by a State against a population.[15]

13.6

Nonetheless, one must understand the provision in Article 33 in the context of the murderous treatment meted out by the Nazis and the Japanese to civilians in territories they invaded and occupied during the Second World War. For instance, the Einsatzgruppen, which operated in countries across Eastern Europe, were, as Prosecutor Benjamin Ferencz declared in the subsequent war crimes trial, special SS paramilitary groups 'established for the specific purpose of massacring human beings because they were Jews, or because they were for some other reason regarded as inferior peoples'.[16] Ferencz

13.7

---

[10] The police and other security forces could also carry out such prohibited acts, potentially even in the context of ostensibly counterterrorism operations.

[11] International Committee of the Red Cross (ICRC), Commentary on Article 33(1), 1949 Geneva Convention IV, 1958, at: http://bit.ly/2LbfkLJ, para. 2.

[12] A. R. Ziegler and S. Wehrenberg, 'Domestic Implementation', in A. Clapham, P. Gaeta, and M. Sassòli (eds.), *The 1949 Geneva Conventions: A Commentary*, 1st Edn, Oxford University Press, Oxford, 2015, p. 662.

[13] D. Kretzmer, 'Terrorism and the International Law of Occupation', Chap. 15 in B. Saul (ed.), *Research Handbook on International Law and Terrorism*, 2nd Edn, Edward Elgar Publishing, Cheltenham, 2021, p. 213.

[14] Art. I(2), Convention for the Prevention and Punishment of Terrorism; adopted at Geneva, 16 November 1937; never entered into force (emphasis added).

[15] The Convention did not envisage such a circumstance, but it did prohibit encouraging terrorist activities against another State and require that they 'prevent and punish activities of this nature'. Art. I(1), 1937 Convention for the Prevention and Punishment of Terrorism.

[16] Opening Statement of Benjamin B. Ferencz, Prosecutor at the Einsatzgruppen trial following the end of the War. Text available at: http://bit.ly/32Bxyvu.

continued: 'Helpless civilians were conveniently labelled "Partisans" or "Partisan-sympathizers" and then executed. In the hospitals and asylums the Einsatzgruppen destroyed the ill and insane, for "useless eaters" could never serve the Third Reich.'[17] Crimes against humanity perpetrated by State agents in occupied territories would today also constitute prohibited measures of terrorism under IHL.

13.8 The prohibition of 'acts of terrorism' under Article 4 of the 1977 Additional Protocol II[18] binds parties to armed conflicts falling within the scope of that Protocol, State and non-State alike. As noted above, the provision is broad in scope, protecting both civilians and all others 'who do not take a direct part or who have ceased to take part in hostilities, whether or not their liberty has been restricted'.[19] The term 'acts of terrorism' is said to cover 'not only acts directed against people, but also acts directed against installations which would cause victims as a side-effect'.[20] Thus, for example, the deliberate destruction of civilian homes, schools, or medical facilities, as well as the murder or torture of civilians or those *hors de combat*, where the intent was to terrorise the population, would be encapsulated by the prohibition.

13.9 The armed conflicts in Sierra Leone in the late 1980s and the 1990s saw widespread use of terror tactics by non-State armed groups, in particular the Revolutionary United Front (RUF) and the Armed Forces Revolutionary Council (AFRC). Charles Taylor, the former President of Liberia, was prosecuted before the Special Court for Sierra Leone for his support to these groups and his complicity in the atrocities they perpetrated. These included widespread amputations of the arms of civilian women and children. In its report on a January 1999 offensive against the Sierra Leonean capital, Freetown, Human Rights Watch stated that: 'Rebel forces in Sierra Leone systematically murdered, mutilated, and raped civilians during their January offensive'.[21] The organisation further documented 'how entire families were gunned down in the street, children and adults had their limbs hacked off with machetes, and girls and young women were taken to rebel bases and sexually abused'.[22]

13.10 In the Special Court's judgment on Mr. Taylor's appeal against his conviction for, among others, the war crime of acts of terrorism, the Appeals Chamber declared itself satisfied that the RUF/AFRC 'used acts of terror as its primary modus operandi', pursuing a strategy to achieve its goals

> through extreme fear by making Sierra Leone 'fearful'. The primary purpose was to spread terror, but it was not aimless terror. Barbaric, brutal violence was purposefully unleashed against civilians because it made them afraid—afraid that there would only

---

[17] Ibid.
[18] Art. 4(2)(d), 1977 Additional Protocol II.
[19] Ibid., Art. 4(1).
[20] ICRC, Commentary on the 1977 Additional Protocols, at: http://bit.ly/2IGhscP, para. 4538.
[21] Human Rights Watch, 'Shocking War Crimes in Sierra Leone. New Testimonies on Mutilation, Rape of Civilians', 24 June 1999, at: http://bit.ly/3bcqDOy.
[22] Ibid.

be more unspeakable violence if they continued to resist in any way, continued to stay in their communities or dared to return to their homes.[23]

13.11 Perhaps surprisingly, the ICRC's customary law study did not find that the prohibition on acts of terrorism perpetrated against persons in the power of the enemy during armed conflict was a distinct rule of customary law. That said, the unlawful acts would clearly fall within the purview of other customary rules, such as the requirement that civilians and persons *hors de combat* be treated humanely,[24] as well as within the prohibition on collective punishments.[25] Murder and torture are war crimes under both conventional and customary international law. Collective punishments are, as the ICRC has clarified, also a war crime under customary international law in both international and non-international armed conflict.[26] Yoram Dinstein has voiced his regret that the prohibition in Article 4(2) of the 1977 Additional Protocol II was not inscribed as a war crime under the jurisdiction of the International Criminal Court.[27]

Acts of violence intended to terrorise the civilian population

13.12 The use of terror tactics against the civilian population in the conduct of hostilities[28] is explicitly prohibited, in identical terms, by the two 1977 Additional Protocols.[29] Thus, it is stipulated that: 'Acts or threats of violence the primary purpose of which is to spread terror among the civilian population are prohibited.'[30] This is a customary rule, applicable to all armed conflicts.[31] The acts proscribed by the prohibition constitute, the ICRC avers, a 'special type of terrorism'.[32] According to the organisation's commentary on the Additional Protocols: 'Air raids have often been used as a means of terrorizing the population', but these are not the only methods. For this reason the text contains a much broader expression, namely 'acts or threats of violence' so as to cover all possible

---

[23] Special Court for Sierra Leone, *Prosecutor* v. *Charles Ghankay Taylor*, Judgment (Appeals Chamber) (Case No. SCSL-03-01-A), 26 September 2013, para. 300.
[24] ICRC, Customary IHL Rule 87: 'Humane Treatment', at: http://bit.ly/380xuqV.
[25] ICRC, Customary IHL Rule 103: 'Collective Punishments', at: http://bit.ly/38nQ8dT.
[26] ICRC, Customary IHL Rule 156: 'Definition of War Crimes', at: http://bit.ly/32HjZb2, paras. ii(ii) and iv(vi), respectively.
[27] Y. Dinstein, *Non-International Armed Conflicts in International Law*, 2nd Edn, Cambridge University Press, Cambridge, 2021, p. 247, para. 703.
[28] Thus, for instance, in the 1977 Additional Protocol I, the relevant rule is inscribed in the Section entitled 'General protection against effects of hostilities'.
[29] In its 1956 Draft Rules, the ICRC had included a provision whereby: 'Attacks directed against the civilian population, as such, whether with the object of terrorizing it or for any other reason, are prohibited.' Art. 6, 'Draft Rules for the Limitation of the Dangers incurred by the Civilian Population in Time of War. ICRC, 1956', at: https://bit.ly/31DEDyv.
[30] Art. 51(2), 1977 Additional Protocol I; and Art. 13(2), 1977 Additional Protocol II.
[31] ICRC, Customary IHL Rule 2: 'Violence Aimed at Spreading Terror among the Civilian Population', at: http://bit.ly/2ONFTT7.
[32] Y. Sandoz, C. Swinarski, and B. Zimmermann (eds.), *Commentary on the Additional Protocols of 8 June 1977 to the Geneva Conventions of 12 August 1949*, Martinus Nijhoff, Geneva, 1987, para. 4538.

circumstances.'[33] The concept of 'terror' has been defined by the International Criminal Tribunal for the former Yugoslavia (ICTY) as 'extreme fear'.[34]

13.13 That said, the ICRC commentary notes that while acts of violence during conflict 'almost always give rise to some degree of terror among the population' and although 'attacks on armed forces are purposely conducted brutally in order to intimidate the enemy soldiers and persuade them to surrender', the Hague Law prohibition on terrorising civilians is limited to acts of violence whose primary purpose is to spread terror among the civilian population 'without offering substantial military advantage'.[35] Thus, as Yoram Dinstein has observed, large-scale aerial bombardments that are 'pounding' military objectives and 'breaking the back of the enemy armed forces' are not unlawful according to this rule, 'even if they lead … to the collapse of civilian morale'.[36] In its 2017 judgment in the *Prlić* case, the Appeals Chamber of the ICTY (Judge Pocar dissenting) held that the Old Bridge at Mostar was a lawful military objective in the circumstances prevailing at the time and thus its destruction could not be the basis for sustaining the conviction at trial for the war crime of unlawful infliction of terror on civilians.[37]

13.14 Certain weapons have been deemed to be 'terror' weapons. This has tended to pertain to inherently indiscriminate weapons, such as missiles that cannot be ordinarily directed at a military objective. In its 2015 *Law of War Manual*, the United States (US) Department of Defense referred to 'indiscriminate terror weapons such as the German V bombs' used in the Second World War.[38] Another example is the first variant of the Soviet Scud missile, which was based on the German V-2 rocket, was expected to miss an intended point target by more than one kilometre.[39] In more recent conflicts, the UN Commission of Inquiry on Syria has affirmed that use of barrel bombs in area bombardment is prohibited 'as a tactic that spreads terror among the civilian population'.[40] This concerns the extent of the blast caused by the detonation of such bombs rather than their inability to be targeted with the requisite accuracy.

---

[33] ICRC, Commentary on the 1977 Additional Protocols, para. 4785.
[34] ICTY, *Prosecutor v. Galić*, Judgment and Opinion (Trial Chamber) (Case No. IT-98-29-T), 5 December 2003, para. 135. This holding was further confirmed in the judgment at trial in the *Blagojević* case two years later. ICTY, *Prosecutor v. Blagojević and Jokić*, Judgment (Trial Chamber) (Case No. IT-02-60-T), 17 January 2005, para. 590.
[35] ICRC, Commentary on the 1977 Additional Protocols, para. 1940.
[36] Y. Dinstein, *The Conduct of Hostilities under the Law of International Armed Conflict*, 3rd Edn, Cambridge University Press, Cambridge, 2016, p. 146, para. 390.
[37] ICTY, *Prosecutor v. Prlić*, Judgment (Appeals Chamber) (Case No. IT-04-74-A), 29 November 2017, paras. 411 and 425–26. In his dissent, Judge Pocar set out his strong disagreement with the Majority, finding rather that the destruction of the Old Bridge of Mostar constituted wanton destruction not justified by military necessity as a violation of the laws or customs of war. Accordingly he also disagreed with the reasoning and the conclusions of the Majority with respect to the destruction of the Old Bridge of Mostar as an underlying act of unlawful infliction of terror on civilians as a violation of the laws of customs of war. Dissenting Opinion of Judge Fausto Pocar, para. 21.
[38] US Department of Defense, *Law of War Manual*, June 2015 (Updated December 2016), §1.4.1, note 54.
[39] See, e.g., S. Casey-Maslen, 'Weapons', Chap. 11 in B. Saul and D. Akande (eds.), *The Oxford Guide to International Humanitarian Law*, Oxford University Press, Oxford, 2020, p. 265.
[40] Report of the independent international commission of inquiry on the Syrian Arab Republic, UN doc. A/HRC/27/60, 13 August 2014, para. 102.

13.15 Under the 1977 Additional Protocol I, an attack by bombardment by any methods or means is indiscriminate where it 'treats as a single military objective a number of clearly separated and distinct military objectives located in a city, town, village or other area containing a similar concentration of civilians or civilian objects'.[41] More tentatively, the UN Commission of Inquiry on the 2014 Gaza conflict noted that, given the impossibility for Palestinian armed groups to direct rockets towards military objectives, it could not 'exclude' that 'the indiscriminate rocket attacks may constitute acts of violence whose primary purpose is to spread terror among the civilian population'.

13.16 Weapons may be used in terror attacks where they are not inherently indiscriminate but have civilians 'as their primary target'. Thus, the UN Commission of Inquiry on Syria has affirmed that a 'massive attack with sarin-filled rockets on eastern Ghutah in August 2013 killed, maimed, injured and terrorized Syrian civilians'.[42] This attack has been ascribed to the Syrian government.[43] The Commission has further affirmed in the past that Jabhat al-Nusra and affiliated groups used suicide bombings and large-scale vehicle-borne improvised explosive devices with a view to terrorising the civilian population. Between 6 March and 24 June 2014, Homs governorate, and in particular Homs city, was hit by multiple car bombings in government-controlled areas. On 24 June 2014, for instance, a car bomb exploded in Homs city, killing two civilians and injuring 20 more. The Commission stated that: 'Such attacks demonstrate a clear intent to spread terror among the civilian population.'[44]

Terrorising civilians as a war crime under customary law

13.17 Whether terrorising civilians in the conduct of hostilities is a distinct war crime under customary international law is not settled. Although incorporated in the Statutes of the International Criminal Tribunal for Rwanda and the Special Court for Sierra Leone, it is not inscribed in the 1998 Rome Statute of the International Criminal Court.[45] In their respective judgments in the *Galić* case, an ICTY Trial Chamber and then the Appeals Chamber declared themselves satisfied, although in each case only by majority decision, that 'a breach of the prohibition of terror against the civilian population gave rise to individual criminal responsibility pursuant to customary international law at the time of the commission of the offences for which Galić was convicted'.[46]

---

[41] Art. 51(5)(a), 1977 Additional Protocol I.
[42] Report of the Independent International Commission of Inquiry on the Syrian Arab Republic, UN doc. A/HRC/46/54, 21 January 2021, para. 9.
[43] The White House, Office of the Press Secretary, 'Government Assessment of the Syrian Government's Use of Chemical Weapons on August 21, 2013', Press release, 30 August 2013, at: https://bit.ly/3xtIdos.
[44] Report of the Independent International Commission of Inquiry on the Syrian Arab Republic, UN doc. A/HRC/27/60, para. 107.
[45] Statute of the International Criminal Court; adopted at Rome, 17 July 1998; entered into force, 1 July 2002.
[46] ICTY, *Prosecutor v. Galić*, Judgment (Appeals Chamber) (Case No. IT-98-29-A), 30 November 2006, para. 86.

13.18 In his Dissenting Opinion at trial, Judge Rafael Nieto-Navia argued that the crime of terror did not fall within the jurisdiction of the ICTY. He believed that the Trial Chamber had failed to establish that the offence of inflicting terror on a civilian population attracted individual criminal responsibility under international customary law.[47] In his Dissenting Opinion in the Appeals Chamber, Judge Wolfgang Schomburg believed that there was no basis to find that 'terrorisation against a civilian population' was penalised 'beyond any doubt under customary international criminal law at the time relevant to the Indictment'.[48] Judge Schomburg agreed that there could be 'no doubt' that the prohibition per se was part of customary international law.[49] But he questioned the State practice on which the Majority of the Appeals Chamber relied, observing, inter alia, that none of the permanent members of the UN Security Council 'or any other prominent State' had penalised terrorisation against a civilian population as a war crime.[50] He considered it relevant that the Rome Statute did not have jurisdiction over such a war crime.[51]

13.19 In its trial judgment against Radovan Karadžić in 2016, the ICTY extended the scope of the crime to potentially encompass also indiscriminate attacks: 'as is the case with unlawful attacks on civilians, the acts or threats of violence constituting terror need not be limited to direct attacks on civilians or threats thereof, but may include indiscriminate or disproportionate attacks'.[52] The Residual Mechanism of the ICTY that followed the Tribunal's formal closure at the end of 2017 once again addressed the issue of whether terrorising civilians in the conduct of hostilities was a war crime under customary law in its adjudication of the appeal of Ratko Mladic in June 2021. Mr. Mladic had asserted that the prohibition of spreading terror among the civilian population did not extend to its criminalisation under customary international law, at least when the Siege of Sarajevo was ongoing, 'due to insufficient evidence of settled, extensive, or uniform state practice'.[53] The Residual Mechanism rejected his assertion.[54]

13.20 The *Galić* case was the first time the ICTY had considered the charge of terror as a war crime. General Stanislav Galić, as commander of the Bosnian Serbs army around Sarajevo, was accused of having 'conducted a protracted campaign of shelling and sniping upon civilian areas of Sarajevo and upon the civilian population thereby inflicting terror and mental suffering upon its civilian population'.[55] The Trial Chamber heard 'reliable evidence that civilians were targeted during funerals, in ambulances, in

---

[47] ICTY, *Prosecutor v. Galić*, Judgment and Opinion (Trial Chamber), Dissenting Opinion of Judge Nieto-Navia, paras. 113, 114.
[48] ICTY, *Prosecutor v. Galić*, Judgment (Appeals Chamber), Dissenting Opinion of Judge Wolfgang Schomburg, para. 2.
[49] Ibid., para. 7.
[50] Ibid., paras. 8–12, 18.
[51] Ibid., para. 20.
[52] ICTY, *Prosecutor v. Radovan Karadžić*, Judgment (Trial Chamber) (Case No. IT-95-5/18-T), 24 March 2016, para. 460.
[53] International Residual Mechanism for Criminal Tribunals, *Prosecutor v. Ratko Mladic*, Judgment (Appeals Chamber) (Case No. MICT-13-56-A), 8 June 2021, para. 280.
[54] Ibid., para. 287.
[55] ICTY, *Prosecutor v. Galić*, Judgment and Opinion (Trial Chamber), paras. 65, 66.

hospitals, on trams, on buses, when driving or cycling, at home, while tending gardens or fires or clearing rubbish in the city'.[56] The Majority at trial were convinced by the evidence that civilians in government-held areas of Sarajevo were 'directly or indiscriminately attacked' from Bosnian Serb-controlled territory, and that, as a result and 'as a minimum, hundreds of civilians were killed and thousands others were injured'.[57]

General Adrianus Van Baal, Chief of Staff of the United Nations Protection Force (UNPROFOR) in Bosnia and Herzegovina in 1994, testified before the Trial Chamber that sniping in Sarajevo was 'without any discrimination, indiscriminately shooting defenceless citizens, women, children, who were unable to protect and defend themselves, at unexpected places and at unexpected times'.[58] This led him to conclude, the Trial Chamber noted, 'that its objective was to cause terror; he specified that women and children were the predominant target'.[59]

13.21

The ICTY Trial Chamber, by Majority, rejected the submissions by both Defence and Prosecution that actual infliction of terror was an element of the war crime of terror. It did so on the 'plain wording of Article 51(2) [of Additional Protocol I], as well as the travaux préparatoires of the Diplomatic Conference'.[60] The key issue was the intent of the perpetrator. Accordingly, the Trial Chamber and the Appeals Chamber found, by Majority, that for the war crime of terror to be established the following specific elements need to be proven:

13.22

1. Acts or threats of violence were directed against the civilian population or individual civilians not taking direct part in hostilities causing death or serious injury to body or health within the civilian population.
2. The offender wilfully made the civilian population or individual civilians not taking direct part in hostilities the object of those acts of violence.
3. The above offence was committed with the primary purpose of spreading terror among the civilian population.[61]

The definition of terrorism under international law

More broadly under international law, there is no consensus as to the definition of 'international terrorism' and thus no definition is reflected in customary law.[62] Indeed, for the last two decades the conclusion of the Comprehensive Convention on International Terrorism has been stymied by, primarily, lack of agreement as to the

13.23

---

[56] Ibid., para. 584.
[57] Ibid., para. 591.
[58] Ibid., para. 573.
[59] Ibid.
[60] Ibid., para. 134.
[61] Ibid., para. 133; ICTY, *Prosecutor* v. *Galić*, Judgment (Appeals Chamber), paras. 100, 101.
[62] See on this issue S. Casey-Maslen, *The Right to Life under International Law: An Interpretive Manual*, Cambridge University Press, Cambridge, 2021, para. 8.12.

precise parameters of the term.[63] Major sticking points include whether the acts of national liberation movements fighting against foreign military occupation or engaged in an armed struggle for independence from colonial rule are to be considered terrorist in nature.[64]

13.24 That said, the 2005 draft of the Comprehensive Convention stipulates that: 'The activities of armed forces during an armed conflict, as those terms are understood under international humanitarian law, which are governed by that law, are not governed by the present Convention.'[65] This reflects a similar provision in the 1997 Terrorist Bombings Convention.[66] The notion of 'armed forces' in these texts encompasses both State armed forces and organised non-State armed groups, where they are party to an armed conflict.[67] This is made clear from the text, which refers to 'armed forces' and then to 'military forces of a State' in the same provision.[68] The narrowing, in the conduct of hostilities, of what one might term the 'peacetime' definition of international terrorism is required because the targeting of objects or personnel that constitute lawful military objectives under IHL (see Chapters 8 and 9 above, respectively) falls within treaty definitions of terrorism, such as that set out in the 1997 Convention.[69]

13.25 For example, the targeting of a military barracks or of combatant members of the armed forces using explosive devices is ordinarily prohibited by law in the territory of the 170 States Parties to the Terrorist Bombings Convention pursuant to its provisions. But a number of States Parties distinguish between criminal actions and legitimate struggle for self-determination outside the conduct of hostilities. In adhering to the 1997 Convention, Pakistan issued a declaration whereby nothing in the Convention 'shall be applicable to struggles, including armed struggle, for the realization of right of self-determination launched against any alien or foreign occupation or domination, in accordance with the rules of international law'. Many States objected to this apparent reservation.[70] Finland, for instance, was 'of the view that the declaration amounts to a reservation as its purpose is to unilaterally limit the scope of the Convention'. Finland further considered the declaration 'to be in contradiction with the object and purpose

---

[63] Ibid., para. 8.06.
[64] See, e.g., M. Hmoud, 'Negotiating the Draft Comprehensive Convention on International Terrorism: Major Bones of Contention', *Journal of International Criminal Justice*, Vol. 4, No. 5 (November 2006), pp. 1031–43.
[65] Art. 20(2), Draft comprehensive convention against international terrorism, Consolidated text prepared by the coordinator for discussion, Appendix II in UN doc. A/59/894 of 12 August 2005.
[66] Art. 19(2), International Convention for the Suppression of Terrorist Bombings; adopted at New York, 15 December 1997; entered into force, 23 May 2001. As of 1 May 2022, 170 States were party to the Convention.
[67] S. Witten, 'The International Convention for the Suppression of Terrorist Bombings', Chap. 8 in B. Saul (ed.), *Research Handbook on International Law and Terrorism*, 2nd Edn, Edward Elgar Publishing, Cheltenham, 2021, p. 117. See also A. R. Perera, 'The draft United Nations Comprehensive Convention on International Terrorism', Chap. 9 in ibid., p. 127.
[68] D. Kretzmer, 'Terrorism and the International Law of Occupation', Chap. 15 in B. Saul (ed.), *Research Handbook on International Law and Terrorism*, 2nd Edn, Edward Elgar Publishing, Cheltenham, 2021, p. 216.
[69] See Art. 2(1), 1997 Terrorist Bombings Convention.
[70] Australia, Austria, Canada, Denmark, Finland, France, Germany, India, Ireland, Israel, Italy, Japan, Moldova, the Netherlands, New Zealand, Norway, Poland, Russia, Spain, Sweden, United Kingdom, and the United States.

of the Convention, namely the suppression of terrorist bombings wherever and by whomever carried out'.[71]

Given the exclusion for the 'activities of armed forces' when governed by IHL, however, as soon as an armed group becomes a party to an armed conflict, the Terrorist Bombings Convention no longer applies to its acts in the conduct of hostilities. This conventional exclusion would not, however, extend to encompass the acts of civilians 'sporadically' participating directly in hostilities,[72] nor would it preclude legal sanction for any crimes committed under domestic criminal law (even where those concerned attacks against lawful military objectives as determined under IHL).[73] **13.26**

Threats to terrorise the civilian population

The primary prohibition in conventional and customary IHL also encompasses *threats* to perpetrate acts of violence with the primary purpose of spreading terror among the civilian population. This is one of the very rare instances in IHL where threats of violence are explicitly outlawed.[74] There is, however, no settled, precise definition of a threat under international law, including in the context of IHL. In the late 1980s, Sadurska described a threat as 'an act that is designed to create a psychological condition in the target of apprehension, anxiety and eventually fear, that will erode the target's resistance to change or will pressure it toward preserving the status quo'.[75] **13.27**

Such a threat could presumably concern the putative use of a weapon of mass destruction against a town or city. Consonant with broader international law, it is likely that such unlawful threats may be made implicitly as well as overtly.[76] Under the 2017 Treaty on the Prohibition of Nuclear Weapons, it is prohibited to each State Party to threaten to use nuclear weapons.[77] In his New-Year's-Day speech of 1 January 2018, the North Korean leader Kim Jong-un stated: 'The entire United States is within range of **13.28**

---

[71] Declaration of Finland, 17 June 2003, at: http://bit.ly/2YbSI1g.

[72] B. Saul, 'Terrorism, Counter-Terrorism, and International Humanitarian Law', Chap. 18 in B. Saul and D. Akande (eds.), *The Oxford Guide to International Humanitarian Law*, Oxford University Press, Oxford, 2020, p. 412. This would imply, for instance, that individual civilians in Ukraine who prepared and/or threw Molotov cocktails at Russian forces would be deemed responsible for international terrorism under the terms of the Convention. On 4 March 2022, Ukraine made a declaration under the Convention stating that it 'is unable to guarantee full implementation of its obligations [under the above Convention] due to the Armed aggression of the Russian Federation and with the imposition of martial law until the complete cessation of encroachment on the sovereignty, territorial integrity and inviolability of Ukraine.' Declaration available at: https://bit.ly/3kIy1og.

[73] *R v. Gul (Appellant)*, [2013] UKSC 64, paras. 46 and 52–54; see Saul, 'Terrorism, Counter-Terrorism, and International Humanitarian Law', p. 417.

[74] For other instances, see Art. 27, 1949 Geneva Convention III; Art. 27, 1949 Geneva Convention IV; Arts. 40 and 75(2), 1977 Additional Protocol I; and Art. 4(2), 1977 Additional Protocol II.

[75] R. Sadurska, 'Threats of Force', *The American Journal of International Law*, Vol. 82, No. 2 (1988), pp. 239–68, at p. 241.

[76] See, e.g., I. Brownlie, *International Law and the Use of Force by States*, Oxford University Press, Oxford, 1963, p. 364.

[77] Art. 1(1)(d), Treaty on the Prohibition of Nuclear Weapons; adopted at New York, 7 July 2017; entered into force, 21 January 2021. As of 1 May 2022, 60 States were party to the Convention.

218 TERRORISM AND ACTS OF TERROR

our nuclear weapons, and a nuclear button is always on my desk. This is reality, not a threat'.[78] On 2 January 2018, in response to that comment, US President Donald Trump tweeted: 'Will someone from his depleted and food starved regime please inform him that I too have a Nuclear Button, but it is a much bigger & more powerful one than his, and my Button works!'[79]

13.29 A clear instance of where acts related to nuclear weapons might amount to a more implicit—yet still potentially unlawful—threat of violence is in the nuclear tests conducted by India and Pakistan in May 1998. India and Pakistan were sending clear signals to each other through the multiple tests each carried out. Indeed, in the subsequent discussions on the tests in the UN Security Council, Ambassador Robert Fowler of Canada said that India and Pakistan had 'returned the world to the dark threat of nuclear terror'.[80]

Counterterrorism operations

13.30 Since 11 September 2001, there has been a growing tendency to refer to counterinsurgency operations or action taken to quell an insurrection as 'counterterrorism' operations. In the aftermath of the 9/11 attacks, US President George W. Bush used the term 'war on terrorism' (on 16 September 2001), and then 'War on Terror' in a speech to Congress (on 20 September 2001). In that speech, George Bush stated, 'Our war on terror begins with Al Qaeda, but it does not end there ... It will not end until every terrorist group of global reach has been found, stopped and defeated.'[81]

13.31 The United States has sought to prosecute and punish leading figures within al-Qaeda who planned the 9/11 attacks. One of these is Khalid Shaikh Mohammed, the alleged mastermind of the attacks. At the time of writing, the selection of the military officers for the jury in his trial on charges of murder in violation of the law of war, attacking civilians, and terrorism had been planned to start on 7 November 2021 at the earliest, more than 20 years after the events in question.[82] But this date came and went without a jury being sworn in.[83] The war crimes trial, should it go ahead as planned, will be heard by a military commission as a hybrid of federal and military courts.[84] Given that the United States is arguing that an armed conflict existed at the time of the

---

[78] '"Nuclear button is always on my desk"', Newshub, 1 January 2018, at: http://bit.ly/2MIjn1l.
[79] Donald J. Trump, Tweet, Twitter, 2 January 2018.
[80] UN, 'United Nations Security Council Condemns Nuclear Tests by India and Pakistan', 6 June 1998, at: http://bit.ly/2VVO0EU.
[81] Address by US President George W. Bush to a joint session of US Congress, Washington, D.C., 20 September 2001, text available at: http://wapo.st/38sNjs9.
[82] C. Rosenberg, 'Pandemic Delays Start of 9/11 Trial Past 20th Anniversary of Attacks', *The New York Times*, 18 December 2020, at: http://nyti.ms/3s9kM1V.
[83] C. Rosenberg, 'Trial Guide: The Sept. 11 Case at Guantánamo Bay', *The New York Times*, 3 December 2021, at: https://nyti.ms/3zhn3wt.
[84] C. Rosenberg, 'Trial for Men Accused of Plotting 9/11 Attacks Is Set for 2021', *The New York Times*, 30 August 2019, at: http://nyti.ms/3q2pEoo.

attacks, the exclusion of the Terrorist Bombings Convention should apply as a matter of international law. Moreover, the attack on the Pentagon concerned a lawful military objective under IHL.

But just as no consensus definition exists of terrorism among States, so there is no universally accepted definition of 'counterterrorism' in international law. In 2006, Javier Ruperez, the Executive Director of the UN Counter-Terrorism Committee Executive Directorate (CTED), observed that 'in order to conclude the accelerating effort to develop a global counter-terrorist policy led by the United Nations, it would be helpful to have both the [Comprehensive] convention and the definition'.[85] As a working definition of counterterrorism, the US Department of Defense uses the following: 'Activities and operations taken to neutralize terrorists and their organizations and networks in order to render them incapable of using violence to instil fear and coerce governments or societies to achieve their goals.'[86]

13.32

The UN Global Counter-Terrorism Strategy was adopted in 2006 under UN General Assembly Resolution 60/288.[87] In the annexed Plan of Action to the Global Counter-Terrorism Strategy, UN Member States resolved: 'To recognize that international co-operation and any measures that we undertake to prevent and combat terrorism must comply with our obligations under international law, including the Charter of the United Nations and relevant international conventions and protocols, in particular human rights law, refugee law and international humanitarian law.'[88]

13.33

Notwithstanding the lack of agreed definitions of terrorism and counterterrorism, there is a duty upon every State to exercise due diligence to seek to prevent manifestations of both international and domestic terrorism. In its General Comment 36 on the right to life, the Human Rights Committee reminds 'all States'—not merely States Parties to the International Covenant on Civil and Political Rights[89] (ICCPR)—of their 'responsibility as members of the international community to protect lives and to oppose widespread or systematic attacks on the right to life', including 'international terrorism'.[90]

13.34

In its 2017 judgment in the *Tagayeva* case,[91] the European Court of Human Rights held that there existed a duty upon States Parties to the European Convention on Human Rights to prevent terrorism. It found for the first time that a State—Russia—had failed to meet its due diligence obligations under the right to life in this regard. The case

13.35

---

[85] J. Ruperez, 'The United Nations in the Fight Against Terrorism', January 2006. CTED conducts expert assessments of each UN Member State and facilitates provision of technical assistance in counterterrorism. UN, 'The United Nations Security Council Counter-Terrorism Committee', at: http://bit.ly/2EdkvHq.
[86] 'Counterterrorism', in US Department of Defense, *DOD Dictionary of Military and Associated Terms*, As of November 2019, Washington, D.C., p. 53.
[87] UN General Assembly Resolution 60/288, adopted without a vote on 20 September 2006.
[88] Plan of Action, annexed to UN General Assembly Resolution 60/288, para. 3.
[89] International Covenant on Civil and Political Rights; adopted at New York, 16 December 1966; entered into force, 23 March 1976. As of 1 May 2022, 173 States were party to the ICCPR.
[90] Human Rights Committee, General Comment No. 36: Article 6: right to life, United Nations (UN) doc. CCPR/C/GC/36, 3 September 2019, para. 70.
[91] European Court of Human Rights, *Tagayeva and others v. Russia*, Judgment (First Section), 13 April 2017 (as rendered final on 18 September 2017).

concerned the siege at the school in Beslan in early September 2004, which ended with the deaths or more than 300 teachers and children as a result of the storming of the school. The pupils and their teachers had been taken hostage by the Riyadus-Salikhin Reconnaissance and Sabotage Battalion of Chechen Martyrs,[92] an Islamist armed group designated as terrorist by the UN Security Council on 4 March 2003.[93]

13.36 The applicants had argued that the Russian authorities had known of a real and immediate threat to life but had failed to take reasonable preventive measures available to them.[94] In its assessment, the Court confirmed that it was 'acutely conscious of the difficulties faced by modern States in the fight against terrorism and the dangers of hindsight analysis'. In its role as the body tasked with supervising the human rights obligations under the European Convention on Human Rights, the Court 'would need to differentiate between the political choices made in the course of fighting terrorism, that remain by their nature outside of such supervision, and other, more operational aspects of the authorities' actions that have a direct bearing on the protected rights'.[95]

13.37 Nonetheless, the Court found that the information known to the authorities before the taking of hostages at Beslan school confirmed the existence of a real and immediate risk to life. At least several days in advance the authorities had sufficiently specific information about a planned terrorist attack in the areas in the vicinity of the Malgobek District in Ingushetia and targeting an educational facility on 1 September.[96] In the face of a threat 'of such magnitude, predictability, and imminence', it could reasonably be expected 'that some preventive and protective measures would cover all educational facilities in the districts concerned and include a range of other security steps, in order to detect, deter and neutralise the terrorists as soon as possible and with minimal risk to life'.[97]

13.38 Although some preventive measures were taken, these were inadequate. The terrorists were, the Court recalled:

> able to successfully gather, prepare, travel to and seize their target, without encountering any preventive security arrangements. No single sufficiently high-level structure was responsible for the handling of the situation, evaluating and allocating resources, creating a defence for the vulnerable target group and ensuring effective containment of the threat and communication with the field teams.[98]

13.39 Counterterrorism operations must of course comply with the right to life, in particular the prohibition on arbitrary deprivation of life. This is especially pertinent to use of

---

[92] Mapping Militant Organizations, 'Riyadus-Salikhin Reconnaissance and Sabotage Battalion of Chechen Martyrs', Center for International Security and Cooperation (CISAC), Stanford University, Last modified August 2018, at: http://stanford.io/321r8F1.
[93] List at: http://bit.ly/321NkyH.
[94] *Tagayeva and others v. Russia*, Judgment, para. 478.
[95] Ibid., para. 481.
[96] Ibid., para. 491.
[97] Ibid., para. 486.
[98] Ibid., para. 491.

firearms and, a fortiori, use of explosive munitions. The standards for use of potentially or intentionally lethal force in all law enforcement operations are set out in the 1990 Basic Principles on the Use of Force and Firearms by Law Enforcement Officials,[99] specifically its Principle 9. This standard, which reflects customary international law applicable to all State use of force in counterterrorism outside the conduct of hostilities in an armed conflict, provides in part that law enforcement officials 'shall not use firearms against persons except in self-defence or defence of others against the imminent threat of death or serious injury'.[100] Solis affirms that, in a non-international armed conflict, 'should government forces come upon an encampment of sleeping enemy fighters, they would be expected to employ the police paradigm'.[101]

Where it is absolutely necessary to kill a terrorist suspect, most notably when he or she is about to detonate a bomb or kill a hostage and no alternative course of action exists to prevent this occurring, it may be lawful to shoot with intent to kill. Intentional lethal use of force may be lawful where it is 'strictly unavoidable in order to protect life'.[102] The use of an explosive munition—mine, grenade, shell, or bomb—is to be considered an intentional lethal use of force.[103] **13.40**

In its General Comment 36 on the right to life, the Human Rights Committee has recalled that Article 6 of the ICCPR continues to apply in situations of armed conflict to which the rules of IHL are applicable, including to the conduct of hostilities.[104] According to the Committee, use of lethal force 'consistent with international humanitarian law and other applicable international law norms is, in general, not arbitrary'.[105] This largely reflects the position advanced by the International Court of Justice in its 1996 Advisory Opinion on the Legality of the Threat or Use of Nuclear Weapons.[106] Therein, the Court has stated that: **13.41**

---

[99] Basic Principles on the Use of Force and Firearms by Law Enforcement Officials; adopted at Havana by the Eighth UN Congress on the Prevention of Crime and the Treatment of Offenders, 7 September 1990 (hereinafter, 1990 Basic Principles). In December 1990, the UN General Assembly welcomed the Basic Principles and invited governments to respect them. UN General Assembly Resolution 45/166, adopted without a vote on 18 December 1990, para. 4.
[100] According to the UN Special Rapporteur on extrajudicial, summary or arbitrary executions, 'an imminent or immediate threat' should be considered 'a matter of seconds, not hours'. Report of the Special Rapporteur on extrajudicial, summary or arbitrary executions, Christof Heyns, UN doc. A/HRC/26/36, 1 April 2014, para. 59.
[101] G. D. Solis, *The Law of Armed Conflict, International Humanitarian Law in War*, 3rd Edn, Cambridge University Press, Cambridge, 2021, p. 429.
[102] Principle 9, 1990 Basic Principles on the Use of Force and Firearms by Law Enforcement Officials.
[103] Thus, for instance, in 2014, the UN Special Rapporteur on extrajudicial, summary or arbitrary executions affirmed that: 'A common sense understanding of the scope of application of Basic Principle 9 suggests that all weapons that are designed and are likely to be lethal should be covered, including heavy weapons such as bombs and (drone) missiles, the use of which constitutes an intentional lethal use of force.' Report of the Special Rapporteur on extrajudicial, summary or arbitrary executions, 1 April 2014, para. 70.
[104] Human Rights Committee, General Comment 36 on the right to life, para. 64, citing General Comment No. 31 (2004) on the nature of the general legal obligation imposed on States parties to the Covenant, para. 11; and General Comment No. 29 (2001) on derogations from provisions of the Covenant during a state of emergency, para. 3.
[105] Human Rights Committee, General Comment 36 on the right to life, para. 64. The use of the words 'in general' by the Human Rights Committee, though, suggests that space may exist to find a violation of the right to life even when IHL rules are complied with, including in a counterterrorism operation in a situation of armed conflict.
[106] International Court of Justice, *Legality of the Threat or Use of Nuclear Weapons*, Advisory Opinion, 8 July 1996, para. 25.

whether a particular loss of life, through the use of a certain weapon in warfare, is to be considered an arbitrary deprivation of life contrary to Article 6 of the Covenant, can only be decided by reference to the law applicable in armed conflict and not deduced from the terms of the Covenant itself.

Thus, counterterrorism operations that amount to the conduct of hostilities must comply with, first and foremost, the principles of distinction and proportionality and employ only lawful weapons.

Concluding remarks and outlook

13.42 It is high time that the Comprehensive Convention on International Terrorism was concluded and entered into force. If there are issues as to the definition, this can be dealt with by States using interpretive declarations and/or reservations. While the 2021 judgment of the International Residual Mechanism for Criminal Tribunals has held that terrorising the civilian population is a war crime under customary law, doubts as to the legal robustness of this determination linger.

14

Starvation and Sieges

Introduction

Although sieges may 'conjure up images of medieval warfare', it is still the case that armed forces and armed groups encircle and besiege populated areas today, in both international and non-international armed conflicts.[1] As Mark Lattimer has observed, how a siege is characterised in legal terms—as an 'attack' or a 'method' of warfare, for example—is 'complicated by the fact that the term "siege" is defined neither in IHL nor in contemporary military doctrine'.[2]

14.1

As this chapter recalls, sieges were a recurrent feature of the myriad armed conflicts in Syria over the past decade. While they are often prosecuted in an indiscriminate manner, sieges are not prohibited per se by international humanitarian law (IHL). That this is the case was implicit from the 1949 Geneva Convention IV, which provides that, in an international armed conflict: 'The Parties to the conflict shall endeavour to conclude local agreements for the removal from besieged or encircled areas, of wounded, sick, infirm, and aged persons, children and maternity cases'.[3]

14.2

The International Committee of the Red Cross (ICRC) affirms that the prohibition of starvation as a method of warfare does not render siege warfare unlawful 'as long as the purpose is to achieve a military objective and not to starve a civilian population'.[4] Accordingly, it is not unlawful to starve combatants into submission. Indeed, as the United States (US) Department of Defense declares in its *Law of War Manual*, encircling enemy forces with a view to inducing their surrender by cutting them off from 'reinforcements, supplies, and communications with the outside world' is a 'legitimate' method of warfare.[5] But while starvation of combatants may often be the intent of a siege, it is rare that all civilians are able or willing to leave, and the civilian population will typically bear a heavy burden during a protracted siege.

14.3

---

[1] E.-C. Gillard, 'Sieges, the Law and Protecting Civilians', Briefing, International Law Programme, Chatham House, London, June 2019, at: https://bit.ly/39e6WEn, p. 1.

[2] M. Lattimer, 'Can Incidental Starvation of Civilians be Lawful under IHL?', *EJIL: Talk!*, 26 March 2019, at: https://bit.ly/3x1rtWh.

[3] Art. 17, Convention (IV) relative to the Protection of Civilian Persons in Time of War; adopted at Geneva, 12 August 1949; entered into force, 21 October 1950 (hereinafter, 1949 Geneva Convention IV).

[4] ICRC Customary IHL Rule 53: 'Starvation as a Method of Warfare', at: http://bit.ly/2BNHBAi, 'Sieges that cause starvation'.

[5] US Department of Defense, *Law of War Manual*, Updated December 2016, Washington, D.C., 2016, §5.19, note 689.

14.4 Starvation of the civilian population as a method of warfare, first outlawed in the Additional Protocols in 1977,[6] is a serious violation of IHL and a war crime in all armed conflict. This is so under both the Rome Statute of the International Criminal Court[7] and customary law.[8] In practice, this renders illegal sieges of towns and cities that contain civilians as soon as food and water supplies are insufficient to meet their needs.

14.5 While adverse claims continue to be made by both certain States[9] and a number of commentators,[10] it is impermissible to starve the enemy into submission where to do so would also result in the starvation of the civilian population. For, as the US Department of Defense has affirmed: 'Military action intended to starve enemy forces ... must not be taken where it is expected to result in incidental harm to the civilian population that is excessive in relation to the military advantage anticipated to be gained.'[11] Allowing civilians to leave the besieged area is not sufficient to allow the siege to be prosecuted should they decline to take advantage of the offer. Reluctance may arise, for instance, from a legitimate fear of either summary execution or arbitrary detention (and likely torture) at the hands of the besieging party.

14.6 More broadly, it is prohibited to attack, destroy, remove, or render useless objects indispensable to the survival of the civilian population. Pertaining to food, crops, livestock, and drinking water installations and supplies, among others, this supplements the general prohibition in customary law on attacking civilian objects. The key rules on sieges and starvation as a method of warfare in the two 1977 Additional Protocols and under customary IHL are summarised in Table 14.1.

The chapter begins by considering in more detail the legality of sieges under contemporary IHL. It then discusses further the prohibition of starvation as a method of warfare and its criminalisation in customary and conventional international law as a war crime.

---

[6] Protocol Additional to the Geneva Conventions of 12 August 1949, and relating to the Protection of Victims of International Armed Conflicts (Protocol I); adopted at Geneva, 8 June 1977; entered into force, 7 December 1978 (hereinafter, 1977 Additional Protocol I); Protocol Additional to the Geneva Conventions of 12 August 1949, and relating to the Protection of Victims of Non-International Armed Conflicts (Protocol II); adopted at Geneva, 8 June 1977; entered into force, 7 December 1978 (hereinafter, 1977 Additional Protocol II).

[7] As discussed further below, under the Rome Statute of the International Criminal Court, 'intentionally using starvation of civilians as a method of warfare' is a war crime in both international and, since December 2019, also non-international armed conflicts. Art. 8(2)(b)(xxv) and (e)(xix), Rome Statute of the International Criminal Court; adopted at Rome, 17 July 1998; entered into force, 1 July 2002. As of 1 May 2022, 123 States were party to the Rome Statute.

[8] ICRC, Customary IHL Rule 156: 'Definition of War Crimes', at: http://bit.ly/32HjZb2, (ii) Other serious violations of international humanitarian law committed during an international armed conflict; and (iv) Other serious violations of international humanitarian law committed during a non-international armed conflict.

[9] The United Kingdom (UK), for instance, states that IHL is not violated 'if military operations are not intended to cause starvation but have that incidental effect'. UK Ministry of Defence, *The Manual of the Law of Armed Conflict*, Oxford University Press, Oxford, 2004, para. 5.27.2.

[10] Y. Dinstein, *The Conduct of Hostilities under the Law of International Armed Conflict*, 3rd Edn, Cambridge University Press, Cambridge, 2016, pp. 253–57, paras. 688–99.

[11] US Department of Defense, *Law of War Manual*, Updated December 2016, §5.20.2.

Table 14.1 Rules on Sieges and Starvation as a Method of Warfare in the Additional Protocols

Prohibited Conduct	AP I	Customary status (IAC)	AP II	Customary status (NIAC)
Attacks on undefended localities	Art. 59(1)	Yes	No	Yes
Starvation as a method of warfare	Art. 54(1)	Yes	Art. 14	Yes
Destruction of objects indispensable to the survival of the civilian population	Art. 54(2)	Yes	Art. 14	Yes

The legality of sieges under international humanitarian law

14.7 IHL has long been concerned with sieges. Two key provisions were incorporated on the issue in both the 1899 and the 1907 Hague Regulations on Land Warfare under a chapter heading of 'On means of injuring the enemy, sieges, and bombardments'.[12] Thus, the Regulations annexed to the 1907 Hague Convention IV declare that: 'The attack or bombardment, by whatever means, of towns, villages, dwellings, or buildings which are undefended is prohibited.'[13] This provision is cited by the ICRC in its first customary rule of IHL on the principle of distinction between civilians and combatants.[14]

14.8 A siege of an undefended locality is prohibited as an unlawful attack both in the 1977 Additional Protocol I and under customary law.[15] In this regard, the Protocol provides simply that: 'It is prohibited for the Parties to the conflict to attack, by any means whatsoever, non-defended localities.'[16] As the United Kingdom explains, it would be 'unlawful to besiege an undefended town since it could be occupied without resistance'.[17] The Additional Protocol I decrees that such a locality must fulfil all of the following conditions: all combatants, as well as mobile weapons and mobile military equipment,

---

[12] See, e.g., S. II, Chap. 1, Regulations concerning the Laws and Customs of War on Land annexed to Convention (II) with Respect to the Laws and Customs of War on Land; adopted at The Hague, 29 July 1899; entered into force, 4 September 1900.

[13] Art. 25, Regulations concerning the Laws and Customs of War on Land, annexed to the Convention (IV) respecting the Laws and Customs of War on Land; adopted at The Hague, 18 October 1907; entered into force, 26 January 1910 (hereinafter 1907 Hague Regulations).

[14] ICRC Customary IHL Rule 1: 'The Principle of Distinction between Civilians and Combatants', at: http://bit.ly/32rIER0.

[15] ICRC, Commentary on Article 59 of the 1977 Additional Protocol I, 1987, at: http://bit.ly/3cM1AB3, para. 2263.

[16] Art. 59(1), 1977 Additional Protocol I.

[17] UK Ministry of Defence, *The Manual of the Law of Armed Conflict*, para. 5.34.1.

must have left the area; no hostile use may made of fixed military installations or establishments; no acts of hostility shall be committed by the authorities or by the population; and no activities in support of military operations may be undertaken.[18] Defended localities, on the other hand, include 'not only fortified towns or those equipped with a fixed defence system, but also localities in or around which troops have taken up position'.[19]

14.9 Where a siege is not unlawful per se, because there are military objectives in the city or town, all offensive and defensive military operations must comply with the principles of distinction and proportionality and the underpinning rule of precautions in attack and defence. In what appears to be a progressive development of the law, Gillard suggests that the 'encirclement dimension of sieges affects the application of the rule of proportionality'. It does so, she affirms, by affecting

> the weight to be given in proportionality assessments to injuries to civilians and damage to civilian property. For example, injuries are likely to be harder to treat in sieges, as medical facilities may be limited and supplies stretched. Damage to civilian residences may have a more severe impact on civilians if alternative shelter is limited. If previous attacks have already damaged water treatment facilities, any further damage will be more significant than if they had been intact.[20]

Such assessment by a commander, however, would demand a level of knowledge of the circumstances in the area under siege that may not be possessed by the besieging party. After all, as she asks: can besieging forces even identify military objectives with the requisite degree of certainty?[21]

14.10 At the same time, Gillard casts doubt on whether a siege can violate the rule of proportionality in attack absent the use of bombardment into the besieged area, casting it as 'a difficult argument to make'.[22] She notes the parallel with cyber operations, in which the effects of a cyber attack are considered salient, rather than merely the 'non-violent' introduction of a virus or worm into a computer network.[23] But perhaps a better parallel to be drawn is one with the 'use' of a firearm. Pointing a gun at someone is still an act of violence even if the firearm is not discharged. This is how it is reported or understood by numerous national jurisdictions.[24] As Judge Chile Eboe-Osuji stated in his partly concurring opinion in the judgment on appeal of Bosco Ntaganda: 'Assailants

---

[18] Art. 59(2), 1977 Additional Protocol I.
[19] ICRC, Commentary on Article 59 of the 1977 Additional Protocol I, 1987, para. 2266.
[20] Gillard, 'Sieges, the Law and Protecting Civilians', pp. 5–6.
[21] Ibid., p. 5.
[22] Ibid., pp. 8, 10.
[23] Rule 92 and associated commentary in M. N. Schmitt (ed.), *Tallinn Manual 2.0 on the International Law Applicable to Cyber Operations*, Cambridge University Press, Cambridge, 2017.
[24] This is the case in Denmark, for instance. See F. R. Olsen, 'The Use of Police Firearms in Denmark', Report, Copenhagen, 2008, at: http://bit.ly/3tDKJXN, p. 2. Similarly, in the United Kingdom, a police officer will be deemed to have used a firearm when it is pointed or aimed at another person as well as when it is fired at another person. College of Policing, 'Armed policing: Use of force, firearms and less lethal weapons', accessed 1 March 2021 at: https://bit.ly/2OV8ID7.

need not shoot to rob their victims. Vocal or silent demand of compliance with force of arms is enough—an understanding that the assailant wants "your money or your life" is enough, whether or not the assailant vocalises that message.'[25]

14.11 Encircling a city or town with heavily armed forces is little different in its effects even if the guns are silent. State practice does not appear to support the more conservative position. The US, for instance, considers that a siege 'must be conducted in accordance with the principles of distinction and proportionality'.[26] Similarly, the United Kingdom stipulates that the 'principles of the law of armed conflict, particularly the rules relating to attacks, apply equally to situations of siege or encirclement'.[27]

14.12 Historically, particular protection was offered to certain civilian objects by international law during the waging of war, rather than imposing a blanket prohibition on targeting such objects, as would be the case beginning with the 1977 Additional Protocol I. In the specific context of a siege or bombardment, the 1907 Hague Regulations stipulated that 'all necessary steps must be taken to spare, as far as possible, buildings dedicated to religion, art, science, or charitable purposes, historic monuments, hospitals, and places where the sick and wounded are collected, provided they are not being used at the time for military purposes'.[28] It is further 'the duty of the besieged', the 1907 Regulations instructed, 'to indicate the presence of such buildings or places by distinctive and visible signs, which shall be notified to the enemy beforehand'.[29] This draws on language from the earlier 1880 *Oxford Manual on the Laws of War on Land*.[30]

14.13 Under the Additional Protocol I, concluded almost a century later, it is prohibited to 'commit any acts of hostility directed against the historic monuments, works of art or places of worship which constitute the cultural or spiritual heritage of peoples'.[31] Moreover, the Protocol specifies that wilfully attacking such objects, where they are clearly recognised and have been accorded special protection by a 'competent international organization', is a war crime.[32] These rules are, of course, additional to the general principles governing the conduct of hostilities set out in the Protocol.

14.14 The risk of attacks being directed against civilians or civilian objects or of indiscriminate attacks is significant in any populated area, but the risks are certainly heightened during a siege in an ethnic conflict. Amid the armed conflicts in Bosnia and Herzegovina in the early 1990s, the so-called Siege of Sarajevo—the 'longest siege of

---

[25] ICC, *Prosecutor v. Bosco Ntaganda*, Judgment (Appeals Chamber) (Case No. ICC-01/04-02/06 A A2), 30 March 2021, Partly concurring opinion of Judge Chile Eboe-Osuji, 29 March 2021, at: https://bit.ly/3rAJmYK, para. 112.
[26] US Department of Defense, *Law of War Manual*, Updated December 2016, §5.20.
[27] UK Ministry of Defence, *The Manual of the Law of Armed Conflict*, para. 5.34.
[28] Art. 27, 1907 Hague Regulations.
[29] Ibid.
[30] Art. 34, *The Laws of War on Land*, Manual published by the Institute of International Law (Oxford Manual), adopted by the Institute of International Law at Oxford, 9 September 1880, available at: https://bit.ly/3vtDYd8.
[31] Art. 53(a), 1977 Additional Protocol I.
[32] Art. 85(4)(d), 1977 Additional Protocol I.

modern history'—involved the widespread commission of war crimes and crimes against humanity. By the end of the siege, 13,352 people are said to have died, of whom 5,434 were civilians.[33]

14.15 In the course of the four-year-long siege, one United Nations (UN) expert estimated that half a million shells were fired at the city, the overwhelming majority from Bosnian Serb positions. Many were targeted at Bosniak civilian areas or fired indiscriminately into the city centre. In 1993–95, some 1,000 shells landed each day in Sarajevo, aside from a lull in 1994 due to a cease-fire.[34] Colonel Andrey Demurenko, Chief of Staff of the UN Protection Force (UNPROFOR) for Sector Sarajevo in 1995, testified before the International Criminal Tribunal for the former Yugoslavia (ICTY) that 'if one looks at the human suffering, then it was a case of a full siege, just like in Leningrad during Second World War'.[35]

14.16 In its judgment in the *Dragomir Milošević* case, an ICTY Trial Chamber found that in the period covered by the Indictment, Sarajevo 'was effectively besieged' by the Bosnian Serb army. While it was

> not a siege in the classical sense of a city being surrounded, it was certainly a siege in the sense that it was a military operation, characterised by a persistent attack or campaign over a period of fourteen months, during which the civilian population was denied regular access to food, water, medicine and other essential supplies, and deprived of its right to leave the city freely at its own will and pace. The purpose of the siege of Sarajevo was to compel the BiH [Bosnia and Herzegovina] Government to capitulate.[36]

The behaviour of the Bosnian Serb troops 'was characterised', the Trial Chamber concluded, 'by indiscriminate shelling of civilian areas and sniping of civilians and civilian objects in the besieged city. As a result of the sniping and shelling, many civilians in Sarajevo were killed or seriously injured'.[37]

14.17 More recently, in Syria, as armed groups gained control over increasing numbers of Syrian population centres between 2012 and 2016, the Syrian Government executed many sieges, often bombarding densely populated civilian areas.[38] The sieges, which were 'the primary method of warfare employed by parties to the conflict', lasted for months and sometimes for years.[39] In its Paper issued in 2018 entitled *Sieges as a*

---

[33] E. Christou, 'What Caused the Siege of Sarajevo and Why Did It Last so Long?', *History Hit*, 4 July 2019, at: http://bit.ly/3923Bbj.
[34] International Criminal Tribunal for the former Yugoslavia (ICTY), *Prosecutor* v. *Dragomir Milošević*, Judgment (Trial Chamber III) (Case No. IT-98-29/1-T), 12 December 2007, para. 415.
[35] Ibid., para. 725.
[36] Ibid., para. 751.
[37] Ibid., para. 991.
[38] Report of the Independent International Commission of Inquiry on the Syrian Arab Republic, UN doc. A/HRC/46/54, 21 January 2021, at: http://bit.ly/3r5GFOm, para. 6.
[39] Independent International Commission of Inquiry on the Syrian Arab Republic, *Sieges as a Weapon of War: Encircle, starve, surrender, evacuate*, Paper, 29 May 2018, at: https://bit.ly/3vKX1Qi, para. 1.

Weapon of War: Encircle, starve, surrender, evacuate, the Independent International Commission of Inquiry on the Syrian Arab Republic stated that the sieges throughout Syria were characterised by 'pervasive war crimes'. They were, the Commission of Inquiry declared, 'repeatedly laid with impunity and in clear breach' of international human rights law and IHL.[40]

In some instances, the Commission of Inquiry reported, 'shortages of food, water, and medicine—often due to the Government's deliberate obstruction of aid access—led to acute malnutrition and deaths among vulnerable groups, including children, the elderly and the infirm'.[41] In 2014, the BBC reported that civilians had been forced by circumstance to eat grass to survive in Homs.[42] The siege of Aleppo in 2016 was another instance of siege warfare where the apparent intent was to starve both rebel fighters and civilians. It was claimed in late November 2016 that Aleppo residents—both combatants and civilians—were ten days away from starvation.[43] On 9 December 2016, with the UN Security Council unable to pass a resolution to address the issue in the face of Russia's implacable opposition, the UN General Assembly adopted a resolution demanding an immediate and complete end to all attacks on civilians and an end to all sieges in the country, 'including in Aleppo'.[44]

14.18

The tactic of sieges without necessarily encircling a city was used by the US in Iraq. An essay by US Army Major Amos C. Fox published in 2018 was entitled 'The Reemergence of the Siege'.[45] In referring to the Siege of Sarajevo, he notes that it was probably seen at the time as an anomaly, 'but in truth it turned out to be a portent of future war'.[46] Indeed, Major Fox suggests that the modern siege, 'perhaps slightly modified from that of a bygone era, is alive and well today'.[47] The 'modern siege' can, he says, be 'terrain-focused, enemy-focused or a blending of the two, depending on the action of the besieged and the goal of the attacker'. He concludes thus:

14.19

> As nations, actors and their proxies continue to clash across the world, the siege is unlikely to fall out of use in the foreseeable future. The continued conflagration in Syria possesses great potential for additional sieges to develop. The Syrian civil war has all but turned into a regional war as Syria, pro-regime forces, anti-regime forces, Kurds, ISIS, Türkiye, Israel, Iran, Russia and the United States all jockey for their own interests within what was once the country of Syria. The Siege of Ghouta is not likely

---

[40] Ibid.
[41] Report of the Independent International Commission of Inquiry on the Syrian Arab Republic, UN doc. A/HRC/46/54, para. 46.
[42] BBC, '"Eating Grass to Survive" in Besieged Homs', 27 January 2014, at: http://bbc.in/3f4JfSi.
[43] See, e.g., 'Syria's War: Aleppo Residents "10 Days from Starvation"', *Aljazeera*, 25 November 2016, at: https://bit.ly/3vIqc6j.
[44] UN General Assembly Resolution 71/130, adopted on 9 December 2016 by 122 votes to 13 with 36 abstentions, operative para. 1.
[45] A. C. Fox, 'The Reemergence of the Siege: An Assessment of Trends in Modern Land Warfare', Landpower Essay, Institute of Land Warfare, No. 18-2, June 2018, at: https://bit.ly/3eZ5pWn.
[46] Ibid.
[47] Ibid., p. 2.

to be the last siege of the Syrian civil war, nor is it likely to be the last siege of modern warfare.[48]

The prohibition on starvation of civilians as a method of warfare

14.20 The prohibition on the starvation of civilians as a method of warfare was first codified in the two 1977 Additional Protocols. While it was considered a new rule at the time of their adoption, the customary status of the norm in all armed conflict has since been confirmed.[49] It was incorporated as a war crime under the jurisdiction of the International Criminal Court in 1998 (although at that time only in the context of international armed conflict).[50] In 2018, for the first time the UN Security Council adopted a resolution strongly condemning the starvation of civilians as a method of warfare.[51] A year later, the surprising omission from the Rome Statute of the war crime in non-international armed conflict was duly rectified by the States Parties.[52] In this regard, the amendment to Article 8(2)(e) of the Statute stipulates that the crime consists of: 'Intentionally using starvation of civilians as a method of warfare by depriving them of objects indispensable to their survival, including willfully impeding relief supplies'.[53]

14.21 In its commentary on the provision in the Additional Protocol I,[54] the ICRC interpreted the rule narrowly as being limited to action 'deliberately' undertaken to provoke starvation. This mental element appears to be reflected in the elements of the war crime under the Rome Statute, which demands that the alleged perpetrator be proven to have 'intended to starve civilians as a method of warfare'.[55] It is probably the case, however, that intent can be inferred from the act of 'causing the population to suffer hunger, particularly by depriving it of its sources of food or of supplies'.[56] After all, the general provision on mental elements in the Rome Statute, which requires both intent and knowledge, explains that intent in relation to conduct demands that the accused 'means to engage in the conduct' and, in relation to a consequence, that the accused 'means to cause that consequence *or is aware that it will occur in the ordinary course of events*'.[57] France's *Law of Armed Conflict Manual* thus explains that attacks on objects indispensable to the

---

[48] Ibid., p. 6.
[49] ICRC, Customary IHL Rule 53: 'Starvation as a Method of Warfare'.
[50] Art. 8(2)(b)(xxv), Rome Statute.
[51] UN Security Council Resolution 2417, adopted on 24 May 2018 by unanimous vote in favour, operative para. 5.
[52] Amendment to Article 8 of the Rome Statute of the International Criminal Court (Intentionally using starvation of civilians); adopted at The Hague, 6 December 2019; entered into force, 14 October 2021.
[53] Art. 8(2)(e)(xix), Rome Statute. In comparison to the provision in the context of international armed conflict in the Statute, the words 'as provided for under the Geneva Conventions' are omitted after 'willfully impeding relief supplies', to reflect the legislative difference in a situation of non-international armed conflict.
[54] Art. 54(1), 1977 Additional Protocol I.
[55] Element 2, Elements of Crime for Article 8(2)(b)(xxv) of the Rome Statute.
[56] ICRC, Commentary on Article 54 of the 1977 Additional Protocol I, 1987, at: https://bit.ly/3iXSdzA, para. 2089.
[57] Art. 30(2)(a) and (b), Rome Statute (emphasis added).

survival of the civilian population are prohibited where this 'would result in the starvation of the population or force it to displace'.[58]

14.22 The prohibition of deprivation of sources of food or supplies that are critical to the civilian population is elucidated by the provisions in the two Additional Protocols. For instance, in the relevant article in the 1977 Additional Protocol II, it is stipulated that it is 'prohibited to attack, destroy, remove or render useless, for that purpose [starvation of the civilian population], objects indispensable to the survival of the civilian population, such as food stuffs, agricultural areas for the production of foodstuffs, crops, livestock, drinking water installations and supplies and irrigation works'.[59] In its commentary on the corresponding war crime under customary law, the ICRC notes that:

> Destroying objects indispensable to the survival of the civilian population also reflects a customary prohibition. There had, in fact, been a prosecution relating to a case of destruction of crops in a scorched earth operation during World War II, although the basis of the prosecution was the destruction of property not required by military necessity.[60]

14.23 According to the United Kingdom Ministry of Defence, as a result of the prohibition of starvation of civilians as a method of warfare, the customary law rule that permitted measures to dry up springs and to divert rivers and aqueducts must now be considered as applying only to water sources used exclusively by military personnel or for military purposes.[61] In contrast, as the US Department of Defense argues, the rule in the Protocol that prohibits attacking, destroying, removing or rendering useless objects indispensable to the survival of the civilian population would not apply to attacks carried out for specific purposes other than to deny sustenance. It cites as an example of permitted conduct destroying a field of crops to prevent it from being used as concealment by the enemy, or destroying a supply route that is used to move military supplies but which is also used to supply the civilian population with food.[62] This is subject to the prohibition whereby 'in no event shall actions against these objects be taken which may be expected to leave the civilian population with such inadequate food or water as to cause its starvation or force its movement'.[63] An exception is also foreseen in the Additional Protocol I that allows a State to engage in a 'scorched earth' defence of a party's own territory.[64]

---

[58] In the original: 'qui auraient pour conséquence d'affamer la population ou de la forcer à se déplacer'. French Ministry of Defence, *Manuel de droit des conflits armés*, Paris, 2012, p. 25.
[59] Art. 14, 1977 Additional Protocol II.
[60] ICRC, Customary IHL Rule 156: 'Definition of War Crimes'.
[61] UK Ministry of Defence, *The Manual of the Law of Armed Conflict*, para. 5.27.2.
[62] US Department of Defense, *Law of War Manual*, Updated December 2016, §5.20.4.
[63] Art. 54(3), 1977 Additional Protocol I.
[64] Article 54(5) allows such action 'by a Party to the conflict within such territory under its own control where required by imperative military necessity'.

Concluding remarks and outlook

14.24 Sieges are a likely future for the conduct of military operations, as the war in Ukraine in 2022 has so tragically demonstrated. They are typically devastating for civilians. It is therefore surprising how little attention has been paid in military doctrine to how to minimise the impact on the civilian population while pursuing legitimate military objectives. In a strong critique of inaction within the North Atlantic Treaty Organization (NATO), Michel Yakovleff accuses the Alliance of failing to prepare for the next war. While he acknowledges that 'No one knows where the next NATO war will be fought, nor when, nor against whom, nor for what reason', 'we all know where it will be decided: in a city'.[65] Even in the leading academic guidelines on humanitarian assistance during armed conflict,[66] relieving humanitarian suffering during a siege is scarcely mentioned. In any event, the duty on States and armed groups to not arbitrarily withhold consent to humanitarian relief for a starving civilian population in a besieged area demands clear and urgent confirmation in international law. One way to do this would be to draft and pass a UN General Assembly resolution on the issue.[67]

---

[65] M. Yakovleff, 'NATO Is Not Preparing for the Next War', NATO Briefs Series No. 02/2021, 10 June 2021, at: https://bit.ly/3zHU2cf, p. 1.

[66] D. Akande and E.-C. Gillard, *Oxford Guidance on the Law Relating to Humanitarian Relief Operations in Situations of Armed Conflict*, Commissioned by the United Nations Office for the Coordination of Humanitarian Affairs (OCHA), University of Oxford and OCHA, 2016, at: https://bit.ly/3krAXXI.

[67] S. Casey-Maslen, 'Protecting civilians in siege warfare: Constraints on military action', Policy Paper, Ceasefire, London, 2022, at: https://bit.ly/3oRAkaD.

15

Reprisals

Introduction

In situations of armed conflict, reprisals were for a long time the primary means of enforcing respect for the laws of war. For, as Shane Darcy has observed, it is still the case today that: 'One of the major shortcomings of the laws of armed conflict is the failure of that regime to provide for adequate means of enforcing those laws.'[1] Developed in the nineteenth and early twentieth centuries, 'belligerent' reprisals[2] are acts by a party to an armed conflict that would ordinarily violate international humanitarian law (IHL) but which, in exceptional cases and under strict conditions, are permissible as 'an enforcement measure in reaction to unlawful acts of an adversary'.[3]

15.1

Such means of 'self-help' are, as the *Oxford Manual on the Laws of War on Land* opined back in 1880, 'an exception to the general rule of equity, that an innocent person ought not to suffer for the guilty'.[4] But while there is a 'trend' in IHL to outlaw reprisals altogether—one that continued apace in the Additional Protocol I of 1977[5]—a comprehensive prohibition has not yet been incorporated in treaty law, nor has one crystallised in custom.[6] That said, as the International Committee of the Red Cross (ICRC) has duly observed, those reprisals that remain lawful are subject to 'stringent conditions'.[7] These conditions are reflected in customary law.

15.2

A prohibition of reprisals against prisoners of war was first incorporated in a situation of international armed conflict under the 1929 Geneva Convention on Prisoners of War[8] and then later, against protected persons, in each of the four

15.3

---

[1] S. Darcy, 'The Evolution of the Law of Belligerent Reprisals', *Military Law Review*, Vol. 175 (2003), pp. 184–251, at p. 184.

[2] Under *jus in bello*, 'reprisals' and 'belligerent reprisals' are synonyms.

[3] International Committee of the Red Cross (ICRC), Customary international humanitarian law (IHL) Rule 145: 'Reprisals', at: http://bit.ly/2OUWdae. See also F. Kalshoven, *Constraints on the Waging of War*, ICRC, Geneva, 1987, p. 65.

[4] Art. 84, *The Laws of War on Land*, Manual published by the Institute of International Law (Oxford Manual), adopted by the Institute of International Law at Oxford, 9 September 1880, available at: https://bit.ly/3vtDYd8.

[5] Arts. 20, 51(6), 52(1), 53(c), 54(4), 55(2), and 56(4), Protocol Additional to the Geneva Conventions of 12 August 1949, and relating to the Protection of Victims of International Armed Conflicts (Protocol I); adopted at Geneva, 8 June 1977; entered into force, 7 December 1978 (hereinafter, 1977 Additional Protocol I).

[6] ICRC commentary on Article 46 of 1949 Geneva Convention I, 2016, at: http://bit.ly/3lkDGRa, para. 2748; G. Gaggioli and N. Melzer, 'Methods of Warfare', Chap. 10 in B. Saul and D. Akande (eds.), *The Oxford Guide to International Humanitarian Law*, Oxford University Press, Oxford, 2020, p. 249.

[7] ICRC, Customary IHL Rule 145: 'Reprisals'.

[8] Art. 2, Convention relative to the Treatment of Prisoners of War; adopted at Geneva, 27 July 1929; entered into force, 19 June 1931, at: http://bit.ly/2OYclI1.

Table 15.1 Prohibitions in the Additional Protocols on Reprisals

Prohibition	AP I	Customary status (IAC)	AP II	Customary status (NIAC)
Reprisals against sick or wounded combatants	Art. 20	Yes	N/A	N/A
Reprisals against POWs	Art. 13, GC III	Yes	N/A	N/A
Reprisals against civilians	Art. 51(6)	No	No	No
Reprisals against civilian objects	Arts. 52(1), 53(c), 54(4), 55(2), and 56(4)	No	No	No

1949 Geneva Conventions. A number of new rules were laid down in the 1977 Additional Protocol I. These generally amounted to the progressive development of international law. No specific provisions on belligerent reprisals were included in the Additional Protocol II of 1977, however, and the status of reprisals in non-international armed conflict is disputed.[9] The key rules and their customary status are summarised in Table 15.1.

15.4 This chapter discusses the interpretation and application of the rules governing reprisals in the Geneva Conventions, the 1977 Additional Protocols, and under corresponding rules of customary law. The chapter first defines the concept of a belligerent reprisal along with the conditions for their lawful exercise under general international law. It then summarises the prohibitions in the Geneva Conventions, including Convention III on the protection of prisoners of war[10] and Convention IV on the protection of civilians,[11] since both categories of protected person are especially at risk of being subjected to reprisals. It moves to consider the new treaty rules in the Additional Protocol I of 1977 in the light of customary IHL. Whether reprisals may ever be lawful in non-international armed conflict is then discussed. Finally, reprisals under international criminal law, and specifically the Rome Statute of the International Criminal Court[12] are addressed. Given that action ostensibly taken in reprisal amounts, by design, to unlawful conduct, when such acts do not meet all of the criteria for a lawful reprisal, they

---

[9] Protocol Additional to the Geneva Conventions of 12 August 1949, and relating to the Protection of Victims of Non-International Armed Conflicts (Protocol II); adopted at Geneva, 8 June 1977; entered into force, 7 December 1978 (hereinafter, 1977 Additional Protocol II).

[10] Convention (III) relative to the Treatment of Prisoners of War; adopted at Geneva, 12 August 1949; entered into force, 21 October 1950 (hereinafter, 1949 Geneva Convention III).

[11] Convention (IV) relative to the Protection of Civilian Persons in Time of War; adopted at Geneva, 12 August 1949; entered into force, 21 October 1950 (hereinafter, 1949 Geneva Convention IV).

[12] Rome Statute of the International Criminal Court; adopted at Rome, 17 July 1998; entered into force, 1 July 2002. As of 1 May 2022, 123 States were party to the Rome Statute.

are highly likely to constitute war crimes. This is so, whether they are committed in international or in non-international armed conflict.

The definition of reprisals and their exercise under customary law

IHL instruments neither formally define reprisals nor do they outline the conditions for their lawful exercise. This has been done through international custom and judicial interpretation. The United States (US) Department of Defense describes reprisals in the most recent version of its *Law of War Manual* (of December 2016) as 'extreme measures of coercion used to help enforce the law of war by seeking to persuade an adversary to cease violations'.[13] Its 2019 *Commander's Handbook on the Law of Land Warfare* terms reprisals 'measures that are otherwise prohibited' which are taken by one State in response to another State's violations of the law of armed conflict 'in order to encourage future compliance'.[14] **15.5**

In its 2016 commentary on the prohibition of reprisals in the First Geneva Convention of 1949,[15] the ICRC described reprisals as 'measures taken in the context of an international armed conflict by a Party in reaction to a violation of international humanitarian law by an adversary'.[16] Reprisals 'may not be carried out for the purpose of revenge or punishment, but only with the aim of putting an end to such violations and inducing the adversary to comply with the law'.[17] The key issues are that reprisals would ordinarily be unlawful under IHL. If they are lawful—although unfriendly—countermeasures, they are termed retorsion.[18] **15.6**

To be lawful, acts committed in the name of reprisals must comply with six cumulative conditions. First, an act of claimed reprisal by one party must be—by definition—in response to a prior unlawful act by an adverse party. Reprisals cannot be preventive in nature. Secondly, an act of reprisal must be in response to *serious* violations of IHL, meaning, in effect, war crimes.[19] Thirdly, recourse to a reprisal must be necessary in the circumstances, meaning that no reasonable alternative is open to the injured party to bring an end to the violations. In this regard, the ICRC has observed that there is 'much more support these days for the notion of ensuring respect for international **15.7**

---

[13] US Department of Defense, *Law of War Manual*, June 2015 (Updated December 2016), Washington, D.C., 2016, §18.18.

[14] US Department of the Army, *The Commander's Handbook on the Law of Land Warfare*, FM 6-27/MCTP 11-10C, Washington, D.C., 7 August 2019, at: https://bit.ly/3eKG9ml, §6-175.

[15] Art. 46, Convention (I) for the Amelioration of the Condition of the Wounded and Sick in Armed Forces in the Field; adopted at Geneva, 12 August 1949; entered into force, 21 October 1950 (hereinafter, 1949 Geneva Convention I).

[16] ICRC, Commentary on Article 46 of 1949 Geneva Convention I, 2016, at: http://bit.ly/38GpGvX, para. 2731.

[17] Ibid.

[18] See generally T. Giegerich, 'Retorsion', *Max Planck Encyclopedias of International Law*, Last updated September 2020, at: http://bit.ly/2OZc5c7.

[19] United Kingdom (UK) Ministry of Defence, *The Manual of the Law of Armed Conflict*, Oxford University Press, Oxford, 2004, para. 16.17.

humanitarian law through diplomatic channels'; they are, in its words, 'a measure of last resort'.[20] Of course, once the prior unlawful acts have ceased, so must the reprisals (as they are, by definition, no longer necessary).[21]

15.8 Fourthly, the *primary* intent of the reprisal must be to end the adverse party's serious violations of IHL.[22] Fifthly, the act of reprisal must be proportionate in nature and extent to the prior serious violations.[23] Sixthly, and finally, reprisals must not be perpetrated against targets which are prohibited by international law to the party that is committing the salient acts ostensibly as a reprisal.[24]

Reprisals under the 1949 Geneva Conventions

15.9 Each of the four Geneva Conventions of 1949 incorporates prohibitions on reprisals against protected persons. As every State is bound by the four Conventions,[25] these rules apply as a matter of treaty law, although they also codify international custom. Thus, one of the customary rules of IHL identified by the ICRC stipulates simply: 'Belligerent reprisals against persons protected by the Geneva Conventions are prohibited.'[26]

15.10 The First Geneva Convention provides that: 'Reprisals against the wounded, sick, personnel, buildings or equipment protected by the Convention are prohibited.'[27] There is no possibility to derogate from this rule.[28] The following are the persons protected under the Convention:[29] the wounded and sick;[30] the dead;[31] medical and religious personnel attached to the armed forces;[32] auxiliary medical personnel;[33] personnel of

---

[20] ICRC, Customary IHL Rule 145: 'Reprisals'.
[21] International Criminal Tribunal for the former Yugoslavia (ICTY), *Prosecutor v. Zoran Kupreškić and others*, Judgment (Trial Chamber) (Case No. IT-95-16-T), 14 January 2000, para. 535.
[22] S. Sivakumaran, *The Law of Non-International Armed Conflict*, Oxford University Press, Oxford, 2012, p. 455.
[23] International Court of Justice, *Legality of the Threat or Use of Nuclear Weapons*, Advisory Opinion, 8 July 1996, para. 46.
[24] It is also suggested that reprisals may only be lawful if they are authorised at the highest political or military level. The ICRC, for instance, affirms that a decision to resort to reprisals 'must be taken at the highest level of government'. ICRC Customary IHL Rule 145: 'Reprisals'. This appears to confuse policy positions of certain States with *opinio juris*. See D. Turns, 'Implementation of International Humanitarian Law', Chap. 16 in B. Saul and D. Akande (eds.), *The Oxford Guide to International Humanitarian Law*, Oxford University Press, Oxford, 2020, p. 366. There is no reason why a field commander could not authorise a reprisal as long as he or she was certain of the facts and had the mandate from his/her hierarchical superior to do so.
[25] There are formally 196 States Parties to the Geneva Conventions of the 197 States recognised by the United Nations (UN) Secretary-General. While Niue is not formally a State Party, according to the ICRC it remains bound by New Zealand's ratification of the 1949 Geneva Conventions, 'until such time as Niue accedes to the Conventions in its own right'. ICRC, States Parties to International Humanitarian Law and Other Related Treaties (as of 1 February 2022), available at: http://bit.ly/2OSD7Sg, p. 6.
[26] ICRC Customary IHL Rule 146: 'Reprisals against Protected Persons', at: http://bit.ly/2OQoMFY.
[27] Art. 46, 1949 Geneva Convention I.
[28] ICRC, Commentary on Article 46 of 1949 Geneva Convention I, 2016, at: http://bit.ly/3lkDGRa, para. 2744. Should they commit acts harmful to the enemy, however, they lose their protection, at least for as long as they commit such acts. Ibid., note 32.
[29] Ibid., paras. 2742, 2743.
[30] Art. 13, 1949 Geneva Convention I.
[31] Ibid., Art. 15.
[32] Ibid., Art. 24.
[33] Ibid., Art. 25.

aid societies;[34] and medical personnel of societies of neutral countries. The following objects are similarly protected against reprisals: fixed medical establishments and mobile medical units;[35] hospital ships;[36] and means of medical transport, including medical aircraft.[37]

The Second Geneva Convention of 1949 provides, in similar language to Convention I, that: 'Reprisals against the wounded, sick and shipwrecked persons, the personnel, the vessels or the equipment protected by the Convention are prohibited.'[38] There is no possibility to derogate from this rule.[39] The persons protected under the Convention are, analogous to those in the First Convention: the wounded, sick, and shipwrecked;[40] the dead;[41] religious, medical, and hospital personnel of hospital ships and their crews;[42] and designated religious, medical, and hospital personnel caring for the wounded, sick, or shipwrecked.[43] The following objects are protected against reprisals: hospital ships;[44] neutral vessels assisting with rescue;[45] medical establishments ashore;[46] coastal rescue craft and fixed coastal installations used exclusively by these craft for their humanitarian missions;[47] sick-bays of warships;[48] and means of medical transport, including medical aircraft.[49]

15.11

The ICRC underlines in its commentary on the Second Convention that the prohibition of reprisals is not limited to measures that would amount to an 'attack' against protected persons or property, but also includes omissions by States to perform particular acts, 'such as omitting to provide medical assistance and care to the wounded, sick or shipwrecked at sea, or to ensure proper burial of the dead at sea'.[50] The prohibition on reprisals in the Second Geneva Convention is, the ICRC affirms, 'well established' and has been 'largely respected since 1949'.[51]

15.12

The 1949 Geneva Convention III reiterated an unequivocal prohibition on reprisals against prisoners of war that had, as noted above, been incorporated in the

15.13

---

[34] Ibid., Art. 26.
[35] Ibid., Arts. 19, 33, and 34.
[36] Ibid., Art. 20.
[37] Ibid., Arts. 35 and 36.
[38] Art. 47, Convention (II) for the Amelioration of the Condition of Wounded, Sick and Shipwrecked Members of Armed Forces at Sea; adopted at Geneva, 12 August 1949; entered into force, 21 October 1950 (hereinafter, 1949 Geneva Convention II).
[39] ICRC commentary on Article 47 of 1949 Geneva Convention II, 2017, at: http://bit.ly/3qMjSqJ, para. 2856. Should they commit acts harmful to the enemy, however, they lose their protection, at least for as long as they commit such acts. Ibid., para. 2854.
[40] Arts. 12 and 13, 1949 Geneva Convention II.
[41] Ibid., Art. 18.
[42] Ibid., Art. 36.
[43] Ibid., Art. 37.
[44] Ibid., Arts. 22, 24, 25, and 33.
[45] Ibid., Art. 21.
[46] Ibid., Art. 23.
[47] Ibid., Art. 27.
[48] Ibid., Art. 28.
[49] Ibid., Arts. 38 and 39.
[50] ICRC, Commentary on Article 47 of 1949 Geneva Convention II, 2017, para. 2858 (notes omitted).
[51] Ibid., para. 2860.

corresponding 1929 Geneva Convention. Thus, it is stipulated in the Third Geneva Convention that: 'Measures of reprisal against prisoners of war are prohibited.'[52] The provision not only excludes violence against a prisoner of war but also covers omissions by the Detaining Power, such as withholding medical assistance[53] or denying him or her food and water. The ICRC observes that among the 'numerous instances of ill-treatment of prisoners of war in conflicts since 1949', many amounted to 'retaliation or revenge for similar conduct carried out by the other Party towards its prisoners, rather than reprisals'.[54] They are thus not lawful reprisals as they were perpetrated out of revenge or for the purpose of punishment rather than with the aim of 'putting an end to a violation and inducing the adversary to comply with the law'.[55]

15.14 In the aftermath of its conflict against Ethiopia in 1998–2000, Eritrea claimed to have suspended the repatriation of Ethiopian prisoners of war in reprisal for similar conduct by Ethiopia.[56] The issue was subjected to adjudication by the Eritrea-Ethiopia Claims Commission, an international arbitration body created under the 2000 Algiers Agreement that brought a legal end to the war.[57] In its Partial Award, the Commission noted that on 29 November 2002, shortly before the hearing in the claim, Ethiopia released all the Eritrean prisoners of war registered by the ICRC as remaining in its custody. Hostilities were deemed to have ceased between the two States on 12 December 2000 (the date of signature of the Algiers Agreement), with the obligation in Convention III to repatriate 'without delay' all prisoners of war[58] coming into operation at that time.[59]

15.15 Even though there is no notion of reciprocity in either the treaty or customary duty to repatriate after the cessation of active hostilities, the Commission declared that: 'it is proper to expect that each Party's conduct with respect to the repatriation of POWs will be reasonable and broadly commensurate with the conduct of the other'.[60] Eritrea pointed out, citing specifically the relevant provision in the Third Geneva Convention, that delaying 'for a year or more' the release and repatriation of nearly 1,300 prisoners of war was not permissible.[61] Controversially, however, the Commission was 'not prepared to conclude' that Ethiopia had violated its obligations under the Convention. It considered that 'suspending temporarily further repatriations pending a response to a seemingly reasonable request for clarification of the fate of a number of missing

---

[52] Art. 13(3), 1949 Geneva Convention III.
[53] ICRC, Commentary on Article 13 of 1949 Geneva Convention III, 2020, at: http://bit.ly/38GUZXw, para. 1647.
[54] Ibid., para. 1650. The ICRC directs readers to Geoffrey Wallace's 2015 work on G. P. R. Wallace, *Life and Death in Captivity: The Abuse of Prisoners during War*, Cornell University Press, Ithaca, 16 April 2015, esp. pp. 84–90.
[55] ICRC, Commentary on Article 13 of 1949 Geneva Convention III, 2020, para. 1650.
[56] Eritrea-Ethiopia Claims Commission, *Prisoners of War, Eritrea's Claim*, Partial Award, 2003, paras. 143–63.
[57] Permanent Court of Arbitration, 'Eritrea-Ethiopia Claims Commission', at: http://bit.ly/30MSgap.
[58] Art. 118, 1949 Geneva Convention III.
[59] Eritrea-Ethiopia Claims Commission, *Prisoners of War, Eritrea's Claim*, Partial Award, 2003, paras. 143, 146.
[60] Ibid., para. 149.
[61] Ibid., para. 159.

combatants' was itself not unlawful.[62] This decision and its reasoning have been justly criticised by leading IHL authorities.[63]

The 1949 Geneva Convention IV, the first IHL treaty dedicated to the protection of civilians, also outlaws all reprisals against 'protected persons and their property'.[64] This concerns aliens in the territory of a party to an international armed conflict and civilians in occupied territories. The application of reprisals against civilians in occupied Europe by the Nazis was a common occurrence in the Second World War.[65] The ICRC had, at the beginning of the War, secured agreement that enemy civilians interned in the territory of a belligerent 'should benefit by analogy' from the provisions of the 1929 Convention on Prisoners of War. All reprisals against these internees were consequently prohibited, but it 'proved impossible to obtain the same decision in regard to civilians in occupied territory'.[66]

15.16

In a number of war crimes trials following the end of the Second World War, officers were held criminally responsible for the commission of unlawful reprisals.[67] In the trial of *Wilhelm List and others* (the so-called Hostages Trial), the US Military Tribunal at Nuremberg discussed at length criminal responsibility for the killing of civilians as a possible reprisal. In its judgment, the Tribunal criticised the 'complete failure on the part of the nations of the world to limit or mitigate the practice by conventional rule'.[68] It further stated that no conventional prohibitions had been invoked 'to outlaw this barbarous practice' but declared that the extent to which the practice had been employed by the Germans exceeded 'the most elementary notions of humanity and justice'.[69] It concluded that the 'shooting of innocent members of the population as a reprisal measure' may not 'exceed in severity the unlawful acts it is designed to correct'. Excessive reprisals are in themselves criminal, the Tribunal held, 'and guilt attaches to the persons responsible for their commission'.[70]

15.17

In passing sentence upon the convicted Nazi generals, the US Military Tribunal said that the failure of the world to deal specifically with the problem of reprisals 'by convention, treaty, or otherwise' since the First World War, had created a situation 'that mitigates to some extent the seriousness of the offence'.[71] Some of the Tribunal's concerns

15.18

---

[62] Ibid., para. 160.
[63] See in particular M. Sassòli, 'The Approach of the Eritrea-Ethiopia Claims Commission towards the Treatment of Protected Persons in International Humanitarian Law', in A. de Guttry, H. H. G. Post, and G. Venturini (eds.), *The 1998-2000 War between Eritrea and Ethiopia*, TMC Asser, The Hague, 2009, pp. 342–44.
[64] Art. 33, 1949 Geneva Convention IV.
[65] See, e.g., C. Neumaier, 'The Escalation of German Reprisal Policy in Occupied France, 1941–42', *Journal of Contemporary History*, Vol. 41, No. 1 (January 2006), pp. 113–31, at: https://bit.ly/3rQCYxe.
[66] ICRC, Commentary on Article 33 of 1949 Geneva Convention IV, 1958, at: https://bit.ly/2LbfkLJ, pp. 227–28.
[67] See, e.g., R. Albrecht, 'War Reprisals in the War Crimes Trials and in the Geneva Conventions', *American Journal of International Law*, Vol. 47, No. 4 (October 1953), pp. 590–614.
[68] US Military Tribunal, Nuremberg, *Trial of Wilhelm List and others* (*The Hostages Trial*), Case No. 47, 1948, in UN War Crimes Commission, *Law Reports of Trials of War Crimes*, Vol. VIII, HMSO, London, 1949, at: https://bit.ly/38HHy9q, p. 63.
[69] Ibid.
[70] Ibid., p. 64.
[71] Ibid., p. 92.

were resolved just a year later under the Fourth Geneva Convention, but the broader issue of reprisals in enemy territory during the conduct of hostilities would take another three decades to address.

Reprisals under the 1977 Additional Protocol I

15.19 Thus, the 1977 Additional Protocol I included several new rules regulating the conduct of hostilities and prohibiting reprisals against both civilians and civilian objects. Certain remain controversial. The rules laid down in Geneva Convention IV concerned civilians in the power of the enemy. But aerial bombardment in particular had brought populated areas within the scope of attacks and the destruction of entire cities in the Second World War had shown that all parties were ready to inflict—and justify— a huge civilian toll of lives. In the late 1960s and early 1970s, widely indiscriminate US bombing across Indochina, particularly Laos and Vietnam, not only seemed counterproductive from a strategic military perspective[72] but also clearly demonstrated the need for new treaty regulation.

15.20 Uncontroversial—as it was effectively a reiteration of the rules set out across the four Conventions of 1949—was the provision in Article 20 of the 1977 Additional Protocol I. Therein it is stipulated that reprisals against the sick, wounded, or shipwrecked or other protected persons and objects in the power of the enemy, as well as against medical personnel are prohibited. As Yves Sandoz observed in the ICRC commentary on Article 20, negotiations at the diplomatic conference that aimed to elaborate a single article on reprisals in the Protocol were not successful.[73] The 'wounded' and 'sick' are defined broadly in the Protocol to mean 'persons, whether military or civilian, who, because of trauma, disease or other physical or mental disorder or disability, are in need of medical assistance or care and who refrain from any act of hostility'.[74] The provision does not specifically protect prisoners of war, against whom reprisals are prohibited in all circumstances in accordance with Geneva Convention III and customary law.

15.21 The most controversial provision on reprisals in the Additional Protocol I by far is that in Article 51(6). It provides simply that: 'Attacks against the civilian population or civilians by way of reprisals are prohibited.' In its 1987 commentary on this provision, the ICRC asserted that this prohibition 'is not subject to any conditions and it therefore has a peremptory character; in particular it leaves out the possibility of derogating from this rule by invoking military necessity'.[75] But the ICRC overstates the case for the

---

[72] M. A. Kocher, T. B. Pepinsky, and S. N. Kalyvas, 'Aerial Bombing and Counterinsurgency in the Vietnam War', *American Journal of Political Science*, Vol. 55, No. 2 (April 2011), pp. 201–18, at: https://bit.ly/3trlOqC.
[73] ICRC, Commentary on Article 20 of the 1977 Additional Protocol I, 1987, at: http://bit.ly/3qRqqo6, p. 242, para. 810.
[74] Art. 8(a), 1977 Additional Protocol I.
[75] ICRC commentary on Article 51 of the 1977 Additional Protocol I, 1987, at: https://bit.ly/30PnnD8, para. 1984.

'peremptory character' of the prohibition on reprisals. The provision was much debated during the negotiations, and its tenet remains opposed by a small number of 'specially affected' States. The United States, for instance, has expressed the view that the provisions in the 1977 Additional Protocol I on reprisals are 'counterproductive', and that 'they remove a significant deterrent that protects civilians and war victims on all sides of a conflict'.[76]

In 1998, the United Kingdom attached the following understanding to its ratification of the Protocol, which clarifies its position with regard to reprisals more generally:

15.22

> If an adverse party makes serious and deliberate attacks, in violation of Article 51 or Article 52 against the civilian population or civilians or against civilian objects, ... the United Kingdom will regard itself as entitled to take measures otherwise prohibited by the Articles in question to the extent that it considers such measures necessary for the sole purpose of compelling the adverse party to cease committing violations under those Articles, but only after formal warning to the adverse party requiring cessation of the violations has been disregarded and then only after a decision taken at the highest level of government. Any measures thus taken by the United Kingdom will not be disproportionate to the violations giving rise thereto and will not involve any action prohibited by the Geneva Conventions of 1949 nor will such measures be continued after the violations have ceased.[77]

In addition, Egypt, Germany, and Italy have expressly reserved the right to react to serious violations of the Protocol with any means permitted by international law to prevent further violations.[78]

In 2005, the ICRC Study of Customary IHL concluded with respect to the legality of reprisals:

15.23

> Because of existing contrary practice, albeit limited, it is difficult to conclude that there has yet crystallized a customary rule specifically prohibiting reprisals against civilians during the conduct of hostilities. Nevertheless, it is also difficult to assert that a right to resort to such reprisals continues to exist based on the practice of only a limited number of States, some of which is also ambiguous. Hence, there appears, at a minimum, to exist a trend in favour of prohibiting such reprisals.

---

[76] A. D. Sofaer, 'The Position of the United States on Current Law of War Agreements: Remarks of Judge Abraham D Sofaer, Legal Adviser, US Department of State, 22 January 1987', *American University Journal of International Law and Policy*, Vol. 2 (1987), p. 460, at p. 469.

[77] Declaration of the United Kingdom of 28 January 1998, point (m), at: http://bit.ly/2PC0crS.

[78] Gaggioli and Melzer note that Egypt and Germany have since made contradictory statements, suggesting that they may no longer support the legality of reprisals against civilian populations under any conditions. Gaggioli and Melzer, 'Methods of Warfare', p. 251, note 133; and see, e.g., International Court of Justice, *Legality of the Threat or Use of Nuclear Weapons*, Advisory Opinion, Written Comments of the Government of Egypt, September 1995, at: https://bit.ly/2Qehi0l, para. 43. That said, the formal reservations of both States to the First Additional Protocol remain and have not been withdrawn.

242 REPRISALS

In fact, as Louise Doswald-Beck, formerly the Head of the ICRC's Legal Division, has suggested, in the case of reprisals against civilian populations in the opposing party's territory, there may simply be no customary rule at all.[79]

15.24 Other prohibitions on reprisals in the Additional Protocol I of 1977 concern civilian objects. Article 52(1) provides generally that civilian objects shall not be the object of reprisals. This general prohibition is buttressed by specific prohibitions on reprisals against 'historic monuments, works of art or places of worship which constitute the cultural or spiritual heritage of peoples';[80] objects 'indispensable to the survival of the civilian population, such as foodstuffs, agricultural areas for the production of foodstuffs, crops, livestock, drinking water installations and supplies and irrigation works';[81] against the natural environment;[82] and 'works or installations containing dangerous forces, namely dams, dykes and nuclear electrical generating stations'.[83]

15.25 In its 1987 commentary on the latter provision, the ICRC stated that its importance 'should be underlined and the prohibition on reprisals which it contains should be welcomed'.[84] The prohibition of reprisals against dykes, dams, and nuclear electrical generating stations went beyond the ICRC proposal in its draft of the Protocol. While some delegations at the diplomatic conference in 1977 had expressed doubts regarding the advisability of such a comprehensive prohibition on reprisals in this area, a 'large majority' supported the prohibitions'.[85]

15.26 For States Parties to the Additional Protocol I that have not entered a reservation to Article 51(6) or more broadly to the prohibition on reprisals against civilians and civilian objects, their scope for reprisals in time of war has indeed considerably reduced.[86] At most, the ICRC states, 'such measures could now be envisaged in the choice of weapons and in methods of combat used against military objectives'.[87] This could potentially concern expanding or exploding ammunition.

15.27 Such reprisals may not, however, involve the use of landmines. In the Protocol II to the 1980 Convention on Certain Conventional Weapons, an instrument negotiated within United Nations (UN) auspices following the failure to agree upon regulation of specific weapons in the Additional Protocol I of 1977, it is explicitly prohibited to direct mines or booby-traps 'by way of reprisals, against the civilian population as such or against individual civilians'.[88] No State Party has entered any reservation with respect to this

---

[79] Remarks to experts meeting, Oslo, 17 June 2013; author's notes.
[80] Art. 53(c), 1977 Additional Protocol I.
[81] Ibid., Art. 54(4).
[82] Ibid., Art. 55(2).
[83] Ibid., Art. 56(4).
[84] ICRC, Commentary on Article 56 of the 1977 Additional Protocol I, 1987, at: http://bit.ly/3eOleiw, para. 2145.
[85] Ibid., para. 2171.
[86] ICRC, Commentary on Article 51 of the 1977 Additional Protocol I, para. 1985.
[87] Ibid.
[88] Art. 3(2), Protocol on Prohibitions or Restrictions on the Use of Mines, Booby-Traps and Other Devices (Protocol II) annexed to the Convention on Prohibitions or Restrictions on the Use of Certain Conventional Weapons which May Be Deemed to Be Excessively Injurious or to Have Indiscriminate Effects; adopted at

provision, including those that object to the sweeping prohibition on reprisals in the 1977 Protocol, and the rule may be taken to codify custom.

The original Protocol II applied only in international armed conflict. But the rule is repeated in the 1996 Amended Protocol II where it applies also to situations of non-international armed conflict.[89] Again, no State Party to the Amended Protocol has entered any reservation with respect to this provision so the customary rule may reasonably be considered to apply in all armed conflict. Moreover, the 164 States Parties to the 1997 Anti-Personnel Mine Ban Convention have all undertaken 'never under any circumstances' to use anti-personnel mines.[90] This is a comprehensive prohibition that admits of no exception whatsoever, with no reservations permissible to any of the Convention's provisions.[91]

15.28

The application of IHL to UN Forces is discussed in Chapter 18. But it is noteworthy that reprisals are specifically prohibited in the Secretary-General's 1999 Bulletin on Observance by United Nations forces of international humanitarian law.[92] Therein, it is stipulated that a UN Force 'shall not engage in reprisals against civilians or civilian objects' nor against objects 'indispensable to the survival of the civilian population' or installations containing dangerous forces, 'namely dams, dikes and nuclear electrical generating stations'.[93] All forms of reprisals are prohibited against persons who are not, or no longer, 'taking part in military operations, including civilians' and against the wounded, the sick, or other protected personnel, establishments, and equipment, including those of a medical nature.[94]

15.29

Reprisals in non-international armed conflict

The issue of whether reprisals may ever be conducted in non-international armed conflict continues to be disputed.[95] The International Criminal Tribunal for the former Yugoslavia (ICTY) held in its judgment in the *Kupreškić* case that reprisals were per se unlawful in non-international armed conflict.[96] France, which had objected to the

15.30

Geneva, 10 October 1980; entered into force, 2 December 1983 (CCW). As of 1 May 2022, 95 States were party to Protocol II.

[89] Art. 3(7), Protocol on Prohibitions or Restrictions on the Use of Mines, Booby-Traps and Other Devices as amended on 3 May 1996 annexed to the CCW; adopted at Geneva, 3 May 1996; entered into force, 3 December 1998. As of 1 May 2022, 106 States were party to the 1996 Amended Protocol II.
[90] Art. 1(1)(a), Convention on the Prohibition of the Use, Stockpiling, Production and Transfer of Anti-Personnel Mines and on Their Destruction; adopted at Oslo, 18 September 1997; entered into force, 1 March 1999.
[91] Art. 19, 1997 Anti-Personnel Mine Ban Convention.
[92] 'Observance by United Nations forces of international humanitarian law', Secretary-General's Bulletin, UN doc. ST/SGB/1999/13, 6 August 1999.
[93] Ibid., §§5.6 and 6.9.
[94] Ibid., §§7.2 and 9.6.
[95] Y. Dinstein, *Non-International Armed Conflict in International Law*, 2nd Edn, Cambridge University Press, Cambridge, 2021, p. 187, para. 520. See *contra* A. Clapham, *War*, Oxford University Press, Oxford, 2021, p. 510.
[96] ICTY, *Prosecutor v. Zoran Kupreškić and others*, Judgment (Trial Chamber) (Case No. IT-95-16-T), 14 January 2000, para. 534.

prohibition on reprisals in the Additional Protocol I, states simply in its *Manual on the Law of Armed Conflict* that: 'Reprisals are a notion that belongs only to the law of international armed conflict.'[97]

15.31 But the arguments offered by the ICTY Trial Chamber for the customary prohibition of reprisals against civilians in enemy territory were unpersuasive. For instance, it suggested that 'the demands of humanity and the dictates of public conscience' had acted to render reprisals unlawful.[98] It further declared that reprisals were prohibited under Common Article 3,[99] without noting that the provision does not apply to the conduct of hostilities.[100] It cited the ICTY's own decision on the indictment in the *Martić* case,[101] even though the Trial Chamber in that case would go on to find that such reprisals *could* be lawfully conducted—albeit 'to the extent possible, in keeping with the principle of the protection of the civilian population in armed conflict and the general prohibition of targeting civilians'—in non-international armed conflict.[102] It also referred to the 'profound transformation of humanitarian law under the pervasive influence of human rights',[103] indicating that human rights law had intervened in this area not to interpret human rights in accordance with IHL or to supplement IHL stipulations but simply to override IHL rules.[104]

15.32 Weakest of all, the ICTY suggested that a means of inducing compliance with international law was 'beginning to prove fairly efficacious: the prosecution and punishment of war crimes and crimes against humanity by national or international courts'.[105] There are many Afghanis, Iraqis, Syrians, and Yemenis and others who would feel rightly insulted by that claim. What is, however, unquestionably true is the Trial Chamber's observation that 'reprisals against civilians are inherently a barbarous means of seeking compliance with international law'.[106]

15.33 The position in the International Criminal Court is, we would submit, not yet fully settled. As Gaggioli and Melzer recall,[107] a chamber of the Court, in its 2011 decision on

---

[97] French Ministry of Defence, *Manuel de droit des conflits armés*, Paris, 2012, at: https://bit.ly/2OUpxxM, p. 82.
[98] ICTY, *Prosecutor v. Zoran Kupreškić and others*, Judgment (Trial Chamber), paras. 531, 533.
[99] Ibid., para. 534.
[100] The same point would pertain to Article 4 of the Second Additional Protocol of 1977, which specifies that persons not or no longer taking a direct part in hostilities 'shall in all circumstances be treated humanely, without any adverse distinction'. These fundamental guarantees do not pertain to the protection of the civilian population in Part IV of the Protocol. Article 13 stipulates that the rules that follow 'shall be observed in all circumstances' but this does not amount to a prohibition on reprisals in the conduct of hostilities. After all, under Article 1 common to the four Geneva Conventions, the States Parties similarly 'undertake to respect and to ensure respect for the present Convention in all circumstances' but specific prohibitions on reprisals were still required to be incorporated in each of the four treaties.
[101] ICTY, *Prosecutor v. Milan Martić*, Review of Indictment Pursuant to Rule 61 (Trial Chamber) (Case No. IT-95-11-R61), 8 March 1996, paras. 10–18.
[102] ICTY, *Prosecutor v. Milan Martić*, Judgment (Trial Chamber) (Case No. IT-95-11-T), 12 June 2007, para. 467. See further ICTY, *Prosecutor v. Milan Martić*, Judgment (Appeals Chamber) (Case No. IT-95-11-A), 8 October 2008, para. 242.
[103] ICTY, *Prosecutor v. Zoran Kupreškić and others*, Judgment (Trial Chamber), para. 529.
[104] See *e contrario* International Court of Justice, *Legality of the Threat or Use of Nuclear Weapons*, Advisory Opinion, para. 25.
[105] Ibid., para. 530.
[106] Ibid., para. 528.
[107] Gaggioli and Melzer, 'Methods of Warfare', p. 252.

the confirmation of charges in the *Mbarushimana* case noted that 'reprisals against the civilian population as such, or individual civilians, are prohibited in all circumstances, regardless of the behaviour of the other party, since 'no circumstances would legitimise an attack against civilians even if it were a response proportionate to a similar violation perpetrated by the other party'.[108] But the Court's citation harks back to the 1996 decision on charges in the *Martić* case rather than to the later judgment at trial, and thus the ICTY's starkly different conclusion. This is far from being a sufficient hook on which to hang such a broad and sweeping assertion.

Sivakumaran expounded a more reflective position in his 2012 work, *The Law of Non-International Armed Conflict*. Noting that the UK Ministry of Defence contests the Trial Chamber's claim in the *Kupreškić* case of the existence of a customary law prohibition on reprisals,[109] he argues, justly, that the view that belligerent reprisals are prohibited in non-international armed conflicts as a matter of customary IHL 'may be overstating the existing position'.[110] Dinstein is less equivocal. Beyond a small number of treaty provisions (on reprisals against cultural property and using landmines), he finds 'no evidence' that belligerent reprisals are unlawful in non-international armed conflicts.[111]

15.34

Reprisals and defences to war crimes charges

The Rome Statute does not provide for a lawful reprisal as a defence to individual criminal responsibility. Perhaps the closest the Statute comes is in its Article 31, which concerns grounds for excluding international criminal responsibility. Therein it is stipulated that a person shall not be criminally responsible if, at the time of his or her conduct he or she 'acts reasonably to defend himself or herself or another person or, in the case of war crimes, property which is essential for the survival of the person or another person or property which is essential for accomplishing a military mission, against an imminent and unlawful use of force in a manner proportionate to the degree of danger to the person or the other person or property protected'.[112] This is not, per se, a belligerent reprisal but it is at least an arguable case for defence counsel should the cumulative criteria for such action otherwise be fulfilled.

15.35

---

[108] ICC, *Prosecutor* v. *Callixte Mbarushimana*, Decision on the Confirmation of Charges (Trial Chamber) (Case No. ICC-01/04-01/10), 16 December 2011, para. 143.
[109] UK Ministry of Defence, *The Manual of the Law of Armed Conflict*, Oxford University Press, Oxford, 2004, para. 16.19.2, note 62.
[110] Sivakumaran, *The Law of Non-International Armed Conflict*, p. 452.
[111] Dinstein, *Non-International Armed Conflict in International Law*, 2nd Edn, p. 188, para. 523.
[112] Article 31(1)(c), Rome Statute.

Concluding remarks and outlook

15.36 Given the markedly differing views on the issue, whether belligerent reprisals are, or can be, lawful in a non-international armed conflict needs clarification. Jurisprudence on the issue, in particular in the ICTY, is unpersuasive and even seemingly contradictory. It is true that reprisals are inherently barbaric and unjust for their victims. But without regulation and circumscription, the risk of spiralling vengeance is only accentuated. It is one more issue that would need to be addressed in a new Additional Protocol to the Geneva Conventions governing all non-international armed conflict.

16

National Implementation

Introduction

It is surprising how little attention is explicitly accorded to domestic implementation of the rules set out in the two 1977 Additional Protocols.[1] The lack of national implementation provisions is especially marked in the Additional Protocol II, which refers only to the duty to disseminate the Protocol 'as widely as possible'.[2] The Additional Protocol I contains considerably more relevant consideration, including through the duty to prosecute war crimes and to 'suppress' other violations, as well as the duty upon commanders to make known and enforce the rules. But whereas disarmament and human rights law treaties ordinarily make domestic incorporation of treaty obligations through national legislation and other measures the subject of a clear, dedicated provision,[3] this is not the case under international humanitarian law (IHL). The closest it comes is in the duty to enact legislation to provide for the prosecution of war crimes[4] and in the requirement under the 1977 Additional Protocol I that, 'without delay', States Parties (and other parties to the conflict: i.e. national liberation movements) take 'all necessary measures for the execution of their obligations' under the Geneva Conventions and the Additional Protocol.[5]

16.1

The International Committee of the Red Cross (ICRC) treats the concept of 'implementation' in a broad manner, understanding it as encompassing respect for the rules of IHL. Thus, in its study of customary IHL encompassed within Part VI on

16.2

---

[1] Protocol Additional to the Geneva Conventions of 12 August 1949, and relating to the Protection of Victims of International Armed Conflicts (Protocol I); adopted at Geneva, 8 June 1977; entered into force, 7 December 1978 (hereinafter, 1977 Additional Protocol I); Protocol Additional to the Geneva Conventions of 12 August 1949, and relating to the Protection of Victims of Non-International Armed Conflicts (Protocol II); adopted at Geneva, 8 June 1977; entered into force, 7 December 1978 (hereinafter, 1977 Additional Protocol II).

[2] Art. 19, 1977 Additional Protocol II.

[3] See, e.g., Art. VII, Convention on the Prohibition of the Development, Production, Stockpiling and Use of Chemical Weapons and on their Destruction; adopted at Geneva, 3 September 1992; entered into force, 29 April 1997 (hereinafter, 1992 Chemical Weapons Convention); and Art. 2(2), International Covenant on Civil and Political Rights; adopted at New York, 16 December 1966; entered into force, 23 March 1976: 'Where not already provided for by existing legislative or other measures, each State Party to the present Covenant undertakes to take the necessary steps, in accordance with its constitutional processes and with the provisions of the present Covenant, to adopt such laws or other measures as may be necessary to give effect to the rights recognized in the present Covenant.'

[4] See, e.g. Art. 49, Convention (I) for the Amelioration of the Condition of the Wounded and Sick in Armed Forces in the Field; adopted at Geneva, 12 August 1949; entered into force, 21 October 1950.

[5] Art. 80(1), 1977 Additional Protocol I.

248   NATIONAL IMPLEMENTATION

Table 16.1 The Duties of National Implementation in the 1977 Additional Protocols

Rule	AP I	Customary status (IAC)	AP II	Customary status (NIAC)
Duty to adopt national measures	Arts. 1(1) and 80(1)	Yes	No	Yes
Duty to disseminate IHL	Art. 83	Yes	Art. 19	Yes
Orders to the armed forces to comply	Art. 80(2)	Yes	No	Yes
Duty to appoint legal advisers in the armed forces	Art. 82	Yes (Arguably)	No	Yes (Arguably)
Duty to investigate possible breaches	Arts. 1(1) and 86(1)	Yes	No	Yes
Duty to suppress breaches	Arts. 1(1) and 86(1)	Yes	No	Yes

Implementation are not only instruction in IHL, the appointment of legal advisers within the armed forces, and dissemination of the rules among the civilian population but also respect for IHL, ensuring respect for IHL 'erga omnes', amnesties, international cooperation, and the exercise of belligerent reprisals.[6] This chapter focuses on domestic implementation of the two 1977 Additional Protocols, which is construed more narrowly (see Table 16.1). The implementation of the 2005 Additional Protocol III[7] was addressed in Chapter 7.

16.3   This chapter addresses first the need for national legislation to give effect to the tenets of the 1977 Additional Protocols. It then considers the dissemination of the rules, followed by the requisite instructions to the armed forces, and then the appointment of legal advisers within the armed forces. The duty to suppress other breaches, including as a result of effective investigation of allegations or reasonable suspicion, closes the present chapter. The duty to establish a national mechanism to review new weapons was considered in Chapter 12 and is not repeated here. The nature of the duty to prosecute war crimes is addressed in Chapter 19.

---

[6] See ICRC, Customary IHL Rules 139–61, at: https://bit.ly/2YV20ST.
[7] Protocol additional to the Geneva Conventions of 12 August 1949, and relating to the Adoption of an Additional Distinctive Emblem (Protocol III); adopted at Geneva, 8 December 2005; entered into force, 14 January 2007.

The duty to adopt national implementing legislation

As noted above, there is a general obligation upon States Parties to the Additional Protocol I to take 'all necessary measures' to ensure the 'execution of their obligations' under the Geneva Conventions and the Protocol. This duty, which is set out in Article 80(1) of the 1977 Additional Protocol I, combines with the broader duty to respect and ensure respect for the Protocol 'in all circumstances' in Article 1(1). In its commentary of 1987 on Article 80(1), the ICRC correctly distinguishes between legislative incorporation and practical application of the Protocol. The former 'covers measures introducing all or the relevant parts of the treaty into the legal order of each Contracting Party'.[8] The commentary notes that this should be conducted in accordance with the rules of the State's Constitution 'which certainly in all cases prescribe the publication of such a treaty',[9] but the commentary does not go beyond that. **16.4**

It is to be regretted that no general duty to adopt implementing national legislation was imposed by each of the two 1977 Additional Protocols. If one looks at the Anti-Personnel Mine Ban Convention, for instance, adopted 20 years later, a dedicated provision imposes on each State Party the obligation to 'take all appropriate legal, administrative and other measures, including the imposition of penal sanctions, to prevent and suppress any activity prohibited to a State Party under this Convention undertaken by persons or on territory under its jurisdiction or control'.[10] Even more detailed prescription had been included in the 1992 Chemical Weapons Convention, which included the obligation to '[p]rohibit natural and legal persons anywhere on its territory or in any other place under its jurisdiction as recognized by international law from undertaking any activity prohibited to a State Party under this Convention, including enacting penal legislation with respect to such activity'.[11] A simple, direct duty to adopt national legislation upon every State Party, whether monist or dualist, and whether of a civil law or common law tradition, would surely have benefited the broader implementation of the Additional Protocols. **16.5**

Indeed, the ICRC's concern about the lack of national implementation of IHL led the organisation to set up its 'Advisory Service' in 1996 in order to 'step up its support to States committed to implementing IHL'.[12] The Advisory Service provides specialised tools for IHL implementation, including model laws and a comprehensive manual on domestic implementation of IHL.[13] The manual, published in 2015,[14] observes that **16.6**

---

[8] ICRC, Commentary on Article 80 of the 1977 Additional Protocol I, 1987, at: https://bit.ly/3jci3lQ, para. 3288.
[9] Ibid.
[10] Art. 9, Convention on the Prohibition of the Use, Stockpiling, Production and Transfer of Anti-Personnel Mines and on Their Destruction; adopted at Oslo, 18 September 1997; entered into force, 1 March 1999.
[11] Art. 7(1)(a), 1992 Chemical Weapons Convention.
[12] 'ICRC, Advisory Services on International Humanitarian Law', *How Does Law Protect in War*, at: https://bit.ly/3n2H1pd.
[13] ICRC, 'International Humanitarian Law in Domestic Law', Article, 1 January 2015, at: https://bit.ly/3vo3YXB.
[14] ICRC, *The Domestic Implementation of International Humanitarian Law: A Manual*, Geneva, 2015, at: https://bit.ly/3ARPP6f.

the requirement for implementing legislation is 'even more evident' in dualist States, 'as without it treaties have no direct effect in domestic law'.[15] The ICRC has a model law for the 1949 Geneva Conventions for the benefit of common law States,[16] but not separately (at the time of writing) for the Additional Protocols. It does, however, have a useful consolidated law that covers the 1949 Conventions and all three Additional Protocols, again focused on States with a common law tradition.[17]

16.7 In May 2021, the ICRC issued new guidance on national implementation of IHL, entitled *Bringing IHL Home: Guidelines on the National Implementation of International Humanitarian Law*.[18] The checklists provided in the guidelines are recommendations and not legally binding.[19] But they include valuable guidance for States prior to and following adherence to an IHL treaty, including on administrative and practical measures, such as measures related to the identification and marking of persons and objects protected under IHL. A further section of the guidelines concerns criminal repression and suppression of violations of IHL.[20] As the ICRC notes, States should adopt legislation detailing and criminalising grave breaches committed in international armed conflict, as well as other serious violations of IHL committed in both international and non-international armed conflict. This can be done, the ICRC argues, 'by passing a new piece of legislation (such as a "Geneva Conventions Act" or a "War Crimes Act") or by including grave breaches and other serious violations of IHL in the existing criminal code'.[21]

16.8 The duty to enact legislation to prosecute war crimes is set out in each of the four Geneva Conventions of 1949. Thus, for instance, Article 49 of the first Geneva Convention provides that: 'The High Contracting Parties undertake to enact any legislation necessary to provide effective penal sanctions for persons committing, or ordering to be committed, any of the grave breaches of the present Convention defined in the following Article.' This duty of *aut dedere aut iudicare* is limited to war crimes perpetrated in an international armed conflict.[22] Its seriousness should be reflected in the severity of the punishments foreseen for those convicted of war crimes. In its 2016 commentary on the provision, the ICRC observes that:

> The implementing legislation ought to provide for penal sanctions that are appropriate and can be strictly applied. Penal sanctions, as opposed to disciplinary ones, will be

---

[15] Ibid., p. 24.
[16] ICRC, 'Model Geneva Conventions Act (for Common Law States)', 21 February 2003, at: https://bit.ly/3jbXINK.
[17] 'Geneva Conventions (Consolidation) Act—Model law', Legal factsheet, 31 August 2008, available at: https://bit.ly/3vmSe7x.
[18] ICRC, *Bringing IHL Home: Guidelines on the National Implementation of International Humanitarian Law*, Geneva, May 2021, at: https://bit.ly/3u3FVyt.
[19] 'Bringing IHL Home: Guidelines on the National Implementation of International Humanitarian Law', in *International Review of the Red Cross*, Vol. 102, No. 915 (2020), 1327–30, at p. 1329.
[20] ICRC, *Bringing IHL Home: Guidelines on the National Implementation of International Humanitarian Law*, Checklist 5.
[21] Ibid., p. 29.
[22] Art. 85(5), 1977 Additional Protocol I.

issued by judicial institutions, be they military or civilian, and will usually lead to the imprisonment of the perpetrators, or to the imposition of fines. Because of their seriousness, imprisonment is widely recognized as a central element in punishing grave breaches and other serious violations of humanitarian law.[23]

Article 85(1) of the 1977 Additional Protocol I does not reiterate the stipulation that legislation must be enacted to give effect to the duty to prosecute war crimes, but it does explicitly apply the provisions of the Geneva Conventions relating to the repression of breaches and grave breaches to the corresponding repression of all breaches of the Protocol. This means, in effect, that legislation must be enacted to allow prosecution of the war crimes newly set out in the Protocol.[24] Prosecution of certain war crimes, such as pertaining to disproportionate attacks, is challenging, as Chapter 10 describes. In negotiating the Protocol, however, a number of States regretted that the 'lack of precision' of certain rules instituted in the Protocol 'would make their introduction in national legislation, as well as their application, difficult and possibly not very uniform'.[25] 16.9

Legislation is ordinarily required for the implementation of the duty to prosecute war criminals not only because of the compulsory nature of the duty but also and especially by virtue of the universal scope of geographical jurisdiction incorporated in the obligation to prosecute or hand over war criminals for prosecution. The issue is not where in the world a war crime was allegedly committed but whether the alleged criminal was in the jurisdiction of a State Party. Failure to comply with the *aut dedere aut iudicare* obligation with respect to grave breaches of the Conventions and Additional Protocols—all too often the case in practice—engages the international responsibility for the commission of an internationally wrongful act of the State on whose territory the individual finds himself or herself.[26] 16.10

This is so, at least where the alleged war crime was perpetrated during and in connection with an international armed conflict. But there may be legitimate dispute as to the classification of an armed conflict. In October 2021, it was reported that 'Guernica 37',[27] an international justice chambers based in the United Kingdom specialising in transnational litigation enforcing human rights and international criminal norms, was filing a legal complaint in the United Kingdom accusing key figures in Saudi Arabia and the United Arab Emirates of being involved in war crimes and crimes against humanity relating to the war in Yemen. The dossier, which was being submitted to British police and prosecutors, would call for the immediate arrest of some 20 senior members of the 16.11

---

[23] ICRC, Commentary on Article 49 of the 1949 Geneva Convention I, 2016, at: https://bit.ly/3mXUKgS, para. 2841.
[24] Arts. 11(4) and 85(2), (3), and (4), 1977 Additional Protocol I. See further Chapter 19.
[25] ICRC, Commentary on Article 85 of the 1977 Additional Protocol I, 1987, at: https://bit.ly/3ciLeQ9, para. 3466.
[26] Article 2 of the 2001 International Law Commission Draft Articles on State Responsibility stipulates that there is an internationally wrongful act of a State when conduct consisting of an action *or omission* is attributable to the State under international law; and constitutes a breach of an international obligation of the State. Draft Article 2, 2001 ILC Draft Articles on State Responsibility (emphasis added).
[27] 'Guernica 37 International Justice Chambers', at: https://bit.ly/3pdXEAW.

political and military elite of Saudi Arabia and the United Arab Emirates.[28] It was not known whether the group would affirm that the conflict against the Houthis in Yemen was international or of a non-international character; each was an arguable case.[29]

16.12 The obligation to ensure that national implementing legislation applies to the conduct of a State Party's armed forces in a situation of non-international armed conflict concerns, at least, every State Party to the 1998 Rome Statute of the International Criminal Court, although this obligation is limited to war crimes. The 1977 Additional Protocol II has no provision demanding national implementation of its provisions. In 2016, the ICRC found it difficult to conclude that extension of the compulsory universal jurisdiction regime to non-international armed conflicts 'has materialized in customary international law in the light of the relative dearth of State practice and opinio juris supporting such extension'.[30] With respect to State practice, the ICRC observed in its commentary of 2016 on the first Geneva Convention first that the 'large majority of national implementing legislation has not extended the regime of grave breaches to non-international armed conflicts'.[31] Later in the same paragraph, however, it declared that 'a growing number of States have now equipped themselves with the means to exercise universal jurisdiction over such war crimes'.[32] The ICRC's study of customary IHL, first completed in 2005, led to the organisation discerning a rule whereby States have a 'right to vest universal jurisdiction in their national courts over war crimes', including in non-international armed conflicts, but not a duty to do so.[33]

The duty to disseminate international humanitarian law

16.13 Naturally, if they are to be respected, the rules of IHL must be known to soldier and civilian alike, given that all can be bound by them.[34] But predictably, the obligation to disseminate is more specific in the case of the military. Thus, the 1977 Additional Protocol I provides that States Parties will, 'in time of peace as in time of armed conflict', disseminate IHL 'as widely as possible', but will 'in particular', include its study 'in their programmes of military instruction'.[35] With respect to the civilian population, the duty is merely one to 'encourage' their study of IHL.[36] But it is further stipulated that any military or civilian authorities who, in time of armed conflict, 'assume responsibilities'

---

[28] D. Sabbagh, 'Lawyers to Submit Yemen War Crimes Dossier to UK Police', *The Guardian*, 20 October 2021, at: https://bit.ly/2Z98AFj.
[29] For a discussion of the legal issues surrounding classification, see, e.g., S. Casey-Maslen, *Jus ad Bellum: The Law on Inter-State Use of Force*, Hart Publishing, Oxford, 2020, pp. 48–50.
[30] ICRC Commentary on Article 49 of the 1949 Geneva Convention I, 2016, para. 2905.
[31] Ibid.
[32] Ibid.
[33] ICRC, Customary IHL Rule 157: 'Jurisdiction over War Crimes', at: https://bit.ly/3n4tP31.
[34] ICRC, *Bringing IHL Home: Guidelines on the National Implementation of International Humanitarian Law*, p. 38.
[35] Art. 83(1), 1977 Additional Protocol I.
[36] Ibid.

for the application of the Geneva Conventions and the Additional Protocol I 'shall be fully acquainted with the text thereof'.[37]

The ICRC found that it is a customary rule for all States and parties to the conflict to provide instruction in IHL to their armed forces.[38] State practice, the ICRC has determined, establishes the rule as a customary norm applicable to States whether in time of peace or when they are parties to international or non-international armed conflicts. The State practice the ICRC collected did not find any distinction between instruction in IHL applicable in international armed conflicts or that applicable in non-international armed conflicts.[39] **16.14**

The method of instruction inevitably determines, in large part, its effectiveness. Scholarly lecture has its place, but is, in and of itself, inadequate. The practice collected for the ICRC customary law study suggested that 'much of the teaching is primarily or exclusively in the form of written instruction or classroom teaching, which may not be sufficient to ensure effective compliance during the stress of combat'.[40] South Africa's *Manual on the Law of Armed Conflict*, cited by the ICRC in this regard, specified that 'in the circumstances of combat, soldiers may often not have time to consider the principles of the LOAC [Law of Armed Conflict] before acting. Soldiers must therefore not only know these principles but must be trained so that the proper response to specific situations is second nature'.[41] **16.15**

The corresponding customary IHL rule for teaching those outside the armed forces provides that States 'must encourage' the teaching of IHL to the civilian population. Again, the rule seemingly applies in all armed conflict, as well as during peacetime.[42] Under the 1977 Additional Protocol II, however, it is provided only that the Protocol 'shall be disseminated as widely as possible'.[43] According to the Statutes of the International Red Cross and Red Crescent Movement, National Societies 'disseminate and assist their governments in disseminating international humanitarian law; they take initiatives in this respect'.[44] Within academia, in Switzerland the Geneva Academy of International Humanitarian Law and Human Rights offers an international executive masters' degree in international humanitarian law and human rights in armed conflict,[45] as well as short courses on the basic principles of IHL.[46] **16.16**

---

[37] Ibid., Art. 83(2),.
[38] ICRC, Customary IHL Rule 142: 'Instruction in International Humanitarian Law within Armed Forces', at: https://bit.ly/3vp8IMM.
[39] Ibid.
[40] Ibid.
[41] South African National Defence Force, *Manual on the Law of Armed Conflict*, Pretoria, 1996, para. 14.
[42] ICRC, Customary IHL Rule 143: 'Dissemination of International Humanitarian Law among the Civilian Population', at: https://bit.ly/3jcSfGe.
[43] Art. 19, 1977 Additional Protocol II.
[44] Art. 3(2), Statutes of the International Red Cross and Red Crescent Movement; adopted by the 25th International Conference of the Red Cross at Geneva in 1986 (as amended in 1995 and 2006), at: https://bit.ly/3n7rFzs.
[45] Geneva Academy of International Humanitarian Law and Human Rights, 'LLM in International Humanitarian Law and Human Rights: An Overview', at: https://bit.ly/3FVRFXi.
[46] Geneva Academy of International Humanitarian Law and Human Rights, 'Basic Principles of International Humanitarian Law', at: https://bit.ly/3DOX0Oj.

Orders to armed forces

16.17 The 1977 Additional Protocol I obligates States Parties to 'give orders and instructions to ensure observance' of the Geneva Conventions and the Protocol, and to 'supervise their execution'.[47] The obligation upon States to issue orders and instructions to their armed forces to ensure respect for IHL was first codified in the 1899 Hague Convention II and the 1907 Hague Convention IV. Article 1 of this latter treaty stipulates that: 'The Contracting Powers shall issue instructions to their armed land forces which shall be in conformity with the Regulations respecting the laws and customs of war on land, annexed to the present Convention.'[48] At customary law, the ICRC subsumes the duty to issue orders and instructions to the armed forces within the broader rule whereby: 'Each party to the conflict must respect and ensure respect for international humanitarian law by its armed forces.'[49]

16.18 In the United States, Field Manual (FM) 27-2, published in November 1984, was entitled 'Your Conduct in Combat under the Law of War'.[50] Among many instructions in the booklet, it ordered US soldiers not to attack 'non-combatants' and to treat all detainees humanely. It does not appear to have been updated.[51] In January 2020, Lieutenant-General Charles N. Pede, the US Judge Advocate General, formally announced the publication of FM 6-27: *The Commander's Handbook on the Law of Land Warfare*.[52] The handbook stipulates that commanders 'have a duty to take appropriate measures as are within their power to control the forces under their command for the prevention of violations' of IHL.[53] Such measures 'may include: training subordinates, issuing command guidance or procedures; investigating allegations or incidents; instituting administrative or disciplinary action; and taking other appropriate corrective action'.[54] Orders to combat troops may also include a small flashcard for soldiers to carry with them, reiterating the key principles and rules of IHL.[55]

---

[47] Art. 83(2), 1977 Additional Protocol I.
[48] Art. 1, Regulations concerning the Laws and Customs of War on Land annexed to Convention (II) with Respect to the Laws and Customs of War on Land; adopted at The Hague, 29 July 1899; entered into force, 4 September 1900; and Art. 1, Regulations concerning the Laws and Customs of War on Land annexed to 1907 Hague Convention (IV) respecting the Laws and Customs of War on Land; adopted at The Hague, 18 October 1907; entered into force, 26 January 1910.
[49] ICRC, Customary IHL Rule 139: 'Respect for International Humanitarian Law', at: https://bit.ly/3jaRAVU.
[50] United States Department of Defense, 'Your Conduct in Combat under the Law of War', FM 27-2, November 1984, at: https://bit.ly/3lQMEar.
[51] See US Army Publishing Directorate's current list of field manuals, at: https://bit.ly/2Z2g7VO.
[52] Lt.-Gen. C. N. Pede, 'Part I: Why the FM 6-27 Update is Vital for Judge Advocates', *The Army Lawyer*, Issue No. 2, 2020, pp. 22–24, at: https://bit.ly/3G7obWG.
[53] US Army and US Marine Corps, *The Commander's Handbook on the Law of Land Warfare*, FM 6-27/MCTP 11-10C, Washington, D.C., August 2019, at: https://bit.ly/3vwMyrY, §8.2.
[54] Ibid.
[55] For one proposed set of such cards, see Brainscape, 'Soldier's Rules Flashcards Preview', at: https://bit.ly/3aTGRux.

Legal advisers in the armed forces

The 1977 Additional Protocol I obligates States Parties to ensure 'at all times' that legal advisers are available as and when necessary to 'advise military commanders at the appropriate level on the application' of the Geneva Conventions and the Protocol, as well as on the appropriate instruction to be given to the armed forces on IHL.[56] This rule is, the ICRC affirms, also a norm of customary law for State armed forces, seemingly in all armed conflicts. Thus, State practice collected by the organisation for its study of customary IHL 'does not indicate' that any distinction is made between advice on IHL applicable in international and non-international armed conflicts.[57]

16.19

The extent to which legal advisers are incorporated in the armed forces varies widely. Practice in this regard certainly does not amount to a general practice among States, but rather is largely confined to Western militaries. Accordingly, Dinstein is perhaps overly confident in his assertion that the 'prevalence of germane States' practice cannot be gainsaid'.[58] As the ICRC notes, the United States, which is not a party to the 1977 Additional Protocol I, 'has specifically stated that it supports this rule'. But this is not the same as believing that it is binding upon all States, as *opinio juris* requires.[59] Indeed, the evidence on which the ICRC appears to rely concerns remarks made in 1987 by a deputy legal adviser of the US Department of State, referring to Articles 80–85 of the Additional Protocol I. Michael Matheson affirmed then: 'We support the principle that legal advisers be made available, when necessary, to advise military commanders at the appropriate level on the application of these principles.'[60] Dinstein does acknowledge a potential problem with the requisite *opinio juris* for a customary rule to exist.[61]

16.20

The role of the legal adviser is a 'preventive' one.[62] During the conduct of hostilities, the task of legal advisers is, particularly, to advise on targeting, in particular giving their view as to whether proposed means and methods of warfare for an attack are lawful and whether the rule of proportionality in attack is being complied with. This advice is not merely provided on request, but 'even *proprio motu*' in the ICRC's words.[63] But despite their important function in upholding the application of IHL, legal advisers are not immune from being targeted themselves during the conduct of hostilities. As members of the armed forces, which they typically are, legal advisers are lawful military targets even though their principal task is to advise, not to participate directly in hostilities.

16.21

---

[56] Art. 82, 1977 Additional Protocol I.
[57] ICRC, Customary IHL Rule 141: 'Legal Advisers for Armed Forces', at: https://bit.ly/3n80O6D.
[58] Y. Dinstein, 'Legal Advisers in the Field During Armed Conflict', The Howard S. Levie Distinguished Essay, *International Legal Studies*, Vol. 97 (2021), pp. 917–36, at pp. 918–19, at: https://bit.ly/3lRgkV4.
[59] See, e.g., D. Turns, 'Implementation and Compliance', in E. Wilmshurst and S. Breau (eds.), *Perspectives on the ICRC Study on Customary International Humanitarian Law*, Cambridge University Press, Cambridge, 2007, 354, at p. 362.
[60] ICRC, Practice relating to Rule 141: United States of America, at: https://bit.ly/3jfoq8g.
[61] Dinstein, 'Legal Advisers in the Field During Armed Conflict', pp. 918–19.
[62] ICRC, Commentary on Article 82 of the 1977 Additional Protocol I, 1987, at: https://bit.ly/3AUiNST, para. 3356.
[63] Ibid., para. 3356(a).

256   NATIONAL IMPLEMENTATION

16.22 In a complex theatre, the task of the legal adviser is especially demanding and stressful.[64] The occasional comic effect in the film *Eye in the Sky* (concerning evolving discussions of the legality of a putative US/UK drone strike in Kenya) does serve to illustrate the pressure under which a legal adviser may be operating. A member of the British Army Legal Service, Lieutenant Colonel Stephanie Beazley, recalled in 2020 how things have changed over the years: 'In the past, lawyers would only be asked for when things had gone wrong. You'd turn up to a meeting and people would joke "Here's the lawyer again—here to tell us what we can't do".'[65] Speaking to the situation of the judge advocates in the United States, Richard DiMeglio notes that they 'find themselves operating in areas of extreme legal complexity, where political and strategic implications are often at the forefront, and where black letter law is rarely sufficient to render competent advice'.[66]

16.23 Incorrect advice to a commander by a legal adviser may obviate a war crimes charge against the commander, but place the legal adviser in a difficult position personnally, especially if the advice was recklessly given. In Dinstein's words: 'Can it be averred that a military commander, who has been assured by a legal adviser that a concrete object constitutes a *military* objective, acted with knowledge and intent to direct an attack against a *civilian* object?'[67] Conversely, it would be a reckless commander who pushed ahead with an attack, having been informed by a legal adviser that it would amount to a war crime or even just a violation of the primary rule.

Duty to investigate possible breaches

16.24 Beyond the duty to prosecute war crimes (and therefore to investigate alleged or reasonably suspected instances of such crimes),[68] there is a duty to suppress other breaches of IHL. This is set out in each of the four Geneva Conventions of 1949, a duty that is incorporated by Article 85(1) of the 1977 Additional Protocol I. Under the Protocol, the States Parties are also obligated to 'take measures necessary' in order to suppress all breaches of the Conventions or of the Protocol 'which result from a failure to act when under a duty to do so'.[69] The ICRC's commentary of 1987 observed that the fact that 'a breach of the rules of applicable international law may consist of an omission,

---

[64] See, e.g., C. Jones, '"Almost Divine Power": the Lawyers who Sign Off who Lives and who DIES in Modern War Zones', *The Conversation*, 12 May 2021, at: https://bit.ly/3n5Mbke.
[65] C. Baksi, 'Military Mettle', *The Law Society Gazette*, 22 June 2020, at: https://bit.ly/3jbuC0U.
[66] Lt.-Col. R. P. DiMeglio, 'Training Army Judge Advocates to Advise Commanders as Operational Law Attorneys', *Boston College Law Review*, Vol. 54, No. 3 (2013), https://bit.ly/3BXhQKK, 1185–206, at p. 1188.
[67] Dinstein, 'Legal Advisers in the Field During Armed Conflict', p. 934 (original emphasis).
[68] ICRC Customary IHL Rule 158: 'Prosecution of War Crimes', at: http://bit.ly/37FdYin; see also N. Lubell, J. Pejic, and C. Simmons, *Guidelines on Investigating Violations of IHL: Law, Policy and Good Practice*, ICRC and Geneva Academy of International Humanitarian Law and Human Rights, Geneva, 2019 (hereinafter, *Guidelines on Investigating Violations of IHL: Law, Policy and Good Practice*), at: https://bit.ly/3jdr6mU, para. 12.
[69] Art. 86(1), 1977 Additional Protocol I.

i.e., a failure to act, just as well as an act by a State organ, is uncontested nowadays'.[70] Indeed, as noted above, this position was firmly endorsed by the International Law Commission in its 2001 Draft Articles on the Responsibility of States for International Wrongful Acts.[71]

One such obligation inherent in the duty to suppress breaches of IHL other than grave breaches is the duty to investigate possible violations of IHL. Such investigations 'are recognised as critical for the proper application of this body of norms in both international and non-international armed conflict'.[72] In 2017, the Office of the UN High Commissioner for Human Rights published a revised version of the 1991 Minnesota Protocol on the Investigation of Potentially Unlawful Death (the Minnesota Protocol),[73] a set of international guidelines on the duty to investigate under the right to life. It stipulates that all deaths occurring in custody, which include those occurring during and in connection with an armed conflict, must be effectively and impartially investigated.[74] A distinct set of obligations pertains to deaths caused during the conduct of hostilities given the differing rules on the use of lethal force:

16.25

> Where, during the conduct of hostilities, it appears that casualties have resulted from an attack, a post-operation assessment should be conducted to establish the facts, including the accuracy of the targeting ... Where any death is suspected or alleged to have resulted from a violation of IHL that would not amount to a war crime, and where an investigation ('official inquiry') into the death is not specifically required under IHL, at a minimum further inquiry is necessary. In any event, where evidence of unlawful conduct is identified, a full investigation should be conducted.[75]

This stipulation was cited by the Grand Chamber of the European Court of Human Rights in its 2021 judgment in *Hanan* v. *Germany*.[76] The case concerned the effectiveness of the investigation into the legality of an air strike by the German Air Force in Kunduz in Afghanistan in 2009. At issue was the rule of proportionality in attack. It was generally agreed that armed Taliban fighters were at the scene of two hijacked tankers and were siphoning off the fuel.[77] These individuals were lawful targets in the conduct of hostilities. An important question at issue was whether the German colonel who authorised the air strike knew or should have known that civilians were also present. The

16.26

---

[70] ICRC, Commentary on Article 86 of the 1977 Additional Protocol I, 1987, at: https://bit.ly/2Zcife9, para. 3529.
[71] Draft Article 2, 2001 ILC Draft Articles on State Responsibility.
[72] *Guidelines on Investigating Violations of IHL: Law, Policy and Good Practice*, para. 12.
[73] Minnesota Protocol on the Investigation of Potentially Unlawful Death (2016), Office of the United Nations High Commissioner for Human Rights, New York/Geneva, 2017, at: https://bit.ly/3aH8Yh7.
[74] Ibid., paras. 16, 17.
[75] Ibid., para. 21. See also in this regard Guideline 12, *Guidelines on Investigating Violations of IHL: Law, Policy and Good Practice*.
[76] European Court of Human Rights, *Hanan* v. *Germany*, Judgment (Grand Chamber), 16 February 2021.
[77] Ibid., paras. 22–23.

German military concluded that 91 people were killed and a further 11 injured by the strike, while other casualty estimates were even higher.[78]

16.27 The European Court concluded that the investigation into the deaths of the applicant's two sons by the German authorities complied with the requirements of an effective investigation under Article 2 of the 1950 European Convention on Human Rights.[79] In so doing, the Court noted that 'there is no substantive normative conflict in respect of the requirements of an effective investigation between the rules of international humanitarian law ... and those under the Convention'.[80] This is an important holding. In their third-party comments in the case between Georgia and Russia, adjudged in 2021, the Human Rights Centre of the University of Essex had averred that, although IHL could require investigations in certain circumstances, there could be perceived differences between IHL and international human rights law in this regard, implying that the duty to investigate under IHL was somehow narrower than that under human rights law.[81]

Duty to suppress breaches of international humanitarian law

16.28 Whenever a violation of IHL is identified, it must be 'suppressed'. The ICRC and the Geneva Academy of International Humanitarian Law and Human Rights argue that the notion of suppressing breaches offers avenues for remedial action beyond a criminal prosecution. Thus, the guidelines they elaborated in 2019 provide as follows:

> The term to 'suppress' usually denotes the wide range of measures that States may take to address all other violations of the laws and customs of war, including violations that do not give rise to individual criminal responsibility, so as to ensure they cease, are prevented and that their reoccurrence is precluded. The notion of suppression also comprises administrative measures that States may take to deal with violations not amounting to war crimes.[82]

A commander or other authority responsible for an internal investigation 'should be able to sanction those liable, i.e. must be superior in rank and be able to take other measures that may be necessary to suppress a violation'.[83]

16.29 Such measures are broad in scope. In 2020, with respect to the corresponding duty to suppress breaches of the 1949 Geneva Convention III, the ICRC suggested that: 'States Parties will determine the best way to fulfil these obligations, for example by instituting

---

[78] Report on deadly German-ordered air raid in Kunduz is inconclusive', *Deutsche Welle*, 28 October 2011, http://bit.ly/3011y2l.
[79] European Court of Human Rights, *Hanan* v. *Germany*, Judgment (Grand Chamber), para. 236.
[80] Ibid., para. 199.
[81] European Court of Human Rights, *Georgia* v. *Russia (II)*, Judgment (Grand Chamber), 21 January 2021, para. 318; see also para. 325.
[82] *Guidelines on Investigating Violations of IHL: Law, Policy and Good Practice*, 2019, para. 16.
[83] Ibid., para. 165.

judicial or disciplinary proceedings … or by taking a range of administrative or other regulatory measures or issuing instructions to subordinates.'[84] The measures chosen, the commentary continues, 'will depend on the gravity and the circumstances of the violation in question, in accordance with the general principle that every punishment should be proportional to the severity of the breach'.[85] An officer may be demoted, for instance.[86] Following a bombing of a hospital at Kunduz by the US Air Force in 2015, described in Chapter 11, administrative measures ranged from 'suspension and removal from command, letters of reprimand, formal counseling and extensive retraining'.[87] In very serious cases, a dishonourable discharge from the armed forces may be warranted. In the United States, a dishonourable discharge can only be handed down to an enlisted member by a general court-martial.[88]

Concluding remarks and outlook

Every State should have national legislation in place to give effect to its obligations under IHL, even though this is not a general obligation under either the Geneva Conventions or their Additional Protocols. Such legislation should not be limited to a State's duty to prosecute or hand over for prosecution individuals suspected to have committed war crimes in an international armed conflict, but should reflect the gamut of the State's IHL obligations under customary and conventional law, including in non-international armed conflict. And while the customary law status of the obligation to have legal advisers in the armed forces remains unsettled, the practice of including such advisers is unquestionably of benefit to all.   16.30

It is not possible to 'suppress' breaches unless all reasonable suspicions or allegations are examined carefully. Battle damage assessments and drone footage can enable a preliminary investigation to take place even when the party concerned does not control the death scene. Greater clarity of the nature of the duty to investigate suspected violations of IHL other than apparent war crimes would thus also be of benefit. The holding by the European Court of Human Rights in *Hanan* that the duty to investigate suspicious death in a non-international armed conflict is the same under IHL as it is under human rights law is a valuable normative statement. Confirmation of this by key actors, such as the ICRC, would also be of value.   16.31

---

[84] ICRC Commentary on Article 129 of the 1949 Geneva Convention III, 2020, para. 5162.
[85] Ibid.
[86] In the British Army, for instance, the ordering of a reduction in rank is made under the authority of section 332 of the 2006 Armed Forces Act (as amended by section 19 of the 2011 Armed Forces Act).
[87] B. L. Cox, 'Five Years On: Military Accountability and the Attack on the MSF Trauma Center in Kunduz', *Just Security*, 3 October 2020, at: https://bit.ly/3mjZGhg.
[88] VetVerify, 'Military Discharge in the United States', 2017, at: https://bit.ly/3lUECgL.

17

Application and Implementation by Armed Non-State Actors

Introduction

17.1 For many years now, non-international armed conflicts (non-international armed conflict) that involve armed non-State actors (ANSAs) fighting against the armed forces of a State or against each other, have been the predominant type of armed conflict.[1] This means, in other words, that ANSAs are the most prevalent actors operating in contemporary situations of armed violence. Against this background, how and to what extent their behaviour is regulated by international humanitarian law (IHL), and how we can enhance their respect of IHL norms to better protect civilians in armed conflicts has been one of the main contemporary policy concerns for the international community.

17.2 The umbrella terms 'armed non-State actors', also sometimes referred to as 'armed groups', 'insurgents', 'rebels', 'freedom fighters', or even 'terrorists' are not defined in international treaties or international customary law. While they potentially depict the same or at least a similar reality—a group of individuals using armed force to achieve certain goals—they convey markedly different perceptions of what they may in fact represent. In that sense, these are subjective terms, which may, depending on the context, mean, in Andrew Clapham's words, 'different things to different people'.[2]

17.3 There are several types of ANSAs, with various aims and ideologies, which may or may not match IHL requirements to be a party to an armed conflict.[3] IHL, however, has a

---

[1] See A. Bellal, *The War Report* 2018, Geneva Academy of International Humanitarian Law and Human Rights, Geneva, 2019, at: https://bit.ly/3onS8dN; see also the Geneva Academy's Rule of Law in Armed Conflicts (RULAC) Project, available at: www.rulac.org.

[2] A. Clapham, 'Non-State Actors (in Postconflict Peace-building)', in V. Chetail (ed.), *Postconflict Peacebuilding: A Lexicon*, Oxford University Press, Oxford, 2009, pp. 200–12, at p. 200.

[3] Political science literature, for instance, classifies ANSAs in different categories, such as: 'armed opposition groups', 'paramilitaries', 'militias', 'criminal organizations', and 'terrorist organizations'. See, e.g., P. G. Thompson, *Armed Groups: The 21st Century Threat*, Rowman and Littlefield, London, 2014; A. H. Sinno, 'Armed Groups' Organizational Structure and Their Strategic Options', *International Review of the Red Cross*, Vol. 93, No. 882 (2011), pp. 311–32; R. H. Shultz, D. Farah, and V. Lochard, 'Armed Groups: A Tier-One Security Priority', Institute for National Security Studies (INSS) Occasional Paper 57, USAF Academy, Colorado, 2004. This chapter will use the term 'Armed Non-State Actors' as covering all these different types of actors. It will not, however, consider mercenaries as a category of armed non-State actor. Mercenaries are not considered as an 'armed group' under IHL, but are regulated as individuals not belonging to an organised armed group or any other party to an armed conflict, and who do not benefit from prisoner of war status. Art. 47, Protocol Additional to the Geneva Conventions of 12 August 1949, and relating to the Protection of Victims of International Armed Conflicts (Protocol I); adopted at Geneva, 8 June 1977; entered into force, 7 December 1978 (hereinafter, 1977 Additional Protocol I).

less than nuanced approach to ANSAs. As long as any given ANSA reaches a 'minimum degree of organization'[4] that enables it to respect and implement IHL norms, its structure is largely irrelevant. This approach may be justified in order to cast the IHL net as broadly as possible and ensure the maximum protection possible for the civilians. For engagement purposes, however, and more particularly if respect for international norms by these actors is to be enhanced, a deeper interdisciplinary inquiry into the typologies, ideologies, and aims of ANSAs is necessary if all the issues they raise in situations of armed conflict are to be tackled in some way.[5]

Furthermore, other bodies of international law have focused on the issue of ANSAs. For example, international human rights law touches upon the issue of the administration of civilian life by non-State 'de facto' authorities.[6] General public international law addresses the use of force by ANSAs and self-defence issues.[7] International criminal law covers notions such as command responsibility and the commission of war crimes by a member of an ANSA.[8] And finally, counterterrorism and domestic law are also obviously relevant when it comes to the regulation and repression of ANSAs.[9]

17.4

Historically, the development of the law applicable to ANSAs has been very gradual. In 1949, one single provision, Article 3 Common to the four Geneva Conventions ('Common Article 3') was deemed applicable to situations of non-international armed conflict. Almost 20 years later, the 1977 Additional Protocol I was negotiated to complement the Geneva Conventions and the law applicable in international armed conflict, but included one particular type of ANSA in its scope of application: so-called 'national liberation movements'. The 1977 Additional Protocol II, which is entirely devoted to a certain form of non-international armed conflict, is relevant to a wider range of ANSAs operating in such conflicts. Finally, in parallel, customary IHL has developed to cover the many legal issues that were not addressed in treaty law pertaining to non-international armed conflict, particularly the conduct of hostilities.

17.5

---

[4] International Committee of the Red Cross (ICRC), 'How Is the Term "Armed Conflict" Defined in International Humanitarian Law?', ICRC Opinion Paper, Geneva, 2008, available at: https://bit.ly/3B27U34.

[5] See, e.g., ICRC, The Roots of Restraint in War, Report, Geneva, 2020, available at: https://bit.ly/3uutEmR; H. Jo, *Compliant Rebels: Rebel Groups and International Law in World Politics*, Cambridge University Press, Cambridge, 2015; A. Bellal, 'What Are Armed Non-State Actors? A Legal and Semantic Approach', in E. Heffes, M. Kotlik, and M. Ventura (eds.), *International Humanitarian Law and Non-State Actors: Debates, Law and Practice*, TMC Asser/Springer, The Hague, 2020, pp. 21–46.

[6] See notably K. Fortin, 'The Application of Human Rights Law to Everyday Civilian Life Under Rebel Control', *Netherlands International Law Review*, Vol. 63, No. 2 (2016), pp. 161–81; see also M. Kotlik, 'Armed Non-State Actors', in C. Binder, M. Nowak, J. A. Hofbauer, and P. Janig (eds.), *Elgar Encyclopedia of Human Rights*, Edward Elgar Publishing, Cheltenham, 2022.

[7] See, e.g., C. Antonopoulos, 'Force by Armed Groups as Armed Attack and the Broadening of Self-Defence', *Netherlands International Law Review*, Vol. 55, No. 2 (August 2008), pp. 159–80.

[8] A. Spadaro, 'Punish and Be Punished? The Paradox of Command Responsibility in Armed Groups', *Journal of International Criminal Justice*, Vol. 18, No. 1 (2020), pp. 1–30.

[9] See, e.g., J. H. Norwitz, *Armed Groups: Studies in National Security, Counterterrorism, and Counterinsurgency*, Naval War College, United States, 2008.

Table 17.1 Summary of key Rules on ANSA in API

Rule	AP I	Customary status (IAC)
Armed forces	Art. 43	Yes
Combatant and prisoners of war status	Art. 44(3)	No
Treaty relations upon entry into force of the Protocol	Art. 96(3)	No

17.6 Because ANSAs are not technically 'party' to treaties, as they do not sign them nor (ordinarily) participate in their drafting, the precise legal means by which ANSA are actually bound by IHL treaty law has been persistently questioned.[10] State practice, international case law, and scholarship have, however, confirmed that Common Article 3, as well as other relevant treaty provisions, apply to ANSAs directly.[11] In fact, one of the issues discussed now by scholarship is not so much whether IHL is binding on ANSAs or not, but to what extent their practice and understanding of humanitarian norms should be considered for law-making purposes.[12]

17.7 The key rules mentioning ANSAs in the 1977 Additional Protocol I are summarised in Table 17.1. All 18 substantive rules of the 1977 Additional Protocol II are applicable in non-international armed conflict and therefore also binding on ANSAs (but see on this issue Paragraph 1.44) and will not be summarised here. (The ten procedural rules in the Protocol, pertaining among other things to the signature or entry into force of the treaty, are not directly applicable to ANSAs.)

---

[10] First, to what extent Common Article 3 *directly* addressed ANSAs has been debated. As the article states that 'each Party to the conflict shall be bound to apply, as a minimum' its provisions, it has been claimed that the term 'each Party' does not apply to ANSAs, but only to governmental armed forces. One of the arguments put forward has been that 'Party' (with a capital 'p') meant 'High Contracting Party', i.e. states, and that it was used in a contracted form merely to avoid repetition. See, e.g., S. Zasova, 'L'applicabilité du droit international humanitaire aux groupes armés organisés', in J. Sorel and C. Popescu (eds.), *La protection des personnes vulnérables en temps de conflits armés*, Bruylant, Brussels, 2010, pp. 47–85, at p. 58. For the different theories on the applicability of IHL to ANSAs, see notably S. Sivakumaran, 'Binding Armed Opposition Groups', *International and Comparative Law Quarterly*, Vol. 55, No. 2 (2006), pp. 369–94.

[11] In its judgment in *Nicaragua* v. *United States of America*, for example, the International Court of Justice (ICJ) confirmed that Common Article 3 was applicable to the Contras, the ANSA fighting the government: 'The conflict between the contras' forces and those of the Government of Nicaragua is an armed conflict which is 'not of an international character''. The acts of the contras towards the Nicaraguan Government are therefore governed by the law applicable to conflicts of that character'. ICJ, *Case Concerning Military and Paramilitary Activities in and against Nicaragua (Nicaragua v. United States)*, Judgment, 27 June 1986, para. 219. In 2004, the Appeals Chamber of the Special Court for Sierra Leone (SCSL) held that 'it is well settled that all parties to an armed conflict, whether states or non-state actors, are bound by international humanitarian law, even though only states may become parties to international treaties'. SCSL, *Prosecutor* v. *Sam Hinga Norman*, Decision on Preliminary Motion Based on Lack of Jurisdiction (Child Recruitment) (Appeals Chamber) (Case No. SCSL-2004-14-AR72(E)), 31 May 2004, para. 22.

[12] See, e.g., A. Roberts and S. Sivakumaran, 'Lawmaking by Non-State Actors: Engaging Armed Groups in the Creation of International Humanitarian Law', *Yale Journal of International Law*, Vol. 37, No. 1 (2012), pp. 107–52, at: https://bit.ly/3HBRPn9.

Armed non-State actors under the 1977 Additional Protocol I

17.8 As specified in Article 1 of the 1977 Additional Protocol I, which in turn refers to Article 2 common to the 1949 Geneva Conventions, the treaty applies in situations of international armed conflicts. That is to say, to all conflicts 'which may arise between two or more of the High Contracting Parties' and to 'all cases of partial or total occupation of the territory of a High Contracting Party'. As stated in paragraph 4 of Article 1, these situations also include armed conflicts:

> [i]n which peoples are fighting against colonial domination and alien occupation and against racist regimes in the exercise of their right of self-determination, as enshrined in the Charter of the United Nations and the Declaration on Principles of International Law concerning Friendly Relations and Co-operation among States in accordance with the Charter of the United Nations.

17.9 Despite its applicability in international armed conflict, the Additional Protocol I may be relevant for ANSAs, albeit of a certain type. Indeed, the Protocol specifies that combatants who have the right to participate directly in hostilities (and who may accordingly be entitled to prisoner-of-war status) are notably 'the armed forces' of a party to a conflict, which:

> consist of all organized armed forces, groups and units which are under a command responsible to that Party for the conduct of its subordinates, even if that Party is represented by a government *or an authority not recognized by an adverse Party*. Such armed forces shall be subject to an internal disciplinary system, which, 'inter alia', shall enforce compliance with the rules of international law applicable in armed conflict.[13]

The armed actors alluded to here are 'militias' and 'organized resistance movements' as well as so-called 'national liberation movements', which meet the conditions of Articles 1(4) and 44(3) of the Protocol.

17.10 Militias and organised resistance movements are both mentioned in the 1949 Geneva Conventions, notably in Article 4 of the Geneva Convention relative to the Treatment of Prisoners of War (1949 Geneva Convention III) While the term *militia* is not defined in IHL, it can be understood as a 'military or paramilitary unit or group, which is not composed of professional soldiers but of regular citizens who are trained for their military duty in cases of emergency to support regular troops'.[14] They are not usually part of a State's regular armed forces, even if they play a supplementary role to them. 'Resistance movements' similarly do not form part of the official armed forces of a Party to a conflict, but nevertheless 'belong' to such a Party.[15] On the one hand, because of

---

[13] Art. 43, 1977 Additional Protocol I (emphasis added).
[14] J. Gebhard, 'Militias', in *Max Planck Encyclopedia of Public International Law*, 2010, at: https://bit.ly/3B0p40Z, para. 1.
[15] R. Barnidge, 'Resistance Movements', *Max Planck Encyclopedia of Public International Law*, 2011, at: https://bit.ly/3HIPKpm, para. 1. See Art. 4(1) and 4(2) of the 1949 Geneva Convention III.

their de facto relationship with the armed forces of a State that is party to a conflict, both militias and resistance movements are entitled to enjoy prisoner-of-war (POW) status. On the other hand, one can hardly consider 'national liberation movements' to be linked to the armed forces of the State against which they are fighting. They are thus ANSAs which benefit from certain privileges usually not afforded to non-State actors.

17.11 National liberation movements can be defined 'by their objective (self-determination), the quality of their constituency (peoples) and the conduct and/or quality of the opposing government'.[16] To what extent national liberation movements can be defined accurately as ANSAs, in the same sense than other insurgents, is debatable. As remarked by Clapham:

> In some ways it is clumsy to list NLMs [National liberation movements] as non-state actors. Their representatives may reject the label of non-state actor as, not only may they wish to stress their putative state-like aspirations and status, but they may sometimes already be recognized as a state member in certain regional inter-governmental organizations.[17]

Indeed, some of these movements have enjoyed observer status in international organisations for some time. An obvious example is the Palestinian Liberation Organization, which held that status at the United Nations until the formal recognition by the UN General Assembly of the existence of the State of Palestine.[18]

17.12 Be that as it may, national liberation movements benefit from a special regime in IHL, since they are considered parties to an international armed conflict if they meet the conditions of Article 1(4) of the 1977 Additional Protocol I, that is, if they are fighting 'against colonial domination and alien occupation and against racist regimes in the exercise of their right of self-determination' (and providing of course that the State against which they are fighting is a party to the Protocol). Members of national liberation movements may also enjoy POW status, as long as they respect the conditions stipulated in Article 44(3) of the Additional Protocol.[19] In addition, through a unilateral declaration under Article 96(3) of the 1977 Additional Protocol I, which is transmitted to the depositary (the Swiss Federal Council), such movements can undertake to apply to the conflict not only the Protocol, but also all four Geneva Conventions of 1949.

---

[16] K. Mastorodimos, 'National Liberation Movements: Still a Valid Concept (with Special Reference to International Humanitarian Law)?', *Oregon Review of International Law*, Vol.17 (2015), pp. 71–110, at p. 71.
[17] A. Clapham, *Human Rights Obligations of Non-State Actors*, Oxford University Press, Oxford, 2006, p. 273.
[18] UN General Assembly Resolution 43/177, adopted on 29 November 2012 by 138 votes to 9 (Canada, Czechia, Israel, the Marshall Islands, Micronesia, Nauru, Panama, Palau, and the United States), with 41 abstentions.
[19] The relevant text provides that: 'In order to promote the protection of the civilian population from the effects of hostilities, combatants are obliged to distinguish themselves from the civilian population while they are engaged in an attack or in a military operation preparatory to an attack. Recognizing, however, that there are situations in armed conflicts where, owing to the nature of the hostilities an armed combatant cannot so distinguish himself, he shall retain his status as a combatant, provided that, in such situations, he carries his arms openly: (a) during each military engagement, and (b) during such time as he is visible to the adversary while he is engaged in a military deployment preceding the launching of an attack in which he is to participate'.

17.13 Owing to the scope of these provisions, it is crucial to distinguish which ANSAs can be qualified as a national liberation movement. The problem lies in the fact that the term is not defined in treaty law and that UN resolutions on self-determination and the 1977 Additional Protocol only speak of 'peoples', without any further specification:[20]

> Since decolonization is essentially complete, it is hard to identify likely additional candidates for coverage under that provision. While there are a number of separatist movements that remain active within peoples such as Kurds in Iraq, Turkey, and Iran, the dissolution of post-colonial States seems outside the scope of these provisions.[21]

17.14 In fact—and unsurprisingly—many ANSAs consider themselves to be 'national liberation movements' and 'authorities representing a people' (a notion also undefined in treaty) fighting for the liberation of a territory from colonial or foreign occupation. A number of these actors made a declaration under Article 96(3) of the 1977 Additional Protocol I to proclaim their willingness to be bound by it along with the 1949 Geneva Conventions. For example, the National Democratic Front of the Philippines (NDFP), an umbrella body for different ANSAs active in the conflict in the Philippines that started in 1968 and whose aim was to overthrow the Government of the Philippines and replace it with a revolutionary one,[22] issued a declaration under 96(3) in 1996.[23] Asserting that there was 'persistent foreign domination and national oppression', the NDFP characterised the Government of the Philippines as a 'puppet government in the service of the United States government' and argued that this meant that Article 1(4) of the Protocol applied.[24] At the time of the declaration, the Philippines was not a party to the protocol, but it acceded to it in 2012.[25] Switzerland, as the depositary of the Geneva Conventions and their Additional Protocols did not react to the NDFP declaration. We can assume it considered the treaty was not applicable since the Philippines was not a party to the Additional Protocol I and thus that the provisions of Article 1(4) and 96(3) were not relevant at the time.

17.15 A few years later, in June 2015, the Polisario Front issued a unilateral declaration under Article 96(3) of the Protocol on behalf of the people of Western Sahara and undertook to apply the Geneva Conventions and their Additional Protocol I to its conflict with Morocco. This time, Switzerland informed the States Parties to the Geneva Conventions

---

[20] The ICRC's 1987 commentary on Article 1(4) notes that: 'In international law there is no definition of what constitutes a people; there are only instruments listing the rights it is recognized all peoples hold. Nor is there an objective or infallible criterion which makes it possible to recognize a group as a people: apart from a defined territory, other criteria could be taken into account such as that of a common language, common culture or ethnic lies'. ICRC Commentary at: https://bit.ly/3Ja8r5E, para. 103.
[21] D. Glazier, 'Wars of National Liberation' in *Max Planck Encyclopedia of Public International Law*, 2009, para. 18.
[22] 'Communist Party of the Philippines—New People's Army (CPP-NPA)', Mapping Militants, Stanford Center for international Security and Cooperation, at: https://stanford.io/3shPNlS.
[23] NDFP Declaration of Undertaking to Apply the Geneva Conventions of 1949 and Protocol I of 1977, available at: https://bit.ly/3BJG51N.
[24] Ibid, p. 9.
[25] See ICRC database at: https://bit.ly/3uAhKrT.

of the communication it had received, affirming that the declaration had, as of 23 June 2015, 'the effects mentioned in Article 96, paragraph 3, of Protocol I'.[26] No State apart from Morocco reacted to this declaration, which was thereby successful. The Polisario Front is perhaps one of the last remaining ANSAs that could fulfil the conditions laid down in the 1977 Additional Protocol I.

Armed non-State actors under the 1977 Additional Protocol II

17.16 In contrast to Common Article 3, which requires that an armed group possess only a minimum degree of organisation,[27] the criteria for application of the 1977 Additional Protocol II are more restrictive. In addition to the existence of an armed conflict between the insurgency and the government taking place in the territory of a State Party,[28] three cumulative material conditions are set out under Article 1(1) for the Protocol to be applicable to an ANSA. First, the organised armed group(s) must be under responsible command; secondly, it must exercise such control over a part of the national territory as to enable it to carry out sustained and concerted military operations; and thirdly, its territorial control must be such as to enable the group to implement the Protocol. Where these criteria for application of the Protocol are objectively met, it becomes 'immediately and automatically applicable', irrespective of the views of the parties to that conflict.[29]

17.17 Given this high threshold, there was some discussion as to whether the 1977 Additional Protocol II would realistically be applicable to most non-international armed conflicts.[30] It was feared that the Protocol would require that an organised armed group

---

[26] See Swiss Confederation, Notification to the Governments of the States parties to the Geneva Conventions of 12 August 1949 for the Protection of War Victims, 26 June 2015, at: https://bit.ly/31YZwRR.

[27] The judgment of the International Criminal Tribunal for the former Yugoslavia (ICTY) in the *Boškoski and Tarčulovski* case held that a group would need to have 'some hierarchical structure' and that, as a minimum, it must be able to implement the basic obligations of Common Article 3. It noted five elements that could help to identify the degree of organization of an ANSA: the existence of a command structure; the fact that the group could carry out operations in an organised manner; elements indicating a level of sophistication with respect to logistics; the existence of internal discipline; and the ability to speak with 'one voice'. ICTY, *Prosecutor v. Boškoski and Tarčulovski*, Judgment (Trial Chamber) (Case No. IT-04-82-T), 10 July 2008, para. 195 *et seq*.

[28] In contrast to the 1977 Additional Protocol II, Common Article 3 also regulates armed conflicts that take place only between ANSAs, for example in a failed State.

[29] See ICRC commentary on Art. 1 of the Protocol, at p. 1353; and International Criminal Tribunal for Rwanda (ICTR), *Prosecutor v. Jean-Paul Akayesu*, Judgment (Trial Chamber) (Case No. ICTR-96-4-T), 2 September 1998, para. 624. Article 1(1) of the Protocol reads as follows: 'This Protocol, which develops and supplements Article 3 common to the Geneva Conventions of 12 August 1949 without modifying its existing conditions of applications, shall apply to all armed conflicts which are not covered by Article 1 of the Protocol Additional to the Geneva Conventions of 12 August 1949, and relating to the Protection of Victims of International Armed Conflicts (Protocol I) and which take place in the territory of a High Contracting Party between its armed forces and dissident armed forces or other organized armed groups which, under responsible command, exercise such control over a part of its territory as to enable them to carry out sustained and concerted military operations and to implement this Protocol.'

[30] See T. Rodenhäuser, *Organizing Rebellion, Non-State Armed Groups under International Humanitarian Law, Human Rights Law, and International Criminal Law*, Oxford University Press, Oxford, 2018, p. 46.

fully attain the degree of organisation of regular forces. These concerns have been partially addressed through interpretation. The ICRC Commentary on Article 1 of the Protocol thus highlights that while the control of the territory would need to be sufficient to allow sustained and concerted military operations to be carried out, only '*some degree of stability* in the control of even a *modest* area of land [is needed] for them to be capable of effectively applying the rules of the Protocol'.[31] Further, as it would appear that the Protocol does not require 'at all times the capacity to implement each and every rule',[32] the degree of organisation an ANSA would need to fulfil to be bound by the Protocol 'is not necessarily as high as many have suggested or feared'.[33]

The problematic absence of a definition of 'organized armed groups'

While the 1977 Additional Protocol II refers to 'dissident armed forces or other organized armed groups', it does not define these terms. In view of the silence of treaty and customary IHL, the ICRC's 2009 *Interpretative Guidance on the Notion of Direct Participation in Hostilities* proposed that, for the purposes of the principle of distinction: 'organized armed groups constitute the armed forces of a non-State party to the conflict and consist only of individuals whose continuous function it is to take a direct part in hostilities ("continuous combat function")'.[34] In other words, the persons who assume exclusively political, administrative, or other non-combat functions are not considered to be members of the organised armed group, but are civilians protected by the principle of distinction.[35]   **17.18**

The ICRC, in its Online Case book, adopted a similar approach to the concept of armed groups falling within the scope of application of IHL: **17.19**

> An 'organized armed group' is the armed wing of a non-state party to a non-international armed conflict, and may be comprised of either: dissident armed forces (for example, breakaway parts of state armed forces); or other organized armed groups which recruit their members primarily from the civilian population but have developed a sufficient degree of military organization to conduct hostilities on behalf of a party to the conflict. The term organized armed group refers exclusively to the armed or military wing of a non-state party to a non-international armed conflict. It does not include those segments of the civilian population that are supportive of the non-state party such as its political wing.[36]

Many organised armed groups possess a civilian/political wing, such as the autonomous region of Rojava in Northern Syria, of which the Syrian Democratic Forces (SDF)

---

[31] ICRC, Commentary on Article 1 of the 1977 Additional Protocol II, para. 4467 (emphasis added).
[32] Rodenhäuser, *Organizing Rebellion, Non-State Armed Groups under International Humanitarian Law*, p. 54.
[33] Ibid.
[34] N. Melzer, *Interpretive Guidance on the Notion of Direct Participation in Hostilities*, ICRC, Geneva, 2009, p. 27.
[35] See on the issue of continuous combat function *supra* Paragraphs 9.13–9.18.
[36] How Does Law Protect in War, 'Armed Groups', ICRC Online Case book, at: https://bit.ly/3J7lRiV.

constitute the 'armed forces';[37] or Hamas in Gaza and its armed wing, the Izz ad-Din al-Qassam Brigades.[38]

17.20 The issue lies in the fact that some of the rules in the 1977 Additional Protocol II are likely to be implemented by the 'civilian wing' of the group. For instance, Article 4(3) of the Protocol stipulates that children 'shall be provided with the care and aid they require, and in particular: a) they shall receive an education, including religious and moral education, in keeping with the wishes of their parents, or in the absence of parents, of those responsible for their care'. Another example is Article 6, which covers the rules on the prosecution and punishment of criminal offences related to the armed conflict. Articles 4 and 6 thus relate to the work of teachers, judges, or lawyers, rather than combatants.

17.21 Furthermore, the Protocol gives little indication as to the precise addresses of the obligations. The norms are generally formulated in a 'passive' mode ('persons shall be respected' and not 'armed groups shall respect'). One exception can be found in the provision on amnesties, which provides that: 'At the end of hostilities, the *authorities in power shall endeavour* to grant the broadest possible amnesty to persons who have participated in the armed conflict, or those deprived of their liberty for reasons related to the armed conflict, whether they are interned or detained.'[39] Here again, neither the treaty nor the commentary defines what is meant by 'authorities'. The commentary only defines the term 'amnesty' as an 'an act by the legislative power which eliminates the consequences of certain punishable offences, stops prosecutions and quashes convictions'.[40] It is thus unclear whether the reference to 'legislative power' would also include the 'legislative power' of an 'authority' understood as the armed wing or the civilian wing of an armed group.

17.22 That said, some of the wording in the article 6, such as the one requiring the establishment of 'a court offering the essential guarantees of independence and impartiality' rather than a 'regularly constituted court' has been chosen to adapt to the reality of armed groups' 'courts'.[41] In reference to Article 6(c), which deals with the criminal law principle of *nullum crimen, nullum poena sine lege*,[42] the commentary also notes that 'the possible co-existence of two sorts of national legislation, namely, that of the State and that of the insurgents, makes the concept of national law rather complicated in this context'.[43]

---

[37] See W. van Wilgenburg, 'Syrian Democratic Forces', European Council on Foreign Relations, at: https://bit.ly/35InW6u.
[38] BBC, 'Profile: Hamas Palestinian Movement', at: https://bbc.in/3buPorK.
[39] Art. 6(5), 1977 Additional Protocol II (emphasis added).
[40] ICRC, Commentary on Art. 6(5), para. 4617.
[41] ICRC, Commentary on Art. 6, para. 4600. See also R. Provost, *Rebel Courts*, Oxford University Press, Oxford, 2021.
[42] This sub-paragraph reads: 'No one shall be held guilty of any criminal offence on account of any act or omission which did not constitute a criminal offence, under the law, at the time when it was committed; nor shall a heavier penalty be imposed than that which was applicable at the time when the criminal offence was committed; if, after the commission of the offence, provision is made by law for the imposition of a lighter penalty, the offender shall benefit thereby'.
[43] ICRC, Commentary on Art. 6, para. 4605.

Thus, it would seem that, at a minimum, it was envisaged that the 1977 Additional Protocol II *did not exclude* the possibility that its provisions generally apply to 'organised armed groups' defined broadly, which would include civilian components charged notably of administering justice, delivering education or health care.[44] If that is the case however, one needs to assume that the acts committed by the 'civilian' wing of the armed group can be attributed to the military wing.[45] Unfortunately, in the absence of any international law rules on the responsibility of 'organised armed groups' as a collective non-State actor, this process of attribution might be arbitrary and could even be perceived as itself contrary to the rule of law.[46]

17.23

Core rules and noteworthy normative silences

Among the core obligations applicable in non-international armed conflicts regulated by the Protocol, ANSAs must respect the fundamental guarantees of the persons within their power, including ensuring that children benefit from specific care and protection (Article 4). Persons in detention or whose liberty has been restricted must be provided with basic necessities and must be judged for any alleged criminal activities in accordance with fair trial guarantees (Articles 5 and 6).[47] Wounded and sick persons must be collected and cared for (Articles 7–12) and as discussed in Chapter 6 of this book, the Protocol also regulates humanitarian relief operations (Article 18).

17.24

In addition, as is well known, the Protocol, and indeed the law of non-international armed conflict in general, does not grant combatant immunity and POW status to members of ANSAs.[48] As a consequence, any member of an armed group can be put on trial in national courts for the mere fact of having participated in hostilities, whether or not they have killed or injured someone, or even fired a gun. However, despite being considered 'equal belligerents', it would not be legal under IHL for ANSAs to hold equivalent trials.[49] Admittedly, while IHL does not explicitly *prohibit* armed groups

17.25

---

[44] See also K. Fortin, 'Civilian Wings Of Armed Groups: Included Within the Concept of "Non-State Party" under IHL?' in Armed Groups and International Law blog, 13 October 2020, at: https://bit.ly/3osBGJl.

[45] See A. Bellal, 'Establishing the Direct Responsibility of Non-State Armed Groups for Violations of International Norms: Issues of Attribution', in N. Gal-Or, C. Ryngaert, and M. Noortman (eds.), *Responsibilities of the Non-State Actor in Armed Conflict and the Market Place: Theoretical Considerations and Empirical Findings*, Brill/Nijhoff, Leiden, 2015, pp. 304–22.

[46] For Jann Kleffner, the absence of clear rules of accountability is contrary to an international order based on the rule of law, which include principles such as legal certainty, avoidance of arbitrariness, and procedural and legal transparency. See J. Kleffner, 'The Collective Accountability of Organized Armed Groups for System Crimes', in H. Wilt and A. Nollkaemper (eds.), *System Criminality in International Law*, Cambridge University Press, Cambridge, 2009, p. 259; see also L. Inigo Alvarez, *Towards a Regime of Responsibility of Armed Groups in International Law*, Intersentia, Cambridge, 2020.

[47] See notably E. Heffes, *Detention by Non-State Armed Groups under International Law*, Cambridge University Press, Cambridge, 2022.

[48] See, inter alia, Arts. 4 and 118 of the 1949 Geneva Convention III; ICRC Customary IHL Rule 106: 'Conditions for Prisoner-of-War Status', at: https://bit.ly/3aXJwlc; and M. N. Schmitt, 'The Status of Opposition Fighters in a Non-International Armed Conflict', *International Legal Studies*, Vol. 42 (2012), p. 121.

[49] As cogently explained by Sean Watts: 'The well-known criteria used to evaluate combatant status in IAC appear nowhere in the positive law of NIAC. And while some States' military manuals address NIAC, none of those reviewed acknowledges international legal input to government forces' status. Instead, most emphasize that the

from prosecuting government soldiers in their own courts for the mere fact of having participated in hostilities, the effect of the judicial guarantee of the principle of legality render such prosecutions unlikely to occur.[50] In light of this, some have suggested that the combatant immunity rule be also applicable to armed groups' members in non-international armed conflict.[51] States, however, are not ready to go down that route, especially in the current context of counterterrorism approach to non-international armed conflicts, as discussed below.

17.26 It is in this context that the reading of Article 6(5) of the 1977 Additional Protocol II on amnesties might take on another colour. The quite succinct ICRC commentary on that sub-paragraph notes that its object 'is to encourage gestures of reconciliation which can contribute to re-establishing normal relations in the life of a nation which has been divided'.[52] One can, however, muse as to whether the amnesty clause was not included also to compensate in some manner for the absence of combatant immunity in non-international armed conflict.

17.27 Indeed, it has been noted that that '(b)oth the drafting history of the proposal and the construction of the initial language (of Article 6(5)) indicate that the provision was drawn up in respect of persons "merely" taking a part in the armed conflict. The amnesty provision was designed to mitigate the effects of the lack of combatant immunity in non-international armed conflicts'.[53] For Frédéric Mégret,

> the normative context within which the argument must unfold is one in which on the one hand there is no privilege of belligerency in non-international armed conflicts, but on the other hand Protocol II encourages the granting of amnesties. It is not hard to see how the granting of such amnesties amounts analytically to something very similar to retrospectively granting a privilege of belligerency, effectively relieving rebels of their criminal responsibility.[54]

---

existing law of NIAC has no effect on the legal status of the parties to the conflict. Finally, there is there no evidence of internationally based prosecutions of government actors for their mere participation in NIAC or based on the nature or composition of such forces. States thus appear to be free from international regulation of the status or nature of government actors they employ against rebels in NIAC.' S. Watts, 'Present and Future Conceptions of the Status of Government Forces in Non-International Armed Conflict', *International Legal Studies*, 2019, pp. 145–80, at p. 149.

[50] As noted by Sassòli: 'State legislation obviously does not prohibit government soldiers from fighting, and it is unclear why—and appears unfair that—they should be bound by any 'legislation' adopted by the non-State armed group before they fall under its control.' M. Sassòli, *Rules, Controversies, and Solutions to Problems Arising in Warfare*, Edward Elgar Publishing, Cheltenham, 2019, p. 585.

[51] See, e.g., E. Crawford, *The Treatment of Combatants and Insurgents under the Law of Armed Conflict* Oxford University Press, Oxford, 2010, p. 173; G. S. Corn, 'Thinking the Unthinkable: Has the Time Come to Offer Combatant Immunity to Non-State Actors?', *Stanford Law & Policy Review*, Vol. 22, No. 1 (2011), p. 253; B. Saul, 'Defending "Terrorism": Justifications and Excuses for Terrorism in International Criminal Law', *Legal Studies Research Paper* 26, 2008.

[52] ICRC, Commentary on Art. 6(5), 1977 Additional Protocol II, para. 4618.

[53] S. Sivakumaran, *The Law of Non-International Armed Conflict*, Oxford University Press, Oxford, 2011, p. 507.

[54] F. Mégret, 'Should Rebels be Amnestied', in C. Stahn, J. S. Easterday, and J. Iverson (eds.), *Jus Post Bellum*, Oxford University Press, Oxford, 2014, p. 519.

In negotiating this clause, it seems that some States at least were conscious that granting partial amnesties could address indirectly the complicated issue of the status of non-State armed groups in non-international armed conflict.

In fact, research has shown that amnesties for merely participating in hostilities have been frequently granted. According to a study conducted in 2018: **17.28**

> 22 per cent of amnesties included in the dataset grant immunity for international crimes (i.e. genocide, war crimes, crimes against humanity and serious human rights violations). In contrast, 23 per cent of amnesties identified exclude international crimes. Taken together, less than half of the amnesties in the dataset relate to international crimes. Political offences are by far the most commonly amnestied category of crime.[55]

Armed non-State actors under customary international humanitarian law

Common Article 3 does not include any provisions that regulates the conduct of hostilities while Article 13 of the 1977 Additional Protocol II contains valuable but limited provisions on the protection of the civilian population. These are certainly modest in comparison to the far more detailed norms on the conduct of hostilities in the Additional Protocol I.[56] The applicability of the norms on conduct of hostilities in non-international armed conflict has been established through rather customary IHL as confirmed by case law. It has been argued that, by virtue of the principle of humanity, the norms on conduct of hostilities and means and methods of warfare applicable in international armed conflict were bound to apply in both types of armed conflicts. As famously stated by the International Criminal Tribunal for the former Yugoslavia (ICTY) in the *Tadić* case: **17.29**

---

[55] Political offences/crimes are defined in this context as 'crimes such as treason, sedition, subversive, rebellion, using false documents, forgery, propaganda, possessing illegal weapons, espionage, membership of banned political or religious organizations, desertion, and defamation'. The crime of rebellion can be understood as mere 'participation in hostilities' in the IHL sense and thus considered as a political offence. L. Malinder, 'Amnesties and Inclusive Political Settlements', PA-X Report, Transitional Justice Series, Global Justice Academy, University of Edinburgh, 2018, at: https://bit.ly/3rr63BD, pp. 2 and 31. As explained in the codebook of the 'Amnesties, Conflict and Peace Agreement Database' (ACPA) (https://www.peaceagreements.org/amnesties/), the dataset referred in the article 'contains qualitative data on 289 amnesties that are introduced during ongoing conflict, as part of peace negotiations, or in post-conflict periods from 1990-2016 in all world regions and the dataset concerns armed conflict as broadly defined in the Uppsala Conflict Data Program (see https://www.peaceagreements.org/amnesties/ACPA_Codebook.pdf)

[56] Article 13 of the Protocol stipulates that: '1. The civilian population and individual civilians shall enjoy general protection against the dangers arising from military operations. To give effect to this protection, the following rules shall be observed in all circumstances. 2. The civilian population as such, as well as individual civilians, shall not be the object of attack. Acts or threats of violence the primary purpose of which is to spread terror among the civilian population are prohibited. 3. Civilians shall enjoy the protection afforded by this Part, unless and for such time as they take a direct part in hostilities.'

elementary considerations of humanity and common sense make it preposterous that the use by States of weapons prohibited in armed conflicts between themselves be allowed when States try to put down rebellion by their own nationals on their own territory. What is inhumane, and consequently proscribed, in international wars, cannot but be inhumane and inadmissible in civil strife.[57]

17.30 More generally, apart from conduct of hostilities rules, the development of customary IHL has filled many of the gaps left by treaty law of non-international armed conflict. Indeed, of the 161 rules identified in the ICRC study on customary IHL, 141 are said to apply equally in international and non-international armed conflict.[58] This 'migration of laws'[59] developed to regulate international armed conflict into non-international armed conflict, while undoubtedly positive for a better protection of civilians, raises challenges for the implementation of IHL.

Challenges

Lack of compliance

17.31 According to the United Nations, every year in different situations of armed conflicts, thousands of civilians are killed, physically injured, or traumatised; millions of people are forcibly displaced from their homes; and women and girls, in particular, are subject to sexual and gender-based violence; while direct or indiscriminate attacks by parties to armed conflict damage or destroy homes, schools, hospitals, markets, places of worship, and essential civilian infrastructure, such as electricity and water systems.[60] Both ANSAs and States are the cause of this reality, but ANSAs' behaviour is clearly problematic in many instances.

17.32 Since 2009, the UN Secretary-General has repeatedly recalled the importance of engaging with ANSAs for humanitarian purposes. In one of his latest reports, he encouraged the international community to move beyond the rhetoric of demanding respect for the law and highlighted that:

> strengthening respect for the law by non-State armed groups requires principled, sustained and strategic engagement with such groups by humanitarian and other relevant actors. It confers no legitimacy on the groups concerned, but reflects the reality that engagement with non-State armed groups is a sine qua non for achieving

---

[57] In particular ICTY, *Prosecutor* v. *Tadić a/k/a 'Dule'*, Decision on the Defence Motion for Interlocutory Appeal on Jurisdiction (Appeals Chamber) (Case No. IT-94-1), 2 October 1995, para. 119.
[58] See ICRC, Customary IHL Database, available at: http://bit.ly/2kBwJQD.
[59] G. S. Corn, 'Regulating Hostilities in Non-International Armed Conflicts: Thoughts on Bridging the Divide between the Tadić Aspiration and Conflict Realities', *International Legal Studies*, Vol. 91 (2015), p. 283.
[60] See, e.g., Protection of Civilians in Armed Conflict, Report of the Secretary-General, UN doc. S/2020/366, 6 May 2020, available at: https://bit.ly/3HyipxB, para. 6. Yearly reports of the UNSG on the protection of civilians in armed conflict are available at: https://bit.ly/3ovquLM.

compliance with the law, negotiating humanitarian access and carrying out humanitarian activities.[61]

Given the intrinsic inequality in structure, legal personality, and capacity between ANSAs and States, holding ANSAs accountable for the implementation and respect of rules that were designed and negotiated by States is, however, problematic. First, ANSAs might not be capable of implementing certain rules which are capacity intensive. Second, ANSAs may not interpret the norms in the same way as States do, let alone agree with them. In that sense, it has been reminded that the effectivity of any legal system depends also on the norms reflecting the needs and characteristics of the actors that they are supposed to govern.[62] In that sense, any efforts to include ANSAs' views in the application and elaboration of IHL norms is also of paramount importance if one wishes to enhance IHL compliance by these actors.[63] **17.33**

The counterterrorism narrative

Mostly for military or political reasons, armed groups are often labelled as 'terrorists', usually by the States against which they are fighting. This is so, whether or not they are listed as terrorist organisations at the international level. Under IHL, in the conduct of hostilities in all armed conflicts, only 'acts or threats of violence the primary purpose of which is to spread terror among the civilian population'[64] can be considered as falling into the category of an 'act of terrorism' which entails individual criminal responsibility under customary international law.[65] In other words, attacks that exclusively target military objectives do not fall into this category.[66] At a political and policy level, the UN Security Council Resolution 1566 of 2004 considers as terrorist those criminal acts **17.34**

> including against civilians, committed with the intent to cause death or serious bodily injury, or taking of hostages, with the purpose to provoke a state of terror in the general public or in a group of persons or particular persons, intimidate a population or

---

[61] Protection of Civilians in Armed Conflict, Report of the Secretary-General, UN doc. S/2020/366, para. 53.
[62] M. Sassòli, 'Taking Armed Groups Seriously: Ways to Improve Their Compliance with International Humanitarian Law', *Journal of International Humanitarian Legal Studies*, Vol. 1, No. 1 (2010), pp. 5–51.
[63] See also A. Bellal, N. Badawi, P. Bongard, and E. Heffez, 'From Words to Deeds: A Study of Armed Non-State Actors' Practice and Interpretation of International Humanitarian and Human Rights Norms', Research Project, 2020–2022, available at: https://words2deeds.org.
[64] See Art. 51(2), 1977 Additional Protocol I; and Art. 13(2), 1977 Additional Protocol II.
[65] ICTY, *Prosecutor* v. *Stanislav Galić*, Judgment (Trial Chamber) (Case No. IT-98-29-T), 5 December 2003, paras. 113–29. See supra Chapter 13 of this book.
[66] While the main UN treaties on terrorism include a saving clause referring to IHL, the relationship between IHL and counterterrorism law is complicated, in particular because acts committed by parties to an armed conflict might be prohibited by counterterrorism legislation, but not by IHL. See Art. 19, International Convention for the Suppression of Terrorist Bombings; adopted at New York, 15 December 1997; entered into force, 23 May 2001; Art. 4, International Convention for the Suppression of Acts of Nuclear Terrorism; adopted at New York, 13 April 2005; entered into force, 7 July 2007; and Art. 21, International Convention for the Suppression of the Financing of Terrorism; adopted at New York, 9 December 1999; entered into force, 10 April 2002.

compel a government or an international organization to do or to abstain from doing any act, which constitute offences within the scope of and as defined in the international conventions and protocols relating to terrorism.[67]

17.35 At a policy level, putting all ANSAs 'in the same basket', even when they respect the rules is counterproductive, as it will lower the incentive for them to comply with IHL and will ultimately preclude the protection of civilians. Furthermore, considering all ANSAs as terrorists may result in critical groups or individuals being excluded from peace negotiations. For instance, the association of ANSAs with terrorists is said to have had 'a direct impact on the EU and the international community's capacity for mediation and dialogue in transition processes'.[68]

Concluding remarks and outlook

17.36 In the years to come, ANSAs are likely to remain alive and powerful actors in geopolitics and armed conflicts.[69] The combination of the four Geneva Conventions, the Additional Protocols and customary IHL do provide for broad protection and taken together the rules seem to be able to adapt to the realities of contemporary forms of non-international armed conflict. That said, national liberation movements or guerrilla groups are not the most prevalent types of ANSAs existing today. Combinations of armed and civilian wings, de facto (non-State) authorities, organised drug cartels, or powerful private military companies could all fall within the ambit of the law of non-international armed conflict.

17.37 While the 1977 Additional Protocol I with regard to ANSAs has a very limited scope of application, due to its historical development, it can be discussed whether the 1977 Additional Protocol II is sufficient to tackle the challenges these actors raise for the international community. Elaborating on the definition and concept of ANSAs; considering their perception and impact on law-making and interpretation of key humanitarian norms; and clarifying the secondary norms on responsibility are among the key issues that should be addressed. Only relying on customary international law, a body of norms the elaboration of which ANSAs has not participated in, and might not feel bound by, may not be enough. In that regard, it is perhaps time to consider drafting a

---

[67] UN Security Council Resolution 1566 (2004), adopted by unanimous vote in favour on 8 October 2004, operative para. 3.

[68] European Union (EU) External Action, 'Mediation and Dialogue in Transitional Processes from Non-State Armed Groups to Political Movements/Political Parties', Factsheet, 2011, at: https://bit.ly/3J1nKO6; see also V. Dudouet and K. Göldner-Ebenthal, 'Challenges and Opportunities for Conflict Resolution with Salafi jihadi Armed Groups', Policy Brief No. 10, Berghof Foundation, Germany, 31 March 2020, at: https://bit.ly/32ZJURs.

[69] V. Felbab-Brown, 'Nonstate Armed Actors in 2022: Alive and Powerful in the New Geopolitics', *Brookings*, 1 February 2022, at: https://brook.gs/3HvrIOQ.

more detailed and inclusive set of norms applicable in non-international conflicts and ANSAs. It remains to be seen whether the time is ripe for this kind of endeavour. In any case, and at a minimum, it is essential the international community adopt a more complex and nuanced approach when it comes to regulation of and engagement with all ANSAs.

18

Application of International Humanitarian Law to United Nations Operations

Introduction

18.1 As a Senior Adviser of the International Committee of the Red Cross (ICRC) observed in 1995,[1] the Charter of the United Nations[2] (UN) does not mention international humanitarian law (IHL) at all. The application to UN operations of the rules laid down in the two Additional Protocols[3] continues to be debated. There is widespread agreement that IHL is directly applicable, at least on the basis of custom, to a UN force when it is a party to an armed conflict,[4] although precisely when that occurs is unsettled. The application of IHL by treaty is contested, with the Secretariat declining for many decades now to see the United Nations formally adhere to the Geneva Conventions and their Additional Protocols. But a 1999 Bulletin issued by the UN Secretary-General—the '*de facto* Commander-in-Chief of UN Blue Helmet operations'[5]—declared that: 'The fundamental principles and rules of international humanitarian law ... are applicable to United Nations forces when in situations of armed conflict they are actively engaged therein as combatants.'[6]

18.2 Two types of UN forces are potentially covered by this chapter. One is UN peacekeeping operations, in particular those with a Chapter VII mandate from the UN Security Council to use force to protect civilians, and especially when a peacekeeping force is tasked to 'neutralise' armed groups as is the case in the Democratic Republic of Congo.[7]

---

[1] H.-P. Gasser, 'The United Nations and International Humanitarian Law: The International Committee of the Red Cross and the United Nations' involvement in the implementation of international humanitarian law', Paper presented at the International Symposium on the occasion of the fiftieth anniversary of the United Nations, Geneva, 19–21 October 1995, 19 October 1995, at: http://bit.ly/30QvPkG.

[2] Charter of the United Nations; adopted at San Francisco, 26 June 1945; entered into force, 24 October 1945. As of 1 May 2022, 193 States were formally bound by the UN Charter: 49 as States Parties and 144 on the basis of a Declaration of Acceptance of the Obligations contained in the Charter.

[3] Protocol Additional to the Geneva Conventions of 12 August 1949, and relating to the Protection of Victims of International Armed Conflicts (Protocol I); adopted at Geneva, 8 June 1977; entered into force, 7 December 1978 (hereinafter, 1977 Additional Protocol I); Protocol Additional to the Geneva Conventions of 12 August 1949, and relating to the Protection of Victims of Non-International Armed Conflicts (Protocol II); adopted at Geneva, 8 June 1977; entered into force, 7 December 1978 (hereinafter, 1977 Additional Protocol II).

[4] C. Greenwood, 'International Humanitarian Law and United Nations Military Operations', *Yearbook of International Humanitarian Law*, Vol. 1 (December 1998), 3–34, at p. 3; P. C. Szasz, 'UN Forces and International Humanitarian Law', *International Law Studies*, Vol. 75 (2000), pp. 507–37, at p. 512.

[5] Szasz, 'UN Forces and International Humanitarian Law', p. 519.

[6] 'Observance by United Nations Forces of International Humanitarian Law', Secretary-General's Bulletin, UN doc. ST/SGB/1999/13, 6 August 1999 (hereinafter, 1999 Secretary-General's Bulletin), §1.

[7] In 2013, the Council tasked an Intervention Brigade under direct command of the United Nations Organization Stabilization Mission in the Democratic Republic of the Congo (MONUSCO) Force Commander

The second type of UN force—a most improbable scenario these days—is one operating directly under the control of the UN Security Council. This occurred in Korea in the 1950s (and continues to this day).[8] But a similar operation under UN Command will, in all likelihood, not be repeated and the prospect will not be further discussed in this chapter.

A key issue to determine the responsibility of the United Nations under international law for an internationally wrongful act by its forces is whether any given peacekeeping or peace-enforcement operation is placed at the disposal of, or under the effective control, of the organisation.[9] As the International Law Commission states in its commentary on the relevant provision in the 2011 Draft Articles on the responsibility of international organisations: 'The United Nations assumes that in principle it has exclusive control of the deployment of national contingents in a peacekeeping force.'[10] States and regional bodies authorised by the Security Council to use force are not to be considered UN forces.

18.3

Accordingly, the chapter discusses the application of the rules set out in the 1977 Additional Protocols and under customary law to United Nations operations, focusing on UN peacekeeping operations. It first discusses when a UN force becomes a party to an armed conflict. The chapter then moves to consider the application of the most important rules to such a circumstance. The key rules most pertinent to UN peacekeeping forces and the customary status of the rules are summarised in Table 18.1. A final section considers the implementation of those rules in practice.

18.4

When do United Nations forces become party to an armed conflict?

As Katarina Grenfell, a Legal Officer in the UN Office of Legal Affairs (OLA), noted in a 2013 article in the *International Review of the Red Cross*: 'While it is clear that IHL

18.5

'with the responsibility of neutralizing armed groups'. UN Security Council Resolution 2098, adopted by unanimous vote on 28 March 2013, operative para. 9.

[8] Following North Korean aggression against South Korea, United Nations Command (UNC) was established on 24 July 1950. UNC was the first attempt at collective security under the UN system. UN Security Council Resolutions 83 and 84 provided the international legal authority for member States to restore peace on the Korean Peninsula, designating the United States as the leader of the unified command. In 1950–53, twenty-two countries contributed either combat forces or medical units to support South Korea under a UN flag. UNC continues to enforce the Armistice Agreement between the Democratic People's Republic of Korea and the Republic of Korea. United Nations Command, 'Under One Flag', at: http://bit.ly/39dwyRN.

[9] D. Akande, 'Classification of Armed Conflicts', Chap. 1 in B. Saul and D. Akande (eds.), *The Oxford Guide to International Humanitarian Law*, Oxford University Press, Oxford, 2020, p. 49. See Art. 7, International Law Commission (ILC), Draft articles on the responsibility of international organizations, adopted by the ILC at its sixty-third session, in 2011, and submitted to the UN General Assembly as a part of the Commission's report covering the work of that session, in UN doc. A/66/10, at: http://bit.ly/2YOKPz7 (hereinafter, 2011 Draft Articles).

[10] Commentary para. 6 on Draft Article 7, 2011 Draft Articles.

Table 18.1 Rules in the Additional Protocols Relevant for UN Operations

Rule	AP I	Customary status (IAC)	AP II	Customary status (NIAC)
Prohibition of inhumane treatment	Art. 77	Yes	Art. 4	Yes
Rule of Distinction	Art. 45	Yes	Art. 13(2)	Yes
Rule of Proportionality in Attack	Art. 51(5)(b)	Yes	No	Yes
Rule of Precautions in Attack	Art. 57	Yes	No	Yes
Prohibition of unnecessary suffering	Art. 35(2)	Yes	No	Yes
Prohibition of indiscriminate weapons	Art. 51(4)(b) and (c)	Yes	No	Yes

applies whenever the factual conditions for its application arise, it is not always apparent, as a practical matter, when that threshold has been met.'[11] She cites as an example of the challenge a situation where peacekeepers provide support to State armed forces involved in an armed conflict with non-State armed groups, and asks 'what level of support would be required to render the UN operation a "party to a conflict" with those non-state armed groups?'[12]

18.6 In a similar vein, Dapo Akande observes that it is 'difficult to determine when peacekeepers become direct participants in hostilities'.[13] This is indeed the case. Most UN peacekeeping missions today are imbued with a mandate to use force to protect civilians. In the contemporary era, this began with Security Council Resolution 1270 (1999), in which the Council, acting under Chapter VII of the UN Charter, granted to the UN peacekeeping mission in Sierra Leone an explicit mandate to protect civilians 'under imminent threat of physical violence'. The mandate was backed by authority to use force when it was deemed necessary and feasible to do so.[14]

18.7 The fact that the Council has authorised the use of force to protect civilians does not preclude the existence of an armed conflict. But the exercise of force pursuant to such an authorisation, even when employed against a party to an armed conflict, does not

---

[11] K. Grenfell, 'Perspective on the Applicability and Application of International Humanitarian Law: The UN Context', *International Review of the Red Cross*, Vol. 95, Nos. 891/892 (2013), pp. 645–52, at: https://bit.ly/2Qa0rLQ, at p. 650.
[12] Ibid., p. 651.
[13] Akande, 'Classification of Armed Conflicts', p. 51.
[14] UN Security Council Resolution 1270 (1999), adopted unanimously on 22 October 1999, operative para. 14.

automatically draw the peacekeeping force into the conflict as an adverse party either. This is because a reasonable use of force in individual self-defence or defence of others against unlawful violence is permissible at all times and in all situations as a general principle of international law.[15] In a situation of armed conflict, the ICRC affirms that such a use of force does not constitute direct participation in hostilities on the basis that the 'causation of harm in individual self-defence or defence of others against violence prohibited under IHL lacks belligerent nexus'.[16] Indeed, as the organisation further observes:

> If individual self-defence against prohibited violence were to entail loss of protection against direct attack, this would have the absurd consequence of legitimizing a previously unlawful attack. Therefore, the use of necessary and proportionate force in such situations cannot be regarded as direct participation in hostilities.[17]

In 2009, with specific respect to peacekeeping operations, the Special Court for Sierra Leone held that 'the use of force by peacekeepers in self-defence in the discharge of their mandate, provided that it is limited to such use, would not alter or diminish the protection afforded to peacekeepers'.[18] This holding was cited and effectively endorsed by a Pre-Trial Chamber of the International Criminal Court a year later. In declining to confirm charges against Bahar Idriss Abu Garda for his actions with respect to international crimes committed in Darfur, Sudan, a majority of the Chamber declared that 'personnel involved in peacekeeping missions enjoy protection from attacks unless and for such time as they take a direct part in hostilities'. This protection, the Majority of the Court averred, 'does not cease if such persons only use armed force in exercise of their right to self-defence'.[19]   **18.8**

Akande suggests that a UN force is engaged in an armed conflict when it uses force against another entity, but not when the other entity has targeted the UN force. In that latter scenario, the UN force 'is acting in self-defence, is not involved in an armed conflict, and its members are protected as civilians'.[20] This implies, he affirms, that in such a circumstance the 'other entity' (for instance, a non-State armed group) is committing a war crime by attacking UN forces if they act in the context of an armed conflict (such as the one the UN force is trying to bring an end to). 'In this way, the UN's special role has an impact on the application of IHL.'[21]   **18.9**

---

[15] See generally J. A. Hessbruegge, *Human Rights and Personal Self-Defense in International Law*, Oxford University Press, New York, 2017.
[16] N. Melzer, *Interpretive Guidance on the Notion of Direct Participation in Hostilities under International Humanitarian Law*, ICRC, Geneva, 2009, p. 61.
[17] Ibid.
[18] Special Court for Sierra Leone, *Prosecutor v. Sesay, Kallon, and Gbao*, Judgment (Trial Chamber I) (Case No. SCSL-04-15-T), 2 March 2009, para. 233.
[19] International Criminal Court, *Prosecutor v. Bahar Idriss Abu Garda*, Decision on the Confirmation of Charges, (Trial Chamber I) (Case No. ICC-02/05-02/09), 8 February 2010, para. 83.
[20] Akande, 'Classification of Armed Conflicts', p. 51.
[21] Ibid. See further on this issue A. Clapham, *War*, Oxford University Press, Oxford, 2021, p. 259.

280   APPLICATION OF IHL TO UN OPERATIONS

18.10   Should, on the other hand, the UN force be or become a party to the armed conflict, they would be a lawful military objective under IHL. In such a case, the peacekeeping mission would no longer be, in the words of the Rome Statute of the International Criminal Court, 'entitled to the protection given to civilians or civilian objects under the international law of armed conflict'.[22] Thus, when pursuing an armed group engaged in a non-international armed conflict, a UN force unquestionably loses its civilian immunity and becomes party to that armed conflict. (The civilian personnel of the UN force and the personnel of UN agencies, of course, fully retain their civilian immunity and special protection under the 1994 Convention on the Safety of United Nations and Associated Personnel[23] and its Optional Protocol[24] even in such circumstances.)

18.11   While the most likely scenario is that offensive UN peacekeeping operations will bring the relevant UN force into conflict with a non-State armed group (and thus engage the force in a non-international armed conflict),[25] a Chapter VII mandate to protect civilians is not ostensibly limited to such actions. Indeed, as the UN's Department of Peace Operations (DPO) stipulates in its 2019 Policy Paper on the protection of civilians: 'The mission will, as far as possible, support the host state's protection efforts but may act independently to protect civilians when the host state is deemed unable or unwilling to do so or where government forces themselves pose a threat to civilians.'[26] Thus, it is conceivable that operations to protect civilians might pit the UN force against the armed forces of the territorial State. Were this to occur, an international armed conflict would exist between the UN force and the territorial State. An alternative scenario, perhaps more probable in occurrence, is that the armed group could be acting on behalf of a foreign State.[27] This was the case, for instance, during occupation by Ugandan forces of parts of the east of the Democratic Republic of Congo from 1999 until 2002.[28] Offensive operations to neutralise a proxy armed group could thus involve an international armed conflict with a foreign State.

18.12   It is indeed in the Democratic Republic of the Congo that the loss of civilian immunity by a UN force has occurred most starkly. This occurred with respect to the

---

[22] Art. 7(2)(b)(iii) and (e)(iii), Rome Statute of the International Criminal Court; adopted at Rome, 17 July 1998; entered into force, 1 July 2002. As of 1 May 2022, 123 States were party to the Rome Statute.

[23] Art. 7(1), Convention on the Safety of United Nations and Associated Personnel; adopted at New York, 9 December 1994; entered into force, 15 January 1999. As of 1 May 2022, 95 States were party to the Convention.

[24] Optional Protocol to the Convention on the Safety of United Nations and Associated Personnel; adopted at New York, 8 December 2005; entered into force, 19 August 2010. The Optional Protocol expands the scope of protection to include operations conducted under UN authority and control that deliver 'humanitarian, political or development assistance in peacebuilding' or 'emergency humanitarian assistance'. As of 1 May 2022, 33 States were party to the Optional Protocol.

[25] Grenfell, 'Perspective on the Applicability and Application of International Humanitarian Law: The UN Context', p. 650.

[26] United Nations Department of Peace Operations (DPO), *DPO Policy on The Protection of Civilians in United Nations Peacekeeping*, UN DPO Ref. 2019.17, 1 November 2019 (hereinafter, *UN DPO 2019 Policy on The Protection of Civilians in UN Peacekeeping*), para. 29.

[27] International Criminal Court, *Prosecutor* v. *Dominic Ongwen*, Judgment (Trial Chamber IX) (Case No. ICC-02/04-01/15, 4 February 2021, para. 2687.

[28] International Criminal Court, *Prosecutor* v. *Germain Katanga*, Judgment (Trial Chamber II) (Case No. ICC-01/04-01/07), 7 March 2014, para. 1213.

UN's MONUSCO peacekeeping mission as a result of a broad mandate, granted by the UN Security Council, to use force offensively against armed groups in the east of the country. Resolution 2098, adopted by the Council by unanimous vote in March 2013, decided that the United Nations Organization Stabilization Mission in the Democratic Republic of the Congo (MONUSCO) would deploy an 'Intervention Brigade' explicitly tasked with the responsibility of 'neutralizing armed groups'.[29] The Resolution authorised MONUSCO, through the Brigade, to take 'all necessary measures' to 'carry out targeted offensive operations' in pursuing this action 'in a robust, highly mobile and versatile manner'. It further stipulated that such action must occur 'in strict compliance with international law, including international humanitarian law'.[30]

Most of the criticisms against MONUSCO, however, concern rather its absence from the battlefield, and not the use of force in violation of IHL. Indeed, in August 2020, a piece published by the Institute for Security Studies headlined that the problem with the 'Force Intervention Brigade' was that it 'no longer aggressively pursues rebel groups in eastern DRC'.[31] In early September of the same year, an article in *The Economist* described an interview with an individual who had helped to burn down MONUSCO's offices in Beni on 25 November 2019. 'We have suffered years of massacres', he told the journalist. 'We see UN soldiers all over town, but when the rebels are killing us, they never come.'[32] That does not mean, however, that MONUSCO troops have not committed serious violations of international law. This issue is revisited below.

18.13

What rules apply to United Nations forces that are party to an armed conflict?

As Paul Szasz has noted, the United Nations 'is not a party to any of the multilateral treaties in which the principles and rules of IHL are expressed'.[33] Over the course of many years, the ICRC encouraged the global organisation to become a party to the 1949 Geneva Conventions, especially the Fourth Convention on the Protection of Civilians, but the UN Secretariat demurred. Arguments proffered in justification of such reluctance focused on the fact that the Conventions, as set out in their final clauses, were intended for adherence by States. The UN Secretariat also pointed out that numerous provisions, especially of Convention IV, could only apply to States, such as the arrest, prosecution, trial, and imprisonment of individual violators.[34] Neither

18.14

---

[29] UN Security Council Resolution 2098 (2013), operative para. 9.
[30] Ibid., operative para. 12(b).
[31] P. Fabricius, 'Asking the Right Questions about the Force Intervention Brigade', Institute for Security Studies, 21 August 2020, at: http://bit.ly/3r1sLgn.
[32] 'All Helmet and No Mettle: The UN's Peacekeepers Are under Pressure to Quit Congo', *The Economist*, 3 September 2020, at: http://econ.st/3bWq4Xy.
[33] Szasz, 'UN Forces and International Humanitarian Law', p. 510.
[34] 'Question of the Possible Accession of Intergovernmental Organizations to the Geneva Conventions for the Protection of War Victims', Legal Opinion issued by the UN Office of Legal Affairs to the Under-Secretary- General

argument persuades and both obstacles could be overcome, should the requisite political will be present. It was also, however, considered 'somewhat unseemly' to suggest that the United Nations might be a 'party' to an armed conflict.[35] Given the actions of the UN Command in the 1950s and the UN Operation in the Congo in the early 1960s, and then more recent operations in the east of the Democratic Republic of Congo, this line of thought is not sustained by weight of evidence.

18.15 In 1972, proposals were made that the Additional Protocol I then under preliminary discussion should include a provision according to which the Geneva Conventions would be open for accession by the UN.[36] These treaties would apply 'each time the forces of the United Nations are engaged in operations'.[37] However, the proposals were ultimately not adopted following an explanation on behalf of the Secretary-General that such 'accession would raise questions as to the legal capacity of the Organisation to become a party to multilateral treaties'. The primary obstacles were said to be 'the lack of certain competences, including the lack of territorial jurisdiction and of disciplinary and penal authority, would make it impossible for the Organisation to discharge many of the obligations laid down in the Geneva Conventions'.[38]

18.16 That does not imply, however, that the Secretariat believes the United Nations as an international organisation is above the law. In the 2009 document by the UN Office of Legal Affairs cited above, the Office referred to 'the Organization's obligations under customary international law and from the Charter to uphold, promote and encourage respect for human rights, international humanitarian law and refugee law'.[39] The question thus is which customary rules apply to a UN force that is party to an armed conflict.[40] The 2019 Department of Peace Operations Policy on the Protection of Civilians, citing the 1999 Secretary-General's Bulletin, stipulates that: 'When international humanitarian law applies to UN forces, they must comply with it, including the principles of distinction, proportionality and precaution.'[41] The peremptory principles of distinction and proportionality in attack are, of course, set out in the 1977 Additional Protocol I. Only the principle of distinction, however, is formally incorporated in the 1977 Additional Protocol II.

18.17 On the status of the Secretary-General's Bulletin, Szasz declares that: 'There is no doubt that as Commander-in-Chief, the Secretary-General is authorized to express such

---

for Special Political Affairs on 15 June 1972, reproduced in *United Nations Juridical Yearbook 1972*, UN doc. ST/LEG/SER.C/10, 1972, at: https://bit.ly/2OEKqgO, pp. 153–54.

[35] Szasz, 'UN Forces and International Humanitarian Law', p. 511.
[36] Grenfell, 'Perspective on the Applicability and Application of International Humanitarian Law: The UN Context', p. 646.
[37] Report of the Secretary-General, UN doc. A/8781, 20 September 1972.
[38] Ibid., para. 218.
[39] Paragraph 12 in Attachment to Note of 12 October 2009 by Ms Patricia O'Brien, Under-Secretary-General for Legal Affairs and UN Legal Counsel, OLA, to Mr Alain Le Roy, Under Secretary-General for Peacekeeping Operations.
[40] A. Clapham, *War*, Oxford University Press, Oxford, 2021, p. 258.
[41] *UN DPO 2019 Policy on The Protection of Civilians in UN Peacekeeping*, para. 22 [footnote omitted].

commands and that if any troop-contributing State should object to such rules, it may not cause its troops to defy or disregard the Bulletin but can only withdraw them from UN operations.'[42] With respect to the principle of distinction, the 1999 Bulletin stipulated that: 'The United Nations force shall make a clear distinction at all times between civilians and combatants and between civilian objects and military objectives. Military operations shall be directed only against combatants and military objectives. Attacks on civilians or civilian objects are prohibited.'[43] Both indiscriminate and disproportionate attacks are prohibited. Thus, it is stipulated that a UN force 'is prohibited from launching operations of a nature likely to strike military objectives and civilians in an indiscriminate manner'. It shall also not launch operations 'that may be expected to cause incidental loss of life among the civilian population or damage to civilian objects which would be excessive in relation to the concrete and direct military advantage anticipated'.[44]

With respect to means and methods of warfare, it is stipulated that a UN force 'is prohibited from using weapons or methods of combat of a nature to cause unnecessary suffering'.[45] Specific prohibitions and restrictions on the use of certain weapons 'under the relevant instruments of international humanitarian law' are also to be respected. These include, in particular:

18.18

> the prohibition on the use of asphyxiating, poisonous or other gases and biological methods of warfare; bullets which explode, expand or flatten easily in the human body; and certain explosive projectiles. The use of certain conventional weapons, such as non-detectable fragments, anti-personnel mines, booby traps and incendiary weapons, is prohibited.[46]

Although the Bulletin has not been formally updated, one may consider that today a UN force may similarly not use cluster munitions. A total of 110 of 197 States were party to the 2008 Convention on Cluster Munitions[47] at the time of writing. Although it is not a UN treaty, as it was negotiated by States outside UN auspices, the UN Secretary-General is nonetheless its depositary. A further omission in the Bulletin's non-exhaustive list is the prohibition, by treaty and in custom, of the use of blinding laser weapons.[48]

With respect to Geneva Law rules, it is stipulated that civilians and persons placed *hors de combat* by reason of sickness, wounds, or detention, 'shall, in all circumstances, be treated humanely and without any adverse distinction based on race, sex, religious convictions or any other ground'.[49] Acts 'prohibited at any time and in any place' include violence to life or physical integrity; murder as well as cruel treatment such as torture,

18.19

---

[42] Szasz, 'UN Forces and International Humanitarian Law', p. 519.
[43] 1999 Secretary-General's Bulletin, §5.1.
[44] Ibid., §5.5.
[45] Ibid., §6.4.
[46] Ibid., §6.2.
[47] Convention on Cluster Munitions; adopted at Dublin, 30 May 2008; entered into force, 1 August 2010.
[48] Szasz, 'UN Forces and International Humanitarian Law', p. 520.
[49] 1999 Secretary-General's Bulletin, §7.1.

mutilation, or any form of corporal punishment; collective punishment; reprisals; the taking of hostages; rape; enforced prostitution; any form of sexual assault; and humiliation and degrading treatment.[50] It is further provided that women 'shall be especially protected against any attack, in particular against rape, enforced prostitution or any other form of indecent assault'.[51]

Implementation of international humanitarian law rules binding United Nations forces

18.20   While the prospects of the war crimes provisions of the Rome Statute being applied to UN peacekeepers are slim, the possibility cannot be completely discounted. This possibility exists, notwithstanding the stipulation in the Secretary-General's Bulletin that: 'In case of violations of international humanitarian law, members of the military personnel of a United Nations force are subject to prosecution in their national courts.'[52] Should a senior commander order the commission of a war crime, however, and should his or her national authorities wilfully decline to prosecute, the issue could be taken up by the Prosecutor of the International Criminal Court if other jurisdictional requirements are met.

18.21   Grenfell asks for clarity on the temporal and geographical scope of application of IHL once the threshold for its application has been met. She asks whether IHL applies in respect of peacekeepers in areas where they are not engaged in actual combat, noting that this is 'particularly relevant in situations where peacekeepers may be deployed throughout a large territory and are carrying out a range of tasks, including purely humanitarian ones, under their mandate'.[53] The better view is that Geneva Law applies throughout the territory to a UN peacekeeping mission once the force, or a section of it, is party to an armed conflict. This is implicit in the Secretary-General's Bulletin, which provides that certain acts are prohibited 'at any time and in any place' to persons in the power of a UN force.[54] But, at the least in a non-international armed conflict, the rules governing the conduct of hostilities are geographically limited to those areas and those units that are engaged in intense and regular combat with an organised armed group.

18.22   Dozens of women in the east of the Democratic Republic of Congo have alleged that they have been raped by UN peacekeepers.[55] Such acts, if confirmed by independent investigation, are thus war crimes falling within the jurisdiction of the International

---

[50] Ibid., §7.2.
[51] Ibid., §7.3.
[52] Ibid., §4.
[53] Grenfell, 'Perspective on the Applicability and Application of International Humanitarian Law: The UN Context', p. 651.
[54] 1999 Secretary-General's Bulletin, §7.2.
[55] Ibid.

Criminal Court.⁵⁶ In 2017, the BBC had reported that more than 100 allegations had been made of sexual abuse and exploitation by UN and French peacekeepers in the Central African Republic.⁵⁷ Each and every allegation of a war crime must be independently investigated and the offenders prosecuted. The fact of belonging to a UN peacekeeping force does not offer immunity from prosecution for international crimes.

Crimes committed by peacekeepers are, of course, without prejudice to any violations of international law that the United Nations may have committed in its operations. This includes international responsibility through complicity in the illegal actions of any State armed forces engaged in a non-international armed conflict. Such complicity may occur whether or not the UN force is itself party to the salient armed conflict. Thus, back in 2011 the International Law Commission cited as an example of practice of potentially prohibited aid or assistance the support given by the United Nations Organization Mission in the Democratic Republic of the Congo (MONUC: MONUSCO's predecessor) to the Forces armées de la République démocratique du Congo (FARDC), and the risk of aiding or assisting violations of IHL, human rights law, and refugee law by the FARDC.⁵⁸ **18.23**

These risks were laid bare in an internal document issued on 12 October 2009 by the UN Office of Legal Affairs. Therein, it was stated that: **18.24**

> If MONUC has reason to believe that FARDC units involved in an operation are violating one or the other of those bodies of law and if, despite MONUC's intercession with the FARDC and with the Government of the DRC, MONUC has reason to believe that such violations are still being committed, then MONUC may not lawfully continue to support that operation, but must cease its participation in it completely.⁵⁹

The document added that 'MONUC may not lawfully provide logistic or "service" support to any FARDC operation if it has reason to believe that the FARDC units involved are violating any of those bodies of law'.⁶⁰ As Szasz concludes in his article on UN forces and IHL: 'Even in the sorry business of war, the United Nations should establish the highest legal standard and set the best example.'⁶¹

---

⁵⁶ Art. 8(2)(e)(vi), Rome Statute.
⁵⁷ F. Keane, 'UN Promises to Stamp Out Abuse after Child Rape Allegations', BBC, 24 February 2017, at: http://bbc.in/3cOtMTI.
⁵⁸ ILC, Commentary para. 6 on Article 14, 2011 Draft Articles.
⁵⁹ Para. 11 in Attachment to Note of 12 October 2009 by Ms Patricia O'Brien, Under-Secretary-General for Legal Affairs and UN Legal Counsel, OLA, to Mr Alain Le Roy, Under Secretary-General for Peacekeeping Operations. The document was 'provided' to a journalist of *The New York Times*, which has made a copy available at: http://nyti.ms/2Ry52VO. See also J. Gettleman, 'U.N. Told Not to Join Congo Army in Operation', *The New York Times*, 9 December 2009, at: http://nyti.ms/35FVsYZ.
⁶⁰ Para. 12 in Attachment to Note of 12 October 2009 by Ms Patricia O'Brien to Mr Alain Le Roy.
⁶¹ Szasz, 'UN Forces and International Humanitarian Law', p. 526.

Concluding remarks and outlook

18.25 The extent to which UN forces are subject to IHL as a matter of law rather than policy is unsettled. In light of this, allowing the United Nations to adhere to the Geneva Conventions and all their Additional Protocols is long overdue. Objections within the UN Secretariat to such accession are unpersuasive from both a legal and a policy perspective. And with more robust peacekeeping operations often crossing the line into peace enforcement, typically through efforts to better protect civilians, clarity on the application of the law, and far better accountability are sorely needed.

19

International Criminal Law

Introduction

International criminal law governs the criminal responsibility of individuals for the perpetration of international crimes. One set of such crimes—war crimes—comprises serious violations of international humanitarian law (IHL) that are perpetrated during and in connection with an armed conflict and which entail individual criminal responsibility under international law. War crimes, as with other international crimes, are *jus cogens* norms from which no derogation is lawful.[1] Gary Solis draws a distinction between grave breaches of the Geneva Conventions and war crimes.[2] But in practice and in law, the distinction is narrow. As the 1977 Additional Protocol I stipulates: 'Without prejudice to the application of the Conventions and of this Protocol, grave breaches of these instruments shall be regarded as war crimes.'[3] Moreover, under customary law, 'States must investigate war crimes allegedly committed by their nationals or armed forces, or on their territory, and, if appropriate, prosecute the suspects.'[4]

19.1

Crimes against humanity[5] and genocide may also be committed during armed conflict: indeed the same acts or conduct may constitute not only war crimes but also either crimes against humanity or even genocide. An act of aggression may also involve the commission of war crimes. The key issues to determine are, first whether an armed conflict exists under international humanitarian law—the same criteria being applicable under international criminal law—and second, whether the conduct in question is directly linked to that conflict. For this purpose, it does not matter what term the belligerents employ to the violence, it is an objective assessment of the prevailing circumstances. Thus, for instance, the fact that the Ethiopian government described their armed forces' actions in Tigray in late 2020 and during 2021 as 'law enforcement' did not preclude the reality that war crimes had been perpetrated on a wide scale.[6]

19.2

---

[1] See, e.g., International Law Commission (ILC), 'Fourth report on peremptory norms of general international law (*jus cogens*) by Dire Tladi, Special Rapporteur', UN doc. A/CN.4/727, 31 January 2019, para. 117. See also Annex, para. (d) to ILC, 'Peremptory norms of general international law (*jus cogens*)', UN doc. 74/10, 2019.

[2] G. D. Solis, *The Law of Armed Conflict: International Humanitarian Law in War*, 3rd Edn, Cambridge University Press, Cambridge, 2021, p. 85.

[3] Art. 85(5), Protocol Additional to the Geneva Conventions of 12 August 1949, and relating to the Protection of Victims of International Armed Conflicts (Protocol I); adopted at Geneva, 8 June 1977; entered into force, 7 December 1978 (hereinafter, 1977 Additional Protocol I).

[4] International Committee of the Red Cross (ICRC), Customary IHL Rule 158: 'Prosecution of War Crimes', at: https://bit.ly/3JP0aFD.

[5] Crimes against humanity were first recognised in the Charter of the International Military Tribunal that was established to try individuals accused of international crimes leading up to and during the Second World War. See, e.g., Solis, *The Law of Armed Conflict: International Humanitarian Law in War*, 3rd Edn, p. 90.

[6] 'Ethiopia Is Deliberately Starving Its Own Citizens', *The Economist*, 9 October 2021.

Table 19.1 Selected War Crimes in the Additional Protocol I

War Crime	AP I	Customary status (IAC)	Customary status (NIAC)
Attacking Civilians	Art. 85(3)(a)	Yes	Yes
Disproportionate attacks	Art. 85(3)(b)	Yes	Yes
Attacking a person who is *hors de combat*	Art. 85(3)(e)	Yes	Yes
Perfidious use of the red cross or red crescent emblems	Art. 85(3)(f)	Yes	Yes
Unjustifiable delay in the repatriation of prisoners of war	Art. 85(4)(b)	Yes (Arguably)	N/A
Depriving a protected person of the right to fair trial	Art. 85(4)(e)	Yes	Yes

19.3 The 1977 Additional Protocol I explicitly provides for, and defines, a number of specific war crimes,[7] but the 1977 Additional Protocol II does not.[8] That said, several of the rules set out in the Additional Protocol II codify prohibitions that have become war crimes under customary international law, as summarised in Table 19.1. With respect to international armed conflict, what were arguably newly established war crimes in 1977 include certain unlawful acts committed in the conduct of hostilities, such as the perfidious use of protective emblems (e.g. the red cross or red crescent),[9] as well as other conduct, such as unjustifiable delay in the repatriation of prisoners of war (which most usually, but not necessarily, occurs after the cessation of active hostilities).[10] This latter crime has not been made subject to the jurisdiction of the International Criminal Court, although the International Committee of the Red Cross (ICRC) has concluded it constitutes a war crime under customary international law.[11]

19.4 The provisions laid down in the four Geneva Conventions of 1949[12] on compulsory universal jurisdiction—*aut dedere aut iudicare*: the duty to prosecute or hand over for

---

[7] Art. 85, 1977 Additional Protocol I.
[8] Protocol Additional to the Geneva Conventions of 12 August 1949, and relating to the Protection of Victims of Non-International Armed Conflicts (Protocol II); adopted at Geneva, 8 June 1977; entered into force, 7 December 1978 (hereinafter, 1977 Additional Protocol II).
[9] Art. 85(3)(f), 1977 Additional Protocol I. ICRC, Commentary on Article 85 of the Additional Protocol I, at: https://bit.ly/3ciLeQ9, para. 3461.
[10] Art. 85(4)(b), 1977 Additional Protocol I. See Art. 118, 1949 Geneva Convention III.
[11] ICRC, Customary IHL Study Rule 156: 'Definition of War Crimes', at: http://bit.ly/32HjZb2, point (ii): 'Other serious violations of international humanitarian law committed during an international armed conflict'.
[12] Art. 49, 1949 Geneva Convention I; Art. 50, 1949 Geneva Convention II; Art. 129, 1949 Geneva Convention III; and Art. 146, 1949 Geneva Convention IV.

prosecution—are applied in the Additional Protocol I, subject of course to the proviso that the unlawful conduct must pertain to protected persons. Such persons include refugees and stateless persons; prisoners of war; persons in the power of an adverse Party who have participated directly in hostilities but who are not entitled to POW status; the wounded, sick, and shipwrecked of the enemy who are protected under the Protocol, and medical or religious personnel, medical units, or medical transports under the control of the enemy and which are protected by the Protocol.[13] In any event, there must be a connection between the criminal act and an armed conflict. Gary Solis gives the example of Staff Sergeant Frank Ronghi, a US Army peacekeeper who kidnapped, raped, and murdered an 11-year-old Kosovar girl in January 2000. As the armed conflict over Kosovo had ended, this was not a war crime but one under domestic and military law.[14]

19.5 To be successfully prosecuted, all international crimes, including war crimes, must involve proof beyond reasonable doubt of the commission by the accused of a culpable act (*actus reus*) and an associated mental state (*mens rea*).[15] The 1977 Additional Protocol I incorporates specific requirements in this regard for the prosecution of the war crimes it lays down: the acts must be committed 'wilfully'; they must violate the Protocol; and they must cause death or serious injury to body or health.[16] These conditions, especially the last, may be more restrictive than is the case under customary international law, as this chapter explores. War crimes are most often committed by soldiers but may also be perpetrated by civilians.[17]

19.6 The Protocol does not address modes of liability beyond the responsibility of commanders or others further up the hierarchy of authority. As the Protocol makes clear, the fact that a grave breach of its provisions was committed by a subordinate does not absolve his or her superiors from penal responsibility 'if they knew, or had information which should have enabled them to conclude in the circumstances at the time, that he was committing or was going to commit such a breach and if they did not take all feasible measures within their power to prevent or repress the breach'.[18] Naturally, ordering that a war crime be committed engages the criminal responsibility of the commander.[19] Other modes of liability provided for under the Rome Statute of the International Criminal Court include attempting (but failing) to commit a crime, aiding or abetting the commission or attempted commission of a crime, and intentionally contributing to its commission or attempted commission by 'a group of persons acting with a common purpose'.[20]

---

[13] Art. 85(2), 1977 Additional Protocol I.
[14] Solis, *The Law of Armed Conflict: International Humanitarian Law in War*, 3rd Edn, p. 251.
[15] Arts. 30(1) and 66(3), Rome Statute of the International Criminal Court; adopted at Rome, 17 July 1998; entered into force, 1 July 2002 (hereinafter, Rome Statute).
[16] Art. 85(3), 1977 Additional Protocol I.
[17] Solis, *The Law of Armed Conflict: International Humanitarian Law in War*, 3rd Edn, p. 275. He offers the significant example of the *Zyklon B* case in the trials of war criminals after the Second World War. Ibid., pp. 277–78.
[18] Art. 86(1), 1977 Additional Protocol I.
[19] Art. 25(3)(b), Rome Statute.
[20] Ibid., Art. 25(3)(f), (c), and (d).

War crimes in the conduct of hostilities

19.7 The 1977 Additional Protocol I laid down, for the first time, war crimes governing the conduct of hostilities. That is not to say that international law had not already criminalised certain conduct during combat—the International Military Tribunal had already considered that prohibitions in the Hague Regulations of 1907 formed part of customary international criminal law[21]—but the express criminalisation of certain acts in the conduct of hostilities in an IHL treaty was a progressive development of the law.[22] Four war crimes in the conduct of hostilities laid down by the Additional Protocol I of 1977 are considered in this chapter: that of directly attacking civilians; disproportionate attacks affecting civilians; attacking a person who is *hors de combat*; and perfidious use of the red cross or red crescent emblems. These are considered in turn.

The war crime of attacking civilians

19.8 The 1977 Additional Protocol I states that 'making the civilian population or individual civilians the object of attack' is a grave breach of the Protocol[23] and thus a war crime.[24] The principle of distinction is the most fundamental of IHL rules: a 'cardinal principle' in the words of the International Court of Justice.[25] The war crime as set out in the Protocol concerns such an act where the attacker knows the status of the individual(s) he or she is attacking; when the attack is 'wilfully' directed against one or more civilians; and when death or serious injury to body or health is caused by the attack. It is implicit but not explicit that the war crime cannot be committed against a civilian who is, at the salient time, directly participating in hostilities.[26]

19.9 The war crime of attacking civilians thus mirrors the corresponding war crime under the jurisdiction of the International Criminal Court: 'Intentionally directing attacks against the civilian population as such or against individual civilians not taking direct part in hostilities'.[27] In the relevant elements of crime, the following constituents of actus reus and mens rea are laid down: the perpetrator directed an attack; the object

---

[21] 'The rules of land warfare expressed in the Convention undoubtedly represented an advance over existing International Law at the time of their adoption ... but by 1939 these rules ... were recognized by all civilized nations and were regarded as being declaratory of the laws and customs of war'. Judgment of the International Military Tribunal, *Trial of the Major War Criminals before the International Military Tribunal*, reprinted in *American Journal of International Law*, Vol. 41 (1947), pp. 248–49.

[22] Article 7 of the 1907 Hague Convention IV addressed the responsibility of the State rather than the individual members of its armed forces: 'A belligerent party which violates the provisions of the said Regulations shall, if the case demands, be liable to pay compensation. It shall be responsible for all acts committed by persons forming part of its armed forces.'

[23] Art. 85(3)(a), 1977 Additional Protocol I.

[24] Ibid., Art. 85(5).

[25] International Court of Justice, *Legality of the Threat or Use of Nuclear Weapons*, Advisory Opinion, para. 78.

[26] As Article 51(3) of the Protocol stipulates in its Section I (General Protection Against Effects of Hostilities): 'Civilians shall enjoy the protection afforded by this Section, unless and for such time as they take a direct part in hostilities.'

[27] Art. 8(2)(b)(i), Rome Statute.

of the attack was a civilian population as such or individual civilians not taking direct part in hostilities; and the perpetrator intended the civilian population as such or individual civilians not taking direct part in hostilities to be the object of the attack.[28] But in contrast to the Additional Protocol I, successful prosecution of the crime before the International Criminal Court does not require death, injury, or damage: it is a crime of conduct.[29]

19.10 As Chapter 9 discussed, in earlier case law, first, the International Criminal Tribunal for the former Yugoslavia (ICTY), and later the International Criminal Court, the crime of attacking civilians has seemingly been conflated with that of indiscriminate attacks. In its trial judgment and opinion in *Galić*, the ICTY concluded that 'indiscriminate attacks, that is to say, attacks which strike civilians or civilian objects and military objectives without distinction, may qualify as direct attacks against civilians'.[30] In its judgment on appeal, the ICTY held that: 'In principle, the Trial Chamber was entitled to determine on a case-by-case basis that the indiscriminate character of an attack can assist it in determining whether the attack was directed against the civilian population'.[31]

19.11 In 2019, in relation to the corresponding war crime in non-international armed conflict, a Trial Chamber of the International Criminal Court found Mr Ntaganda criminally responsible for a direct attack on civilians, declaring that the crime under the Rome Statute 'may encompass attacks that are carried out in an indiscriminate manner, that is by targeting an area, as opposed to specific objects, or not targeting specific military objects or persons taking a direct part in hostilities, so long as the perpetrator was aware of the presence of civilians in the relevant area'.[32] 'Therefore', the Trial Chamber asserted, 'the use of weapons that have inherently indiscriminate effects in an area where civilians are present may constitute an attack directed at the civilian population or individual civilians'.[33]

The war crime of disproportionate attacks affecting civilians

19.12 The 1977 Additional Protocol I not only defined different forms of indiscriminate attack, but it also criminalised certain of these. In particular, 'launching an indiscriminate attack affecting the civilian population or civilian objects' and 'launching an attack against works or installations containing dangerous forces' where these occur 'in the knowledge that such attack will cause excessive loss of life, injury to civilians or

---

[28] Elements of Crime for Article 8(2)(b)(i) of the Rome Statute.
[29] C. Stahn, *A Critical Introduction to International Criminal Law*, Cambridge University Press, Cambridge, 2019, p. 83.
[30] ICTY, *Prosecutor v. Galić*, Judgment and Opinion (Trial Chamber I) (Case No. IT-98-29-T), 5 December 2003, para. 57.
[31] ICTY, *Prosecutor v. Galić*, Judgment (Appeals Chamber) (Case No. IT-98-29-A), 30 November 2006, paras. 131, 132.
[32] International Criminal Court, *Prosecutor v. Bosco Ntaganda*, Judgment (Trial Chamber VI) (Case No. ICC-01/04-02/06), 8 July 2019, para. 921.
[33] Ibid.

damage to civilian objects' are war crimes.[34] In addition, the crimes must be committed wilfully, in violation of the Protocol, and they must in fact cause death or serious injury to body or health.[35] This implies that an indiscriminate attack affecting one or more civilian objects but which does not also directly harm civilians does not fall within the purview of the crime under the Protocol. That said, the notion of health is deemed to cover mental as well as physical health,[36] potentially broadening the ambit of the actus reus of the crime.

19.13 An indiscriminate attack is first and foremost one that is not directed at a specific objective, or which uses a means or method of warfare that cannot be directed at a specific objective (i.e. an inherently indiscriminate weapon, such as an unguided rocket). The primary rule in the Protocol declares that indiscriminate attacks are prohibited.[37] But the corresponding war crime is explicitly limited to those indiscriminate attacks where the civilian harm 'would' be 'excessive in relation to the concrete and direct military advantage anticipated'[38] and only where the person or persons launching the attack knew that excessive loss of life, injury to civilians, or damage to civilian objects would occur.[39] Thus, as the ICRC observed in its commentary on the provision, 'there is only a grave breach if the person committing the act knew with certainty that the described results would ensue', which 'would not cover recklessness'.[40]

19.14 In this case, however, one element of the war crime's actus reus is narrower in the Rome Statute and, at least in the view of the ICRC, in the customary law crime in an international armed conflict. The Rome Statute stipulates that the corresponding war crime is one where an attack is intentionally launched in the knowledge that it will cause incidental loss of life or injury to civilians or damage to civilian objects which would be *clearly* excessive in relation to the concrete and direct overall military advantage anticipated.[41] With respect to the crime under customary law, the ICRC notes that its similar formulation follows more closely the wording in the Rome Statute (to which 123 States were party as of writing) but not the Additional Protocol I (to which 174 States were party as of writing).[42] This is hard to justify. Moreover, in customary law, the wording of the corresponding war crime in non-international armed conflict does not include the modifier 'clearly', suggesting a broader scope in such conflicts than in international armed conflict.

19.15 Cryer and others observed that the inclusion of the modifier 'may well be seen as an unwarranted restriction' on the standard in the Additional Protocol I. 'Alternatively',

---

[34] Art. 85(3)(b) and (c), 1977 Additional Protocol I.
[35] Ibid., Chapeau to Art. 85(3).
[36] ICRC, Commentary on Article 85 of the Additional Protocol I, para. 3474.
[37] Art. 51(4), 1977 Additional Protocol I.
[38] Ibid., Art. 57(2)(a)(iii).
[39] Ibid., Art. 85(3)(b) and (c).
[40] ICRC, Commentary on Article 85 of the Additional Protocol I, para. 3479.
[41] Art. 8(2)(b)(iv), Rome Statute (emphasis added).
[42] ICRC, Customary IHL Study Rule 156: 'Definition of War Crimes', at: http://bit.ly/32HjZb2, point (ii): 'Other serious violations of international humanitarian law committed during an international armed conflict'.

they affirm, 'it may be seen as an appropriate clarification given that the Statute deals not with civil liability of the parties to a conflict, but rather with the criminalization of individual behaviour'.[43] This is not persuasive. The requisite mens rea performs that necessary function and does so adequately. The narrowing of the actus reus of the war crime of a disproportionate attack under the Rome Statute has meant that the distinction between directly attacking civilians and launching an indiscriminate attack that disproportionately affects civilian is slender to say the least. This may help to explain why it has yet not been charged against a defendant (as does the absence altogether of the war crime in non-international armed conflict under the Statute).

19.16 In its judgment in the *Ntaganda* case, the International Criminal Court found that the crime of attacking civilians 'may also include attacks that are launched without taking necessary precautions to spare the civilian population or individual civilians'.[44] This would potentially cover disproportionate attacks, as set out in Article 57(2)(a)(iii) of the Protocol: 'those who plan or decide upon an attack shall ... refrain from deciding to launch any attack which may be expected to cause incidental loss of civilian life, injury to civilians, damage to civilian objects, or a combination thereof, which would be excessive in relation to the concrete and direct military advantage anticipated'.

The war crime of attacking a person *hors de combat*

19.17 The 1977 Additional Protocol I codified long-standing customary law whereunder a person *hors de combat* may not be attacked.[45] A narrow formulation of the rule was already incorporated in the Hague Regulations. Thus, the 1907 Regulations 'especially' forbade to 'kill or wound an enemy who, having laid down his arms, or having no longer means of defence, has surrendered at discretion'.[46] The primary rule set out in Article 41 of the Protocol stipulates that: 'A person who is recognized or who, in the circumstances, should be recognized to be *hors de combat* shall not be made the object of attack'.[47] Constructive knowledge of the status of the object of attack is thus sufficient to ground a violation of the Protocol.

19.18 it is further clarified in the Protocol that a person is deemed to be *hors de combat* if he or she is in the power of the enemy; if he or she clearly expresses an intention to surrender; or if he or she has been rendered unconscious or otherwise incapacitated by wounds or sickness, and is therefore incapable of defending him- or herself. This is so, provided that in any of the three cases the person abstains from any hostile act and does not

---

[43] R. Cryer, D. Robinson, and S. Vasiliev, *An Introduction to International Criminal Law and Procedure*, 4th Edn, Cambridge University Press, Cambridge, 2019, p. 287.
[44] International Criminal Court, *Prosecutor* v. *Bosco Ntaganda*, Judgment (Trial Chamber VI), para. 921.
[45] ICRC Customary IHL Rule 47: 'Attacks against Persons Hors de Combat', at: https://bit.ly/30rn0hg.
[46] Art. 23(c), Regulations concerning the Laws and Customs of War on Land, annexed to the Convention (IV) respecting the Laws and Customs of War on Land; adopted at The Hague, 18 October 1907; entered into force, 26 January 1910 (hereinafter, 1907 Hague Regulations).
[47] Art. 41(1), 1977 Additional Protocol I.

attempt to escape.[48] Accordingly, and in contradistinction to the Hague Regulations, it is not necessary under the Additional Protocol I that the combatant has in fact sought to surrender.

19.19 The corresponding war crime in the Protocol, however, is narrower than is the primary rule. It is limited to a situation where a person is attacked 'in the knowledge that he is *hors de combat*'.[49] This excludes constructive knowledge—a situation where the attacker should have known that the person he or she was assailing was *hors de combat*. Again, the chapeau to the paragraph makes it explicit that death or serious injury must have been caused to body or health.[50] Thus, as the ICRC observes, the war crime is committed 'when someone wilfully attacks a person he knows to be "hors de combat", causing his death or serious injury to his body or health.'[51]

19.20 Under the Rome Statute, the International Criminal Court is accorded jurisdiction in international armed conflict over the war crime of 'Killing or wounding a combatant who, having laid down his arms or having no longer means of defence, has surrendered at discretion'.[52] This mirrors the provision in the Hague Regulations rather than the Additional Protocol I. The corresponding elements of crime determine that the accused must have killed or injured one or more persons who were *hors de combat* and the perpetrator must have been aware of the factual circumstances that established this status.[53] There is no similar specific war crime under the jurisdiction of the Court in a situation of non-international armed conflict, but the relevant conduct is covered by the prohibition on violence to life and person against 'members of armed forces who have laid down their arms and those placed hors de combat by sickness, wounds, detention or any other cause'.[54]

19.21 The only serving British officer to have been convicted of war crimes since the Second World War was, in effect, charged with just such an offence (in the context of a non-international armed conflict). Sergeant Alexander Blackman, a Royal Marine, was given an eight-year prison sentence (reduced on appeal from 15 years) following his conviction at court-martial for the murder of a seriously wounded Taliban fighter in Afghanistan.[55] On 15 September 2011, while on patrol in Helmand province, he shot an unknown, seriously wounded Afghan insurgent in the chest and killed him. The Afghan fighter had been 'engaged lawfully by an Apache Helicopter' (i.e. during the conduct of hostilities), but when Sergeant Blackman found him, he was 'no longer a threat'. Indeed, after his action, Sergeant Blackman explicitly acknowledged that he

---

[48] Art. 41(2), 1977 Additional Protocol I.
[49] Ibid., Art. 85(3)(d).
[50] Ibid., Chapeau to Art. 85(3).
[51] ICRC, Commentary on Article 85 of the Additional Protocol I, para. 3493.
[52] Art. 8(2)(b)(vi), Rome Statute.
[53] Elements of Crime for Article 8(2)(b)(vi) of the Rome Statute.
[54] Art. 8(2)(c)(i), Rome Statute.
[55] Court Martial Appeal Court, *R v. Alexander Wayne Blackman*, Judgment (Case No. 2014/00049/B5), 22 May 2014, at: https://bit.ly/3z2QVfi, para. 77.

had just violated the Geneva Conventions.[56] In sentencing him, the Court Martial stated that: 'That Afghan man, as an injured enemy combatant, was entitled to be treated with dignity, respect and humanity.'[57] Sergeant Blackman's conviction for murder was subsequently reduced to manslaughter on further appeal, on the basis of his diminished responsibility at the time of the killing.[58] He was released in April 2017 after serving three-and-a-half years in prison.[59]

The war crime of making perfidious use of the red cross or red crescent emblems

It is prohibited to kill, injure or capture an adversary by resort to perfidy. This is also a long-standing rule of IHL, with the 1907 Hague Regulations 'especially' forbidding a party to an international armed conflict to 'kill or wound treacherously individuals belonging to the hostile nation or army'.[60] Perfidy involves a number of unlawful acts that are intended to lead an enemy to believe, wrongly, that a person is entitled to protection from attack under IHL.[61] One such unlawful act is the use of the red cross or red crescent or other protected emblems.[62] Where the underlying purpose of the act is to kill, injure, or capture an adversary, and where death or serious injury is caused to body or health,[63] this amounts to a war crime under the Additional Protocol I.[64] Prior to this, there was limited case law indicating that such use was criminalised, although the prohibition per se was undoubtedly a rule of customary law.[65]

19.22

Under the Rome Statute, making improper use of the distinctive emblems of the Geneva Conventions in an international armed conflict is a specific war crime under the jurisdiction of the International Criminal Court, where such use results in death or serious personal injury.[66] The corresponding elements of crime are particularly detailed. The perpetrator must have used the distinctive emblems of the Geneva Conventions for 'combatant purposes' (defined as those directly related to hostilities, and not including medical, religious, or similar activities) and such use must have occurred in a manner

19.23

---

[56] Court Martial (Bulford), *R v. Alexander Blackman*, Sentencing Remarks (Case No. 2012CM00442), at: https://bit.ly/3mmCL50, p. 1.
[57] Ibid.
[58] Court Martial Appeal Court, *R v. Alexander Wayne Blackman*, Judgment, [2017] EW CA Crim 190, 15 March 2017.
[59] See, e.g., S. Morris, 'Marine A, Who Killed Wounded Taliban Fighter, Released from Prison', *The Guardian*, 28 April 2017, at: https://bit.ly/3kdirQK.
[60] Art. 23(b), 1907 Hague Regulations.
[61] Art. 37(1), 1977 Additional Protocol I.
[62] Ibid., Art. 37(1)(d).
[63] Ibid., Chapeau to Art. 85(3).
[64] Ibid., Art. 85(3)(f).
[65] The ICRC's customary law study cites the judgment by the United States' Intermediate Military Government Court at Dachau in the *Hagendorf* case on 9 August 1946. ICRC Customary IHL Study Rule 156: 'Definition of War Crimes', 'Violations entailing individual criminal responsibility under international law'. The case concerned a German soldier who was charged with having 'wrongfully used the Red Cross emblem in a combat zone by firing a weapon at American soldiers from an enemy ambulance displaying such emblem'. The accused was found guilty. United States Practice Relating to Customary IHL Rule 65: 'Perfidy', at: https://bit.ly/3D3jVpy.
[66] Art. 8(2)(b)(viii), Rome Statute.

that is prohibited under IHL. The conduct must further have resulted in death or serious personal injury. As to the mental element of the crime, the perpetrator either must have, or should have, known of the prohibited nature of the use and he or she must also have known that the conduct could result in death or serious personal injury.[67]

19.24 In 2008, in one of the then ongoing non-international armed conflicts in Colombia, Colombian military intelligence used the red cross emblem in a rescue operation in which guerrillas were duped into handing over 15 hostages.[68] In a rare public statement criticising a party to an armed conflict for a specific violation of IHL, the ICRC expressed serious concern over a seemingly deliberate misuse of the red cross emblem during the operation. The organisation observed that the use of the red cross, red crescent, and red crystal emblems 'is governed by the Geneva Conventions and their Additional Protocols. These emblems may not be used by bodies or persons not entitled to do so under international humanitarian law'.[69]

19.25 The then Colombian President Alvaro Uribe apologised to the ICRC for the incident, describing it as an unauthorised error by a nervous soldier. The ICRC accepted the apology, but said that it was up to the Colombian government to take action against those responsible for misusing the symbol.[70] No one was seemingly killed in the operation, but a number of the guerrillas appear to have been captured. Under the 1977 Additional Protocol II, it is stipulated that the distinctive emblem of the red cross and red crescent 'shall not be used improperly'.[71] A violation of the provision is not criminalised under the Additional Protocol II, but is a war crime under customary law and the Rome Statute in non-international armed conflict. This is so, by virtue of the broader war crime of 'killing or wounding treacherously a combatant adversary'.[72]

Other war crimes

The war crime of unjustifiable delay in the repatriation of prisoners of war

19.26 The Additional Protocol I of 1977 made the 'unjustifiable delay in the repatriation of prisoners of war' a specific war crime.[73] Despite the very widespread adherence to the

---

[67] Elements of Crime for Article 8(2)(b)(vii) of the Rome Statute.
[68] K. Penhaul, 'Colombian Military Used Red Cross Emblem In Rescue', *CNN*, 6 August 2008, at: https://cnn.it/3AZ5PDE.
[69] ICRC, 'Colombia: ICRC Deplores Improper Use of Red Cross Emblem', News Release 08/139, Geneva, 6 August 2008, at: https://bit.ly/3z5AAqb.
[70] Associated Press, 'Red Cross: Colombia Lied about Using Emblem', NBC News, 6 August 2008, at: https://nbcnews.to/3sw49yF.
[71] Art. 12, 1977 Additional Protocol II.
[72] ICRC, Customary IHL Study Rule 156: 'Definition of War Crimes', (iv) 'Other serious violations of international humanitarian law committed during a non-international armed conflict'; and Art. 8(2)(e)(ix), Rome Statute.
[73] Art. 85(4)(b), 1977 Additional Protocol I.

Protocol, it is not certain that this is also a war crime under customary law.[74] There are two distinct scenarios requiring the repatriation of a POW: one during the conduct of hostilities and the other following the cessation of active hostilities. Where a prisoner is 'seriously wounded' or 'seriously sick' and is fit to travel, he or she should be repatriated while hostilities persist. This is the case, unless the prisoner opposes such a return.[75] The ICRC has observed that failure to repatriate has occurred on a number of occasions. In its 1983 Memorandum of Understanding concerning the Iran-Iraq Conflict, the organisation stated that, although some severely wounded and sick prisoners of war had been repatriated, 'most of the severely wounded and sick prisoners of war [had] not been repatriated, as required by the Convention'.[76]

19.27 Once active hostilities have effectively ended, all POWs should be repatriated 'without delay'.[77] The corresponding war crime concerns a failure to repatriate 'without valid and lawful reasons justifying the delay'.[78] The crime must be committed 'wilfully' but does not need to lead to death or serious injury to a prisoner.[79] While there is no explicit exception in the salient provision in the 1949 Geneva Convention III, as the ICRC has explained, 'the obligation to repatriate must be understood as subject to an exception where the prisoners face a real risk of a violation of fundamental rights by their own country. This interpretation is reflected in State practice and statements made by the UN and other international bodies.... It also accords with the principle of *non-refoulement* under international law'.[80]

19.28 The crime established under the Additional Protocol may also exist under customary law[81] (although this is not certainly the case). The ICRC notes in this regard that even States not party to the Protocol have criminalised an unjustifiable delay in repatriating POWs, citing the specific example of Azerbaijan.[82] There is of course no corresponding crime in a non-international armed conflict as the concept of combatantcy and entitlement to prisoner-of-war status does not exist in such a situation. There is, however, an underlying concern about the war crime instituted under the Additional Protocol I. Even where the circumstances exist for a possible prosecution, who in practice is to be held criminally responsible for an unjustified failure to repatriate POWs? Is it the

---

[74] Indeed, as the ICRC acknowledges in its customary law study: 'So far, no prosecutions of this war crime have been noted, nor is this crime specifically listed in the Statute of the International Criminal Court.' ICRC Customary IHL Study Rule 156, (ii) 'Other serious violations of international humanitarian law committed during an international armed conflict (continued):', point (v).

[75] Art. 109, 1949 Geneva Convention III.

[76] ICRC, Commentary on Article 109 of 1949 Geneva Convention III, 2020, at: https://bit.ly/3ziKyUY, para. 4269 and note 29.

[77] Art. 118, 1949 Geneva Convention III.

[78] ICRC, Commentary on Article 85 of the Additional Protocol I, para. 3508.

[79] Chapeau to Art. 85(4), 1977 Additional Protocol I.

[80] ICRC, Commentary on Article 118 of 1949 Geneva Convention III, 2020, at: https://bit.ly/3j5rlkg, para. 4469.

[81] ICRC, Customary IHL Study Rule 156: 'Definition of War Crimes', (ii) Other serious violations of international humanitarian law committed during an international armed conflict.

[82] Art. 116.0.15 of the 1999 Criminal Code of Azerbaijan provides that unjustified delay in repatriating prisoners of war and civilians to their country constitutes a crime. Unofficial translation of the provision available at: https://bit.ly/3CZmcCh. See Chapter 5 with respect to practice in Azerbaijan in the 2020 armed conflict with Armenia.

commander of the camp or barracks where the prisoners are being held? Is it the head of the army? The president or prime minister?

The war crime of an unfair trial

19.29 Similar issues arise with respect to the war crime of unfair trial of a protected person. This crime is long-standing, having been instituted in the 1949 Geneva Convention III with respect to prisoners of war[83] and in the 1949 Geneva Convention IV with respect to protected civilians under that treaty[84].[85] The Additional Protocol I confirms that it is a war crime to deprive a person protected by the Geneva Conventions or the Protocol of '[t]he rights of fair and regular trial'.[86] The crime must be committed 'wilfully', but does not need to lead to death or serious injury to the accused.[87] The question arises, however, as to who may commit the war crime. Is it, for instance, the presiding judge at trial? A woefully inadequate defence counsel?

19.30 The International Criminal Court has jurisdiction over the war crime in international armed conflict of '[w]ilfully depriving a prisoner of war or other protected person of the rights of fair and regular trial'.[88] The corresponding elements of crime determines that the perpetrator deprived one or more persons of a fair and regular trial by denying judicial guarantees as defined, in particular, in the 1949 Geneva Conventions III or IV, to a person or persons protected under one or more of the 1949 Conventions. The perpetrator must have been 'aware of the factual circumstances that established that protected status'.[89] But no indication is given as to who such a perpetrator might be.

19.31 More narrowly, with respect to non-international armed conflict the Rome Statute reflects the wording of Article 3 common to the 1949 Geneva Conventions whereby it is a war crime to pass sentences or carry out executions 'without previous judgment pronounced by a regularly constituted court, affording all judicial guarantees which are generally recognized as indispensable'.[90] The corresponding elements of crime demonstrate the awkwardness of the war crime. The perpetrator must have either passed sentence (i.e. have been the judge) or have executed one or more persons (i.e. the executioner or executioners). In addition, the victims must have been either *hors de combat*, or have been civilians, medical personnel, or religious personnel taking no active part in the hostilities and the perpetrator must have been aware of the factual circumstances that established this status. There must further have been no previous judgement

---

[83] Art. 130, 1949 Geneva Convention III.
[84] Art. 147, 1949 Geneva Convention IV.
[85] See, e.g., J. Pejic, 'Detention in Armed Conflict', Chap. 12 in B. Saul and D. Akande (eds.), *The Oxford Guide to International Humanitarian Law*, Oxford University Press, Oxford, 2020, pp. 294–96.
[86] Art. 85(4)(e), 1977 Additional Protocol I.
[87] Ibid., Chapeau to Art. 85(4).
[88] Art. 8(2)(a)(vi), Rome Statute.
[89] Elements of Crime for Article 8(2)(a)(vi) of the Rome Statute.
[90] Art. 8(2)(c)(iv), Rome Statute.

pronounced by a court, or the court that rendered judgement was not 'regularly constituted', that is, it did not afford the essential guarantees of independence and impartiality, or the court that rendered judgment did not afford all other judicial guarantees generally recognised as indispensable under international law. Finally, the perpetrator must have been aware of the absence of a previous judgment or of the denial of relevant guarantees and the fact that they are essential or indispensable to a fair trial.[91]

The war crime also exists under customary law. Thus, Rule 100 of the ICRC's study of customary IHL provides that no one may be convicted or sentenced, except pursuant to a fair trial affording all essential judicial guarantees.[92] This primary rule is criminalised on the basis that the conduct 'breaches important values', even if the lack of a fair trial does not physically endanger a person objects directly.[93] As of writing, no one had been prosecuted before an international criminal tribunal for the war crime of denial of the rights of fair trial to an accused, although trials of foreign nationals serving in the Ukrainian armed forces as 'mercenaries'[94] would seem to qualify for such a prosecution.

19.32

Alleged war crimes

As Chapter 13 describes, both the 1977 Additional Protocols prohibit acts of terrorism against civilians in the power of the enemy and violence whose primary purpose is to terrorise civilians. Convictions for the corresponding war crimes have been secured before the Special Court for Sierra Leone and the International Criminal Tribunal for the former Yugoslavia. The United States Congress, however, articulated two different war crimes concerning terrorism: material support for terrorism and conspiracy to commit terrorist acts.[95] These were based not on IHL or international criminal law, but on US domestic law provisions, including the PATRIOT Act adopted in the aftermath of the 9/11 attacks. While a number of convictions were secured before US military commissions, as Solis further documents, appellate courts in the United States subsequently held—correctly—that these were not internationally recognised as war crimes. In 2012, for instance, the US Court of Appeals for the District of Columbia vacated a prior conviction by a military commission of material support for terrorism against Salim Ahmed Hamdan, the erstwhile driver for Osama bin Laden.[96]

19.33

---

[91] Elements of Crime for Article 8(2)(c)(iv) of the Rome Statute.
[92] ICRC, Customary IHL Rule 100: 'Fair Trial Guarantees', at: https://bit.ly/2N7nPFj.
[93] ICRC, Customary IHL Study Rule 156: 'Definition of War Crimes', 'Serious Nature of the Violation'.
[94] M. Cursino and C. Cooney, 'Families of condemned Britons Aiden Aslin and Shaun Pinner call for help', *BBC News*, 10 June 2022, at: https://bbc.in/3zr3gLA.
[95] G. D. Solis, *The Law of Armed Conflict: International Humanitarian Law in War*, 3rd Edn, Cambridge University Press, Cambridge, 2021, p. 252.
[96] J. H. Cushman, 'Appeals Court Overturn Terrorism Conviction of Bin Laden's Driver', *The New York Times*, 16 October 2012.

Concluding remarks and outlook

19.34 The inclusion of grave breaches provisions in the 1977 Additional Protocol I continued the tradition that had first been established in the four Geneva Conventions of 1949. What was progressive at the time was both the explicit criminalisation of certain acts in the conduct of hostilities and of the broadening of the list of crimes under the Geneva branch of IHL. The requirement that physical harm be inflicted narrowed the ambit of the crimes unnecessarily, but this has not prevented international law from developing to criminalise inchoate offences nor to impose individual criminal responsibility for those actions that do not, by happenstance, kill or harm civilians.

19.35 The absence of grave breaches provisions in the 1977 Additional Protocol II is thus a matter of regret. When, as must surely occur one day, a new IHL treaty is concluded to govern in a comprehensive manner non-international armed conflicts, such a significant lacuna must not be permitted to occur again. With most armed conflicts likely to be of a non-international character for the foreseeable future, clarifying not only IHL but also international criminal law is necessary.

20

The Role of the International Committee of the Red Cross

Introduction

On 17 February 1863, the Swiss businessman Henry Dunant, who had witnessed the terrible suffering of those wounded and dying as a result of the Battle of Solferino four years earlier founded the International Committee for the Relief of Wounded in the Event of War in Geneva, along with Gustave Moynier, Guillaume-Henri Dufour, Louis Appia, and Théodor Maunoir. The creation of what was to become the International Committee of the Red Cross (ICRC)[1] thus predates the elaboration of the first Geneva Convention of 1864. Although this treaty mentions the ICRC, it did not create the organisation. Rather, the Committee acted as the driving force which led to the elaboration of the first Geneva Convention.[2] Ever since, the ICRC has safeguarded its role as the impetus and critical supporter of new international humanitarian law (IHL) treaties and norms.

20.1

The ICRC is neither a non-governmental organisation nor an intergovernmental one, although it shares some of the attributes of both (its 'non-State' membership for the former and the enjoyment of certain privileges usually afforded to international organisations for the latter). According to its Statute:

20.2

1. The ICRC is an association governed by Article 60 and following of the Swiss Civil Code.
2. In order to fulfil its humanitarian mandate and mission, the ICRC enjoys a status equivalent to that of an international organisation and has international legal personality in carrying out its work.[3]

For these reasons, the ICRC is often referred as a *sui generis* organisation, which does not fall into a traditional categorisation under international law. Indeed, for some,

---

[1] The International Committee for the Relief of Wounded in the Event of War was renamed the International Committee of the Red Cross in 1875.

[2] R. Giladi and S. R. Ratner, 'The Role of the International Committee of the Red Cross', in A. Clapham, P. Gaeta, and M. Sassòli (eds.), *The 1949 Geneva Conventions: A Commentary*, Oxford University Press, Oxford, 2015, p. 526.

[3] Article 2, Legal Status, Statute of the International Committee of the Red Cross, available at: https://bit.ly/3FXjL3f.

with its large secretariat and many field missions, 'it has as much in common with a foreign ministry as with an NGO'.[4]

20.3 While the organisation's role is today predominantly operational, it was not originally the Committee's vocation to collect and care for the wounded and sick in the field. Rather, national committees were created for that purpose in 1863.[5] It came to be progressively involved in field activities when 'the National Societies of countries in conflict—viewed as too close to the authorities—asked the ICRC to send its own relief workers, believing that humanitarian work in times of conflict needed to offer guarantees of neutrality and independence acceptable to all parties, which only the ICRC could do'.[6]

20.4 The ICRC also acts as the 'guardian' of IHL.[7] In contrast to human rights treaties, there is no formal implementation mechanisms for IHL, such as the one played by the human rights treaty bodies in overseeing implementation of their treaty obligations by States.[8] As a consequence, the ICRC has played an important role in the implementation of IHL, such as through its interpretations of the four Geneva Conventions[9] (three of which had been fully revised at the time of writing); the identification of customary IHL;[10] and the drafting of legal texts; as well as helping States to implement the norms that bind them.[11]

20.5 From an operational point of view, the organisation has a broad scope of action. It does not only operate in situations of armed conflicts regulated by IHL. Thus, it supports humanitarian operations in the context of natural and environmental disasters while also acting in so-called 'other situations of violence', that is, situations that fall below the threshold of armed conflicts as defined by IHL. In that regard, one could argue that, from an institutional point of view, the ICRC and the United Nations (UN), and more specifically the Office of the UN High Commissioner for Human Rights (OHCHR), sometimes work in similar, and indeed overlapping contexts.

20.6 In its more than 150 years of existence, it is obvious that the ICRC has faced criticisms and challenges. Its silence during the Holocaust, for instance, has been heavily

---

[4] S. R. Ratner, 'Law Promotion beyond Law Talk: the Red Cross, Persuasion, and the Laws of War', *European Journal of International Law*, Vol. 22, No. 2 (May 2011), pp. 459–506, at p. 460.
[5] Giladi and Ratner, 'The Role of the International Committee of the Red Cross', p. 526.
[6] ICRC, *The ICRC, Its Mission, Its Work*, Geneva, 2009, at: https://bit.ly/3KCNTVa, p. 3.
[7] 'What is the ICRC's role in developing and ensuring respect for IHL?', ICRC Blog, 14 August 2017, at: https://bit.ly/343XAuN. The depositary of the Geneva Conventions is not the ICRC, but the Government of Switzerland. See the Swiss Federal Department of Foreign Affairs webpage on its role as depositary, at: https://bit.ly/3nUcf34.
[8] For more information on the human rights treaty bodies, see the webpage of the Office of the United Nations High Commissioner for Human Rights, at: https://bit.ly/3r3MPlD.
[9] See, e.g., L. Cameron, E. La Haye, H. Niebergall-Lackner, J.-M. Henckaerts, and B. Demeyere, 'The Updated Commentary on the First Geneva Convention—A New Tool for Generating Respect for International Humanitarian Law', *International Review of the Red Cross*, Vol. 97, No. 900 (November 2016), pp. 1209–26, at: https://bit.ly/35jErG3.
[10] ICRC, Customary Law Study and online database, available at: http://bit.ly/2kBwJQD.
[11] See the ICRC National Implementation Database, available at: https://bit.ly/3H8uZTK, and Chapter 16 of this book.

Table 20.1 Summary of Key Rules on the Role of the ICRC

Rule	AP I	Customary status (IAC)	AP II	Customary status (NIAC)
Appointment of Protecting Powers	Art. 5(3) and (4)	Yes	No	N/A
Missing persons	Art. 33	Yes	No	No
Activities of the Red Cross	Art. 81	Yes	Art. 18	Yes

criticised,[12] while its controversial rule of confidentiality when encountering serious violations of IHL has prompted the creation of other humanitarian organisations with a markedly different operational policy.[13]

20.7 The key rules mentioning the ICRC in the protocols illustrate the different facets of the organisation's role and functions under IHL (see Table 20.1). Most of them are to be found in the 1977 Additional Protocol I.[14] That said, the ICRC's role in non-international armed conflict is grounded in Common Article 3 of the Geneva Conventions while humanitarian relief operations are explicitly regulated by Article 18 of the 1977 Additional Protocol II.[15]

The humanitarian activities of the International Committee of the Red Cross under international humanitarian law

20.8 In the context of international armed conflict, Article 9 of the 1949 Geneva Convention I mentions the ICRC's humanitarian activities. A common clause can be found in the three other conventions (Article 9, 1949 Geneva Convention II; Article 9, 1949 Geneva Convention III; and Article 10, 1949 Geneva Convention IV). These stipulate that:

> The provisions of the present Convention constitute no obstacle to the humanitarian activities which the International Committee of the Red Cross or any other impartial

---

[12] As explained by Giladi and Ratner, 'its preference for confidential communications, combined with fear among its Swiss leaders concerning the implications for Switzerland of the ICRC's activities, contributed to a failure to speak publicly about the Holocaust, despite knowledge of the conditions in concentration camps and the fate of those deported for extermination', Giladi and Ratner, The Role of the International Committee of the Red Cross', p. 526.

[13] R. Brauman, 'Médecins Sans Frontières and the ICRC: Matters of Principle', Crash, 2013, at: https://bit.ly/3qTuirO, in which the author and former President of Médecins Sans Frontières explains how MSF was established in response to the commitment to remain silent by French Red Cross personnel working under the auspices of the ICRC during the armed conflict in Biafra (1967–70).

[14] Protocol Additional to the Geneva Conventions of 12 August 1949, and relating to the Protection of Victims of International Armed Conflicts (Protocol I); adopted at Geneva, 8 June 1977; entered into force, 7 December 1978 (hereinafter, 1977 Additional Protocol I).

[15] Protocol Additional to the Geneva Conventions of 12 August 1949, and relating to the Protection of Victims of Non-International Armed Conflicts (Protocol II); adopted at Geneva, 8 June 1977; entered into force, 7 December 1978 (hereinafter, 1977 Additional Protocol II).

humanitarian organization may, subject to the consent of the Parties to the conflict concerned, undertake for the protection of wounded and sick, medical personnel and chaplains, and for their relief.

20.9 These provisions make clear that the concerned State must consent to the humanitarian activities undertaken by the ICRC in a particular context. Consent cannot, however, be denied for arbitrary reasons. As the ICRC's 2016 Commentary of Article 9 of the 1949 Geneva Convention I observes:

> at all times, the Party must assess the offer in good faith and in line with its international legal obligations with regard to humanitarian needs. Thus, where a Party is unable or unwilling to address the humanitarian needs of such persons, international law requires it to respond positively to an offer by an impartial humanitarian organization to do so in its place.[16]

20.10 Among core ICRC activities, the right to visit prisoners of war and protected persons in detention is recognised in Article 126 of the 1949 Geneva Convention III and Article 143 of the 1949 Geneva Convention IV. Furthermore, the Central Tracing Agency—in practice the ICRC itself—has the essential objective of tracing the missing, identifying the dead, informing the families of the fate of their loved ones, and reuniting those separated by conflict, violence, or migration.[17] Here too, although not specifically mentioned in the provisions, the ICRC needs to obtain consent from the parties to a conflict at a *practical* level to implement these activities.[18]

20.11 The role of the ICRC in the 1977 Additional Protocol I is further spelled out in different provisions. Most notably, Article 81(1) declares that:

> The Parties to the conflict shall grant to the International Committee of the Red Cross all facilities within their power so as to enable it to carry out the humanitarian functions assigned to it by the Conventions and this Protocol in order to ensure protection and assistance to the victims of conflicts; the International Committee of the Red Cross may also carry out any other humanitarian activities in favour of these victims, subject to the consent of the of the Parties to the conflict concerned.

20.12 What were, at the time, new tasks are set out in Article 5(3) and (4) of the Additional Protocol I. They authorise the ICRC to propose its good offices with regard to the designation of a Protecting Power. Furthermore, Article 33 of the Protocol reiterates the responsibility of the Central Tracing Agency with regard to missing persons.[19]

---

[16] ICRC, Commentary of Article 9 of the 1949 Geneva Convention I, 2016, para. 1159, at: https://bit.ly/341wF34. For further information on the issue of consent and humanitarian relief, see Chapter 6 above.

[17] Art. 16(2), 1949 Geneva Convention I; Art. 126, 1949 Geneva Convention III; and Art. 140, 1949 Geneva Convention IV. See also ICRC Blog Cross-Files, 'The Central Tracing Agency', 30 August 2020, at: https://bit.ly/3IN03cv.

[18] M. Sassòli, *International Humanitarian Law: Rules, Controversies, and Solutions to Problems Arising in Warfare*, Edward Elgar Publishing, Cheltenham, 2019, p. 139, para. 5.175.

[19] See further on this issue, ICRC, Missing Persons, at: https://bit.ly/3rNYV1n.

20.13 In the context of non-international armed conflicts, the ICRC's right of initiative, i.e. the right of impartial humanitarian organisations to offer their services to parties without such an offer being deemed interference in the internal affairs of the State in question,[20] is recognised in Common Article 3 of the 1949 Geneva Conventions.[21]

20.14 In the 1977 Additional Protocol II, the emphasis is rather put on the work of national relief societies. Article 18(1) and (2) of the Protocol thus stipulates that:

> Relief societies located in the territory of the High Contracting Party, such as Red Cross (Red Crescent, Red Lion and Sun) organizations, may offer their services for the performance of their traditional functions in relation to the victims of the armed conflict. The civilian population may, even on its own initiative, offer to collect and care for the wounded, sick and shipwrecked.
>
> If the civilian population is suffering undue hardship owing to a lack of the supplies essential for its survival, such as foodstuffs and medical supplies, relief actions for the civilian population which are of an exclusively humanitarian and impartial nature and which are conducted without any adverse distinction shall be undertaken subject to the consent of the High Contracting Party concerned.

20.15 The emphasis placed on national relief societies is not happenstance. Indeed, in the early years of the humanitarian movement, the ICRC was rather ambiguous about its role in non-international armed conflicts. Thus:

> It was not until 1938, during the 16th International Conference of the Red Cross and Red Crescent, that the right of initiative, as we now know it, started to emerge. Partly due, perhaps, to its rather traumatic experience in Russia (1917–21), where its activities were challenged as interference in internal affairs, as well as its experiences in Upper Silesia, Ireland, and Spain, the ICRC submitted a Draft Resolution to the 16th International Conference, which addressed the issue of ICRC activities in situations outside of international armed conflict.[22]

20.16 Of no doubt today, the ICRC's role is of great relevance in non-international armed conflicts, as its statutes confirm:

> The role of the ICRC shall be in particular: … to endeavour at all times—as a neutral institution whose humanitarian work is carried out particularly in time of international and other armed conflicts or internal strife—to ensure the protection of and assistance to military and civilian victims of such events and of their direct results.[23]

---

[20] N. Nishat, 'The Right of Initiative of the ICRC and Other Impartial Humanitarian Bodies', in A. Clapham, P. Gaeta, and M. Sassòli (eds.), *The 1949 Geneva Conventions: A Commentary*, Oxford University Press, Oxford, 2015, para. 1, p. 496.

[21] Common Article 3, paragraph 2 states that: 'an impartial humanitarian body, such as the International Committee of the Red Cross, may offer its services to the Parties to the conflict'.

[22] Nishat, The Right of Initiative of the ICRC and Other Impartial Humanitarian Bodies'. para. 2, p. 496.

[23] Article 4(1)(d) of the Statutes of the International Committee of the Red Cross, adopted on 21 December 2017, available at: https://bit.ly/3FXjL3f.

Within this framework, the ICRC has systematically offered to parties to non-international armed conflict to visit persons in detention (while it has a *right* to visit detainees in international armed conflict[24]). Other bodies, such as the UN Security Council as well as the European Parliament and the Organization for Security and Co-operation in Europe (OSCE), have also requested that ICRC visit detainees in the context of several non-international armed conflicts, in particular in Afghanistan, Chechnya, Rwanda, Tajikistan, and the former Yugoslavia.[25]

20.17 Promoting the respect and implementation of IHL by armed groups is another core ICRC activity in non-international armed conflict. In 2020, for example,

> the ICRC counted 614 armed groups of concern to the organization's humanitarian operations around the world. As part of its impartial humanitarian work, the ICRC had contact with roughly three quarters of these groups—irrespective of the countries in which they operate, their ideology, religion, motivation or any other characteristic.[26]

The ICRC's work in this context includes for instance conducting confidential bilateral dialogue and representations, reminding each party to conflict of its obligations and commitments, while also conducting monitoring and reporting, as well as providing training and capacity-building.[27] In such contexts, however, the ICRC's work might be compromised by State resistance to engaging armed groups they generally consider to be 'terrorist organisations'.[28]

The action of the International Committee of the Red Cross in 'other situations of violence'

20.18 It would be wrong to assume that the ICRC only works in situations of armed conflicts regulated by IHL. As a matter of fact, the organisation has, since its inception, intervened in situations falling below the threshold of armed conflicts as legally defined, otherwise referred to as 'other situations of violence' (OSV). While the applicable legal regimes in OSV are international human rights law and domestic law, ICRC's

---

[24] Article 126 of the 1949 Geneva Convention III stipulates that: 'Representatives or delegates of the Protecting Powers *shall* have permission to go to all places where prisoners of war may be, particularly to places of internment, imprisonment and labour, and shall have access to all premises occupied by prisoners of war; they shall also be allowed to go to the places of departure, passage and arrival of prisoners who are being transferred. They shall be able to interview the prisoners, and in particular the prisoners' representatives, without witnesses, either personally or through an interpreter ... The delegates of the International Committee of the Red Cross shall enjoy the same prerogatives.'
[25] Commentary to Customary IHL Rule 124: 'ICRC Access to Persons Deprived of Their Liberty', at: https://bit.ly/3fP7UK7.
[26] J. Pejic, I. Herbert, and T. Rodenhäuser, 'ICRC Engagement with Non-State Armed Groups: Why and How', *Humanitarian Law and Policy Blog*, 4 March 2021, at: https://bit.ly/3AtaBKw.
[27] M. Mack with J. Pejic, *Increasing Respect for International Humanitarian Law in Non-International Armed Conflicts*, ICRC, 2008, p. 14.
[28] On the issue of armed groups, see supra Chapter 17.

interventions in such contexts are also guided by so-called 'Red Cross law', i.e. the law of the Movement of the Red Cross and Red Crescent.[29]

Thus, the Statutes of the Movement as well as the ICRC's own Statutes foresee that, in addition to endeavouring to carry its work in 'internal strife',[30] the ICRC may also 'take any humanitarian initiative which comes within its role as a specifically neutral and independent institution and intermediary, and may consider any question requiring examination by such an institution'.[31] 20.19

Through the years, specific conditions have emerged to identify when ICRC action in OSV is justified. This is the case when the situation of violence has significant humanitarian consequences and when ICRC humanitarian action can constitute a relevant response to alleviate the victims' suffering. In these scenarios, the ICRC decides whether to act directly or in support of the National Society.[32] 20.20

ICRC's annual reports contain numerous examples of such interventions. For instance, in the context of the military coup in Chile in 1974, with the Chilean authorities having permitted ICRC delegates to visit most places of detention, the ICRC had, by 31 December 1973 'made 114 visits to sixty-one places of detention and met several thousand detainees held by the military authorities ... Not only was ICRC action continued in 1974 but its field of activity was considerably extended, particularly with regard to relief. The number of delegates increased accordingly'.[33] In 2005, in the context of the general elections taking place in Haiti, who faced persistent instability for several years, the ICRC also 'helped the Haitian Red Cross evacuate hundreds of wounded people from Cité Soleil, one of the most violence-prone shantytowns, where a water and sanitation project initiated with the National Society in 2005 reversed to some extent the increasing marginalization of its residents'.[34] 20.21

In OSV in particular, but also generally in situations of armed conflicts, to which international human rights law and domestic law apply, ICRC interventions might overlap with the work of the OHCHR. The mandate of each organisation is different—the ICRC is more involved in purely humanitarian activities while the OHCHR's mandate is to promote and protect human rights.[35] But both organisations are sometimes called 20.22

---

[29] The Movement of the Red Cross and Red Crescent is composed of three components: the National Red Cross and Red Crescent Societies; the International Federation of Red Cross and Red Crescent Societies; and the ICRC. Red Cross law comprises all the legal and regulatory texts adopted at the Movement's statutory meetings.

[30] Art. 4(1)(d) of the Statutes of the Movement.

[31] Art. 5(2)(d) and 5(3) of the Statutes of the International Red Cross and Red Crescent Movement, adopted by consensus by the 25th International Conference of the Red Cross, available at: https://bit.ly/33ZAtBJ, and Article 4(1)(d) and 4(2) of the Statutes of the International Committee of the Red Cross (see supra para. 20.16).

[32] 'The International Committee of the Red Cross's (ICRC's) Role in Situations of Violence below the Threshold of Armed Conflict', Policy document, February 2014, *International Review of the Red Cross*, Vol. 96, No. 893 (2014), p. 289.

[33] ICRC, Annual Report for 1973, available at: https://bit.ly/3tT2Zjf, p. 42.

[34] ICRC, Annual Report for 2005, p. 215.

[35] In particular, the OHCHR 'works with and assists Governments in fulfilling their human rights obligations; speaks out objectively in the face of human rights violations worldwide; provides a forum for identifying, highlighting and developing responses to today's human rights challenges and acts as the principal focal point of

upon to take similar actions operationally. For example, in the context of the conflict in Mali, it was agreed that OHCHR and ICRC had both to be granted access to detained persons by G5-S forces.[36]

20.23 In situations of armed conflicts and violence, the OHCHR works closely with other UN entities, such as the Department of Peacekeeping Operations (DPKO), the Department of Political and Peacebuilding Affairs (DPPA), and the Office for the Coordination of Humanitarian Affairs (OCHA).[37] The extent to which there is systemic collaboration more generally between the OHCHR (or UN agencies) and the ICRC intervening in the same contexts is unclear. If, on the one hand, the UN, including the OHCHR, promotes integrated approach to humanitarian action,[38] the ICRC, on the other, in order to ensure its independence and impartiality, 'refuses to be coordinated by anyone, included by the host country'.[39]

Controversies and challenges

20.24 Perhaps one of the most controversial operational practices adopted by the ICRC is the 'confidentiality policy'. It means that the ICRC 'requires confidential and bilateral communications, including written submissions, with the relevant authorities, and that it expects such authorities to respect and protect the confidential nature of its communications'.[40] Derived from the principles of neutrality (the ICRC does not take side in hostilities); independence (it does not work under the direction or coordination from States or international organisations); and impartiality (it makes no discrimination as to nationality, race, religious beliefs, class or political opinions), the purpose of the confidentiality policy is to gain safe access to conflict zones, to protect staff in the field, and also to 'ensure that violations of IHL are addressed by those responsible as they are happening, rather than only in a later, ex post facto manner'.[41]

---

human rights research, education, public information, and advocacy activities'. See OHCHR, 'What We Do', accessed 1 January 2022 at: https://bit.ly/35iZV5W.

[36] OHCHR, 'Status Report: OHCHR Project supporting the G5 Sahel Joint Force with Implementation of the Human Rights and International Humanitarian Law Compliance Framework 1 May 2018–31 March 2020', at: https://bit.ly/3qVHU6b, para. 88.

[37] A. Bellal, 'Building Respect for the Rule of Law in Violent Contexts: The Office of the High Commissioner for Human Rights' Experience and Approach', *International Review of the Red Cross*, Vol. 96, Nos. 895/896 (2015), p. 885, available at: https://bit.ly/3Izmhi2.

[38] It was for example noted that 'given the variety of actors, involved in humanitarian response including NGOs, concerted efforts should be made to ensure that methods and approaches are used complementarily to obtain optimal protection outcomes'. See 'The Protection of Human Rights in Humanitarian Crises', Joint Background Paper by OHCHR and UNHCR IASC Principals, 8 May 2013, para. 4, available at: https://bit.ly/3ArSNiX.

[39] M. Sassòli, *International Humanitarian Law: Rules, Controversies, and Solutions to Problems Arising in Warfare*, Edward Elgar Publishing, Cheltenham, 2019, para. 5.174, p. 138.

[40] 'Memorandum, The ICRC's Privilege of Non-Disclosure of Confidential Information', *International Review of the Red Cross*, Vol. 97, Nos. 897/898 (2016), p. 434.

[41] Ibid., p. 435.

20.25 The confidentiality policy has also been recognised as granting the ICRC the privilege not to disclose confidential information to international criminal courts and tribunals.[42] Rule 73(4) of the ICC Rules of Procedure and Evidence thus requires from the Court to:

> regard as privileged, and consequently not subject to disclosure, including by way of testimony of any present or past official or employee of the International Committee of the Red Cross (ICRC), any information, documents or other evidence which it came into the possession of in the course, or as a consequence, of the performance by ICRC of its functions under the Statutes of the International Red Cross and Red Crescent Movement, unless: [the] ICRC does not object in writing to such disclosure, or otherwise has waived this privilege; or [s]uch information, documents or other evidence is contained in public statements and documents of ICRC.

20.26 The confidentiality policy is closely linked to the legal status of the ICRC. Indeed, and similar to an intergovernmental organisation, the ICRC enjoys immunity from judicial proceedings at the domestic and international levels. The ICRC thus regularly concludes with individual States bilateral status agreements granting it privileges and immunities.[43] Such immunity enables the ICRC to carry out the mandate or functions entrusted to it by the Geneva Conventions effectively, with regard notably to its commitment of confidentiality. For instance, immunity means that the ICRC premises, property, and assets are inviolable and that ICRC staff and representatives have freedom of movement and travel to, from, and throughout the relevant national territory.[44]

20.27 The confidentiality policy is not, however, absolute and there are instances where the ICRC will disclose publicly violations of IHL committed by a party to an armed conflict. This will be the case when:

(1) the violations are major and repeated or likely to be repeated
(2) delegates have witnessed the violations with their own eyes, or the existence and extent of those violations have been established on the basis of reliable and verifiable sources
(3) bilateral confidential representations and, when attempted, humanitarian mobilisation efforts have failed to put an end to the violations
(4) such publicity is in the interest of the persons or populations affected or threatened.[45]

---

[42] See notably International Criminal Tribunal for the former Yugoslavia (ICTY), *Prosecutor v. Simić*, Decision on the Prosecution Motion Under Rule 73 for a Ruling Concerning the Testimony of a Witness (Case No. IT-95-9), 27 July 1999, paras. 72–74; ICTY, *Prosecutor v. Brdjanin*, Decision on Interlocutory Appeal (Appeals Chamber) (Case No. IT-99-36), 11 December 2002, para. 32; and International Criminal Tribunal for Rwanda (ICTR), *Prosecutor v. Muvunyi*, Reasons for the Chamber's Decision on the Accused's Motion to Exclude Witness TQ (Case No. ICTR-2000-55), 15 July 2005, paras. 14–16.

[43] E. Debuf, 'Tools to Do the Job: The ICRC's Legal Status, Privileges and Immunities', *International Review of the Red Cross*, Vol. 97, Nos. 897/898 (2016), p. 327.

[44] Ibid., pp. 339–40 with further examples.

[45] 'Action by the International Committee of the Red Cross in the Event of Violations of International Humanitarian Law or of Other Fundamental Rules Protecting Persons in Situations of Violence', *International Review of the Red Cross*, Vol. 87, No. 858 (June 2005), p. 397.

However, by privileging soft persuasion over denunciation of IHL violations in most cases, the ICRC has often opened itself to criticism. It has, for instance, been argued that 'as it is thus often impossible to know the ICRC's legal characterization in specific cases, its self-professed role as an authoritative interpreter of and voice for international humanitarian law seems undermined'.[46]

20.28   Finally, as 'guardian' of IHL, the ICRC must not only 'work for the faithful application of international humanitarian law applicable in armed conflicts and to take cognizance of any complaints based on alleged breaches of that law',[47] but must also 'work for the understanding and dissemination of knowledge of international humanitarian law applicable in armed conflicts and to prepare any development 'thereof'.[48] In this role as well, the ICRC's work has not been unquestioned. In particular, methodological concerns over the ICRC's customary law study have been voiced by States and scholars,[49] and when it comes to the development of IHL, the organisation has been accused of not taking sufficiently into consideration the perspectives of armed groups, partially out of fear of frustrating States' views on the overriding importance of sovereignty.[50]

Concluding remarks and outlook

20.29   The ICRC is truly a 'unique protagonist'[51] in international relations. Four times a Nobel Peace Prize winner, untold numbers of victims of armed conflict as well as IHL have benefited very greatly from its work and engagement throughout history. Indeed, it would be difficult to imagine the world without it. But the ICRC has also been caught in its own seemingly conflicting goals to protect victims and protect IHL at the same time. Because of its pivotal role in the system in supporting IHL implementation, the ICRC's challenge to find a better equilibrium can be problematic: 'if the ICRC is actually choosing protection of victims over guardianship of IHL rather than reconciling these two functions, then we confront a situation where a critical enforcer of the law

---

[46] Ratner, 'Law Promotion Beyond Law Talk', p. 461. For Marco Sassòli, holding discussions on legal issues 'behind the scenes increases the public perception that law does not matter', M. Sassòli, *International Humanitarian Law: Rules, Controversies, and Solutions to Problems Arising in Warfare*, Edward Elgar Publishing, Cheltenham, 2019, para. 5.187, p. 144.

[47] Art. 4(1)(c) of the ICRC Statutes.

[48] Art. 4(1)(g) of the Statutes of the ICRC. See also Y. Sandoz, 'The International Committee of the Red Cross as Guardian of International Humanitarian Law', 31 December 1998, available at: https://bit.ly/3e4rr7a; and ICRC, 'What is the ICRC's role in developing and ensuring respect for IHL?', ICRC Blog, 14 August 2017, at: https://bit.ly/343XAuN.

[49] See, e.g., J. B. Bellinger III and W. J. Haynes II, 'A US Government Response to the International Committee of the Red Cross Study Customary International Humanitarian Law', *International Review of the Red Cross*, Vol. 89, No. 866 (June 2007), pp. 443–71. See also E. Wilmshurst and S. Breau (eds.), *Perspectives on the ICRC Study on Customary International Humanitarian Law*, Cambridge University Press, Cambridge, 2007.

[50] M. Sassòli, *International Humanitarian Law: Rules, Controversies, and Solutions to Problems Arising in Warfare*, Edward Elgar Publishing, Cheltenham, 2019, para. 5.188, p. 145.

[51] D. P. Forsythe, 'The ICRC: A Unique Humanitarian Protagonist', *International Review of the Red Cross*, Vol. 89, No. 865 (March 2007), pp. 63–96.

(in a loose sense) appears ready to sacrifice promoting that law for the sake of other values'.[52] In addition, its 'obsession to be independent'[53] and its preference for a confidential approach to denouncing more systematically IHL violations has led to the perception that the ICRC is not always in line with the more contemporary goals of fight against impunity for the commission of international crimes and even seems 'to contradict an empowering rights-based approach under which the punishment of violations is viewed as essential'.[54]

Also of very great concern, the ICRC's core mission has been rendered more fragile by increasing attacks of different natures against it. Thus, between 1997 and 2020, there were 198 attacks against ICRC staff in different contexts.[55] In January 2022, a major cyber-attack targeted data held by the ICRC on 500,000 people.[56] The ICRC will surely need to consider carefully what these recurring threats and new challenges imply for its future.

20.30

---

[52] Ratner, 'Law Promotion Beyond Law Talk', p. 461.
[53] M. Sassòli, *International Humanitarian Law: Rules, Controversies, and Solutions to Problems Arising in Warfare*, Edward Elgar Publishing, Cheltenham, 2019, p. 522, para. 10.81 and p. 141, para. 5.181.
[54] Ibid., p. 142, para. 5.182.
[55] Aid Worker Security Database, 'Major Attacks on Aid Workers: Summary Statistics', Last updated 3 January 2022, at: https://bit.ly/3AsUsoD.
[56] ICRC, 'Sophisticated cyber-attack targets Red Cross Red Crescent data on 500,000 people', News Release, 19 January 2022, at: https://bit.ly/3vBe5K4.

Bibliography

Books

Blackman, A.
  Marine A: 'my Toughest Battle', Mirror Books, London, October 2019.
Boothby, W.
  Weapons and the Law of Armed Conflict, 1st Edn, Oxford University Press, Oxford, 2009.
  Conflict Law: The Influence of New Weapons Technology, Human Rights and Emerging Actors, TMC Asser Press, The Hague, 2014.
Bothe M., K. J. Partsch, and W. A. Solf, with M. Eaton
  New Rules for Victims of Armed Conflicts: Commentary on the Two 1977 Protocols Additional to the Geneva Conventions of 1949, Martinus Nijhoff, The Hague, 1982.
  New Rules for Victims of Armed Conflicts: Commentary on the Two 1977 Protocols Additional to the Geneva Conventions of 1949, 2nd Edn, Martinus Nijhoff, Leiden, 2013.
Brownlie, I.
  International Law and the Use of Force by States, Oxford University Press, Oxford, 1963.
Casey-Maslen, S.
  Jus ad Bellum: The Law on Inter-State Use of Force, Hart Publishing, Oxford, 2020.
  The Right to Life under International Law: An Interpretive Manual, Cambridge University Press, Cambridge, 2021.
  Treaty on the Prohibition of Nuclear Weapons: A Commentary, Oxford University Press, Oxford, 2019.
Casey-Maslen, S. with S. Haines
  Hague Law Interpreted: The Conduct of Hostilities under the Law of Armed Conflict, Hart Publishing, Oxford, 2018.
Casey-Maslen, S. and T. Vestner
  A Guide to International Disarmament Law, Routledge, Abingdon, 2019.
Casey-Maslen, S. (ed.)
  Weapons Under International Human Rights Law, Cambridge University Press, Cambridge, 2014.
Clapham, A.
  War, Oxford University Press, Oxford, 2021.
  Human Rights Obligations of Non-State Actors, Oxford University Press, Oxford, 2006.
  'Non-State Actors (in Postconflict Peace-building)', in V. Chetail (ed.), *Postconflict Peacebuilding: A Lexicon*, Oxford University Press, Oxford, 2009, 200–12.
  Commentary on the Harvard Manual on International Law Applicable to Air and Missile Warfare, Cambridge University Press, Cambridge, 2013.
Crawford, E.
  The Treatment of Combatants and Insurgents under the Law of Armed Conflict, Oxford University Press, Oxford, 2010.
Crawford, E. and A. Pert
  International Humanitarian Law, 2nd Edn, Cambridge University Press, Cambridge, 2020.
Cryer, R., H. Friman, D. Robinson, and E. Wilmshurst
  An Introduction to International Criminal Law and Procedure, Cambridge University Press, Cambridge, 2010.
Cryer, R., H. Friman, D. Robinson, and E. Wilmshurst
  An Introduction to International Criminal Law and Procedure, 3rd Edn, Cambridge University Press, Cambridge, 2014.

Cryer, R., D. Robinson, and S. Vasiliev
> *An Introduction to International Criminal Law and Procedure*, 4th Edn, Cambridge University Press, Cambridge, 2019.

Dinstein, Y.
> *The Conduct of Hostilities under the Law of International Armed Conflict*, 3rd Edn, Cambridge University Press, Cambridge, 2016.
> *Non-International Armed Conflicts in International Law*, 2nd Edn, Cambridge University Press, Cambridge, 2021.

Duffy, H.
> *The 'War on Terror' and the Framework of International Law*, 2nd Edn, Cambridge University Press, Cambridge, 2015.

Fortin, K.
> *The Accountability of Armed Groups under Human Rights Law*, Oxford University Press, Oxford, 2017.

Heffes, E.
> *Detention by Non-State Armed Groups under International Law*, Cambridge University Press, Cambridge, 2022.

Heller, K. J. and M. D. Dubber (eds.)
> *The Handbook of Comparative Criminal Law*, Stanford University Press, Stanford CA, 2010.

Henckaerts, J.-M. and L. Doswald-Beck (eds.)
> *Customary International Humanitarian Law—Volume 1: Rules*, Cambridge University Press, Cambridge, 2005.

Hessbruegge, J. A.
> *Human Rights and Personal Self-Defense in International Law*, Oxford University Press, New York, 2017.

Inigo Alvarez, L.
> *Towards a Regime of Responsibility of Armed Groups in International Law*, Intersentia, Cambridge, 2020.

Irving, D.
> *The Mare's Nest*, Panther Books, London, 1985.

Jo, H.
> *Compliant Rebels: Rebel Groups and International Law in World Politics*, Cambridge University Press, Cambridge, 2015.

Kalshoven, F.
> *Constraints on the Waging of War*, ICRC, Geneva, 1987.

Kalshoven, F. and L. Zegveld
> *Constraints on the Waging of War: An Introduction to International Humanitarian Law*, 3rd Edn, ICRC, Geneva, 2001.

Moir, L.
> *The Law of Internal Armed Conflict*, Cambridge University Press, Cambridge, 2002.

Neufeld, M. J.
> *The Rocket and the Reich: Peenemünde and the Coming of the Ballistic Missile Era*, The Free Press, New York, 1995.

Pictet, J.
> *Commentary on 1949 Geneva Convention I*, ICRC, Geneva, 1952.
> *Commentary on 1949 Geneva Convention II*, ICRC, Geneva, 1960.

Provost, R.
> *Rebel Courts*, Oxford University Press, Oxford, 2021.

Rodenhäuser, T.
> *Organizing Rebellion, Non-State Armed Groups under International Humanitarian Law, Human Rights Law, and International Criminal Law*, Oxford University Press, Oxford, 2018.

Rogers, A. P. V.
> *Law on the Battlefield*, 3rd Edn, Manchester University Press, Manchester, 2012.
> *Law on the Battlefield*, 2nd Edn, Manchester University Press, Manchester, 2004.

Sandoz Y., C. Swinarski, and B. Zimmermann (eds.)
   Commentary on the Additional Protocols of 8 June 1977 to the Geneva Conventions of 12 August 1949, ICRC/Martinus Nijhoff, Geneva, 1987.
Sassòli, M.
   International Humanitarian Law: Rules, Controversies, and Solutions to Problems Arising in Warfare, Edward Elgar Publishing, Cheltenham, 2019.
Saul, B. (ed.)
   Research Handbook on International Law and Terrorism, Edward Elgar Publishing, Cheltenham, 2021.
Schabas, W. A.
   Genocide in International Law: The Crime of Crimes, 2nd Edn, Cambridge University Press, Cambridge, 2009.
Schmitt, M. N. (ed.)
   Tallinn Manual on the International Law Applicable to Cyber Warfare, 1st Edn, Cambridge University Press, Cambridge, 2013.
   Tallinn Manual 2.0 on the International Law Applicable to Cyber Operations, 2nd Edn, Cambridge University Press, Cambridge, 2017.
Sivakumaran, S.
   The Law of Non-International Armed Conflict, Oxford University Press, Oxford, 2012.
Solis, G. D.
   The Law of Armed Conflict, International Humanitarian Law in War, 3rd Edn, Cambridge University Press, Cambridge, 2021.
   The Law of Armed Conflict, 1st Edn, Cambridge University Press, Cambridge, 2010.
Spaight, J. M.
   Air Power and War Rights, 3rd Edn, Longman's, London, 1924.
Stahn, C.
   A Critical Introduction to International Criminal Law, Cambridge University Press, Cambridge, 2019.
The Laws of War on Land
   Manual published by the Institute of International Law (Oxford Manual), adopted by the Institute of International Law at Oxford, 9 September 1880, available at: https://bit.ly/3pAH0KQ.
Thompson, P. G.
   Armed Groups, The 21st Century Threat, Rowman and Littlefield, London, 2014.
Verini, J.
   They Will Have to Die Now: Mosul and the Fall of the Caliphate, They Will Have to Die Now: Mosul and the Fall of the Caliphate, OneWorld Publications, London, 2019.
Wallace, G. P. R.
   Life and Death in Captivity: The Abuse of Prisoners during War, Cornell University Press, Ithaca, NY, 16 April 2015.
Wilmshurst, E. and S. Breau (eds.)
   Perspectives on the ICRC Study on Customary International Humanitarian Law, Cambridge University Press, Cambridge, 2007.
Zaloga, S.
   The Scud and Other Russian Ballistic Missiles, Concord Publications, Hong Kong, 2000.

Articles, Chapters, and Monographs

Abu Sa'Da, C., F. Duroch, and B. Taith
   'Attacks on Medical Missions: Overview of a Polymorphous Reality: the Case of Médecins Sans Frontières', *International Review of the Red Cross*, Vol. 95, No. 890 (2013), 309–33.
African Child Policy Forum
   The African Report on Violence against Children, 2014.

Akande, D.

'Classification of Armed Conflicts', Chap. 1 in B. Saul and D. Akande (eds.), *The Oxford Guide to International Humanitarian Law*, Oxford University Press, Oxford, 2020.

Akande, D. and Gillard, E.-C.

Oxford Guidance on the Law Relating to Humanitarian Relief Operations in Situations of Armed Conflicts, University of Oxford and OCHA, 2016.

Albrecht, R.

'War Reprisals in the War Crimes Trials and in the Geneva Conventions', *American Journal of International Law*, Vol. 47, No. 4 (October 1953), 590–614.

Altunjan, T.

'The International Criminal Court and Sexual Violence: Between Aspirations and Reality', *German Law Journal*, Vol. 22, No. 5 (2021), 878–93.

Amnesty International

Unlawful and Deadly. Rocket and Mortar Attacks by Palestinian Armed Groups during the 2014 Gaza/Israel Conflict, March 2015.

Antonopoulos, C.

'Force by Armed Groups as Armed Attack and the Broadening of Self-Defence', *Netherlands International Law Review*, Vol. 55, No. 2 (August 2008), 159–80.

Baksi, C.

'Military Mettle', *The Law Society Gazette*, 22 June 2020, at: https://bit.ly/3jbuC0U.

Barnidge, R.

'Resistance Movements', *Max Planck Encyclopedia of Public International Law*, 2011, available at: https://bit.ly/3HIPKpm.

Bartels, R.

'Denying Humanitarian Access as an International Crime in Times of Non-International Armed Conflict: The Challenges to Prosecute and Some Proposals for the Future', *Israel Law Review*, Vol. 48, No. 3 (2015) 281–307.

Bellal, A.

'Building Respect for the Rule of Law in Violent Contexts: The Office of the High Commissioner for Human Rights' Experience and Approach', *International Review of the Red Cross*, Vol. 96, Nos. 895/896 (2015), 881–900.

The War Report 2018, Geneva Academy of International Humanitarian Law and Human Rights, Geneva, 2019, at: https://bit.ly/3onS8dN.

'What Are Armed Non-State Actors? A Legal and Semantic Approach', in E. Heffes, M. Kotlik, and M. Ventura (eds.), *International Humanitarian Law and Non-State Actors: Debates, Law and Practice*, TMC Asser/Springer, The Hague, 2020, 21–46.

'Establishing the Direct Responsibility of Non-State Armed Groups for Violations of International Norms: Issues of Attribution', in N. Gal-Or, C. Ryngaert, and M. Noortman (eds.), *Responsibilities of the Non-State Actor in Armed Conflict and the Market Place: Theoretical Considerations and Empirical Findings*, Brill/Nijhoff, Leiden, 2015, 304–22.

Bellal, A., Badawi, N., Bongard, P., and Heffes, E.

'From Words to Deeds: A Study of Armed Non-State Actors' Practice and Interpretation of International Humanitarian and Human Rights Norms', Research Project, 2020–2022, available at: https://words2deeds.org.

Bellinger III, J. B. and Haynes II, W. J.

'A US Government Response to the International Committee of the Red Cross Study Customary International Humanitarian Law', *International Review of the Red Cross*, Vol. 89, No. 866 (June 2007), 443–71.

Letter to Dr Jacob Kellenberger, President, ICRC, Regarding Customary International Humanitarian Law Study, 3 November 2006, reprinted in *International Legal Materials*, Vol. 46 (2007), 514.

Bialke, J. P.

'Al-Qaeda & Taliban—Unlawful Combatant Detainees, Unlawful Belligerency, and the International Laws of Armed Conflict', *Air Force Law Review*, Vol. 55 (2004), 1.

Bouchet-Saulnier, F.
- 'Consent to Humanitarian Access: An Obligation Triggered by Territorial Control, Not States' Rights', *International Review of the Red Cross*, Vol. 96, No. 893 (2014), 207–17.

Bradley, M. M.
- 'Additional Protocol II: Elevating the Minimum Threshold of Intensity?', *International Review of the Red Cross*, Vol. 102, No. 915 (2020), 1125–52.
- 'Classifying Non-International Armed Conflicts: The "Territorial Control" Requirement under Additional Protocol II in an Era of Complex Conflicts', *Journal of International Humanitarian Legal Studies*, Vol. 11, No. 2 (2020), 349–84.

Brehm, M.
- *Defending the Boundary: Constraints and Requirements on the Use of Autonomous Weapon systems under International Humanitarian and Human Rights Law*, Academy Briefing No. 9, Geneva Academy of International Humanitarian Law and Human Rights, Geneva, May 2017.

Breitegger, A.
- 'The Legal Framework Applicable to Insecurity and Violence Affecting the Delivery of Health Care in Armed Conflicts and Other Emergencies', *International Review of the Red Cross*, Vol. 95, No. 889 (2013), 83–127.

Cameron, L., Demeyere, B. Henckaerts, J.-M. La Haye, E., and Niebergall-Lackner, H.
- 'The Updated Commentary on the First Geneva Convention—A New Tool for Generating Respect for International Humanitarian Law', *International Review of the Red Cross*, Vol. 97, No. 900 (2015), 1209–26.

Canada Ministry of National Defence
- *Manual of the Law of Armed Conflict at the Operational and Tactical Levels*, Joint Doctrine Manual, Doc. B-GJ-005-104/FP-021, Ottawa, 2001.

Casey-Maslen, S.
- 'Weapons', Chap. 11 in B. Saul and D. Akande (eds.), *The Oxford Guide to International Humanitarian Law*, Oxford University Press, Oxford, 2020.

Casey-Maslen, S., Corney, N., and Dymond-Bass, A.
- 'The Review of Weapons under International Humanitarian Law and Human Rights Law', Chap. 14 in Casey-Maslen (ed.), *Weapons Under International Human Rights Law*, Cambridge University Press, Cambridge, 2014.

Conte, A.
- 'The Legality of Detention in Armed Conflict', in A. Bellal and S. Casey-Maslen (eds.), *The War Report 2014*, Oxford University Press, Oxford, 2015.

Corn, G. S.
- 'Thinking the Unthinkable: Has the Time Come to Offer Combatant Immunity to Non-State Actors?', *Stanford Law & Policy Review*, Vol. 22, No. 1 (2011), 253–94, at: http://stanford.io/3oxIG5d.
- 'Regulating Hostilities in Non-International Armed Conflicts: Thoughts on Bridging the Divide between the Tadić Aspiration and Conflict Realities', *International Legal Studies*, Vol. 91 (2015), 281–322.

Crawford, E.
- 'The Temporal and Geographic Reach of International Humanitarian Law', Chap. 3 in B. Saul and D. Akande (eds.), *The Oxford Guide to International Humanitarian Law*, Oxford University Press, Oxford, 2020.

Darcy, S.
- 'The Evolution of the Law of Belligerent Reprisals', *Military Law Review*, Vol. 175 (2003), 184–251.

Debuf, E.
- 'Tools to Do the Job: The ICRC's Legal Status, Privileges and Immunities', *International Review of the Red Cross*, Vol. 97, Nos. 897/898 (2016).

DiMeglio, Lt.-Col. R. P.
- 'Training Army Judge Advocates to Advise Commanders as Operational Law Attorneys', *Boston College Law Review*, Vol. 54, No. 3 (2013), 1185–1206, at: https://bit.ly/3BXhQKK,.

Dinstein, Y.
    'Legal Advisers in the Field During Armed Conflict', The Howard S. Levie Distinguished Essay, *International Legal Studies*, Vol. 97 (2021), 917–36, at: https://bit.ly/3lRgkV4.

Dörmann, K.
    'The Legal Situation of "Unlawful/Unprivileged Combatants"', *International Review of the Red Cross*, Vol. 85, No. 849 (2003), 45–74.

Dudouet, V. and Göldner-Ebenthal, K.
    'Challenges and Opportunities for Conflict Resolution with Salafi jihadi Armed Groups', Policy Brief No. 10, Berghof Foundation, Germany, 31 March 2020, at: https://bit.ly/32ZJURs.

European Union (EU External Action)
    'Mediation and Dialogue in Transitional Processes from Non-State Armed Groups to Political Movements/Political Parties', Factsheet, 2011, at: https://bit.ly/3J1nKO6.

Ferencz, B. B.
    Opening Statement of Prosecutor at the Einsatzgruppen trial following the end of the War. Text available at: http://bit.ly/32Bxyvu.

Forsythe, D. P.
    'The ICRC: A Unique Humanitarian Protagonist', *International Review of the Red Cross*, Vol. 89, No. 865 (March 2007), 63–96.

Fortin, K.
    'The Application of Human Rights Law to Everyday Civilian Life Under Rebel Control', *Netherlands International Law Review*, Vol. 63 (2016), 161–81.

Fox, A. C.
    'The Reemergence of the Siege: An Assessment of Trends in Modern Land Warfare', Landpower Essay, Institute of Land Warfare, No. 18-2, June 2018, at: https://bit.ly/3eZ5pWn.

French Ministry of Defence
    Manuel de Droit des Conflits Armés, Ministère de la Défense, Paris, 2012.

Gaggioli, G. and Melzer, N.
    'Methods of Warfare', Chap. 10 in B. Saul and D. Akande (eds.), *The Oxford Guide to International Humanitarian Law*, Oxford University Press, Oxford, 2020.

Gal, T.
    'Territorial Control by Armed Groups and the Regulation of Access to Humanitarian Assistance', *Israel Law Review*, Vol. 50, No. 1 (2017), 25–47.

Gebhard, J.
    'Militias', in *Max Planck Encyclopedia of Public International Law*, 2010, at: https://bit.ly/3B0p40Z.

Geiss, R. and Siegrist, M.
    'Has the Armed Conflict in Afghanistan Affected the Rules on the Conduct of Hostilities?', *International Review of the Red Cross*, Vol. 93, No. 881 (2011), 11–46.

German Ministry of Defence
    Law of Armed Conflict Manual, Joint Service Regulation (ZDv) 15/2, Berlin, 2013.

Giacca, G.
    Economic, Social, and Cultural Rights in Armed Conflict, Oxford University Press, Oxford, 2014.

Giladi, R. and Ratner, S. R.
    'The Role of the International Committee of the Red Cross', in A. Clapham, P. Gaeta, and M. Sassòli (eds.), *The 1949 Geneva Conventions: A Commentary*, Oxford University Press, Oxford, 2015.

Gillard, E.-C.
    'Sieges, the Law and Protecting Civilians', Briefing, International Law Programme, Chatham House, London, June 2019, at: https://bit.ly/39e6WEn.

Glazier, D.
    'Wars of National Liberation', in *Max Planck Encyclopedia of Public International Law*, 2009.

Graham, L.
    'Prosecuting Starvation Crimes in Yemen's Civil War', *Case Western Reserve Journal of International Law*, Vol. 52, No. 1 (2020), 267–86, available at: https://bit.ly/3EMdAPh.

Greenwood, C.
    'International Humanitarian Law and United Nations Military Operations', *Yearbook of International Humanitarian Law*, Vol. 1 (December 1998), 3–34.

Grenfell, K.
: 'Perspective on the Applicability and Application of International Humanitarian Law: The UN Context', *International Review of the Red Cross*, Vol. 95, Nos. 891/892 (2013), 645–52, at: https://bit.ly/2Qa0rLQ.

Haines, S.
: 'Developing International Guidelines for Protecting Schools and Universities from Military Use During Armed Conflict', *International Legal Studies*, Vol. 97 (2021), 573–620, at: https://bit.ly/3lCdZva.

Hays Parks, A.
: 'Air War and the Law of War', *Air Force Law Review*, Vol. 32, No. 1 (1990), 1.

Henckaerts, J.-M. and Wiesener, C.
: 'Human Rights Obligations of Non-State Armed Groups: An Assessment Based on Recent Practice', in E. Heffes, M. D. Kotlik, and M. J. Ventura (eds.), *International Humanitarian Law and Non-State Actors: Debates, Law and Practice*, Springer, The Hague, 2020, 195–227.

Hill-Cawthorne, L.
: 'Persons Covered by International Humanitarian Law: Main Categories', Chap. 5 in B. Saul and D. Akande (eds.), *The Oxford Guide to International Humanitarian Law*, Oxford University Press, Oxford, 2020.

Hmoud, M.
: 'Negotiating the Draft Comprehensive Convention on International Terrorism: Major Bones of Contention', *Journal of International Criminal Justice*, Vol. 4, No. 5 (November 2006), 1031–43.

Hoffberger-Pippan, E.
: 'Non-Lethal Weapons and International Law: A Three-Dimensional Perspective', PhD Thesis, Johannes Kepler University, Linz, Austria, 2018.

Hughes K. and others,
: 'Prevalence and Risk of Violence against Adults with Disabilities: A Systematic Review and Meta-Analysis of Observational Studies', *The Lancet*, Vol. 379, No. 9826 (2012), 1621–29, at: http://bit.ly/3rLt0xn.

Irish Department of Foreign Affairs
: *Draft Political Declaration on Strengthening the Protection of Civilians from the Humanitarian Consequences that can arise from the use of Explosive Weapons with Wide Area Effects in Populated Areas*, Draft REV 1, 29 January 2021, at: https://bit.ly/3CGj3Xl.

Israeli Ministry of Foreign Affairs
: *IDF Conduct of Operations during the 2014 Gaza Conflict*, at: https://bit.ly/3ybru9Q.

Jackson, A.
: *In their Words: Perceptions of Armed Non-State Actors on Humanitarian Action*, Geneva, 2016, at: https://bit.ly/3BHtqZC.

Junod, S.
: 'Additional Protocol II: History and Scope', *American University Law Review*, Vol. 33 (1983), 30.

Kleffner J. K.
: 'The Legal Fog of an Illusion: Three Reflections on "Organization" and "Intensity" as Criteria for the Temporal Scope of the Law of Non-International Armed Conflict', *International Legal Studies*, Vol. 95 (2019), 161–78.

: 'The Collective Accountability of Organized Armed Groups for System Crimes', in H. Wilt and A. Nollkaemper (eds.), *System Criminality in International Law*, Cambridge University Press, Cambridge, 2009.

Kleinlein, T.
: 'Jus Cogens as the "Highest Law"? Peremptory Norms and Legal Hierarchies', *Netherlands Yearbook of International Law*, Vol. 46 (2015), 173–210.

Kocher, M. A., Pepinsky, T. B., and Kalyvas, S. N.
: 'Aerial Bombing and Counterinsurgency in the Vietnam War', *American Journal of Political Science*, Vol. 55, No. 2 (April 2011), 201–18, at: https://bit.ly/3trlOqC.

Kotlik, M.
: 'Armed Non-State Actors', in C. Binder, M. Nowak, J. A. Hofbauer, and P. Janig (eds.), *Elgar Encyclopedia of Human Rights*, Edward Elgar Publishing, Cheltenham, 2022.

Kretzmer, D.
> 'Terrorism and the International Law of Occupation', Chap. 15 in B. Saul (ed.), *Research Handbook on International Law and Terrorism*, 2nd Edn, Edward Elgar Publishing, Cheltenham, 2021.

Lattanzi, F.
> 'Humanitarian Assistance', in A. Clapham, P. Gaeta, and M. Sassòli (eds.), *The 1949 Geneva Conventions: A Commentary*, Oxford University Press, Oxford, 2015.

Leonard Cheshire Disability
> *Still Left Behind: Pathways to Inclusive Education for Girls with Disabilities*, 2017.

Lubell, N., Pejic, J., and Simmons, C.
> *Guidelines on Investigating Violations of IHL: Law, Policy and Good Practice*, ICRC and Geneva Academy of International Humanitarian Law and Human Rights, Geneva, 2019, at: https://bit.ly/3jdr6mU.

Massingham, E. and Thynne, K.
> 'Humanitarian Relief Operations', in B. Saul and D. Akande (eds.), *The Oxford Guide to International Humanitarian Law*, Oxford University Press, Oxford, 2020.

Matheson, M.
> 'Additional Protocol I as Expressions of Customary International Law', *American University Journal of International Law and Policy*, Vol. 2, No. 2 (Fall 1987), 415.

Megret, F.
> 'Should Rebels be Amnestied', in C. Stahn, J. S. Easterday, and J. Iverson (eds.), *Jus Post Bellum*, Oxford University Press, Oxford, 2014.

Malinder, L.
> 'Amnesties and Inclusive Political Settlements' (2018) PA-X Report, Transitional Justice Series, Global Justice Academy, University of Edinburgh, at: https://bit.ly/3rr63BD.

Melzer, N.
> *Interpretive Guidance on the Notion of Direct Participation in Hostilities*, ICRC, Geneva, 2009.

Mettraux, G.
> 'Crimes Against Humanity in the Jurisprudence of the International Criminal Tribunals for the former Yugoslavia and for Rwanda', *Harvard International Law Journal*, Vol. 43, No. 1 (2002), 237–316.

Mikos-Skuza, E.
> 'Hospitals' in A. Clapham, P. Gaeta, and M. Sassòli (eds.), *The Geneva Conventions in Context: A Commentary*, Oxford University Press, Oxford, 2015, 207–29.

Mastorodimos, K.
> 'National Liberation Movements: Still a Valid Concept (with Special Reference to International Humanitarian Law)?', *Oregon Review of International Law*, 2015, 71–110.

Moxley Jr, C. J., Burroughs, J., and Granoff, J.
> 'Nuclear Weapons and Compliance with International Humanitarian Law and the Nuclear Non-Proliferation Treaty', *Fordham International Law Journal*, Vol. 34, No. 4 (2011), 595–696, at: http://bit.ly/354K855.

Murphy, D. T.
> 'The Restatement (Third)'s Human Rights Provisions: Nothing New, but Very Welcome', *International Lawyer*, Vol. 24 (1990), 917.

Neumaier, C.
> 'The Escalation of German Reprisal Policy in Occupied France, 1941–42', *Journal of Contemporary History*, Vol. 41, No. 1 (January 2006), 113–31, at: https://bit.ly/3rQCYxe.

New Zealand
> *Manual of Armed Forces Law, Vol. 4: Law of Armed Conflict*, 2019.

Nishat, N.
> 'The Right of Initiative of the ICRC and Other Impartial Humanitarian Bodies', in A. Clapham, P. Gaeta, and M. Sassòli (eds.), *The 1949 Geneva Conventions: A Commentary*.

Norwitz, J. H.
> *Armed Groups: Studies in National Security, Counterterrorism, and Counterinsurgency*, Naval War College, United States, 2008.

O'Connor, S.
'Nuclear Weapons and the Unnecessary Suffering Rule', in G. Nystuen and others (eds.), *Nuclear Weapons under International Law*, Cambridge University Press, Cambridge, 2014, 128–47.

Payne, C.
'Protection of the Natural Environment', Chap. 9 in B. Saul and D. Akande (eds.), *The Oxford Guide to International Humanitarian Law*, Oxford University Press, Oxford, 2020.

Pede, Lt.-Gen. C. N.
'Part I: Why the FM 6-27 Update is Vital for Judge Advocates', *The Army Lawyer*, Issue 2, 2020, 22–24, at: https://bit.ly/3G7obWG.

Pedrazzi, M.
'Additional Protocol II and threshold of application' in F. Pocar and G. L. Berute (eds.), *International Institute of Humanitarian Law: The Additional Protocols 40 Years Later: New Conflicts, New Actors, New Perspectives*, 40th Round Table on Current Issues of International Humanitarian Law, Franco Angeli, 2018.

Pejic, J.
'Detention in Armed Conflict', Chap. 12 in B. Saul and D. Akande (eds.), *The Oxford Guide to International Humanitarian Law*, Oxford University Press, Oxford, 2020.

Peterson, N.
'Life, Right to, International Protection', *Max Planck Encyclopedia of Public International Law*, Last updated October 2012.

Priddy, A.
'Sexual Violence against Men and Boys in Armed Conflict', Chap. 2 in S. Casey-Maslen (ed.), *The War Report: Armed Conflict in 2013*, Oxford University Press, Oxford, 2014, 271–96.

Program on Humanitarian Policy and Conflict Research at Harvard University
HPCR Manual on International Law Applicable to Air and Missile Warfare, 1st Edn, Cambridge University Press, New York, 2013.

Quéguiner, J.-F.
'Commentary on the Protocol Additional to the Geneva Conventions of 12 August 1949, and Relating to the Adoption of an Additional Distinctive Emblem (Protocol III)', *International Review of the Red Cross*, Vol. 89, No. 865 (March 2007).
'Precautions under the Law Governing the Conduct of Hostilities', *International Review of the Red Cross*, Vol. 88 No. 864 (December 2006), 801–802.

Ratner, S. R.
'Law Promotion beyond Law Talk: the Red Cross, Persuasion, and the Laws of War', *European Journal of International Law*, Vol. 22, No. 2 (May 2011), 459–506, at 460.

Roberts, A. and Sivakumaran, S.
'Lawmaking by Non-State Actors: Engaging Armed Groups in the Creation of International Humanitarian Law', *Yale Journal of International Law*, Vol. 37, No. 1 (2012), 107–52, at: https://bit.ly/3HBRPn9.

Rolle, B. and Lafontaine, E.
'The Emblem that Cried Wolf: ICRC Study on the Use of the Emblems', *International Review of the Red Cross*, Vol. 91, No. 876 (December 2009), 759–78.

Sadurska, R Zelada
'Threats of Force', *The American Journal of International Law*, Vol. 82, No. 2 (1988), 239–68.

Sassòli, M.
'The Approach of the Eritrea-Ethiopia Claims Commission towards the Treatment of Protected Persons in International Humanitarian Law', in A. de Guttry, H. H. G. Post, and G. Venturini (eds.), *The 1998–2000 War between Eritrea and Ethiopia*, TMC Asser, The Hague, 2009.
M. Sassòli, 'Taking Armed Groups Seriously: Ways to Improve Their Compliance with International Humanitarian Law', *Journal of International Humanitarian Legal Studies*, Vol. 1, No. 1 (2010).

Saul, B.
'Defending "Terrorism": Justifications and Excuses for Terrorism in International Criminal Law', *Australian Year Book of International Law*, Vol. 25 (2006), 177.

Schmitt, M.,
- 'Law of Cyber Warfare: *Quo Vadis?*', *Stanford Law and Policy Review*, Vol. 25, No. 2 (June 2014), 269–99, at: https://stanford.io/3sWsJLc.
- 'The Status of Opposition Fighters in a Non-International Armed Conflict', *International Legal Studies*, Vol. 88 (2012), 119–44.
- 'International Humanitarian Law and the Conduct of Hostilities', Chap. 7 in B. Saul and D. Akande (eds.), *The Oxford Guide to International Humanitarian Law*, Oxford University Press, Oxford, 2020.
- 'Autonomous Weapon Systems and International Humanitarian Law: A Reply to the Critics', *Harvard National Security Journal*, Features Online, 2013.

Short, J. M.,
- 'Sexual Violence as Genocide: The Developing Law of the International Criminal Tribunals and the International Criminal Court', *Michigan Journal of Race and Law*, Vol. 8 (2003), 503–27.

Shultz, R. H., Farah, D., and Lochard, V.
- 'Armed Groups: A Tier-One Security Priority', Institute for National Security Studies (INSS) Occasional Paper 57, United States Air Force (USAF) Academy, Colorado, 2004.

Sinno, A. H.
- 'Armed Groups' Organizational Structure and Their Strategic Options', *International Review of the Red Cross*, Vol. 93 (2011), 311–32.

Sivakumaran, S.
- 'Binding Armed Opposition Groups', *International and Comparative Law Quarterly*, Vol. 55 (2006), 369–94.

Sofaer, A. D.
- 'The Rationale for the United States Decision', *American Journal of International Law*, Vol. 82 (1988), 784.
- 'The Position of the United States on Current Law of War Agreements: Remarks of Judge Abraham D Sofaer, Legal Adviser, US Department of State, 22 January 1987', *American University Journal of International Law and Policy*, Vol. 2 (1987), 460.

Sommaruga, C.
- 'Unity and Plurality of the Emblems', *International Review of the Red Cross*, Vol. 32, No. 289 (1992), at: https://bit.ly/3HlIaR4.

South African National Defence Force
- *Manual on the Law of Armed Conflict*, Pretoria, 1996.

Spadaro, A.
- 'Punish and Be Punished? The Paradox of Command Responsibility in Armed Groups', *Journal of International Criminal Justice*, Vol. 18, No. 1 (2020), 1–30.

Swiss Federal Department of Foreign Affairs
- *ABC of International Humanitarian Law*, Bern, 2009.

Szasz, P. C.
- 'UN Forces and International Humanitarian Law', *International Law Studies*, Vol. 75 (2000), 507–37.

Turns, D.
- 'Implementation and Compliance', in E. Wilmshurst and S. Breau (eds.), *Perspectives on the ICRC Study on Customary International Humanitarian Law*, Cambridge University Press, Cambridge, 2007.

United Kingdom Ministry of Defence
- *The Manual of the Law of Armed Conflict*, Oxford University Press, Oxford, 2004.

United States Army and US Marine Corps
- *The Commander's Handbook on the Law of Land Warfare*, FM 6-27/MCTP 11-10C, Washington, D.C., August 2019, at: https://bit.ly/3vwMyrY.

United States Department of the Army
- *The Commander's Handbook on the Law of Land Warfare*, FM 6-27/MCTP 11-10C, Washington, D.C., 7 August 2019, at: https://bit.ly/3eKG9ml.

United States Department of Justice
 'Application of Treaties and Laws to al Qaeda and Taliban Detainees', Memorandum for Alberto R. Gonzales, Counsel to the President, and William J. Haynes II, General Counsel of the Department of Defense, Washington, D.C., 22 January 2002.
United States Department of Defense
 Department of Defense Law of War Manual, Washington, D.C., June 2015 (Updated December 2016).
 DOD Dictionary of Military and Associated Terms, As of November 2019, Washington, D.C., at: http://bit.ly/34cGg58.
 Autonomy in Weapons Systems, Directive 3000.09 (as amended).
United States Senate
 Afghanistan's Narco War: Breaking the Link Between Drug Traffickers and Insurgents. A Report to the Committee on Foreign Relations, US Senate, 10 August 2009, at: https://bit.ly/3r6k1sq.
Vité, S.
 'Typology of Armed Conflicts in International Humanitarian Law: Legal Concepts and Actual Situations', *International Review of the Red Cross*, Vol. 91, No. 873 (March 2009), 69–94.
Watts, S.
 'Present and Future Conceptions of the Status of Government Forces in Non-International Armed Conflict', *International Legal Studies*, 2019, 145–80.
Witten, S.
 'The International Convention for the Suppression of Terrorist Bombings', Chap. 8 in B. Saul (ed.), *Research Handbook on International Law and Terrorism*, 2nd Edn, Edward Elgar Publishing, Cheltenham, 2021.
Yakovleff, M.
 'NATO Is Not Preparing for the Next War', NATO Briefs Series No. 02/2021, 10 June 2021, at: https://bit.ly/3zHU2cf.
Weizmann, N. and Costas Trascasas, M.
 Autonomous Weapon Systems under International Law, Academy Briefing No. 8, Geneva Academy of International Humanitarian Law and Human Rights, Geneva, November 2014.
Zasova, S.
 'L'applicabilité du droit international humanitaire aux groupes armés organisés', in J. Sorel and C. Popescu (eds.), *La protection des personnes vulnérables en temps de conflits armés*, Bruylant, Brussels, 2010, 47–85.
Ziegler, A. R. and Wehrenberg, S.
 'Domestic Implementation', in A. Clapham, P. Gaeta, and M. Sassòli (eds.), *The 1949 Geneva Conventions: A Commentary*, 1st Edn, Oxford University Press, Oxford, 2015.

ICRC documents

Bugnion, F.
 Red Cross, Red Crescent, Red Crystal, ICRC, Geneva, 2007.
Gasser, H.-P.
 'The United Nations and International Humanitarian Law: The International Committee of the Red Cross and the United Nations' Involvement in the Implementation of International Humanitarian Law', Paper presented at the International Symposium on the occasion of the fiftieth anniversary of the United Nations, Geneva, 19-21 October 1995, 19 October 1995, at: http://bit.ly/30QvPkG.
Gisel, L.
 The Principle of Proportionality in the Rules Governing the Conduct of Hostilities under International Humanitarian Law, Report of an International Expert Meeting in Quebec, 22–23 June 2016, ICRC, Geneva, August 2018, at: http://bit.ly/397bsor.

International Committee of the Red Cross (ICRC)
  'Action by the International Committee of the Red Cross in the Event of Violations of International Humanitarian Law or of Other Fundamental Rules Protecting Persons in Situations of Violence', *International Review of the Red Cross*, Vol. 87, No. 858 (June 2005).
  Blog Cross-Files, 'The Central Tracing Agency', 30 August 2020, at: https://bit.ly/3IN03cv.
  'Bringing IHL Home: Guidelines on the National Implementation of International Humanitarian Law', *International Review of the Red Cross*, Vol. 102, No. 915 (2020), 1327–30.
  Bringing IHL Home: Guidelines on the National Implementation of International Humanitarian Law, Geneva, May 2021, at: https://bit.ly/3u3FVyt.
  'Colombia: ICRC Deplores Improper Use of Red Cross Emblem', News Release 08/139, Geneva, 6 August 2008, at: https://bit.ly/3z5AAqb.
  'Draft Rules for the Limitation of the Dangers incurred by the Civilian Population in Time of War. ICRC, 1956', at: https://bit.ly/31DEDyv.
  Explosive Weapons With Wide Area Effects: A Deadly Choice in Populated Areas, Geneva, January 2022, at: https://bit.ly/3H6VBo9.
  'Geneva Conventions (Consolidation) Act—Model Law', Legal factsheet, 31 August 2008', available at: https://bit.ly/3vmSe7x.
  'How Is the Term "Armed Conflict" Defined in International Humanitarian Law?', ICRC Opinion Paper, March 2008.
  How Does Law Protect in War, 'Armed Groups', ICRC Online Case book, at: https://bit.ly/3J7lRiV.
  'ICRC, Advisory Services on International Humanitarian Law', *How Does Law Protect in War*, at: https://bit.ly/3n2H1pd.
  'International Committee of the Red Cross (ICRC) Position on Autonomous Weapon Systems: ICRC Position and Background Paper', *International Review of the Red Cross*, Vol. 102, No. 915 (2020), 1335–49.
  International Humanitarian Law and the Challenges of Contemporary Armed Conflicts, Report for the 32nd International Conference of the Red Cross and Red Crescent, Geneva, October 2015.
  'Internment in Armed Conflict: Basic Rules and Challenges', Opinion Paper, Geneva, November 2014.
  'International Humanitarian Law in Domestic Law', Article, 1 January 2015, at: https://bit.ly/3vo3YXB.
  'Memorandum, The ICRC's Privilege of Non-Disclosure of Confidential Information', *International Review of the Red Cross*, Vol. 97, Nos. 897/898 (2016).
  Missing Persons, at: https://bit.ly/3rNYV1n.
  'Model Geneva Conventions Act (for Common Law States)', 21 February 2003, at: https://bit.ly/3jbXINK.
  National Implementation Database, at: https://bit.ly/3H8uZTK.
  'Second Protocol to the Hague Convention of 1954 for the Protection of Cultural Property in the Event of Armed Conflict. The Hague, 26 March 1999', at: http://bit.ly/2NK9Dmb.
  Statutes of the International Committee of the Red Cross, adopted on 21 December 2017, available at: https://bit.ly/3FXjL3f.
  Study on the Use of the Emblems, Geneva, 2009, at: https://bit.ly/34ePK1J.
  The Domestic Implementation of International Humanitarian Law: A Manual, Geneva, 2015, at: https://bit.ly/3ARPP6f.
  The ICRC, Its Mission, Its Work, Geneva, 2009, at: https://bit.ly/3KCNTVa, p. 3.
  'The International Committee and the Vietnam Conflict', *International Review of the Red Cross*, Vol. 6, No. 65 (1966), 399–418.
  The International Committee of the Red Cross's (ICRC's) Role in Situations of Violence below the Threshold of Armed Conflict, Policy document, February 2014, *International Review of the Red Cross*, Vol. 96, No. 893 (2014).
  The Roots of Restraint in War, Report, Geneva, 2020, available at: https://bit.ly/3uutEmR.
  The SIrUS Project: Towards a Determination of Which Weapons Cause 'Superfluous Injury or Unnecessary Suffering, Geneva, 1997.

'What Is the ICRC's Role in Developing and Ensuring Respect for IHL?', ICRC Blog, 14 August 2017, at: https://bit.ly/343XAuN.

Lawand, K. with R. Coupland and P. Herby

A Guide to the Legal Review of New Weapons, Means and Methods of Warfare, Measures to Implement Article 36 of Additional Protocol I of 1977, ICRC, Geneva, January 2006.

Sandoz, Y.

'The International Committee of the Red Cross as Guardian of International Humanitarian Law', 31 December 1998, available at: https://bit.ly/3e4rr7a.

United Nations documents

Basic Principles on the Use of Force and Firearms by Law Enforcement Officials; adopted by the Eighth UN Congress on the Prevention of Crime and the Treatment of Offenders at Havana, 27 August to 7 September 1990.

'Capital Punishment and the Implementation of the Safeguards Guaranteeing Protection of the Rights of Those Facing the Death Penalty: Yearly Supplement of the Secretary-General to his Quinquennial Report on Capital Punishment', 2015.

Committee on the Rights of the Child

General Comment No. 24 (2019) on Children's Rights in the Child Justice System, UN doc. CRC/C/GC/24, 18 September 2019 (reissued for technical reasons on 11 November 2019).

Conflict-Related Sexual Violence, Report of the UN Secretary General, UN doc. S/2019/280, 29 March 2019.

Conflict-Related Sexual Violence, Report of the UN Secretary-General, UN doc. S/2020/487, 3 June 2020.

Department of Peace Operations (DPO), *DPO Policy on The Protection of Civilians in United Nations Peacekeeping*, UN DPO Ref. 2019.17, 1 November 2019.

'Draft International Covenants on Human Rights', UN doc. A/2929, 1 July 1955.

Human Rights Committee

General Comment No. 36: Article 6: Right to Life, UN doc. CCPR/C/GC/36, 3 September 2019.

General Comment No. 35: Article 9 (Liberty and Security of Person), UN doc. CCPR/C/GC/35, 16 December 2014.

General Comment No. 29 on States of Emergency (Article 4 of the ICCPR), UN doc. CCPR/C/21/Rev.1/Add.11, 31 August 2001.

'Impact of Armed Conflict on Children', UN doc. A/51/306, 26 August 1996.

Independent International Commission of Inquiry on the Syrian Arab Republic

Sieges as a Weapon of War: Encircle, starve, surrender, evacuate, Paper, 29 May 2018, at: https://bit.ly/3vKX1Qi.

Integrated Disarmament, Demobilization and Reintegration Standards (IDDRS)

Standard 5.30: Children and DDR, 1 August 2006.

International Law Commission (ILC)

Draft Conclusions on Peremptory Norms of General International Law (*Jus Cogens*), adopted by the ILC on first reading, in UN doc. A/74/10, 2019.

Text of the draft principles on protection of the environment in relation to armed conflicts, adopted by the Commission on first reading, in UN doc. A/74/10, 2019.

Draft articles on Prevention and Punishment of Crimes Against Humanity, with commentaries, in UN doc. A/74/10, 2019.

'Fourth report on peremptory norms of general international law (*jus cogens*) by Dire Tladi, Special Rapporteur', UN doc. A/CN.4/727, 31 January 2019.

Draft articles on the responsibility of international organizations, adopted by the ILC at its sixty-third session, in 2011, and submitted to the UN General Assembly as a part of the Commission's report covering the work of that session, in UN doc. A/66/10, at: http://bit.ly/2YOKPz7.

Note of 12 October 2009 by Ms Patricia O'Brien, Under-Secretary-General for Legal Affairs and UN Legal Counsel, OLA, to Mr Alain Le Roy, Under Secretary-General for Peacekeeping Operations.

Observance by United Nations Forces of International Humanitarian Law, Secretary-General's Bulletin, UN doc. ST/SGB/1999/13, 6 August 1999.

OCHA
   Global Humanitarian Overview 2021, New York, 2021, available at: https://bit.ly/2ZXDGQ4.
   'Explosive Weapons in Populated Areas', at: https://bit.ly/2UFDzXf.

Office of the High Commissioner for Human Rights (OHCHR),
   'The United Nations Independent International Commission of Inquiry on the Occupied Palestinian Territory, including East Jerusalem, and in Israel', at: https://bit.ly/3DbvPhh.

Office of the Special Representative of the Secretary-General for Children and Armed Conflict
   'Global Coalition for Reintegration of Child Soldiers', undated but accessed 1 March 2021 at: http://bit.ly/3l0xiOQ.

Principles and Guidelines on Children Associated with Armed Forces or Armed Groups (Paris Principles), Paris, February 2007.

'Question of the Possible Accession of Intergovernmental Organizations to the Geneva Conventions for the Protection of War Victims', Legal Opinion issued by the UN Office of Legal Affairs to the Under-Secretary- General for Special Political Affairs on 15 June 1972, reproduced in *United Nations Juridical Yearbook 1972,* UN doc. ST/LEG/SER.C/10, 1972, at: https://bit.ly/2OEKqgO, 153–54.

Protection of Civilians in Armed Conflict, Report of the Secretary-General, UN doc. S/2020/366, 6 May 2020, available at: https://bit.ly/3HyipxB.

Report of the detailed findings of the independent international Commission of inquiry on the protests in the Occupied Palestinian Territory, UN doc. A/HRC/40/CRP.2, 18 March 2019.

Report of the Independent International Commission of Inquiry on the Syrian Arab Republic, UN doc. A/HRC/27/60, 13 August 2014.

Report of the Independent International Commission of Inquiry on the Syrian Arab Republic, UN doc. A/HRC/46/54, 21 January 2021.

Report of the Special Rapporteur on Extrajudicial, Summary or Arbitrary Executions, Christof Heyns, UN doc. A/HRC/26/36, 1 April 2014.

Report of the Special Rapporteur on Extrajudicial, Summary or Arbitrary Executions, Philip Alston, Addendum, UN doc. A/HRC/14/24/Add.6, 28 May 2010.

Report of the Special Rapporteur on Extrajudicial, Summary or Arbitrary Executions, UN doc. A/HRC/23/47, 9 April 2013.

Report of the UN Secretary-General on the Protection of Civilians in Armed Conflicts, UN doc. S/2021/423, May 2021.

Report of the Working Group on Arbitrary Detention, 'Deliberation No. 9 Concerning the Definition and Scope of Arbitrary Deprivation of Liberty under Customary International Law', UN doc. A/HRC/22/44, 24 December 2012.

'The United Nations Security Council Counter-Terrorism Committee', at: http://bit.ly/2EdkvHq.

The Minnesota Protocol on the Investigation of Potentially Unlawful Death (2016), Office of the United Nations High Commissioner for Human Rights, New York/Geneva, 2017, at: https://bit.ly/3aH8Yh7.

UN Protection Cluster
   Protection Analysis Report, Protection Sector North-East, June 2021.

UNAMA
   Protection of Civilians in Armed Conflict, Annual Report 2020, Kabul, February 2021, at: https://bit.ly/3eoqMjh.

UN Assistance Mission for Iraq (UNAMI) and OHCHR
   Report on the Protection of Civilians in the context of the Ninewa Operations and the retaking of Mosul City, 17 October 2016–10 July 2017, Baghdad, 2017, at: https://bit.ly/3hXp2hi.

UNICEF
   State of the World's Children: Children with Disabilities, 2013.

United Nations Human Rights Guidance on Less-Lethal Weapons in Law Enforcement, Geneva, 2020, at: http://bit.ly/367c0ac.

Voices of Survivors of Conflict-Related Sexual Violence and Service-Providers, Office of the Special Representative of the Secretary-General on Sexual Violence in Conflict, New York, September 2021, at: https://bit.ly/3nMcwny.

Blog Entries, Online Articles and Press Releases

AFP
'"Roof Knocking": Israel Warning System under Scrutiny in Gaza Conflict', *France24*, 20 May 2021, at: https://bit.ly/3B4pke9.

Aid Worker Security Database
'Major Attacks on Aid Workers: Summary Statistics', Last updated 3 January 2022, at: https://bit.ly/3AsUsoD.

Albright, D., P. Brannan, and C. Walrond
'Did Stuxnet Take Out 1,000 Centrifuges at the Natanz Enrichment Plant? Preliminary Assessment', Report, Institute for Science and International Security, 22 December 2010, at: https://bit.ly/3qW5m1J.

Ali, I.
'US Strike on Afghan Hospital in 2015 Not a War Crime: Pentagon', Reuters Canada, 29 April 2016, at: https://reut.rs/3mplwjw.

'All Helmet and No Mettle: The UN's Peacekeepers Are under Pressure to Quit Congo', *The Economist*, 3 September 2020, at: http://econ.st/3bWq4Xy.

Amnesty International, 'South Sudan's Man-Made Hunger Crisis', February 2016, at: https://bit.ly/3CQfIF1.

Arnold, Maj. T. D. and Maj. Nicolas Fiore
'Five Operational Lessons from the Battle for Mosul', *Military Review*, January–February 2019, at: https://bit.ly/3kmFQRE, p. 58.

Associated Press
'Red Cross: Colombia Lied about Using Emblem', NBC News, 6 August 2008, at: https://nbcnews.to/3sw49yF.

Avedian, L.
'Armenian POWs Stand Trial', *The Armenian Weekly*, 30 June 2021, at: https://bit.ly/3AJoTFP.

Azerbaijan State Security Service
'Joint Information of the Press Services of the State Security Service and the Prosecutor General's Office', 10 June 2021, at: https://bit.ly/3g1GaCr.

BBC
'"Eating Grass to Survive" in Besieged Homs', 27 January 2014, at: http://bbc.in/3f4JfSi.
'How the Battle for Mosul Unfolded', 10 July 2017.
'Profile: Hamas Palestinian Movement', at: https://bbc.in/3osCygQ.

Blume, R.
'The 'Children and Armed Conflict' Report on Grave Violations Is Vital in Protecting Children, and Here's Why', *War Child*, 26 June 2018, at: http://bit.ly/32mLWX6.

Brauman, R.
'Médecins Sans Frontières and the ICRC: Matters of Principle', *Crash*, 2013, at: https://bit.ly/3qTuirO.

Bright, A.
'India Uses Death Penalty: 5 other Places Where It's Legal But Rare', *Christian Science Monitor*, 29 August 2012, at: http://bit.ly/325oxLY.

Christou, E.
'What Caused the Siege of Sarajevo and Why Did It Last So Long?', *History Hit*, 4 July 2019, at: http://bit.ly/3923Bbj.

Clemmer, C.
'Beyond The Definition: What Does "Sexual And Gender Based Violence" Really Mean?', *WeWillSpeakOut.US*, at: http://bit.ly/399Zhaq.

'Coalition "Failing to Protect Civilians" in Mosul', Forces.net, 28 March 2017, at: https://bit.ly/3zJdu8q.
Commentary on the Guidelines for Protecting Schools and Universities from Military Use During Armed Conflict, at: http://bit.ly/2m6212t.

Conte, A.
'The UK Court of Appeal in Serdar Mohammed: Treaty and Customary IHL Provides No Authority for Detention in Non-international Armed Conflicts', *EJIL: Talk!*, 6 August 2015, at: http://bit.ly/3gHWozG.

Cornell Center on the Death Penalty Worldwide
'Pregnant Women', Last updated 25 January 2012, no longer available online.

Cox, B. L.
'Five Years On: Military Accountability and the Attack on the MSF Trauma Center in Kunduz', *Just Security*, 3 October 2020, at: https://bit.ly/3mjZGhg.

Crown Prosecution Service
'Homicide: Murder and Manslaughter', Legal Guidance, Last updated 18 March 2019, at: https://bit.ly/3o8Wrqh.

Cushman, J. H.
'Appeals Court Overturn Terrorism Conviction of Bin Laden's Driver', *The New York Times*, 16 October 2012.

Dunlap, C.
'No, the Law of War Does Not Always Require the Use of Precision Munitions—and That's a Good Thing for the US', *Lawfare*, 25 February 2016, at: http://bit.ly/2Oocelt.

'Ethiopia Is Deliberately Starving Its Own Citizens', *The Economist*, 9 October 2021.

Euronews with AFP
'German IS Bride Jailed in One of World's First Trials for War Crimes against Yazidis', Euronews, Updated 25 October 2021, at: https://bit.ly/3mDRmIX.

Fabricius, P.
'Asking the Right Questions about the Force Intervention Brigade', Institute for Security Studies, 21 August 2020, at: http://bit.ly/3r1sLgn.

Feith, D.
'Law in the Service of Terror—the Strange Case of the Additional Protocol', *National Interest*, Vol. 1 (1985), 36–47.

Felbab-Brown, V.
'Nonstate Armed Actors in 2022: Alive and Powerful in the New Geopolitics', *Brookings*, 1 February 2022, at: https://brook.gs/3HvrIOQ.

Fortin, K.
'Unilateral Declaration by Polisario Under API Accepted by Swiss Federal Council', 2 September 2015, at: http://bit.ly/2NcA0lb.
'Civilian Wings Of Armed Groups: Included Within the Concept of "Non-State Party" under IHL?' under IHL?' in Armed Groups and International Law blog, 13 October 2020, at: https://bit.ly/3osBGJl.

Gannon, K.
'Pakistan, Saudis, UAE Join US–Taliban Talks', *AP News*, 17 December 2018, at: http://bit.ly/2y9tMtO.

Gardner, F.
'Afghanistan Airport Attack: Who Are IS-K?', BBC, 27 August 2021, at: https://bbc.in/3yjS7tz.

Gettleman, J.
'U.N. Told Not to Join Congo Army in Operation', *The New York Times*, 9 December 2009, at: http://nyti.ms/35FVsYZ.
'German IS Bride Sentenced to 10 Years in Prison for Fatal Neglect of Yazidi Girl', *France24*, 25 October 2021, at: https://bit.ly/3GMDjcg.

Giampietro, R.
'The Red Crystal', 2005, at: https://bit.ly/2WB6xIS.

Giegerich, T.

'Retorsion', *Max Planck Encyclopedias of International Law*, Last updated September 2020, at: http://bit.ly/2OZc5c7.

Global Coalition to Protect Education from Attack (GCPEA),
'The Safe Schools Declaration', 2020, at: http://bit.ly/2TDzWy3.

Global Coalition for Reintegration of Child Soldiers
'Improving Support to Child Reintegration: Summary of Findings from Three Reports', New York, 2020, at: https://bit.ly/2OfMjjF.

Goodman, R.
'Clear Error in the Defense Department's Law of War Manual: On Presumptions of Civilian Status', *Just Security*, 9 February 2022, at: https://bit.ly/3Lz9Apu.

Heller, K. J.
'Bad Criminal Law in the Alexander Blackman Case (With Addendum)', *Opinio Juris*, 31 March 2017, at: https://bit.ly/2XZDMpR.

Hiemstra, H. and V. Murphy
'GCIII Commentary: I'm a Woman and a POW in a Pandemic. What Does the Third Geneva Convention Mean for Me?', ICRC Blog, 8 December 2020, at: http://bit.ly/3f5bVuz.

Horowitz, J.
'Joint Blog Series: Precautionary Measures in Urban Warfare: A Commander's Obligation to Obtain Information', ICRC Joint Blog Series, 10 January 2019, at: https://bit.ly/383cQqT.

Human Rights Watch
'Azerbaijan: Armenian POWs Abused in Custody', 19 March 2021, at: https://bit.ly/3iRw2hv.
'Shocking War Crimes in Sierra Leone. New Testimonies on Mutilation, Rape of Civilians', 24 June 1999, at: http://bit.ly/3bcqDOy.

Iaria, A.
'E-Emblems: Protective Emblems and the Legal Challenges of Cyber Warfare', Instituto Affari Internazionali, 18 June 2018, at: https://bit.ly/3qHLXBp.

'Is It Time for "Ecocide" to Become an International Crime?', *The Economist*, 28 February 2021, at: http://econ.st/3crovS9.

Jones, C.
'"Almost Divine Power": the Lawyers who Sign Off who Lives and who DIES in Modern War Zones', *The Conversation*, 12 May 2021, at: https://bit.ly/3n5Mbke.

Katz, Y.
'How the IDF Invented "Roof Knocking", the Tactic that Saves Lives in Gaza', *The Jerusalem Post*, 25 March 2021, at: https://bit.ly/3z9OVlb.

Keane, F.
'UN Promises to Stamp Out Abuse after Child Rape Allegations', BBC, 24 February 2017, at: http://bbc.in/3cOtMTI.

Kucera, J.
'Post-war Report: Armenia Accuses Azerbaijan of Dragging Feet on POWs", *EurasiaNet*, 5 March 2021, at: https://bit.ly/3sk5eta.
'Prisoners of the Caucasus: Post-War Report', *EurasiaNet*, 23 April 2021, at: https://bit.ly/3z0tYsU.

Lattimer, M.
'Can Incidental Starvation of Civilians be Lawful under IHL?', *EJIL: Talk!*, 26 March 2019, at: https://bit.ly/3x1rtWh.

McCormack, T.
'Negotiating the Two Additional Protocols of 1977: Interview with the Right Honourable Sir Kenneth Keith' in S. Linton, T. McCormack, and S Sivakumaran (eds.), *Asia-Pacific Perspectives on International Humanitarian Law*, Cambridge University Press, Cambridge, 18 October 2019, 17–35, at: https://bit.ly/3Ga4gpF.

Mack, M. with J. Pejic,
Increasing Respect for International Humanitarian Law In non-International Armed Conflicts, ICRC, 2008.

Mapping Militant Organizations
'Riyadus-Salikhin Reconnaissance and Sabotage Battalion of Chechen Martyrs', Center for International Security and Cooperation (CISAC), Stanford University, Last modified August 2018, at: http://stanford.io/321r8F1.

Michaels, J.
'Iraqi Forces in Mosul See Deadliest Urban Combat Since World War II', *USA Today*, 29 March 2017, at: https://bit.ly/3klGxea.

Mirasola, C.
'Last Week in the Military Commissions, 12/4-12/8: Was There an Armed Conflict Pre-9/11?', Lawfare, 14 December 2017, at: https://bit.ly/3AEl0Dq.

Morris, S.
'Alexander Blackman Shoots Wounded Taliban Fighter—Transcript', *The Guardian*, 15 March 2017, at: https://bit.ly/3nCZQiM.
'Marine A, Who Killed Wounded Taliban Fighter, Released from Prison', *The Guardian*, 28 April 2017, at: https://bit.ly/3kdirQK.

MSF
Initial MSF Internal Review: Attack on Kunduz Trauma Centre, Afghanistan', November 2015.

Mundy, M.
'The Strategies of the Coalition in the Yemen War: Aerial Bombardment and Food War', World Peace Foundation, 2018, available at: https://bit.ly/3wjnyEH.

Nebehay, S.
'Islamic State Using Tens of Thousands as Human Shields in Mosul: U.N.', *Reuters*, 28 October 2016, at: https://reut.rs/2UK9GVy.

Norton-Taylor, R.
'Serb TV Station Was Legitimate Target, Says Blair', *The Guardian*, 24 April 1999, at: http://bit.ly/3692RwJ.

'New Power Plant Opens in Massawa', *The New Humanitarian*, 28 March 2003, at: http://bit.ly/2Rd8QfQ.

'News Transcript: Department of Defense Press Briefing by Army General Joseph Votel, commander, US Central Command, Press Operations, Army General Joseph Votel, commander, US Central Command', 29 April 2016.

O'Rourke, C.
'Geneva Convention III Commentary: What Significance for Women's Rights?', *Just Security*, 21 October 2020, at: http://bit.ly/3gFMKxz.

OHCHR
'Status Report: OHCHR Project supporting the G5 Sahel Joint Force with Implementation of the Human Rights and International Humanitarian Law Compliance Framework 1 May 2018–31 March 2020', accessed 1 January 2022 at: https://bit.ly/3qVHU6b.

Olsen, F. R.
'The Use of Police Firearms in Denmark', Copenhagen, 2008, at: http://bit.ly/3tDKJXN.

Pannier, B.
'First Firefight: Turkmen, Taliban Engage in Border Shoot-Out', *Ghandara*, 5 January 2022, at: https://bit.ly/3qNuVC6.

Pejic, J., I. Herbert, and T. Rodenhäuser
'ICRC Engagement with Non-State Armed Groups: Why and How', *Humanitarian Law and Policy Blog*, 4 March 2021, at: https://bit.ly/3AtaBKw.

Penhaul, K.
'Colombian Military Used Red Cross Emblem in Rescue', *CNN*, 6 August 2008, at: https://cnn.it/3AZ5PDE.
'Uribe: Betancourt Rescuers Used Red Cross', *CNN*, 16 July 2008, at: https://cnn.it/3pHSpJs.

Pileggi, T.
'Red Cross Asked to Expel MDA over Emblem Violation', *Times of Israel*, 20 September 2015, at: https://bit.ly/3EK09z1.

Pribbenow, M.
- 'Treatment of American POWs in North Vietnam', Research Paper, Cold War International History Project, Wilson Center, Washington, D.C., at: http://bit.ly/340NTuj.

Radio Free Europe/Radio Liberty
- 'Azerbaijan, Armenia Swap Prisoners as Part of Nagorno-Karabakh Truce Deal', 14 December 2020, at: http://bit.ly/3ndXbd6.
- 'Which Countries Have Troops In Afghanistan?', 21 December 2018, at: https://bit.ly/3zo9URz.

Report on Deadly German-Ordered Air Raid in Kunduz is Inconclusive', *Deutsche Welle*, 28 October 2011, http://bit.ly/3011y2l.

Reuters
- 'Fears Grow of New Western Sahara War between Morocco and Polisario Front', 13 November 2020, at: http://reut.rs/2Wdk5Xm.

Riedel, B.
- 'Saudi Arabia and the UAE Consolidating Strategic Positions in Yemen's East and Islands', The Brookings Institution, Washington, D.C., 28 May 2021, at: https://brook.gs/3yiQpIW.

Rosenberg, C.
- 'Pandemic Delays Start of 9/11 Trial Past 20th Anniversary of Attacks', *The New York Times*, 18 December 2020, at: http://nyti.ms/3s9kM1V.
- 'Trial Guide: The Sept. 11 Case at Guantánamo Bay', *The New York Times*, 3 December 2021, at: https://nyti.ms/3zhn3wt.
- 'Trial for Men Accused of Plotting 9/11 Attacks Is Set for 2021', *The New York Times*, 30 August 2019, at: http://nyti.ms/3q2pEoo.

Ruperez, J.
- 'The United Nations in the Fight Against Terrorism', January 2006, at: http://bit.ly/3h8XHqH.

Sabbagh, D.
- 'Lawyers to Submit Yemen War Crimes Dossier to UK Police', *The Guardian*, 20 October 2021, at: https://bit.ly/2Z98AFj.

Siddique, H.
- 'Legal Experts Worldwide Draw Up "Historic" Definition of Ecocide', *The Guardian*, 22 June 2021, at: https://bit.ly/3wDMWUu.

Stop Ecocide Foundation
- 'Top International Lawyers to Draft Definition of 'Ecocide'', undated but accessed 1 March 2021, at: http://bit.ly/3rHyrx5.

'Syria's War: Aleppo Residents "10 Days from Starvation"', *Aljazeera*, 25 November 2016, at: https://bit.ly/3vIqc6j.

Swissinfo.ch
- 'People from Western Sahara Deemed Stateless in Switzerland', 20 August 2021, at: https://bit.ly/3yoQqLe.

Syria Justice and Accountability Centre
- 'One Year after Banning the Practice, the SDF Is Still Recruiting Children', 23 July 2020, at: https://bit.ly/3fFvx87.

'The Protection of Human Rights in Humanitarian Crises', Joint Background Paper by OHCHR and UNHCR IASC Principals, 8 May 2013, available at: https://bit.ly/3ArSNiX.

'The Unspeakable Truth about Slavery in Mauritania', *The Guardian*, 8 June 2018, at: http://bit.ly/2Jrgjqd.

The White House, Office of the Press Secretary, 'Government Assessment of the Syrian Government's Use of Chemical Weapons on August 21, 2013', Press release, 30 August 2013, at: https://bit.ly/3xtIdos.

'UN Warns Mosul Civilians in Grave Danger', Forces.net, 27 May 2017, at: https://bit.ly/2VhrOpN.

'United Nations Security Council Condemns Nuclear Tests by India and Pakistan', 6 June 1998, at: http://bit.ly/2VVO0EU.

'UN again Blacklists Saudi-led forces for Yemen Child Killings. Coalition Blacklisted for Third Year over Killing and Wounding of 729 Children but Critics Say Measure Is Not Enough', *Aljazeera*, 28 July 2019, at: http://bit.ly/2w0rM9r.

UNICEF
'Education under Attack', 18 February 2021, at: http://uni.cf/3bvd7oO.
UNICEF UK,
'15 Children Associated With Armed Forces, Released in South Sudan', 26 February 2020, at: http://bit.ly/3melWpg.
United States Library of Congress
'The SIrUS Project: Towards a Determination of Which Weapons Cause "Superfluous Injury or Unnecessary Suffering"', 16 July 2010, at: http://bit.ly/34U0MEO.
van Wilgenburg, W.
'Syrian Democratic Forces', European Council on Foreign Relations, at: https://bit.ly/35InW6u.
Zelada, S.
'A Controversial Emblem', ICRC blog cross-files, 21 April 2021, available at: https://bit.ly/342urjI.

Diplomatic Records

Elements of Crimes under the Rome Statute of the International Criminal Court, reproduced from *Official Records of the Assembly of States Parties to the Rome Statute of the International Criminal Court*, First Session, New York, 3–10 September 2002.

Official Records of the Diplomatic Conference on the Reaffirmation and Development of International Humanitarian Law Applicable in Armed Conflicts, Geneva (1974–1977), Vol. IV, at: https://bit.ly/3zAkJAZ.

Final Record of the Diplomatic Conference of Geneva of 1949, Bern, 1949.

Index

For the benefit of digital users, indexed terms that span two pages (e.g., 52–53) may, on occasion, appear on only one of those pages.

9/11 attacks 1.30, 1.31, 1.32, 13.4, 13.30, 13.31, 19.33

actus reus 2.9, 2.16, 2.24, 3.11, 4.8, 4.11, 9.35, 10.23, 10.24, 19.5, 19.9, 19.12, 19.14, 19.15
Afghanistan 1.2, 1.31, 1.32, 1.45, 1.46, 1.49, 2.11, 4.33, 5.28, 5.29, 6.28, 9.42, 10.12, 10.13, 11.10, 12.19, 16.26, 19.21, 20.16
African Commission on Human and Peoples' Rights 2.8
African National Congress (ANC) 0.4
African Union (AU) 1.22, 10.28
Aggression 1.10, 1.15, 18.2, 19.2
Akande, Dapo 6.14, 14.24, 18.6, 18.9
Aleppo 14.18
All necessary measures 4.7, 16.1, 16.4, 18.12
al-Qaeda 1.30, 1.31, 1.32, 6.28, 13.30, 13.31
al-Shabaab 6.28
American Civil War 12.9
Amnesty International 6.21, 11.20, 12.35
Anti-personnel mines 5.24, 12.44, 15.28, 18.18
Apartheid 2.21
Armed non-State actors (ANSAs) *See* Non-State armed groups
Armenia 1.10, 1.14, 5.43, 5.44, 5.45
Autonomous weapons 12.46 – 12.47
Azerbaijan 1.10, 1.14, 5.43, 5.44, 5.45

Barrel bombs 13.14
Belgium 5.27, 4.40, 8.22, 11.5, 12.19
Biological weapons 12.38–12.39
Blackman, Alexander 2.11, 19.21
Blackwater 5.39
Bombardment 1.15, 8.39, 8.43, 10.42, 11.17, 12.34, 13.13, 13.14, 13.15, 14.7, 14.10, 14.12, 15.19
Boothby, William 12.12, 12.58
Bosnia and Herzegovina 8.12, 8.13, 9.26, 13.21, 14.14, 14.16
Bradley, Martha 1.40, 1.43
Brazil 0.12, 4.29
Brunei 5.9

Burkina Faso 0.12
Burma *see* Myanmar
Burundi 3.22

Canada 0.12, 8.7, 12.7, 12.8, 12.38, 13.29
Central African Republic 18.22
Central Tracing Agency 20.10
Chemical weapons, use of 1.13, 5.23, 12.40
Child (see also Children)
   Soldiers 4.4–4.31, 4.40, 9.19
Children **4.1–4.48**
   and the death penalty 4.46–4.47
   with disabilities 4.38–4.39
   Protection of 11.26
Chile 20.21
China 1.10, 4.29, 4.40, 5.9, 5.28, 12.17, 12.43
Churchill, Winston 12.33
Circular error probable (CEP) 8.30, 8.31
Civilian object **8.1–8.49**, 12.49, 12.57, 14.6, 14.12, 14.14, 15.19, 15.24, 15.29, 16.23, 18.17, 19.12
   Definition 8.3–8.20
Civilians **9.1–9.44**
   Definition 9.19
   Direct attack on 9.37, 12.29, 19.11
   In the power of the enemy 0.3, 1.42, 2.34, 5.31, 8.34, 13.11, 15.19, 15.20, 19.18, 19.33
Clapham, Andrew 1.22, 1.40, 5.1, 5.56, 17.11
Cluster munition 8.30, 12.6, 12.28, 12.60, 18.18
Collective punishments 2.4, **2.25–2.28**, 13.11
Combatant **9.1–9.44**
   Definition 9.6–9.18
Combatant's privilege 2.33, 5.1, 5.16
Commission on Human Rights 4.41
Committee on the Rights of the Child 4.31, 4.41
Continuous combat function 9.14–9.19, 9.44
Corn, Geoffrey 5.29, 17.25, 17.30
Coupland, Robin 12.21
Crawford, Emily 1.41, 1.49, 5.36, 5.37, 17.25
Crimes against humanity 3.9, 3.13, 3.14, 3.15, 4.18, 13.7, 14.14, 16.11, 19.2
   Definition 3.13
Croatia 8.8, 8.43

334 INDEX

Cultural objects, special protection of 8.39–8.45
Cyber operations 12.47–12.48
Czechia 0.12, 1.46, 12.19, 12.39

Darcy, Shane 15.1
Darfur 18.8
Democratic Republic of Congo 4.12, 6.23, 6.31, 9.28, 18.2, 18.11, 18.12, 18.14, 18.22, 18.23
Denial of quarter 2.12–2.13
Dinstein, Yoram 1.38, 1.40, 2.12, 2.21, 2.27, 2.29, 2.30, 5.36, 8.5, 8.6, 8.15, 8.18, 8.46, 8.47, 9.19, 8.18, 10.19, 11.31, 12.53, 13.11, 13.13, 15.34, 16.20, 16.23
Direct participation in hostilities 4.15, 4.17, 4.21, 4.22, 4.29, 5.1, 5.16, 5.19, 9.14, **9.38–9.43**, 9.44
Disarmament law 1.6
Dissemination, duty of 1.4, 1.5, **16.13–16.16**
Doswald-Beck, Louise 15.23
Duffy, Helen 1.30, 1.31, 8.1
Dunant, Henry 20.1
Duty to investigate 16.24–16.27
Duty to prosecute 2.30, 16.1, 16.10, 16.24, 19.4
Duty to respect and ensure respect 1.7, 1.19, 16.4, 16.17

Education 4.35, 4.36
Educational establishments, protection of 4.37
Effective control test 1.18, 1.19
Elderly (see also Older persons) 10.19, 11.26
Environmental protection 10.38–10.46, 12.
Eritrea 5.41, 8.16, 15.14, 15.15
Eritrea-Ethiopia Claims Commission 5.41, 8.16
Ethiopia 5.41, 8.16
European Court of Human Rights 9.13, 10.12, 13.35, 16.26, 16.31
Expanding bullets 12.18, 12.23
Exploding bullets 8.23, 9.20, 12.23
Explosive weapons in populated areas 10.47, 11.32

Fair trial, right of 2.31–2.33
Fajr-5109 rockets 12.35
Ferencz, Benjamin 13.7
Firearms 5.22, 13.39
First shot theory 1.12
First World War 2.25, 10.42, 12.50
Fortin, Katharine 1.22, 6.2, 17.4, 17.23
France 1.46, 4.29, 5.27, 8.7, 8.47, 9.6, 10.14, 10.42, 14.21, 15.30
Fundamental guarantees **2.1–2.35**, 3.4, 5.13, 5.30, 5.51, 15.31
Furundžija, Anto 2.18

Gaggioli, Gloria 15.33
Galić, Stanislav 9.26, 13.20
Gaza 8.30, 9.15, 11.18, 11.20, 11.22, 12.35, 13.15
Geneva Academy of International Humanitarian Law and Human Rights 12.44, 16.16, 16.28
Geneva Call 7.22
Genocide 3.17, 19.2
Georgia 1.10, 1.46, 9.9
Guatemala 0.12

Hamas 17.19
Heffes, Ezequiel 16.2, 17.3, 17.24
Heller, Kevin Jon 2.9, 2.11
Hospitals, special protection of 6.27, 7.5, 8.2, **8.34–8.38**, 10.17, 14.12
Hostage taking **2.29–2.30**, 13.35, 13.37, 15.17, 18.19
Humanitarian personnel, protection of 6.23–6.27
Humanity, principle of 2.26, 6.28, 10.10, 15.31
Human Rights Committee 2.8, 5.9, 5.13, 13.34, 13.41
Human Rights Council 4.41, 11.19, 11.22, 12.35
Human Rights Watch 5.44, 13.9
Human shields 2.29, 4.15, 4.31, 11.29
Humane treatment, duty of 5.13–5.14, 5.47, 5.51–5.56, 11.16

Immunity from attack, loss of see Direct participation in hostilities
Impartiality, principle of 6.28, 6.30, 20.24
India 0.7, 4.29, 5.12, 5.36, 12.58, 13.29
Indiscriminate attack 8.24, 9.3, 9.22, **9.32–9.37**, 10.9, 10.11, 10.23, 10.24, 10.28, 10.47, 12.25, 12.26, 12.29, 12.30, 12.31, 12.36, 12.46, 12.57, 13.19, 14.14, 19.10, 19.12, 19.13, 19.15
Inherently indiscriminate weapons 12.25–12.
Inter-American Court of Human Rights 3.14, 9.18, 11.16
Internally displaced persons (IDPs) 3.21, 6.1
International Committee of the Red Cross (ICRC) 0.13, 1.7, 1.25, 1.27, 1.39, 1.48, 2.2, 2.9, 2.22, 2.27, 2.29, 3.1, 3.6, 3.7, 4.4, 4.5, 4.6, 4.7, 4.9, 4.10, 4.24, 4.36, 4.47, 5.11, 5.15, 5.16, 5.21, 5.22, 5.24, 5.26, 5.29, 5.30, 5.31, 5.37, 5.40, 5.43, 5.46, 5.47, 5.49, 5.50, 5.55, 6.9, 6.12, 6.14, 6.17, 7.9, 7.14, 7.20, 7.31, 8.6, 8.7, 8.21, 8.25, 8.46, 9.8, 9.13, 9.14, 9.19, 9.30, 9.39, 9.41, 10.7, 10.9, 10.16, 10.19, 10.25, 10.26, 10.27, 10.28, 10.39, 10.47, 11.2, 11.13, 11.17, 11.23, 12.6, 12.8, 12.18, 12.19,

INDEX

12.20, 12.21, 12.22, 12.23, 12.24, 12.31,
12.34, 12.37, 12.40, 12.43, 12.44, 12.45,
12.49, 12.51, 12.55, 12.57, 12.59, 13.11,
13.12, 13.13, 14.3, 14.21, 15.2, 15.6, 15.7,
15.12, 15.13, 15.14, 15.16, 15.20, 15.21,
15.23, 15.25, 15.26, 16.2, 16.4, 16.6, 16.7,
16.8, 16.12, 16.14, 16.17, 16.19, 16.20,
16.21, 16.28, 16.29, 16.31, 18.1, 18.14,
19.3, 19.13, 19.14, 19.19, 19.24, 19.25,
19.26, 19.27, 19.28, **20.1–20.30**

Customary IHL study
Rule 1 9.30, 11.8, 13.2, 14.7
  Rule 2 13.3, 13.12
  Rule 3 9.6, 9.13
  Rule 5 9.19
  Rule 6 9.43
  Rule 7 8.32, 11.8
  Rule 8 8.3
  Rule 9 8.3
  Rule 10 8.21
  Rule 11 10.9
  Rule 12 8.1, 9.2
  Rule 14 10.9, 10.10, 10.14
  Rule 15 10.1, 11.2
  Rule 22 11.23
  Rule 28 8.35, 8.38
  Rule 38 8.41, 8.42, 8.45
  Rule 42 0.9, 8.46
  Rule 43 10.40, 10.44
  Rule 45 0.9, 10.40, 12.51, 12.54
  Rule 46 2.13
  Rule 47 19.17
  Rule 53 6.20, 14.3, 14.20
  Rule 55 6.7, 6.9, 6.12
  Rule 56 6.9
  Rule 70 11.13, 12.13, 12.15, 12.19
  Rule 71 12.27
  Rule 72 12.40
  Rule 85 12.20
  Rule 87 5.47, 13.11
  Rule 89 2.7
  Rule 97 4.31
  Rule 100 19.32
  Rule 103 13.11
  Rule 106 5.30, 5.37, 17.25
  Rule 108 0.9
  Rule 113 1.10
  Rule 118 5.14
  Rule 119 3.5, 5.55
  Rule 124 20.16
  Rule 134 3.1, 3.6, 3.7
  Rule 136 4.24
  Rule 139 16.17
  Rule 141 16.19, 16.20
  Rule 142 16.14
  Rule 143 16.16
  Rule 145 15.1, 15.2, 15.7, 15.8
  Rule 146 15.9
  Rule 156 2.9, 5.43, 7.28, 9.3, 9.31, 10.26,
    10.28, 12.31, 13.11, 14.4, 14.22, 19.3,
    19.14, 19.22, 19.25, 19.26, 19.28, 19.32
  Rule 157 16.12
  Rule 158 16.24, 19.1
Draft Rules for the Limitation of the Dangers
  incurred by the Civilian Population in
  Time of War 0.3
International Court of Justice 1.17, 1.18, 1.19,
  6.13, 9.34, 10.15, 10.40, 12.15, 12.27,
  12.51, 13.41, 19.8
International Criminal Court 1.17, 1.34, 3.14,
  3.16, 4.12, 4.17, 4.18, 8.44, 9.28, 9.32,
  9.36, 9.37, 9.40, 10.11, 10.43, 11.7, 12.30,
  15.33, 18.8, 19.11, 19.16
International Criminal Tribunal for Rwanda
  (ICTR) 2.19, 9.40, 13.17
International Criminal Tribunal for the former
  Yugoslavia (ICTY) 0.10, 1.11, 2.9, 9.26,
  11.7, 13.12, 14.15, 15.30, 19.10
  Committee 8.5, 10.20
  Statute 12.16
International human rights law 2.5, 2.34, 4.2,
  4.3, 4.25–4.31, 4.40, 5.8, 5.9, 5.11, 5.19,
  5.46, 5.56, 5.57, 6.2, 6.6, 6.14, 9.16, 9.18,
  11.22, 13.4, 13.33, 14.17, 15.31, 16.1,
  16.27, 16.31, 18.23, 20.18, 20.22
International Law Commission (ILC) 2.8, 2.21,
  3.14, 5.42, 8.33, 10.44, 16.24, 18.3, 18.23
International Military Tribunal 19.2, 19.7
Iran 0.7, 0.12, 1.51, 7.11, 12.48
Iran–Iraq War 19.26
Iraq 2.9, 2.23, 2.30, 5.39, 8.14, 11.27, 11.28,
  12.53, 14.19
Ireland 10.47
Islamic State 2.9, 2.23, 2.30, 6.28, 11.27,
  11.28, 11.29
Islamic State Khorasan Province (ISIS-K) 1.49
Israel 1.20, 5.36, 7.10, 7.11, 7.12, 7.16, 9.17,
  11.18, 11.21, 12.47
Italy 1.46, 8.7, 8.22, 11.5, 15.22
Izz ad-Din al-Qassam Brigades 17.19

jus ad bellum 1.9, 1.10, 1.15, 1.31, 10.34
jus cogens 2.5, 2.8, 2.18, 2.21, 2.22, 5.46, 8.33,
  9.18, 9.31, 10.15, 11.13, 12.6, 12.8, 15.21,
  18.16, 19.1

Karadžić, Radovan 13.19
Khalid Sheikh Mohammed 1.30, 1.31

336 INDEX

Kleffner, Jann 1.35, 17.23
Kosovo 1.35, 8.11, 19.4
Kosovo conflict 1.35, 8.9, 11.34, 19.4
Kuwait 12.53

Laos 15.19
Lattimer, Mark 14.1
Law enforcement
  bodies (incorporation in armed forces) 5.27, 9.6
    Rules 1.42, 5.21, 5.22, 13.4, 13.39
    Use of firearms 5.21, 5.22, 13.39
Lebanon 4.40
Legal advisors 1.4
Levée en masse 9.9
Libya 1.41
Lieber Code 12.9
Lord's Resistance Army (LRA) 3.15
Lubanga Dyilo, Thomas 4.12

Mali 8.44, 20.22
Martens clause 12.3
Matheson, Michael 0.8, 16.20
Mauritania 2.23
Médecins sans Frontières 6.32, 11.10, 20.6
Medical personnel 5.17, 6.24, 7.17–7.20, 7.24, 9.10, 10.18, 10.19, 15.10, 15.20
Mégret, Frédéric 17.27
mens rea 2.9, 2.24, 3.11, 4.11, 9.35, 10.23, 10.24, 10.25, 19.5, 19.9, 19.15
Mercenaries 0.8, 0.9, 5.30
Military necessity 6.9, 8.6, 8.36, 8.40, 8.41, 8.45, 8.48, 9.42, 10.45, 11.13, 12.6, 12.20, 14.22, 15.21
Military objective 8.3–8.22, 8.24, 8.27, 8.31, 8.40, 8.48, 9.25, 10.31, 10.32, 10.41, 11.8–11.10, 11.30–11.31, 12.28, 12.46, 13.15, 13.31, 14.9, 18.10
  Definition **8.3–8.22**, 10.31, 10.32, 12.46
Military occupation 1.9–1.10
  as international armed conflict 1.9
Militias 17.10
Minnesota Protocol on the Investigation of Potentially Unlawful Death (2016) 6.25
Mladic, Ratko 13.19
Moldova 0.12, 1.10, 13.25
Monaco 1.34
MONUC 18.23, 18.24
MONUSCO (*see also* MONUC) 18.12, 18.13, 18.23
Morocco 1.10, 1.22, 5.38, 17.15
Mortar(s) 8.31, 8.37, 9.26, 9.33, 12.35
  Homemade/artisanal 9.33
Mosul 2.23, 11.27, 11.28, 11.29

Moynier, Gustave 20.1
Murder, prohibition of **2.7–2.11**, 2.12, 13.8, 13.11, 13.31, 18.19, 19.4, 19.21
  as *jus cogens* 2.8
  definition in the law in force in England and Wales 2.10
Myanmar 0.7, 6.23, 6.29

National Democratic Front of the Philippines (NDFP) 17.14
National liberation movement 17.4, 17.9, 17.11, 17.12
NATO 8.5, 8.9, 8.11, 11.34, 14.24
Nepal 0.7
Netherlands, the 0.12, 1.46, 5.36, 6.27, 8.22, 8.39, 8.42
Nieto-Navia, Rafael 10.32, 13.18
Nigeria 3.21
Non-combatants 9.10, 9.12
Non-discrimination, principle of **2.20–2.21**, 3.20
Non-refoulement, principle of 19.27
Non-State armed groups (*see also* Organised armed groups) 1.15, 1.33, 3.3, 4.26, 4.30, 4.48, 5.49, 9.11, 11.16, 13.1, 13.9, 13.24, **17.1–17.37**, 18.5, 18.11
North Macedonia 0.12
Norway 0.12, 1.46, 6.27, 8.10, 12.19
Ntaganda, Bosco 3.16, 9.29, 9.37
Nuclear power stations, special protection of 0.8, 0.9, 8.2, 8.46, 8.47
Nuclear weapons 12.41–12.43

Obama, Barack 0.7
Older persons 10.19, 11.26, 14.18
Ongwen, Dominic 3.15, 4.18, 4.19
Organised armed groups 1.33, 1.37, 7.21, 9.16,
Osama bin Laden 1.32
Overall control test (see also Effective control test) 1.16, 1.17, 1.19
Oxford Guidance on the Law relating to Humanitarian Relief Operations in Situations of Armed Conflicts (2016) 6.9, 6.14, 6.19, 6.23, 14.24

Pakistan 0.6, 0.7, 5.28, 5.36, 9.4, 13.25, 13.29
Palestine 7.9, 9.15, 11.22
Palestine Liberation Organization (PLO) 0.4
Payne, Cymie 10.38, 10.39
Pedrazzi, Marco 1.43
Pejic, Jelena 19.29
Peremptory *see* jus cogens
Persons with disabilities 4.38, 4.39
Philippines, the 0.12, 4.29, 17.14

Pictet, Jean 1.34
Poison 12.40
Polisario Front 1.22, 17.15
Power to detain 5.2, 5.49, 5.50
Precautions in attack, rule of **11.8–11.22**, 14.9
Precision-guided ('smart')
    munitions 11.15, 12.48
Priddy, Alice 3.4, 3.12
Prisoner of war
    Application to national liberation
        movements 17.12
    Repatriation of 1.25, 4.9, 5.13, 5.19, **5.40–5.46**, 15.14–15.15
    Status of 0.8, **5.1–5.47**, 15.13, 19.30
Proportionality in attack, rule of (*see also* ICRC Customary IHL Rule 14) 9.15, 9.17, **10.1–10.47**, 11.1, 11.31, 11.34, 12.6, 12.44, 14.10, 16.21, 16.26

Rape 2.18, 2.19, 3.2, 3.3, 3.8, 3.10, 3.11, 3.13, 3.15, 3.16, 3.17, 3.22, 13.9, 18.19, 18.22, 19.4
    as genocide 3.17
    as torture 2.19
    definition in international criminal law 3.11
Ratner, Steve 20.1, 20.2, 20.29
Red Crystal 0.12, 1.51, **7.2 *et seq.***
Refugee(s) 6.1, 6.31, 10.20, 19.4
Reprisals, belligerent 0.8, 2.27, 5.15, 8.24, **15.1–15.36**, 16.2
Right to life 2.2, 6.2
Rodenhäuser, Tilman 17.17, 20.17
'Roof knocking' 11.18
Russia 1.10, 1.13, 5.45, 9.9, 13.35, 13.36, 14.18, 16.27
Rwanda 6.31, 12.17, 20.16

Sahrawi Arab Democratic Republic 1.22
Sands, Philippe 10.46
Sarajevo 8.12, 8.37, 9.26, 10.30, 13.19, 13.20, 13.21, 14.14–14.16, 14.19
Sarin 13.16
Sassòli, Marco 1.15, 5.6, 6.14, 7.24, 12.46, 12.47
Saudi Arabia 1.10, 1.14, 4.29, 4.40, 4.45, 5.9, 5.28, 16.11
Saul, Ben 2.29, 9.10, 9.42, 9.43, 13.26, 17.25
Schabas, William 3.17
Schomburg, Wolfgang 13.18
Schools (*see also* Educational establishments) 4.37, 4.43, 8.10
    Protection
    Safe Schools Declaration 4.37, 8.10
Schmitt, Michael 9.43, 10.6, 10.21, 10.22, 12.58

Second World War 5.29, 8.30, 8.39, 11.16, 11.27, 12.33, 12.34, 13.7, 13.14, 14.15, 14.22, 15.16, 15.17, 15.19, 19.21
Self-determination, right of peoples to 1.3, 1.20, 5.36, 5.38, 5.57, 13.25
Sexual violence **3.4–3.17**, 3.20, 3.21
Sieges 0.15, 6.26, 8.39, 10.47, 14.1, 14.2, 14.4, 14.6, **14.7–14.19**, 14.24,
Sierra Leone 2.28, 13.9, 13.10, 18.6
Sivakumaran, Sandesh 15.34, 17.6, 17.27
Slavery **2.22–2.24**, 3.12,
    as *jus cogens* 2.22
    sexual 3.8, 3.12, 3.13, 3.15, 3.16
Solferino, Battle of 20.1
Solis, Gary D. 1.13, 1.36, 2.35, 5.39, 8.6, 8.40, 9.9, 9.14, 9.18, 9.23, 10.21, 12.45, 12.46, 13.39, 19.1, 19.4, 19.33
Somalia 0.7, 6.28
South Africa 1.20, 16.15
South Sudan 0.12, 5.9, 5.19, 6.23, 6.26
Special Court for Sierra Leone 2.24, 4.15, 13.9, 18.8, 19.33
    Statute 13.17
Stahn, Carsten 3.8, 4.18, 19.9
Starvation of civilians as a method of warfare 14.20–14.23
Stop Ecocide Foundation 10.46
Sudan 6.30
Superfluous injury 12.9–12.24
Sweden 0.12, 7.16, 10.46, 12.19
Switzerland 0.2, 0.4, 0.12, 1.21, 1.22, 7.7, 7.16, 12.19, 12.39, 20.4, 20.6
Syria 2.30, 6.15, 6.23, 6.29, 13.14, 13.16, 14.2, 14.17, 14.19
Syrian Democratic Forces (SDF) 17.19
Szasz, Paul 18.14, 18.17, 18.24

Taliban 1.12, 1.32, 1.49, 5.28, 5.29, 6.28, 9.42, 10.13, 16.26, 19.21
Tear gas 5.23
Terrorism 1.35, 2.6, 2.30, 4.20, 4.30, 5.45, **13.1–13.42**, 19.33
Threats of violence 2.1, 2.12, 2.13, **13.27–13.29**
Torture, prohibition of 2.2, 2.14–2.19, 2.20, 5.15, 13.8, 13.11, 14.5, 18.19
    as *jus cogens* 2.18
Turkey 0.7, 4.40, 14.19
Turkmenistan 1.12, 4.29

Uganda 0.12, 4.19, 18.11
Ukraine 0.12, 12.10
UNESCO 8.39
UNHCR 20.23
UNICEF 4.42, 5.19

INDEX

United Arab Emirates 1.10, 16.11
United Kingdom 1.13, 1.20, 1.21, 1.46, 2.10, 4.27, 4.29, 8.7, 9.24, 15.22, 16.11
   Manual of the Law of Armed Conflict 9.9, 10.41, 12.7, 14.8, 14.11, 14.23,
United Nations (UN) (*see also* MONUSCO; UNESCO; UNHCR; UNICEF)
   Assistance Mission in Afghanistan (UNAMA) 4.33, 10.13
   Commission of Inquiry on Syria 13.14, 13.16
   General Assembly 2.15, 4.5, 4.41, 9.21, 10.44, 11.22, 12.5, 12.39, 13.33, 14.18, 14.28
     Resolution 1386 (XIV) 4.5
     Resolution 2444 (XXIII) 9.21, 12.5
     Resolution 2603A (XXIV) 12.39
     Resolution 3314 (XXIX) 1.15
     Resolution 3452 (XXX) 2.15
     Resolution 51/77 4.41
     Resolution 60/288 13.33
     Resolution 71/130 14.18
   Office for the Coordination of Humanitarian Affairs (OCHA) 6.1, 6.14, 20.23
   Office of Legal Affairs 18.5, 18.16, 18.24
   Office of the High Commissioner for Human Rights (OHCHR) 11.29, 20.5, 20.22, 20.23
   Secretary-General 1.22, 3.2, 3.3, 3.20, 3.21, 4.44, 4.45, 11.32, 15.29, 18.1, 18.5, 18.18
     1999 Bulletin 15.29, 18.1, 18.16–18.18, 18.20, 18.21
   Security Council 1.10, 3.2, 3.9, 4.29, 4.44, 5.28, 6.15, 6.24, 13.29, 13.35, 14.18, 14.20, 18.2, 18.3, 18.6, 18.12, 20.16
     Resolution 1261 4.43
     Resolution 1267 3.3
     Resolution 1270 18.6
     Resolution 1325 3.2
     Resolution 1333 1.10, 5.28
     Resolution 1566 17.34
     Resolution 1612 4.44
     Resolution 1888 3.3
     Resolution 1960 3.3
     Resolution 1989 3.3
     Resolution 2098 18.2, 18.12
     Resolution 2106 2.6
     Resolution 2139 6.15
     Resolution 2165 6.15
     Resolution 2216 1.10
     Resolution 2253 3.3
     Resolution 2286 6.24
     Resolution 2427 4.29, 4.30
   Working Group on Children and Armed Conflict 4.44
   Six Grave Violations (against children) 4.43
   Special Rapporteur on extrajudicial, summary or arbitrary executions 9.14, 13.39
   Special Representative of the Secretary-General on Sexual Violence in Conflict 3.3
   Special Representative of the UN Secretary-General for Children and Armed Conflict 4.41, 4.42
United States (US) 0.3, 0.8, 0.9, 1.20, 1.30, 1.31, 1.32, 4.27, 5.29, 8.2, 8.14, 9.43, 10.21, 10.40, 12.19, 12.20, 12.42, 12.46, 12.51, 12.54, 12.58, 13.28, 13.31, 14.19, 19.33
   Department of Defense 1.23, 5.39
     DOD Dictionary of Military and Associated Terms 13.26
     Law of War Manual 9.23, 9.24, 9.42, 10.1, 10.17, 10.21, 12.8, 12.12, 12.15, 12.20, 12.26, 12.27, 12.33, 12.38, 12.41, 13.14, 14.3, 14.5, 14.23, 15.5
   Department of State 0.8, 5.39, 10.21, 16.20
   Supreme Court 2.5

V-1 flying bombs 12.33
V-2 rockets 12.33, 12.34, 13.14
Van Baal, Adrianus 13.21
Vietnam War 0.3, 5.15

War crimes **9.1–9.44**
Wars of national liberation 0.8, 1.20–1.22
'War on Terror' 1.32
Waterboarding 2.13
Watts, Sean 1.31, 17.25
Weapons
   Duty to review the legality of 1.6, **12.55–12.58**
   Transfer of 1.7
Weapons of mass destruction 12.2, 13.28
Western Sahara (*see also* Sahrawi Arab Democratic Republic) 1.10, 1.22, 1.46, 5.38, 17.15
Women **3.1–3.22**
   and the death penalty 3.18–3.20
   detention of 3.5

Yazidi 2.9, 2.23
Yemen 1.10, 1.14, 4.45, 6.23, 6.26, 16.11
Yugoslavia, Federal Republic of 8.5, 8.9, 8.43